Missouri historical review

(Volume VIII) Octorber 1913- July, 1914

Editor: F. A. Sampson

Alpha Editions

This edition published in 2020

ISBN : 9789354049309 (Hardback)
ISBN : 9789354049804 (Paperback)

Design and Setting By
Alpha Editions
www.alphaedis.com
email - alphaedis@gmail.com

As per information held with us this book is in Public Domain.
This book is a reproduction of an important historical work. Alpha Editions uses the best technology to reproduce historical work in the same manner it was first published to preserve its original nature. Any marks or number seen are left intentionally to preserve its true form.

CONTENTS.

Book Notices.................................65, 105, 164
Civil War in Missouri, by Capt. Geo. S. Grover..................   1
Death Notices from Missouri Intelligencer, April, 1819, to Dec., 1835 113
Early Missouri Roads, by G. C. Broadhead...................... 90
Echoes of Indian Emigration, by David W. Eaton..........93, 142, 198
Famous Goose Case, by N. T. Gentry.......................... 100
First Soldier Paper, by Edgar White............................ 223
First Threshing Machine Across the Mountains, by H. F. Grinstead. 54
Fort Orleans, the First French Post on the Missouri, by M. F. Stipes. 121
From Senator Doolittle's Papers, by Duane Mowry............... 227
Glance Over the Field of Music in Missouri, by Mrs. Susan A. Arnold
    McCausland.. 206
Historical Sketch of Shelby County, by W. O. L. Jewett............ 154
Hon. David Barton, by Samuel W. Ravenel...................... 216
Monumental Inscriptions in Missouri Cemeteries, Twelfth Paper.... 55
    Thirteenth Paper... 111
Mormon Troubles in Carroll County, by Susan H. Whiteman...... 220
Necrology...66, 110, 173, 243
Notes...63, 102, 170, 230
Old Missouri Town, Napton, by Rollins Bingham................. 211
Old Town of Elizabeth, by Ovid Bell........................... 86
Recollections of Thomas H. Benton, by L. T. Collier.............. 136
Report of the Committee on Old Landmarks of Jefferson County, by
    John L. Thomas... 29
Schuyler Letters, Duane Mowry................................ 44
Sketches of Livingston County, No. 4, by L. T. Collier............ 35
Wetmore's Diary of a Journey to Santa Fe, by F. F. Stephens...... 177
Value and Sale of the Missouri Slave, by Harrison A. Trexler....... 69

CONTRIBUTORS TO VOLUME VIII.

OVID BELL, Fulton, Editor of the Gazette.
BROADHEAD, G. C., former State Geologist, Professor in the State University, Late of Columbia, Mo.
L. T. COLLIER, Attorney at Law, Kansas City.
DAVID W. EATON, Versailles, U. S. Coast Survey.
H. F. GRINSTEAD.
CAPT. GEO. S. GROVER of Law Department of Wabash Railroad, St. Louis.
W. O. L. JEWETT, Shelbina, Editor of Democrat, Ex-President of the State Historical Society of Missouri.
MRS. SUSAN A. ARNOLD McCAUSLAND, Lexington, Mo.
DUANE MOWRY, Milwaukee, Wis.
CAPT. SAMUEL W. RAVENEL, Boonville, Mo.
ROLLINS BINGHAM, Deceased.
DR. F. F. STEPHENS, Professor of History, University of Missouri.
M. F. STIPES, Jamesport, Missouri, Editor of the ————.
JUDGE JOHN L. THOMAS, Washington, formerly Judge of the Supreme Court of Missouri.
DR. HARRISON A. TREXLER, Professor of History in the University of Montana.
EDGAR WHITE, Macon, Mo.
SUSAN H. WHITEMAN, Carrollton, Mo.

MISSOURI HISTORICAL REVIEW.

VOL. 8   OCTOBER, 1913.   NO. 1

CIVIL WAR IN MISSOURI.[1]

Commander, comrades, ladies and gentlemen:
It has been well said, and that, too, by an American, that

"We may build more splendid habitations,
Fill our rooms with paintings and with sculptures,
But we cannot buy with gold the old associations."

It is a comforting thought to many of us, for whom "'life's shadows are growing long," that there yet remains, in this commercial age, a few things too precious by far to be estimated upon a money basis. And of these, the most priceless heritage of all, next to the love of a good woman, is the memory of the stirring days of 1861, when, in the springtime of youth and vigor, we wore the blue uniform of the volunteer army of the United States, and helped to destroy forever, upon her soil, the dogma of secession and the right of property in man.

And what part or lot had the great commonwealth of Missouri in this memorable struggle? It is high time that her glorious history was better understood, especially by the generation which has come upon the stage of active life since that time.

In the census of 1860, the great states of New York, Pennsylvania, Ohio, Illinois, Indiana, Massachusetts and

---

1. Address of Capt. Geo. S. Grover before the Col. Grover Post, No. 78, G. A. R. at Warrensburg, Missouri, November 4, 1893.

Missouri ranked in the order named as to population, Missouri having the seventh place.

It might be well, at the risk of exhausting your patience, to refer briefly to the slavery question, the real cause of our civil war.

We of America are indebted to England and Holland for the origin of this gigantic evil, as it was introduced upon this continent by these two maritime nations. It existed in New England, and in New York and Pennsylvania, as well as in the South, during the war of the Revolution, and no issue was then raised concerning it. But the Puritans in New England, the Holland Dutch in New York, and the Quakers in Pennsylvania, soon destroyed it within their respective boundaries after achieving their independence.

When the Northwestern Territory, now the states of Ohio, Michigan, Indiana, Illinois and Wisconsin, was formed in 1787, after a bitter struggle, the proviso was inserted, and passed both houses of Congress, "that there should be neither slavery nor involuntary servitude, except as a punishment for crime, whereof the party shall have been duly convicted" there. Thus those great states came into the Union free. By reason of the purchase from France, in 1803, of that vast domain then known as the Louisiana Territory, the question of the further continuation of slavery there, brought on the contest which terminated only in Lee's surrender at Appomattox, in 1865. The states of Louisiana, Arkansas, Mississippi, Alabama and Florida came into the Union as slave territory; but in 1820, when Missouri applied for admission, the controversy as to whether she should be slave or free shook the nation from center to circumference. It was finally settled by a compromise, which inflicted the curse of slavery upon the great state of Missouri, but which admitted Iowa and Minnesota as free states. Like all compromises, however, upon great moral questions, it satisfied nobody, and left wounds behind it which time could never heal. The annexation of Texas as slave territory then followed, with the admission of California and Oregon as free states. Then came the struggle over Kansas and Nebraska. These two territories were fairly debatable ground, as they were both south of thirty-six degrees and thirty minutes of latitude, the boundary fixed in the Missouri compromise as the "dead line" between freedom and slavery.

Emigrants from both North and South poured into these territories, especially into Kansas, and "chaos came again" upon that unhappy land between 1856 and 1861. The followers of freedom prevailed, and then the haughty Southern Oligarchy realized at last, what they had long feared, that slavery could not be maintained in the new territories beyond the Missouri river, and that its end was only a question of time. Then came the scheme of secession, to which the Democratic party in the South was fully committed, as well as to the maintenance of slavery in the new territories as well as in the South. The northern democracy attempted to evade the question, by adopting the elusive theory of Stephen A. Douglas, then United States senator from Illinois, called popular sovereignty, which referred this issue to each territory to decide for itself.

The Whig party attempted to ignore this issue, and perished ignobly in such attempt, for the brains and the conscience of that organization immediately deserted it, founding the Republican party, which was pledged to the destruction of slavery.

Such was the condition of affairs in 1856, when John C. Fremont, a Republican, became the standard-bearer of freedom, and was defeated for president by James Buchanan, the Democratic nominee.

During thirty consecutive years of this struggle Missouri was represented in the United States senate by Thomas H. Benton, a North Carolinian by birth, and a slaveholder by inheritance, who never once wavered in his support of all measures looking toward the ultimate destruction of slavery.

In 1858 there arose to national prominence that wonderful statesman, whose name and career will illuminate the pages of history until time shall be no more, Abraham Lincoln, of Illinois, whose masterly debate with Douglas foreshadowed his entrance into public life the following year. He became the Republican candidate for president in 1860, having been nominated at Chicago, as hereafter stated, and was supported with enthusiasm by Francis P. Blair and Edward Bates of

Missouri, the latter afterwards entering the cabinet as attorney general.

The Democratic party divided at Charleston in 1860, both wings afterwards re-assembling at Baltimore, where Stephen A. Douglas was nominated by the northern and John C. Breckenridge by the southern faction.

In the same year the remnant of the old Whig party, then calling themselves the Constitutional Union men, met at Baltimore, and nominated John Bell of Tennessee for president.

In the presidential contest of that year, Abraham Lincoln, a native of Kentucky, and citizen of Illinois, the greatest statesman America has yet produced, was the candidate of the Republican party; Stephen A. Douglas, the "Little Giant," of Illinois, then in the United States senate from that state, of the union wing of the Democratic party, John C. Breckenridge of Kentucky, of the secession wing of the same organization, and John Bell of Tennessee, of the Whig party.

In the electoral college the entire vote of California, Connecticut, Illinois, Indiana, Iowa, Maine, Massachusetts, Michigan, Minnesota, New York, New Hampshire, Ohio, Oregon, Pennsylvania, Rhode Island, Vermont, Wisconsin, and four votes of New Jersey, one hundred and eighty votes in all, were cast for Lincoln.

Alabama, Arkansas, Delaware, Florida, Georgia, Louisiana, Maryland, Mississippi, North Carolina, South Carolina and Texas, seventy-two votes in all, were cast for Breckenridge.

Kentucky, Tennessee and Virginia, thirty-nine votes in all, were cast for Bell. The entire vote of Missouri and three votes of New Jersey, twelve votes in all, were cast for Douglas. In the following year, by a majority of 80,000, the people of Missouri decided against secession. Not a single member of that party was returned to the convention called to determine that question, though there were a number of the delegates who were believers in the doctrine of state rights, or, as it is now termed, local self-government.

Of the whole number of members, eighty-one were born in the slave states, fourteen in the North, three in Europe, and one in the District of Columbia. This convention, when it assembled, adhered firmly to the Union from beginning to end, and when Claiborne F. Jackson, with a party of state officials, and a minority of the general assembly, fled from the state in 1861, Hamilton R. Gamble, an eminent lawyer and unswerving Union man, was appointed as provisional governor in his stead, and a legislature elected, which was as steadfastly devoted to the government of the United States as any corresponding body in the North.

In the spring of 1861 the states of Alabama, Arkansas, Florida, Georgia, Louisiana, Mississippi, the two Carolinas, Tennessee, Virginia and Texas, eleven in all, attempted to secede. And thus was born the ill-starred and ill-fated Southern Confederacy. By this time Kansas was admitted into the Union and conspicuous among the loyal states, twenty-three in number, stood the grand old state of Missouri. This is clearly demonstrated by the number of Union soldiers furnished by each state in the four years beginning in 1861 and ending in 1865. I have taken pains to obtain this information from official sources, and the roll of honor down to and including Missouri, as follows:

New York, 445,959; Pennsylvania, 338,155; Ohio, 310,654; Illinois, 258,162; Indiana, 194,363; Massachusetts, 146,467; Missouri, 109,162; total, 1,802,922.

Thus it is that Missouri, seventh among the Empire States in point of population in 1860, was seventh also among her sisters in the struggle for human freedom, although, unlike them, every mile of her territory almost was a battle ground over which armies marched and countermarched for four long years in the most gigantic civil war ever known in the world's history.

There is another fact well nigh forgotten also, but also of record, as to this eventful period, and that is that while drafts were ordered and executed in all of the six states above named which exceeded Missouri in the number of soldiers furnished, Missouri alone of them all furnished her full quota in every call made by the president or his subordinates for troops to suppress the slaveholders' rebellion. And while it is true that a draft was ordered in Missouri in 1863, it is also a fact that the order was countermanded as soon as it was shown that Missouri's quota was full.

Nor is this all. The entire vote of Missouri for president in 1860 was 165,518 and sixty per cent of this number wore the blue uniform of the United States and lent efficient aid in the destruction of slavery forever on this continent.

This, too, when Missouri's quota in the Confederate army was also full, and while no official records survive from which the exact number of such troops can be obtained yet, it has been stated upon the best authority that at the close of the war there were more men from Missouri in the Confederate army than from any of the seceding states.

This is further exemplified by the fact that the three presidential candidates in 1860, who stood distinctively for the Union, differing only on the question of further extension of slavery in the territories, Mr. Lincoln being opposed to such extension, Mr. Bell believing in the idea of non-interference, and Mr. Douglas being in favor of each territory determining that question for itself, those three candidates had, combined, in Missouri, a majority of 102,884, in a total vote of 165,518, over the followers of Breckenridge, who were disunionists and in favor of the absolute right of the slaveholder to take his slaves into the territories, and keep them there unaffected by any territorial legislation, the vote being as follows:

Lincoln,	17,028
Douglas,	58,801
Bell,	58,372
	134,201
Breckenridge,	31,317
	102,884

The accuracy of the foregoing statement as to the relative positions of the respective political parties in the campaign of 1860, is verified by the following quotations taken from those platforms, as they appear in the Political Text Book for 1860, compiled by Horace Greeley and John F. Cleveland, and published in New York by the Tribune Association in that year.

REPUBLICAN PLATFORM

On Which Lincoln Was Nominated, May 18, 1860.

3. "That to the Union of the states this nation owes its unprecedented increase in population, its surprising development of material resources, its rapid augmentation of wealth, its happiness at home and its honor abroad; and we hold in abhorrence all schemes for disunion, come from whatever source they may: And we congratulate the country that no Republican member of congress has uttered or countenanced the threats of disunion so often made by Democratic members, without rebuke and with applause from their political associates; and we denounce those threats of disunion, in case of a popular overthrow of their ascendency, as denying the vital principles of a free government, and as an avowal of contemplated treason, which it is the imperative duty of an indignant people sternly to rebuke and forever silence." * * *

7. "That the new dogma, that the Constitution of its own force carries slavery into any or all of the territories of the United States, is a dangerous political heresy, at variance with the explicit provisions of that instrument itself, with contemporaneous exposition, and with legislative and judicial precedent: is revolutionary in its tendency, and subversive of the peace and harmony of the country."

8. "That the normal condition of the territory of the United States is that of freedom: That as our Republican fathers, when they had abolished slavery in all our national territory, ordained that 'no person should be deprived of life, liberty, or property, without the process of law,' it becomes our duty, by legislation, whenever such legislation is necessary, to maintain this provision of the Constitution against all attempts to violate it: and we deny the authority of congress, of a territorial legislature, or of any individuals, to give legal existence to slavery in any territory in the United States."

CONSTITUTIONAL UNION PLATFORM

ON WHICH BELL WAS NOMINATED, MAY 9, 1860.

"2. *Resolved:* That it is both the part of patriotism and of duty to recognize no political principle other than the *Constitution of the country, the Union of the states, and the enforcement of the laws*, and that, as representatives of the Constitutional Union men of the country in national convention assembled, we hereby pledge ourselves to maintain, protect and defend, separately and unitedly, these great principles of public liberty and national safety, against all enemies at home and abroad, believing that thereby peace may once more be restored to the country, the rights of the people and states re-established, and the government again placed in that condition of justice, fraternity and equality, which, under the example and Constitution of our fathers, has solemnly bound every citizen of the United States to maintain a more perfect union, establish justice, insure domestic tranquility, provide for the common defense, promote the general welfare, and secure the blessings of liberty to ourselves and our posterity."

DEMOCRATIC CONVENTION, DOUGLAS WING

PLATFORM UPON WHICH DOUGLAS WAS NOMINATED AT BALTIMORE, MD., JUNE 22, 1860.

1. "*Resolved:* That we, the Democracy of the Union, in convention assembled, hereby declare our affirmance of the resolutions unanimously adopted and declared as a platform of principles by the Democratic convention, at Cincinnati, in the year 1856, believing that Democratic principles are unchanging in their nature when applied to the same subject matters; and we recommend, as the only further resolution, the following:

Inasmuch as differences of opinion exist in the Democratic party as to the nature and extent of the powers of a territorial legislature, and as to the powers and duties of congress, under the Constitution of the United States, over the institution of slavery within the territories:

2. *Resolved:* That the Democratic party will abide by the decisions of the supreme court of the United States on the questions of constitutional law."

From Platform of 1856.

1. "*Resolved:* That, claiming fellowship with and desiring the co-operation of all who regard the preservation of the Union under the Constitution as the paramount issue, and repudiating all sectional parties and platforms concerning domestic slavery, which seek to embroil the states and incite to treason and armed resistance to law in the territories, and whose avowed purpose, if consummated, must end in civil war and disunion, the American Democracy recognize and adopt the principles contained in the organic laws establishing the territories of Nebraska and Kansas, as embodying the only sound and safe solution of the slavery question, upon which the great national idea of the people of this whole country can repose in its determined conservation of the Union and non-interference of Congress with slavery in the territories or in the District of Columbia.

2. That this was the basis of the Compromise of 1850, confirmed by both the Democratic and the Whig parties in National Conventions, ratified by the people in the election of 1852, and rightly applied to the organization of the territories of 1854.

3. That by the uniform application of the Democratic principle to the organization of territories, and the admission of new states with or without domestic slavery, as they may elect, the equal rights of all the states will be preserved intact, the original compacts of the Constitution maintained inviolate, and the perpetuity and expansion of the Union insured to its utmost capacity of embracing, in peace and harmony, every future American state that may be constituted or annexed with a Republican form of government.

Resolved: That we recognize the right of the people of all the territories, including Kansas and Nebraska, acting through the legally and fairly expressed will of the majority of the actual residents, and whenever the number of their inhabitants justifies it, to form a Constitution, with or without domestic slavery, and be admitted into the Union upon terms of perfect equality with the other states."

PLATFORM ON WHICH BRECKENRIDGE WAS NOMINATED

At Baltimore, June 28, 1860.

"*Resolved:* That the platform adopted at Cincinnati be affirmed, with the following resolutions:

That the National Democracy of the United States hold these cardinal principles on the subject of slavery in the territories: First, that congress has no power to abolish slavery in the territories; second, that the territorial legislature has no power to abolish slavery in the territories, nor to prohibit the introduction of slaves therein, nor any power to destroy or impair the right of property in slaves by any legislation whatever.

Resolved: That the enactments of state legislatures to defeat the faithful execution of the Fugitive Slave Law are hostile in character, subversive to the Constitution and revolutionary in their effects."

Thus it appears, that while the Republican party was absolutely opposed to the extension of slavery, or to its further existence, it was as resolutely opposed to any scheme of disunion. And this was true also of the Douglas wing of the Democratic party as well as the remnant of the Whig party, then known as the Constitutional Union party. While the Breckenridge wing of the Democratic party were not only disunionists, but resolved to force the institution of slavery upon the free people of the new states then forming in the West and Northwest, without the consent of the inhabitants of such territories. Failing in this, they drew the sword for the purpose of perpetuating the curse of slavery on this continent, and of upholding the dogma of secession, and in their case, for once, the Scriptures were fulfilled, for the adherents of this dogma, having drawn the sword, perished by it.

Indeed, if a line be drawn one county wide on the west side of the Mississippi from the northern to the southern boundary of the state of Missouri, and one county wide on each side of the Missouri river from the city of St. Louis to the northwestern boundary of this state, within that line of demarkation will be found the great recruiting ground for the Confederate army as well as the strongholds of both slavery and secession in Missouri; while outside of these lines the great heart of her people beat as firmly for the cause of the Union as it did in similar communities in any of the northern states. So that any claim now made by any one, whether in official life or out of it, that Missouri ever belonged in sentiment to the South is an unmerited slander, promulgated only by those who are totally unacquainted with the imperial resources and densely ignorant of the glorious history of our great commonwealth. "Poor Old Missouri" she is not and never was. Union Missouri she was, is and always will be. Brave Old Missouri she was in her heroic past. Great Old Missouri she is in her boundless present, and Rich Old Missouri she will be, as I fully believe, in her transcendent future.

There is no reason to doubt that if Thomas H. Benton, who represented Missouri in the United States senate for thirty consecutive years, had lived, his overshadowing influence and massive intellect would have been on the side of the Union, as the Democracy of Missouri was really divided on that issue, and that wing of it which bore the name of that great statesman, was opposed to slavery, and unconditionally and almost unanimously arrayed on the side of freedom. Two of Benton's most devoted lieutenants, Francis P. Blair, and B. Gratz Brown, were striking illustrations of this truth. Blair and Brown were cousins, both natives of Kentucky, both slaveholders by inheritance, both voluntarily manumitted their slaves, and at the beginning of the civil war, Blair was a free-soil or anti-slavery member of congress from the city of St.

Louis, and Brown was the able editor of the Missouri Democrat, a Benton paper, whose owner, William McKee, was an ardent and outspoken Union man, and whose paper never once faltered in its support of the United States government in the darkest hours of its death-grapple with secession.

The lamented death of Stephen A. Douglas occurring as it did early in the civil war, deprived the Union cause of a leader, who would have been a host in himself.

It became apparent to the Union men of Missouri, before the end of the year 1860, that the desperate and unscrupulous secession minority, although defeated at the polls, would resort to extreme measures at any cost to enroll Missouri among the defenders of slavery and secession. So such men as Blair, Brown, Bates, Broadhead, Fletcher, Gamble, Glover, How, Filley, Krekel, Edwards, Dyer, Draper, Lovelace, Wagner, Rollins, Hall, Pretorious, McKee, Boyd, Phelps, McClurg, Guitar, Geo. R. Smith, and B. W. Grover, with many others in various portions of the state, resolved to keep Missouri in her proper place among the loyal states or perish in the effort.

The people of Johnson county were almost evenly divided between the Whig and Democratic parties. The location of the county was outside of the great slaveholding belt of the country along the Missouri river, and, therefore, there was a large number of substantial small farmers settled there from the mountain regions of East Tennessee, Kentucky and the Carolinas, as well as a small number from the free states, who refused to own slaves and who were at heart opposed to that institution. The majority of these men were uncompromising Whigs. On the other hand the Democrats were mainly large land owners and slaveholders, and were chiefly from Virginia, Kentucky, Georgia and the other slave states. The prestige of wealth and social position was largely on the Democratic and also the secession side, but the Whigs, and Union men as well, were an uncompromising and numerous body of men, whose undaunted spirit could be depended upon in any emergency.

In 1861, by a decisive majority, Johnson county elected the Union candidate, Aikman Welch, a native of Missouri, and one of the ablest lawyers then in the state, as a delegate to the constitutional convention. Welch soon so distinguished himself in that body, as to secure the appointment of attorney-general, and died in that office during the war. His opponent was M. C. Goodlett, a young man then, who had recently emigrated to the county from Tennessee, and a prominent secessionist. Among the Union men of the county Benjamin W. Grover was the recognized leader, as he was afterwards the representative Union soldier. A native of Ohio, of Welsh ancestry, he came to the county in 1844, and was a life-long Whig and opponent of both slavery and secession. He was a member of the state senate of Missouri from 1852 to 1856, and was one of the early directors of the Missouri Pacific Railroad, and, in furtherance of that enterprise, devoted many of the best years of his life. He took an active part in the election of Aikman Welch, whose intimate personal friend he was, and when the war clouds began to lower, gave early public notice of his intention to enter the military service of the United States on the first opportunity.

Among his intimate friends, all strong Union men, were Robert A. Foster, John L. Rogers, A. H. Gilkeson, W. B. Moody, Thomas Evans, William and David Marr, Geo. W. and Thos. D. Houts, D. W. Reed, John Brown, James K. Farr, Thomas Ijams, Robert, John and Baxter Morrow, John H. McCluney, William Parman, Samuel Maguire, William E. Applegate, William E. Chester, Thomas Foster, William Fisher, Andrew Granger, Samuel Workman, Henry Hays, Daniel Adams, James Shumate, Jacob Knaus, Leroy C. Duncan, Samuel Bird, Stephen J. Burnett, A. M. Christian, Ingram Starkey, James Isaminger, Brinkley Hornsby, John J. Welshans, Alfred Duffield, William Zoll, Jesse and Harvey Harrison, and many others, whom want of time and space alone prevent present mention.

Robert A. Foster was a minister of the Gospel, a Southern Methodist, and the only minister of that denomination in the state who was for the Union, and a native of South Carolina, but he early chose the Union side, though past the age of military service, entered the volunteer army of the United States with his three sons, and served four years, as hereinafter described. The sons of Henry Hays, Daniel Adams, James Shumate, Andrew Granger, A. M. Christian, Geo. W. Houts, William Marr, Brinkley Hornsby, John J. Welshans, John L. Rogers, the Harrison brothers, and many others, were afterwards gallant soldiers for the Union. Brinkley Hornsby, a native of East Tennessee, openly voted for Fremont in 1856, and for Lincoln in 1860, in Johnson county. Marsh Foster, the eldest son of Robert A. Foster, was the ablest young man by long odds in Johnson county at that time. In 1860 he was an independent Democratic candidate for county clerk, and was elected after a remarkable canvass, defeating both the regular Democratic nominee, James McCown, and the Whig candidate, F. S. Poston, for that office. When secession became the issue, he supported the Union candidate, Welch, for delegate to the constitutional convention, and on the afternoon of election day, February 18, 1861, was assassinated in the most cowardly manner at the polls in Warrensburg by the two McCowns, father and son. Had his life been spared, Marsh Foster would soon have entered the Union army, and would undoubtedly have risen to a high rank in the service. As it was, he was the first martyr to the Union cause in Johnson county and also in the United States, and as such will ever be held in loving and tender remembrance.

After the unprovoked murder of Marsh Foster, the two McCowns fled to the jail for refuge, where they would have been hanged by a band of young men led by Thos. W. and W. L. Houts, but their lives were saved by B. W. Grover and Emory S. Foster, the second son of R. A. Foster, who persuaded them to let the law take its course. A packed grand jury of secessionists afterwards refused to indict the McCowns for murder, which but intensified the feeling against them. Both of them served in the Confederate army, though not with credit either to themselves or to that cause.

Early in 1861 an independent military company was organized in Warrensburg, for the avowed purpose of serving in the Union army. Emory S. Foster was the captain and Thos. W. Houts its first lieutenant. No military clothing was obtainable, and of necessity a uniform was adopted of red shirts and black pants, so the company was known as the "Red Shirt Company."

At that time there was stored in a room in the courthouse at Warrensburg one hundred muskets belonging to the state, which had been furnished to the county under the militia law of 1857, then in force. These arms were intended by the secession leaders to be used in overawing the Union men. But Foster and his men secured possession of them, and stood guard over them day and night. A demand was made on Foster for these arms, and he was threatened with prosecution if it was not acceded to, but he kept them fully loaded all the time for the use of his company, and afterwards turned them over to Col. Grover, who used them in arming his regiment.

At the same time F. M. Cockrell, now our United States Senator, afterwards a brave and distinguished soldier, was recruiting a company for the Confederate army, which he soon afterwards entered. Foster's company drilled daily on the east side of town and Cockrell's on the west side. On several occasions Cockrell and his men drilled with Foster and Foster and his men with Cockrell. Cockrell went south before Foster could get mustered into the Union army, but the utmost good feeling always prevailed between the two commands until the last.

The legislature of Missouri was at that time controlled by the secession element, and passed a conscription law, known as the Harris Military Bill, with the avowed purpose of raising an army to force Missouri out of the Union, a plan successfully adopted in many of the slave states. As soon as the bill passed, B. W. Grover made arrangements to canvass Johnson county in opposition to it, with a view of organizing the Union men. In this work he was joined by James D. Eads, a lifelong Democrat, who had recently removed to Missouri from Iowa, and was then the editor of the "Warrensburg Missourian," the Democratic organ. Eads was an educated physician and had served in the Mexican war. But he was a follower of Douglas, and when the secession tendencies of Johnson county Democracy became apparent, he became an outspoken Union man, resigned his place on the paper, and joined Grover in the canvass of the county, speaking in every school district. For this both Eads and Grover were proscribed, and a reward of five hundred dollars offered to any man who would kill them. But Foster and Houts, with a picked guard of the red shirt company, escorted the speakers in safety from one end of the county to the other, and so overawed the secessionists, that after one feeble interruption at Chilhowee they relinquished all idea of either interruptions or assassination.

By this time the Union men in Johnson county were fully organized, and what was afterwards the Twenty-seventh regiment of Missouri Mounted Infantry, United States Volunteers, was formed. B. W. Grover was unanimously chosen colonel, but declined the place in favor of his friend, Jacob Knaus. Grover was then chosen lieutenant-colonel; Emory S. Foster, major; Thomas W. Houts, quartermaster; and John J. Welshans, commissary.

Captains McGuire, Isaminger, M. U. Foster, Duncan, Applegate, Turley, Parker, Miller, McCluney, Ijams, Taylor, and Brown; and Lieuts. Shanks, Hall, Box, Starkey, Pease, W. L. Christian, Bird, Burnett, Gallaher, Keaton, Smiley, McCabe and Van Beek, with a thousand of the best and bravest young men in Johnson and Pettis counties, were organized into a regiment, which was called, for want of a better name, the Johnson County Home Guards. There were no United States mustering officers nearer than St. Louis, and no communication with them by rail nearer than Otterville, in Cooper county, with the state government in secession hands, so that nothing could be done but appoint rallying places and devise a code of signals, leaving each company in the neighborhood where it had been recruited. Captains McGuire and Applegate were, therefore, stationed in what is now Grover township, in the northeastern part of the county, Capt. M. U. Foster at Warrensburg, Capt. Duncan at Kingsville, Capt. Turley at Dunksburg, Capt. Parker at Sedalia, Capt. Miller at Windsor, Capt. McCluney at Fayetteville, Capt. Isaminger in the southeastern part of the county on Clear Fork south of Knob Nos-ter, Capt. Ijams at Cornelia, and Capts. Taylor and Brown at Chilhowee and Rose Hill. Such was the situation when Fort Sumter fell and also when Camp Jackson was taken on the 10th of May, 1861, by General Nathaniel Lyon and Colonel Frank P. Blair.

Then came a change in affairs. The crisis had come, and the Union army found its general in Nathaniel Lyon, who, had his life been spared, would have ranked among the greatest soldiers of the war. After capturing Camp Jackson, Lyon immediately organized a small command in St. Louis, and proceeded with it up the Missouri river.

Claiborne F. Jackson, then Governor, a secessionist, abandoned Jefferson City and fled south, first taking the precaution to empty the state treasury, and steal all the blankets from the state lunatic asylum at Fulton.

On the 17th of June, 1861, General Lyon reached Boonville with a small infantry and artillery force recruited in St. Louis, and there attacked and defeated a large number of secessionists, who were commanded by John S. Marmaduke, afterwards a Confederate general.

By this time, though the Twenty-seventh regiment had been enrolled, organized, and in active service, since the latter part of April, it had not been mustered in by any one possessing any authority from the United States to perform that act. In order to get into the service properly and regularly, Col. Grover rode alone across the country from Warrensburg to Boonville, a distance of seventy-five miles, to meet Gen. Lyon and procure the necessary authority from him to muster in his command. He arrived in time to act as volunteer aide to Gen. Lyon in the battle of Boonville, and received authority from that officer to immediately muster the Twenty-seventh into the service of the United States. While he was thus absent, Gen. Sterling Price, then in command of the Missouri State Guards, as the secession troops were then called, arrived in Warrensburg on his way south from Lexington, retreating from Gen. Lyon's advance. Gen. Price was accompanied by only a small escort and was very sick, necessitating his riding in an ambulance. He remained in Warrensburg during the afternoon of June 18th, at the Bolton House in Old Town. Major Foster, Capt. Foster and Lieutenant Houts were in town that day with about twenty-eight men, but none of them had any legal authority to order the men. All matters were at that time submitted to a vote and the majority ruled, the ranking officer simply carrying out the will of the majority. The younger men in the command proposed to capture Price at dusk and hurry off with him to Lyon, but the older men would not agree to it, fearing reprisals from the large rebel force then retreating south. In the twilight, in the Colburn pasture in Old Town at Warrensburg, a vote was taken in Major Foster's hat. Thirteen voted yes, the three officers above named being among that number, and fifteen, no. Not long afterwards, Gen. Price and his escort left town in a hurry. Col. Grover arrived about midnight that night with ample authority, and at once ordered a pursuit. We chased that ambulance to the Henry county line, where, in the gray dawn of the 19th, it safely reached a rebel camp too large for our little squadron to attack. So passed away a great opportunity.

As soon as the men could be collected from the various parts of the county, a work requiring nearly two weeks' time, the entire regiment assembled in New Town, at Warrensburg, in the grove east of where Land, Fike & Co's mill now stands, and there, on the 4th day of July, 1861, it was mustered into the United States service by Col. Grover, for "three years or during the war." It then marched to Lexington, thirty-five miles distant, to meet a detachment from St. Louis of Gen. Lyon's rear guard and procure arms. Upon arriving there, it was found that the troops then due had not arrived, so Col. Knaus encamped the regiment near the Fair grounds south of town, and remained there several days, without tents or camp equipage, officers and men alike sleeping on the bare ground, in a drenching rain storm, with a scant supply of food, arms and ammunition. In the meantime the rebels in Lexington, who could still muster a large force, formed a plan to capture the camp, and did seize and hold Capt. Foster, James M. Shepherd and several others who had gone into town for supplies. But, upon the appearance of two squadrons galloping into town, on parallel streets, one led by Col. Grover and the other by Major Foster, the prisoners were quickly released and their captors fled to the brush without firing a shot.

The storm, perhaps, prevented the attack on the camp that night, but on the next day Col. Chas. G. Stiefel arrived on a steamboat with a regiment of infantry from St. Louis, and supplied Col. Knaus with a lot of Belgian muskets, of an antiquated pattern, far more dangerous to the men using them than to the foe. A report was circulated over the rebel "grapevine telegraph" that Col. Knaus had received no arms, so when the command arrived the next day but one, at Atkinson's, fifteen miles from Lexington, on the Warrensburg road, it was fired on from the brush by a large rebel force, and several men wounded. But the line soon formed, Col. Knaus leading the center, Col. Grover the right, and Major Foster and Captain Fred. Neet, of the Fourteenth Missouri, the left. The rapid fire and spirited charge of Col. Knaus and his men soon dislodged the enemy, who broke and ran in all directions, closely pursued all that afternoon as far as Chapel Hill by Capt. Foster and Lieut. Box, with detachments of the mounted men. Upon arriving in Warrensburg the regiment went into camp at Camp Lyon, three miles southeast of town, in the Bear Creek valley, and there remained on active duty, scouting incessantly day and night until about August 20th, when it was ordered to Jefferson City. It marched to Sedalia, and there the main portion, under Col. Grover, went east by rail, while Col. Knaus followed with the mounted detachment *via* the wagon road. While passing Lookout Station, or Centretown, on the railroad, while the train was moving through a deep cut, a band of rebel guerrillas fired from behind piles of cordwood on the edges of the cut on both sides down upon the heads of the men who were closely packed in stockcars. Several men were badly wounded, and one, Dan. Cecil, one of the best and bravest boys in Foster's Company, mortally.

Col. Grover, who was on the engine, rallied and formed the men as soon as possible, but the guerrillas, being well mounted, escaped, with the exception of three, whose horses broke loose before they could mount. These three were captured and shot, and several houses where the guerrillas had harbored were burned, and the train then moved on, reaching Jefferson City the same afternoon. On the next day but one, Col. Knaus arrived, not having been molested en route.

Soon after his arrival in Jefferson City, Col. Knaus, then advanced in years, resigned and went home. Col. Grover succeeded to the command of the regiment and was again tendered the colonelcy by an unanimous vote, but declined it in favor of his friend, James D. Eads. Major Foster recruited a picked detachment from the regiment under the personal supervision of Gen. Grant, and called it the Fremont Scouts. He was ordered into active service with this detachment in western Missouri, and Capt. William Beck succeeded him as Major. Col. U. S. Grant was then in command of the post at Jefferson City, and to him Col. Grover reported for duty. A strong friendship sprang up between them and there was also a marked personal resemblance, as they were almost exactly the same size, with the same complexion and the same colored hair and eyes. So, when Col. Grant received notice of his promotion to Brigadier-General, he gave to Col. Grover his uniform coat, which he had never worn, which the latter wore all through the battle and siege of Lexington, and was afterwards buried in it. By order of Gen. Grant, the regiment was fully mounted, uniformed and equipped on the 1st day of September, 1861, and its proper name and number recorded, the Twenty-seventh Mounted Infantry Missouri Volunteers. It remained at Jefferson City, doing active and incessant service in the field as scouts, until Col. Mulligan, of the Twenty-third Illinois Infantry, who had succeeded Gen. Grant as post commander at Jefferson City, was ordered to Lexington by Gen. Fremont, who then commanded the department of Missouri. Col. Grover was detailed with parts of five companies, commanded by Capts. Maguire, Duncan, Applegate, Parker and McCluney, about three hundred men in all, to accompany Col. Mulligan to Lexington. On the march, about one hundred men were cut off from the command at Dunksburg, and were dispersed and a large number captured by an overpowering rebel force, so that less than two hundred of the Twenty-seventh actually participated in the battles and siege of Lexington from Sept. 12 to Sept. 20, 1861. These men, however, were at the front, and led by their brave officers, fought Price's advance, themselves forming Mulligan's rear guard all the way from Georgetown, *via* Warrensburg, to Lexington, a distance of sixty-five miles, without rest or rations, and without dismounting a man, except those who were killed and wounded in the repeated and sharp engagements. When the heroic Mulligan fortified Lexington in order to hold it, as he was directed to do, the Twenty-seventh were stationed, with the Thirteenth and Fourteenth Missouri and the First Illinois Cavalry, on the bluff overlooking the river, while the Twenty-third Illinois Infantry occupied the works surrounding the college. The most desperate hand-to-hand fighting then ensued around these works, between the little band of less than three thousand Union soldiers, every man a hero, and Price's army of more then twenty thousand men. For eight days and nights, without cessation, this unequal contest raged. It was terminated at last by the capture of the brave Mulligan and his devoted men, through the cowardice of an officer who did *not* belong to either the Twenty-seventh, Thirteenth or Fourteenth Missouri, the First Illinois Cavalry or the Twenty-third Illinois Infantry, who, without any orders, ran up a white flag, and let the enemy into a commanding position inside of the works. No better fighting was ever done by any soldiers, in any war, than by the Twenty-seventh at Lexington. Of its officers, Col. Grover and Capt. McCluney received mortal wounds, from which Col. Grover died in St. Louis on the 31st of October, 1861, and Capt. McCluney at his home in Johnson county afterwards. Captains Duncan, Maguire, Parker and Applegate were all wounded, and about one-half of the command were either killed or wounded in this siege. Long before the surrender, the whole force had been completely surrounded and cut off from water, so that, when Col. Grover fell, never to rise again, in the thickest of the fight, on the afternoon of September 20, he had been continuously on duty and in the battle for sixty consecutive hours, during all of which time not a morsel of food nor a drop of water had passed his lips.

While their brave comrades were thus being overpowered at Lexington, Col. Eads, in command of the remaining seven companies of the Twenty-seventh, formed the advance guard of Veatch's brigade of Hovey's division of the army of the west, afterwards the frontier, then being organized, and marched to Lamine bridge, near Otterville, where it was encamped. Col. Eads was detailed as Post Commander at Syracuse, and Major Beck sent to Sedalia, leaving Capt. Isaminger in command of the regiment.

There were, at this time, two splendid divisions of Indiana Infantry with Cockifair's Battery of four twelve-pound Napoleon guns, all under the command of Col. Jeff. C. Davis, at the Lamine bridge. The regimental officers were such men as Cols. Davis, Veatch, Hovey and Benton, who afterwards rose to high rank in the service. With these were the seven companies of the Twenty-seventh, under Col. Eads, well drilled, mounted and equipped, and thoroughly familiar with the country, the whole command numbering nearly eight thousand men. That these troops would have raised the siege at Lexington and defeated Price, there can be no question. So eager were they to go that their officers could scarcely restrain them. Major Foster, at the head of the Fremont Scouts, drove in the enemy's pickets on the Warrensburg road, close to Lexington, a week before the surrender, and sent one of his men, Frank Johnson, of Warrensburg, into the entrenchments with a message to Col. Mulligan concealed in the sole of his shoe. Johnson went in and out safely, and brought a message back in the same manner from Mulligan to Fremont, stating that he, Mulligan, was surrounded by an overwhelming force, but was "holding the fort," as ordered, and would do so until overpowered, and calling for immediate re-inforcements.

Major Foster took that message to St. Louis, and was turned away from the door of Fremont's headquarters by his Hungarian guard, to whom the English language was an unknown tongue. He then hunted up Col. Frank P. Blair, who was an intimate friend of Col. Grover, and the two were finally admitted to Gen. Fremont's presence, and the whole situation laid before him.

Col. Davis, on the 16th, sent two scouting parties of the Twenty-seventh, under the command of Capt. Foster and Lieut. Box, from Lamine bridge to see if the roads to Lexington were clear. Foster chased in the enemy's pickets five miles from Lexington, on the Sedalia road, and Box did the same thing on the River road, and both returned on the morning of the 18th to Sedalia, and reported those facts to Col. Davis. Davis almost burnt the telegraph wire down with repeated messages to Fremont, beseeching him for marching orders, yet they never came. Had they been issued as late as the 18th, the siege would have been raised, and Mulligan saved on the morning of the 20th beyond a doubt, as the surrender did not take place until late in the afternoon of that day. This useless sacrifice of these brave men at Lexington is a stain upon the military record of John C. Fremont that time will never efface.

The distance between Lamine bridge and Lexington was only sixty-five miles. The roads were in good condition, and the country abounded with ample supply of both food and forage. Blair, who up to this time had been the friend of Fremont, now became his relentless foe. The speech of Blair in Congress, entitled: "Fremont's one hundred days in Missouri," aroused the country and drove Fremont from power. It has no rival in English literature, except the great arraignment of Warren Hastings, by Edward Burke, in the English Parliament. The survivors at Lexington in the Twenty-seventh could not be exchanged at that early day, so their services were lost to that regiment.

Col. Eads was then assigned to duty as Post Commander at Georgetown, and the regiment remained in the field under Major Beck and Capt. Isaminger, taking part in the vainglorious march and inglorious retreat of Fremont from Sedalia to Springfield and return. No one in the army or out of it were more heartily rejoiced over the downfall of Fremont than the remnant of the gallant Twenty-seventh, when that news reached them on the road between those two places.

The Fremont Scouts were engaged in a number of brilliant fights with the enemy in the Fall of 1861. They met the Whitley family of guerrillas, in a hand-to-hand set to, on Clear Fork, and completely routed them, driving them into Henry county in wild confusion. In this fight Morris Foster's horse ran away with him, causing him to outrun his comrades, and overtake and capture the Rebel Captain, who was acting as rear guard for his retreating companions. They went to the relief of Col. Hough at the California ford, west of Warrensburg, riding the forty-two miles from Sedalia to that place in less than six hours, and rescued that brave officer, after he had received a disabling wound and had been completely surrounded by a superior force. Foster, with ten of them, captured Col. Lewis, a Confederate officer on recruiting service, and fifteen of his men, at Holden, and brought the whole party safely into our lines. They joined forces with a squadron of the First Missouri Cavalry under Major Henry J. Stierlein, and recaptured 1,200 cattle belonging to a government train, the wagons having been burned before their arrival, rescued the guard, put the guerrillas engaged in the affair to flight after a sharp encounter, in which Dave Greenlee, a former resident of Warrensburg, was killed, and drove the herd overland to Fort Leavenworth, there turning over to the United States quartermaster at that post 1440 head of work oxen in tip-top condition.

The remainder of the regiment fought guerrillas, from the Missouri to the Osage rivers, almost every day in the week. In December, 1861, it took part in the Pope expedition, and participated in the engagement at Milford, where a part of two of its companies (Isaminger's and Foster's), with four companies of regular United States Cavalry, under Col. J. C. Davis, and without either infantry or artillery support, surprised and captured a recruiting camp of 1300 rebels, under Col. Alexander, and marched the whole of that long line under guard to Sedalia, sleeping most of the time on the bare ground in the snow, with the temperature near zero.

In this campaign Capt. Foster, with seventeen men of Company C of the Twenty-seventh, attacked a picket of thirty-three Confederates near Bear Creek, on the Sedalia road, one night, and chased them more than three miles to the outskirts of Warrensburg, killing five and wounding several more, without the loss of a man. He surprised the "Johnnies" around their camp fire, and they fled pell-mell into town at the first fire, with the report that Pope's whole army was coming and not far away.

Col. Clarkson (Confederate) had 1500 men at Warrensburg, but he immediately struck out for Rose Hill, and thus escaped capture by Pope's advance guard, who were moving up the Fort Scott road, some twelve miles south of Warrensburg. Instead of receiving any credit for this exploit, Foster was sharply reprimanded for flushing the game before it could be bagged. But if the First Cavalry on the Fort Scott road had moved as promptly according to orders as Foster did, Clarkson would have been surely captured at Warrensburg.

Upon its return to Sedalia the regiment was ordered to Benton Barracks, St. Louis. Upon its arrival there it found Gen. W. T. Sherman in command. This great soldier was temporarily shelved, because in an unguarded moment he had said that it would require a force of 600,000 men to suppress the rebellion. There, on the 27th of January, 1862, the remnant of the Twenty-seventh Missouri was mustered out. So continuous and severe had been its service since April, 1861, that only 469 men answered to their names on the muster-out roll, as the remaining 531 had been killed, wounded or captured while serving in the field and at the front.

The subsequent military history of the men who formed this splendid regiment is worthy of note. Four full companies, all from the Twenty-seventh, were recruited by Major Foster at Warrensburg, in January, February and March, 1862 and commanded by Capts. T. W. Houts, M. U. Foster, Maguire and Box, and Lieuts. Jewell, Peak, W. L. and A. W. Christian, Marr, Maguire and Daly, served in the Seventh Cavalry M. S. M. for three years, fighting constantly and bravely in the field. Part of them, led by the heroic Foster, were at Lone Jack in August, 1862, in one of the bloodiest and hardest fights, for the numbers engaged, of the whole war.

Capt. Duncan and Lieuts. Shanks and Chester recruited another detachment from the Twenty-seventh, which enlisted in the Fiftieth E. M. M. and did good service. Lieuts. Van

Beek and Burnett, afterwards Major Van Beek and Capt. Burnett, with another portion, entered Company A, of the Thirty-third Mo. Volunteers, and served with distinction in the Sixteenth Army Corps, under Gen. A. J. Smith, at Vicksburg, Helena, Red River Expedition, Franklin, Nashville, and finally at the capture of Mobile in 1865. Capt. or Col. Isaminger of the Sixty-third Illinois, as he was then, was in Libby Prison when Richmond fell, in April, 1865, and was one of the last officers set free there by Gen. Weitzel. With him marched to the sea, Capts. Starkey and Short and many brave boys of the old Twenty-seventh.

Other large detachments served on the plains in the Thirteenth and Fourteenth Mo. Cavalry, under Capt. Turley and Lieut. W. L. Christian, until 1866, and others in Tennessee in the Forty-fifth and Forty-eighth Mo. Infantry, under Capt. Faulke and Col. Blodgett, in 1865.

Another large detachment, after having served for three years from the Cumberland to the Gulf, returned to Warrensburg in 1864 in time to enlist in Foster's Cavalry Battalion, then recruited there, and under Capts. Foster, Grover, Parman and Fisher, and Lieuts. Creek, Bird, Reavis, Allen, Marshall, Bondurant and Fisher, joined Jennison's Brigade of Blunt's Division of the Army of the Border, and served in that historic campaign and aided in driving their ancient enemy, Gen. Sterling Price, from the state, and in the defeat and capture of Gen. Marmaduke's Division at Mine Creek, and thus once more received honorable mention for "coolness under fire and bravery in action."

Time has thinned and is thinning the ranks of this noble command, so that few now remain, and those few are scattered far and wide, and may never all meet again on earth.

Cols. Eads and Grover, Capts. Duncan, McCluney, Applegate and Parker, and Lieuts. Van Beek, Jewell, Daly and many others have long ago crossed the "shining river," and now await their reunion with their brave and beloved comrades of the Twenty-seventh in heaven, to part nevermore.

Comrades of the Potomac, we share with you your just pride in your glorious achievements, but may we not remind you that your last and greatest Commander, U. S. Grant, served with us in Missouri long before you followed him to victory. While Ohio claims the world's greatest soldier as her son, and Illinois as her citizen, may we not all say,

> "When asked what State he hails from,
> Our sole reply will be,
> He comes from Appomattox,
> And its famous apple tree."

Comrades of the Cumberland, the names of some of Missouri's best and bravest are on your rolls, and we revere with you the name of Geo. H. Thomas, Virginia's greatest soldier since Washington, the one Union general who never disobeyed an order, or made a mistake, whose fame will ever increase,

> "'Till the sun grows cold,
> 'Till the stars are old,
> And the leaves of the judgment book unfold."

Comrades of the Tennessee, we are of near "kin" to you. Our own matchless Sherman was a Missouri soldier, for his first volunteer command, the Thirteenth Regulars, was recruited in St. Louis and accredited to this state. He sleeps his last sleep in Calvary Cemetery in St. Louis, overlooking the "Father of Waters," surrounded by all that is mortal of Blair, Harding, Hassendeubel, Boomer, Cornyn, and a host of other Missouri heroes, who followed him from Donelson to the sea.

Comrades of the Gulf, the Stonewall Jackson of the Union army, brave old A. J. Smith, still lives, an honored citizen of St. Louis, his eye still as bright and his step as firm, despite the weight of seventy-five years, as when he checked the rebel advance with a Missouri brigade, and saved the day at Pleasant Hill.

Comrades of the Shenandoah, your beloved Sheridan, the greatest cavalry commander the world has yet seen, served with us in the army of the frontier before you knew him and ere his star had risen.

Comrades of the Frontier and the Border, we of the Missouri Cavalry belong to you evermore, as side by side with you, under Curtis, Blunt, Herron, Steele, and Davidson, we fought with Hindman, Price, Van Dorn, Marmaduke, Shelby, Fagan and Standwatie, for four long and weary years, until all the pathways between the Missouri and the Arkansas rivers were as familiar to us as the bronzed faces in our lines.

Comrades of the regular army, your present heroic commander, John M. Schofield, entered the volunteer service from Missouri in 1861, and won his first promotion by gallant service, as Major of the immortal First Missouri Light Artillery, on the battle field of Wilson's Creek.

Comrades of the navy, it was that noble patriot, James B. Eads, of St. Louis, the great engineer, who built the gunboats Osage, Carondelet and St. Louis, whose timely aid turned defeat into victory at Shiloh, and who met the dauntless Farragut at Port Hudson, and thus opened the Mississippi to the Gulf.

Survivors of the Twenty-seventh, so near and dear to me, let us, some time in the near future, form a regimental organization to perpetuate forever the memory of the heroes who served with us, and to whom it was not given to see the glorious end of our struggle.

"Theirs the cross and ours the crown."

Ladies, in my dreams I sometimes see a marble shaft arise in the beautiful cemetery in this city, bearing an inscription like this:

"To the memory of the Union soldiers of Johnson county, Missouri, who died that this nation might live forever free."

I believe that some day you will build it, and that then will be said of it, as was so fitly spoken long ago of a similar monument,

"Let it rise till it meet the sun in his coming; let the earliest rays of the morning gild it, and parting day linger and play on its summit."

REPORT OF THE COMMITTEE ON OLD LANDMARKS.

The Telegraph Line Through Jefferson County.

The first telegraph line in Missouri and west of the Mississippi river ran through Jefferson county, but it has been out of commission so long only a few people in the county know it ever existed. The electric telegraph is not old. The first message sent over such a wire, for any distance at least, was sent from Baltimore to Washington, in 1844, by Prof. S. F. B. Morse, which was: "See what God hath wrought." McMaster, in his school history, speaking of the telegraph, says: "Samuel F. B. Morse got his patent in 1837, and for seven years, helped by Alfred Vail, he struggled on against poverty. In 1842 he had but 37 cents in the world. But perseverence conquered all things, and with $30,000 granted by congress the first telegraph line in the world was built in 1844 from Baltimore to Washington." Congress hesitated long before acting. Morse traveled all over Europe to raise money to test his invention without avail. It took him seven years to convince congress that intelligence could successfully be sent by electric wire, but it finally made the appropriation, and when that message went over the Baltimore-Washington line the problem was solved and arrangements were soon made to erect telegraph wires in all directions from Washington City.

In 1845 the wire extended to Jersey City, on the Hudson river, and on the 22d day of December, 1847, it reached East St. Louis, but as wires could not then be made to work under water messages had to be carried across the river in boats. This was ten years before the railroad reached East St. Louis.

In October, 1850, the line was extended into St. Louis by submerged wire across the Mississippi. The year 1850 is an epochal year for the history of Missouri. This year saw telegraphic connection between St. Louis and all cities east, and it was that year that Thomas Allen, John O'Fallon and others organized the St. Louis and Pacific Railroad Company (now the Missouri Pacific), and the construction of the first railroad west of the Mississippi was made certain.

THE FIRST TELEGRAPH LINE IN MISSOURI.

It was also in 1850 that the first telegraph line was constructed and put in operation west of the Mississippi. A company known as "The St. Louis and New Orleans Telegraphy Company," constructed lines to Nashville, Tenn., and thence to New Orleans, south, and to Paducah, Cape Girardeau, Ste. Genevieve and St. Louis on the north. Tol. P. Schaffner of Kentucky was president of the company, and D. A. Given, Adam Rankin, L. M. Flournoy, J. W. Jones, S. A. Sawyer, R. Sturtivant, Isaac M. Veitch and Joseph Powell were the directors. Several of these directors were of St. Louis. The work on this line in Missouri was begun probably in the winter or spring of 1850, and was superintended by Dr. John Lee of Ste. Genevieve. The line from Cape Girardeau to St. Louis followed the old King's Trace with only an occasional divergence from it. It ran by Perryville and Ste. Genevieve and entered Jefferson county at Mead's farm on Isle au Bois creek, and ran thence along the King's Trace route by Judge Howe's, the old Horine farm, now owned by John Thompson, to Gamel's place, west of Festus. At the latter place the line diverged from the King's Trace and ran by Charles G. Warne's and David Bryant's to Dr. Clarke's and thence through the present site of Pevely to the old State Road, or King's Trace, at Joshua Herrington's house, and from there along the same road by way of Sulphur Springs and the Paul Franklin place, subsequently J. G. Crow's, just west of Windsor Harbor, where the first Sulphur Springs postoffice was kept, to St. Louis, crossing the Joachim west of the bridge at Bryant's place, and the Meramec at the Lower Ferry.

The wires of this line were attached very largely to trees instead of poles, as growing timber in abundance was found along almost the entire line.

The superintendent, Dr. Lee, married a sister of Dr. Clarke, very much against the latter's consent, and in 1856 he was living in the Stone House at Plattin Rock. Lee and Miss Clarke eloped to marry, and this enraged Dr. Clarke so much he sought Lee out and they had a personal altercation, the particulars of which are not known to this committee.

First Message West of the Mississippi.

July 27, 1850, the first message by electric telegraph was sent over this line from St. Louis, via Ste. Genevieve, Cape Girardeau, Paducah and Nashville to New Orleans.

The company that constructed that line was not incorporated in Missouri till March 3, 1851, when a special act of the legislature was passed for that purpose, the above parties being named as incorporators. This company had, prior to the latter date, been chartered by the states of Kentucky and Tennessee. The annual meetings of the company were to be "held at Paducah, Kentucky, or at such other places as may be determined on from time to time." On the same day (March 3, 1851), the Missouri legislature passed an act to incorporate a company to "erect a telegraph line from St. Louis to Jefferson City, Boonville, Lexington, Weston and St. Joseph, and a lateral connecting with Brunswick, Glasgow, Columbia and Fulton, and such other towns on or near the Missouri river, as Schaffner and Veitch (the sole incorporators), may elect." The act recites these men "had acquired, or may acquire, from Prof. Samuel F. B. Morse the right to use his electro-magnetic telegraph, chemical or printing-telegraph system, by him invented and patented."

On the same day (March 3, 1851), "The Santa Fe, New Mexico, and Missouri Telegraph Company" was incorporated by an act of the Missouri legislature, Tol. P. Schaffner and his associates being named as incorporators to "erect a line of telegraph connecting with the great St. Louis and Missouri river telegraph line at or near Independence, in this state."

The stock of these companies was not limited, and that held by the citizens of Missouri was to be exempt from taxation until the company paid dividends, thus throwing the door to watering stock wide open. But the people of that period had to grant all sorts of privileges and exemptions to get capitalists to invest their money in public utilities of this sort. Sixty years ago we patted men with money on the back and by that means through the past we induced them to invest their means to build up the country and push the frontier line farther and farther to the west, until that line entirely disappeared from the map of our country. The policy of 1851 has been reversed and now we call the large owners of the stocks of all public utilities all sorts of vile names, and constantly throw obstacles in their way in the use of the utilities they have already constructed, which has brought a halt in the construction of more, and still we are not happy.

July 27, 1850.

This day ought to be a memorable one in the history of Jefferson county, of Missouri and all the trans-Mississippi states, the noblest portion of our national domain. We of Jefferson county especially ought to inscribe that epochal date in golden letters in our records, public and private. But we, with the whole country, have forgotten if we ever knew it. We celebrate the days of the great battles of our country, in some of which brothers drenched the land in fraternal blood, but no one mentions July 27, 1850, the day on which the greatest civilizing agency of the world was installed west of the Mississippi. The message sent from St. Louis to New Orleans that day marked in silence the triumph of man over distance and intervening space—marked the triumph of science over matter. That day was a peaceful one. The roar of cannon, the rattle of musketry, the clash of swords, the wild cries of the wounded and dying, the heart wails of widows and sisters and parents, were not heard; and yet we have forgotten the great event of that day and that epoch. Why is it man is so prone to celebrate bloody battles, and erect costly monuments to military heroes, and forget and remit to oblivion the silent triumphs of science over matter and space? Who cares for Dr. Lee, who put up that wire at least through Jefferson county, or for Tol. P. Schaffner and his colleagues, who financed the enterprise? Or who cares much for Prof. Morse, the father of the electro-magnetic telegraph? These men were pioneers in telegraphy, and behold today what their efforts have brought to the world! The telegraph penetrates every nook and corner of our broad land, and of all civilized lands. Ocean cables, so far as the transmission of messages for business or pleasure or love is concerned, have abolished the waters that cover three-fourths of the earth's surface, and the wireless telegraph system has almost blotted out distance and space on land and sea. The telephone has become such a common medium of communication between neighbor and neighbor, business man and business man, and between states and cities, that it has long since ceased to be a wonder. Electricity is doing a large part of the work of the world. But, alas, we let the day come and go unnoticed.

The Only Memorial of the St. Louis-Ste. Genevieve Telegraph Line.

The only memorial of this line anywhere in this state is "The Telegraph School House," a short distance from Judge Madison's farm on the Plattin.

When the Illinois Central Railroad was finished from Chicago to the Ohio river the telegraph line from St. Louis to Cape Girardeau disappeared from the map, which was about 1857 or 1858, or it may be earlier.

Since the above was written the committee has been informed by Judge Charles that his wife thinks the Lee who put up the wires of the telegraph through Jefferson county in 1850 was not the same Lee who married Dr. Clarke's sister. The committee has a letter from Mr. Jewett, in which he says he had interviewed Mr. John M. Bailey on the history of that old telegraph line, and he then goes on to say that the Lee who put up the wires and the one who married Dr. Clarke's sister was the same, though he does not say he got that information from Mr. Bailey. It may be he got that item from Dr. Lee himself, for he says when he came to Plattin Rock in 1856 Dr. Lee was then living in the Stone House there.

So far as the committee can learn no telegraph office on the St. Louis and Ste. Genevieve telegraph line was ever kept within the borders of Jefferson county, due probably to the fact that it ran through no town in our county and there was no demand for such an office to justify its establishment and maintenance.

JOHN L. THOMAS,
Sept. 27, 1912. Chairman.

SKETCHES OF LIVINGSTON COUNTY.

No. 4.

In previous papers relating to the early history of Livingston county, its pioneer settlers, the location of Chillicothe as the county seat, and other towns then existing or afterwards laid out and founded, nothing was said about the administration of justice in the courts as then constituted.

It may here be observed that the first term of the circuit court was held at the residence of Joseph Cox, about four miles north of the present site of Chillicothe, on Monday, July 5, 1837, Judge Austin A. King of Ray County (afterwards governor), presiding, with Thomas R. Bryan, clerk; W. O. Jennings, sheriff; E. Pearl, deputy clerk, and Thomas C. Burch, prosecuting attorney. The second term was held at Cox's on Tuesday, November 7, 1837, and the July term, 1838, was held at Chillicothe, the established county seat. At the April term, 1839, Thomas C. Burch having received his appointment and commission from Governor Lilburn W. Boggs, took his seat as judge, but in December following was succeeded by James A. Clark of Chariton county, B. F. Stringfellow being the prosecuting attorney for the circuit.

Judge Clark continued in office until about the year 1860, when the judicial district was changed and Livingston county passed into the new circuit composed of Davies and adjacent counties, and at the ensuing election James McFerran of Gallatin was chosen judge of the new circuit, and continued in office till the end of his term in 1866. His successors in office in regular order were Jonas J. Clark, E. J. Broaddus (late of the Kansas City Court of Appeals), James M. Davis, who resigned after several years service, and Judge Broaddus was appointed by Governor Francis to fill the vacancy, afterwards elected for a full term when Joshua W. Alexander of Gallatin, Missouri (now member of Congress), became judge, who was succeeded by Francis M. Trimble (recently elected a member of the Kansas City Court of Appeals). Judge Arch. B. Davis, the present incumbent becoming his successor.

In 1852, when the writer located at Chillicothe, JamesA. Clark was still judge of the circuit. He was a brother of Gen. John B. Clark of Howard county, a distinguished lawyer, and member of Congress from his district for two or three terms prior to the war. The judicial district at that time embraced the counties of Livingston, Chariton, Linn, Sullivan, Putman, Mercer and Grundy. The judge in his rounds over the circuit was accompanied by many of the lawyers from the different counties, following the custom to "ride the circuit," as observed by the pioneer Methodist preachers of that day.

Judge James A. Clark (long on the bench of that circuit), was an able and upright jurist. He was not, however, extensively learned as a lawyer. He had read but few law books, but these he had studied well, and with his strong common sense and practical knowledge of men and affairs, he was well enough equipped to dispense justice with an even hand and gave general satisfaction. Few cases tried before him were appealed, and rarely were his rulings reversed. His dockets, however, in Livingston county were not burdened with cases, and the terms rarely continued a week, usually lasting two or three days. The litigation was light, and did not involve large amounts. The criminal cases usually involved minor offenses, such as horse racing, betting at cards, and now and then a case of homicide.

The county was still sparsely settled and the people in the main were law-abiding and ever ready to lend a helping hand in ferreting out and bringing to justice offenders of every description.

In 1852 (when the writer came to Chillicothe), William Y. Slack, William C. Samuel, and J. H. B. Manning, were the resident attorneys. Slack, (during the war was a confederate general, and was killed in the battle of Pea Ridge), located in the county soon after its organization in 1837, coming from Boone county, where he was raised and educated. As a lawyer he was honest, attentive to business and had the confidence of the community in which he had cast his lot. He was an active and useful citizen, sparing no pains and begrudging no sacrifice for the development and progress of the county of his choice.

W. C. Samuel located in Chillicothe about the year 1848, and closed a long life only two or three years ago. As a lawyer he was in some respects rather unique, endowed with good native ability, sound judgment, and good memory, he became a good and safe lawyer, and by his practice was enabled to support a large family, and strange to say that during his long practice he was never known to make or attempt to make a speech to court or jury. He was essentially a counselor at law, and his brethren of the bar often consulted him, and were pleased to have him in their cases as advisory counsel.

J. H. B. Manning (as I believe), never engaged in the regular and orderly study of the law, but his native tact, shrewdness, and intimate acquaintance with men, enabled him to achieve reasonable success in the line of his practice.

At the time indicated (1852), the largest part of the business intrusted to the lawyers consisted of mercantile collections. There being no banks and the retail merchants usually buying their goods on time, the result was that overdue paper was, in the first instance, placed in the hands of lawyers for collection, and the lawyer receiving such collections reaped a harvest that now goes to the local banks, and only the claims that the banks now fail to realize on are turned over to lawyers for suit.

Outside of such collections the business then was confined to cases of minor importance, and the fees coming to the lawyers were small. It then required but little knowledge of the law besides the statutes to conduct the cases in court, and when this knowledge was lacking, attorneys had recourse to their native resources, and their cases were won by methods not laid down in the books or sanctioned by the better ethics of the profession.

This is illustrated by one of the earliest cases in which the writer appeared after coming to Chillicothe. One, Sidney Kilgore, had been committed to jail charged with horse stealing, and awaiting action of the grand jury at the ensuing term of the circuit court. Manning, attorney for the prisoner, apprehensive that his client would have no chance for acquittal on a regular trial in court, concluded that his only show of success lay in a resort to the writ of habeas corpus. The writ was accordingly issued by George Pace, presiding justice of the county court, and on full hearing it became quite apparent that the prisoner would be committed to jail, but Manning was equal to the emergency. Anticipating an adverse decision, he arranged to have a horse tied to the court house fence, and he instructed his client, at the crucial moment to slip out at the door or through a window, mount the horse and make good his escape. The instructions so given was carried out to the letter, and Kilgore left for parts unknown.

Another case illustrating the course of justice in those days was one where the aid of lawyers was dispensed with altogether.

About a mile south of Spring Hill, a small town some eight miles northwest of Chillicothe, a resident citizen by the name of William Avery was waylaid and shot down by a neighbor named Samuel Husher. It was a case of cold-blooded and deliberate murder, and was the culmination of a feud previously existing in the neighborhood. The attending circumstances strongly pointed to Husher as the guilty party, and the evidence disclosed before the examining court established his guilt beyond a reasonable doubt. Husher was charged with the killing, and he was arrested and brought before two justices of Jackson township, Pepper and Lewis, as the examining court, or as it turned out to be, the *trial court*. Without warrant of law, a jury of twelve men were empanelled and sworn to try the case. From a list of twenty-four men the prisoner was allowed to select twelve men as the jury to try his case, and to conduct his own defense. He had sent a courier to Chillicothe to procure counsel; accordingly the writer accompanied by Charley H. Mansur and Col. R. S. Moore, hastened to the rescue, but on our arrival, at the scene of action, the trial was already in progress, and we were advised that neither the court or assembled crowd would permit lawyers to appear or interfere in any way with the proceedings then on hand. The verdict of the jury was, "Guilty, death by hanging within the next twenty-four hours." This sentence was carried out the next morning and the accused accordingly hanged at or near Simpson's Spring on the east side of town. The leading actors in this mob transaction were afterwards indicted, but owing to the disturbed conditions incident to the war, they were never tried, and finally discharged.

A notable case of the miscarriage of justice was that of the State against Henry Martin.

William Gordon, a well-to-do farmer living about seven miles northeast of Chillicothe, was killed by Henry Martin on the 6th day of April, 1858. They were both farmers and neighbors living a few miles north of Chillicothe. On the fatal day they were both in town. Gordon late in the evening left for home accompanied by Thomas Musselman. Martin, with one Sapp, followed soon after and overtook Gordon a mile out from town. They were all on horse back. An altercation at once ensued, when Martin dismounted, and drawing a revolver, shot Gordon from his horse, killing him instantly. Martin went on home. That night he was arrested by the sheriff, taken to Chillicothe and lodged in jail. The next day a preliminary examination was held before a justice of the peace and Martin was retained in custody to await further proceedings at the ensuing term of the circuit court. A day or two afterward the committing magistrate, on information that the Chillicothe jail was unsafe, ordered that the prisoner be taken to the Linneus jail for safe keeping. Thither C. H. Mansur, then a young attorney (and who had appeared for Martin at the preliminary hearing), accompanied the sheriff, and on arrival there, no time was lost in suing out a writ of habeas corpus before Judge French of the county court. Mansur in connection with Jacob Smith, a resident attorney, presented the application, claiming defect and irregularities in the papers made out by the justice, and on an *ex parte* hearing, Martin was released, and mounting a horse already provided by his friends made good his escape from the state. The people of Chillicothe were aroused to a high pitch of indignation. A mass meeting was at once called. Speeches were made and resolutions passed strongly denouncing what they considered a travesty on justice. The whereabouts of Martin were kept concealed, and I believe that it is not known to this day where he went or may now be found.

From 1837 (the date of organization), up to the year 1858, there were few homicides committed in the county, but after that such cases became of frequent occurrence. It would, however, extend these papers to unreasonable length to enter into full details and it must here suffice to note the cases as they occurred, omitting a full narrative of the facts involved in each particular case.

On the 19th of April, 1853, Joseph Slagle killed Benjamin Collins, his brother-in-law. Slagle's fifth wife was a sister of Collins. Slagle was indicted, tried, and acquitted on the ground of self defense. Gen. John B. Clarke of Howard county conducted his defense. The trial was had at the October term 1854 of the circuit court.

September 6, 1864, D. Morrison was killed at the military hospital by Frank Bradford and others.

On September 4, 1865, Jacob Crouch shot George Cross in Bell & Coopers saloon in Chillicothe.

A negro named Sam was shot and killed by Jourdan a short distance east of Spring Hill on January 27, 1866. Sam had served in the Federal army, and Jourdan as a Confederate soldier.

December 24, 1867, W. H. Dudley, a constable, shot a young man named Thomas M. Bayles under arrest for stealing clothes, and in an attempt to escape.

September 23, 1872, Thomas Fox killed Thomas K. Conn in Hale's saloon, Chillicothe. This was the result of a feud previously existing. Fox was indicted, tried and acquitted on the ground of self-defense.

In the southern part of the county, and on August 14, 1875, Thomas Florence was killed by George F. Bell. Bell was indicted and acquitted in the circuit court of Carroll county where the case had been taken by change of venue.

On the 10th day of September, 1876, Henry Gamble was killed by John A. Wingo at Caldwell's house in Spring Hill. Wingo was indicted and tried in the circuit court, January 25, 1877, and the verdict of the jury was ten years in the penitentiary. Wingo appealed to the supreme court and the judgment of the circuit court was reversed, and a new trial awarded. On the second trial Wingo was again convicted of murder in the second degree with a ten year's sentence in the penitentiary, but Judge Broaddus, before whom the case was tried, granted a new trial. The case was then continued from term to term, until under the law, the prisoner was entitled to, and had to be discharged.

On October 6, 1877, Jesse Offield killed his cousin, Newton J. Eads. In May, 1878, Offield was tried and convicted of murder in the second degree and sentenced to fifteen years in the penitentiary. Judge Broaddus set the verdict aside and in February, 1879, the case was again tried and the evidence tended to show guilt of murder in the first degree, and under the instruction of the court, the jury returned a verdict of acquittal.

December 25, 1883, Green Shepherd was stabbed to death at a negro dance in Chillicothe by Lewis Waller, who was tried and convicted of murder in the second degree and sentenced to the penitentiary for 99 years.

For thirty-five years, and during the writer's residence in Chillicothe, only one case is remembered in which there was a conviction for murder in the first degree by regular trial in the circuit court, and this was the case of the State against one Adams. A man by the name of Mathias, coming from Ohio a few years previously, bought a farm on the Trenton road, and about one mile north of the town of Farmersville. He was a quiet man, and highly respected in his community, and doing well on his farm. One night about 11 o'clock some one knocked at the door and informed him that a wagon was mired down a short distance from his house, and that his help was needed. Mathias, suspecting nothing wrong, immediately dressed himself, and hurried to the place indicated. He found no wagon and at once some one of the crowd opened fire upon him and killed him on the spot. The circumstances of the case were mysterious. A thorough search was made by officers and neighbors of the murdered man for some days, but without result, until finally after the lapse of two or three weeks, facts came to light that pointed strongly to a young man of the neighborhood by the name of Adams as the guilty party. He was indicted and tried in the circuit court, and the jury returned a verdict of guilty of murder in the first degree, and sentence passed accordingly—the day for his execution being fixed. Adams was taken to jail, but while awaiting the day of execution he fell sick and died. He was vigorously prosecuted by Judge John Dixon (an old Ohio friend of Mathias, the murdered man), who aided the prosecuting attorney and his forceful speech in the case contributed much to the conviction of the accused.

On the 21st of June, 1873, a bold and daring attempt was made to rob the People's Savings Bank of Chillicothe, of which Major Sidney McWilliams was then the president. Smith Rambo, living across Grand River, and about eight miles south of Chillicothe, conceived and planned the raid. He lived on his farm and up to that time bore a fair reputation in his community. He called to his assistance three young men—Manso, Monroe, and Brunk. The latter was a schoolteacher and boarded at Rambo's. Being advised of the intended robbery, and of all the plans therefor, he notified McWilliams of the conspiracy and the night when the attack would be made. It was planned that Rambo on the evening fixed was to stop with a neighbor who lived near town as if on a friendly visit—then leaving, to meet his confederates at a designated spot about 11 o'clock at night and thence proceed to McWilliams' home north of the town limits, seize McWilliams, compel him to open the bank safe and thus accomplish the robbery. McWilliams, having been forewarned, made full preparations for defense. Seven men were stationed at his house, well armed; Joseph Cooper, cashier of the Bank, W. B. Leach, assistant cashier, W. H. Gaunt, Ben Grant, J. H. Ware, Major McWilliams, and a colored man then in the Major's employ. Other citizens were stationed outside, and in the vicinity. It was arranged by Rambo that Brunk was to act as spokesman when McWilliams appeared at the window upstairs in answer to Brunk's summons; Rambo came up to the front door and knocked. Brunk had gone inside through a raised window as it had been arranged. Rambo's knock at the door was the signal for the firing. The first shots came from the inside. The robbers returned the fire. Manso, and Monroe fled, but Rambo was shot down dead—three balls having entered his body. Manso and Monroe were indicted and plead guilty, and sentenced to the penitentiary for a term of years.

Major McWilliams in full appreciation of the kind services of Brunk as rendered in this affair, took him into his family, sent him to college and aided him in his preparation for the practice of law. On receiving his license, Brunk located in Neosho, Missouri, where he pursued his profession up to the time of his death some years ago.

Major McWilliams removed to Kansas City in 1873 or 1874, and after twenty years or more of active business departed this life some three years ago.

L. T. COLLIER.

SCHUYLER LETTERS.[1]

Geneva, Nov. 3d, 1831.

Friend Chum:

Life, as has justly been observed, is fraught with misery and woe. Such has been emphatically the condition of us for the last few weeks. Doolittle, I have again returned and with the promise that you would quickly return. The students are all eager and desirous for your return. Our old chumship I hope will not be dissolved. John Barker's earnest is for your return and I hope will soon be answered. Write soon and tell if the faculty have written for you.

I remain your friend,

MONTGOMERY SCHUYLER.

Note.—The above letter concerns the college life of Mr. Schuyler and his life-long friend, Judge James R. Doolittle, afterward a senator from Wisconsin. The college, of course, was located at Geneva, N. Y.

DUANE MOWRY.

Ovid, December 26, 1832.

My Dear Friend,

I must own that I have not followed the arrangement to write as soon as I was fairly settled at home, for time has slipped away faster than I was aware. But if I have not written it has not been because I have not thought of you. No, Doolittle, if ever there was one whom I could strictly call a friend, whom feelings and heart accorded so nearly with my own and whom from these circumstances I *must love, it is you.* Never will I forget, though time and space may intervene, though the cold-hearted world may tear from me every comfort and reduce me to the condition of the meanest beggar that roams through the world, "unnoticed and unknown," never

---

1. The following letters of Rev. Dr. Montgomery Schuyler, later of Christ Church, St. Louis, are from the collection of Duane Mowry, Milwaukee, Wis.

will I forget the pleasant, yes, the most pleasant days I ever enjoyed with you. My old chum, we have been participants for some time in the same pleasures in the same sorrows and we have experienced like misfortunes. It was a source of sorrow to be dismissed from college, considering that by the world we were thought idle and profligate, for we know it is very common, if the question is asked, was he ever dismissed from college? and it is answered in the affirmative to set that person down as a useless if not worse than useless member to (the) community. But with regard to myself it has, giving the above mentioned reason all its weight it has, though painful, still been beneficial. It has made me more active and diligent and caused me to resolve if it is in my power that Geneva College shall never be ashamed at least, if she is not proud, of classing me among her sons. I have often endeavored to ascertain in what I would be most likely to succeed should I pay all my attention and direct what little talents I have to that point. "Perseverantia vincit omnia" would then be my motto and if there was any truth in the maxim I would find it by experience. Chum, it is my opinion the laurel that Fame gives and the unfading wreath she weaves should not be despised and that none ought to stand quietly by who wish the prize without making an effort to obtain it. Fame, Fame, who would not labour to obtain thy reward. We cannot, no, we cannot obtain the ever-blooming laurel without climbing a steep and rugged way, without removing many an obstinate rock from our path. But as glittering, as precious, as may be the prize, yet I would not sacrifice my happiness to obtain it. As glorious, as immortal as may be the name of Byron, yet who would be willing to desert friends and home, or who would be willing to lead Byron's life to possess Byron's power. No, Glory is not always the reward of vice and unhappiness for virtue's path lead to her temple and among those who have become famous and still enjoyed that domestic happiness which ever attends virtue may be classed a Washington and a Henry. And I would ask you this question: Would you be willing to have another call Adelia's heart his own, to give up all claim to her affections and become wedded to ambition alone, for all the glory even of a Demosthenes or a Cicero? I can answer for you and I know it will be exactly your opinion—that all the world can bestow could not compensate me for Adelia's love. How long and how far distant the time seems before we can engage in the active business of life before we can enjoy all the happiness of seeing our most earnest desires fulfilled. Chum, you know my opinion well enough that the choice of a companion through life should not be the business of a few months. But I believe my choice is made and nothing shall change my purpose. To be sure it is a long time before the happy period can roll around, but to love and be beloved will sweeten its every moment. I think, I am almost sure, Sarah loves me, and to know that she sometimes thinks of me and perhaps, too, when I am thinking of her alone, will never fail to afford me real happiness. Yesterday as we were coming from church it happened that from some turn of the conversation my mother remarked to me that I had a good many years to make my choice in and that there was plenty time to think of such things "bime bye." Thinks I to myself, I have effected the work of many years in a short time and to my satisfaction. To be sure there are a great many things to render the fulfillment of my wishes uncertain. She may not always love me, (though this I can not believe unless I render myself unworthy of her love; unless I forget my duty to her, myself and friends.) Her friends may oppose it, for you know friends or those who *pretend* to be friends sometimes meddle with things that do not concern them, but from my friends, those whom I should wish and think it my duty to obey, I am afraid of no opposition. But should I be doomed to disappointment, should death mark her for his victim—O, is there a possibility of such an event? Can death lay his icy fingers on those bright eyes and close them forever; can he forbid that tongue to speak which has uttered naught but love and affection? My heart sickens at the thought. Should anything intervene thus to destroy my happiness one of two things remains, to yield at once to the keen dart of affliction or determine to acquire fame, reckless and careless of the miseries that attend its pursuit. For to love another I can not. It seems as impossible that there can be more than one object of love as it seems certain that fame can not be obtained without an effort. This is not the first time I have declared my opinion to you on this subject and it will be always the same. I can imagine you swelling through fields but yet the marks of a new settlement and having the wild appearance exactly suitable to my taste, or as wandering along the banks of that little fairy lake which you have so oft described to me, and enjoying (shall I say perfect happiness?). No, she does not accompany you. But I can imagine you somewhere else, seated by the side of her with whom your happiness resides and enjoying all the pleasure of her delightful conversation. But poor me, I am deprived of that happiness. All that I can do is to imagine the pleasure I might have received. She is not coming home this vacation, but she did not stay from her own wish. I can spend my time pleasantly at home, for my brothers and sisters and mother are all here, but would it not pass doubly pleasant was Sarah home also? You know it would. But I must dismiss this subject on which I could write for ages could my feelings find expressions for them. Even as young as I am my happiness depends on the success or failure of one single act. But to know that she loves me, of which I am almost certain, will add half to my present happiness. Yes, chum, she has a heart that would not despise even the exaggerated expressions which I have made use of in the course of this letter. That is exaggerated in the opinion of the cold-hearted for I know you would not call them so. What I have written were some to hear would be a source of ridicule, but I have too much confidence in your sincerity to think you would be so devoid of feeling. Perhaps this last sentence may lead you to doubt my confidence in you, but do not for a moment imagine it—never harbor such an idea. When you write tell me your feelings and express your opinion without the least degree of reserve. I have done so to you. I have unfolded my whole heart to you and will always do so whenever I write. I am certain your vacation thus far has been a pleasant one and no doubt will continue to be so. We had a very unpleasant ride home as it was cold and bad roads. By the way, we were six hours on the way. Write soon and believe me ever your constant friend

M. SCHUYLER.

Note.—A most interesting and confidential letter from one college chum to another—Schuyler to Doolittle.

DUANE MOWRY.

Ovid, Jan. 1834.

My Old Chum,

Though I believe you owe me a letter, yet I will not be ceremonious, especially as I wish you to do me a favor. Please send by the stage driver, directed to be left at "Eagle's Hotel, Ovid," my chemistry, mechanics, optics and Butler. And tell Geer, if you please, not to forget to bring my German books with him. Well, the miscellaneous business transacted, I will now proceed to other things. During the latter part of last term I could but notice in your actions toward me something like coldness, and I always felt a restraint in expressing my feelings freely, presuming that in the state of mind I then believed you in, an expression of them would not be *over grateful* to you. This my chum also noticed and we frequently talked together on this same subject. Perhaps you will recollect a remark I made in your room with respect to leaving, toward the close of last term (viz.), "that there were not so many friends to me in college as there once were." I would have told my suspicions to you then, but my pride revolted at the idea. I never will court anyone's favor and when I had almost come to the resolution of avowing my thoughts to you plainly, such ideas as these would be sure to insinuate themselves into my mind: "If he is tired of my friendship, though I truly regret the loss of such a friend as he once was, yet shall he never know it." "I will show that I can be as indifferent as he is." These were my feelings when I left at the close of last term. When I returned again you were not so distant, but more familiar, though that open familiarity, that unrestrained freedom, which once existed between us, was very far from being restored. Yet the attention was so great as to induce me as I have already done to tell you plainly my thoughts in the hopes that our former intimacy might be restored. Perhaps this opinion may have no foundation in reality. I hope it has not, yet I thought it my duty to express it so that there should be none of that mistrust existing between us which saps the very life's blood of friendship. Doolittle, we have separated perhaps never to spend any length of time again together. The many happy hours, days and nights we have passed in the same room have fled never more to be enjoyed. For this there would be some consolation were we certain that still we had like hours to spend together. Yes, Memory, as she wanders back into the past will often dwell with rapturous delight on those days as the fairest spots on the barren pathway of life. In old number 9 we have indeed been happy together, we were happy when, locked in each others' arms ,we told of those we loved, formed our plans for the future and in fancy were acting the scenes which we had just sketched in imagination. But I must close. Tell me, Doolittle, if your feelings towards me have ever been such as I have described. If not, forgive me for even entertaining such an opinion. I know to harbor such a thought is wrong, but suspicion, I fear, may be reckoned among my many disagreeable qualities. Write if you have time and send the letter with the books if not soon after I arrive at Union.

Your firm friend,
M. Schuyler.

Note.—This letter is postmarked, "Lodi, N. Y., Jan'y 24," evidently in 1834. It is directed to "James R. Doolittle, Geneva College, Geneva." We have no means of knowing the real significance of this letter. But it is thought that the friendship formed at college continued during the lives of these two admirable characters. Possibly, "suspicion" was one of the "disagreeable qualities" possessed by Mr. Schuyler. Nevertheless, there is a warmth of feeling manifest in this letter which is altogether too rare in college chums.

Duane Mowry.

Union College, May 15, 1834.

Dear Chum,

I have delayed too long answering your letter and I am afraid you will draw wrong conclusions from my silence. But little things ought not to affect a friendship laid too deep (I did hope) to be easily shaken. As to your resolution, which you mentioned as effecting so great a change in your actions, permit me to say a few things, and I shall say them with a view to your good though perhaps they may not deserve your attention. It is of importance for every young man to acquire a set of friends before going into the world on whose fidelity he can rely with perfect confidence. When thrown upon our own resources, no matter how much talent we possess, yet there is always a chain of circumstances binding us down which genius alone can never break. Friends then come in to our assistance; mere acquaintances are not enough and friends are only to be acquired by that mutual confidence which reposes trust and seeks it in return. In this way a friend becomes as it were a part of self and we almost by intention rush to his assistance when needed. Respect for talent is not sufficient to obtain what is called the favor of any one. Had you, Doolittle, told those whom you had considered your friends candidly your intention that you had determined to be more studious and that though you liked to receive visits from your friends, yet if they were not so frequent they would be more acceptable, I am sure they would have been as warmly your friends and would have done all in their power to give you opportunity for "solitary reflection" if you chose, by using their influence to dissuade others from visiting you too frequently. I can assure you my affection cooled greatly toward you during the last term as you seemed to avoid that reposing of confidence which *he who would* be my friend must observe towards me. I speak thus plainly because my pride was a little touched by your neglect. It may be my imagination presented the construction I put upon your conduct, yet I must say you seemed to part with Thompson with much more reluctance and a greater demonstration of affection than with me. But I'll not trouble myself with the thought. If you have altered your opinion of me I'll not shove myself upon your regard and will cut the tie that once bound us together, though I'd do it in sorrow not in anger. We once were intimate and you have read the secret emotions of my heart. I'll shut the page if you wish and we will be strangers to each other hereafter. But if this construction is incorrect only say it and we will again be more true and firmer friends than ever. There is one expression in your last letter I have read again and again, still the same feeling of doubt comes over me; it is this: "that there was a change in my actions towards you in private my feelings can *hardly* be persuaded to believe." As much as if you were to say I cannot tell whether my feelings would lead me to esteem you or not. But enough of this till you give me an explanation of your feelings. *Now* to me mine are those of friendship and esteem towards you. I would not be back to Geneva for any consideration. It has been the making of me coming here. Here you can feel yourself a man and act in accordance with your feelings. If you have talents and possess generous sentiments your society will be courted. Your resources are drawn out and as old Prex says, "College is a world in miniature in which you may learn how to mould your conduct when you go out into the world." We have a paper in opposition to the Parthenon and should you feel a disposition to write something for it we will receive it gladly. I wish you would conclude to take it. You may have the back numbers or commence the year with the next number. Try and see if you can get any one in college to take it. It is only $1.00 a year. Geer, Dick, Taber and Platt are all well pleased with old Union and only regret, as we all do, that we did not come before. Taber wishes you to send on his papers if you will. They all send their respects. Tell Bates and Smith I shall write to them very soon, and believe as ever,

Your firm friend,
M. SCHUYLER.

Thompson sends his respects and says he will write soon.

P. S.—Enclosed is $2 which I have shamefully neglected sending you before.
M. S.

St. Louis, April 28, 1866.

My dear old friend:

I have been watching your course in the Senate the past winter with a good deal of interest. I can assure you I am proud of the noble stand you have taken in supporting the President in his wise and conservative measures he has recommended and as far as he has been permitted, has carried out. It does seem to me that the honour and prosperity, if not the very life of the nation, depends upon his being sustained. I have no party predilections to influence my judgment. When I had anything to do with politics, I was an old Whig, and had, therefore, an *inherent dislike* to the Democratic party.

But in the present emergency, they seem to have taken the right position, and had I anything to do with public affairs now I should lay all prejudice aside and give them or whoever stands by the President my hearty support. We have had bitter and revengeful feelings enough among the people of the various sections of the country and it is time now that we should forget and forgive. In my humble sphere as a minister of Christ I try to preach and to practice this teaching.

I go over frequently and talk with Judge Bates, the former attorney-general, and we agree perfectly in the course which the President seems to have marked out. I love my country next to my God and desire her honour, peace and prosperity, and I can but believe that she has yet a glorious future before her. But in my humble estimation Sumner and Stevens are not the men to bear her onward in the right path. Nor do I believe that the people will sustain them.

I have written this letter as the outgush of my feelings and because I have vanity enough to believe that *even my good opinion* of your course would not be without its value.

Praying for God's blessing upon you and yours, I am, as ever, Truly your friend,

M. Schuyler.

St. Louis, April 13, 1889.

My Dear old friend:

Yours of the 11th just rec'd. I am sorry I can not recall the incident to which you refer. There certainly can be no objection in the mention of it, as the author need not give his authority, and your memory, as it naturally would be, would be very distinct on that point.

But the sentiment, "Liberty—Liberty," was eminently characteristic of you at that period of your life. I remember well your devotion to Jeffersonian Democracy. Thomas Jefferson, I might almost say, was your idol. This was one of the subjects on which we did not agree. I was a Whig, and I must say my opinions as far as I had any, inclined to Federalism, and to the extermination of the evils of slavery, as those of an institution not sinful "per se." But your opinions were decidedly Anti-Slavery, and your subsequent connection with the Republican party was what I would have anticipated.

I am happy to say that as I look back, your whole political course commends itself to me as one of which you may well be proud.

I am glad to hear that there is a volume of your speeches to be published and with it a sketch of your life.

I shall certainly procure a copy when published.

By the way, I believe our old friend, James Smith, will remember your *maiden speech*.

With cherished memories of our early friendship, and with the assurance that it has not grown cold, I am as ever,

Sincerely yours,
M. SCHUYLER.

HON'L JAS. R. DOOLITTLE.

FIRST THRESHING MACHINE ACROSS THE MOUNTAINS.

The first threshing machine ever transported across the plains by ox-train was taken across in 1859 by the freighting company of Russell, Majors & Waddell. It went via Old Oregon Trail to Fort Bridger, Wyoming, though it was then in the vast unorganized territory. Judge Carter, a government trader and contractor who owned a ranch near Bridger, had begun raising wheat on a scale too large for the old method of tramping out with oxen, and ordered a small separator and treadmill power of the "Groundhog" type. The separator was loaded on a freight wagon, and put in charge of William Grinstead, who had been wagon-master for this company of freighters for several years.

The machine was loaded at Leavenworth, Kansas, and presented a striking spectacle when the train was viewed from a distance. Freighters and immigrants who had taken the road on the opposite side of the Platte river came across at the first opportunity to see whether or not it was a steamboat they had seen being towed across the plains by ten yoke of oxen.

A premium of $75 was given the wagon-master for getting the machine safely across 1500-mile trip and unloaded at its destination. At all rough places on the road, ropes were tied to the machine, and with five men on each side it was held on the wagon.

The little station of Carter was named in honor of this pioneer ranchman, near whose ranch the Union Pacific was built a number of years later.

H. F. GRINSTEAD,
Morrisville, Mo.

MONUMENTAL INSCRIPTIONS IN MISSOURI CEMETERIES.

TWELFTH PAPER.

With some additions the following data is of inscriptions in the new cemetery at Warrensburg, of persons who died previous to 1876, and of later deaths of persons more than 75 years old:

Mary Ann, wife of Henry Albin, born in Harrison County, Ind., Dec. 27, 1832; died Dec. 13, 1881.
Mary Allison, born Nov. 27, 1794; died Dec. 28, 1884.
Henry B. Anderson, Dec. 27, 1852; June 10, 1891.
Newton H. Baxter, Co. C, 18th Reg. Ky., Vol. Inf., b. Dec. 13, 1828.
Sallie, wife of N. H. Baxter, b. Oct. 15, 1827.
L. M. Berry, D. D., Apr. 12, 1828; Mch. 25, 1902.
Martha B., his wife, Sept. 13, 1823; Aug. 10, 1907.
Josiah D. Biser, b. in Frederick County, Md., Feb. 26, 1833; d. Feb. 28, 1894.
F. M. Bixby, b. Feb. 23, 1839; d. Feb. 3, 1885.
James Bales, Co. F, 61st Ill. Inf.
Rebecca Brinkerhoff, wife of G. S. Brinkerhoff; b. July 12, 1836; d. Nov. 19, 1893.
Frederick Brock, b. in Germany, May 29, 1827; d. June 19, 1892.
Barbara Willner Brock, b. in Germany, Sept. 7, 1819; d. May 19, 1879.
Annie M., dau. of F. and A. Brock, b. Oct. 26, 1865; d. July 21, 1879.
Chas. D. Brookes, b. Jan. 27, 1818; d. July 30, 1906.
Susan Barnes, his wife, b. Feb. 15, 1820; d. July 31, 1906.
James L. Brown, b. Jan. 11, 1847; d. Oct. 10, 1897; Co. H, 125th Ill. Inf.
John Burns, b. County Wicklow, Ireland; d. Jan. 13, 1886, aged 82 years.
Sarah Burns, b. in County Wicklow, Ireland; d. Jan 12, 1886; aged 75 years.

R. S. Campbell, b. Sept. 25, 1844; d. May 1, 1893.
Diana, wife of Dr. F. A. Carter, b. May 26, 1839; d. Apr. 26, 1892.
John T. Cheatham, b. Mar. 8, 1836; d. Mar. 23, 1901.
Israel Christian, d. Oct. 6, 1875, aged 80 years, 2 months and 15 days. "By strangers honored and by strangers mourned."
Abraham Cole, b. Dec. 3, 1816; d. Jan. 22, 1888.
Minerva, his wife, b. Nov. 28, 1820; d. Dec. 15, 1890.
Isabella, wife of Bennet Crook, b. June 10, 1821; d. Jan. 19, 1880.
Jeremiah Crowley, b. in County Cork, Ireland, Jan 1, 1822; d. Jan. 19, 1890.
John Culp, b. Oct 6, 1846; d. Dec. 31, 1905.
Hannah, wife of W. Cummings, d. July 26, 1865; aged 68 years, 4 months, 2 days.
John Cummings, d. Sept. 26, 1864, aged 40 years, 1 month, 19 days.
Ambrose Daly, b. in County Limerick, Ireland, Aug 11, 1827; d. Sept. 13, 1867.
James Daly, b. in County Limerick, Ireland, Jan. 1, 1830; d. Feb. 20, 1883.
Mary R. Delaplain, b. Jan. 15, 1849; d. June 27, 1908.
Jane S., wife of J. W. Delaplain, d. Dec. 21, 1893; aged 85 years, 4 months, 17 days.
Willard J. Ditler, b. Feb. 10, 1840; d. June 27, 1899.
Emma Morrison Ditler, b. Sept. 30, 1850.
Emily, wife of J. E. Dodds, d. Nov. 1, 1869; aged 55 years, 7 months, 3 days.
John E. Dodds, d. Apr. 15, 1888; aged 74 years, 2 months, 20 days.
Granville A. Douglass, b. Mch. 10, 1838.
Emma Pyle, his wife, b. Jan. 31, 1833; d. June 23, 1907.
Ebbyline Lydia Drake, b. 1829; d. 1899.
Zachariah H. Emerson, b. in Kentucky, May 15, 1824; d. Aug. 1, 1890.
Sarah A., wife of Z. H. Emerson, b. in Kentucky, Oct. 16, 1822; d. June 3, 1905.

Wm. W., Sarah E., John H., Mary E., children of L. H. and
S. A. Emerson.
Anthony Fisher, b. Feb. 28, 1831.
Martha A. Edwards, wife of Anthony Fisher, b. Oct. 25, 1832;
d. Mch. 7, 1904.
James M. Foster, b. Aug. 17, 1819; d. Aug. 24, 1878.
Peter Fox, d. Aug. 12, 1872; aged 66 years.
Rebecca M., wife of James Gilliland, d. Jan 8, 1871; aged 39
years, 5 months, 21 days.
Naomi A., daughter of Jas. and Rebecca M. Gilliland, d. Nov.
19, 1888, aged 32 years, 2 months, 21 days.
Wm. M. Grainger, d. Feb. 25, 1909; aged 64 years.
Rebecca Grainger, d. Oct. 10, 1899, aged 39 years.
A. B. Grainger, b. Dec. 5, 1812; d. Feb. 8, 1894.
Susanna Eagan, his wife, b. Sept. 10, 1818; d. Dec. 27, 1893.
W. M. Greenup, d. Sept. 9, 1872; aged 37 years, 8 months, 1
day.
Henry M. Green, b. Sept. 22, 1840; d. Apr. 5, 1897.
Maggie Reichle, his wife, b. Dec. 7, 1845; d. Aug. 10, 1895.
John Green, b. July 1, 1838; d. Oct. 10, 1878.
Margaret L., wife of John Goens, b. Nov. 25, 1839; d. Nov.
29, 1880.
Alice C., wife of John A. Graham, b. Aug. 21, 1865; d. Apr.
29, 1895.
James P. Grinstead, b. July 9, 1856; d. Jan. 4, 1894.
Samuel Grinstead, b. Dec. 18, 1818; d. Mch. 10, 1900.
Helen M., wife of S. Grinstead, b. June 12, 1830; d. Feb. 24,
1906.
Caroline E., wife of P. Halfert, d. Apr. 21, 1871; aged 23 years,
4 days.
S. Z. Hamm, d. Apr. 7, 1882 in seventh-second year.
Wm. Harmon, 1818-1892.
Mary M., his wife, 1825-1898.
Elizabeth Bashore, wife of F. Harmoney, d. Nov. 7, 1883;
aged 71 years, 8 months, 29 days.
S. Y. Harris, b. Oct. 12, 1826; d. Sept. 18, 1884.
Jas. L. Hickman, b. May 31, 1831; d. May 21, 1870.
Junius B. Hildreth, b. Mch. 22, 1833; d. Oct. 18, 1899.

Elizabeth Baird, b. May 12, 1842.
Sarah E. Hinson, b. June 18, 1828; d. Feb. 27, 1906.
Sarah E. Hinson, daughter of W. W. and L. Doak, b. Aug. 29, 1868; d. Sept. 8, 1887.
John Hughes, b. in Columbia, Ky., Apr. 27, 1800; d. Feb. 5, 1883.
Mary Diddle, wife of J. Hughes, b. in Columbia, Ky., June 10, 1816; d. Dec. 10, 1882.
Children of J. & M. Hughes; Wm. D. Hughes, d. Nov. 30, 1859; aged 17 years, 7 months, 16 days.
John B. Hughes, d. Apr. 16, 1858, aged 9 years, 2 months, 7 days.
James C. T. Hughes, d. Nov. 18, 1856; aged 2 years, 9 months, 24 days.
Sallie S., wife of H. Y. Hughes, b. in Adair County, Ky., Apr. 22, 1841; d. May 6, 1889.
Harvey Y. Hughes, b. in Jackson County, Tenn., June 27, 1827; d. May 31, 1899.
Thos Hughes, d. July 30, 1888; aged 60 years, 10 months, 7 days.
Calvin C. Hunter, b. May 4, 1835.
Martha J., his wife, b. Mch. 28, 1832; d. July 1, 1907.
Preston Isaacs, b. Mch. 5, 1834.
Elizabeth Isaacs, b. Aug. 4, 1840; d. Feb. 25, 1899.
David W. Johnson, d. Oct. 1, 1851, aged 52 years.
Vir Jane Johnston, b. Mch. 11, 1828.
Joel Prewitt, b. Nov. 13, 1824; d. June 10, 1896.
Rosana N., wife of Thos Kane, d. Mch. 10, 1884, aged 63 years.
Magdalene, wife of J. H. Kemmerly, d. Sept. 8, 1869; aged 35 years.
Henry Kemmerly, d. June 10, 1885, aged 67 years, 6 months, 13 days.
Garrett Crownover Land, b. in St. Clair County, Ill., Aug. 3, 1846; graduated in McKendree College, June 7, 1868; graduated in Law Department of Harvard University, June 26, 1872; d. Nov. 4, 1882.
Minerva Primm, wife of Nathan Land, b. in St. Clair County, Ill., Mch. 21, 1822; d. Sept. 29, 1899.

MONUMENTAL INSCRIPTIONS.

Mary Joan Lancaster, b. in St. Clair County, Ill., June 11, 1854; d. Apr. 12, 1879. Niece of Mrs. Land.

Nathan Land, Capt. Co. K, 117th Ill. Vol. Inf., b. in St. Clair County, Ill., May 4, 1817; d. Aug. 8, 1885.

S. J. Larue, Co. 11, 3d Pa. Res.

T. J. Leake, b. July 31, 1862; d. Apr. 20, 1899.

John L. Lobban, b. in Charlottesville, Va., June 18, 1836; d. Apr. 29, 1895.

Hannah, wife of Sylvenis Lockard, b. Jan. 25, 1845; d. Sept. 6, 1869.

Conrad Loun, Co. C, 27th Mo. Mtd. Inf.

W. S. McCoy, d. Oct. 7, 1892; aged 49 years.

Elizabeth, his wife, b. June 15, 1842; d. June 6, 1880.

Sarah, wife of Hugh McCoy, d. Mch. 18, 1884; aged 81 years.

Robt. Wm. McGinnis, M. D., b. Nov. 30, 1862; d. Feb. 21, 1899.

Dan McNair, b. May 19, 1842; d. Oct. 12, 1903.

John C. Macon, b. Mch. 6, 1830; d. Nov. 15, 1903.

Josephine, his wife, b. Oct. 18, 1840; d. Nov. 27, 1905.

Rev. B. G. Manard, D. D., b. Oct. 9, 1841; d. Jan. 27, 1899.

Lilly A., wife of Wm. S. Mikel, d. Jan. 1, 1870; aged 29 years, 29 days.

Wm. S. Mikel, b. in Wilkesboro, N. C., Jan. 9, 1827; d. Feb. 28, 1903.

Nancy J., his wife, d. Apr. 8, 1866, aged 31 years, 3 months, 4 days.

Willson Moore, b. May 24, 1834; d. Mch. 13, 1899.

James C. Morrow, d. Mch. 15, 1875; aged 62 years, 11 months, 9 days.

Margaret W. Morrow, b. Apr. 16. 1892; aged 79 years, 10 months, 26 days.

Jno. Murphy, Co. E, 1st Mo. Cav., b. in County Cork, Ireland, Dec. 21, 1823; d. Mch. 9, 1904.

Eliza, his wife, b. in County Cork, Ireland, 1830; d. Feb. 7, 1902.

Abraham Newcomer, d. Mch. 21, 1909; aged 73 years, 10 months, 21 days.

Agnes Newcomer, d. Mch. 27, 1897; aged 54 years.

Sarah Ann Creese, wife of John Norris, b. May 21, 1828; d. May 23, 1899.
Mary, wife of J. W. Ogburn, b. Nov. 1, 1824; d. July 30, 1906.
G. W. O'Neal, d. May 20, 1881; aged 62 years, 9 months, 4 days.
Augustus H. Osgood, d. May 8, 1875; aged 41 years, 4 months, 16 days.
Chas. N. Palmer, M. D., b. Feb. 25, 1831; d. July 21, 1899.
M. J. Pennock, d. Mch. 19, 1869; aged 38 years, 3 months, 7 days.
Amos R. Phelps, b. Jan. 5, 1854; d. Mch. 23, 1906.
Sarah Hoover, wife of M. A. Plumer, b. Nov. 16, 1838; d. Jan. 9, 1907.
M. A. Plumer, b. Feb. 28, 1834; d. Dec. 18, 1907.
Alex S. Porter, d. July 31, 1870; aged 46 years, 5 months, 4 days.
Andrew Powell, b. Mch. 15, 1840; d. Nov. 24, 1907; Co. H, 116th Ohio Inf.
Rachel, his wife, b. Mch. 1, 1841.
Maria Louisa, wife of John A. Powers, b. July 30, 1829; d. Apr. 4, 1902.
Elizabeth, wife of Robert Price, d. May 26, 1873; aged 70 years.
James Lester Prouty, b. Nov. 13, 1851. While on his way to attend the Normal School he perished in the fire which destroyed Mings Hotel, Nov. 29, 1873.
Phoebe G., wife of Noah Redford, b. May 30, 1804; d. Aug. 20, 1885.
Noah Redford, b. Jan. 13, 1805; d. Dec. 18, 1888.
James Reed, b. Sept. 25, 1827; d. Jan. 10, 1906.
Mary, his wife, b. Aug. 2, 1817; d. July 24, 1870.
A. Remison, d. Nov. 24, 1876; aged 55 years, 8 months, 11 days.
John M. Rice, b. Jan. 12, 1833; d. Oct. 8, 1904.
Rev. Geo. V. Ridley, b. July 3, 1811; d. Oct. 21, 1892.
Emma C., his wife, b. Apr. 22, 1812; d. Jan. 21, 1892.
Joseph Rittman, b. Oct. 12, 1844; d. Feb. 7, 1907.
Eliza E. Sampsal, b. Mch. 17, 1844.
Dr. Chas. Robinson, d. Aug. 31, 1889; aged 56 years.

H. H. Robinson, Co. E, 149th Ohio Inf.
J. H. Rowley, b. Apr. 14, 1834; d. Nov. 15, 1879.
Chas. E., son of J. H. and N. J. Rowley, b. Apr. 20, 1870; d. Aug. 22, 1870.
Maud M., daughter of same, b. May 12, 1868; d. Aug. 29, 1881.
Fannie D. Russell, b. Aug. 31, 1792; d. Feb. 1, 1879.
Henry Russell, b. June 28, 1788; d. Oct. 8, 1876.
James Ryan, b. Feb. 15, 1860. Killed on Easter Sunday, Apr. 19, 1908, while performing his official duty as city marshal.
J. W. Schnegelsiepen, Co. E, 33d Ill. Inf.
Stella Morrow, wife of L. J. Schofield, b. June 30, 1867; d. Mch. 20, 1896.
Wm. G. Scott, b. Apr. 7, 1832; d. July 26, 1899.
Wm. Sensenderfer, b. Apr. 13, 1814; d. Aug. 16, 1895.
Arminda C., his wife, b. Apr. 2, 1824; d. Feb. 6, 1899.
John Sumati, b. Jan. 1, 1842; Co. G, 7th Reg. Mo. S. M. Cav.
Sarah J. Sumati, b. Apr. 2, 1841; d. July 30, 1898.
Stephen Sims, b. Jan. 9, 1819; d. May 23, 1893.
Wm. F. Sperling, b. Nov. 21, 1826.
Minna J., his wife, b. June 26, 1826; d. Feb. 2, 1901.
Joseph D. Stanver, b. Jan. 17, 1835; d. Feb. 26, 1905.
Elizabeth, his wife, b. Nov. 30, 1839; d. Dec. 10, 1892.
John C. Steele, b. Dec. 22, 1812; d. Dec. 10, 1887.
Joseph Taylor, son of John and Lousa Steele, b. Jan. 6, 1849; d. Oct. 25, 1880.
Lousa Pressly, wife of John C. Steele, b. June 13, 1818; d. Mch. 12, 1890.
Lucie A. M., wife of J. D. Steele, d. Dec. 17, 1866, in her thirty-first year.
Nancy W., wife of Geo. Stepper, d. Sept. 7, 1877; aged, 38 years, 9 months, 6 days.
Dr. Chas. P. Stevenson, b. Mch. 6, 1817, in Lewis County, Ky.; d. July 30, 1873.
J. B. Stillwell, Co. L, 11th Mo. Cav.
Oliver M. Stone, b. June 5, 1833; Co. H, 6th Mo. Cav.
Elizabeth A. Stone, b. June 4, 1834; d. Sept. 5, 1896.

Oscar R. Stone, b. Oct. 9, 1870; d. June 23, 1898. Co. L. 4th Reg. Mo. Vol. Inf, Spanish American War.
Emma L. Strait, b. June 13, 1837; d. Apr. 4, 1909.
Maggie J. Kirby, b. Mch. 14, 1837; d. Apr. 7, 1909.
James D. Sullivan, b. Mch. 28, 1867; d. Mch. 23, 1902.
Kate Jay Sullivan, b. Mch. 28, 1835; d. June 7, 1903.
Clifton Thomson, b. Feb. 14, 1845; d. July 19, 1897.
Susan Vanarsdale, b. Aug. 26, 1812; d. Apr. 18, 1891.
G. T. Wilson, b. Feb. 24, 1841; d. June 30, 1899.
Alexander Wilson, b. Oct. 11, 1822; d. Oct. 6, 1877.
Eliza A., wife of S. Woolsey, d. Oct. 23, 1879; aged 49 years, 10 months, 6 days.
Adaline, daughter of S. and E. A. Woolsey, d. Jan. 3, 1877; aged 27 years, 3 months, 11 days.

NOTES.

PRESERVATION OF MISSOURI PUBLICATIONS.

The secretary of the State Historical Society frequently learns of the wanton destruction of publications of historical value and of great enough importance, that one on learning of it cannot repress the feelings of disgust that the destructor had ever been placed in a position where it was possible for the destruction to take place. When it is done by some one who has not the education to allow him to appreciate what he does, we pity his ignorance, but when the destruction is done by a college man of education we wonder why dense ignorance can be combined with college education, and regret that the person ever got in a position above that of a section hand on a railroad. What will the reader think of the following case:

"Our . . . President, . . . desiring to have additional room for his own office, kept a fire burning on the campus for several days, destroying the 'trash' that we had collected. With this went duplicate unbound sets of Scribner's, Century, Popular Science Monthly, Harper's, old college pamphlets, catalogues, miscellaneous papers and many things, valuable historically, which were all consigned to the flames. The only complete file of the Missouri House and Senate Journals and Reports and Laws of Missouri were dumped by the wheelbarrow load, helter skelter, into a damp basement room in another building, where for all I know, they remain a prey to mildew and mice."

Degradation from office and a jail sentence would be the only adequate punishment for such conduct!

Mr. WM. E. WALTON, of Butler, Missouri, an old time friend of the editor, in a letter with some very commendatory references to the REVIEW, states that his grandfather, Samuel

Turley, moved from Madison County, Kentucky, to Cooper County, Missouri, in 1813, and with his wife lived sixty years on the land they settled. His mother was born on that farm in 1824, and he was born in 1842 and reared within a mile of it. Mr. Walton is the president of the Old Settlers' Association, of Bates County, and is interested in all matters of Missouri history. He is also president of the Walton Trust Company of Butler, and in that connection has been known by the editor for many years.

REVOLUTIONARY GRAVE. The D. A. R. at Independence, Missouri, have obtained from the government a marker for the grave of Isaac Drake, a soldier of the Revolutionary war, who died in 1837. The grave is on the Jackson farm, ten miles east of Independence, and not far from old Six Mile Church.

BOOK NOTICES.

A BETRAYED TRUST. A story of our own times and country. A romance of the middle west. By W. T. McClure. Publishing House of the M. E. Church, South, 1903.

The author of this story was born near Washburn, Barry County, Missouri, and for some years was a teacher and afterwards a Methodist minister. While presiding elder of the Boonville district he wrote the above book, while waiting in depots and riding on cars.

The book was written as a character study for the Epworth Leaguers of the Methodist church, and pleads for fidelity in the keeping of vows whose motives and purposes are good.

We are obliged to the reverend doctor for adding the book to our collection of Missouri authors.

SAINT PAUL METHODIST EPISCOPAL CHURCH, SOUTH. Brief history with list of charter members, 1831 and 1868, together with the names of present membership. By GEO. M. JONES. 1904. Springfield, Mo., 41 pp., 4 plates.

The Society would be glad to acknowledge the receipt of several publications similar to above, in each number of the Review.

DEUTSCHE GESCHICHTSFORSCHUNG FUER MISSOURI. (German Historical Researches of Missouri.) We welcome the first number of the above quarterly, of which our friend, Chas. Botz of Sedalia, is one of the editors.

NECROLOGY.

THOMAS F. LOCKHART, forty-three years of age, of which twenty-seven had been spent in bed, welcomed death on the 6th of August, last.

He took to his bed Christmas night, 1886, following a long ride through a cold rain, and for more than a quarter of a century remained in it, his joints so ossified that he could only slightly shrug one shoulder, and the middle joints of two fingers, and yet with such a handicap, he wrote several books from the proceeds of which he supported himself and paid for a constant nurse. He resided at Wellington, Missouri.

HARRY H. MITCHELL, a member of this Society, died July 24, 1913, while on a train on the M. K. & T. Railroad, enroute to St. Louis from Boonville. He was born in England about 64 years ago, and came to Polk county in this State, where he was reared and educated. He began newspaper work at Bolivar, and went from there to Springfield, where he became chief of the fire department. At a fire he received an injury causing the amputation of a leg. From Springfield he went to Clinton and established the Henry County Republican, and was later appointed postmaster. When Hon. John M. Swanger was Secretary of State he gave Mr. Mitchell a place in his office, and while there Mr. Mitchell compiled the Official Manual, or Blue Book. During the past sixteen years he was an active worker in the campaigns of the Republican party, and of the Republican Editorial Association, he had been secretary from its organization fifteen years ago. In 1912 he was elected its secretary and treasurer for life. He was for a time clerk of the Springfield Court of Appeals.

While a boy he enlisted in the Union army and served till the close of the war. He is survived by his widow and six children.

REV. W. J. PATRICK, of Bowling Green, a member of this Society and the oldest Baptist minister in his part of the State, fell dead August 18, 1913. In the morning he had preached a funeral sermon, and in the afternoon had attended another funeral.

Hon. H. J. Simmons, a Democratic representative in the Forty-first, Forty-second, Forty-third and Forty-fourth General Assemblies of Missouri from Shelby county, former editor of the Clarence Courier in that county, for four years a mayor of Clarence, and chairman of the State Board of Mediation and Arbitration, and editor of the Kirksville Democrat and Kirksville Morning News, committed suicide at Kirksville, July 11, 1913. While in the legislature he was floor leader of his party.

He was born at Coldwater, Branch county, Michigan, and came to Missouri when one year old. He was educated in the public schools and at college at Glasgow, Missouri. He left a note to his wife saying that his act was for the best, and that he would meet her in Heaven, indicating that his mind had become unbalanced.

MISSOURI HISTORICAL REVIEW.

VOL. 8 JANUARY, 1914. No. 2.

THE VALUE AND THE SALE OF THE MISSOURI SLAVE.

No problem concerning the slave is more difficult to handle than the value of this form of property. The selling price of individual negroes, and of lots of them, can be found in the county records and in the newspapers. But to generalize on these figures for any particular period, or to compare values in different periods, would be most misleading. For example, if a male slave twenty years of age sold for $500 in 1820, and another of the same age sold for $1,400 in 1860 we learn little. The negro in the first instance may have been less healthy, less tractable, and less intelligent than the other. Therefore the $900 difference could not fairly represent the general rise in prices nor the increased value of slave labor. To illustrate this point concretely—two slaves were sold in Ray county in 1854, both were twenty-six years of age, yet one brought $1,295 and the other but $670.[1] This shows how unsafe it is to compare specific sales.

However, by comparing the prices brought by a lot of negroes about the same age and in the same locality we gain an approximately sound conclusion. In general it can be said that a gradual rise in slave values is apparent up to the Civil War. It was exceptional indeed when a negro brought over

---

1. Notice of the sale of the slaves of the Estate of Thomas Reeves (Richmond Weekly Mirror, Jan. 5, 1855).

$500 before 1830,[2] a prime male servant from eighteen to thirty-five years of age was in this early period worth from $450 to $500, and the women about a fourth less.[3] When Auguste Chouteau's negroes were appraised in 1829, the eleven men among them who were between the ages of sixteen and thirty-five averaged $486.35 each, the highest being worth $500 and the lowest $300. The eleven women between the ages of sixteen and thirty-nine averaged $316.35, the highest valuation being $350 and the lowest $130.[4]

From the third decade of the century on there is an increase in values. Men brought considerably more by the late thirties.

2. The following representative examples of slave values for the Territorial period are taken from the St. Louis Probate Records. In the will of the Widow Quenel of March, 1805, we find four slaves listed and valued as follows: Two women at 376 and 641 "piastres", respectively; Sophie, age 13, at 900 piastres; Alexander, age 5, at 300; and a cow at 10 piastres. If the latter was a normal animal we get some idea of the comparative value of the negroes (MS. Probate Records, St. Louis county, Estate No. 7). Joseph Robidoux's estate was probated in August, 1810. His slaves were listed as follows: Felecite, with child at breast, 200 piastres; her daughter of 8 years at 150, a girl of 6 at 125, and "Une autre petite Negrette," 100 piastres, (ibid, Estate No. 50). In 1817 the following values were attached to slaves in Cape Girardeau county: Two men, $900; a woman and two children, $800; a woman and child, $550; a woman, $350, and five men at $2700 (MS. Probate Records, Cape Girardeau county, Appraisement of the Estate of Elijah Betty, Filed June 2, 1817, Estate No. 628). H. R. Schoolcraft, writing in 1820 or 1821, stated that a good slave sold for $600 in Missouri (Travels in the Central Portion of the Mississippi Valley (New York 1825), p. 232).

3. In 1830 the following values were given in St. Louis: Charles, age 32, $450; Anthony, age 30, $400; Antrim, age 24, $450; Allen, age 24, $500 (Estate of John C. Sullivan, MS. Probate Records, St. Louis County, Estate No. 882, Appraisement filed Oct. 9, 1830). By comparing the appraisements and sale bills it was found that they correspond very closely, in some cases negroes selling for more than the appraisal and in some for less. In Pike county in 1835 a negress aged 22 and her three children, aged four years, three years and three months respectively, sold for $650 (MS. Receipt of sale dated May 2, 1835, Dougherty Papers, Missouri Historical Society).

4. MS. Copy of appraisement dated May 11, 1829, Missouri Historical Society.

In 1838 prime hands were bringing from $600 to $900 in St. Louis.[5]

Up to 1840 female slaves were worth from $300 to $350 when men were bringing from $500 to $600. Children from two to five years of age were sold for from $100 to $200. In 1838 W. H. Ashley's women and children were valued as follows in St. Louis: Berril (boy), age 12, $350; Celia, age 9, $250; Lucy, age 9, $250; Catherine, age 7, $200; Betsy, age 30 and her infant son, $500.[6]

For the golden age of slave values we must turn to the fifties. The prime male slave of Missouri in 1860 was worth around $1,300 and the negresses about $1,000. The fabled $2000 negro is more often found in story than in record. "Uncle" Eph Sanders of Platte City, still a very active and intelligent negro, claims that his master refused $2000 for him in 1859 when he was twenty-three.[7] But contemporaries put the normal limit at about $1500. Mr. Paxton says that stout, hemp-breaking negroes "sold readily for from $1200 to $1400" in the heyday of Platte county hemp culture.[8] Dr. John Doy claims

---

5. In this year the estate of Thomas Withington received $800 each for two men, aged 22 and 25, and $600 each for one 16 and one 23, (MS. Probate Records, St. Louis County, Estate No. 1374, bill of sale dated June 14, 1838). This same year a man of 21 was rated at $650, and one of 35 at $900 (ibid, Estate of W. H. Ashley, Estate No. 1377, Inventory and appraisement, filed June 20, 1838). In 1844, in Saline county good hands brought around the same figures. Thomas Smith's blacks were valued as follows: $500 each for three men, $550 each for two others, and another for $600 (MS. Probate Records, Saline county, Box No. 248, Inventory and Appraisement, filed Nov. 11, 1844).

6. MS. Probate Records, St. Louis County, Estate No. 1377, Inventory and Appraisement, filed June 20, 1838.

7. Mr. Hunter B. Jenkins of St. Louis claims that a good sound black brought from $1500 to $2000 in the late fifties.

8. William M. Paxton, Annals of Platte County, Missouri (Kansas City, 1897), p. 37). G. B. Merrick says that while on the Mississippi as a boatman in the late fifties a male slave sold for from $800 to $1500, (Old Times on the Upper Mississippi, 1854-1863 (Cleveland, 1909), p. 64). At the Lexington Pro-Slavery Convention of 1855, President James Shannon of the State University declared that the average Missouri slave was worth $600, and that field hands "will now readily sell for $1200" (Pro-

that a slave sold in Weston in the late fifties for $1800.[9]

If the above figures are exceptional we nevertheless have plenty of evidence that negroes were very valuable in these years. In 1854, the slaves of Thomas Reeves were sold in Richmond for fine prices. The ages and price of these negroes were as follows:[10]

                Man,   age 23, price $1440.
                Man,   age 26, price 1295.
                Man,   age 23, price 1249.
                Man,   age 40, price 1115.
                Man,   age 31, price   911.
                Man,   age 33, price   904.
                Man,   age 26, price   670.
                Man,   age 58, price   115.
                Boy,   age 13, price   851.
                Boy,   age 14, price   825.
                Boy,   age 11, price   795.
                Boy,   age 13, price   775.
                Woman, age 49, price   510.
                Girl, age 12, price   942.

ceedings and Resolutions of the Pro-Slavery Convention, held at Lexington, July 13 to 15, 1855 (St. Louis, Republican Office, 1855), p. 7).

9. Narrative of John Doy of Lawrence, Kansas (New York, 1860), p. 59.

10. Richmond Weekly Mirror, Jan. 5, 1855. $1000 to $1200 seems to have been the common figure for good men in the late fifties. In 1858 in Boone county, four men were valued at $1200 each, one at $1100, and another at $1000. Two women were rated at $900 each (MS. Probate Records, Boone County, Inventories, Appraisements and Sales, Book B, p. 87-8, filed Dec. 30, 1858). The following year in Greene county two men were valued at $1100 each (Estate of Jonathan Carthel, MS. Probate Records, Greene County, Inventories and Appraisements, Book A, p. 31, filed Aug. 4, 1859). In 1860 in the same county a man was listed at $1200 (Estate of Jacob Rodenkamer, ibid, p. 160, filed May 18, 1860). The same year a woman was sold for $1100, and two men for $1150 and $1260 respectively (Estate of James Boaldin, ibid, p. 202, sale bill not dated). In Henry county in 1860, a man aged 29 was valued at $1250, a girl of twelve at $1000, and one of fifteen at the same figure. A girl of nine and two boys of seven were valued at $800 each, and a boy of five at $600 (MS. Estate of A. Embry, MS. Probate Records, Henry County, Inventories, Appraisements and Sales, p. 126, filed Sept. 26, 1860).

In the same issue of the Richmond Weekly Mirror which published the above is an account of the sale of the negroes of Charity Creason, which were sold on January 1, 1855. They brought the following prices: A man, age 23, $1439; another, age 38, $1031; a woman, age 26, and her 18-month-old child, $1102.50; a girl, age 3, $400; and a woman of 59 for $1.

During the middle and late fifties all classes of negroes were priced high. In 1856 a lot of children were sold in Saline county. A boy of nine went for $550, one of seven for $500, and another of five for $300.[11] A Saline county inventory of 1859 shows what good prices negroes in general were commanding in the closing years of the slavery regime.[12]

Henry, age 17, value $1300.
Daniel, age 36, value 1200.
George, age 13, value 950.
Stephen, age 8, value 650.
Addison, age 8, value 550.
Thomas, age 5, value 440.
Ellen, age 20, value $1300.
Mary, age 21,
  (and child of
  14 months) value 1250.
Susan, age 15, value 1150.
Eliza, age 17, value 1050.
Francis, age 10, value 800.
Minerva, age 12, value 800.
Marie, age 35,
  (and son

---

11. Estate of Benjamin Moberly, (MS. Probate Records, Saline County, Appraisements and Sales, 1855-1861, vol. 1, p. 118-9, filed Jan. 26, 1856). At Hannibal on April 15, 1855, a girl of nine sold for $450, and a boy of four for $321 (St. Louis Weekly Pilot, Apr. 21, 1855).

12. Estate of H. Eustace (MS. Probate Records, Saline County, Appraisements and Sales, 1855-61, vol. i, p. 602-3, filed Apr. 4, 1859). In this same year, two men, ages not given, were appraised in Saline county at $1300 each, and another at $1100. A mother and child were together valued at $1100 (Estate of Samuel M. McDonald, ibid, Probate files, Box No. 169, Inventory filed Nov. 20, 1859). In these Records there are many similar valuations.

18 months)   value   775.
Delia,   age 46, value   500.
Julia,   age 4, value   400.
A girl, age 6 mos., value   50.

But for top prices we turn to Boone county where in 1860 George W. Gordon's blacks brought superior valuations:[13]

Lou,   age 25, value $1500.
Horace,   age 30, value   1500.
Charles,   age 34, value   1600.
Roger,   age 36, value   1500.

It appears from the foregoing pages that the highest official valuation placed upon a negro man was $1600, and upon a woman, $1300. A difficulty in finding the exact price of slave women is the fact that small children were often included with them.

When the Civil War opened and escapes became more numerous the value of slave property began to decline. Compared with the above figures we have the following appraisement of the estate of Lawson Calvin of Saline county, filed July 11, 1861, after the war had engulfed the State in a torrent of strife:[14]

Lewis,   age 18, value $800.
George,   age 12, value   600.
Lewis,   age 47, value   500.
Henry,   age 7, value   300.
Narcissa,   age 16, value   600.
Mag,   age 40, value   275.

Nevertheless it is surprising how slaves persisted as property in the State during the War. The prices kept fairly high.

---

13. MS. Probate Records, Boone County, Inventories, Appraisements and Sales, Book B, p. 287, Inventory filed Dec. 25, 1860). In 1859, William W. Hudson's negro named Beverley, age 29, was valued at $1500, three other men at $1200 each, and four men at $1000 each, (ibid, p. 170, filed Sept. 12, 1859).

14. MS. Probate Records, Saline County, Inventories and Appraisements, 1855-61, vol. i, p. 677. The appraisement of the estate of Elizabeth Huff of July 7, 1861, bears similar testimony to the effect of the War on slave property (ibid).

VALUES OF SLAVES IN MISSOURI 75

The probate records of Lafayette, Missouri's greatest slave county, bear witness to this fact. Two men were actually appraised at $1100 and $800, respectively, and a woman at $1000 in November, 1861.[15] In January, 1862, a woman was valued at $650 and another at $550, and a boy of seventeen at $650, while one of the eleven was rated at $500.[16] By the last of July, 1863, the price had further decreased. But although Gettysburg had been fought and the State was overrun by bushwhackers, the price dropped but did not fall, as one conversant with conditions in the border-states in those years would expect. In the above month two women, aged 23 and 16 were appraised at $300 each, and a boy of eight at $400.[17] But slaves were not merely appraised this late. On June 3, 1863, the negroes of Samuel F. Taylor of Lafayette county were actually sold as follows: Amanda, $380; Milky (girl), $370; Jack, $305; Georgetta, $300; William, $250; Eunis, $200; and Sam, $200.[18] There is an appraisal of an estate in Lafayette county made on October 2, 1863, but the slaves listed are not assigned value.[19] Nevertheless over a month later, on November 5, 1863, negroes were still appraised, but it is the last official valuation of slave property in Lafayette county records. On that date a ''boy'' named Charles was appraised at $300 and a girl of fourteen at $200.[20]

The total value of slave property is of course very difficult to find. Contemporaries were far from agreeing on this point.

15. The Estate of Col. John Brown, Appraisement filed Nov. 18, 1861 (MS. Probate Records, Lafayette County, Inventories, Appraisements and Sales, vol. ii, p. 24).
16. Estate of John D. Bailey, Inventory filed Jan. 2, 1862 (ibid, p. 18).
17. Estate of Randell Latamer, Appraisement filed July (?), 1863 (ibid, p. 261.)
18. Estate of Samuel F. Taylor, Bill of Sale, filed June 6, 1863 (MS. Probate Records, Lafayette County, Inventories and Sale Bills, Book D, p. 69). Several slaves appraised in the fore part of this year are found in these records. The values show a gradual decline.
19. Estate of Western Woolard (ibid, Inventories, Appraisements and Sales, vol. ii, p. 267).
20. Estate of F. U. Talliferro (ibid, p. 262).

For instance in 1854 John Hogan of the "Republican," in an article to boom St. Louis and Missouri, placed the average value at $300.[21] Contrasted with this low estimate the "Address to the People of the United States," prepared by a committee of the Lexington Proslavery Convention of 1855, valued the 50,000 slaves of western Missouri at $25,000,000, or $500 each.[22] Governor Jackson in his inaugural address of January 3, 1861, estimated the 114,931 slaves of the State to be worth $100,-000,000.[23] Of course the Governor was speaking in general terms, but his average would be nearly $700 the slave.

The above figures are in excess to those of the county assessors of the period. Tax values are usually considered lower than market values. The Jackson county tax average for 1860 was $483.05 per slave,[24] and that of Boone county $372.30.[25] The average in Pike county in 1859 was $434.78.[26] In 1856 in Buchanan county it was $450.92,[27] and that of the 170 slaves of its county seat, St. Joseph, was $434.70.[28] Evidently the assessors of the various counties had no uniform standard in rating slave values.

Despite the fact that the above figures vary they at least show that slave property was increasing in price. In 1828 the 239 slaves of Lafayette county were taxed at an average of

21. Thoughts about the City of St. Louis, pamphlet, p. 65 (Republican Office, 1854).

22. Proceedings of the Convention, p. 3, or in the Missouri Weekly Sentinel, Oct. 5, 1855. This address was signed by W. B. Napton, Governor Sterling Price, and others.

23. Pamphlet, p. 7 (Jefferson City, 1861).

24. MS. Tax Book, Jackson County, 1860; 3316 slaves, tax value, $1,452,591.

25. MS. Tax Book, Boone County, 1860; 4354 slaves, tax value, $1,721,000.

26. MS. Tax Book, Pike County, 1859; 3733 slaves, tax value, $1,623,085.

27. MS. Tax Book, Buchanan County, 1856; 1534 slaves, tax value, $691,825.

28. M. H. Nash, City Registrar, valued the 170 slaves of the town at $73,900 (St. Joseph Commercial Cycle, Sept. 7, 1855).

$249.68.[29] This is at the least a third less than the average rate in the counties above mentioned in the years around 1860. In comparing these values the decreasing purchasing power of money should be taken into consideration.

A very bitter experience which the slave might at any time be forced to undergo was his removal to a strange region far from his family and old associations. This disruption of the negro family was entirely dependent upon the humanity of the individual owner. The sale of the slave south was practiced in Missouri as in the other border states. But the Missourians deny that it was ever practised save where financial reverses, an excess of hands, or a chronic spirit of viciousness or of absconding on the part of the slave necessitated it.[30]

Whether to mollify the new antislavery party which developed during the Compromise struggle, or through pure conviction, the constitution of 1820 provided that the Legislature might pass laws to prohibit the introduction of slaves into the State as "an article of commerce."[31] The provision was not taken seriously and the General Assembly never acted upon the suggestion.

The slave trader is generally pictured as the brutal, conscienceless, necessary evil, of the slavery system, detested even by those with whom he dealt. In Missouri he held no very enviable position. "Slave-traders and whiskey-sellers were equally hated by many," wrote one anti-slavery clergyman of

---

29. The History of Lafayette County (St. Louis, 1881), p. 306. The total valuation was $59,665, as copied by the author of the above work from the tax book.

30. "I never heard of any Missourian who consciously raised slaves for the southern market. I feel sure it was never done," said Lieutenant Governor R. A. Campbell of Bowling Green. Mr. Robert B. Price of Columbia denied that slaves were consciously bred for the southern market. Mr. J. W. Beatty of Mexico stated that there was a general feeling that the sale of negroes south was not right. Old residents and slaveholders in all parts of the state were corresponded with and all denied that in Missouri, at least, slave breeding was ever engaged in as the antislavery people so often charged. The better classes at any rate frowned upon the practise.

31. Art. III, sec. 26.

St. Louis,[32] while another maintained that "large fortunes were made by the trade; and some of those who made them were held as fit associates for the best men on 'change'."[33] Dr. John Doy, the Kansas Abolitionist, who had a personal grievance against the Missouri slaveholder, claims that Gen. Dorris, whom he described as a brutal dealer, was highly respected and "belonged to the aristocracy of Platte county."[34]

Some of the slaveholders who were interviewed declared that the slave trader and the saloon keeper were tolerated as necessary evils, but that they were personally loathed and socially ostracized. Others, however, stated that it was a question of the individual trader, some being liked and some disliked.[35]

If the slave trader was a hard man and detested, he at least had the satisfaction of knowing that the wisest and gentlest of men would be hated by many if plying his trade. The very nature of the business made it contemptible. If the Missouri system was as patriarchal and the tie between the master and man as close as we are led to believe it was, the dealer who higgled and bargained even for the most unruly servant must have been disliked. This feeling would naturally be enhanced if financial reverses compelled the sale of familyslaves.[36]

32. Galusha Anderson, A Border City During the War, p. 171. (Boston, 1908).
33. William G. Eliot, The Story of Archer Alexander, p. 100 (Boston, 1885).
34. Narrative, p. 59.
35. Captain J. A. Wilson of Lexington declared that slave traders were considered worse than saloon keepers, many of them about Lafayette county being gamblers. Mr. R. B. Price of Columbia stated that they were considered a questionable class in Boone county. Messrs. J. H. Sallee and J. W. Beatty of Mexico said that like any other class of people some were respected and some were detested. James Aull of Lexington, a prominent merchant and slaveholder, wrote in 1835, "—a traffic in slaves we never could consent to embark in. No hope of gain could induce us to do it—we entirely and forever abandon the least share in the purchase of negroes for sale again." (MS. Aull to Siter, Price & Company of Philadelphia, June 15; Aull Papers, in the collection of E. U. Hopkins and John Chamberlain of Lexington, Mo.).
36. Many dealers were undoubtedly brutal men. An escaped Missouri slave later wrote that he was once hired to a dealer named Walker,

In addition to the vicious, the runaway, and the slave of the financially depressed owner, there was a surplus from the natural increase. Consequently quite a local negro exchange existed. Besides this there was the itinerant buyer for the southern markets. The smaller towns seem to have been regularly visited, while the larger centers had permanent dealers. There were two such in Lexington in 1861, but they are said to have had difficulty in getting sufficiently large gangs to make the business pay.[37] There was at least one permanently located firm of dealers in St. Joseph in 1856.[38] John Doy claims many were shipped from St. Joseph while he was imprisoned there, to Bernard Lynch, Corbin Thompson, and other large St. Louis buyers.[39] Columbia and Marshall were regularly visited, and Platte City had quite a thriving trade.[40] John R.

who collected Missouri slaves for the Gulf markets. This Walker forced a beautiful mulatto slave into concubinage, and after years sold her and his four children by her into slavery before marrying a white woman (William B. Brown, Narrative, p. 47). Once while on a negro buying expedition Walker was annoyed at the continual wailing of an infant in the gang. He seized it from the mother and ran into a wayside house with the child hanging by one leg. Despite the shrieks of the mother he gave it to a woman who thankfully received it. The gang then marched on to St. Louis (ibid, p. 49). John Doy says that while a prisoner in Platte City he met many brutal dealers. He thus describes a slave gang: "At midnight Gen. Dorris, his son and assistants, came to the jail and ordered the slaves to get ready to leave. As it was quite cold a pair of sox were drawn over the fists and wrists of the men, in place of mittens, they were then handcuffed together in pairs and driven into the street, where they were formed into marching order behind the wagons containing the women and children—some of the former tied with ropes when considered unruly . . . " (Narrative, p. 64).

37. Captain J. A. Wilson has a map of Lexington executed by Jos. C. Jennings in 1861. It also contains a business directory in which are given two slave traders, A. Alexander at the City Hotel, and R. J. White at the Laurel Hotel. The latter, Captain Wilson remembers, had a three story building he used as a slave pen, but found it difficult to collect many negroes.

38. Wright and Carter who were "Located permanently at the Empire on Second Street" (St. Joseph Commercial Cycle, Aug. 15, 1856).

39. Narrative, p. 98.

40. Mr. R. B. Price remembers that dealers came regularly to Columbia. "Uncle" Henry Napper said that buyers came regularly to Mar-

White of Howard county was a wealthy farmer of good repute who dealt in slaves. He lived on a farm of 1,053 acres and was taxed with 46 negroes in 1856.[41] The slave trader like the stock dealer undoubtedly plied his trade wherever he could obtain his commodity.

St. Louis became quite a market for shipping gangs down the Mississippi. One Reuben Bartlett openly advertised for negroes for the "Memphis and Louisiana Markets."[42] "St. Louis was fast becoming a slave market," wrote the Reverend W. G. Eliot, an antislavery clergyman, "and the supply was increasing with the demand. Often have I seen gangs of negroes handcuffed together, two and two, going through the open street like dumb cattle, on the way to the steamboat for the South. Large fortunes were made by the trade."[43] "I had to prepare the old slaves for the market," states William Brown, a slave who worked for a trader on a boat from St. Louis south on the Mississippi, "I was ordered to have the old men's whiskers shaved off, and the grey hairs plucked out where they were not too numerous, in which case he (the trader) had a preparation of blacking to color it, and with a blacking brush we put it on. . . . These slaves were then taught how old they were. . . . After going through the blacking process

shall and picked up unruly slaves and those of hard-up masters. John Doy wrote, "During our imprisonment [in Platte City in the fifties] numbers of slaves were lodged in the jail by different traders, who were making up gangs to take or send to the south. Every slave when brought in, was ordered to strip naked, and was minutely examined for marks, which with the condition of the teeth and other details, were carefully noted by the trader in his memorandum book. Many facts connected with these examinations were too disgusting to mention." (Narrative, p. 59.) J. G. Haskell states that, unless unruly, the slave had little danger of being sold to a distant market, "the oldest inhabitant remembers no such thing as a market auction block in western Missouri." "The Passing of Slavery in Western Missouri," Kansas Historical Society Collections, vol. vii, p. 31.

 41. MS. Tax Book, Howard County, 1856. Mr. George Carson of Fayette gave the above description of White's character.
 42. Republican, Apr. 23, 1852.
 43. The Life of Archer Alexander, p. 100.

they looked fifteen years younger. . . ."[44] In one issue of the Republican three firms, perhaps to imply great prosperity or to outdo one another, advertised for five hundred, one thousand, and twenty-five hundred slaves respectively.[45] The St. Louis Directory of 1859 lists two "Slave Dealers" among the classified places of business. These were Bernard M. Lynch of 100 Locust St., and Corbin Thompson, 3 South Sixth street.[46] As a type of the great Missouri slave dealer we will take the former. Bernard M. Lynch, as we have seen, had his correspondents in western Missouri. His historic slave-pen was afterwards used as a military prison.[47] By means of the newspapers, he, like other dealers, advertised his business. Lynch posted a placard in his office, giving his rates, and the conditions under which he handled negroes. This broadside reads as follows:[48]

44. Narrative, p. 43. Brown claims that "Missouri, though a comparatively new State is (1847) very much engaged in raising slaves to supply the southern market," (ibid, p. 81). On the other hand the anti-slavery clergyman, Frederick Starr, said in 1863, "It is true that our papers are defiled by the advertisements of slave traders, but they are few. Our Courthouse witnesses the sale (of slaves) . . . and yet, this is emphatically a free city . . . most of the sales are for debt, or to close estates in accordance with the statute law . . . " (Letters to the People, No. 1, Slavery in Missouri, p. 8 (New York, 1853). He wrote under the pseudonym "Lynceus".
45. Issue of Jan. 7, 1854.
46. Published by L. and A. Carr, p. 131. In the Directory of 1859, published by R. V. Kennedy and Company, this same list appears by Lynch's address is given as 109 Locust St. (p. 615.). In a letter to S. P. Sublette of Jan. 19. 1853, Lynch gave his address as 104 Locust St. (MS. Sublette Papers).
47. An account of this building can be found in the Encyclopedia of Missouri History, vol. III, p. 1333. There was also a slave pen at Broadway and Clark Streets (J. L. Foy, "Slavery and Emancipation in Missouri," ibid, vol. IV, p. 2079). Another was located at Fifth and Myrtle streets (Galusha Anderson, A Border City During the War, p. 184). Lucy Delaney states that her mother was sold at an "auction room on Main street." (From the Darkness Cometh the Light, or Struggles for Freedom (St. Louis, 1892(?) p. 22). Father D. S. Phelan of St. Louis remembers seeing slaves sold at the block on the northeast corner of Fifth and Elm streets.
48. Photofacsimile copy in the Missouri Historical Society.

"RULES

"No charge less than one dollar

"All negroes entrusted to my care for sale or otherwise must be at the Risk of the Owners,

"A charge of 37½ cents will be made per day for board of negroes 2½ per cent on all sales of slaves,

"My usual care will be taken to avoid escape, or accidents, but will not be made Responsible should they occur. I only promise to give the same protection to other negroes that I do to my own I bar all pretext to want of diligence.

"These must be the acknowledge terms of all Negroes found in my care, as they will not be received on any other.—As these rules will be placed in my Office, so That all can see that will see, the pretence of ignorance shall not be a plea.

"1st January, 1858

B. M. LYNCH
No. 100 Locust St."

Lynch could not have been the terror-inspiring genius that the slave dealer is usually pictured. On two different occasions slaves ran for refuge to his door.[49] He was evidently clever enough to empty his "pen" on tax assessment day. In 1852 Lynch was taxed with three slaves,[50] on the same number in 1857,[51] and on four in 1860.[52]

The slave dealer had his troubles and was perhaps a little prone to horse "swapping" methods. His commodity at times fell back upon his hands. "I received your letter yesterday," runs a note from John S. Bishop to S. P. Sublette in 1854, "in reference to the negro girl I sold you. I will be on my way south by the last of October . . . and will take the negro

---

49. On Dec. 16, 1852, Lynch wrote Solomon P. Sublette, "Your negro woman Sarah came to the gate for admittance. She is here and will be held subject to your order. Very respectively, B. M. Lynch." (MS. Sublette Papers). On Jan. 19, 1852, Lynch wrote Sublette, "Your negro woman with child rang about 4 o'clock this morning for admittance and will be retained subject to your order." (Ibid.)
50. MS. Tax Book, St. Louis City, 1852, Second District p. 117.
51. MS. Tax Book, St. Louis City, 1857, vol. II, p. 96.
52. MS. Tax Book, St. Louis City, 1860, Book L to O, p. 74.

and pay you the money—or if you should see my brother J. B. Bishop he perhaps will pay you the money, and request him if he does to leave the girl at Mullhall's at the stock yards."[53] In February, 1855, Bishop wrote Sublette, "I received yours of February 8 and was rather surprised . . . times is hard and money scarce. I would of taken her as I was going south but do not want her now in hard times as negroes have fallen. I bought her above here and paid $600 for her as a Sound Negro and a very good one and will have my recourse where I bought her so you will know how to proceed according to law."[54]

In some respects the slave trade was unique. In the earlier period the negro was frequently used as a medium of exchange, being traded for land in the early days of the State.[55] Some dealers bought up horses and slaves.[56] Others handled negroes, real estate, and loans.[57] In some cases slaves were taken on trial.[58] Some dealers sold negroes on commission, boarding them till sold at the owner's risk and at his expense.[59]

53. MS., dated Mexico. Mo., Sept. 26, 1852 (Sublette Papers).
54. MS., dated February 14, 1855 (Ibid). A guarantee of soundness for a slave sale reads as follows: "Franklin County, Mo. March 1, 1856. Received of Mr. Solomon P. Sublette Eight Hundred and Fifty Dollars in full payment for a negro girl Eliza, aged 17 years, the above described negro girl, I warrant sound in body and mind a Slave for life & free from all claims. W. G. Nally." (Ibid.)
55. In the Farmers' and Mechanics' Advocate (St. Louis), of Nov. 21, 1833, is an example of this. Such advertisements are common.
56. Advertisement of George Buchanan in the Republican of March. 19, 1849.
57. "I. B. Burbbayge, General Agent, and proprietor of the old established Real Estate, Negro Slave, Money Agency and Intelligence Office, Third St., between Chestnut and Market Streets." (Daily Missourian (St. Louis), May 1, 1845).
58. We find this Advertisement in the Richmond Weekly Mirror of Oct. 20, 1854 "Negro woman for Sale—She can be taken on trial if preferred."
59. See the advertisements of Blakey and McAfee (Republican, Mar. 6 1849); B. M. Lynch (St. Louis Daily Union, Feb. 6, 1849); of R. Bartlett (Republican, Jan. 7, 1854), and of Wright and Carter in the St. Joseph Commercial Cycle of Aug. 15, 1856.

Many sorrows were undoubtedly suffered by bereaved slave families, and much misery borne by negroes in the hands of traders. But the master at times endeavored to make his departing bondman confortable. In the Republican of January 7, 1854, we read, "For Sale—A good negro man, 32 years old, and not to be taken from the city." In the same issue a dealer offered to find homes for negroes within the city or State if requested. Either these provisions were to prevent a separation of slave families or to insure the master that his negro would not be sold south.

The official negro block of St. Louis was the eastern door of the Courthouse.[60] Some of these sales, especially when negresses were on the block may have been accompanied by obscene jibes and comment. The frequency of this is denied by contemporaries. "I have often," said a citizen of Lexington, "heard the auctioneer cry, 'a sound wench, sixteen years old, good to cook, iron, bake, and work. Warranted a slave for life.' Crowds would flock to the courthouse to see the sight. I never heard or saw any indecency on such an occasion."[61] William Brown stated it was common in St. Louis to hear a negress on the block thus described: "How much is offered for this woman? She is a good cook, good washer, and a good obedient servant. She has got religion."[62]

But at its best the slave traffic was perhaps the worst feature of the system. Unruly slaves were continually threatened with being "sold south" as a means of encouraging industry or of enforcing discipline. Families were separated and obedient slaves often sold into a life of misery "down the river", either because of callousness on the part of the owner or because financial straits demanded it.[63]

---

60. Most of the notices of official slave sales state that the bidding would take place at the east door of the courthouse. Slaves were also sold at the north door.
61. Captain J. A. Wilson.
62. Narrative, p. 83.
63. Lucy Delaney states that she was continually threatened with being sold south. Her father was sent south despite the will of his late master. Lucy herself escaped this fate by hiding with friends in St. Louis

Many sad incidents occurred at the block. Children were at times wrung from their parents. Professor Peter H. Clark of St. Louis remembers a house on the southwest corner of Morgan and Garrison streets in which lived a woman who bought up infants from the mothers' arms at the slave markets of St. Louis and raised them for profit.

On the other hand a little good was inadvertently done by some dealers. The story of the finding of Wharton Blanton's slave pen near Wright City, Warren county, is most interesting. The mounds, some two score in number, were supposed to mark the resting place of some ill-fated Spanish expedition, or of an Indian tribe. After exhuming the bodies they were found to be those of negroes. Eventually it was learned that one Blanton had bought up diseased negroes about St. Louis and taken them to the above place for recuperation. Those dying on his hands were buried as above described.[64]

The incidental and often exceptional results of the system were juicy morsels for the gleaning of anti slavery agitators. The public too often generalized on these exceptions which were perhaps only too numerous.

HARRISON A. TRESLER.

University of Montana.

(Out of the Darkness Cometh the Light, p. 14, 22). Undoubtedly the sale of slaves was discouraged by the better classes. We read the following letter dated St. Joseph, Nov. 26, 1850: "I must Know tell you what I have done with Kitty. I found her two expensive and I sold here for one hundred and fifty dollars which money started me House Keeping it was through necessity I sold here." (MS. Wm. S. Hereford to S. P. Sublette, Sublette Papers.) The separation of families was also described. "I have a Negro Woman in St. Louis," runs a letter of Nov. 1, 1848, "she should remain (in St. Louis) if she prefers it—She may have a child or children, if so, dispose of the whole family to the same person . . . " (MS. Captain G. Morris to W. F. Darby, Darby Papers.)

64. This information was gained by Mr. T. C. Wilson of Columbia, Mo. Mr. Wilson was one of the excavators of this cemetery. His knowledge of the above traffic of Blanton was gained from old residents of the neighborhood. He also learned a great deal from Mr. Emil Pollien of Warrenton, Mo., the present possessor of this property. According to Mr. Pollien's papers the land came into the Blanton family's possession in 1829.

THE OLD TOWN OF ELIZABETH.

WAS CALLAWAY'S FIRST COUNTY SEAT—LOCATED ON HAM'S PRAIRIE.

Elizabeth, the first county seat of Callaway county, was located at the northwest edge of Ham's Prairie, in section 9, township 46, range 9, on 100 acres of ground donated to the county by Judge Benjamin Young and Thomas Smith. The exact location of the site cannot be determined from the records now in existence, but the impression among old citizens is that it was just west of the Rupert or Ratekin place, and immediately south of the east-and-west lane on the Mokane road, a little more than a mile northwest of the village of Ham's Prairie.

The statute of the general assembly of November, 25, 1820, which created Callaway county, appointed Josiah Ramsey, Jr., Henry Brite, William McLaughlin, Samuel Miller and Enoch Fruit members of a commission to locate the permanent seat of government of the county, and on March 8, 1821, the commissioners reported to the county court that they had chosen Elizabeth.

The report was signed by Brite, McLaughlin and Miller. Fruit dissented, making a note on the report which said: "I do hereby enter my protest against the foregoing county seat, in consequence of its not being nearer the center of the county. Enoch Fruit." Ramsey did not sign the report, and on October 1 of the same year resigned from the board. James Nevins was named as his successor by Rufus Pettibone, of St. Charles, who was the first judge of the circuit court of Callaway county.

Fruit's objection to the location of the county seat evidently was shared by the people of the county, for in 1824 a majority of the citizens of the county petitioned the general assembly to re-locate the county seat. In consequence of that petition Fulton became the county seat.

Elizabeth was named for the wife of Henry Brite, one of the commissioners. He kept a tavern on Ham's Prairie, just east of Elizabeth, in the house now owned and occupied by C. F. Shiffler, and during the time that the county seat remained at Elizabeth his tavern was used as the meeting place of all the courts. The original house was built of logs and was one story high. Many changes have been made in it, among them being the erection of a second story. All trace of Brite and his family has been lost.

Elizabeth was platted, lots were sold, and at least a jail built. The jail was burned just about the time the county seat was moved to Fulton. The proceeds from the sale of lots was $705.50, and the whole sum was spent in the erection of the jail. The first sale of lots was at public auction on May 14, 1821, when 17 were sold for $345.50.

The purchasers of lots in the town of Elizabeth were the following: William Cowherd, Samuel Miller, Thomas Smith, Henry Brite, William McLaughlin, Bethel Allen, Joseph T. Sitton, Thomas G. Rankin, Wharton R. Moore, Benjamin Young, Samuel T. Moore, Lafayette Collins, William F. Dunnica, William Coats, James Goodridge, Robert Taylor, John Coats, James Humphreys, Patrick Ewing, John Pratt, William Martin, James Nevins, Johathan Crow, Simon Riggs, Robert Humphreys, Thomas Kitchens, Daniel McLaughlin, Joseph Aud, Fontaine Marr and John Hayes.

Several lots sold as low as $5, while William Cowherd, who got lot No. 4 in block No. 7 for $40, paid the highest price. Cowherd was a tanner, and later had a tanyard on the creek in Fulton. It is possible that he was a remote relative of William S. Cowherd, Democratic nominee for governor of Missouri in 1908.

Nothing is on record to show that any houses were built in Elizabeth. Most of the men who bought lots were owners of farm lands in the county, and it is not probable that they erected houses in Elizabeth when they had no use for them. Judge Young and Mr. Smith both lived near by, and they, with the Brite tavern folks, probably constituted the settlement at the county seat.

Judge Young was a man of large consequence in the county during his life time. Governor McNair appointed him a member of the first county court, and when the court met he was chosen as presiding justice. After serving on the court about a year, Judge Young resigned, and Samuel T. Moore, who lived on Ham's Prairie and was founder of one branch of the Moore family in Callaway county, was appointed to take his place. Judge Young was elected a member of the state senate in 1822 and continued in that office through the year 1832. Subsequently he represented the county in the general assembly in 1838 and 1840. He also was a member of the state constitutional convention of 1845. Judge Young died in 1851 and is buried in the old family graveyard on Ham's Prairie. He was quite wealthy, having more than 1,100 acres of land at the time of his death, and also a dozen negroes and a lot of personal property, including considerable money that was loaned out. His will, written by Judge Irvine O. Hockaday, father of the late Judge John A. Hockaday, is on file in the office of the probate court. He was married twice, and at the time of his death his second wife and four married daughters were living. The daughters were Mrs. Mary C. Layson, mother of Samuel Layson, of Fulton; Mrs. Elizabeth A. Guthrie, Mrs. Ann E. George and Mrs. Martha V. Moore. Mrs. Young afterward married Elder Theodrick Boulware, father of I. W. Boulware, Fulton's venerable lawyer, and was his third wife. The will tells that he had given his daughters 11 negroes. His son-in-law, William M. George, was the executor of his will. Young's creek is named for Judge Young.

Many of the men who bought lots in Elizabeth have descendants living in the county today. Samuel Miller lived near Miller's Creek Methodist church, and Miller's creek was named for him. His wife, Polly Miller, was a pioneer Methodist, and they were the parents of the Rev. Dr. Wesley Green Miller, the most eminent Methodist minister Callaway county has ever produced. Joseph T. Sitton afterward moved to Fulton and kept a tavern, which was used as a meeting place for the courts until the court house was erected. All of the Moores have descendants in the county. William Coats was a Primitive Baptist preacher and the man who in 1818 established Old Salem Baptist church on Coat's Prairie, the first Protestant church in the county. John Pratt was the father of James W. Pratt, of this city, and of John and Robert Pratt, of McCredie.

John Yates, father of Dr. Martin Yates, of this city, and the man who built the first house in the original town of Fulton, kept a store at Brite's tavern during Elizabeth days. The store was owned first by Collier & Company, of St. Charles, but soon after it was opened Mr. Yates bought an interest in it. He moved the store to Fulton in 1825 and was a merchant here many years. The store at Elizabeth was the second in the county, the first being at Cote Sans Dessein and owned by Daniel Colgan, Jr.

When the county seat was moved from Elizabeth to Fulton, the ground on which Elizabeth was located reverted back to the original owners. The purchasers of lots in Elizabeth were given permission by law to buy lots in Fulton to take the place of those owned in Elizabeth, and several availed themselves of the privilege. The commissioners who built the court house and jail in Fulton, however, had to pay out $688.50 for Elizabeth claims.

The last courts at Elizabeth were held in 1825. No one is living who remembers the place, but the records of the various courts of the county tell much concerning it. Many documents in connection with its official history are still on file in the office of the clerk of the county court, among them being the reports made by the commissioners to the county court, including one giving an account of the sale of lots.

Ovid Bell.

EARLY MISSOURI ROADS.

Many of our native wild animals had their regular trails. The rabbit knew his narrow path. The deer had his, and his route was known to the hunters. When the hunter put his hounds on the trail of a deer, other persons would take positions behind trees along the known trail, and would shoot the deer as he passed. The buffalo had a well marked trail worn by the tramping of hundreds. In Ralls county I have seen an old buffalo trail 50 feet wide and 5 feet deep. This I traced for several hundred yards. I have noticed a similar trail in Newton county, Missouri. At several places in Mitchell county, Texas, I have seen well marked buffalo trails.

Our early settlers selected good land convenient to streams, but they needed neighbors. As they were often some distance apart, paths had to be made or roads cleared out. On the plains west a pile of rocks would be formed on a hilltop. Further along the route other piles would be formed. These were guides for the traveler.

Hence, our early legislatures occupied much time in passing acts authorizing certain roads. As this took up much time the matter was finally left to the counties.

Well-marked roads generally connected the nearby county seats. Campbell's maps of Missouri counties show many roads.

Before railroads were built there were well-marked and well-worn roads leading across the State. The Boonslick was probably the best traveled of our early roads. It started at St. Charles and followed the ridge most of the way to Howard county. It passed Cottleville, Pittmans, Naylor's store, Pondfort, Pauldingville (where Kemer kept), Hickory Grove, Warrenton, Camp Branch, Jones, Danville, Williamsburgh, seven miles north of Fulton, and as far north of Columbia, thence through Thralls Prairie, to Franklin and to Boonslick. This was the main route prior to 1822. Missouri becoming a State, Fulton and Columbia became county seats. This affected the travel. So, from Williamsburgh the road was opened by way of Fulton, Millersburgh, and Columbia, thence to Rocheport and Franklin. Trade at this time was much directed to Santa Fe, and the road continued westwardly from the old town of Franklin by Arrow Rock, Marshall, Malta Bend, Grand Pass, Fort Osage, to Independence. The Salt River road passed out from St. Charles to St. Peters, thence along the Mississippi bluffs to Burkles', thence by Wellsburgh, Flint Hill to Troy thence by Alexandria, Auburn, Prairieville (now Eolia), Bowling Green, New London, to Palmyra. In St. Charles county there were tributaries of this road, one known as the Middle Salt River, passing from St. Peters by Gilmores, Thos. Pierce's to Flint Hill.

From St. Louis the Manchester Road passed out northwest by Manchester, Gray's Gap, Moseley's and further across the State was known as the Springfield Road. It passed right by Wishong's and Weber's (now Rolla), thence by Lebanon, Marshfield, Springfield, Mt. Vernon, to Neosho and beyond.

From Gray's Gap on the Manchester Road, a main traveled road passed west by Union, Mt. Sterling, Lisle and Osage, to Jefferson City. From Jefferson City a road passed south by Hickory Hill and Tuscumbia to Lebanon. A well traveled stage route from Jefferson City, by Russellville, Versailles, Cole Camp, Warsaw, and Bolivar to Springfield. From Jefferson City west by Centertown, Tipton, Georgetown, Knobnoster, Warrensburg, Centre Knob, Pleasant Hill, to Independence.

All the principal roads leading out from St. Louis had names which they still keep. The Bellefontaine passed northwardly. The Natural Bridge Road and the St. Charles Rock Road both reached a point on the Missouri river opposite St. Charles. The Olive Street Road, the Manchester Road extended to Manchester and beyond, the Clayton Road passing west, the Gravois Road southwest.

In Boone there were well marked roads in different directions; from Columbia to Rocheport, Columbia to Sturgeon, the Paris Road, the Mexico Road, Providence Road, to Ashland and Jefferson City.

An important road was one from Louisiana to Bowling Green, Ashley, Middletown and Danville. Well-marked roads from Louisiana to Frankfort, Clarksville to Paynesville, Clarksville to Prairieville.

I have been over the most of the above roads, and speak from personal knowledge.

Plank roads were considered before the railroads and were built in St. Genevieve, St. Louis, Pike and Boone. They very soon were abandoned because they wore out too soon. They were not renewed and the people began to think of railroads. In 1836 railroads were first talked of. In 1836 the Legislature incorporated eighteen railroad companies, but few of which ever built roads. In 1848 the Legislature granted charters to three railroads companies. In 1852 the first few miles of the Pacific Railroad of Missouri were built. After that, railroad building progressed in Missouri.

G. C. BROADHEAD.

December, 1912.

ECHOES OF INDIAN EMIGRATION.

William Clark was Governor of Missouri Territory after its organization as a territory, from 1813, until its organization as a state in 1820. He was ex-officio superintendent of Indian Affairs during this time, and Richard Graham was Indian agent of the Osage nation. Clark continued to act as superintendent of Indian affairs until June 30, 1821, to which time he was allowed to settle his accounts, and after which, his superintendency ceased.

There were several persons who acted as interpreters, and at St. Louis there were the following official interpreters: L. T. Honore (of several languages); Paul Loise, Osage and other Indians in Missouri; P. Fournier, Osages in Missouri. In Richard Graham's Agency at St. Louis there was Philip Cramer, blacksmith, and one assistant. Also there was one blacksmith and gunsmith for the Osages, in Missouri at $550 per annum, and one for the Delawares at $550 per annum, and one for the Osages at $200 per annum.

John Kennerly was transportation agent at St. Louis receiving $400 per annum. At Fort Clark, George C. Sibley was factor, L. W. Boggs, assistant factor, and Joseph Renoe was interpreter. Paul Ballio was factor at Osage branch factory.

Preparatory to removing several of the Indian tribes from the lands purchased from them by treaty in the Ohio valley, sites were selected for them in the then far west. Dr. McCoy was the surveyor selected to mark out the limits of some of their reservations. Dr. McCoy ran the western line of Arkansas from the southwestern corner of the state of Missouri to Fort Smith, as the following letter shows, which was written by Isaac McCoy, a brother of Dr. McCoy, who was also a surveyor engaged in the surveys of the public lands.

Aug. 18th, 1831.
Station Camp, Neosho River.

Sir:

I have just completed a tour of 33 days. I first accompanied the surveyors to the southwest corner of the state of Missouri, whence Mr. Donaldson proceeded on, and has completed a traverse line from that place to Fort Smith (about 77 miles) between the Cherokee and territory of Arkansas. It remains for that line to be corrected and marked back to the corner of Missouri.

Dr. McCoy proceeded northerly from the corner of Missouri, marked the line between the Cherokees and that state, and establish the northeast corner of the Cherokee lands as I shall describe below; and thence proceeded on the line of Missouri 22 miles further, marking distinctly every five miles, in order to facilitate subsequent surveys on the Indian side.

Mr. Donaldson's instructions embraced the completion of his line. Dr. McCoy was directed to note the crossing of the first water of the Neosho, north of the corner of Missouri (which is a small creek and only about a mile and a half north of the corner of Missouri) and to proceed until he had crossed all the waters on that line which run into Neosho; to note this northern termination of his line, and then measure west until he reached the Osage reservation marking every five miles.

(Signed)   ISAAC MCCOY, Surveyor.

(See Emigrant Indians) Vol. 2—Page 561.

* * * * *

St. Louis, Dec. 13th, 1831.

Henry C. Brish, Sub Indian agent, in removing the Seneca Indians from Ohio to their lands west of Missouri arrived with them in St. Charles at this time, and found a considerable number of them were too sick to be taken farther, and one woman died. Fourteen were left. With the remainder he continued to Troy. There two others died, and nearly the whole number became sick. A number of children had their feet and hands frozen. An encampment was pitched on the Quiver Creek until better weather obtained.

"Messrs. David and Samuel Bailey, contractors to remove the Seneca Indians to their lands, were both taken ill soon after they reached Troy. Myself and the friends who accompanied me have all been sick, and have suffered much from the cold. The services of either Col. Bailey or his brother, would have been absolutely necessary to me in the trip.

"I have made an arrangement with Col. Bailey to furnish the necessary provisions to my Indians during their stay at their present encampment, and have also contracted with him to supply them for the first six months after they arrrive upon their lands, on terms which I consider reasonable. I beg leave, respectfully, to submit those reasons for the course pursued in this matter, to your consideration.

"Your Obedient Servant,
(Signed) Henry C. Brish.
Sub Indian Agent."

"Gen. Wm. Clark,
"Superintendent Indian Affairs St. Louis.

In a letter from Wm. Clark, the Secretary of War, dated St. Louis, Dec. 20, 1831, he explains that Mr. Brish contracted with Bailey, "to supply the Senecas, encamped near Troy, with provisions, at ten cents per ration, and to procure, (while provisions can be obtained), a supply for six months to be delivered on their lands at sixteen cents per ration. This is, I believe, as reasonable as provisions can be procured and transported." There were 232 Senecas.

When the Shawnees crossed the state of Missouri they were under Lieutenant Col. J. J. Abert, special commissioner of Emigration. They crossed the Mississippi into Missouri at Alton on Nov. 1, and 2, 1832. They had followed the same route as the Senecas as far as Vandalia and here Clark's advice was for them to avoid St. Louis. They were going to their lands on the Kansas river and hence this northern route. A small detachment of Ottawas were with them as part of the emigration. This band was connected by intermarriages with the Shawnees, and looked up to them as elder brothers. The cholera attacked the Ottawas, but with no serious results. On the 16th of November they arrived at the Missouri, at Arrow Rock, and here a storm delayed them, and they were five days in crossing the Missouri. Here, at Arrow Rock, they received twenty-three new rifles, which had been provided for in treaty with the Shawnees.[1] The Shawnee village, twenty miles west of Independence, Mo., was reached during the afternoon of November 30th. The Shawnees in this band numbered about 450, and the Ottawas about 100.

In a letter from James B. Gardiner to Hon. Lewis Cass, Secretary of War, bearing date of Feb. 25, 1833, he says:[2] "For the sake of convenience, as well as to avoid collisions and quarrels on the way, each tribe or band was marched separately, and as nearly as circumstances would permit, from ten to twenty miles apart. While passing through the populous setttlements, it was found impossible to prevent the Indians from obtaining ardent spirits in such quantities as produced some serious disturbances and numerous detentions.

"The most of these travelled on horseback. A few had carriages and wagons of their own. The sick, the aged, and the decrepit, who were unable to ride on horses, were carried in the public baggage wagons in a comfortable manner."

Gardiner, under date Dec. 1, 1832, writes Lewis Cass, that he has just received a letter from Col. Abert, dated at Franklin, Mo., which "gives him the gratifying intelligence that the cholera had entirely subsided among the Ohio Emigrating Indians. No new cases had occurred for the, then, last six days, and those slightly attacked were all convalescent. The Indians had crossed the Missouri at Arrow Rock ferry, and were pushing on to their destination with all possible speed." Delaware Indians from Little Sandusky, Ohio, were also removed but were only about thirty in number.

DAVID W. EATON,
Versailles, Mo.

---

[1]. See Indian Treaties, 1778 to 1837, p. 483, Art., 12.
[2]. Emigrant Indians, Vol. III, p. 111.

JOURNAL ACROSS MISSOURI, OF BAND OF OHIO INDIANS TO THE INDIAN TERRITORY.

The following is an excerpt from a "Journal of occurrences kept by the conducting officer of the Seneca and Shawnee emigrating Ohio Indians to their lands west of Missouri." These Indians lived in the vicinity of Lewistown, Logan county, Ohio, and numbered 220 persons. They assembled at Lewistown on August 20, 1832 as they had been previously notified to do, and were prepared for the trip by first being vaccinated. They were also requested to choose their own method of transportation, whether by horseback, wagon or by steamboat, these being the only means of transportation then in use in this part of the country. They were to be removed to the Neosho River in the Indian Territory. They chose to travel by horseback, many of the squaws refusing to travel either by wagon or steamboat. After some delays as to making a start they finally got under way, September 19th, and the progress of the party is given day by day until its arrival at the Mississippi, after which date I will quote the Journal word for word. Upon reaching Vandalia, Ill., news was brought them that the cholera was prevalent in St. Louis, and the conductor sent a messenger to report to Governor Clark, and ask as to the truth of the information, and to get his advice as to the best route to take to reach the Indian Territory, as it had evidently been the plan to have gone via St. Louis. Clark advised crossing the river at Kaskaskia, which was on the Illinois side opposite St. Genevieve county, Missouri. They arrived at Kaskaskia on the evening of Thursday, November 6th, but the wind being strong, they did not cross. From this date the Journal was as follows:

"Wednesday, 7th (Nov.) Today about two-thirds of them were taken over, which occupied their time until dark.

"Thursday, 8th—The remaining part of the Indians were taken over to day.

"Friday, 9th—The Indians remained in camp for the purpose of getting their horses shod.

"Saturday, 10th—The Indians had considerable difficulty in finding their horses. We started late, and only travelled eight miles.

"Sunday 11th—We travelled eighteen miles.

"Monday 12th—We travelled seventeen miles.

"Tuesday 13th—We travelled four miles, one mile west of mine of Burton where we camped for the purpose of having the remainder of the horses shod.

"Wednesday 14th—We remained today for the purpose of getting horses shod, and giving the squaws an opportunity of washing their clothes and blankets.

"Thursday 15th—It was late this morning before the Indians could collect all their horses; we travelled only eight miles.

"Friday, 16th—We travelled sixteen miles to the Merimack River.

"Saturday, 17th—A family was left behind a day or two ago, which the Indians say they intend waiting for at this place.

"Sunday, 18th—Rained all day so much that the Indians would not start.

"Monday, 19th—It was so cold that the Indians refused to travel. It snowed and blowed terribly.

"Tuesday, 20th—A child died this morning (the only death which has occurred in this tribe), which detained us until late. Some horses strayed away, which added to the delay. We travelled seven miles.

"Wednesday, 21st—We travelled eighteen miles.

"Thursday, 22d—It rained and snowed so much that the Indians could not travel.

"Friday, 23d—We marched fifteen miles.

"Saturday, 24th—We struck our tents at 8 o'clock, and marched until about 5. We made the distance of sixteen miles. The horses of two of the teamsters ran away, and their wagons were consequently left behind.

"Sunday, 25th—A part of the detachment travelled ten miles, and the remainder continued stationary. The wagons which were left behind yesterday arrived in the evening.

"Monday, 26th—The Indians who remained behind yesterday, waiting for the teams, joined those in front.

"Thursday, 27th—We marched ten miles.

"Wednesday, 28th—We struck our tents at 8 o'clock and continued travelling until late in the evening, by which means we made the distance of eighteen miles.

"Thursday, 29th—We travelled thirteen miles to the Gasconade.

"Friday, 30th—The Indians remained today for the purpose of waiting for some of their brethern, who are behind.

"Saturday, December 1st, 1832. Commenced raining in the night and continued all day so that the detachment could not travel.

"Sunday, 2d—We were compelled to cross the streams several times to day, which nearly swam the horses, so that we were detained along the road so much that we travelled but eight miles.

"Monday, 3d—We travelled fourteen miles. One keg of powder and one hundred pounds of lead were given to the Indians to day, by First Lieutenant Lane, upon condition that they should pay for it in game, which should be divided among all as other supplies of provision.

"Thursday, 4th—We travelled twenty miles to day. We started early and had a good road, and travelled late.

"Wednesday, 5th—We travelled thirteen miles today, which brought us to White River.

"Thursday, 6th—We remained at the encampment for the purpose of refreshing the detachment.

"Friday, 7th—About 10 o'clock we left the encampment and crossed White River, and marched nine miles beyond it, making ten miles today.

"Saturday, 8th—We travelled twelve miles to Gibson's fork of the Neosho.

"Sunday, 9th—We travelled fifteen miles..

"Monday, 10th—We travelled seven miles today. We could have gone farther, but it was necessary to halt to get corn and meat.

"Tuesday, 11th—We travelled thirteen miles.

"Wednesday, 12th—We travelled eighteen miles.

"Thursday, 13th—We travelled twelve miles to the Seneca Agency. Here the Indians were delivered to Major Kennerly, the agent for the Senecas.

(Signed) Daniel M. Workman, conductor of Lewistown Emigrating Indians.

DAVID W. EATON,
Versailles, Mo.

FAMOUS GOOSE CASE.

First Missouri Justice of the Peace to Deliver Written Opinion —Forty Years Ago.

As far as known the first justice of the peace in Missouri to deliver a written opinion was Thomas B. Gentry, of Columbia, the father of Ex-Assistant Attorney-General N. T. Gentry. Not far from the historic Bonne Femme Baptist Church, and near the banks of a little stream, now called "Goose Creek," two women had a difficulty, which resulted in the name for the creek, a bruised head for one woman, and a criminal prosecution in the magistrate's court for the other woman. The time consumed in the trial of this little case was five days; three days in the taking of testimony, one day in argument and the justice took one day to consider the case. Six of Boone county's leading attorneys, Odon Guitar, Squire Turner, A. J. Harbinson, J. D. W. Robinson, F. F. C. Triplet and H. C. Pierce, took part in this noted trial; and a host of witnesses and many spectators thronged the old courthouse. The written opinion of Justice Gentry is as follows, and the same was read by him to the eager crowd in the court room:

"State of Missouri vs. Rachael Scott. The defendant is charged with feloniously assaulting, with a dangerous weapon, and maiming, wounding, disfiguring, causing great bodily harm and endangering the life of Sarah P. Gans, under such circumstances as would have constituted murder or man-slaughter, if death had ensued. The defendant entered a plea of not guilty; —she admits the striking but claims that it was done in the defense of her own property, to-wit two geese.

"From the evidence in this case, it appears that for some time previous to the 28th of February 1872, Mrs Rachel Scott, the defendant, and Mrs Sarah P. Gans had been living on neighboring farms South of Columbia; and that for a long time they had not been on friendly terms. On that day, Mrs Gans entered upon the premises and within the enclosure of the defendant, without permission or invitation, and began driving four of her own and one or two of Mrs Scott's geese. The testimony also shows that the defendant warned Mrs Gans to let the geese alone, stating to her in a loud tone of voice that two of those geese belonged to her (defendant), but that Mrs. Gans continued to drive all of the geese toward the front gate, which she had previously proped open. She was in the act of driving them through said gate and onto the Columbia & Ashland gravel road, when the defendant struck her.

"I regard the entry of Mrs Gans upon the defendant's premises, under the circumstances, as a trespass; and the attempt to drive off defendant's geese, or goose, as the case may be, without permission as a still further trespass. Mrs Gans was clearly in the wrong place, where she had no right to be, and engaged in the commission of an unlawful act and must be considered a trespasser. Under these circumstances, she was assaulted by defendant with a pine stick twenty-two and one-half inches in length, one inch and a quarter in thickness and two inches wide, which stick was picked up by the defendant after she started out from her house to where Mrs Gans was driving the geese. The wounds produced by this stick upon the person of Mrs Gans were not shown to be dangerous wounds, or disfiguring wounds, and it was not shown that her life was endangered thereby. The assault made by defendant, under such circumstances, viewed in the light of human law, I regard as justifiable. The battery, however, which was proved to be considerable, and was not resisted, was perhaps excessive, and went beyond what was necessary for the defendant to make in order to keep possession of her personal property. Yet considering the results and effects of this battery, as they appear in the testimony, I cannot regard them as sufficiently great to constitute a violation of Section 33 of Chapter 42 of Criminal Code of Missouri. In other words, if the defendant had intended to kill Mrs Gans, I do not believe she would have selected this little pine stick. The offense then, in my opinion, is reduced to a simple assault and battery; which until properly charged and sworn to, I shall not feel called upon to have investigated. I therefore discharge the defendant from custody.

T. B. GENTRY, J. P."

Soldiers of War of 1812.

In 1857 a petition was signed by the soldiers of the war of 1812, living in Boone county, for a pension to be granted to the serving soldiers of that war. Below are the names of those who signed it, the state where born and the age at the time of signing the petition. It does not state the regiment in which the service was performed:

John Barclay, Kentucky, 66 years.
John Barnes, Kentucky, 64 years, 8 months.
Henry Berry, Kentucky, 60 years.
Benjamin Brookshire, North Carolina, 61 years.
John Caruthers, Virginia, 64 years.
Allen Coats, North Carolina, 87 years.
Abraham Davenport, Virginia, 77 years.
John Davenport, Virginia, 64 years.
Berkley Estes, Virginia, 60 years.
James Green, Kentucky, 71 years.
John Green, Kentucky, 67 years.
Thompson Hardin, Virginia, 72 years.
Fleetwood Herndon, Virginia, 67 years, 2 months.
Greenbury Jacobs, Virginia, 73 years.
James King, Kentucky, 62 years.
Cyrus Lusk, Kentucky, 61 years, 3 months.
Hugh Melvin, Kentucky, 73 years.
Gabriel Parker, Maryland, 66 years.
Hiram Phillips, Virginia, 66 years, 6 months.
Daniel G. Searcy, Kentucky, 63 years.
Williams Simmes, Kentucky, 67 years.
Norborne B. Spottswood, Virginia, 67 years, 2 months.
Elijah Stephens, North Carolina, 75 years.
James Thomas, Virginia, 65 years, 5 months.
David Todd, Kentucky, 71 years, 6 months.
Samuel B. Todd, Kentucky, 64 years, 6 months.
Cornelius Vanansdal, Virginia, 65 years.
James Willer, Virginia, 67 years.
Isaac Williams, Pennsylvania, 66 years, 7 months.

Manuscripts Saved.

The Third Biennial Report of the Society gave an account of the donation of a very valuable collection of manuscript made by the grandchildren of Gen. Thomas A. Smith, of Saline county. Since the donation was made to the Society the residence of Dr. George P. Smith in Saline county, where the collection was given to the Society was burned with the loss of his entire library. The General's heirs decided wisely when they gave the collection to a place of safety and permanent preservation.

St. Louis Nights Wi' Burns.

"Burns and Religion," by Rev. W. C. Bitting; "Burns, The World Poet," by William Marion Reedy; "Burns and English Poetry," by Professor J. L. Lowes; "Burns and the Prophet Isaiah," by Judge M. N. Sale; "Burns and the 'Auld Clay Biggin,' " by Frederick W. Lehmann; "The Club, the Room, the Burnsiana, the Nights," by Walter B. Stevens. Printed for private distribution to lovers of Burns by the Burns Club of St. Louis, 1913.

The Burns Club of St. Louis headed by W. K. Bixby, who has made himself and St. Louis known among lovers of books, and especially of privately printed books, has issued this fine little work, with excellent papers on various phases of Burns and of his works. This club has a membership of twenty-one members who have given a fine memento of their love of Burns, and the Society is under obligations to the Club for a copy.

$50.00 REWARD.

Ran away this morning, my negro man David. He is a black man, about six feet two or three inches high, stout made fond of whiskey, getting drunk whenever he can procure it. Had on when he went off, a good hat, blue cloth coat, velvet collar, brown broad cloth pantaloons, vest, etc., not recollected. He is pretty well known about this place, and there is little doubt but he will be found lurking about H. Gratiot's or Papin's old place. The above reward will be given to any person who will lodge him in the St. Louis gaol, or delever him to me well pinioned and secured.

The cause of my man's running off, was a knowledge of my intention to move down to the Chickasaw purchase; together with an apprehension of being chastised for disobeying and giving me insolent and abusive language, in Col. Benton's yard, as he went off. I have owned said fellow for several years, and never molested him; nor should I have had a pretence for undertaking it when he ran off, if he had not been spirited up. He has been instigated to give me abusive language, and to leave me, by two or three persons within and about this place. I presume that the said fellow is either in this place at this time, or in its vicinity; and that he may be found in St. Louis or Papin's old house, half a dozen miles from this place, as soon as my departure is announced. I hereby forewarn all persons from employing, harboring, or affording him any protection, aid, or the like, under the penalty of the law. I will empower a man in this case, who understands and has the spirit to assert his rights. I have been told that I had a list doomed to death; this I say is not true; and that I do not owe but one or two fellows that much harm; and even them I shall not turn out of my course to find, for the poor devils will die of fear. At any rate my man David is not among the proscribed.

One hundred dollars in silver will be given to any person who will deliver him to me or my agent, at the Chickasaw Bluffs.

NATH BENTON.

N. B. No person within the Missouri territory has any authority from me, neither to sell, hire, employ or control the said negro David; and any one offending in these particulars, besides other inconveniences, will be posted for a rascal.

N. G.

—Missouri Gazette and Public Advertisers, March 29, 1820.

WISCONSIN'S LOSS.

Reuben Gold Thwaites, beyond question the most widely known secretary of any Historical Society in the United States, the editor of the "Jesuit Relations," in more than sixty volumes, the "Early Western Travels," in thirty-two volumes, and "Lewis and Clark Travels," in fifteen volumes, died suddenly since our last issue. Dr. Frederick Jackson Turner, of Harvard University, delivered a memorial address in the Assembly Chamber of the State Capitol at Madison, Wisconsin, December 19, 1913.

BOOK NOTICES.

OLD TAVERN. Arrow Rock, Missouri. Established on Santa Fe Trail, 1830. Compiled by J. P. BIGGS, Arrow Rock, 1913.

From the portraits of the tavern given in the booklet, the present name from the sign at the door, seems to be "Old Tavern." What it originally was called is not stated, but probably it was without name, or was known as "Arrow Rock Tavern." In its continuous use, from 1830 to the present, it has had many of the prominent men of early days as guests, and in 1912 the local Women's National Old Trails Road Association fitted up a rest room in the hotel for the comfort and entertainment of the present day travelers. This room has a portrait of George C. Bingham, and lithographs of ten of Bingham's paintings. The State Historical Society ought to be able to say this about its collection, but unfortunately it cannot do it. The room has also many historic relics, which are of interest to all now passing over the old Santa Fe Trail.

The booklet gives an interesting history of the town of Arrow Rock, where Capt. Geo. Sibley built a substantial log house in 1807; the first plat of the town, then called Philadelphia was filed in 1829. Credit for the compilation and publication of the booklet is due to Mr. Biggs, cashier of the Arrow Rock Stock Bank, and it is to be hoped that many others will publish similar local memorials.

NOTES ON THE LIFE OF NOAH WEBSTER, compiled by EMILY ELLSWORTH FOWLER FORD. Edited by Emily Ellsworth Ford Skeel, two volumes. New York, Privately printed, 1912.

The society is endebted for the above privately printed work to the editor, Mrs. Roswell Skeel, Jr. The principal part of the work was prepared by her mother twenty years before, and was enlarged from its original scope by the publication of the life of Webster by Horace E. Scudder in the American Men of Letters Series, which seemed to the compiler, Webster's daughter, to be very unjust and incorrect. In philology Webster began his studies in 1783, and the oldest claim of comparative philology in Europe dates from the formation of the Oriental Society in 1784, so he was the pioneer in Europe as well as in America.

Dr. Johnson wrought seven years with six amanuenses, and with a certainty of a final recompense as five firms of booksellers agreed to take the huge scheme in hand and give Johnson £1575 for his share of the work. But Webster wrought single handed for forty-three years at the study of language, and for twenty-eight years at the making of the Dictionary, never condescending to an amanuensis until he was eighty years of age, with but few means of support outside of his own personal earnings, and but small promise of help from any source.

His was a wonderful achievement, and one that Americans ought to know and honor.

THE INJUSTICE OF HISTORY. A neglected patriot. By Companion Captain WILLIAM R. HODGES.

This paper on Thomas Paine was read before the Commandery of Missouri of the Military Order of the Loyal Region, October 4, 1913, and printed by order of the Commandery, of which the author is the secretary.

THE FUNDAMENTAL LAWS OF HUMAN BEHAVIOR. Lectures on the foundations of any mental or social science, by MAX MEYER, Professor of Experimental Psychology in the University of Missouri, Boston, Richard G. Badger, (C. 1911.)

This work is intended to describe the complete dependence of all human activity on the functional properties of the nervous system, on the changes which these functional properties undergo during life, and particularly the way in which these changes come about.

What the book proposes to do is essentially an investigation into the problem contained in the inquiry, What are the simplest assumptions, necessary and sufficient, to explain hypothetically the facts of human behavior as dependent on the function of the nervous system? Having answered this question, it attempts to illuminate the deep-rooted habit of describing human behavior as dependent on subjective states, on states of consciousness, a habit which still largely governs the sciences of human society, preventing them from throwing off the shackles of subjectivity.

The work has been adopted by Columbia University and the University of Missouri.

A SYSTEM OF PHONETICS applied to the English language for the use of singers and speakers by HOMER MOORE,
St. Louis, (C. 1913.)

The author is a teacher of speaking and of music, and quotes a sentence from Shakespeare, that should be quoted frequently to all public speakers and singers: "Speak the speech, I pray you, as I pronounced it to you—trippingly on the tongue; but if you mouth it, as many of our players do, I had as lief the town-crier spoke my lines."

THE PROCEEDINGS OF THE NANTUCKET HISTORICAL ASSOCIATION at its nineteenth annual meeting held during the past year, shows the fact that the local historical societies of the east are better supported and create more general interest than do those in the west. This Society has a present membership of 338, the total number from the start being 609. Among the manuscripts acquired during the year was a deed of manumission of Hiram Reed, a slave in St. Louis, and afterwards a resident of Nantucket. He was freed by Gen. Fremont, and the deed was signed by Fremont, September 12, 1861.

The proceedings give an account of a meeting of the Bay State Historical League of the Historical Societies of the State of Massachusetts. At the meeting there were sixty delegates from twenty historical societies of the State. The Association preserves old account books, diaries, inventories, copies of family bible records, cemetery records and other things that might have a bearing on historical or genealogical subjects.

An account is given of a visit to a little burial ground whose broken head stones were piled around the walls, but by the aid of a man to handle the stones every inscription was copied by the enterprising young lady who was looking up data.

A notice of the meeting of the American Historical Association at Boston, mentions a meeting in the hall of the Massachusetts Historical Society, a hall that was not large, but the voices of the speakers were so low and indistinct that it was difficult to understand them. The editor is sorry to say that he notices that fault at every meeting of the Association.

THE KEEPER OF THE VINEYARD. A tale of the Ozarks, by CAROLINE ABBOT STANLEY, New York, Fleming H. Revell Company, (C. 1813.)

This story of a "return to nature" lies in the Missouri Ozarks, and the events are told so naturally and true to life that the reader feels a companionship with the characters, and an interest in all the efforts of the heroine of the story in her struggle to overcome obstacles unexpectedly encountered.

Eleanor Dinwoody, a successful teacher, is suddenly confronted with the problem not only of the maintenance of her brother's family of five, but of the proper care of a girl budding into young womanhood and of a boy hardly beyond the years of infancy. The story of how she got them to Missouri and how she maintained them there, and at the same time was an almost unconscious leader in the uplift of the entire neighborhood holds the unfailing interest of the readers who are open to the appeal to men and women of like sympathy and aims and passions.

The Society is under obligations to the authoress and publisher for this addition to the Society Collection of Missouri authors, and to Mrs. Stanley for a set of her other works.

THE HUGH STEPHENS IMPRINT, Published by the Hugh Stephens Printing Co., Jefferson City, Mo.

This booklet was issued as a reminder of the good printing and illustrating work by this well known Company. It has a printing plant of a capacity of more than a half million pages of book presswork daily. Its output of commercial work and of bound books is very great; its facilities are of the best with an expanse of 24,000 square feet, and 125 workmen.

A SHEAF OF MEMORIES. Address by R. F. WALKER at a meeting of the Old Settlers Association of Morgan County, Missouri.

If all of the old settlers associations of the state would have some competent person deliver interesting addresses like the above they would perform a great benefit in preserving local history.

BRIEF BIOGRAPHY and popular account of the unparalleled discoveries of T. J. J. SEE. BY W. L. WEBB, Lynn, Mass., 1913.

The author shows that Prof. See has done what no one before him ever did—laid the foundations for two great physical sciences; Cosmogony, dealing with the creation of the Heavens; and Geogony, which treats of the creation of the earth. The accomplishment of this by Prof. See, while yet a young man, has placed him at the head of living natural philosophers.

Prof. See was born in Montgomery County, Missouri, February, 19, 1866, and took his first University degree in 1889. Since that time degrees and positions of honor and of learning have been held by him, and since 1903 he has been pursuing his investigations while in charge of the Naval Observatory at Mare Island, California.

The octavo work of about 300 pages, with many illustrations gives a popular account of the work that has been accomplished by Professor See, and it will furnish pleasure and information to the reader.

NECROLOGY.

MAJOR WILLIAM HENRY CURRENT died in St. Louis, August 24, 1913, and was buried by Ransom Post in the National Cemetery at Jefferson Barracks. During the civil war he was Major of the 134th Indiana Infantry, and later came to Pettis county, Missouri. He studied law with Sampson & Bro., at Sedalia and after his admission to the bar he was engaged on several newspapers, and was married there. He moved to St. Louis and for some time was connected with the office of the Metropolitan Insurance Company, and in his later years was a writer for insurance periodicals.

HON. ADOLPH E. METHUDY, member of the Senate in the Forty-fourth, Forth-fifth and Forty-sixth General Assemblies of Missouri, died at Highland, North Carolina, December 16, 1913. He was born in St. Louis in 1876, and was a graduate from Smith Academy, Manual Training School, Washington University and St. Louis Law School. On account of failing health he was compelled to withdraw from the Senate.

JUDGE LUTHER C. SLAVENS was born in Indiana seventy-seven years ago, and a graduate of De Pauw University. Soon after the civil war he came to Kansas City, and in the Republican Presidential Convention of 1880 he was one of the 306 who remained staunch for a third term for General Grant.

He served a term as circuit judge, and was city Counselor of Kansas City at the time when the city succeeded in becoming the owner of the waterworks. Judge Slavens suddenly died while sitting in a chair in a hotel in Kansas City, October 23, 1913.

HON. WESLEY A. VIA aged 71 years, a member of the Thirty-Sixth General Assembly in 1882, died December 17, 1913 at Rolla of which place he was one of the oldest residents. He served in the Confederate army under Col. Early A. Steen.

MONUMENTAL INSCRIPTIONS IN MISSOURI CEMETERIES.

THIRTEENTH PAPER.

The following is a partial list from the cemetery in Columbia, and is, with some exceptions, of persons who died before 1876, or of persons who died since who were more than 75 years old:

Stephen Bedford, born April 20, 1823; died Oct. 20, 1875.
Caroline L. Bedford, born Aug. 22, 1828; died April 24, 1897.
William, son of Robert S. and Mary M. Barr, born Nov. 11, 1838; died Dec. 3, 1858.
James T. Barr, died Nov. —, 1830, aged six years and seven months.
Daniel D. Barr, died Sept. —, 1831, aged one year, nine months.
Robert N. Barr, died May 10, 1837, aged three years, eleven months, fourteen days.
  (Children of Robt. S. and Mary M. Barr.)
Robert Steele Barr, died Sept. 24, 1852, aged 55 years, 7 months and 15 days.
Mary M., wife of Robert S. Barr, died April 22, 1881, aged 78 years, 6 months and 13 days.
Alexander Douglass, died February 10, 1866, aged 47 years.
Albert M. Elston, died March 21, 1868, aged 29 years, 11 month and 1 day.
Sue M. Elston, wife of Albert M. Elston, died Oct. 25, 1868, aged 28 years, 1 month and 17 days.
James Ferguson, born May 15, 1812; died July 11, 1888.
Mary E. Ferguson, died Sept. 12, 1870, aged 43 years, 6 months and 7 days.
James Hickman, born June 5, 1764; died April 25, 1825.
William T. Hickman, born in Bourbon county, Kentucky, September 2, 1819; died January 31, 1897.
Sophia W. Hickman, born January 1, 1801; died April 29, 1843.
Mary F. Woods, wife of William T. Hickman, born in Boone county, Missouri, June 1, 1829; died August 23, 1905.

David H. Hickman, born November 11, 1821; died June 25, 1869.

Annie Bryan, wife of David H. Hickman, born January 28, 1839; died July 9, 1867.

Eliza K. Hickman, wife of David M. Hickman, born November 7, 1802; died June 14, 1827.

David M. Hickman, born August 10, 1788; died June 14, 1851.

Milton Hickman, son of David M. and Cornelia A. Hickman, born August 25, 1835; died August 13, 1836.

Dr. George R. Jacobs, born in Nelson county, Virginia, Feb. 20, 1802; died February 24, 1877.

Laura H. Jacobs, wife of J. T. Jacobs, and daughter of J. M. and B. M. Huston, born December 27, 1836; died August 8, 1872.

Jeremiah Orear, born July 15, 1799; died April 28, 1875.

Mary Orear, born July 4, 1796; died December 12, 1864.

Nannie L., wife of John W. Rollins, and only daughter of Richard Stowers of Kentucky, born December 17, 1827; died July 16, 1862.

Sallie Rodes, wife of A. W. Rollins, born in Madison county, Kentucky, June 7, 1787; died July 12, 1856.

Robert R. Rollins, born in Madison county Kentucky, May 7, 1818; died March 2, 1864.

Anthony W. Rollins, born in Westmorland county, Pennsylvania, March 5, 1783; died October 9, 1845.

A model citizen, an able physician, a sterling patriot, a Christian philanthropist, just and upright in all the relations of life, he commanded universal respect and died lamented by all who knew him.

Sallie W. Rollins, born February 24, 1849; died in Denver, Colorado, November 20, 1872.

James S. Rollins, born in Richmond, Madison county Kentucky, April 19, 1812; died January 9, 1888.

Mary E. Hickman Rollins, wife of James S. Rollins, born in Howard county, Missouri, October 10, 1820; died May 1, 1907.

Annie E., wife of G. W. Rogers, died Oct. 13, 1870, aged 27 years, 6 months 13 days.

James Shannon, LL. D., born in Monaghan county, Ireland April 23, 1799; died February 25, 1859.

A Christian philanthropist and teacher has gone to receive the crown of the faithful.

James Ways, son of James and Francis C. Shannon, born in Jackson, Louisiana, March 24, 1839; died July 20, 1859.

Emeline A. Staten, died January 11, 1867, aged 33 years.

Dr. Archibald Young, died February 23, 1869, aged 41 years, 4 months, 23 days.

DEATH NOTICES.

In "*Missouri Intelligencer and Boon's Lick Advertiser,*" published at Franklin, Howard county, Missouri, April 23, 1819, to June 16, 1826; at Fayette same county, June 29, 1826 to June 9, 1830; and Columbia, Boone county, May 4, 1830 to December 5, 1835, when the paper became the "*Columbia Patriot.*"

When the deaths did not occur at the place of publication or its vicinity, the place is stated. The first date give is the date of death, and the second the date of publication.

Dr. William Baldwin. Sept. 1, 1819; Sept. 3, 1819. Of U. S. Navy.

Capt. Aaron T. Crane. Sept. 26, 1819; Oct. 15, 1819. At St. L. Ex. P. M.

Christine Wilt. Oct. 11, 1819; Oct. 15, 1819.

Peter Ferguson. Feb. 16, 1820; Feb. 18, 1820.

Henry Carroll. Feb. 28, 1820; Mch. 4, 1820. Murdered.

Wm. Jucket, 6th Inf. Reg. Apr. 6, 1820; Apr. 22, 1820. At Cantonment, Missouri.

Maj. Chas. M. Phierson. June 29, 1820; July 1, 1820.

John S. Bristow. July 25, 1820; July 29, 1820. Of Ky.

Col. Daniel Boone. Sept. 26, 1820; Oct. 14, 1820. At Charette village.

Geo. Holliday. Sept. 30, 1820; Oct. 14, 1820.

Miss Elizabeth Shaw. Nov. 5, 1820; Nov. 16, 1820.

Heron Corum. Oct. 26, 1820; Nov. 16, 1820.

John Short. Dec. 17, 1820; Jan. 1, 1821.
Wm. Chisham. Dec. 28, 1820; Jan. 1, 1821.
Wm. Chisham. Dec. 29, 1820; Jan. 15, 1821.
Jesse B. Boone. Dec. 22, 1820; Jan. 1, 1821. At. St. Louis.
Mrs. Charlotte C. L. Riske. May 19, 1821; May 21, 1819.
Charlotte Chambers Ludlow Risk. Aug. 28, 1821.
Col. Samuel Williams, Aug. 11, 1821; Aug. 28, 1821. At Chariton Co. Member Legislature.
Dr. Chas. Kavenaugh. Aug. 27, 1821; Aug. 28, 1821.
Mrs. Elizabeth Waserman. Aug. 27, 1821; Aug. 28, 1821.
John Payne. Sept. 15, 1821; Sept. 25, 1821.
Capt. Asa Morgan. Sept. 21, 1821; Sept. 25, 1821. At Boonville.
Miss Margaret Dodd, Sept. 18, 1821; Sept. 25, 1821.
James D. Miller. Sept. 23, 1821; Sept. 25, 1821.
    By lightning.
Miss Mary B. Patten. Sept. 8, 1821; Oct. 9, 1821.
Robert P. Barr. ———; Oct. 9, 1821.
Robert Shaw. Nov. 12, 1821; Nov. 13, 1821.
Mrs. Martha Clark. June 21, 1822; July 2, 1822.
Andrew McClure. Aug. 8, 1822; Aug. 13, 1822.
Mrs. Nancy Mullens. Aug. 11, 1822; Aug. 13, 1822.
Jno. W. Scudder. Aug. 11, 1822; Aug. 13, 1822. In Boonville.
Dabney Carr. Aug. 6, 1822; Aug. 13, 1822. In St. Louis.
Miss Caroline I. Barr. July 8, 1822; Aug. 13, 1822.
Capt. Baxter M. Ewing. Aug. 13, 1822; Sept. 3, 1822 In Cooper county.
Col. Elias Rector, Aug. 7, 1822; Sept. 3, 1822. In St. Louis. P. M. and State Senator.
John Gaw. Sept. 11, 1822; Sept. 17, 1822.
James Donaldson. Sept. 26, 1822; Oct. 1, 1822.
John S. Peebels. Aug. 1822; Oct. 15, 1822. At St. Francisville.
James Barnes. Oct. 13, 1822; Oct. 22, 1822.
Mrs. Cynthia Jewell. Oct. 18. 1822; Oct. 22, 1822. Wife of Dr. Wm. Jewell. At Columbia.

DEATH NOTICES

Armsted S. Grundy. Feb. 14, 1823; Feb. 18, 1823.
Franklin Chrissman. April 11, 1823; Apr. 15, 1823.
James Finney. Apr. 2, 1823; May 20, 1823. Of Howard county. At St. Louis.
Wm. S. Edwards. May 21, 1823; May 27, 1823. In Saline county.
Baylor Banks. July 14, 1823; July 22, 1823. Near Chariton.
J. H. Handy. Dec. 8, 1823; Dec. 23, 1823. Killed in duel at Potosi.
Henry V. Bingham. Dec. 26, 1823; Dec. 30, 1823.
Rev. Thos. Hubbard. Dec. 25, 1823; Dec. 30, 1823.
Chas. Carroll. Oct. 28, 1283; Jan. 6, 1824. At Williamsburg, N. Y. Formerly Register, Land Office, Franklin, Mo.
Daniel Chriesman and Bartlett Hall. Feb. 1, 1824; Feb. 5, 1824. Drowned below Boonville.
Dr. Jabez Hubbard. Feb. 4, 1824; Feb. 5, 1824.
Hon. John Rice Jones. Feb. 1, 1824; Feb. 14, 1824. At St. Louis. Judge Supreme Court.
Mrs. Jane Hughes. Feb. 5, 1824; Feb. 21, 1824.
James McMunn. Aug. 19, 1824; Aug. 21, 1824.
Mary Jane Todd. Aug. 24; 1824, Aug. 28, 1824.
Mrs. Mary Mahan. Aug. 30, 1824; Sept. 4, 1824.
John Shaw. Sept. 12, 1824; Sept. 18, 1824.
Cynthia Smith Berry. Oct. 4, 1824; Oct. 23, 1824.
Maj. Taylor Berry. Sept. 22, 1824; Nov. 6, 1824.
Mrs. John Shaw. Feb. 17, 1825; Mch. 1, 1825.
Peter B. Harris. May 2, 1825; May 7, 1825.
Elizabeth S. Hood, May 25, 1825; July 2, 1825.
Martha McGirk. July 8, 1825; July 16, 1825.
Frederick Bates. Aug. 4, 1825; Aug. 12, 1825. Gov. of Mo. At St. Louis.
Judge Rufus Pettibone. July 31, 1825; Aug. 12, 1825. Of Supreme Court. At St. Charles.
Matthias Haywood. Aug. 4, 1825; Aug. 12, 1825.
George McGirk. Apr. 6, 1826; Apr. 7, 1826.
Alex McNair. ———; Apr. 7, 1826. Late Governor.

Mrs. Abr. Groom. Apr. 7, 1826; Apr. 14, 1826. Clay county.

Joseph Cooley. April 3, 1826; Apr. 14, 1826. Formerly of Howard county.

Mrs. Elizabeth Monroe. Mch. 31, 1826; Apr. 14, 1826. Of Saline county.

John Munro. May 13, 1826; May 26, 1826.

Mrs. Margaret Dargen. June 21, 1826; July 13, 1826.

Robert Patrick. Aug. 13, 1826; Aug. 7, 1826.

Capt. James Hickman. Sept. 13, 1826; Sept. 21, 1826. In Boone county.

Hugh Lunard. Sept. 2, 1826; Sept. 28, 1826. In Cooper county.

Mrs. Col. Jno. M. (Eliz.) Bell. Oct. 2, 1826; Oct. 12, 1826. In Chariton county.

Mrs. David (Mary) Workman. Sept. 30, 1826; Oct. 12, 1826. At Franklin.

Jane Peebles. Oct. 1, 1826; Oct. 12, 1826. At Franklin.

Bennet H. Clark. Oct. 29, 1826; Nov. 2, 1826.

Dr. John Holman. Nov. 27, 1826; Nov. 30, 1826. In Chariton.

James Scott. Mch. 13, 1827; Mch. 15, 1827.

Miss Harriet L. Lientz. May 20, 1827; May 24, 1827.

Mrs. Eliz. Crawley. Sept. 19, 1827; Sept. 20, 1827.

Austin Martin.———; Sept. 20, 1827. Of Howard county. At Bluffton.

Mrs. Lucy Ann Green. Oct. 3, 1827; Oct. 12, 1827. At Chariton.

Mrs. Ann Williams. Oct. 10, 1827; Oct. 12, 1827. At Chariton.

William Wilson. Oct. 14, 1827; Nov. 9, 1827.

Joseph Simpson. Feb. 12, 1828; Feb. 22, 1828.

Rev. Samuel Giddings. Feb. 1828; Feb. 22, 1828. At St. Louis. By accident.

William Hughes. Jan. 10, 1828; Jan. 25, 1828.

William Witt. Dec. 25, 1827; Jan. 4, 1828. At Fayette. A Revolutionary Soldier.

Mrs. Elvira Thomson. May 29, 1828; May 30, 1828.

Maj. Daniel Ketchum. Aug. 31, 1828; Sept. 12, 1828. At Jefferson Barracks. 6th Reg. U. S. Inf.
Samuel Shepherd. Sept. 15, 1828; Sept. 26, 1828. At Liberty.
Capt. Christopher Burckhardt. Oct. 13, 1828; Nov. 14, 1828. In St. Louis county. Revolutionary officer.
Capt. E. B. Witt. Feb. 24, 1829; Feb. 27, 1829.
Col. Auguste Chouteau. Feb. 24, 1829; Mch. 13, 1829. At St. Louis.
John Ferry. Apr. 1829; May 22, 1829. Near Alexandria, Lincoln county.
Peter Bass. May 18, 1829; June 12, 1829. Of Boone county. At Smithland, Kentucky.
Joseph Higbee. Aug. 9, 1829; Aug. 14, 1829.
Anderson Higbee. Aug. 14, 1829; Aug. 21, 1829.
Capt. John Hardeman. Recently; Oct. 2, 1829. Of Howard county. At New Orleans.
Wm. V. Rector. Sept. 16, 1829; Oct. 23, 1829. Ex-Auditor of Missouri. Near Little Rock, Arkansas.
Benj. Ayers. Sept. 10, 1829; Oct. 23, 1829. At St. Louis.
Mrs. Martha Reeves. Nov. 14, 1829; Nov. 20, 1829.
Mrs. Matilda Patten. Dec. 27, 1829; Jan. 1, 1830.
Mrs. Matilda Patton. Dec. 27, 1829; Jan. 8, 1830.
Mrs. Augustus H. (Mildred) Evans. Feb. 1, 1830; Feb. 12, 1830. At St. Louis.
Isaac C. McGirk. Feb. 5, 1830; Feb. 19, 1830. At St. Louis.
Mrs. Abner (Frances) Cornelius. Mch. 18, 1830; Apr. 2, 1830.
Jacob Stuart. Apr. 8, 1830; Apr. 9, 1830. (Hanged) Columbia.
Thos. Patton. May 17, 1830; May 22, 1830.
David Todd. June 6, 1830; June 12, 1830.
Matilda Jane Todd. June, 1830; June 12, 1830.
Mrs. Gen. W. H. (Eliza B.) Ashley. June 1, 1830; June 12, 1830. At St. Louis.
Wm. Peerce. July 25, 1830; July 31, 1830.
Charles Hardin. Aug. 20, 1830; Aug. 21, 1830.
Thos. Crosthwaite. Sept. 9, 1830; Sept. 18, 1830.

William Jones. Oct. 5, 1830; Oct. 9, 1830.
Lt. James H. Wright. Sept. 20, 1830; Oct. 16, 1830. At Jefferson Barracks.
Samuel Conway. Sept. 17, 1830; Oct. 16, 1830. In Marion county. A Revolutionary soldier.
Elvira Bibb. Nov. 23, 1830; Nov. 30, 1830.
Col. Robert P. Farris. Dec. 27, 1830; Jan. 15, 1831. At St. Louis.
Henry Reily. Dec. 24, 1830; Feb. 5, 1831. At St. Louis
Dr. Daniel P. Wilcox. Feb. 10, 1831; Feb. 19, 1831. Representative House.
Mrs. Charity Hinch. Jan. 31, 1831; Mch. 5, 1831. In Howard county.
Mrs. Marshall B. (Mary) Smith. Aug. 9, 1831; Sept. 10, 1831.
Chas. Wahrendorff. Aug. 27, 1831; Sept. 10, 1831. At St. Louis.
Rev. James Bankson. Sept. 4, 1831; Sept. 10, 1831.
Daniel Barr. Sept. 21, 1831; Sept. 24, 1831.
Wm. Lemon. Sept. 25, 1831; Oct. 1, 1831.
Thos. Chevis. Oct. 2, 1831; Oct. 8, 1831.
Mrs. Hutchens (Mary) Barnett. Oct. 4, 1831; Oct. 8, 1831.
Stephen Hempstead. Oct. 3, 1831; Oct. 15, 1831. At St. Louis. Revolutionary soldier.
Mrs. Rev. Hoxey. Apr. 5, 1831; Apr. 7, 1832. At Fulton.
Mr. Napier. Mch. 25, 1831; Apr. 7, 1832. At Fulton.
Thos. Greenalge. May 23, 1831; June 2, 1832.
Nathaniel Ford. Recently; July 14, 1832. Sheriff Howard county. At New Orleans.
Mrs. Polly Ewing. Sept. 18, 1832; Sept. 29, 1832. In Lafayette county.
Joel L. Musick. Sept. 25, 1832; Oct. 6, 1832. Near Florissant. Represent. elect.
Maj. Jonathan Smith Findlay. Sept. 21, 1832; Nov. 1, 1832. Near Lexington.
Robert Johnston. Dec. 19, 1832; Dec. 29, 1832. At Fayette.
Jno. P. Thomas. Dec. 31, 1832; Jan. 5, 1833.
Alex. Stuart. Dec. 9, 1832; Jan. 12, 1833. Ex Speaker

House and Judge Circuit Court, St. Louis. In
   Staunton, Virginia.
Thos. Jefferson Miller. Jan. 15, 1833; Jan. 26, 1833. In
   St. Louis.
Mary Frances Cornelius. Feb. 19, 1833; Feb. 23, 1833.
Geo. D. Woods. Mch. 27, 1833; Apr. 20, 1833.
Perlina Roberts. Apr. 19, 1833; Apr. 27, 1833.
Col. Wm. McRee. May 15, 1833; May 25, 1833. At
   St. Louis.
Hon. Alex Buckner. June, 1833; June 29, 1833.
Mrs. Alex. Buckner. June, 1833; June 29, 1833.
Col. James McClelland. July 8, 1833; July 13, 1833.
Mrs. Wm. R. (Eliza J.) Morton. ———; Aug. 24, 1833.
   At Lexington.
Saml. Hall, Mrs. S. Wells, Mrs. Joseph Smith, Capt
   Joseph McCann, Capt. Harvey Bledsoe. Aug. 24,
   1833. Above five of cholera at Fayette.
Francis W. Hawley. Aug. 9, 1833; Aug. 24, 1833. At
   St. Louis.
Bartholomew Walsh. ———; Aug. 24, 1833. At St. Louis.
Robert Hood. Aug. 13, 1833; Aug. 24, 1833. At Boonville.
Benj. B. Ray. Aug. 31, 1833; Sept. 7, 1833. In St. Louis
   County. Ex Representative.
Margaret Bass. Sept. 12, 1833; Sept. 14, 1833.
Amelia Ann. Sept. 9, 1833; Sept. 14, 1833. Sister of
   Charity. At St. Louis.
Jane Amanda McAffee. Oct. 23, 1833; Oct. 26, 1833.
Geo. Compton Jewell. Nov. 12, 1833; Nov. 23, 1833.
Mary Melvina Bryan. Dec. 18, 1833; Dec. 21, 1833.
Gen. Danl. Bissell. Dec. 15, 1833; Jan. 4, 1834. At St.
   Louis.
Rev. David M. Kirkpatrick. Jan. 12, 1834; Jan. 18, 1834.
Mrs. R. W. (Harriet Amanda) Wells. Feb. 3, 1834; Feb.
   15, 1834.
Catherine Ann Mullins. Feb. 17, 1834; Feb. 22, 1834.
   Suicide.
Mrs. Nathan Glasgow. Mch. 6, 1834; Mch. 15, 1834.
Mrs. Andrew (Elizabeth Irvine) McGirk. Mch. 29, 1834;
   Apr. 19, 1834.

Col. Nicholas S. Burckhartt. June 13, 1834; June 20, 1834. In Howard county. Of cholera.
Col. Rufus Easton. July 5, 1834; July 12, 1834. At St. Charles, of Cholera.
John Mason. July 5, 1834; July 12, 1834. At St. Louis.
Capt. Thos. B. Williams. July 3, 1834; July 19, 1834. Near Richmond.
Mrs. Eliz. Williams. July 10, 1834; July 19, 1834. In Chariton county.
James M. McClelland. Aug. 10, 1834; Aug. 16, 1834; In Callaway county.
Maj. Thos. Wright. Nov. 9, 1834; Nov. 15, 1834. Near St. Louis.
Wm. G. Owens. ———; Dec. 6, 1834. Clerk Franklin Circuit Court. Shot.
Wm. C. Farrar. Feb. 20, 1835; Mch. 7, 1835. At St. Louis. By accident.
Rev. Allen McGuire. Mch. 30, 1835; Apr. 4, 1835.
Dr. Lloyd B. Giddings. Mch. 24, 1835; Apr. 4, 1835. At Fayette.
Mrs. Col. Wm. (Nancy) Boon. Mch. 22, 1835; Apr. 4, 1835. At Fayette.
Mrs. Thos. J. (Sarah) Givens. Apr. 2, 1835; Apr. 4, 1835. In Jackson county.
Mrs. Benj. H. (Patsey) Reeves. May 9, 1835; May 16, 1835. At Fayette.
Judge Thos. Shackelford. June 17, 1835; June 27, 1835. Of Saline. At St. Louis. Cholera.
Jesse Hart. Aug. 4, 1835; Aug. 8, 1835.
Gen. I. P. Owen. Aug. 26, 1835; Aug. 29, 1835. At Fayette. Shot.
Elijah Hook. ———; Sept. 5, 1835. On Steamboat Far West.
Mrs. James (Susan) Cunningham. Sept. 4, 1835; Sept. 19, 1835.
Mrs. Capt. A. W. (Matilda R.) Turner. Aug. 13, 1835; Sept. 19, 1835.
Thos. J. Givens. Sept. 9, 1835; Sept. 26, 1835. At Potosi.
Lazarus Wilcox. Oct. 23, 1855; Nov. 7, 1835.

MISSOURI HISTORICAL REVIEW.

FORT ORLEANS, THE FIRST FRENCH POST ON THE MISSOURI.

One who makes a careful study of the explorations and efforts at colonization made in the Mississippi Valley by the Spanish and the French is struck by the marked difference in the purposes by which the two nations were animated, The efforts of each were by professed Catholics, and priests invariably accompanied every expedition of any importance. The French made commercialism a secondary matter; the glory of discovery and the conversion of such peoples as were found in the new lands to the true religion were of first importance. With the Spanish, the wild scramble for gold is seen in the history of every expedition. None save the black-robed priests seemed to be actuated by any desire to lead the red aborigines to the light of the Gospel. The Frenchman was willing to profit by a barter, more or less legitimate, with the red men for furs and skins; the Spaniard sought yellow gold, with the determination, when found, to wrest it, if necessary, from its possessors.

About the beginning of the eighteenth century there were afloat stories of the fabulous wealth in gold and other mines in the valley of the Missouri. The French nation was slowly penetrating the region in the prosecution of its purpose of exploring all the territory—or at least so much thereof as possible—of the unknown interior of the new continent. The Illinois region east of the Mississippi was known and occupied, but no settlement or fort existed on the west side of that great stream north of the gulf region. The belief that wonderful deposits of precious metals existed in the great Missouri Valley, and the intelligence that the French were gradually encroaching upon this territory, had aroused the cupidity of the Spaniards at the southwest. The result was the Great Caravan of 1720, which ended so disastrously for all the participants excepting one priest, who effected his escape by the fleetness of his horse, and carried to civilization the news of the fate of his companions. (1) While one may pity the sad end of the ill-starred adventurers who accompanied the soldiers, there is some mitigation in the fact that the fate of the caravan was the result of an endeavor to mete out a similar fate to the French of the locality.

In order that a better understanding of the conditions existant in the Mississippi Valley at the opening of the eighteenth century may be had, a brief *resume* of the enterprises and expeditions immediately preceding that to which this paper is devoted follows:

It seems that the French made several efforts to establish commercial relations with the Spaniards in the southwest, stimulated, doubtless, by the reports above mentioned of great mineral wealth in that region. The hope, too, that a water or other easy outlet to the Pacific Ocean (Mer de l' Ouest) existed somewhere in that direction gave a strong impetus to their spirit of exploration. (2) Hardy *voyageurs* pushed into dense wildernesses and across vast prairies. No danger was great enough to awe them. To this indomitable spirit France owed much of her claim to the great stretches of American soil. La Seuer, as early as 1683, had penetrated the unexplored wilds of Minnesota; Perrot, ten years later, had visited the Sioux country, and, in 1700, sailed up the Missis-

---

1. Charlevoix's Letters, p. 204; Stoddard's Sketches of Louisiana, p. 46.
2. The French had become possessed of the idea, due to Indian reports, that the Missouri, in its upper course, bent so far to the south that a waterway to New Mexico was formed thereby.

sippi with a party of twenty-five to its upper reaches, opening trade with this tribe. (3) In 1703 twenty Canadians tried to find their way from the Illinois to New Mexico, in the hope of stimulating trade. A year later Bienville wrote that one hundred Canadians, in small parties, were scattered along the Mississippi and the Missouri. In 1717 one Hubert proposed a scheme for following the Missouri to its source, saying, "Not only may we find the mines worked by the Spaniards, but also discover the great river that is said to rise in the mountains where the Missouri has its source, and is believed to flow to the Western sea." (4) However this report of the sources of these rivers had its origin, Lewis and Clark, nearly a century later, were able to verify it. In 1714 Saint Denis pushed up Red River to a point some seventy leagues above Natchitoches. Two years later, venturing again toward the Mexican borders, he was seized and his goods confiscated. (5) In 1719 Benard de la Harpe attempted to ascend Red River, but became entangled in the jungle of trees and driftwood, and much alarmed at the numerous snakes and alligators abounding therein. But he reached the navigable water above, turned to the northwest and traversed the prairies about the Arkansas River. The only end accomplished by this expedition of La Harpe was the confirmation of the report that the Comanches and the Spaniards had commercial interchange by this route. (6)

---

3. Penecant's Relation, Margry VI. Nearly all the original documents relative to the French in the Mississippi Valley are contained in "Decouvertes et Etablissements des Francais dans l' Ouest et dans le Sud do l'Amerique Septentrionale (1614-1754)," a collection in six volumes by M. Pierre Margry, Director of the Archives of the Marine and Colonies at Paris. The collection was published, through the efforts of Francis Parkman, in 1874, in the French language, the United States Government paying for 500 copies. The work, as a whole, has never been printed in English. The writer has a manuscript copy of a translation of Bourgmont's Relation, his instructions, some letters pertaining to his enterprise, and the Memoires of Renaudiere, all of which are found in the sixth volume of Margry. This translation is the work of Edward A. Kilian of Manhattan, Kansas, Secretary of the Quivira Historical Society. Said translation, almost entire, can be found in Stipes' "Fort Orleans on the Missouri."

4. Hubert, Memoires encoyean Conseil de la Marine.
5. Margry, vi, 193.
6. La Harpe, in Margry vi, 264.

The erection of Fort Orleans in 1723 has been ascribed by Amos Stoddard, (7) and by many subsequent writers, to the advent of the Spanish caravan of 1720 into the Missouri Valley. But the news of this event did not reach Bienville, the governor-general at New Orleans, until the middle of 1721, and his report thereof was dispatched to Paris on November 21st of the same year. (8) Hence, when one remembers the length of time required at that day for a voyage across the Atlantic, it will be realized that the news could not have been known at the French capital until about the first of February, 1722. And it is necessary to give a few words to the condition of affairs in France at this date, in order that a clear understanding of subsequent events may be had.

Sieur Etienne Venguard de Bourgmont had resided for some years among the Indians of the Missouri Valley, being engaged in barter with them. In 1718 he returned to France, and laid before the directory of the John Law Company the advantages to be derived from trade with these Indians, and advised the establishment of a post among them. Bourgmont, in common with the other Frenchmen of the Upper Illinois, believed that the region abounded in mineral wealth. He reached France at the time of the great financial distress, and found the officials eager to grasp at any scheme that promised to refill the coffers of the bankrupted kingdom. Hence Bourgmont was, on August 12, 1720, commissioned captain and commandant of the Missouri (9)—probably at about the time the great caravan met its fate. Therefore it is not possible that the Spanish caravan to the Missouri was

---

7. Sketches of Louisiana.
8. Bienville to Council of Regents, Margry vi.
9. In the library of the Missouri Historical Society, at St. Louis, is the original commission of Bourgmont from the Company of the Indies. The writer, in 1906, had it translated for his "Fort Orleans on the Missouri." The document is in a dilapidated condition and some words thereof are not legible. Following is the translation, as nearly complete as possible. It will be noticed that the Captain's name therein is spelled "Bourmont."

"Commission of Captain of Infantry in Louisiana, for the Sieur de Bourmont.

"The Directors of the Company of the Indies to the Sieur de Bourmont, Greeting: Taking into consideration the services which you have rendered

responsible for the plan to establish a post or fort on the Missouri River. The French were aware of the Spanish claim to the region because of DeSoto's explorations west of the Mississippi in 1542, and it was plainly seen that if the fleur-de-lis was to be permanently established there, and if their nation was to profit from the representations of the great wealth, by Bourgmont and others (for which France was so much in need just then), it was high time they were taking steps to supplant their rivals.

When Marquette and Jolliet, in 1673, paddled down the Mississippi, they found near the mouth of the Missouri River a tribe of Indians bearing the same name. Later the ravages of the Sacs, Foxes and other predatory tribes forced the Missouris to abandon that locality, and they established their village on the Bowling Green prairie, a few miles below the mouth of Grand River, and on the north bank of the Big Muddy. Some writers state that at the time of the Spanish caravan the tribe still occupied this prairie, but there seems to be no warrant for such a claim, as we shall

to the King and to the Company in the country of Louisiana, both by the discoveries which you have made and by your acts of war which have caused the French nation to be respected and honored amongst the savages, and wishing to show you our satisfaction in giving you among the troops which are or may afterwards be sent to the said country a rank above that which you have until the present held;

"For these causes, and other good considerations, we, in virtue of the power accorded by His Majesty, have named you, commissioned and established you, name, commission, and establish you, to take and hold the rank of captain in the troops of infantry that the Company sends or will send in future to the colony of Louisiana, from the day and date present, *taut amsi?* (the same as if?) you held the chief command under the authority of the commandant general of the colony and of other superior officers (of the service?). We have given and give power, commission, authority, special mandamus. We give order to the Sieur de Bienville, Commandant-General of the colony, and in his absence to whoever may be in command, to receive you into service, recognizing (manuscript blurred) quality of captain and to (?) which he belongs to obey and hear all that you shall order for the glory of the name of His Majesty and the good of the service of the Company and the advantage of its commerce in the said colony of Louisiana. These letters are the (?) of the Company in the faith of what you have done. Sealed in presence with the seal of the Company and countersigned by the Directors of the same.

"Done in Paris, in (the hotel?) of the Company of the Indies, the 26th day of the month of July, 1720." The signatures to the commission are: Mouchard, Fromaget, Corneau, Castanier, D'Artaguette, Diron, Lallemant de Bet, Remy—as deciphered by the translator.

show. Dutisne, who ascended the Missouri in 1719, records (10) that his further advance was barred by the Missouri tribe of Indians, whose village was at a "distance of 80 leagues from the mouth of the river Missouri. The prairie begins 10 leagues beyond their village. This would be a good place to make an establishment. The Missouris are jealous because the French go to other nations. One league southwest of them is a village of the Osages, which is thirty leagues from their great village." This great village, which Dutisne later visited, was situated on the Osage River, in what is now Vernon County. The first village of the Osages stood on what was afterward known as Petitesas (Petite Osage) Plains, near the present town of Malta Bend. Adjoined to a letter by M. Perry, written September 1, 1723, as quoted by Sieur de la Renaudiere, (11) is a statement in which it is said: "Continuing to ascend the Missouri, there is another river called Grand River, coming from the north. From there you go to the village of the Missouris, which is not more than six leagues to the southward." The remains of these two Indian villages are still to be seen on the Petitesas Plains, about three miles apart as stated by Dutisne. In Coues' Lewis and Clark, (12) it is said, "The sites of both these Indian tribes (Little Osages and Missouris) are plainly marked on D'Anville's map of 1752, and also on Perrin du Lac's, 1802. The location is very near the present town of Malta Bend, in Saline County, and a little above this place is the large island of Du Pratz, where was old Fort Orleans."

It will be remembered that the Spanish, in 1720, were attacked and destroyed by the Missouris on the south side of the river of the same name, says the narrative. Had the great village of this nation stood on the Bowling Green prairie at that date, it is not probable that a force of two thousand warriors would have been gathered on the south side of the stream in so short a time after the appearance

10. Dutisne a Bienville, Margry vi, 309-313.
11. Margry vi, 393.

of the expedition. Just where its destruction took place is not known, but it must have been near the Missouri, and not far from the Petitesas Plains.

The responsibility for the claim that Fort Orleans was built on an island opposite Bowling Green prairie is attributed to Le Page du Pratz. Here is all that a careful examination of his "History of Louisiana" reveals on the subject: (13) "There was a French post for some time in an island a few leagues in length, over against the Missouris; the French settled in this post at the east point, and called it Fort Orleans." If it is established that the Missouris had been driven from the Bowling Green prairie some years prior to the founding of Fort Orleans (probably about 1700), it is easy to reconcile this statement of Du Pratz with the additional fact that the fort stood on an island in the Missouri, or on the north bank thereof, "vis-a-vis" (opposite) the village of the Missouris, at *Le Grande Passe*, at the upper end of the Petitesas Plains.

It is upon the foregoing statements that we base our conclusion that the establishment of the village of the Missouris in these plains, three miles northwest of the village of the Little Osages, was antecedent to the erection of Fort Orleans. As far as our researches have extended, it seems conclusive that to Lewis and Clark is due the statement that Le Page du Pratz located the fort on an island some five miles below the mouth of Grand River, being thus misled by placing an erroneous construction on the statement of Du Pratz, who had reference to the later location of the tribe, and not to the Bowling Green prairie. Bradbury and Brackenridge, who ascended the Missouri in 1811, both repeat the statement of Lewis and Clark, though none of the three claims to have seen any ruins or other evidences of the fort.

12. Coues's Lewis and Clark, i, 26.
13. Le Page du Pratz, English edition of 1763, vol. i, 296-297. In this volume is a map, showing, in the Missouri at about the mouth of the Grand River, an island, larger than an ordidary county, with Fort Orleans placed on the east end thereof.

Having reached a conclusion as to the location of the Missouri tribe in 1723, we can proceed to the history of the fort itself, which stood "over against" the village of these Indians.

In the instructions to Bourgmont from the Council of the India Company, (14) he was directed to embark on the first vessel sailing to Louisiana; to apply to Bienville for aid and instructions; then proceed to the Illinois where he would receive the instructions of Boisbriant; thence to ascend the Missouri to the site chosen. In pursuance of these instructions, Bourgmont sailed from L'Orient in the summer of 1722, reaching Biloxi about the first of September. Thence he repaired to New Orleans, where Bienville supplied him with three boat loads of provisions, arms, merchandise and other requisites for his proposed enterprise; also some soldiers to serve first as boatmen, and later to garrison the projected fort. Thence he proceeded to stem the current of the Mississippi until Fort Chartres, on the Illinois bank of that river, some sixty miles below the present site of St. Louis, was reached. There the expedition spent the winter.

In the spring of 1723 Bourgmont proceeded up the Missouri, and was well received by his former friends, the Missouri Indians. A site near their village was given him for his establishment. A palisade fort was erected, within it a cabin for the officers and another as barracks for the soldiers. (15) The post was designated Fort Orleans, in honor of the Duke of Orleans.

Bourgmont made reports to the Council of Louisiana on November 27, 1723, and on January 11, 1724. In the latter he speaks of the necessity of more merchandise to carry on traffic with the natives, and adds, "I doubt if M. de Boisbriant will be able to hold this fort," which was prophetic of its fate.

14. In Margry, vi, bearing date of January 17, 1722.
15. Dumont's Memoires Historiques sur le Louisane, ii.

The last duty enjoined upon Bourgmont was to effect a treaty with the Padouca (Comanche) Indians. (16) This predatory and warlike tribe at that time roamed the vast prairies from the headwaters of the Kansas to the Great Rockies, and from the Platte River to Texas and Mexico. In 1724 their main village stood some seven or eight miles southeast of the present town of Salina. (17) This tribe was on terms of friendship with the Spaniards, and effectually barred not only the French, but also those tribes friendly with the latter people, from all intercourse in that direction. But Bourgmont was directed "to open a profitable inland trade for the French, to approach the Spaniards and establish commercial relations with them, and induce the Padoucas to enter into a treaty of peace with all the Indian nations allied with the French and enter into an alliance with them." (18)

The latter part of the summer and the autumn of 1723 were doubtless spent in the erection of Fort Orleans and in effecting treaties with the neighboring tribes. In the ensuing spring preparations for the expedition to the Padoucas began. The director-general of mines for the Province of Louisiana, Philip Francois de la Renaudiere, together with several soldiers and helpers in his employ, had arrived for the purpose of accompanying the cavalcade. (19)

On June 25, 1724, some boats laden with merchandise, in charge of Lieutenant Saint-Ange and eleven soldiers, departed from Fort Orleans for the village of the Kansas Indians, at or near the site of Doniphan, Kansas. (20)

Bourgmont, on Monday, July 3, departed with the land force. This consisted of Ensign Saint Ange de Bellrive, five soldiers, three Canadians and servants, who had come with Renaudiere; one hundred Missouris, in command of their grand chief and eight war chiefs; sixty-four Osages, in command of four war chiefs. The Relation states that the

16. Instructions au Sieur de Bourgmont, 17 January, 1722, Margry vi, 389.
17. Edward A. Kilian, newspaper article.
18. Instructions, Margry vi, 389.
19. Bourgmont's Relation, Juln-November, 1724, Margry vi, 398.
20. Edward A. Kilian, newspaper article.

party traveled "west and a quarter northwest," after leaving the fort. On the 7th they reached the river again, opposite the village of the Kansas, having marched 30 leagues or some 83 miles. On the 8th the party crossed the Missouri, the white men in pirogues, the Indians on rafts, while the horses swam. Much sickness prevailed. Bourgmont himself was among those sick, and Saint Ange with the boats was detained until the 16th, Bourgmont sending him assistance.

On July 24th the march was resumed. Many Kansas and other Indians had joined the expedition, and a few of those from the Petitesas Plains, on account of sickness, returned. On the 27th, the Relation states, "Sieur Renaudiere was posted on the road where the people passed by. He counted 300 warriors, 14 war chiefs, about 300 women and 500 children, and at least 300 dogs. The women carried loads which astonished the Frenchmen, who had not yet seen this nation. Everyone carried as much as one dog dragged. Girls of ten or twelve years of age carried more than 100 pounds. But it is true that with such burdens they do not make more than two or three leagues a day." (21)

On the 31st the expedition reached the Vermillion River, in what is now Potawattomie County, Kansas. Captain Bourgmont was seized by an attack of fever and the project had to be abandoned, the commandant being carried to the Kansas village on a litter. From there he traveled to Fort Orleans in a canoe. But he first sent to the Padoucas a woman aged about 22 and a boy of about 16 (whom the captain ransomed from the Kansas who held them as prisoners), with one of the Frenchmen named Gaillard, with a message that the captain would visit their village as soon as he was able.

On September 6th word came to Bourgmont that his messenger to the Padoucas had returned to the Kansas village (where Sergeant Dubois and a soldier had been left to await Gaillard), and that said messenger had been amicably re-

21. Renaudiere's Memoires, Margry vi.

ceived by that tribe. Although far from being entirely recovered from his attack of fever, Bourgmont prepared to renew his effort to visit the Padoucas, and departed by water from Fort Orleans on September 20th with a much smaller company. He left the Kansas village on October 8th, reaching the village of the Padoucas ten days later, where the Frenchmen and their red companions were received with much cordiality and ceremony and the desired treaty duly effected. Bourgmont's party consisted of Saint-Ange, Bourgmont's son, Renaudiere, a sergeant and eleven soldiers, Gaillard, Sieur Quesnal, Prichard, and one helper, with ten horses to carry the merchandise. Of the Indians there were five Padoucas who had returned to the Kansas village with Gaillard, the grand chief of the Kansas, with four war chiefs of this nation, four war chiefs of the Othos and three of the Agovis. The women of the Padouca village made much ado over Bourgmont's son, and the chiefs made him valuable presents. The ceremonies and feasts continued from the 18th to the 22nd, when the return began. Fort Orleans was reached on November 5th, the commandant being there received with a discharge of firearms, the flags were run aloft and a Te Deum sang. (22)

One duty enjoined upon Bourgmont was to return to France within two years, bringing with him some Indian chiefs, "in order to give them an idea of the might and power of the French." (23) On the 19th of November, 1724, a general council of the nations of the Missouris, Osages and Othos was held "on the subject of choice of those whom they deputed to go to France." The Missouris sent four chiefs and the daughter of their grand chief, the Osages sent four chiefs, the Othos one warrior. So leaving his lieutenant in charge at Fort Orleans, Bourgmont set out early in 1725. Several prominent Indian chiefs joined the party at Kaskaskia. At New Orleans the ship on which the party em-

22. This account of Bourgmont's expedition is condensed from his Relation and from Renaudiere's Memoires, as found in the sixth volume of Margry.
23. Instructions, Margry vi, 389.

barked sank, and after that misfortune only Chicagou (chief of the Metchigami), Manatouensa (chief of the Kaskaskias), two Osages and the girl proceeded on the journey. In due time the party reached Paris, where the Indians were royally entertained and feted, the chief's daughter being called "The Missouri Princess." She embraced Christianity, was baptized in the famous Notre Dame church, and later married Sergeant Dubois. The latter was promoted to captain, and after his return to America had command at Fort Orleans. Bourgmont remained in France, being created a Knight of St. Louis, and afterward married a rich widow. The Indians came home loaded with presents.

There was great rejoicing among the Indians at Petitesas Plains on the return of their friends. When the last boat of the season (1725) started down the river from the fort, peace and good will reigned supreme in that locality. In the instructions given to M. Perier, under date of September 30, 1726, appears the following: "A fort on the Missouri River, about 180 leagues from the Illinois, is kept up in maintenance; where there are actually twelve or fifteen men, although the whole should be reduced to eight. Whenever this expense appears unneccessary to M. Perier, it has to cease, and he will send to this place the missionary who is assigned them." (24)

But already an end had come to the fort and its little garrison. When the first boats came up the river in the season of 1726, they found only blackened ruins at its site. None of the white men were ever found. Dubois' Indian wife had renounced Christianity and was living with her tribe. She told nothing of the massacre. In Bossu's "Travels Through Louisiana," (25) the fate of the fort is tersely told: "Baron Porneuf, who has been governor of Fort Orleans, established in that nation [the Missouris], and who knows their genius perfectly well, has informed me that

24. Margry vi.
25. Bossu's "Travels Through Louisiana, vol. i, 145; Dumont's "Memoires sur le Louisiane," ii, 74-78.

they were formerly very warlike and good, but that the French hunters had corrupted them by their bad conduct, and by some disunions among them; they had made themselves contemptible by frauds in trade; they seduced and carried off the Indian women, which, among these people, is a great crime. All these irregularities of these bad Frenchmen irritated the Missouris against them; and, therefore, during M. de Bienville's government, they massacred the Sieur Dubois and the little garrison under his command; and, as no soldier escaped, we have never been able to know who was right and who was wrong."

At "Le Grande Passe" was the crossing of all the predatory tribes of Indians whose homes were on the north side of the river, in their forays or visits to the south side. It was in the midst of a veritable hunters' paradise. On the south side were the villages of two of the dominant tribes. This, then, would seem like an ideal place for the establishment of Fort Orleans. It was probably located on the north bank of the broad Missouri, or on an island in that stream, with the main current on the south side thereof. The evidence we have presented supports that contention, and the relation of Bourgmont's expedition by land seems to add additional weight. This Relation fully harmonizes with our conclusion. Nothing is said of his expedition crossing the Missouri on July 3, 1724, and the route followed from the fort will lead with singular directness to the location of the Kansas village. The party certainly did not start from a spot below the mouth of Grand River, as any one can determine by a few minutes' study of a map of that region. The site of the fort probably washed into the river years prior to the expedition of Lewis and Clark. The fort was opposite (vis-a-vis) the village of the Missouris, and the creeks (rivieres) mentioned in the Relation correspond remarkably with what would be encountered today should one start in the south part of Carroll County, opposite the site of the old Indian villages, and travel in the direction indicated in Bourgmont's Relation.

Before the writer is a fac-simile copy of Perrin du Lac's

map of the Missouri Valley, bearing the date 1802. On it, at a longitude of about 96 degrees and 30 minutes, are "Anciens villages des petite Os et Missouris," on the south side of the Missouri River. Opposite (on the north side of the river) is a square labeled, "Vieux Fort." This is placed at some distance above the mouth of Wakenda Creek.

It is singular that while the French writers of the eighteenth century often gave much space to what would usually be considered as minor and insignificant details, at the same time they failed to chronicle matters that seem to be of prime importance. Not one of them, for instance, states whether Fort Orleans stood on the north or the south side of the Missouri. It is said to have been opposite the Missouri village, which seems to indicate that it was on the north side, and the fact that evidences of this village and that of the Little Osages were plainly visible at the advent of the first white settlers leaves no doubt as to the location of these tribes. Du Pratz locates the fort on an island, as shown above, while Perrin du Lac puts it on the north bank of the river. Contemporary evidence seems to leave little doubt as to the correctness of this map. The bottom land of this locality is, on the north side of the river, several miles in width, the current of the Missouri is constantly changing in position, hence the site of this early French fort may have tumbled into the Missouri many years prior to the journey of Lewis and Clark.

From the number of relics and from other indications it would seem that the Petitesas Plains and the higher lands adjoining were the scene of many sanguinary conflicts between Indian tribes. In several places the ruins of fortifications are plainly visible today. It is believed that the last of the native tribes were driven from this locality about 1775, after many fierce battles. The condition of the relics found show that flames swept bare the tracts upon which the lodges stood. Among these relics, besides Indian flints, are gun barrels, kettles and other iron utensils, all of which bear evidences of fire. Among these relics are two two-pound cannon balls, probably fired from some boat. Some two years ago, in clearing a tract of land about one mile west of Malta Bend, a tract that had never been cultivated theretofore, embankments evidently artificial were found, with ditches and pits, the latter similar to those found elsewhere in the vicinity. Many bones were found, some of which, at least, were human. There were also found about one hundred gun barrels (some inscribed with a French name), several iron hoes and a sort of adze with a circular cutting edge. These finds are similar to earlier ones in that locality. (26)

The land on which these ruins are found is high and comparatively level. To the north or northwest of this high land (which is the western portion of Petitesas Plains) is an abrupt "bluff," in places a hundred feet in height, descending to the real bottom lands along the Missouri River. When the writer visited that locality in 1868 there was, at the base of these bluffs, a long shallow lake or series of lakes, extending from Grande Passe in an eastwardly direction to and below Malta Bend. These lakes were not wide at any point—perhaps from a few yards to not exceeding one-fourth mile. The soil-laden drainage from the tilled uplands was gradually filling them, and it is probable they have now almost, if not entirely, disappeared. The upland was cut occasionallly by a ravine, but otherwise was quite level. The locations of the two Indian villages and the embankments and other pre-historic remains are on the high lands, at or near the edge of this bluff. The Petitesas Plains have a considerable elevation above the bottom lands proper along the river, and before Miami is reached both bottoms and plains disappear. Two miles above that town, however, at the top of the bluff, along the base of which at this point sweeps the turbid waters of the Missouri, are the ruins of ancient fortifications, covering some six acres of land.

M. F. STIPES.

26. This information is obtained from a gentleman who visited the scene shortly subsequent to the discovery of the ruins. A number of the gun barrels and other relics are in possession of the Missouri Historical Society at St. Louis.

RECOLLECTIONS OF THOMAS H. BENTON.

Col. Benton was a Senator in Congress from Missouri for thirty years, and compeer of Webster, Clay and Calhoun, and his record of public service has long been familiar to the American public, and nothing new, of course, can now be added; but as is common with any illustrious man who has played a conspicuous part in the councils of his country, and left his impress upon its legislation for a long period, it is quite natural that attention should be directed to the personal characteristics of such a man; and people generally are always curious to know something of those personal traits and everything relating to his personality, the incidents of his life, his general make-up, size, expression of countenance, bearing, and personal habits, especially after he has passed from the stage of action; and succeeding generations are likely to be interested in the particulars of his life, from the cradle to the grave, and esteem it a special privilege to meet any surviving contemporary who may have known him, seen or heard him speak while he was still in life.

Col. Benton was a remarkable man, of stalwart physique, aggressive, courageous, with talents of high order and great industry, possessing a great fund of information and earning the appellation of the "Walking Library." These qualities were exemplified in his long career of public service. With this preliminary, the writer hereof proceeds to recall some of his own personal recollections of the great man in question.

In the summer of 1843, the writer being a student at our State University, and during its vacation accompanied his father, with two or three of his friends, from his home county of Randolph, on a business trip to New Orleans. On return to St. Louis passage was taken on a steamboat bound for the Missouri River, and having passed Jefferson City during the night, early the following morning a large, robust man of florid complexion was observed sitting in a barber's chair and in the process of being shaved. It was soon known that this man was Col. Thomas H. Benton. After breakfast, accompanied by Dr. John J. Lowry of Howard County, his long personal and political friend, he came out to the bow of the boat, and was introduced to the bystanders. He was dignified, reserved, and by no means familiar or communicative, and simply contended himself with asking some questions as to the different varieties of timber that lined the banks of the river, and soon retired to his state room. Nothing of a political character was broached or discussed in this short interview.

Afterwards, during the same summer, Col. Benton, in his rounds of the State, visited Columbia, the seat of our State University, and, as usual, stopped at Gentry's Hotel, then kept by Mrs. Gentry, widow of Col. Richard Gentry, who was killed in the Florida war. At the hotel the writer, with one or two other students, had rooms and board, and while sitting in the waiting room after breakfast, in strode a grave and dignified gentleman, who stopped a moment and then passed out without saying a word or giving a sign of recognition. This man we understood to be Col. Benton. He remained a day or two, calling on President Lathrop of the University, and conferring with personal and political friends in and around Columbia.

During this visit a religious revival was going on, under auspices of the Presbyterian Church, and at an evening service Col. Benton was in attendance, accompanied by the two Misses Lenoir, in whose family he then was a guest.

During this same visit (as I remember) occurred a serious difficulty between two students, Thomas F. McLean and John H. Moore, and as the facts disclosed that McLean was in the wrong, the faculty had already expelled or was about to expel him. Meanwhile, McLean availed himself of the presence of Col. Benton in Columbia and applied to him for a cadetship at West Point. Col. Benton, on full inquiry, as was doubtless the case, became satisfied of McLean's fitness and gave him the appointment. It was then, and ever since has been, a mystery how McLean managed thus to secure Col. Benton's favor. Of all the students (to the writer's knowledge) McLean was the oddest and most unique one that ever entered the University. He was of stout, muscular build, always dressed in homespun, a close student, rarely went to bed, preferring to study sitting in his chair, with a light burning at all hours at night, and taking but short snatches of sleep to relieve exhaustion, and withal, his hair never touched by shears or beard by razor, he was a young man of strange, uncouth appearance. In spite of these peculiarities, or by reason of them, Col. Benton's favor was won and the appointment made.

In 1849 the Great Railroad Convention was held at St. Louis. It was called for the purpose of inaugurating the movement for the construction of a trans-continental railroad, to run from the seaboard of the Atlantic to the Pacific shore. It was a large and representative body, attended by prominent men from the states of the middle west, north and south. Stephen A. Douglas of Illinois presided. Col. Benton was there, and made his great speech in support of the proposed railway, emphasizing its national importance, and depicting the rich trade that would come to us from India and other nations east, and answering all objections, particularly the one as alleged, that the Rocky Mountains would be an insurmountable barrier. As to this, he declared that when the foot of the Rockies was reached, instead of trying to run over or around them, the plan was to tunnel through them on a common level, and thus clear the way of construction on to the Pacific Coast, and proposing that when the great work was completed a statue should be placed on the highest pinnacle of the mountain with hand pointing towards the Orient—"There is the East— There is India."

The convention bore fruit, but it was not till some time during the war that Congress took up the matter and passed the act authorizing the construction of this national highway.

During the proceedings of the convention Col. Benton again exhibited one of his personal characteristics. Col. James H. Birch of Plattsburg and himself were not on friendly terms. This bad feeling grew out of some alleged slanderous words as used by Benton, charging that Birch had mistreated his wife. A suit for slander then pending or soon after brought by Birch against Benton remained on the court dockets for a number of years.

On this occasion, when Benton had finished his speech and had taken his seat, Birch addressed the chair, and when in the act of addressing the convention, Benton quickly rose, and taking up his hat and cloak, was about to leave the hall, but friends intervened and at last prevailed on him to remain. This feud continued, and it is related that afterwards, during the same year, Benton had an appointment to speak at Platte City, the day being fixed. On his arrival he learned that Birch had spoken there the day before Benton was angered and declared that he would not speak from the platform that Birch had occupied the day before, and persistently refused to speak until his friends arranged a place outside of the town limits, where he at last addressed the crowd assembled.

On March 14th, 1849, the General Assembly of Missouri passed the famous Jackson resolutions relating to the vexed question of slavery and instructing the Missouri Senators in Congress to act in compliance therewith. Benton refused to obey the instructions, and took his celebrated appeal direct to the people of Missouri. The result of the contest thus raised was a split in the Democratic party of Missouri. Benton came home from Washington and entered upon a thorough canvass of the state, everywhere denouncing the Jackson Resolutions as "Fire Brands," and leading directly to secession and disunion.

But the ensuing Legislature, before which Benton was a candidate for re-election to the United States Senate, failed to sustain him, and James S. Green of Lewis County received the majority and was declared Benton's successor. During that celebrated canvass the writer again heard

Benton at Fayette, Missouri, where had been Benton's general headquarters for the State, and here lived Dr. Lowry, Claiborne F. Jackson and others, long personal and political friends, but now bitter enemies, constituting a part of the anti-Benton wing of the democracy. Owing to the embittered feelings engendered by this disruption of the party, it was anticipated that Benton would not be permitted to speak, and if he did, Claiborne F. Jackson was expected to reply. Benton made his speech, denouncing as usual his Democratic opponents and met with no interruption. On its conclusion he left immediately for Boonville, where he was to speak the next day. The late John W. Henry, then a young attorney, and loud in his opposition to Benton, was, in the absence of C. F. Jackson, urged to make reply. This he positively declined to do, saying that if he should make the attempt "Benton would eat him up in a minute." Finally, however, he consented that if they would wait until Benton was known to be half way on the road to Boonville he would "Speak and give him h—ll."

As the result of this exciting campaign, the ensuing Legislature failed to sustain Benton, and James S. Green of Lewis County was elected as his successor in the United States Senate. In 1852 Benton was elected a Representative in Congress from the St. Louis district, but was defeated for re-election by Luther M. Kennett, the Whig candidate.

To conclude these reminiscences, the writer remembers that the last time he had an opportunity to see and hear Col. Benton was at Chillicothe during his canvass for Governor in 1856. He stopped at the Fitzmorris House, a frame building then standing on the present site of the Henrietta Hotel. After dinner, while Benton was sitting on the porch fronting the street, a big crowd gathered, anxious to see the distinguished man, of whom they had heard so much. A farmer, of bushy head and unshorn face, called out to Col. Benton, and inquired to know his age. Promptly the Colonel replied: "According to the calendar, my age is 74, but when anything is to be done I am 35 years old, sir."

Col. Benton's speech on this occasion was mild and conciliatory as compared with his speeches in former campaigns, and at its close he proceeded on his way to Linneus, his next appointment, stopping for the night with Major Seth Botts, a pioneer settler of Linn County.

The ensuing election resulted in the election of Trusten Polk of St. Louis and the defeat of Benton for Governor. At the following session of the General Assembly Col. Benton was again a candidate for the United States Senate, but owing to the division of the Democratic party, and the alliance of the Anti-Benton wing with the Whig members, Henry S. Geyer of St. Louis, long a Whig leader in the State and eminent lawyer of the St. Louis bar, was, after a protracted contest, declared elected for a term of six years as Senator from Missouri.

Thus ends Benton's political career, and the writer's recollections of this distinguished Missourian. That he had faults, infirmities of temper, and outbursts of passion, exhibited often, in a long, and at times, stormy career, must be acknowledged, but these now should be regarded simply as mere specks upon the sun, whose light shall continue to shine undimmed upon the memory of this great man, and the record of his service to the State of his adoption and the country at large.

L. T. COLLIER.

Kansas City, Mo., Feb. 5, 1914.

ECHOES OF INDIAN EMIGRATION.

Second Paper.

When Missouri became a state in 1821, as stated in my previous article on "Echoes of Indian Emigration," and William Clark settled his accounts on June 30th, 1821, as "Ex-officio Superintendent of Indian Affairs," he was not out of this office very long. In a little more than a year he was appointed as "Superintendent of Indian Affairs at St. Louis, Missouri," and this office he administered until his death September 1st, 1838.

When Missouri became a state several tribes of Indians were within its borders. The Shawnees, originally from the "Straits," (1) had become scattered over parts of Ohio, Indiana and Illinois. When they migrated from these homes east of the Mississippi, they settled along the eastern border of Missouri. A few of them settled on the Meramec river, about 30 miles northwest of the lead mines, (2) but the greater number settled in the vicinity of Cape Girardeau. In 1793 Baron de Carondelet granted the Shawnees and Delawares (3) a grant of land near Cape Girardeau. The Delawares left this tract sometime in 1815, scattering to various places, but most of them settled on James' Fork of White River. Some of them went to the Kansas. Those on White River were removed to the lands allotted to the Delawares between the Kansas River and Camp Leavenworth in —— (4). The Shawnees were given land just west of what is now Newton and McDonald counties in the Indian

---

1. Houcks' Spanish Regime in Mo., Vol I, p. 45. "The Shawnees * * come to get presents, although rarely. These tribes belong to the Straits."
2. Lead mines had been worked in Washington, Jefferson and St. Francois counties since 1720.
3. See referenc to in Indian treaties, 1778 to 1837, p. 388.
4. See reference to in Indian treaties, 1778 to 1837, p. 444.

Territory, and this tract was 25 by 100 miles square. (5) The Osages had been for many years near the western part of the State on the upper waters of the Osage; their principal village (The Great Osages) was near the mouth of the Marias de Cygne, and Harmony Mission, near where Papinsville now is, was established for their benefit. The Kickapoos were granted land from the mouth of the Pomme de Terre to its source and westward to include most to the old Osage line due south from Fort Osage (6). An interesting item in Clark's accounts relates to a disturbance in the Kickapoo tribe, then living on the Pomme de Terre, on account of some objectionable settlers among them, and it became necessary to send an officer to settle it.

When the Seneca Indians arrived at Jefferson City they pursued their course westward over what was known about this date as the "Harmony Mission Trail," which passes the present sites of Versailles and Cole Camp and on through Henry county to the Mission on the Marias de Cygne.

Emigrant Indians, Vol. V, p. 102 et seq.

See "While the Seneca Indians were in camp on Quiver Creek, near Troy, the following expenses were incurred:

Dec. 2, (1831), Lawson Levering, ferrying over the Missouri at St. Charles of 16 wagons and teams, engaged in the transportation of the Senecas and sundry Indians and horses, $40.25.

William Eckart, provisions and provender for the Indians and their horses, $28.53.

(Provisions and feed was also bought from Paul Trendler, John Wells, James Taylor and Christopher Clark.)

James H. Audrain, on Dec. 24th, furnished wagon and team in transporting sick Indians from St. Charles to encampment near Troy, $17.50.

Jan. 24th, 1832, Robert C. Mott, corn, $73.00.

April 25th, J. S. Chauvin, horse, wood and coffin, $28.52.

5. See reference to in Indian treaties, 1778 to 1837, p. 388.
6. See Indian treaties, 1778 to 1837.

April 28, R. Payne (sold various articles from store), $56.91.

May 1st, S. T. McKenny, a horse, saddle and bridle for Henry C. Brish, agent for Senecas, $79.00.

May 2nd, Christ Clark, corn for 43 Indian horses during the winter, $132.50.

May 3rd, M. C. Martin, 9 coffins for Senecas and their children who died at their encampment near Troy, $30.00.

M. C. Martin, ferriage of 24 wagons and teams over Quiver River, with Indians and baggage, $30.00.

May 6th, Christ Clark, provender, etc., and for the use of storehouse to deposit ploughs, hoes, axes, etc., due the Indians under treaty, $40.00.

May 7th, Lawson Lovering, ferriage of party from Indiana over the Missouri to St. Charles, $32.50.

May 8th, Block and Snethan, 50 lbs. of tobacco for use of Indians, $10.00.

May 9th, Arington Perkins, a horse for public service, $50.00.

May 9th, J. N. Robbins, necessary groceries for sick Indians at the encampment near Troy, $12.50.

About this last date the Indians broke camp and started for their lands west of Missouri, and on the way the following accounts appear:

May 18, Granville Basye, medicine and attendance on sick Indians forwarded by steamboat to Jefferson City, $5.00.

May 21st, Wm. Kidwell, ferriage of wagons, etc., over Missouri at Jefferson City, $134.50.

May 21, Wm. Kidwell, pasture for Indian and government horses while delayed at the Missouri at Jefferson City, $22.50.

May 21, Thomas Miller & Co., 2 tents, linen for horse covers, and necessary medicine, tea and sugar for use of the sick, $57.75

July 24, Robert E. Mott, attention and nourishment of sick left in camp at Quiver River near Troy, 2 coffins, $46.00.

ECHOES OF INDIAN EMIGRATION. 145

Thomas Rodgers, ferriage of 16 teams over the Missouri on their return from the Seneca lands, $32.00.

* * * * *

Nov. 30, 1831, Alexander Moore, use of 2 wagons and teams in conveying Senecas from St. Louis to about 8 miles from the city, $8.00.

Dec. 1, J. Mullanphy, rent of house, $15.00.

Dec. 2, John Simonds, 10 cords of wood at $3.25, $32.50.

Dec. 9, O. D. Bolster, services with team in moving Seneca Indians from St. Louis to Troy, 55 miles, 6 days going and 3 returning at $4.00 per day, $36.00.

D. Goodfellow, ditto, $36.00.

Dec. 12, J. M. Tomlinson, ditto, 10½ days, $42.00.

Jesse Colbourn, keeping horses, $26.28.

Numerous other items occur in the accounts of Wm. Clark in relation to these removals while passing through Missouri.

* * * * *

The second Auditor in Treasury department complained to Wm. Clark as to the delay on this trip, and the following letters explain the conditions:

Troy, Lincoln Co., Dec. 12, 1831.*

Sir: I presume that you have been informed by Major H. C. Brish, the agent for the Seneca Indians, that I have contracted with him for supplying the Seneca Indians while they remain in the county of Lincoln, and also for the first six months after their arrival on their lands; and as it will require a considerable fund, more than I can command without borrowing, to purchase and lay in the necessary supplies to fill the contract, and which must be expended now immediately before the present killing time passes, or perhaps they could not be purchased in the upper settlements at all. This, therefore, is to solicit the favor of you, if not inconsistent with the public interest and convenience with yourself to advance on the contract. It will be a very great

*Em. Ind. Vol. 5, p. 114.

favor, and I am willing to give any security that may be deemed necessary for the faithful disbursement of said funds so advanced, and for that special purpose. I will stand in need of five or six thousand dollars. Maj. Brish promised to call on you and see if any advance could be made; if so, I was to have the benefit, and he was to inform me of the result; but the time is drawing so near that the meat must be purchased and barrelled, that there is no time for delay, and my health is so impaired, although gaining, I thought it advisable for my brother to go to St. Louis to make the arrangements there if they could be made, so that I can go up the country as soon as I am able to ride. If it should meet your approbation to advance, you can prepare a bond, my brother will sign it and bring it up, and have it filled here with such names as will satisfy you, and send it down.

Mr. Rutland (Ruland) is acquainted with all the responsible men in this county, and I can give any names mentioned, etc. My brother will be the bearer of this, and await the result. I am, most respectfully, with high esteem,

Your obedient servant,

Gen. Wm. Clark,   (Signed)   DAVID BAILEY.
Sup. Indian Affairs.

Gen. Wm. Clark, Supt. Indian Affairs: *1

The subjoined is an estimate of the cost of the rations that will be required for the first six months after their arrival on their lands, viz.:

It will take 182,000 lbs. of freight from Lexington, Mo., to the Seneca lands, will make 81 wagon loads, and twenty days to each load is 1,820 days, at $4.00 per day is $7,280
365 bbls. pork at $9.00 per bbl. is.................. 3,285
375 bbls. flour at $5.00 per bbl. is................ 1,875

$12,440

*   *   *   *   *

*1. Emigrating Indians, Vol. 5, p. 116.

Troy, May 8, 1832.*²

Dear Sir: I have experienced much difficulty and delay in reaching the encampment of the Senecas, who remained here during the winter on account of the high water of Quiver River. We crossed it by swimming the teams with the empty wagons, and after loading proceeded with the Indians and their baggage about five miles up the river, when we had the good fortune to employ a boat, which, although small, has accomplished the object of crossing us. The party which came on last have now joined their friends, and on tomorrow we shall start the whole upon their journey. I have been obliged to leave six of the party which encamped here during the winter in their wigwams, being too ill to be moved, and will no doubt die in a short time. Sixteen others are very sick, but I have made most comfortable arrangements to carry them on, and have employed additional teams for that purpose. The roads are almost impassable, and I apprehend a tardy trip. The small spring branches in this neighborhood were yesterday deep enough to swim a horse. I have the honor to be, with much esteem,

Your obedient servant.

Gen. Wm. Clark,   (Signed) HENRY C. BRISH,
Supt. Indian Affairs.   Agent Emigrating Senecas.

*   *   *   *   *

Camp 15 miles east from Jefferson,

May 16th, 1832.*³

Sir: The Senecas under my charge have been overtaken by two young men of their tribe, belonging to a party (42 in number) which has for some years past resided near Ste. Genevieve. The chief of my party, at their request, solicit their removal to the lands assigned them; for which I refer them to you. Their expenses in coming here have been paid by themselves; they will also have to pay hire for the horses which they are now riding, and they request, as "they are

---

*2. Emigrating Indians, Vol 5, p. 116.
*3. Emigrating Indians, Vol. 5, p. 117.

poor," that the whole amount expended by them may be refunded to them; for their service in performing this errand for their friends they request some "little presents." We are getting along well, considering the excessive badness of the roads and the great number of sick. The measles have broken out among the Indian children, and I fear that many of them will die in consequences of the exposure to which they are unavoidably subjected. In haste I have the honor to be,

Your obedient servant,
Gen. Wm. Clark,   (Signed)   HENRY C. BRISH,
Supt. Indian Affairs, St. Louis.   Agent Senecas.

Encampment, Grand River, June 6, 1832.*2

Sir: Our journey to this place has been very slow in consequence of the almost continual hard rain and the excessive deep state of the roads. The smallest streams and drains upon the prairies have several times delayed us by being swimming deep. We have had much trouble and some delay on account of sickness, which has gone the rounds of the whole tribe. We have been in camp at this place since Saturday last, waiting for the river to fall sufficiently for fording, until yesterday it has been ten feet above that point; it is now falling rapidly, and I am in hopes we shall soon cross. The rivers in advance of us are also out of their banks, and we shall perhaps have some difficulty on account of them.

I am sorry to inform you that Colonel Bailey must lose considerable by his contract to furnish rations for my Indians, in consequence of those failing to comply who had contracted to furnish him with the necessary provisions; compelling him therefore to pay high prices for his supplies and to procure them from more remote points. He has, notwithstanding, procured the quantity contracted for with me for provisioning the Indians during the next six months without a murmur at his loss. Provisions of every kind are high and scarce in this country. Many difficulties exist

*2. Em. Ind., Vol. 5, p. 118.

between the Senecas and Cayuga parties of my Indians; they are constantly quarreling, and at times I am fearful that they will break out into open hostility and give me much trouble.

In haste, I have the honor to be, with much esteem,
Your obedient servant,
Gen. Wm. Clark,   (Signed)   HENRY C. BRISH,
Supt. Indian Affairs.   Agent for Emigrating Senecas.

*   *   *   *   *

Camp at Maries des Signes, near Harmony Mission,
July 12, 1832.[*1]

Sir: We have been here waiting two days for the river to fall sufficiently for us to cross. I was under the impression on my arrival at this place, and until this morning, that we should be compelled to take the route by way of "White Hair's Village," it being the only wagon road; but very fortunately I met with a man this morning who is perfectly acquainted with the country, in a direct line between this and the Seneca lands; he is recommended by the gentlemen of the missionary establishment as worthy of confidence, and I have employed him as a guide. By this route we shall reach our destination four or five days sooner than by "White Hair," and our new guide assures us we shall have a better road. We have found the road to this place deep and muddy, and expect difficulty throughout the journey as the mud stiffens, particularly at the watercourses, which have been very high. We leave here in the morning; the river will be low enough for our wagons to cross empty; our baggage will be carried over on horseback. We are now preparing to bury an Indian woman; several others (children) are at the point of death. We have been delayed much by sickness; it was unavoidable.

I have been informed by the person whom Mr. McCoy employed to survey the Seneca lands that there are not more than 50 to 100 acres of good land in the whole tract; that the

[*1]. Em. Ind., Vol. 5, p. 117.

rest is a bed of flinty rocks, Mr. McCoy's report to the contrary notwithstanding. If this is the fact, God help the poor Senecas; they expect to become agriculturists at their new home. With great respect, I have the honor to be your obedient servant.

      (Signed)   H. C. BRISH,
Gen. Wm. Clark,   Agent for Emigrant Senecas.
Supt. Indian Affairs.

July 16, 1832.[*1]

Sir: I have the honor to inform you that on the fourth day of July (inst.) I succeeded in reaching and placing the Seneca tribe of Indians from Sandusky upon the lands assigned them under treaty of 28th of February, 1831. This, sir, was a laborious duty, and in the discharge of it I have encountered many difficulties which were unlooked for and unexpected. On reaching the encampment of the party which remained in the neighborhood of Troy during the winter I found upwards of a hundred Indians sick of different kinds of disease, principally, however, with measles; most of whom were too ill either to walk or ride on horseback, and I was compelled, being the only alternative, to increase the number of wagons for that party to 24, which, together with those employed with the party which arrived this spring past, made 30. With this number I performed the journey throughout, notwithstanding the increase of sickness and the frequent solicitations of the Indians to employ others, although I was obliged to admit, at the same time, that more were absolutely necessary for the comfort of the sick. But, sir, the number already in service being so much above what was supposed necessary upon the estimate, and consequently the expense incurred so much greater, obliged me to resist all their importunities to employ more, and proceed with the number stated as well as possible. The immense quantity of baggage taken by these people left but little room for the sick in the wagons; and there were several instances on this journey when the sick, the dying and the dead were

[*1]. Em. Ind., Vol. 5, p. 118.

crowded together in the same wagon, and it was unavoidable. I regret to inform you that nine of the tribe (four adults and five children) died between the Osage Mission at Harmony and the Seneca lands. Such as were christians required time to perform the burial rites as they understood them; and such as were pagans solicited the privilege of performing theirs. Neither could be interfered with, and of course much time was spent in this way. For a statement of the extreme distress suffered by these poor creatures, I respectfully refer you to Dr. John T. Fulton, special agent for removal and subsistence of Choctow Indians, who was the bearer of letters to me from the War Department, and subsistence office, Arkansas, and met me previous to my arrival upon the Seneca lands, and who visited the sick at my request and afforded relief to many of the sufferers. In the outset of our journey we had to contend with high water; in some cases we could cross streams by raising our loading in the wagons to a pitch above the water; in others we had to make entire bridges, and in others, where the streams were too large for either, and no means of ferrying offered, we were obliged to wait for the water to fall, which was the case at Grand river (Mo.) and at Maries des Signes, Osage Mission. At both these places, after the water had abated sufficiently, we crossed; there were still difficulties to oversome, for such is the nature of the soils along these streams that immediately and for some time after a high stage of water the banks will mire either horses or oxen in ascending or descending them. All such places required bridging the banks, which not only took up much of our time, but imposed much labor upon the wagoners and others in the service. Difficulty in crossing wet bottom prairies can scarcely be imagined, and we could only cross them by disengaging the oxen and horses from half the wagons and adding them to the other half, and then the whole to those left; this had to be done repeatedly in the course of almost every day, which, of course, was calculated to retard our progress very greatly.

In the last part of our journey the flies attacked our horses and oxen in such immense swarms that we could only travel before daylight or after dark. This severe duty rendered a noble set of horses and oxen almost unfit for service, and I have no doubt that most of them will be lost to the owners.

These, sir, are the plain causes of the protracted journey of the Senecas to their lands. I assure you there has been no unnecessary delay. I charge myself with cruelty, forcing these unfortunate people on at a time when a few days' delay might have prevented some deaths and rendered the sickness of others more light, and have to regret this part of my duty, which, together with the extreme exposure to which I have been subjected, and the sickness consequent upon it, has made the task of removing the Senecas excessively unpleasant to me. It affords me pleasure that the lands given by the government to the Senecas are of the best quality, as it respects water and soil and timber; the streams particularly are the most beautiful I have ever seen—pure and healthy and stored with fish. Their present location, or encampment, is Cow Skin or Elk river, at present called Seneca river, and they manifest a determination to support themselves hereafter by agricultural industry; and I believe that if the government will furnish them with all the necessary means to begin that pursuit, they may be preserved and become a happy and prosperous people. I have the honor to be, with much esteem, your obedient servant,

 (Signed)   HENRY C. BRISH,
              Agent for Senecas.

P. S.—I forgot to mention that we were detained five days in crossing the Missouri at Jefferson City, there being but one boat, which was so small that a wagon could only be taken without the team at a trip, and then the team, making in that way two trips for each wagon and team.

          Yours, etc.,
Gen. Wm. Clark,   H. C. BRISH,
Supt. Indian Affairs.   Agent for Senecas.

August 31, 1832.*1

Sir: When the appointment of superintendent was given me to remove the Senecas of Sandusky, Ohio, to the lands assigned them west of this state, I accepted it with pleasure, as it afforded me an opportunity of aiding in the benevolent policy of removing the Indians to a country better adapted to their habits and necessities, and of providing for those immediately under my charge such comforts upon their journey as they had been accustomed to.

I have discharged the duty assigned me to the best of my ability; and as I have heretofore informed you, the Senecas are upon their lands, comfortably fixed, and pleased with the prospects before them. I am now anxious to return to the comforts of my home, and beg the liberty of offering this through your hands to the Hon. Secretary of War, as a resignation of my appointment as agent for the Senecas of Sandusky.

I have the honor to be, with much esteem, your obedient servant,

(Signed)   HENRY C. BRISH,
Gen. Wm. Clark,
Supt. Indian Affairs, St. Louis.

                                         DAVID W. EATON,
                                             Versailles, Mo.

*1. Em. Ind., Vol 5, p. 120.

HISTORICAL SKETCH OF SHELBY COUNTY, MISSOURI.

Bounded on the east by Marion, on the north by Knox, on the west by Macon, and on the south by Monroe, Shelby is the second county west of the Mississippi and the third south of the Iowa line. The county is small in territory, being 24 miles east and west by 20 miles north and south, except at the southwest corner, where it juts south four miles by six east and west, giving an area of 504 square miles.

When first visited by white people, about half of this territory was covered by timber and the remainder was prairie. Some that was prairie then subsequently grew up in timber, caused, doubtless, by the partial protection from fires. The highest and nearest level land was generally in the center of the prairies; nearer the watercourses the ground is more rolling, sometimes slightly hilly. The timber consisted mainly of various kinds of oak, hickory and elm, but along the streams there were also walnut, ash, soft and, sometimes, hard maples, birch, willow, sycamore and other timber growths. On the bottom lands the soil is often very dark; elsewhere in the tree land it is a yellowish clay loam, and on the prairie a dark gray, all of it producing abundant crops when properly tilled. It is, however, pre-eminently a grass country, a paradise for horses, cattle, sheep and hogs. It is said that blue grass had to be introduced here, but it certainly adopted the country, for nowhere in the world does it flourish better than in Northeast Missouri. Forty-five years ago the prairies were mainly unbroken and covered with wild grass, much of it called blue joint, growing from six to ten feet high. As soon, however, as this land was pastured severely it produced blue grass, and now this most excellent pasture food grows everywhere in abundance. Sow a piece of land to timothy and red clover and pasture

HISTORICAL SKETCH OF SHELBY COUNTY. 155

it, and in a few years blue grass and white clover will root out the other growths.

Shelby is a well watered county, abounding in streams. The north fork of Salt River is the largest, meandering across from near the northwest to near the southeast corner of the county; then there are North River and Tiger Fork, a branch of the same, Black, Crooked, Clear and other creeks.

The county was organized by act of the Legislature in 1835 and was named for General and Ex-Governor Isaac Shelby of Kentucky. The inhabitants then numbered only a few hundred, and here is a list of the names of the heads of seventy of the families:

Geo. Anderson, Josiah Abbott, James Y. Anderson, Thomas J. Bounds, W. B. Broughton, Anthony Blackford, Jas. Blackford, Isaac Blackford, Samuel Bell, Alexander Buford, Silas Boyce, S. Buckner, Thos. H. Clements, W. S. Chinn, Bryant Cochrane, Samuel Cochrane, J. W. Cochrane, C. Christian, Obadiah Dickerson, R. Duncan, Wm. H. Davidson, Levi Dyer, Geo. Eaton, Elisha K. Eaton, John Eaton, Jas. Foley, Benjamin F. Forman, Jesse Gentry, Geo. W. Gentry, Julius C. Gartell, James B. Green, Wm. J. Holliday, Thompson Holliday, E. L. Holliday, Thomas Holeman, Chas. A. Hollyman, Bradford Hunsucker, Wm. B. Hill, Julius C. Jackson, Robt. Joiner, Peter Looney, Oliver Latimer, Michael Law, Russell W. Moss, John H. Milton, W. Moore, Wm. T. Matson (died same year), J. C. Mayes, S. W. Miller, Henry Musgrove, Jno. McAfee, Samuel J. Parker, George Parker, Elijah Pepper, W. H. Payne, Peter Roff, John Ralls, Peter Stice, Montillion H. Smith, Hiram Rookwood, Robert Reed, James Shaw, Cyrus A. Saunders, Henry Saunders, James Swartz, Hill Shaw, John Sparrow, William Sparrow, Major Turner, William S. Townsend, John Thomas, Abraham Vandiver, Dr. Adolphus E. Wood, Nicholas Watkins.

And the following twenty-two men settled in the county within a year after its organization

John Dunn, James Graham, Alexander Gillaspy, Lewis Gillaspy, Stephen Miller, James T. Peake, Samuel Bell,

John Jacobs, Joseph West, James Ford, William Conner, Robert R. Moffit, Wm. Matson, Elisha Moore, J. T. Tingle, G. H. Edmonds, S. O. Van Vactor, M. J. Priest.

One familiar with the people of this county will recognize a majority of these names among the citizens of the county at this time, more than three-quarters of a century after their ancestors settled here.

It is probable that Maj. Obediah Dickerson, who in October, 1831, built a log house on the banks of Salt River, $3\frac{1}{3}$ miles north of where Shelbina now stands, was the first permanent settler. He is said to have been the founder of Palmyra, and it is certain he was the first postmaster there. He carried the office in his hat, and as he went on trips and hunting excursions, delivered the letters from his hat to those to whom they were addressed as he met them, thus instituting the first rural mail delivery.

It is told that one day a man from the frontier came to Palmyra seeking the postoffice, but office and keeper were away. Going in pursuit he found the major, who fished out of his hat half a dozen letters for this man and his neighbors, and also handed out three more, saying: "Take these along with you and see if they belong to any one in your settlement. They have been here two weeks, and I do not know any such names and do not want to be bothered with them longer."

The major was an honored citizen of Shelby county for many years, represented the county in the Legislature, and helped it along in many ways during the pioneer days. His son, John, was three times chosen sheriff and collector of the county, and a number of his grandchildren are now worthy citizens of Shelbina. About the time Maj. Dickerson settled on Salt River, Mrs. Holliday, a widow with seven sons and three daughters, settled on Black Creek, near what is now called Oak Dale. These sons were Richard T., Angus, McDonald, W. J., James M., Elias and Cornelius T. All were prominent citizens. W. J. represented the county, was county clerk and held other important offices. James was for years considered a walking encyclopedia of political knowledge, was employed by Congressman Hatch at Washington, but is now a resident of Sixteen, Montana. Children of others still live in the county. The Vandiver family was prominent in the pioneer days, and, at one time, it was said the Vandiver relatives held the balance of power in the county. W. B. Broughton established a store, and afterward a woolen mill, and thus founded Oak Dale. At his house the first courts were held. His son, W. C., lived there for many years, and his grandson, T. J., now owns the old place, and two other grandsons, B. F. and J. L., live in that vicinity. Russell W. Moss was one of the pioneers of special prominence, represented the county in '44 and held other offices. Robert and Addison Lair and John McAfee were prominent men in pioneer days, and some of their descendants are now worthy citizens of the county.

Dr. Adolphus E. Wood was originally a New Yorker, but he came here from Cuba and settled near Oak Dale. Like most men in that day, he had a large family, and some of his children and many of his grandchildren still live in the county; one son, B. O., lives at Monroe City; also one son, Dr. A. G. Wood, living at Lentner, is quite active at 82. Fernando Wood, at one time mayor of New York, was a brother of the doctor.

Joshua M. Ennis was a man of great influence in the early history of the county, though he came after its organization. He was six times elected sheriff and collector, and four times county treasurer. If one seeking office could get "Josh," as he was familiarly called, on his side, he was pretty sure to win. He was a man who always stood by his friends, and was very hospitable and entertained more people than any other man. His children and grandchildren are still prominent in the county.

John F. Benjamin came from Syracuse, New York, in the forties, and settled near Walkersville on a farm, drove an oxteam, but the gold fever took him to California. However, he returned in time to beat John McAfee for the Legislature in 1850. He studied law and became a strong practitioner. Before the war a Democrat, he became an uncompromising Union man, an officer in the army and was three times elected to Congress as a radical Republican. In 1870 he established at Shelbina the first bank in the county, a national bank, and he was then the wealthiest man in the county. He died in Washington in the spring of 1877.

The Dimmitt family is said to be of French origin, but settled in Maryland at an early day. From there Judge Walter B. came first to Kentucky, then to Marion county in Missouri in 1829, and purchased a large amount of land. His son, Phillip, was born in the Blue Grass State, but was only five when his father settled in Marion county. He studied medicine and practiced in Lewis, Cooper and finally in this county. He raised six sons, five of whom are prominent and respected citizens of the county, three being bankers.

Dr. Anthony Minter was a prominent citizen in the early days, and his nephew, Daniel G. Minter, was prominent up to the time of his death last year. One of his daughters married W. A. Reid, who came from Virginia to Shelbina before the war, and was for years among the foremost business men in the county, and was also prominent in Sunday school and other church work.

There are many more who deserve mention, but lack of space prevents. More of the early settlers came from Kentucky than from any other state. Virginia furnished the next largest number. Some came from Tennessee, some from Maryland, a sprinkling from other southern states and from the north. But during the forties and fifties the number from the north increased, and since the war immigrants from that section have been numerous.

Pioneers here, like those in most all of the country, were a hardy, robust race. In fact, frontier life produces that class of people. There is no place for weaklings among them. Only the strong survive. Their manner of life was simple, compared with that of their descendants. Their houses were built of logs, the cracks filled with split pieces

HISTORICAL SKETCH OF SHELBY COUNTY. 159

plastered with clay. Heat for comfort and cooking was provided in a large fireplace. Some had a little glass in their windows, others did not. Many lived in one room for years, but usually there was an upstairs for sleeping purposes. Where two rooms on the ground were built usually a passageway was left, with a clapboard roof over all. Instead of nails, weights were used to hold the clapboards on. Wooden pins took the place of iron in most places. Floors were made of split logs. These were called puncheon. Furniture was homemade, except what little was brought in the mover wagons from the older states.

From my acquaintance with many of the early settlers and from information gathered during the past forty-five years in the county, my impressions are that there were an unusual number of strong characters among those who founded Shelby county. Perhaps this is true of pioneers everywhere. Weaklings seldom migrate. Then the fact that these men were so much alone gave those inclined to think an opportunity to meditate. As the foundation of a building is the most important part, as all rests upon it, so the character, habits and surroundings of the early settlers of a county should be carefully noted by the historian, since these have much to do in shaping the subsequent history of a community.

For the first 20 years the pioneers settled along the creeks and branches. Few ventured to tackle the prairie, and there was good reason for this. The luxuriant growth of grass made the ground too wet and the sward very hard to break up. Then the flies were so numerous and hungry that neither man nor beast could endure them. It is related that when a settler desired to cross any stretch of prairie in the summer time he went at night to avoid these pests. Then in the timber materials were at hand for buildings, fences and for fuel.

While the life of the pioneers was rough and he had few advantages, he had his pleasures and his virtues, and as a rule he was not destitute of the feelings and promptings of a gentleman. He was kind, generous, hospitable, ready to lend a helping hand, not only to neighbors, but as well to strangers. He had few opportunities to learn of the happenings of his own community or the world at large, except through word of mouth, and this one source of information he usually improved. He went long distances to attend gatherings, and thus he obtained information, made acquaintances and had intercourse with his fellows. There were good and bad people then as now, but these qualities were manifested somewhat differently. The use of whiskey was common, and the article was so cheap there was no temptation to adulterate it. It often retailed at ten and fifteen cents per gallon, and few thought it wrong to drink—indeed, many thought it essential to maintain health; yet excess was condemned, though it was not considered as disgraceful to become intoxicated as now. The principles of honor and honesty were dwelt upon as worthy of the greatest consideration. Finery and luxuries were scorned.

To build a farm in the timber is necessarily a slow and laborious process, and especially was this the case with the poor equipment of the pioneers days. With the exception of the axe, there is scarcely a tool which has not been greatly improved in the past sixty years. Farmers now would think it impossible to make a crop with only a crooked stick or even an iron point with a wooden mould board to stir the ground. Yet the pioneer with such plows raised good crops, though they tilled few acres, compared to the present. Corn was then raised largely for bread; some, however, was fed to the work horses. But oxen were chiefly used on the farm, and these lived on the wild grass and the prairie hay. Hogs grew and fattened on acorns and other nuts called mast. But constant watch was necessary to protect the pigs from wolves and other wild animals. Produce brought little money, and the people needed little, as nearly all they used they produced themselves. The men generally wore buckskin trousers and jackets made of the skins of animals. They made moccasins, but usually went barefooted in summer, as did the women except on dress occasions.

In those days there was little complaint of heat or drouths injuring the crops, but we hear of cold winters and early frosts. It is related that about the middle of May, 1835, there was winter weather freezing the ground to considerable depth, and on the 16th of September of that year a killing frost cut the corn crop short. Chinch bugs first became destructive about 1842, and their last appearance in great numbers was in 1881.

From the organization of the county, in 1835, population rapidly increased, so that the census in 1850 showed 3,744 whites, 498 slaves and 11 free colored persons, and the census of 1860 showed 6,565 whites, 724 slaves and 12 free colored persons.

In the history of a people an account of schools, churches, lodges and other organizations of society should have a prominent place, but in this sketch space is so limited room can be found only for the most general mention of these important things. Though the pioneers had few school opportunities, they were generally alive to the advantages of education, and as soon as a few families settled in a neighborhood a log schoolhouse was built and a teacher employed for a few months each year. There was no public school system then. Before the war a high school of much reputation was established at Shelbyville. At one time Prof. Chas Johnson, remembered by many people in this county, had charge of this school.

Unselfish men came among the pioneers seeking "the lost sheep of the house of Israel." Though they were not learned in the books, they were often fluent and interesting talkers, sometimes really eloquent. They preached in the cabins of the settlers and in the schoolhouses, after these were built. It mattered little to what denomination they belonged, they gathered congregations and laid the foundations for the various churches which now supply the people of the county with places for worship. From these rude beginnings have grown our present school and church systems, our elegant church buildings and schoolhouses. There are now in the county about eighty schools, some of the high schools being of first rank, and more than forty church buildings.

In intelligence and thrift the people of Shelby will compare favorably with the inhabitants of any section of the country, and in morality they are equal to the best. There has not been a saloon in the county for 30 years, and lawsuits are so few that members of the bar seek other occupations. There never has been much crime as compared with other communities.

Lack of space compels the omission of all accounts of the courts, lawyers, offenses against the law, operations during the Civil War, political contests, the establishment of newspapers and many other interesting things connected with the history of the county. However, a sketch would not be complete without mentioning Bethel, the communistic colony established by Dr. Wm. Keil about 1844. A large tract of land was bought and farms, mills and factories were established. All worked under the direction of the leader, and their wants were supplied from a common store house. There were no drones in this hive, but all labored for the common good. It was one of the most successful experiments ever undertaken along this line. For thirty years peace and plenty abounded. It was finally dissolved and the accumulated property divided with little friction.

Eighty-three years ago the territory now comprising Shelby county was without human inhabitants. The land was covered with primeval forests and prairie grass about half each. The deer, wolf, bear, panther, turkey, prairie chicken, quail, beasts and reptiles wandered about unalarmed by the presence of man. There was not a road, a house or an acre of tilled land. See what civilized man has done! Now there are about 500 miles of laid-out roads. Upon some of this little work has been bestowed, and but a small part is really good except in dry weather. Now there are thousands of pleasant homes, some of them really delightful. Nearly every acre of land is more or less utilized,

HISTORICAL SKETCH OF SHELBY COUNTY. 163

though much more might be produced if the land were more thoroughly cultivated. There are three cities, three incorporated towns and several villages. A trip over the county will disclose many charming spots, many highly improved farms and many evidences of culture, taste and refinement. As a rule, the houses and barns show thrift and comfort. Here nearly seventeen thousand people dwell in safety and peace, surrounded with an abundance of the necessaries of life and many encouragements to mental development and moral and spiritual uplift. These people are not an unworthy part of this great and growing republic of which we are all so proud. Shelby will measure up fairly well with the most favored sections of this favored land.

Prior to the war the county had usually chosen democratic officials, and in the fifties it was anti-Benton. But during the civil conflict the large majority of the people were uncompromisingly for the Union. Probably the decided stand taken by such leaders as John F. Benjamin, Joseph Irwin, Alexander McMurtry, Wm. J. Holliday and James M. Collier, nearly all of them being southern men by birth, had much to do in keeping the people so loyal to the Union.

In 1860 there were but 724 slaves in the county, and some who owned negroes were the strongest opponents of secession. Those who lived in the north never could fully comprehend the real situation in the south on the subject of slavery; and many who have grown up here since the war do not understand how good people could own and work slaves. But two hundred years ago few people thought it wrong to bring the uncivilized African to this continent and hold him in bondage. In the border states like Missouri people who owned slaves usually inherited them—few bought. It was an institution handed down from generation to generation, and the owner could hardly do otherwise than hold the negro as a chattel. Free colored men were in disfavor, and they had a harder time than those in bondage. Emancipation was not favored, as it was considered dangerous to have a body of free colored people in any community. Therefore those who were really opposed to this peculiar institution and hoped it would die out felt constrained to simply hold on as the best which could be done for the negro. In this State, and probably generally in other states, most of the negroes were humanely treated, and the colored servant became greatly attached to his master and mistress.

Neither did the South understand the people of the free states, and the abuse of the slaveholder was of course resented. This abuse, however, came from the few, and many of the most abusing had been raised in slave-holding states.

W. O. L. JEWETT.

BOOK NOTICES.

Earmarks of Literature. The things that make good books good. By **Arthur E. Bostwick**, Ph. D., Librarian St. Louis Public Library. Chicago, A. C. McClurg & Co., 1914. The Society is pleased to have a copy of the above work. It opens with a chapter on the nature of literature, studies of grammatical form, clearness, appropriateness and character of style following. The structure, appreciation, preservation and ownership of literature; the makers of literature and other matters are treated in readable and compact form. 12mo., 90 cents, net.

The Invincible. A Magazine of History. Edited by **Anita Calvert Bourgoise.** Vol. 1, Nos. 1-4, April-October, 1913, St. Louis. This new magazine, in addition to its history feature is also largely genealogical and the numbers that have been issued are of special interest to the Thornton and Strother families, and to those whose families date back to dormant, forfeited and extinct peerages of Great Britain. Other numbers will doubtless be of similar interest.

BOOK NOTICES.

Christopher Columbus. Address of **Hon. B. B. Cahoon, Sr.,** before the Knights of Columbus at Fredericktown, Mo., Oct. 12, 1913. n. p. n. d.

The address was published and distributed by the Knights of Columbus, and it was dedicated to Archbishop Glennon of St. Louis, with an explanation of how it came that the author was not controlled by prejudices against the Catholics. On July 4, 1857, an Irish Catholic boy working for a firm to which his father belonged was mortally wounded, and his friends were anxious for him to have the ministrations of a priest. Mr. Cahoon's father—tho it was at the time of very strong Know Nothing prejudices against the Catholics—sent to a distance for a priest and entertained him at his home, saying that he refused to enjoy his religion and deny others the right to enjoy theirs.

Facts, Fancies, Fun and Poems. A book of original poems together with translations from the German and Latin, by **John Fleming Cowan,** D. D.

We find in our catalogs of Westminster College as far back as 1858 at least, that Rev. John F. Cowan was one of the trustees of the College and at that time living at Carondelet. In later years he became the secretary of the board and a resident of Fulton. A few years ago the Society received from him a published book of poems by him, and now the above, which is in typewriting and making a book of 225 pages.

When Frank W. Sneed became pastor of the Presbyterian Church in Columbia in 1888, Rev. Mr. Cowan preached the installation sermon, and at that time it was stated that he had been a pastor for forty years.

The Society is pleased to add this book of poems to its Missouri Author Collection.

The Louisiana-Texas Frontier, by **Isaac Joslin Cox.** Reprint from **The Quarterly** of the Southwestern Historical Association, July-October, 1913.

Thomas Sloo, Jr. A typical politician of early Illinois, by **Isaac J. Cox.** Reprint from Transactions of the Illinois State Historical Library, 1911.

Professor Cox of the University of Cincinnati is one of the most active of the historical workers of the west, and both above papers show the thoroughness of his work. The first paper is the second part on the same subject, and is of 187 pages, with full references to publications and documents. It is a valuable publication relating to the Louisiana Purchase.

The Third Diamond. By **John Breckenridge Ellis,** author of Fran. Yost. (C. 1913.)

Lahoma, by **John Breckenridge Ellis,** author of Fran. With illustrations by W. B. King. Indianapolis. (C. 1913.)

The Little Fiddler of the Ozarks. A novel. By **John Breckenridge Ellis,** author of Fran. Chicago. (C. 1913.)

We have from the author, a native Missouri writer, his last three books. Naturally, they refer to his "Fran", which was the tenth best selling book in America during 1912. The Third Diamond is left in trust with a merchant, and it is found adorning the arm of his wife, tho he did not put it there. The man who left the diamond in trust comes back and finds it.

In the second a girl, reared on the western frontier, is sent from her mountain cabin to a great city to learn its ways, and becomes a fascinating woman with a love story. The scene of this is Oklahoma, but several chapters are staged in Kansas City and the Ozarks. The Third Diamond is a Missouri story, and the last is partly placed in Missouri.

Chronicles of the Civil War in Monroe County, by B. C. M. Farthing and **T. V. Bodine.** n. p. n. d.

The above is a valuable addition to the rather scanty history of the Civil war period of Missouri. The time is fast passing when such accounts can be written, as the participants of that period are becoming fewer each year.

Cold New Years, January 1, 1864. A tale of the Civil War, by **J. West Goodwin**, Company I, 62nd Ohio Volunteer Infantry. Sedalia, 1914.

In the above Col. Goodwin tells his personal experience in camp in Kentucky when the thermometer fell fifty-six degrees in twelve hours, causing suffering and death to soldiers.

Journal of Jean Baptiste Truteau on the Upper Mississippi, "premiere partie," June 7, 1794—March 26, 1795. Reprint from the American Historical Review, January 1, 1914.

This journal is in French, and was discovered in the Archives of the Indies at Seville, Spain, only lately, tho the Part II of the journal was known, and is preserved in the Bureau of Rolls and Library, Department of State at Washington.

Truteau, whose name is sometimes given as Trudeau, was born in Montreal in 1748, and was related to Trudeau, Lieutenant-Governor at St. Louis, 1792—1799. Coming to St. Louis in 1774 he became the first schoolmaster of the village, and died there in 1829. He was chosen to take charge of the expedition to the Mandan villages and while on it he kept a journal with a daily record of events, and this publication is of the trip from St. Louis up the Missouri river to the western present limits of Missouri and beyond.

Proceedings of the Thirty-first Annual Meeting of the Missouri Press Association, at Kansas City, 1913, Springfield, n. d.

The proceedings of the first annual meeting of the above association was a modest pamphlet of 121 pages; the above is a bound book of 329 pages, with seven page plates. The set of proceedings in the library of the State Historical Society is complete except for 1893 and 1902. Donations of these are requested.

Poems, Estelle Johnson Rule (Mrs. Virgil Rule). Nixon-Jones Printing Company, St. Louis, Mo., 1913.

"Do you believe in Fairies?" "The Fairies' Ball" and other pleasing poems make a neat volume, and the Society is under obligations to the authoress for an autograph copy.

The Story of Old St. Louis, by Thomas Edwin Spencer. Prepared for the information of persons who expect to witness the Pageant and Masque of St. Louis in Forest Park, St. Louis, 1914. St. Louis, [1914].

Preparations are being made on a magnificent scale to depict in pageant and masque the history of St. Louis during the celebration of the one hundred and fiftieth anniversary of the founding of the city next May, when the history of the city will be presented in a dramatic form on a scale never before attempted on a similar occasion. This booklet is intended to prepare its readers for a thorough understanding of the scenes that will be presented at the celebration. It has been prepared by Mr. Spencer, the principal of one of the public schools of St. Louis, is a native of Missouri, born in Columbia, Boone county, and has been ably assisted in his work by Judge Walter B. Douglas and William Clark Breckenridge, the latter of whom is one of the most active of the trustees of the State Historical Society of Missouri, and has one of the best libraries of "Missouriana" in the State. Later a more extensive history will be prepared by Mr. Spencer.

The Great River. Poems and Pictures. By **Frederick Oakes Sylvester.** Chicago, 1911.

A magnificently bound autograph copy of the above has been presented to the Society by Mr. and Mrs. C. R. Meston of St. Louis. The flyleaf contains a six verse original poem on "History" signed by Mr. Sylvester, and the book contains an original signed water color by him. There are many platinum photographs of paintings by Mr. Sylvester, one of which, "The Stream of the Ancient Arrow Makers," hangs in the corridor of the Academic Building of the State University of Missouri. There were only 100 copies printed, and the Society is under many obligations to Mr. and Mrs. C. R. Meston of St. Louis for a copy.

A Legislation Program to Restore Business Freedom and Confidence. An address by **Samuel Untermyer** of New York. n. p. n. d.

This address was delivered before the Illinois Manufacturers' Association at Chicago, and whether the reader agrees with all of the conclusions of Mr. Untermyer or not, the paper is a valuable one and from an able man.

Virginia Under the Stuarts. 1607-1688. By **Thomas J. Wertenbaker, Ph. D.** Princeton. Princeton University Press, 1914.

In 1607, after a voyage of more than four months, three small vessels with a party of colonists reached the shores of Virginia, and ascending the James river to lessen the danger of an attack by the Spaniards, they selected a spot and founded Jamestown, the first permanent English settlement of the New World.

The author of the above work, following the line of the many investigators of the present time, has delved into legislative journals, letters, reports and other manuscript, with close examination of conclusions of earlier writers, and these efforts have brought out new light and necessitated new conclusions. The defects of the plan of government for the London Company granted by James I were a continual source of difficulties, the civil contest in England, the overthrow of the King, the hostility of the Virginia government to Parliament, all contributed to dearth of material to be now studied in making out the correct history of the time covered by this work. It will be welcomed by all who may be interested in the history of Virginia, and may be had of the publisher for one dollar and a half.

NOTES.

Historical Data of Bench and Bar of Missouri.— At the meeting of the Missouri Bar Association in September, 1913, the committee on historical data of the bench and bar of the State, among other things reported:

"The library of the State Historical Society at Columbia, Missouri, has in it a mass of material covering biographical matter, including reference to members of the bench and bar of the State. It is altogether a rich collection."

A Good County History. Many county histories have been published purely as money-making schemes, an effort being made to have every one whose biographical sketch is included to subscribe for a copy of the work and possibly pay a large price to have his picture inserted. The general history of the county was merely used as the excuse for publishing the biographies, and usually was written by some employee of the publisher from data hastily gathered up by him. The popular designation of these histories was "Herd books," showing the popular impression of them.

The later county histories, while having very much the same financial aims as the earlier ones, are of a distinctly higher class, and the historical part is printed under the name and by the labor of some person living in the county and acquainted with its history.

In the late "History of Northeast Missouri," the history of Callaway county deserves special commendation. It bears evidence of having been written for a true and correct history, and the foot notes give ample authority for all statements made. It should be taken as a model by other writers of history. It was written by Ovid Bell of Fulton.

The Residence of Mrs. C. L. Vance, widow of a collector of relics, at Joliet, Ill., was lately burned, destroying among other things a bible more than 650 years old. Valuable relics should be in fire-proof buildings.

Sometime ago the women of one of the churches in Fulton got from the Insane Asylum there four wagon loads of newspapers, pamphlets, etc. The church women must be considered as one of the agencies for destroying valuable publications.

The Krefeld Society has been organized to honer the lives and deeds of the First Settlers of Germantown, Pennsylvania, and for securing and preserving information concerning them or their descendants. This was the first permanent settlement made in North America by German subjects, and was made October 25, 1683. There were thirteen heads of families under the leadership of Francis Daniel Pastorius. Any of their descendants can address the Secretary, Dr. J. E. Buckenham, Chestnut Hill, Philadelphia.

The Independent. Missouri University. The Historical Society on checking up "The Independent," and the "M. S. U. Independent," finds that the ninth volume, 1901-1902 is missing. It is possible that some one has borrowed it and forgotton to return it. In the meantime, the Society asks donations of any of the numbers of that volume. It is now about to send to the bindery the 16th and 17th volumes, and four numbers of these volumes are missing. Donations of single numbers of these volumes are also asked.

The Last General Assembly of Illinois created a commission for the purpose of having plans drawn for a building for the use of the State Historical Library, the State Historical Society, the Natural History Museum, the State Superintendent of Public Schools and allied interests.

The commission is composed of the Governor, Secretary of State, Superintendent of Public Instruction, President of Board of Trustees of the State Historical Library, the President of the State Historical Society, the Auditor of Public Accounts and Department Commander of the G. A. R.

The Commission will report to the next General Assembly.

November 5th, 1913, the office of the Atchison County Journal was destroyed by fire, and the files of the paper were burned. It may be a benefit in a hundred cases that the

Society has a file from 1879 to the time of the fire, and it will be glad to give the benefit of them to the publishers and others who may need them.

CEMETARY RECORDS.

The Review has contained thirteen papers of copies of Cemetery inscriptions in various towns of Missouri. The data thus preserved will in the future be of value in genealogical and other investigations, and the editor has been disappointed because his work in this line does not seem to have pleased the Society, or interested the readers of its quarterly. Knowing that eastern historical societies look upon this work as of much value, he has at his individual expense procured about 1402 records from 15 cemeteries, but not a member during the thirteen quarters of publication has given a word of approval, and the local newspapers of the places of the cemeteries recorded have not made even a three-line item about the publication. Under the circumstances the editor does not feel like continuing the work. If, however, enough persons will take up the work, and will copy the records of cemeteries, the publication of such lists may be resumed again, and for commendation, the editor will await that which time is sure to bring.

GENERAL ASSEMBLY JOURNALS.

Some have an idea that there is nothing in the journals of the legislature of any interest, but often an item is found that is of interest to the most casual reader—what would be thought now of the Democrat who should be elected Speaker *pro tem.* and who would resign in favor of a Republican? Now look in the Journal of the House of Representatives in 1861, and see this communication from Nat. Claiborne:

"Jefferson City, January 5, 1861.

To the Hon. John B. McAfee, Speaker of the House of Representatives of Missouri:

Dear Sir: Satisfied that the appointment of Speaker *pro tem.* of this House, as a matter of courtesy, should be given by the party in the majority to some member of the opposition, I would respectfully tender, through you to the House, my resignation of that office.

Yours with great respect,
N. C. CLAIBORNE."

The resignation was accepted and on motion of Mr. Claiborne, Marcus Boyd of Greene County was elected without an opposing vote.

NECROLOGY.

Bishop Thomas Bowman was born in Berwick, Pennsylvania, July 15, 1817, and after studying law under Judge Jeremiah Black of Pennsylvania, he turned to the Ministry, his first pastorate being in 1837. He was well known as an educator, before becoming a bishop, having been president of Dickenson Seminary in Pennsylvania, and for fourteen years president of Asbury College at Greencastle, Indiana, now DePauw University. He was elected bishop of the Methodist Episcopal Church in 1872, and actively held Conferences in this country and Europe till 1898, when he retired from active work. In 1864-65 he was Chaplain of the United State Senate when Lincoln was President. He died at Orange, New Jersey, at the home of a daughter, Mrs. B. B. Caldwell, and was buried at Greencastle, Indiana.

Judge Samuel R. Crockett, a pioneer of Vernon county, Missouri, was born at Frankfort, Kentucky, May 15, 1831, and came to Missouri when a young man. He was married September 11, 1862, in Cooper county, and ten children by that union are now living. In 1868 he moved to Vernon county, and in 1870 was elected circuit clerk. In 1875 he was elected a member of the Constitutional Convention of Missouri. Afterwards, for a time, he resided in Texas, and on returning to Missouri was a resident of Cedar county, and for several years was the Probate Judge there.

He died at Nevada November 11, 1913.

Hon. Jacob F. Gmelich was born at Wurtemberg, Germany, July 23, 1839, came to the United States in 1852, and to Missouri in 1858, and resided in Boonville till 1909. He was a member of the General Assembly from Cooper county in 1895, was twice the nominee of the Republican party for State Treasurer, and was elected to that office in 1904. Four years afterward he was elected Lieutenant-Governor under Governor Hadley. During a serious sickness he went from Jefferson City to his former home at Boonville, and died there February 21, 1914.

Dr. E. S. Holden, astronomer, scientist, educator and librarian died at West Point, March 16, 1914, where he had been librarian since 1902, and where he had graduated in 1870. He had been president of the University of California, and for ten years after that was director of the Lick Observatory. He was the author of quite a number of books, mostly astronomical, and these had brought him recognition and honors from various countries. He was born about 68 years ago in St. Louis and married Miss Mary Chouvenet of that city.

George Washington Martin, next to Reuben Gold Thwaites was the best known Secretary of the Historical Societies of the Country, and did not long survive him. He was born at Hollidaysburg, Pennsylvania, June 30, 1841, and there began his printing and newspaper work. In 1857 he went to Kansas, and from that time became a part of the history of Kansas. He held many positions of trust and responsibility—postmaster of Junction City, register of the land office, assistant assessor of internal revenue, mayor of Junction City, member of the legislature, state printer, grand master of the Odd Fellows, and for fifteen years the efficient Secretary of the State Historical Society. He was present at every session of the legislature from the territorial of 1857 to the present, except that of 1861. On his 72nd birthday he was presented a bound volume containing birthday letters from 250 friends. Like Mr. Thwaites he made his historical society well known, and the possessor of a wonderful collection of valuable historical data, and especially full and complete of the State of Kansas. Col. Martin died March 27, 1914, leaving, perhaps, more personal friends than any other Kansan has had, and a host of friends outside of the State.

Hon. Arthur Phillips Murphy, generally known as "Pat" Murphy, son of Judge W. H. Murphy, was born at Hancock, Missouri, December 19, 1870. He attended the School of Mines at Rolla, and later was admitted to the bar. In 1902 President Roosevelt appointed him attorney for the Creek Nation, and in 1904 he returned to Missouri, and was elected on the Republican ticket to Congress. His opponent then defeated him in 1906, but he was successful again in 1908, and was defeated by Rubey in 1910. He was a candidate for nomination for Governor in 1912, but was defeated by McKinley. He was a member of the Methodist Church, a Knight Templar and Scottish Rite Mason. He died suddenly February 1, 1914 at Rolla.

Hon. R. Steel Ryors died at Linn, Missouri, February 8, 1914. He was elected State Senator four times from the 21st district, 1885 to 1893, and later was judge of the Circuit Court.

Hon. E. O. Stanard was born at Newport, New Hampshire, January 5, 1832, and came west with his parents five years later. The most of his life he was in the milling business, living in St. Louis. In November, 1868 he was elected Lieutenant-Governor of Missouri, and in 1873 elected to Congress from St. Louis. He was a member of the Indianapolis Monetary Conference in 1897-98; president of the Merchants' Exchange in 1868 and served on the directories of the Boatmen's Bank and the St. Louis Union Trust Company. He died suddenly March 10, 1914, in St. Louis.

Hon. Hervey Henry Willsie was born at Burr Oak, Iowa, June 25, 1855, and at the age of fifteen with his parents moved to Atchison County, Missouri, and in 1899 moved to Tarkio, where he died January 8, 1914. He was elected a member of the Forty-first General Assembly of Missouri in 1901, and reelected in 1903. He also served as Judge of the County Court, and was one of the leading business men of the county.

MISSOURI HISTORICAL REVIEW.

VOL. 8.   July, 1914.   No. 4.

MAJOR ALPHONSO WETMORE'S DIARY OF A JOURNEY TO SANTA FE, 1828.

Alphonso Wetmore (1), like several other of our noteworthy early settlers, first became interested in the Territory of Missouri as an official of the National Government, and when he later resigned his office he remained in the new State and became one of its influential citizens.

Born in 1793, he was not yet twenty years of age when the second war with England commenced. He entered the national service at that time and lost his right arm in one of the northern frontier campaigns. He was retained in the service of the United States Army, however, after the war, and was stationed in the Territory of Missouri, being paymaster in the Sixth Regiment, United States Infantry. After leaving the army service some years later, he settled on the extreme frontier, in the Boone's Lick country, where he became a merchant, lawyer, and author. He was one of the original trustees of New Franklin when it was incorporated in 1833, (the former town of Franklin having been destroyed by the Missouri river.)

>   1. For notes on the life of Wetmore, see the following:
>   F. L. Billon, Annals of St. Louis, 1804-1821, p. 96.
>   A. Wetmore, Gazeteer of Missouri, preface.
>   Missouri Statesman, June 22, 1849 (gives obituary notice).
>   J. T. Scharf, History of St. Louis, Vol. II, p. 1615.
>   R. G. Thwaites, Early Western Travels, Vol. XXVI, p. 31.

(177)

Soon after 1833, he seems to have moved to St. Louis, where in 1837 he compiled and published the first Gazeteer of Missouri. For the next twelve years, Wetmore was engaged in the practice of law, and in writing for various periodicals. In the summer of 1849, a terrible visitation of the cholera spread over the Mississippi Valley, and claimed Wetmore as one of its victims, June 13, 1849.

It was when Franklin was the starting point for the "inland trade," and while Major Wetmore was one of its residents, that he became interested in the Santa Fe overland commerce. Various communications from his pen, in regard to the traffic, written either directly for the press or sent to prominent officials from whom it found its way into the papers, appeared from time to time in the Missouri Intelligencer, the famous Boone's Lick country pioneer newspaper. The following history of the trade, however, was written in response to an inquiry from Lewis Cass, Secretary of War in President Jackson's cabinet, and together with the "Diary," appeared as a part of Senate Document 90, 22nd Congress, First Session.

The Missouri Legislature petitioned Congress with more or less regularity for nearly twenty years for aid in carrying on the Santa Fe trade, and particularly for a rebate on foreign goods imported into the United States before being exported to New Mexico. Occasionally one branch or the other of Congress became interested enough to ask the President for more information as to the trade. In this instance, Secretary Cass was collecting information in response to a resolution of the Senate.

F. F. STEPHENS.

LETTER AND DIARY.

FRANKLIN, MISSOURI, October 11, 1831.

SIR: In reply to the queries transmitted under cover of your letter of the 9th ultimo, I have the honor to submit the following history of our trade to Mexico.

Early in the summer of 1821, several citizens of Boonlick made a small outfit at this place, and departed with the avowed purpose of visiting the settlements of New Mexico. The enterprise was at the time, deemed one of infinite peril; and the pecuniary venture was accordingly limited in amount; and the articles of merchandise comprised in it, were suited either to Mexican or Indian taste. In the event of failure to reach the point of destination, it was a part of the plan of the adventurous party to remunerate themselves with the capture of wild horses, or, in the manly and animating sport of the buffalo chase; they returned the same season. In the spring of 1822, an increased number of adventurers packed on mules a small amount of merchandise (valued at $3,000) at this place, with the purpose of making a farther experiment in the Santa Fe trade. In pursuing the route, in their judgment the most direct, they fell upon a sandy desert beyond the Arkansas, where they suffered infinitely from thirst, for more than forty hours. They continued their route and were remunerated for their toil and perils with a profit of about two thousand per cent. Encouraged by this essay, in 1823, the trade assumed a more settled and regular character.

An additional number of respectable citizens, with increased capital, engaged in it, and wagons were employed this year, for the first time, in the transportation of merchandise. This company, too, suffered extremely in the passage of the great *Jornada*, or day's journey, from one watering place to another, beyond the Arkansas river. A safer route across the sands has been since traced out, and is now pursued with little or no inconvenience. The experiment of this year, gave encouragement for an increase of the trade, which has been progressive ever since; and its importance induced Congress to appropriate $30,000 for laying out and making the route. This task had been previously performed by the traders themselves; and no advantage was derived from the expenditure of the money in the summer of 1824. The protection subsequently afforded in 1829 by the troops, is matter of record in the War Department. The whole number of lives lost in the Mexican trade up to this year, is eight souls, to which we may add two of the fur traders, who fell on or near the trace, while the caravan of this year, which has just arrived, was returning. In 1827, the robberies on the Santa Fe trace amounted to 130 head of stock; and, in 1828, the loss was estimated at 825 head of animals of all kinds. Since that year, the losses have been so inconsiderable, that no mention is made of the particulars. The Camanches and Panis are chargeable with these frays. In 1821, the caravan consisted of 21 men, and their merchandise was valued at $3,000. The caravan of last spring numbered 260 men, with 135 wagons, and merchandise to the amount of $270,000. Autumn is not the most favorable season for going through the unsettled tract of country of 800 miles, although it has been several times successfully attempted. A small company went out this fall. The dangers that are encountered in this trade, consist in the hostile operations against the caravans, of the Panis, Chians, Comanches, Kiawas and Arrapaho Indians, all of whom hunt in and claim the country through which the Mexican road leads.

The Blackfeet Indians have this year, for the first time, made their appearance in great force on the trace.

To insure the safety of the caravans it is the custom of the traders, on reaching the rendezvous on the western boundary of Missouri, to elect a caravan bachi, and other officers, who are invested with such authority as may be voluntarily conceded from day to day, or such as they may have the address to enforce. This is greater or less, as the dangers increase or diminish. When on the march, as night approaches, the wagons are thrown into a square, and made to resemble, with much aid of the imagination, a camp fortified by the Roman legions. Guards are always set, and these watch or sleep, as their interest or love of repose may predominate. The capital employed in the trade this year, is about three hundred thousand dollars. The outfits consists [sic] of wagons, mule and ox teams. The arms carried, are generally rifles and pistols, with a light piece of artillery to each caravan. A small supply of provisions is laid in to subsist the company until they reach the buffalo country, where an abundance is always procured by hunting during the march. The returns consist of bullion, Mexican dollars, fine gold, beaver, and horses, mules, and asses. One hundred packs of beaver are embraced in this year's return. The time of departure from the rendezvous on our border, is settled at or about the middle of May, when the prairie grass is sufficiently advanced to forage the teams, and the return caravans reach the same point from the 1st to the 10th of October. The time employed in going, in effecting sales, and in returning, is less than five months.

Those traders who bring their operations within the compass of one season, never penetrate the settlements more than one hundred miles, visiting the towns of Santa Fe and Toas, and some small Pueblos, and Banchos, on Rio Del Norte. Those who remain in the country, extend their operations throughout the State of Senora and as far south as some of the most considerable towns of the State of Chihuahua, (Chiquaqua,) including the city of that name.

When any of these traders may have completed their sales at a season unfavorable for their return by the interior routes, they proceed to the port of Brazos Santiago, near the mouth of Rio del Norte, or Rio Grand, (as it is there called) and return to the United States in one of the New Orleans packets. They likewise travel home through Texas. Thus it is the practice to perform the whole route from Franklin, in Missouri, with wagons, and the same mule team, to the gulf of Mexico, a distance by the coach road of three thousand miles. There is a good coach road from Santa Fe through El Pasos, Chihuahua, El Bayo, Mapomis, Paras, Saltillio, and Monteroy, to Matamoras, the business town for the port of Brazos Santiago. It will be perceived that there is some connection subsisting between the Mexican (interior) and the fur trade. American mountain companies are annually fitted out at Santa Fe, and at Toas, after the arrival of the caravans at these towns; and our traders take into account this branch of business in laying in their goods. In responding to the inquiry "what are the facilities or impediments offered by the Mexican Government," we are led to the most interesting point to which this communication tends. There are no facilities afforded the merchants of the United States who trade to Mexico by the interior route. But great impediments have been always thrown in the way of this class of our citizens, who have, by their risks and daring enterprise, deserved much indulgence. The Mexican Government has always given a preference, strongly marked, to their own merchants. This cannot be objected to. But facilities are afforded to the merchants of Great Britain and France, that are denied to those of the United States. The most grievous exactions have been imposed on our merchants latterly in the form of a per diem tax, for keeping open retailing shops; and an arrival duty of ten dollars on each cargo, or mule load of merchandise, has been collected. State and federal enactments have sometimes conflicted, and these have tended to enhance the impositions.

The suggestion for a remedy for these evils cannot, I presume, with propriety, come within the compass of this communication. But, the merchants of the United States, trading to Mexico, by the interior, if allowed the advantage of debenture, will, on entering the market, be placed on an equal footing with those of all nations trading through the sea ports. With this change the interior trade would assume an importance, which it has never claimed; and it would, probably, advance to several millions per annum. It might then be extended as far south as the city of Durango.

A heavy duty is now collected in our ports on many of the leading articles of the Mexican trade, to which the Mexican duty is added before the goods are offered in market. The articles of foreign manufacture chiefly in demand, and which are not contraband, in the states of Chihuahua, and Senora, and province of New Mexico, are French calico and cotton shawls, English calico, brown and bleached cotton shirtings, and cotton hose, India black silk handkerchiefs, and German linens. If it is in contemplation to do anything for this trade, it is only necessary to allow drawback on all merchandise imported into the United States for the Mexican market, and actually exported by the interior, and our caravans will be strong enough for self defence.

With all the disadvantages which have been encountered, this trade has continued to increase steadily for a period of nine years, and the circulating medium of Missouri now consists principally of Mexican dollars. Many of our citizens are profitably engaged in the trade; horses, mules, and oxen, are employed in carrying it on; the farmers and mechanics derive advantage from the outfits, and our whole community is benefitted by this interesting traffic. It has been remarked that the Government of Mexico evinces an unfriendly disposition towards the citizens of this country engaged in the trade; yet, in the personal intercourse I have had with the Mexicans in their own country, I find nothing to justify a belief that they entertain any but the most friendly, if not kindred feelings, for their republican friends of the north.

The commercial regulations of which we have a right to complain, have been always effected by the deep laid schemes of the English merchants resident in that country. They, too, may have retarded the negotiation of our commercial treaty with Mexico, and its ratification by that Government. The unsettled state of the Mexican Government gives encouragement, and insures success to the machinations of crafty men, who, perhaps, address themselves, on some occasions, to irresponsible and corrupt officers.

The accompanying letter from a respectable merchant in Chih'uah'ua is offered for the information of the War Department; but it would, perhaps, be impolitic to publish its contents.

With the existence of the kind feelings which the people and the Government of this country entertain towards the Mexicans, there can be no occasion for a hint, which, at this moment, occurs to me, but adopting the doctrine which may be applicable, if our just expectations are not realized, that "whom the Lord loveth he chasteneth," it may not be amiss to observe, that a field or battering train would encounter little or no obstruction between the place where I write and the city of Mexico. The provisional government of New Mexico has sometimes facilitated the operations of our traders; and, in 1829, furnished the return caravan with an escort commanded by Colonel Biscarara, a very distinguished officer of the Mexican army.

The following extract from a diary which I kept while traveling from Missouri to New Mexico, may not be inappropriate, and it is accordingly offered for your perusal. In the memoranda made while pursuing my route from Santa Fe to the mouth of the Rio Grande, I find nothing that relates to the subjects embraced in your inquiries, which I have not already noted or alluded to, and the extracts, therefore, end on reaching the former place.

DIARY.

May 28, 1828. Reached the Blue Spring, the rendezvous of the Mexican traders, in season to attend to the election of officers; *ourself* elected captain of the host. "There may be some honor in it," as the deacon remarked on his own promotion, "but not much profit." 29th. In preparation for departure, inspection of arms, fixing ammunition. 30th. The caravan moved at 7 o'clock, a. m. made 16 miles, and encamped early. Formed our wagons into an oblong square, and set a horse guard. 31st. Made ten miles at noon, halted, and prepared for the approaching storm; after dinner, the rain commenced, and continued until sunset.

June 1. (Sunday), a tempest just as we were ready to set forward, the mules disengaged from the wagons in haste, and *double reefs* taken in the wagon covers. All hands employed in detaining the mules, who are disposed to take leave of *nos amigos*. At 9 o'clock under way, reached the 'Big Blue,' all our spades in requisition to make the descent into the river practicable; the wagons eased down the bank by 20 men at a trail rope; encamped in the prairie beyond the river; met here two bee hunters; one of our hunters brought in a deer in the red, and lean of course; one prairie fly discovered today, alarming; my Mexican servant furnished with a gun, proud as Franklin was with his whistle. This character is today mounted on the *verbatim* copy of old Rosinante, caparisoned in character.

June 2. Set off early, and marched 14 miles, and encamped at the Round Grove.

3d. Our route today lies over a fine prairie country, timber at a distance on our right, and a little on our left; encamped at 20 miles distance from last night's camp, at a point of timber opposite Bel Mont. Found today a swarm of bees in our path.

4th. Moving smoothly forward, met an Indian moccasin track; encamped at a little grove on the left of the trace. Made 18 miles.

5th. The road today fine and the country beautiful; nothing wanting but timber; two irregular hills on our right, passed over corn hill, encamped on the right of the trace, one mile from timber. March of the day estimated at 18 miles.

6th. At 5 miles reached Elk creek, where we discovered the corpse of a wagon which had been left by the preceding caravan. O Temperance! O Ditch Water! Crossed Mari De Signe. Made 16 miles.

7th. At ten o'clock reached Rock creek, 8 miles; ate strawberries and caught fish; crossed two other small creeks, and, at 6 o'clock, encamped, after completing 18 miles.

8th. (Sunday). Passed three or four rocky fords, and over a thin rocky soil; rolling ground; took our siesta at an old Indian camp; picked up a soft-shelled turtle;. saw fresh Indian signs. Made 18 miles.

9th. At 2 o'clock, a. m., thunder, lightning, and rain; in motion at ten o'clock; and at six miles arrested by high water. This, and the last stream, fell into the Arkansas river. Ate this morning bacon and goose eggs, and at noon turtle soup. Not an alderman present! ! !

10th. Still waiting for the fall of the small water course in our route.

11th. The small streams are down this morning, and we are in motion at the usual hour. Road muddy; reached Council Grove; the creek Ni Osho too high to ford. Made 8 miles.

12th. Detained by high water; one mess breakfasting on ham and eggs, another dining on alderman soup; met here a return caravan.

13th. Made a bridge to the water edge and crossed the wagons in season to encamp before the storm; rain in the evening, and at midnight a thunder gust.

14th. Rain continues, which detains us until the middle of the day. Made only six miles, and encamped in time to reef wagon cover before a Noah-like tempest descended.

15th. Under way at 8 o'clock; made eight grievous miles, and encamped early at Diamond Spring; a mutinous disposition repressed by *bandit logic.*

16th. With infinite labor, through mud, we reached 8 miles, and slept in the prairie at a spring; no fuel.

17th. In four hours' march made only 8 miles; found weeds and brush sufficient to boil coffee. Our route today is over a roundabout (Irish) cutoff; encamped after marching 14 miles; not a tree in view; enough fuel procured to dress our suppers. These scanty gleanings consist of sumack brush. While suffering with extreme thirst, about the middle of today, one of the party discovered a spring, the water of which bubbled through white sands, at the head of a prairie ravine.

18th. Made a prairie bridge, and marched 12 miles, to Cotton Wood grove.

19th. After having proceeded 10 miles, halted at a place where there are "ferruginous appearances;" our mules found salt here on the surface of the earth. The antelope is a subject of speculation this morning, and one of our hunters has been occupied in decoying, with a flag, one of these nimble-footed animals. He likewise attempted this ruse de guerre to draw a wolf within reach of his rifle: a piece of flesh on the end of his gun-stick would have been more effectual. We find buffalo grass today; and fresh traces of buffalo remind us of the approaching marrow-bone feasts that are to change the monotony of our meals. No fuel; made 18 miles.

20th. Our route today is over a fine tract of table-land; passed several branches of Turkey creek, which runs into the Arkansas; saw one wild horse and a few antelope; encamped at a little creek; without fuel; two men lost; fired a gun, and, late at night, they reached camp. This day's march extended 20 miles.

21st. A little before daylight, the mules made an abortive attempt to raise a stampido; half an hour later an alarm was created by a shot from one of the sentinels, and the cry of Indians, aroused the whole camp. Killed and wounded, blank; alarmed, none.

22d. At 5 o'clock, a. m., after moving quietly forward three hours and a half, a team in rear of the caravan took fright, and, in an instant, more than twenty were coursing over the prairie with Olympic speed. Dined at twelve miles, and dressed our first meal over a fire made of dry buffalo ordure; marched six miles further, and encamped on the branch of Little Arkansas. An Irish sentinel of the horse guard, about 10 o'clock, mistook one of the company for an Indian; he fired, and then challenged. Several fish caught this evening.

23d. At six o'clock commenced a bridge, and completed it at ten. Several fine fish caught this morning; crossed, and put the caravan in motion at 2 o'clock. The road lies over a less fertile country than that which we have passed; a hot wind from the sand hills to the south, and on our left. The ground here, in many places, covered with salt; made 12 miles, and encamped at a branch of Cow creek; timber on its banks.

24th. Dined at a difficult crossing of another branch of Cow creek, which we passed after an interesting entertainment of a wagon race. It is one of the *foibles* of mule teams that, after they have travelled four or five hundred miles, and when it is supposed they are about to tire, to take fright from a profile view of their shadows, and run like the antelope of these plains. After marching 13 miles, reached the main branch of Cow creek, which is barely fordable. Bridged the crossing.

25th. Finished crossing at 10 o'clock; a good supply of fish caught last night, and this morning. Reached the Arkansas at 4 o'clock, encamped and replenished our shot pouches. "Keep your eyes skinned now," said the old trapper. We are now entering upon the most dangerous section of the trace, the war ground of the Panis, Osages and Kansas. This is likewise a fine buffalo country, but we have no hump! no marrow bones! and no tongues, except our own *parts of speech*. Our hunters have brought in an antelope. We have observed in the prairie, during the last six days, the sensitive plant, or, as our Englishman says, "the plant to try maids with." One of our hunters has filled the camp with "smiles" and buffalo meat: the first two buffaloes which we discovered are slain. Netty Bumpo himself would have granted an approving grin on such a hunt.

26th. Our route today lies up the left bank of the Arkansas river. Saw a hare, larger than the English animal of that name. We have bigger thunder here, too. Passed through several prairie-dog villages. Our hunters saw thirty buffalo, and selected two. Made 20 miles. We find the Walnut creek swimming.

27th. A fish resembling a shad caught this morning. Waiting for the high water to recede.

28th. Discovered a shallow ford, and crossed. The prairie on our right and left, and in front, speckled with buffalo. Encamped early near the Arkansas. Our hunters give tongue and hump meat: this our old trapper calls "strong" buffalo signs, and the old Englishman was heard to mutter something about one Sir Loin, whom he had seen once or twice in Cumberland. A strong gale of wind at nightfall. Made six miles today.

29th. Fine short grass prairie; buffalo in immense herds on all sides; selected several fat ones, and encamped, after a march of 19 miles.

30th. At 8 miles, reached the Pani fork of the Arkansas, cut down and bridged the muddy banks, and passed over in a thundergust.

July 1st. Half the day spent in drying, and bringing up arrears of meals. Our route continued over a beautiful inclined plain 15 miles. During this day's march, the caravan bachi shot his own mule through the head in a buffalo chase. Stearne's lament over the dead ass repeated.

2d. Saw two small herds of wild horses; hunters killed five buffalo. Our road lies over a fine buffalo grass plain until noon, when we enter a rolling prairie country. Twenty-one miles today.

3d. Our march today is through a plain and rolling prairie, surrounded with buffalo. A herd of these attempted to break through our column of teams. "It will take a smart skrimmage and a sprinkle of shots," said the old trapper, "to turn them aside," and the leader fell at the flash of his rifle. Marched 20 miles, and encamped without timber —our supper dressed as usual, over buffalo fuel.

4th. Continued our march over the finest natural road in the world, along the left bank of the Arkansas, 18 miles, to Anderson's caches. Saw here the grave of a white man and a broken swivel; two miles farther reached the ford of the river. Encamped.

5th. This day employed in preparation for passing the deep ford.

6th. Doubled teams, and passed the river. Here we take in water for three days' march.

7th. At 4 p. m. we entered *Jornada*. After passing the sand hills, a few buffalo were discovered, which is an indication of water, and at 5 and 7 miles, ponds were discovered; at the last we encamped for the night.

8th. We have found water at 3, 4, and 12 miles; all apprehensions are at rest. Wild horses have approached within four miles of our line of march. Made 22 miles, and encamped without water.

9th. Three miles from camp, on the trace, we observed water; sixteen miles further on several ponds of water were discovered, which had been indicated as we were approached by herds of buffalo and swarms of mosquitoes. Encamped, after a march of 19 miles.

10th. Water in abundance along the trace today. At the pool where we dined, a buffalo approached within gunshot, and was slain. This day's march is estimated at 22 miles.

11th. Our course today was parallel with the Semiron. Crossed Sandy creek, and, at 14 miles, halted. The Semiron here presents a fine view of water, and 8 miles further up, at our camp, not a drop of water appears in the channel. Our course from the Arkansas to the Semiron is generally southwest; along the left bank of the latter, it lies almost due—west.

12th. At 12 o'clock reached water. In the afternoon our course changed to south-southwest; about sunset a hill ahead and buffalo in view: both these indicate water. At 7 o'clock encamped at a small pond, after completing 22 miles.

13th. At 8 miles reached the Semiron, changed our

course up the stream two miles, and dined at a spring which waters a small piece or parcel of *tierra calicante*. In the evening, proceeded up the stream 8 miles: the earth whitened with salt and saltpetre; thunder and wind; the earth thirsting, but not a drink obtained from the clouds. This day's march 18 miles.

14th. Advanced 11 miles up the left bank of the Semiron, and dined. In the evening marched 10 miles, crossing and recrossing the river. Saw two wild horses. Course southwest in the forenoon, and south-southwest in the evening. 21 miles, a stampido at night, with wind and rain.

15th. At 7 miles, reached the Willows, a noted land mark, and at the same time obtained a view of the Sugarloaf mound; the two middle mounds, and the table mound, all above and near the upper Semiron spring. At 12 o'clock, encountered an Indian and squaw of the Kiawa nation. Several teams tired; the road good, but the saltpetre along the river bottom weakens our animals. This might be avoided by keeping out on the plains. Only 17 miles today.

16th. Crossed and filed off from the Semiron, and at 10 miles reached the upper Semiron spring, at the base of a very abrupt rocky hill, on the summit of which is a cross standing over the bones of two white men, who were slain while asleep by the *gallant, high-minded, persecuted, gentlemen Indians.* Saw here the first timber in nine days' march.

17th. At 7 miles a creek; cedars in abundance on the neighboring cliffs; marched 8 miles farther, and encamped at water, in a drain: 15 miles.

18th. After two hours' march, discovered the Rabbit Ears, two high isolated mountains which rise above the plain; since we crossed the Arkansas, the soil is miserably poor; marched 10 miles over hilly ground. In the evening, our road lies up an inclined plain, toward the Rock Mountains; seven miles to our camp, on the bank of a muddy pool, around which one hundred and sixty mules are pressing; a puddle is reserved for ourselves, which is deemed a luxury, after having drank unto pickling the salt waters of the Semiron;

our long-eared stoics opened their konks half an hour before we halted, inviting this humane measure. The chapter of untoward events today, are, the resignation, in disgust, of a guard sergeant, and a gun-broken head of a driver, who held a seditious rein of ill-governed ass colts: at 17 miles we halted, without timber.

19th. The road this morning over rolling ground six miles, to a dry creek; thence up the bed of the creek to a rocky basin of water; the videttes ahead. In the evening discovered three Kiawa Indians, who were at war with a buffalo bull; they hid themselves in clift of a rock; when they came forth, they uttered all the Spanish they were masters of, bellowing lustily *amigo! amigo!* friend! friend! This day's march estimated at fifteen miles.

20th. The road today hilly until noon; in the evening over a plane; passed an excellent spring, and a small creek, *La Madre Loma*, (Mother hill), in our view. Yesterday morning after we encamped, a small party of red gentlemen called on us; smoked, ate, drank, and slept with us; one of them, at the first setting, drank nine pints of water; he was probably a secretary of some cold water conventicle. The chief of this little band claimed the honor for them of being Kiawas. Through the medium of the Pani language, we learned that they had been on a gentleman-like horse stealing expedition against the Chians, in which they were at first successful, but when they believed that had escaped with their booty, the Chians were down upon them, and retook the cavalry and a few scalps. They had walked at double quick step for the last two or three days; finding themselves at ease and secure in our camp, they 'slept fast.' Our march of the day was 15 miles.

21st. This morning, we parted with our guests, with mutual expressions of esteem and good will; our old trapper told them that when he returned their visit, he would leave his card, meaning a ball cartridge. The soil today is improving as we advance. Saw wild horses, deer, and antelope; encamped four miles short of the Round Mound; 15 miles.

22d. Sent a party of 8 men ahead today to make arrangements for payment of duties; the supposed distance from Toas, the nearest settlement, is one hundred miles. This evening our road is fine, and lies over a plane, on all sides of which, detached mountains render the scenery extremely picturesque; a few wild horses in view; the buffalo have been banished their usual range in these plains, by the droughth of the seasons. Recent rains have afforded us a supply; and in the deep rocky branch near where we are tonight encamped, there is really a deficiency. Our mules, during the last few days, have been thriving.

23d. Reached this morning the summit of the ridge which divides the waters of the Semiron and Canadian branch of the Arkansas. From this point, we have a view of a spar of the Rocky Mountains; we observe, likewise, *Cievas las Gallinas*, (Chicken Hills,) which are situated not far from St. Magill. The atmosphere on this mountain region is so clear that we can, with the naked eye, take in incalculable distances; a hill that may seem within an hour's ride, proves to be ten leagues from us.

24th. After four hours' march, we find ourselves at the Point of Rocks. We were today gratified with a full view of the Rocky Mountains ranging along to the right. When our Mexican, from a hill top, caught a distant view of the mountain, he lept for joy, discharged his carabine, and exclaimed, "La luz de mis ojos, mi casa, mi alma;" light of my eyes, my house, my love. Such emotions as these, we call, in Spanish, *amor de la patria*. Marched 17 miles.

25th. In the morning entertained with mule races by several teams; crossed the Canadian branch of the Arkansas; encamped after a march of 15 miles.

26th. Still encamped at the ford of Canadian river; the base of the Rocky Mountains appeared to us not more than six leagues distant; the mountain tops are covered with snow. This evening when threatened with a famine, or a mule feast, two black specks appeared far off, up the ravine leading to the mountains: these were buffalo, and they cost us only two ball cartridges.

27th. Marched today twenty-five miles, and encamped at the *Pilot Knobs*. The only occurrence worthy of note, is a sample of sharpshooting by Maj. Nimrod; he attempted to create a wild mule, and shot him somewhere about the hips.

28th. Timber to the right and left, not far off; the soil sufficiently fertile for growing small grain. Our mules have been recently much benefited by the *gramme grass*, the best pasturage between the Atlantic and Pacific ocean. A heavy shower of rain fell on us as we were about to renew our afternoon march; before we halted for the night, another shower; and, about 9 o'clock, a rain far hung over the hills on our right; the moon was up; encamped near a grove of pines, after completing 20 miles.

29th. At dawn of day the whole caravan of merchants and muleteers resolved themselves into a committee of tar makers, and long before night every tar bucket was filled. Ourself here "bruised a serpent's head;" the snake measured 5 feet 3 inches in length, and one of the tar kill operators killed his brother or cousin, which measured 5 feet 4 inches, inclusive of rattles. This last had swallowed a prairie dog of mature age and full grown.

30th. Resumed our march, and crossed *el Moro* and *el Sapiote*. Timber in all the streams of this region of country.

31st. Waiting the return of our advance party. The Mexicans spinning rope yarn out of the foretops of buffalo.

August 1st. The caravan in motion at the usual time; at one mile from camp, "a horse loose in a cane brake," said the old trapper; turned around and saw twenty teams in full career; the mules had rested one day, and grateful for the indulgence, volunteered this entertainment. About noon saw a party of horsemen on the trace ahead; they were our advance party, with several Mexicans. Continued our march, and encamped at *Rio las Gallinas*.

2d. Left the caravan, which was within a day's march of San Magill, the first Mexican settlement through which the wagon road passes. A guide proposed to lead the light party which I had joined, by a direct route, in one day to Santa Fe; he did so, but over Alps and Appenines. Before we reached the summit of the mountain, in mercy to our mules, we were constrained to dismount. All marvellous, and some scientific, travellers write, "that, on ascending the summit of cloud ridden mountains, they feel great difficulty in respiration, on account of a change in the atmosphere;" never bearing in mind that their impatience to reach the end of the journey, imposes on their lungs the double duty of a blacksmith's bellows.

End of extracts from the diary.

In expressing an opinion that the caravans are competent to self-defense, I have perhaps adopted the impression that prevails among men, with arms in their hands, and impelled by that fearless spirit which animates the people of this country.

But the loss of several valuable lives in this trade has occurred; and this evil may be extended, if the Blackfeet Indians and the Chians continue to infest the route of the traders. These tribes are numerous, warlike, and extremely hostile. Perhaps the War Department may suggest some mode of military protection to this trade, which will meet with the approbation of Congress, so as to prevent a recurrence of the disasters of 1820. [Should be 1828—Ed.]

In the autumn of that year, the largest return caravan was repeatedly attacked, and two lives lost. A smaller company, which returned late in the fall, was defeated, with the loss of one man, all their horses and mules; and they were to a precipitate flight in the night, lighted on the way by the blaze of their wagons. Toiling under the grievous weight of their money packs, feeding on the herbage of the prairies, they marched in this manner more than three hundred miles to our frontier settlements.

The larger company was strong enough, and so prudent as to escape defeat, although two of their number were slain. One of these, with only the faint flickerings of life remaining, was borne along, with great care, two days' march; and when at length the caravan halted in the wilderness, to perform for him the last sacred office, the enemy appeared. A band of the same nation which had enacted the mischief, approached with friendly indications. The grief and indignation which were mingled, and strongly operating at the grave of their companion, rendered abortive all the conciliatory efforts of the commander of the caravan: not from the pipe of peace, but from fifty rifles, a volume of smoke arose. The bloody reprisal was complete; and when the traveller subsequently passed that way, he saw the wolf of the prairie

> "Gorging and growling o'er carcass and limb;
> They were too busy to bark at him;
> From a Panis' scull they had stripped the flesh,
> As ye peel the fig when the fruit is fresh;
> And their white tusks cranched o'er the whiter scull
> As it slipped through their jaws, when their edge grew dull,
> As they lazily mumbled the bones of the dead,
> When they scarce could rise from the spot where they fed."

Permit me to conclude this communication, which, perhaps, has been already extended beyond endurance, with the description of a surgical operation that was performed on the plains beyond the Arkansas. One of the traders had a dangerous gun-shot wound in the arm; he was reduced to the alternative of death or amputation. The last was attempted, with such instruments as could be found in the camp. The operation was performed by one of the hunters of the company, who had attained some celebrity in cutting out hump meat. A small cord twisted around the limb was the tourquet; the cutis was separated from the muscles by the application of the sharpest butcher's knife in camp.

The muscles were divided, and the bone was cut asunder with a carpenter's saw. It was not deemed necessary to take up the arteries, and a large wagon bolt was heated, with which the stump was seared so effectually as to prevent hemorrhage.

The whole operation was concluded by the application of a dressing from the nearest tar bucket. Not a groan nor a sigh was uttered during the operation, and the patient recovered.

This is a lively picture of the shifts to which human ingenuity is sometimes driven; and the fortitude evinced by the sufferer in this case, is a trait of character belonging to the pioneers of the perilous commerce.

I am, very respectfully,
    Sir, your obedient servant,
                      ALPHONSO WETMORE.
HON. LEWIS CASS,
        Secretary of War.

ECHOES OF INDIAN EMIGRATION.

Third Paper.

Of the many tribes of Indians that came to Missouri and remained for a short time, the Kickapoos are among the most interesting. They were residents of Indiana and Illinois in 1819, and, chafing under the encroachments of white settlers on their hunting grounds, they ceded their lands to the United States. A treaty was made and concluded July 30th, 1819, at Edwardsville, Ill., between August Chouteau and Benjamin Stephenson, commissioners in behalf of the United States, and the principal chiefs of the Kickapoo tribe. Their lands in Indiana and Illinois were ceded to the United States and in lieu thereof obtained lands in Missouri as follows:

"Beginning at the confluence of the Rivers Pommes de Terre and Osage; thence, up said river Pommes de Terre to the dividing ridge, which separates the waters of the Osage and White rivers; thence, with said ridge, westwardly, to the Osage line; thence, due north with said line, to Nerve Creek; thence down the same to a point due south of the mouth of White Clay, or Richard Creek; thence, down said river to the beginning." (1)

This treaty and removal to these lands in Missouri were no doubt promoted and welcomed by Chouteau. He was interested in several trading posts in this territory. The trade with the Osages was decreasing. Most of them removed to the Arkansas and Neosho country. The Pomme de Terre was practically unoccupied by either white or Indian. It was a good business venture for Chouteau as the Kickapoos would patronize the trading posts in which he and his friends were more or less interested.

The Osages resented the removal of the Kickapoos of Indiana and Illinois to this part of the State of Missouri. On the arrival of the Kickapoos at the Pomme de Terre the

1. See Indian Treaties, 1778-1837, p. 268.

Osages objected on the ground that their lands had been sold to the United States for the whites, and not for other Indians who would spread over their hunting grounds and kill their game. (2)

Soon the influx of whites began to spread along the rich valleys in this part of the Ozarks and the Kickapoos found themselves in a situation similar to the one they had left in Indiana and Illinois. These Indians began to be a source of trouble to the settlers and a treaty was made with them, concluded October 24, 1832, when they ceded their lands in Missouri and agreed to remove to lands given them in the territory west of the Missouri river at Camp Leavenworth.

Some of the items in the auditor's accounts at the time of this removal are of interest:

James Kennerly, for the removal and subsistence of the Kickapoo Indians emigrating to their lands west of the Missouri up to May 31, 1833, as follows:

Oct. 30, 1832, John F. Hogel, (3) for services in conducting a deputation of Kickapoos from Pomme de Terre to St. Louis, from Sept. 20th to Oct. 5th, at $4.00 per day, $90.00.

Oct. 29, 1832, Kickapoo Prophet, for cash paid him to purchase horses for his people, Kickapoos, under the 11th Art. of Treaty, 24th inst., $1,000.00.

Nov. 1, 1832, Robert Payne, for merchandise furnished Kickapoos under treaty, $5,000.00.

These last two items make the $6,000.00 called for in the treaty. (4)

May 21, 1833, Josiah S. Walton, (5) 20 bu. corn, $10.00; Josiah S. Walton, for one wagon for use of Kickapoos, $60.00.

Oct. 31, 1832, C. Redman, for two horses furnished Kickapoos to aid them in moving west, $65.00.

2. See Houck Hist. Mo. Vol. 1, p. 196.
3. John F. Hogel had a trading post at a very early date on the Osage river at the mouth of Hogel's Creek, in what is now Benton Co.
4. See Indian Treaties, 1778 to 1837, p. 533.
5. Josiah S. Walton built the first grist mill in what is now Morgan County, at James Mill Springs, and court was held in his residence until a court house could be completed in Versailles.

Dec. 19, 1832, Benjamin O'Fallon, for three horses furnished Kickapoos to assist them in moving west, $120.00; W. T. Redman, for catching and delivering two stray Kickapoo horses, $5.00.

Numerous items for catching and delivering horses occur throughout the accounts of the various emigrating tribes. Horses turned out to graze often wandered great distances from the Indian encampments. When found, such strays were returned to the village or encampment to which they belonged. For this service the government paid while the Indians were being removed.

The following names appear in the accounts for supplies or for services rendered and some of them will be recognized as old settlers: W. B. Dunivan, corn; Andrew Ramsey, corn; J. S. Hutchinson, potatoes; Von Pheet and McGill, merchants; Wm. Gennings, Solomon Hoyle, Stephen Howard, N. W. Mack, John R. Huff, Truston Fisher.

"The Prophet" and "Ma-cha-we-na" were the names of two of the Chiefs of the Kickapoos on the Pomme de Terre and on Kickapoo Prairie in what is now Greene county.

"Kickapoo Chiefs" for cash to "Prophet" and "Ma-cha-we-na" for provisions for their people while on their route, $40.00.

Dec. 24, 1832, John M. McCausland, for services and expenditures in conducting Kickapoos from Illinois, from near St. Louis to Osage River, $275.97.

May 2, 1832, paid to P. Chouteau, Jr., for expenses as follows:

John F. Hogel, being due him by the Kickapoos tribe of Indians and provided for by the 3rd Art. of the treaty made with said tribe at Castor Hill, $5,972.00.

G. Kennerly, for the Kickapoo tribe and provided for by treaty as per above, $128.00.

G. S. Hubbard, for a debt due him by the Prophets band, $110.00.

G. E. Walker, in full of a debt due him by the Kickapoos of the Prophet's band, $43.00.

P. Delounoi, as per above, $82.33.

D. Lanston, as per above, $82.00.

W. Crumpton, as per above, $82.34.

Menard and Valle incurred expenses as follows:

William Gillis, amount allowed him by the Kickapoo tribe, and provided for by the 3rd Art. of treaty, $4,865.00.

John Campbell, as per above, $350.00.

Wm. Marshall, as per above, $285.00.

Aug. 14, 1833, Charless and Pascall, for publishing in the Missouri Republican proposals for furnishing provisions for the Kickapoos, $7.75.

Similar bills for advertising the same were allowed the St. Louis Free Press, published by Peach and Ruggles; Missouri Courier, published by Robert Stewart; Western Monitor, published by W. H. Birch; and in the Jeffersonian Republican, published by Calvin Gunn.

Sept. 14, W. Christy, for two bay horses for Kickapoo Prophet, $120.00.

Sept. 14, W. Christy, one yoke of oxen for same, $45.00.

Oct. 2, Kickapoo Prophet, for cash advanced him to pay ferriage, for provisions, etc., for himself and party from St. Louis home, $20.00.

Dec. 1, J. D. Swallows, for pay as teacher Kickapoo's school, Dec. 1833, at $400 per annum, $33.33.

The advertisement referred to in the above accounts appeared in the Jeffersonian Republican from August 3, 1833, to Nov. 9, 1833, and was as follows:

"PROPOSALS FOR FURNISHING RATIONS."

Notice is hereby given, that proposals will be received at this office until the first day of Sept. next, for furnishing and issuing rations to the Kickapoo and Pottawattomie Indians, now on the Kickapoo lands near Fort Leavenworth, at such points (not exceeding two) on or near the Missouri River, as may be designated by the Agent for those tribes, viz.:

To the Kickapoo and Pottawattomie Indians, who are expected to be on the Kickapoo lands as above stated, such quantity of rations as may be required, not exceeding 300 rations per day for one year from the time of their arrival, of which due notice will be given.

The rations to consist of ¼ lb. of fresh beef or fresh pork, or ¾ lbs. of salt pork or bacon, and of ¾ a qt. of corn or corn meal, or 1 lb. of flour, and four quarts of salt to every 100 rations; the government agent having the right to require the issue of such proportion of the bread ration in *flour* as will be equal to at least one-half of said ration; and also to regulate the number of days to be drawn for any one time, as well as the proportion of salt and fresh meat to be issued.

Bond and security will be required for the faithful performance of the contract." (Signed) Wm. Clark.

Office of Superintendent Indian Affairs,
St. Louis, July, 1833.

The Delawares ranged in the Discovery period over Eastern Pennsylvania, New Jersey, and from Sandy Hook to Cape May, and on both shores of the Delaware bay. They roamed north to the Hudson and south as far as the Potomac. It was with this people that Penn made his famous treaty in 1682, under the spreading elm that stood at "Shackamoxon." In the rotunda of the capitol at Washington is an historical fresco recalling that event. It was the Delawares and Shawnees, under the leadership of the French, that defeated Braddock, and it took all the strategy of the then young Washington to save the remnants of an army. These tribes were gradually pushed back across the Allegheny ridges until they occupied scattered outposts from the great lakes to the northern line of Tennessee.

To protect the Spanish settlements from the attacks of the Osages, Carondelet induced the Delawares and Shawnees to emigrate to what was the Spanish domain and settle at

Apple Creek and other places near the eastern border of the State. They afterward scattered over the State in small bands as the hunting became poor at their old camps. They were successful in keeping the Osages confined to the Neosho tribal lands and the plains country. Before the Delawares and Shawnees came a small band of 30 Peorias and Kaskaskias living near Ste. Genevieve, seldom hunted because of their fear of the Osages. (6)

In a supplemental treaty with the Delawares on Sept. 24, 1829, that tribe agreed to "vacate the country on James Fork of White River in the State of Missouri." (7)

George Vashon, U. S. Indian Agent on James Fork of White River in State of Missouri, Sept. 24, 1829, signed the treaty with the Delawares. (8)

In 1806 the Delawares had a village near Forsyth, in what is now Taney county, on the White river, and another village on James' Fork in what is now Christian county, and a village on Wilson Creek in Greene county, near what was afterwards the famous battlefield where Gen. Lyon fell.

"A number (I know not how many, nor what their state and character) of the Delawares, emigrants from east of the Mississippi, settled on the east side of the White river, at the bend, in about Lat. 35, 40 N. Their hunting grounds are in that neighborhood." (9)

It is stated in one of the reports to the Baptist Board of Foreign Missions that there were 1800 of these Delawares. This band lived in what is now Arkansas, hunted near the headwaters of the White, and sometimes made excursions into Missouri up the Current River and other streams.

Some accounts of Delawares:

Oct. 29, 1830, Wm. Clark, for Benjamin Smith, for services as express to Delaware towns on White River, with a message to Chief Anderson in relation to his moving to Kansas, $28.00.

6. See Houck's Hist. Mo. Vol. 1, p. 181, also ibid. 208.
7. Indian Treaties, 1778 to 1837, p——.
8. Indian Treaties, 1778 to 1837, p. —— .
9. Morses' Report, p. 236.

Dec. 31, 1831, Pierre Menard, for expenses on account of Delawares, among other items the following: (10)

To James Wright, for transportation of Delawares from White River to Kansas River, $124.00.

James Pool, ditto, $93.00.

Billy Anderson, ditto, $52.00.

Edward Bradford, for his services driving chief Anderson's wagon, 31 days, $31.00.

The Shawnee tribe was closely associated with the Delawares through intermarriages and constantly being in neighboring territory. Peter Cornstalk, a son of the celebrated Cornstalk of Dunmore war, was among the Shawnees of Apple Creek, in Perry and Ste. Genevieve counties. These tribes lived together on Shawnee and Indian Creeks on the Meramec.

"On the Meramec about 24 warriors of the Shawnees lived, one band on the Fourche-a-Courtois, in Washington county, another between the Bourbeuse and Meramec under Rogers, their chief or head man. A few near Bridgeman, in St. Louis county. About 1803 or 1804, Rogers' band moved to the big spring at the head of the Meramec, but it afterwards came back down the river and settled on Indian prairie, in Franklin county, a few miles south of Union." (11)

A village of Shawnees and Delawares lived on the headwaters of the Gasconade. "Wapepillose, afterward with Dodge on the Missouri, and, in 1835, Chief of the Shawnee village where Bloomfield now stands." (12)

In 1837 the Pottawattomies were removed from northern Indiana to the headwaters of the Osage River in Kansas. N. Clary, wagoner, driving a four horse team, was with a party during the removal and relates that the caravan moved in wagons and on foot, the Indian men walking and hunting as they went. The number of wagons was sixty and the distance made each day was from 7 to 20 miles. Stops for

10. Emigrating Indians, Vol. 5, p. 502.
11. See Houck's Hist. Mo., Vol. 1, p. 209-211.
12. Spanish Regime in Mo., Houck, Vol. 2, p. 74, note.

the night were made where water was plentiful and all slept in tents and wagons. The Indians were well treated by the removing party and did not suffer for food or water. The caravan crossed the Mississippi river at Alton, Ill., in an old shattered steamboat that was unsafe, and it took them two days to cross to the Missouri side. The Grand river was crossed near its mouth and the Missouri was ferried near Independence. After having been 60 days making the journey the Indians were left near the Osage river in Kansas. (13).

DAVID W. EATON,
Versailles, Mo.

13. McDonald, Removal of Pottawattomies, p. 46.

A RUNNING GLANCE OVER THE FIELD OF MUSIC IN MISSOURI.

In the western forests the first music to displace the primitive, rhythmical divisions of the monochord used by the Indians was that of France; chansons, the folksongs of the earliest comers into the territory of Upper Louisiana.

Because there exists no mention of others, the only musical instruments, it seems, in use in the new country were the violin (fiddle), and a mouth harp peculiar to the street players of France. It was not long, however, until mention of flute and harpsichord appeared in the tellings of the time; and, yet, for all dances of record until well on into the next century only fiddles furnished the music. On the night of the Fourth of July, 1778, the English officers at Kaskaskia gave a ball. The music for this occasion was made by two old French fiddlers, and most of the dancers there were from Saint Louis, amongst them Pepita, the beautiful daughter of De Leyba, the newly-appointed Spanish commandant of Upper Louisiana. It was this dance into which irrupted George Rogers Clark, his overland journey of occupation in the name of the State of Virginia being ended there, and at that hour. As he entered the midst of the unwitting and merry dancers he appeared an apparition of terror; but was recognized as the emissary of the new government, and the beautiful Pepita hastened to say for herself, "Sir, I am not of England. I am from Saint Louis, and of Spain." The Virginian needed no further invitation to make himself one of the company, and at once was transformed from a warlike captain into a willing devotee of Terpsichore; also, before the merriment ran out, he was captive to Dan Cupid. Thus we hear of another dance, contrived by him, that he might again look upon the beauty and feel the charm of the presence of Pepita. This was the ball at Prairie du Rocher, in the house of M. Henri Rolaine. Rolaine was, himself, the single fiddler on this occasion. He is described in an old account thus: "In huge slippers, bulging yarn stockings, tight breeches of blue, and a flowing coat of yellow, he was gleefully happy, and ever and anon tuned his violin lovingly."

Fireside songs there were in plenty, brought from over the ocean, and later from New Orleans; folksongs grave and gay, chansons merry and bright, with the minor music of grief and reflection. There, too, was the ronde, always accompanied by the singing of the dancers, never danced to an instrumental accord.

And that one day which was completely filled with song and dance! —That sadly gay, madly merry but tearful day, when the beloved flag of La Belle France again waved over the town after an eclipse of forty years. This fell between Spanish supremacy and that of the United States. On this occasion the agent for the States became a Pooh Bah. It was in order for Amos Stoddard to receive the country from France, so that he named himself a French agent, on one side of the stage, to take over Louisiana from Spain; then, with a run (metaphorical) to the opposite side became again himself that the United States might treat with Spain. So for the one day of French possession the tricolor again waved over Saint Louis. At sight of it the people became wildly happy.

The day was passed underneath the flag, with songs and dancing, and a guard of honor kept watch there all the night. Until the rising of the sun on the 10th of March, 1804, the people waked, singing the dear home songs of France; then at sunrise took down the standard of the sunny land over seas and folded it away, to float in supremacy no more, for all time, over the earth this side the wide sea.

It was the same year that President Jefferson appointed Col. Samuel Hammond commander of the new District of St. Louis. With the coming of his family came also a piano, called then "forte piano." This kind of instrument was fitted with hammers, crude enough in comparison with after advances in construction, but notable then as being better than the reeds of the harpsichord. Mrs. Hammond was a woman of social inclinations and musical taste, and many were the grand entertainments given in the mansion on the corner of Third and Spruce streets. At the commandantorial dances the piano was enforced by two violins, with sometimes a flute. So that here was prophesy of the superb orchestration destined one day to be developed in the future city.

Affairs moved on into the double 'teens, and in 1814 when the village had grown into a town there was organized a "Thespian Society." This was not given over to theatricals alone, but partook largely of the character of a musical club. Concerts were often given by the Thespians, and their plays always featured music in some sort. An old announcement ran, "The Thespian Society will present Monday evening the five-act play of Lovers' Vows. Excellent music provided."

Then there was the "Cafe Chantant," and the "Bowery;" still, upon the coming of La Fayette in 1825 only fiddlers furnished the music for the grand ball given in his honor.

The decade following showed a marked advance in the understanding and appreciation of music, as both an art and a science, as distinguished from its enjoyment, and being a means of entertainment. About the year 1834 an exponent of this forward movement came to the front in the person of Miss Amanda Phillips, whose repertoire included Beethoven, Mozart, and others of the great masters. She was the daughter of a musician, and finely educated; but brilliant and beautiful as she was her life went out in darkness, though not without having left its impress and uplift on local taste for music.

In 1838 came a vocalist from the Malibran Opera Company, Madame Brichter. She was a singer of rare charm and versatility; and remaining to teach, and use her talents for the benefit of the growing city her influence for the best in music cannot be overestimated.

In a series of concerts given in November, December, January, March, April and May of 1838-39 she had the assistance of Therese Weber, a girl of wonderful musical ability, both as a vocalist and pianist. In these concerts Mr. William Robyn was celloist, Mr. Charles Balmer was one violinist, Mr. Fallen another. Martinetz, the famous Spanish guitarist, was amongst these performers, as also was M. Carriese, one of the sweetest of flute players. Madame Brichter and the pure-voiced, clean-throated Therese Weber sang together the great duos from Semiramides, Tancredi, Norma, and many other selections from the Immortals in music. These concerts were for the benefit of the first Episcopal church, then being built and in need of funds for its completion. The building was finished and dedicated in 1840, with Mr. Charles Balmer at the organ, and Miss Therese Weber, the soloist, in "Angels Ever Bright and Fair," and "O, Rejoice ye Daughters of Zion."

'Twas on this night that, after the service, Mr. Balmer displaced Mr. Rene Paul as Miss Weber's escort home, and "Took advantage of this opportunity to propose marriage to the rosy-cheeked young musical enthusiast." So it was that Therese Weber became Mrs. Charles Balmer, and the two together set a deep and enduring impress, a lovely intaglio of musical ideals, upon the young State of Missouri.

In 1839 Mr. Weber organized Saint Louis' first orchestra, in his enthusiasm paying the musicians at his own cost. Then, in a year or two, was given the first Oratorio, with Mr. Balmer its leader.

Long before this time the fast filling State was being vocalized throughout. In every town and hamlet were pioneer musicians gathering together small classes of students of instrumental music, and in every country neighborhood an itinerant music master, (so-called), was teaching singing "by note," as he beat out the time with a movement of his lifted hand. Those old-time singing men did as much for the progress of musical taste and ability in Missouri as was done by the early circuit rider for the cause of religion.

And now came a demand for musical entertainment. This was almost state-wide, and brought such response as the traveling minstrel troupes, and such sweet singers as the quartette vocalists—the Rainey Family, the Hutchinson Family and others. Some time in the forties came Madame Anna Bishop, singing charmingly in all the river towns as far as Independence. At that time there was no Kansas City.

But the crowning event of those days, the apotheosis of musical fulfillment, was the coming to Saint Louis, in 1852, of Jenny Lind. People from all over the State flocked there to hear her marvelous singing. It is not altogether easy now to understand—after all the years have enriched us with the highest and finest powers of the human throat in vocalization—the furore, the enthusiasm, the wild delight with which Jenny Lind's singing was received. And with her coming began a new epoch; the old order changed, and the feeling for, and understanding of the soundless depths, the unreachable heights of the meaning of MUSIC took on a different presentment. So, here endeth the first Lesson. The second Lesson has been so filled with multiplex characteristics, so goldenly interwoven, in and out, with all that is worth while in music, it needs must be that a wise and very knowledgeful recorder should deal with its containment. The present reminiscencer is but taking a swift backward look from the elevation of more than threescore-and-ten years, and must, perforce, leave the second Lesson to some historian of Music in Missouri.

SUSAN A. ARNOLD McCAUSLAND.

AN OLD MISSOURI TOWN. (1)
NAPTON, SALINE COUNTY.

Down the Salt Fork ten miles from Marshall on the "river route" of the Missouri Pacific railroad is the town of Napton. So small and unpretentious is it, so like hundreds of little country villages all over Missouri that the passer-by on the train rarely glances out the window and more rarely ever remembers any such place. Small as it is, however, it is not to be sneezed at according even to present day standard. It is a convenient shipping point for a very rich farming section and its railroad business is larger than many towns five times its size.

To that man who is interested in Missouri's history, especially history of times before the war, little Napton looms up big. There was a time when the town was the largest pumpkin in the garden of Saline. Napton used to be called Jonesboro and, as Jonesboro, was the county seat of Saline county from 1831 to about 1839. Saline has had four county seats since its organization in 1820. First Jefferson on the Missouri river near where is now the town of Cambridge, next Jonesboro, next Arrow Rock and finally Marshall. The name Jonesboro was changed to Napton not many years ago on account of a ruling by the postal department. There was another Jonesboro somewhere in Missouri which the department let keep the name and forced a change on the Saline county town. Nobody cared a great deal though and the town was rechristened Napton in honor of Judge W. B. Napton of Missouri's supreme court who lived near by. Napton to-day, although small, is by no means dead, a mere memory of the past. There is plenty of life there as anyone can see who has the right kind of eyes. In the county seat

---

1. A newspaper article from the Kansas City Star of March 5, 1905, by Rollins Bingham. It contains a good deal of information, not only of this particular town, but of the customs of the early days of the State.

days, however, it was comparatively much more of a town than it has ever been since. It was not only the seat of justice, the place where public business was transacted, but it was a favorite outfitting and starting point for traders, explorers and adventurers bound for the great West and Southwest.

The room where court was held was the upper story of a double log building on the higher elevation of the second bank down near the creek. The lower story was divided into two rooms in one of which was a grocery store and in the other a livery stable. When it was necessary for a jury to retire for deliberation it was taken down into the stable, the horses being first taken outside so that the jurymen might be absolutely undisturbed or not distracted by any kind of presence. Among the lawyers who used to plead in that log court room were some big men. Big they were then and they would be prominent now or at any time should such be born again. Among them were Judge Todd, Abiel Leonard, Hamilton R. Gamble, General Duff Green and John E. Ryland. There was a famous old hotel at Jonesboro in those days. Rather crowded during court sessions it was, but there was always plenty to eat, and, for drinking, a fair article of Kentucky whiskey, unadulterated, uncontaminated and untaxed. Courthouse and hotel have long since passed away and today it would be hard to locate where they stood. No one but the oldest of the old men would know. Near Napton is "Elk Hill," the fine old country home of Judge Napton, still owned by his family. It is said that when the house was being built the judge insisted that the carpenters should shingle the roof *from the comb down*. He got mad because they would not do it his way. One of the workmen remarked:

"The judge may know all the law there is, but he don't know everything. He don't know a derned thing about shingling a roof."

MISSOURI'S OLD MILITIA LAW.

While Jonesboro was a county seat Missouri's old time militia law was in being and rigidly enforced. The town was where the general muster of the whole county was held, Saline's grand maneuvers. Few men are now living who were old enough to come under that law. General muster was a big time, the biggest kind of a time. There have been no days since that begin to compare with general muster day in people's minds. The militia law was passed by the legislature in 1825 and was in force up to about 1840. Its purpose was to prepare the state for Indian wars or any other emergency that might arise. Those exempt from service were civil officers, preachers, teachers, millers and students in school. The civil standing of ministers prior to the adoption of the constitution of 1865 was curious. They were exempt from military service, but were not allowed to hold any civil office. Under the military law they could be chaplains, a position regarded as an honorable distinction and much sought after.

Under the militia law all able-bodied men between the ages of 18 and 45 were required to organize into companies, choose officers and meet at stated times and places for drill and exercise in military evolutions. Company commissioned officers were a captain and lieutenants; companies were organized into battalions; battalions into regiments with colonels, lieutenant colonels, majors and other field officers; regiments into brigades with a brigadier general in command; brigades into divisions under a major general. The whole was under the governor as the commander-in-chief of the military forces of the State. Commissioned officers from colonel down were elected by the votes of the rank and file; the higher officers by the vote of the subordinate commissioned officers. These officers drew no pay, but the titles gave rank and standing and were eagerly sought. There was much electioneering and log-rolling to secure them.

On the first Saturday of April every year the citizens of each township, or, in thinly populated sections, the citizens of each county, came together to be formed into companies and drilled for soldiers. In May companies met for a battalion drill which lasted several days. In October drills were had by regiments and brigades. In Saline, company musters were held regularly in every township at a town or some convenient public place. Battalion musters were held at Miami, Jonesboro, Marshall, Keyser's bridge on Salt Fork and other places. The general muster, the grand yearly round up of the whole county, was at Jonesboro as long as that town remained the county seat.

GOT THEIR OWN EQUIPMENT.

There was no getting around the militia law. Militiamen had to attend musters or they were soaked with a fine. They had to provide and bring arms with them and have the weapons in good order. Every individual militia man did not own a gun, however, and those who did not were allowed to attend with any kind of a substitute which would suffice for going through the manual of arms. Poles, sticks, hoe handles and even cornstalks did martial duty in the stern ranks of war at the musters. It was not every officer who could get hold of a sword. No difference. A sword of wood, a rapier made from a lath did just as well.

As to the drilling, it did not go far towards making an efficient and disciplined body of soldiers. The officers as a rule knew nothing of tactics. Few of them knew "about face" from "grand right and left." The soldiers resented all attempts to make them disciplined machines. They were imbued with the same feeling as a Saline county militia company, at the beginning of the war, which was ordered to march to Boonville. The men refused to march because it looked too much like it was going to rain. As a matter of fact the drilling at the musters was a secondary incident to be got through with as quickly as possible. The "fun" and the "frolic" was the main thing and that drew the crowds.

The soldiers were not in uniform. The officers were compelled to uniform themselves at their own expense, but were allowed to use their own taste in the kind of uniform they wore. The result, one may imagine, was a gorgeous collection. The musters produced one certain result—an abundant supply of military titles. Saline had colonels, majors, captains, etc., enough to supply Napoleon's grand army.

General muster day was a day to which everyone in the county looked forward. The wealthy officers made display of magnificent uniforms and popular heroes were cheered and hurrahed. On that day all the people from the surrounding country came in, looked at the drill, and, as a result of getting together, it was a day when debts were paid, new loans negotiated and trading done. No other day in the year was so generally observed or did so much to get the people acquainted with each other. It also was effective in cultivating a fine feeling of pride in the State and her institutions.

But the fun at the musters was not the least attraction. There was the old darky with his stand loaded with cider, spruce beer and ginger cakes; there was horse racing, foot racing, wrestling matches, climbing poles and catching the greased pig. There were fights, too, rough and tumble, fist and skull, where the woolly wolf from the Blackwater had it out with the ringtailed Painter from the Miami bottoms. Then at night there was the dance. The pigeon wing and the double shuffle, winding up with the ranking colonel leading out the grandest dame of the county into the measured maze of the Virginia reel.

The theory underlying the old time militia law was a good one—in time of peace prepare for war; but in practice the law was cumbersome, inconvenient and unsuited to the people and the times. It failed in its main purpose of creating an efficient militia and was finally repealed by the legislature some time before the breaking out of the Mexican war.

HON. DAVID BARTON. (1)

As one strolls through any "silent city of the dead," how often, alas, does he run across the cold marble shaft marking the resting place of some one prominent, conspicuous and useful in his day, but now only numbered in the long list of those so forgotten that our young men and women of the current day are even unaware that such a person ever lived, and are entirely untaught in the history that oftentime attaches to them even locally.

Such a condition of things should not exist in these days of progressive and easy education, but in some way the local history of those whose deeds or words brought them into worthy prominence in their day and age should be kept fresh in the minds and memory of our young people as they, too, grow up to become more or less useful or prominent in statesmanship, heroism or philanthrophy.

Why should not our public schools set apart a day a year to be devoted to addresses on our local celebrities, whether of the field or forum, the pulpit or the bar, of war or of peace?

Such a thought is aroused in the mind of the writer as his eye rests upon a cold marble shaft in Walnut Grove cemetery, marking the last resting place of David Barton, "the forgotten statesman," who, in life, won such a place in the hearts and minds of his friends and neighbors that they not only erected to his memory, in death, a marble shaft, but inscribed on it, in lasting letters cut in stone, for all mankind forever to read and consider, this beautiful tribute: "A profound jurist, an honest and able statesman, a just and benevolent man."

In order, therefore, that our young people may not grow up in ignorance of so bright and noble a character who lived, labored and was loved in our midst in days gone by, I have written this brief sketch of the life of David

---

1. This sketch of Senator Barton was prepared by Captain Ravenel for and was first published in a newspaper, probably one of the Boonville papers.

Barton, that it may perpetuate in the minds of our people the memory of a man whose worth was so beautifully recognized by his friends, but whose modesty seems to have almost forbidden its most public recognition.

David Barton was a Tennesseean by birth and education, having been born there December the 14th, 1783. He was a lawyer by profession, and in 1809, with two brothers, also limbs of the law, moved to Missouri, the subject of this sketch settling in St. Charles, and the two brothers in St. Louis. His brother Isaac returned to his native state, but Joshua, his other brother, was killed in a duel on "Bloody Island" by Thomas C. Rector, in 1823.

In addition to his professional duties, he for a time taught school in St. Charles.

At the breaking out of the war of 1812 he enlisted in the United States army and at its close settled in St. Louis. In 1813 he became attorney-general of the Territory, which office he held for two years, when he was elected to the circuit judgeship in St. Louis. He next became speaker of the Territorial legislature which met in St. Louis in 1818. In 1820 we again see a great honor and distinction conferred upon him, when he was elected president of the first constitutional convention of Missouri, held during that year in St. Louis. It has been claimed that it was his mind that framed and his hand that wrote the constitution adopted by that convention, and which, be it said to his credit, seemed so replete and complete that it was in force until displaced by the Drake constitution in 1866.

In 1820 another great compliment and honor was paid Mr. Barton in his being elected Missouri's first United States senator by acclamation, in which body he faithfully served his adopted state for ten years.

In the same session, Thomas H. Benton was elected as his colleague, not by acclamation, however, but after a most spirited contest for three days. We mention this incidentally to emphasize the compliment paid the subject of our sketch. Not only that, but history gives credit to Mr. Barton's loyalty and sagacity for consummating this contest in Mr. Benton's favor, whose warm personal friend Mr. Barton was at that time. It was done in this way—at the instigation of Mr. Barton, David Ralls, a very ill member, was brought into the chamber on a litter, and whose vote for Mr. Benton ended the contest.

Mr. Barton was a Whig, while Mr. Benton was a Democrat, and in time they drifted apart politically, until the two former friends became bitter enemies, personally. The breach widened until it culminated on February 9th, 1830, in Senator Barton making such a scathing and excoriating arraignment of his colleague, Senator Benton, in a speech of four hours on the Foote resolution, relating to public school lands and abolishing the office of surveyor-general, that critics have classed it with the famous reply of Webster to Hayne. This speech was considered so powerful a debate that it appears in "Sale and Seaton's Debates in Congress" among the great speeches of that august body. In retaliation for this excoriation it is said that Senator Benton never mentioned Senator Barton's name in his "Thirty Years Review" except to record his vote.

After leaving the United States senate, Mr. Barton became state senator from St. Louis and later circuit judge at Boonville, Mo., where he died September the 22nd, 1837, at the home of his life-long friend, Mr. William Gibson, just east of Walnut Grove cemetery, where his remains are at rest.

The first monument erected by his friends was in the old City cemetery, where all the old families are buried, but his remains were later removed to Walnut Grove cemetery, where the present marble shaft, erected by the state, marks the resting place of this statesman, jurist and honest man. The old shaft that was originally placed over him in the City cemetery was removed to Columbia, where it stands side by side with that of Thomas Jefferson, on the university campus, in that city, and where it was unveiled in 1899 before thousands of people.

Mr. Barton was never married, and has relatives not nearer than nephews and nieces living. His life-size portrait, in recognition of his distinguished and unstinted services to his adopted state, hangs upon the walls of the Hall of Representatives in Jefferson City.

SAMUEL W. RAVENEL.

MORMON TROUBLES IN CARROLL COUNTY.

To the average citizen the name *Mormon* had a sinister sound, and made impressions very far from the truth. I remember during the winter of 1843-44, a Mormon elder on his way from Hydesburg sought shelter from a snow storm at my father's house in Ralls county, and great was the surprise and disappointment of the young folk to see that he was not equipped like Mephistopheles!

The Mormons had some peculiar views, especially as regards marriage. There had been disturbances in Jackson and Caldwell counties; so when the farmers of Carroll found these people buying land in the east end they were filled with alarm. There was the arrogant assumption of their name "Latter Day Saints," which tended towards unfavorable feeling. The sentiment became almost universal that the Mormons must go. A committee was appointed to confer with citizens of Ray, Clay, Howard, Saline and Chariton counties to ascertain what assistance could be had in case the expulsion of the Mormons should be formally determined upon.

Having received assurance of support, it was thought best to notify the Mormon leader at Dewitt of the course to be pursued by the people of Carroll and the other counties. When the ultimatum was communicated to him, Col. Hinkle threatened to exterminate any and all who should seek to disturb him and his people.

About this time the forces of Carroll county were required in Daviess county to aid in suppressing the Mormons there, and on their return they went into camp at Pleasant Park near Dewitt. This was on the 9th of September. The next morning Col. Hinkle was told that he would be given ten days in which to make up his mind to leave the county peaceably. At the end of that time hostilities would begin and he must take the consequences.

He coolly replied that he was ready to assume all responsibility. All this time, by boat and wagon, Mormon recruits were pouring into Dewitt, and the timber was full of their "soldiers." The 20th of September was decided upon as date of attack. The law and order forces were to move down the road to the main town, while skirmishers beat the brush. A volley was fired by the Mormon sharpshooters, and the settlers could hear and see a man encouraging the Mormons and telling them to "shoot low." A steady fire was kept up by both sides until a volunteer party sent a sharp volley into the Mormon works, when the man who had been so active was seen to press his hand to his side and disappear. Soon after the Mormons retired to some log houses where they were safe from attack. The Carroll "troops" also returned to their camp to await reinforcements from Ray, Howard and Clay counties, and the return of Hiram Wilcox, who had been sent to Jackson county for a cannon which was to be used to batter down the stockade.

In the interim every effort was made to cut off the Mormons who were trying to reinforce Dewitt. Guards were posted, pickets stationed to prevent the besieged from obtaining supplies sent them from Far West. Affairs began to look serious. Timber was cut for breast works, projectiles for the cannon fashioned of chains, scrap iron and nails. At this time the besiegers had increased to four or five hundred men. The troops were brigaded, military discipline enforced, war was on in earnest. The needs of the army were supplied by the patriotic farmers around Dewitt. The arrival of Mr. Wilcoxson with his cannon was hailed with satisfaction, and it was immediately mounted on a carriage previously prepared.

On the evening of the ninth day Judge Carickson and other citizens of Howard county reached the camp, seeking permission to try to settle the difference without bloodshed. They were allowed to make this proposition: The citizens of the county to purchase at first cost the lots in Dewitt, and some tracts of land adjoining—the property of the Mormons—the Mormons to pay for all cattle killed by them, and belonging to the citizens. Their wagons to be loaded during the night, ready to move by ten o'clock next morning, and that no further attempt at settlement in Carroll county should be made by the Mormons.

To these stringent terms Col. Hinkle was loth to agree, but he soon became convinced that resistance was useless, and gave orders to load the wagons for departure.

If "the flight of the Tartars was a sight so grievous and piteous as to melt the stoutest heart," the flight of the Mormons was none the less sorrowful.

The lesson of life is endurance—how much the heart may bear and not break, how much the body suffer and not die—sure the sad-eyed Mormon women have learned that lesson well!

SUSAN H. WHITEMAN.

THE FIRST SOLDIER PAPER.

In an interesting letter received from Comrade C. L. Fowler, residing in the National Military Home of Kansas, he tells of the first newspaper printed at the front by the soldiers during the Civil War. Mr. Fowler, who was a soldier with the first Iowa Infantry, was chosen to succeed D. E. H. Johnson, the "Rebel" editor of the Macon, Mo., Register. The Iowa troops and several regiments from Illinois arrived in Macon, June 13, 1861, and found here a red-hot "secesh" newspaper, and a flagpole proudly displaying a rebel banner. A large part of the population hereabouts strongly sympathized with the South, and General Porter's Confederate Army was hovering about town.

The first thing the Yankee soldiers did was to cut down the rebel flagpole, and the next to take charge of the rebel newspaper. When the pole fell it attracted the attention or Dr. F. W. Allen, president of Macon College, who looked out the window and saw the pole topple. Later Governor A. M. Dockery was in the midst of his Latin lesson. Dr. Allen was a strenuous Southerner, a small man but a good one. When he saw that pole fall he didn't take time to put on his coat, but rushed down town and offered to lick the whole Yankee army. The soldiers laughed at him, but one man took it a little serious and he and the Doctor came together. In the fall the Doctor lit on top. But he couldn't whip the whole army by himself, so after expressing his opinion concerning foreign troops he left the scene with his head high in the air.

The previous issue of the Register had prophesied Union disaster, and urged the rallying of the Southerners to drive the invaders from "The Sacred Soil of Missouri." The editor offered to melt his type up into bullets and to handle a gun if the Yankees undertook to disturb the quietude of Macon, but when the bluecoats finally appeared it is said that the fiery editor left town to "hunt his cow," and forgot to come back.

After casting about for talent the Iowa troops voted Mr. Fowler into the editorial chair. The outfit was quite primitive, consisting of an old-fashioned hand press and a few frames of type, but some of the Iowa men knew the business and Editor Fowler took his quill in hand and filled "Our Whole Union" full of loyal literature. The issue was dated June 15, 1861.

The following paragraph describes the tense situation under which the Register was changed from a rebel into a loyal sheet.

"It is not often that one enters a printing office conducted under precisely the circumstances of the one in which 'Our Whole Union' is now being issued. Men in uniform stand at the cases, a row of gleaming muskets is stacked before the door, with a sentinel on guard. The editor's table is ornamented with a revolver, two bottles of—well—something to sustain a drooping spirit; in short, the only resemblance to a printing office is the click of the type and the music of the press."

The Register's enthusiastic account of the raising of the rebel flagpole the week before was reprinted and underneath it was run a line of death's heads, such as are used on poison labels, to indicate what had happened to that pole when the Yankees came to town.

The price of "Our Whole Union" was $1.50 per copy, cash in advance; advertising was $1.00 a square inch or $60 a column per year. There were no society movements chronicled, because the new editor didn't happen to be acquainted with any of the ladies of the vicinity, and none would volunteer to assist him. The following editorial seems to evince considerable interest in the former editor, supposed to be out looking for his cow:

"Johnson, wherever you are—whether lurking in the dim woods, hunting your cow, or a fugitive on the open plains, good-bye! We never saw you, never expect to see you, and never want to see you, but for all of that, old fellow, we are not proud and stuck-up. So, Johnson, good-bye. We are sorry, very sorry, that you would not stay with us, and that you had to skulk away and lose yourself. Johnson, dear unknown enemy, we leave you tonight. We are going where the bullets are thick and mosquitoes thicker. We may never return; if so, old boy, remember us kindly in your dreams. We sat at your table; we stole Latin from your 'Dictionary of Latin Quotations;' we wrote union articles with your rebel pen; printed them with rebel ink on your rebel paper. Our boys set the type, used your galleys, shooting sticks and things. We drank some of your poor whiskey out of your disloyal bottle. Until then we thought of you kindly, but now we swear to lick you on sight. Now, Johnson, after all this you won't forget us, will you? We certainly will not forget you and that awful liquor you left for us to drink. You and your comrades will not be able to disrupt this union with powder and ball, but if you could get together a few barrels of that stuff and distribute it among our loyal soldiers the Lord only knows what might happen to this distracted country."

A diligent inquiry among the older citizens of Macon who lived here in the early days of the war failed to bring to light any information concerning the return of Johnson, and it is presumed that he never came back to claim his newspaper plant. But two copies of "Our Whole Union" are now in existence One is in a glass case in the State House at Des Moines, Iowa. The other is in the possession of an Iowa soldier who helped to get the one issue of the paper out, and who is now living at Muscatine, Iowa. There are no copies to be found here in Macon, where the paper was printed. The advent of the Iowa and Illinois soldiers was regarded with terror by the non-unionists in the vicinity. They supposed that the invaders would ruthlessly slay them on slight provocation and many lit out for the south to escape.

Mr. Fowler states that his experience as a newspaper editor in Macon interested him in the business, and after the war he went into it permanently as a means of livelihood. He founded the Stewartsville, Mo., Independent in 1877 and run it successfully for fifteen years. Afterwards he moved to Nebraska and published the Steele City Standard. He remained in the newspaper business as long as he was able to work, and even now, at the age of 70, invalided as he is, he writes most entertainingly.

Regarding the question of priority in publications at the front, which seems at one time to have evoked quite an animated discussion, the Washington Evening Star stated that an Illinois regiment published an Union paper in the fall of 1863, and that it was the first one. To this statement the Twentieth Michigan Infantry offered evidence to prove that its members had printed the "Union Vidette" in Kentucky in April or May, 1863. Then came the Twenty-Sixth Michigan Infantry with proof that it printed "Our Camp Journal" in February, 1863. All of which is frankly admitted and yet Mr. Fowler seems to have been ahead of the other soldier editors by nearly two years.

EDGAR WHITE.

NOTE—The following other Missouri Soldier papers were printed in the State:
Missouri Army Argus, 1861.
Union Democrat—Extra, 1861.
The Normal Picket, 1862.
Cape Girardeau Eagle, 1862.
The War Eagle and Camp Journal, 1862.

FROM SENATOR DOOLITTLE'S PAPERS.

Some of these letters do not appear to be written by prominent or well-known residents of Missouri. They do, however, touch upon an interesting and vital period of our country's history. And the endorsements received by the friends of President Johnson, as well as the cordial approval of Judge Doolittle's courageous stand in the national halls of legislation, are worthy of something more than passing remark. Few public men, living or dead, would have had the lofty independence and courage of his convictions that possessed the late Senator Doolittle during his entire political career. It is to be noted, to the honor of his memory, that he deliberately severed his public career from his Wisconsin constituents at the behests of conscience. The reconstruction period of our history was a time that tried men's souls. And this great statesman was one whose mental and moral metal was of the purest and the best. His public career is an interesting study for the student of history.

DUANE MOWRY.

Milwaukee, Wis., February 4, 1911.

St. Louis, Mo., September 9th, 1865.

My dear Judge:

By this time, I presume you have digested my letter in answer to your interrogatories. What I said is the result of a long and most intimate association with the Indians. I feel sure that from your disposition, and I trust determination, to better their condition, you will agree with me. I shall be gratified in co-operating with you at all times. To have accompanied you on the journey would have given me great pleasure, but we were just then making preparations for a campaign into Texas. Please present me acceptably to Mrs.

NOTE—Although it does not appear on the letter, this was directed to, and intended for, Senator Doolittle of Wisconsin.   D. M.

Doolittle, and to Miss Doolittle give my affectionate regards. I want to see her and to talk over our triumphs.

Your friend,
JOHN T. SPRAGUE.

To Hon. James R. Doolittle.

St. Louis, November 1, 1865.

Dr. Sir:

I telegraphed you from Chicago yesterday to ascertain if you was at home and rec'd no answer. I am desirous of seeing you. Will you on receipt of this write me when and where I can meet you.

Respectfully,
J. H. LANE.

Hon. Mr. Doolittle, Racine, Wis.

Saint Louis, December 1st, 1865.

Hon. J. R. Doolittle, Washington, D. C.

My Dear Sir:

Mr. Geo. W. Sturgis of Geneva in your state wants to be Post M on the Atlantic & Mississippi Steamship Co's line from here to New Orleans. He is a very worthy man. Was the Agent of the State at this place during a part of the war—stands well here, would make a good officer and ought to have the appointment. If you can help him you will confer a bounty upon a worthy man and a favor upon me. In 1868 I expect to help nominate and elect you to the Presidency. I always had great faith in your conservatism. If I had been in the State Senate as I should have been upon a fair count of the votes cast I should have voted to continue you where you now are. But I am in Missouri now and in state matters in Wisconsin can neither help nor harm you. I was rejoiced when I read your speeches made during the late canvass in Wisconsin. They were sound. My enclosed business card will advise you what I am doing here.

Very truly yours,
JNO. C. TRUESDELL.

Columbia, Mo., January 29th, 1866.

My dear Sir:

The views of yourself and Mr. Cowan of Penn'a accord so perfectly with my own, in regard to the proper policies to be pursued, in getting the Government back upon the old pathway, that I must ask the favor of you to send me a dozen or two copies of your speeches, under your frank, if they have to be and have been put up in Pamphlet form. Missouri will stand firmly by the President in the course which he seems to have worked out for himself, and we rely upon such statesmen as yourself and Mr. Cowan to ward off the blows aimed at him by Sumner, Wilson, Howe, etc.

I am very truly,
Your friend,
JAS. S. ROLLINS.

NOTES.

The Oregon Trails Commission unveiled a monument two miles west of Lanham, Nebraska, at the Kansas-Nebraska State line, which was erected by the State of Nebraska, the people of Washington county, Kansas; Gage and Jefferson counties, Nebraska, and the D. A. R. of Beatrice, Nebraska. The exercises were May 12, 1914, and were participated in by the Governors of both States, Wm. E. Connelly, Secretary of the Kansas State Historical Society, and others.

The Sedalia Capital of May 20, 1914, has an account of marking the grave of Gen. David Thomson, the only veteran of the war of 1812 buried in Pettis county. The grave is two and one-half miles northwest of Georgetown, and the exercises were under the auspices of the Spencer-McClure Chapter of the Daughters of 1812. Gen. Thomson was born August 21, 1775, in Richmond, Virginia, and came to Missouri in 1833, and settled at the place where he was buried. He was the father-in-law of General George R. Smith, the founder of Sedalia, and for whose daughter, Sarah, the city was named.

A memorial monument to three well-known German editors, Emil Preetorius, Carl Schurz and Carl Daenzer, was unveiled and dedicated in Reservoir Park, St. Louis, Sunday, May 24, 1914. The exercises were participated in by the Mayor of the city, Congressman Bartholdt and other prominent persons.

Among the Volumes received from the bindery by the State Historical Society is one containing the catalog of Elizabeth Aull Seminary of Lexington, Missouri, from 1871 to 1899 when the Seminary closed. The catalog for 1898-99 was to be of 34 pages, and the cover and all but the first four pages had been printed, when it was decided to close the school, and all of the catalogs except one were destroyed, so that the copy that the Society has is absolutely unique.

CEMETERY RECORDS.

In the last number of the Review mention was made of apparent indifference of the members and editors to the records of Missouri cemeteries which had been printed in numbers of the Review. The following letter from a genealogist shows what persons in that line of work think:

Hopkinsville, Ky., May 18th, 1914.

Mr. F. A. Sampson,

Dear Sir:

I regret very much that you have concluded to discontinue the cemetery inscriptions. To me they are the most valuable part of the Review, and I am sure other members of the Society must appreciate your work in this line as I do. Hoping for the continuation of these records, I am

Very truly,

NANNIE K. STERLING.

David W. Eaton of the United States Coast Survey writes hoping that the publication of the records will be continued, and says "It is of value to the historian, and such lists as you have been publishing, anything that throws light on the past is of value. Take my own case. My wife was a 'Hook,' great granddaughter of Elijah Hook who died in Boonville, and was part owner of the 'Far West,' one of the first steamboats to run on the Missouri river, and my wife found this history from your list that had been lost to the family."

Captain Louis Benecke of Brunswick and several others offer to make copies from local cemeteries, and volunteers for this work are requested, and the publication of lists will be resumed.

COTTON IN BOONE COUNTY.

In a scrap book made by Professor Broadhead is an article by George Tompkins White of Colorado Springs, taken from the Columbia Herald, the date of which was not preserved, which tells of cotton being formerly grown in Central Missouri. He said that before 1835 it was very common to see persons with large bundles of cotton going up to Howard county to the cotton gin. I understand there were two cotton gins in Howard county that the people went to, but there was none in Boone county. Sometimes after these hard winters, I remember hearing my father say that he met with one of the owners of the cotton gins and he told him that so little cotton had been brought to his gin that he deemed it unnecessary to keep his gin in order for running. * * * * * At my father's place for a number of years it was the habit to have a small cotton patch. My father insisted that when he had a cotton patch he could plant melon seed and in that way was sure to have melons. My mother said she wanted to raise cotton to get her candlewick, for she did not feel disposed to go to the store for it."

Mrs. Tidd, who formerly lived in Columbia, had some cloth that was made from Boone county cotton.

REPRINT OF GOVERNOR'S MESSAGE.

For several years the State Historical Society has been doing necessary preparatory work for the reprinting of the Governor's messages and proclamations, and this work has made prominent the fact that the State does a great amount of printing, but very little towards the preservation of what is printed. Commencing with the 8th General Assembly in 1834 to the 22nd in 1862, there were 38 messages ordered printed in pamphlet form in numbers varying from 200 to 25,000, amounting in all to 390,400 copies in English, 65,600 in German and 1,500 in French, or a total of 457,500 copies. During the past thirty-five years or longer the Secretary has sought for copies of these messages, and has visited most of the court houses in the State, and in all possible ways has tried to get copies of them and yet the Society now has only two of them in English and one in French. To the present time about a million copies have been printed by the State, and by chance a few of them are preserved. For the last twenty years the Secretary has gone to Jefferson City at the close of each session of the Legislature to secure a supply of publications, but if he should be a few hours late, the books and pamphlets left by the members or remaining in the bill rooms, the publications will have already been turned over to the second-hand paper man to be again ground up for printing more things to throw away. Why print five or ten thousand copies and not provide for the preservation of any?

BOUND PAMPHLETS.

The State Historical Society has lately received from the bindery several hundred volumes. In the first shipment delivered were uniformly bound sets of the Revised Statutes of Missouri, the session laws and journals of the Legislature and county histories of the same, and also seventy-three volumes of between sixteen and seventeen thousand bills of the General Assembly of Missouri from 1879 to date, the most of which cannot be found in any other library.

In the last shipment there were 94 volumes of official publications of Missouri, made up of the biennial reports of the various institutions, bureaus and officials, the bulletins issued by some of them, and reports of various kinds; 30 volumes of church minutes, containing more than five hundred separate publications; 14 volumes of annual reports of railroad companies that reach into Missouri; 24 volumes of transactions of the St. Louis Academy of Science, and other societies, including the State Press Association from its organization; and 107 volumes of school board reports, college catalogs and college periodicals. Among the first are complete sets of reports of Sedalia and Hannibal, the former from 1868 and the latter 1878; more than 90 volumes of college and school periodicals, publications that have been preserved in no other library in such numbers. While at present they would perhaps be looked on as of less value than the same number of volumes in other departments, yet it must be remembered that they contain the record of many facts which are a part of the educational history of the State, the biographies of educators, and the doings and portraits of many who in a generation from the time of publishing will be among the rulers of the State and nation.

In the last shipment were 269 volumes, and these contained 1327 pamphlets, 707 parts or bulletins and 1524 numbers of the periodical publications. There is yet in the bindery a large number of volumes, and more than 1,200 volumes of newspapers.

Some libraries have pamphlets on various subjects bound in the same volume, and then label it, perhaps, "Miscellaneous Pamphlets," arranging them in volumes according to size and not subject. The Society in all its volumes does not have any "Miscellaneous" volumes, but adheres strictly to the subject arrangement. In doing this it is compelled to include in a volume many different sizes, so that the book can be trimmed on the top only.

It would be supposed that the State Press Association would have its transactions of uniform size, but of the four volumes bound by the Society, from the 1st to the 37th, there are hardly two consecutive numbers of the same size, and all volumes can be trimmed on top only.

The State Board of Directors of the Missouri State Fair have printed six biennial reports and these six are in five distinct sizes.

Of the thirty volumes of Church Minutes, including more than five hundred pamphlets, those of the West Missouri Diocese of the Episcopal Church in two volumes were the only ones that could be trimmed on all three sides. It looks as if every Secretary or Clerk had no idea that his publication would be worth binding, and that consequently the size or shape was of no consequence.

SOLDIERS MEMORIALS.

Some years ago Missouri and Kansas each received from the general government nearly a half million dollars on old war claims. The State Historical Society of Missouri made an active campaign to have the Missouri fund appropriated to the erection of a Soldiers Memorial Building, to be used by the State Historical Society and the University library. The General Assembly, however, gave the fund to the counties to be divided among all the townships for road purposes, altho every one knew that it was practically throwing away a half million of dollars. Now a minute inspection of the entire State could not find the result of ten thousand dollars of that splendid fund.

Kansas acted with more judgment, and put its half million in the erection of a great marble hall of fame consecrated to the memory of the men who went out from the State and gave their lives to their country's service, and this building was dedicated May 27, 1914, to the credit, the joy and the pride of the entire State. There the soldiers who yet survive may meet, and live over again the days of battle, and may deposit the relics and historical objects for preservation, for the pleasure, the enlightenment and the reverence of future times; there the Kansas State Historical Society finds a safe and permanent home for its library and collections, and there kindred organizations are permanently housed. Such a building erected in Missouri would have been more creditable than would have been a mile or two of good roads in each county if Missouri's fund had been honestly appropriated to that purpose. The building erected by Kansas is 185 by 103 feet, with three full sixteen feet stories, basement and an attic story suitable for museum purposes, and the State has the credit of now having the finest and greatest Soldier Memorial in the world. Missouri refused a memorial to its soldiers. There is no marble hall erected to their memory, and those that are yet living have no such recognition from the State they served, and they have the knowledge that the State refused it to them when it would not have cost it a cent to have so honored them; and that a fine fund was diverted into ten thousand pockets, and now nothing to show for it.

PALMYRA ROAD.

"Mr. William Muldrow has commenced the long-talked of road from Palmyra to Marion City, and intends to prosecute it to completion. His plan is to build a levee from the warehouse running about half a mile up the river, extending thence across the prairie to the bluff, and there joining the present road. This levee will serve the double purpose of protecting Marion City from inundation, and also making a road which in the highest water will be above the surface. The advantages of this road are so apparent, and have been so much, that it is useless for us to say anything on that head. We believe there are none of our citizens who do not admit that it is a matter of the highest consequence. The resources and industry of Mr. Muldrow are adequate to the work, and if any man can do it, he is the man.

We believe it is in contemplation that the subscriptions which have already been obtained will be used as the work progresses."—The Missouri Whig, Palmyra, Nov. 6, 1845.

NOTE—When Dickens was in this country he was told of the unfortunate story of Marion City, and in Martin Chuzzlewit he describes it under the name of Eden. It has been supposed that Colonel Muldrow was the original of his Wilkins Micawber, but this was not so.

BOOK NOTICES.

Augustus Charles Bernays. A Memoir. By **Thekla Bernays**, St. Louis. C. V. Mosby Company, 1912.

Dr. Bernays on the paternal side was of Jewish descent. Previous to the time of Napoleon Jews on the Rhine were known only by their given names. Napoleon decreed that the Jews should adopt family names, and the grandfather of Dr. Bernays, and his brother, both of them Jewish rabbis, formed a word from the name of their father and the town he was from, and adopted that as the family name. Their descendants in the course of a hundred years have scattered almost all over the world. Some have remained orthodox Jews; some are of "reformed" Judaism; some are orthodox Christians. By intermarriage with Anglo-Saxon and French, the racial type of Judea is disappearing from some branches of the family. The subject of this memoir was born October 13, 1854 at Highland, Illinois, and for years was a prominent medical writer and teacher in St. Louis. The memoir written by Miss Tekla Bernays, his sister, is an interesting account of his life and tribute to his memory.

Race Culture; Mother and Child. By **Susanna Way Dodds**, A. M., M. D., author of "Health in the Household," "The Reason Why," etc. New York and Passaic, N. J. The Health Culture Company. (c. 1910.)

The Diet Question, giving the reason why. By **Susanna W. Dodds**, A. M., M. D. St. Louis, 1901.

The two above books have lately been added to our collection of Missouri authors by Dr. Mary Dodds, who was associated with her sister-in-law, Susanna, in the practice of medicine and in the establishment of the St. Louis Hygienic College of Physicians and Surgeons in St. Louis.

Dr. Susanna, **nee** Way, was born in Indiana, November 10, 1830, and died in California, January 20, 1911. The work first above mentioned was written to teach women the secret of health and happiness, and if every mother would read it and learn from it, the race would be benefited physically, morally and intellectually.

Sociology and Modern Social Problems. By **Charles A. Ellwood,** Ph. D., University of Missouri. New York, Cincinnati and Chicago. American Book Company. (c., 1910, 1913.)

This is a revised and enlarged edition of the former publication of Dr. Ellwood. It aims to illustrate the working of the chief factors in social organization and evolution, and shows the elementary principles of sociology, by the study of concrete problems, especially thru the study of the origin, development, structure and functions of the family considered as a typical human institution. To bring out the factors and principles of the social life not illustrated by the family, the author selected mainly from contemporary American society, because the United States affords the greatest sociological laboratory that can possibly be found. The work will be extensively used as a textbook.

Personal reminiscences and fragments of the early history of Springfield and Greene county, Missouri, related by pioneers and their descendants at Old Settlers' dinners given at the home of **Capt. Martin J. Hubble,** March 31, 1907, 1908, 1909, 1910, 1911.

Springfield, Mo., 1914.

If one of our members or other person in each county seat would follow the example of the one above mentioned in Springfield, and then publish the reminiscences of the old settlers as given by them around the dinner table, a great amount of local history that is now being lost would be preserved, and we cannot too strongly commend Capt. Hubble for publishing the pamphlet of 96 pages with the interesting talks that were made at his home.

The Jefferson County Republican, Quarter Century Edition, Vol. XXV, No. 15, DeSoto, Mo., April 2, 1914, **W. E. Crow,** Editor and Publisher.

This is a very creditable issue of more than thirty pages, twelve by nine inches in size, and containing about thirty views in and about DeSoto, with valuable reading matter.

Notable Women of St. Louis, 1914. Edited and published by **Mrs. Chas. P. Johnson.** [St. Louis, 1914.]

This is a delightful book by Anne Andre Johnson, the wife of Ex-Lieut. Gov. Johnson of St. Louis, and contains sketches of about sixty-five women of St. Louis who are notable in some field of work, and their achievements are made known as a tribute to them. Full page portraits are given of many of those of whom sketches are given.

Mirmir. An annual published by the senior class of the Kirksville High School. Kirksville Journal Printing Co., 1914.

Charles Banks, Superintendent of the Kirksville schools and a member of this Society, sends us a copy of the above. It is a bound volume of 146 pages, with many full page plates, and a host of photographs of students of the School, some of whom will in future time be prominent in State or national history, and the volume will be of special value because of having such portraits. The publication is one of the finest issued by the schools of Missouri, and is of much credit to the school, the school officials and the printer.

History of the Watson Family in America, 1760-1914. [By **Dr. Clayton Keith,** Louisiana, Missouri.] n. p., n. d.

We have this addition to our collection of Missouri authors and Missouri biography from Dr. Keith, one of our members. It gives the history of the family from an early day in Scotland to the present, and is dedicated to the seven Watsons, who came to Pike county, Missouri, in 1809.

First Annual Report of the Warehouse Commission of Missouri, April 16, 1913, to December 31, 1913. James T. Bradshaw, State Warehouse Commissioner, Jefferson City. The Hugh Stephens Printing Company. n. d.

The Forty-fourth General Assembly passed a law, approved April 12, 1911, by which the Board of Railroad and Warehouse Commissioners was abolished, and the office of Warehouse Commissioner was created, and James T. Bradshaw was appointed to this office.

The above is the report for 1913, the first report issued in Missouri devoted entirely to the subject of grain inspection and weighing, with a detailed account of the work, and the manner in which it is done, together with the business of the department for the year.

The Society is under obligations for a specially bound copy.

The Story of Old St. Louis by **Thomas Edwin Spencer.** Prepared for the information of persons who expect to witness the Pageant and Masque of St. Louis in Forest Park, St. Louis, 1914. St. Louis (c. 1914.)

The preliminary publication of the above was noticed in the April Review. This has been enlarged to a book of 170 pages, with eight full page plates. Those who saw the pageant should have the book to explain and fix upon the memory the events that were depicted in the celebration of the founding and growth of the city.

Ancestry of John Barber White and of his descendants. Published by **John Barber White** of Kansas City, Missouri. Compiled and edited by **Almira Larken White** of Haverhill, Mass. Press of C. H. Webster, Haverhill, Mass., 1913.

Mr. White was born in Chautauqua county, New York, December 8, 1847, and at an early age engaged in the lumber business, and for years has been a prominent figure in the Missouri and Southern States lumber companies. He is a member of a number of historical societies, and is a student of genealogical and family historical matters. He has prepared or assisted in the publication of a number of genealogies, the last being the one above noticed. It is a well printed work of 355 pages and 67 plates of views and portraits. All the lines of his family connections are run back to early times, and hundreds of families are interested in the work, and will be helped in tracing their family histories.

Minnis Family of Ireland and America. Compiled by **Elizabeth Austin,** Genealogist, 1913. Press of the Republican-Record, Carrollton, Missouri.

This publication of 31 pages and 21 plates by one of our members at Carrollton, is of special interest, because so many of the family live in Missouri. It is a welcome addition to our genealogies by Missouri authors.

Slavery in Missouri, 1804-1865. By **Harrison Anthony Trexler,** Ph. B., Assistant Professor of Economic History, University of Montana. Baltimore, John Hopkins Press, 1914. (Johns Hopkins University Studies.)

The above publication of 259 pages, prepared for the degree of Doctor of Philosophy, is the extended paper of one published in the **Review** for January, 1914, on "The Value and the Sale of the Missouri Slave."

The work is one of the most scholarly and painstaking of all publications relating to facts that have been published about Missouri. Professor Trexler worked in the library of the State Historical Society, and many of the manuscripts, books and newspapers cited in the work were used by him in its library.

Love's Young Dream. By **Maria I. Johnston.** Published by ladies of the St. Louis Chart Club. St. Louis, n. d.

The Siege of Vicksburg. By **Maria I. Johnston.** Boston, 1869.

The two above books have been added to our Missouri author collection by the authoress, now of Hemenway Terrace, Alexandria, Louisiana; but she writes that both were written while she resided in St. Louis. The first is of late date, but the first was written soon after the horrors of cave life at Vicksburg during the Civil War. The Society has another work by a Missouri author dealing of the same time and place: "My Cave Life in Vicksburg," by Mrs. James M. Loughborough, of which the first edition was published anonymously in 1864. The Society has both editions.

The Balkan Wars, 1912-1913. By **Jacob Gould Schurman**, Princeton. Princeton University Press, 1914. 140 pp. $1.00 net.

As early as 1326 the Turks made the great European city of Brusa capitulate to a son of the first Sultan, and other cities in succeeding years were added to the Sultan's empire. In 1389 on the field of Kossovo, the Christian army of Serbs, Bosnians, Albanians, Poles, Magyars and Vlachs were vanquished by the Moslems, and after more than five centuries the Montenegrins continued to wear black on their caps in mourning of that fatal day.

For centuries the Turks ruled their European subjects for tribute and plunder, and during the nineteenth century the independent states of Greece, Servia, Roumania and Bulgaria were established, and these with the aid of the Montenegrins drove the Turks back into Asia, leaving them only the city of Constantinople and the fortifications defending it.

These lectures by President Schurman will be welcomed by all who wish to understand the history and status of these far eastern European countries.

NECROLOGY.

Hon. Arthur Mason Allen was born in Fairfax county, Virginia, January 14, 1831, moved to Kansas City in 1855, and two years later married a daughter of Allen B. H. McGee of Westport. A year later he was made a director of the Westport School, and continued such for thirty years. In 1859 he was appointed principal of the Westport School, and in 1879 became the presiding judge of the Jackson County Court. In 1881 he was a member of the House in the Thirty-first General Assembly of Missouri, and in the Thirty-third and Thirty-fourth General Assemblies he was a member of the Senate and later was a member of the Democratic State Central Committee. He was one of the founders of the Allen Library, Westport avenue and Wyandotte street, Kansas City. After a long illness he died at his home, 4131 Oak street, May 12, 1914.

Hon. George W. Crawford was born near Bangor, Pennsylvania, May 8, 1838. During the Civil War he served in the Fifty-first Pennsylvania Infantry, and at the close of the war located at Marshall, Michigan, where he married. He came to Missouri in 1868, and was elected a member of the Thirty-third General Assembly, 1887, from the western district of Pettis county, where for twenty years he lived upon a farm; later he lived in Lamonte, and the last three years in Sedalia, where he died April 1, 1914, the last survivor of a family of fifteen children.

THE MISSOURI HISTORICAL REVIEW

VOLUME IX

October, 1914-July, 1915

PUBLISHED BY
THE STATE HISTORICAL SOCIETY OF MISSOURI

FLOYD C. SHOEMAKER, Secretary,
EDITOR

COLUMBIA, MISSOURI
1915

CONTENTS.

Bibliography of the Missouri Press Association, by F. A. Sampson	155
Book Notices	51, 135, 212
Books of Early Travel in Missouri—Long-James-by F. A. Sampson	94
Books of Early Travel in Missouri—Bradbury—By F. A. Sampson	177
Cabell Descendants in Missouri, by Joseph A. Mudd	75
Carroll County Marriage Record, 1833-1852, by Mary D. Brown	104
Garland Carr Broadhead, by Darling K. Greger	57
Harmony Mission, from Morse's Report on Indian Affairs, contributed by David W. Eaton	183
Harmony Mission and Methodist Missons, by G. C. Broadhead	102
Historical Articles in Missouri Newspapers, by Floyd C. Shoemaker	248
Historical News and Comments	272
Indian Mode of Life in Missouri and Kansas, by Geo. Sibley	43
"Missouri Day" Programs for Missouri Club Women, by Floyd C. Shoemaker	241
Missouri River Boats in 1841	133
Nathaniel Patten, Pioneer Editor, by F. F. Stephens	139
Necrology	54, 136, 218
Notes	132, 209
Notes and Documents	263
Pike County Marriage Records, 1818-1837, by (Mrs. W. J.) Harriet V. Rowley	119
Origin of "O. K.", by J. W. Baird	50
Six Periods of Missouri History, by Floyd C. Shoemaker	221
Sketch of Missouri Constitutional History During the Territorial Period by Floyd C. Shoemaker	1
Travel into Missouri in October, 1838, by Eduard Zimmermann, translated by W. G. Bek	33

CONTRIBUTORS.

BAIRD, J. W., Louisville, Kentucky.
BEK, DR. W. G., Professor German in the University of North Dakota.
BROADHEAD, G. C., former State Geologist, Professor in the University of Missouri, Late of Columbia, Missouri.
BROWN, MARY G., Carrollton, Missouri.
EATON, DAVID W., U. S. Coast Survey, Versailles, Mo.
GREGER, DARLING K., Professor of Geology in the University of Missouri.
MUDD, JOSEPH A., Author, Hyattsville, Md.
ROWLEY (Mrs. W. J.) HARRIET V., Regent Bowling Green (Mo.) Chapter, D. A. R.
SAMPSON, F. A., Bibliographer of the State Historical Society of Missouri.
SHOEMAKER, FLOYD C., Secretary of the State Historical Society of Missouri.
SIBLEY, GEO.,
STEPHENS, PROFESSOR F. F., Professor of History, University of Missouri.

MISSOURI HISTORICAL REVIEW.

Vol. IX.   October, 1914.   ·   No. 1.

A SKETCH OF MISSOURI CONSTITUTIONAL HISTORY DURING THE TERRITORIAL PERIOD.

In the history of an American commonwealth there appear relatively few dates that chronicle events of commanding importance. Ranking first in the history of Missouri and one of the foremost in that of the United States is April 30, 1803. On that date was concluded the treaty between this nation and France for the cession of Louisiana. The ratification of this treaty was advised by the United States Senate and was made by President Jefferson on October 21, 1803; and on the same day ratifications were exchanged and a proclamation was issued to that effect. (1) By this treaty the United States came into the absolute possession of the largest and most valuable extent of territory that was ever obtained purely through purchase by any nation since the dawn of history. Prior to 1762 France had held legal title to Louisiana, but since the settlements made in that part now included in the State of Missouri had been few, the French law need not receive consideration here. From 1762 to 1800 Spain held legal title to Louisiana. By the treaty of San Ildefonso, October 1, 1800, Louisiana was retroceded by Spain to France, but Spain remained in actual possession almost up to the time of transfer to the United States in 1803. During a period of thirty-four years the Spanish law of Upper Louisiana governed the people within the present

(1) *Treaties & Conventions*, I. 508-11; *Mo. Ter. Laws*, I. 1-4.

limits of Missouri. (2) Nor were these laws of less binding character after the cession of 1803, except as they were expressly annulled, superseded, or amended. (3) However, for our purposes, the provisions of the Spanish laws of Upper Louisiana may be disregarded. The English system of jurisprudence gradually superseded that of the Continent in Upper Louisiana, and today the organic law of Missouri rests entirely on an Anglo-American basis beginning with the Act of Congress of October 31, 1803.

It is important to notice in this connection one of the

(2) Houck, *Hist. Mo.*, I. 287, 298. The secret treaty of Fontainbleau, December 3, 1762, ceded the territory west of the Mississippi to Spain. France officially advised the director-general of Louisiana of this fact in a letter dated April 21, 1764. On the 18th of August, 1769, Spain took possession of Louisiana, and on May 20, 1770, Upper Louisiana was formally surrendered to Spain.

(3) "The return of Louisiana under the dominion of France, and its transfer to the United States, did not, for a moment weaken the Spanish laws in the province. The French, ———, made no alteration in the jurisprudence of the country." "According to the laws of nations, and the treaty between the United States and France, of April 30, 1803, and the acts of Congress of March 26, 1804, March 3, 1805 and June 4, 1812, the Spanish laws in Upper Louisiana were expressly continued in full force, until altered or repealed by the proper legislative authority."

"There was no legislation on this subject, until the 19th of January, 1816, when the territorial legislature of Missouri declared that the common law of England, and the statutes of the British Parliament, made prior to the fourth year of James the First, to supply its defects, should be the rule of decision, so far as the same was not repugnant to, or inconsistent with, the *laws* (omitting to say *statute* laws) of the territory." Casselberry, *The First Laws of the Mississippi Valley.* (*The Western Journal*, I. 191.)

"The Supreme Court of Missouri [Cf. *4 Mo. Reports*, p. 380, and *10 Mo. Reports*, p. 199] seems to have decided, that the act of the territorial legislature of the 19th of January, 1816, did not abolish the Spanish laws, but only introduced the common law, so far as was necessary to supply the *deficiencies* of the Spanish law, and the Missouri District Court of the United States, in the case of Smith vs. Fitzsimmons and Rogers, made a similar decision."

"And as there was no more legislation on this subject, until the act of the legislature of February the 12th, 1825, which went into operation on the 4th of July following, we may safely come to the conclusion, that the main body of the Spanish law continued in full force, until the 4th of July, 1825, when the revised statutes of that year went into operation, which made the English common law the rule of decision, except so far as the same was inconsistent with the *statute* laws of the State." *Ibid.*, p. 192.

By act of the Missouri Territorial Legislature, January 19, 1816, the common law of England and acts of the English Parliament made prior to the 4th year of James I., which were both of a general nature, and which were not contrary to United States Constitution or Missouri Territorial enactment, were made "The rule of decision" in Missouri until altered by the Legislature. *Mo. Ter. Laws*, p. 436.

articles of the treaty of cession of 1803. Article III states thus: "The inhabitants of the ceded territory shall be incorporated in the Union of the United States, and admitted as soon as possible, according to the principles of the federal constitution, to the enjoyment of all the rights, advantages, and immunities of citizens of the United States; and in the meantime they shall be maintained and protected in the free enjoyment of their liberty, property, and the religion which they profess." At the time of Missouri's struggle for admission in 1819 and 1820, it appears from the articles in the territorial newspapers that practically every well-informed Missourian had learned this article by rote and especially that part which guaranteed to them protection "in the free enjoyment of their liberty, property, and the religion," etc. Slaves formed part of the "property" of the people of Upper Louisiana prior to 1803, and also after that time, and Congressional dictation on this subject only served to recall the third article of the treaty of 1803.

Although as far as this work on Missouri is concerned there is no need to study the laws in force here under French and Spanish dominion, it is important to note that under Spanish rule, the Province of Louisiana was divided into a lower and an upper district for the purpose of facilitating governmental administration. There were several reasons for this division, the more important being the great distance separating the two centers of settlement near the mouth of the Mississippi and that of the Missouri. (4) Also, the pop-

(4) Nicollet in his History of St. Louis, page 92, states that in 1763, Laclede, the founder of St. Louis, took three months to come from New Orleans to Ste. Genevieve with his flotilla, a distance of 1,286 miles.
Cf. also Houck, *Hist. Mo.*, II. 4.
It took about three months to ascend the Mississippi at that time as is also evidenced in the Report of Don Pedro Piernas to Gov. O'Reilly dated Oct. 31, 1769, (Houck, *Spanish Regime in Mo.*, I. 66-75.) and in a letter of Fernando De Leyba dated July 11, 1778. (*Ibid.*, pp. 163f.)
Paul Alliot in his *Historical and Political Reflections on Louisiana*, written about 1803, makes the following remark on this point:—
"Although it is reckoned as five hundred leagues from St. Louis to New Orleans, yet with the river high, it only takes twenty days to reach the latter place."
He further adds that the merchants "generally take three months in taking their merchandise up the river."
(Robertson, *Louisiana*, 1785-1807, I. 139, 141.)

ulation around New Orleans, which was the seat of government of Lower Louisiana, was greater and represented a higher stage of development than we find in Upper Louisiana. The governor-general at New Orleans exercised direct jurisdiction over Lower Louisiana and appellate jurisdiction over the upper district; and a lieutenant-governor at St. Louis exercised direct jurisdiction over Upper Louisiana. (5)

At the time of the cession the population of Upper Louisiana was over ten thousand, (6) of which over one-half were Americans. (7) Not only did Spanish law give place to English law, but even Spanish and French influence as represented by the population had already greatly diminished and was soon to become a negligible quantity as far as legislation was concerned. Excepting some of the large Spanish land grantees and a part of the American settlers, especially those around Cape Girardeau and Mine à Breton, the inhabitants of Upper Louisiana neither rejoiced nor were they even reconciled either at the time when the treaty of cession became known or later when the actual transfer was made. (8)

---

(5) Stoddard, *Sketches of Louisiana*, chap. VIII. Loeb, *Beginning of Mo. Leg.*, in *Mo. Hist. R.*, I. 53f.

(6) Stoddard, *op. cit.*, p. 226, gives the population in 1804 as 10,340,—9,020 whites and 1,320 slaves.

(7) *Ibid.*, p. 225, states that three-fifths of the population were "English Americans."

Perkins and Peck, *Annals of the West*, pp. 543f., gives the total population of Upper Louisiana in 1804 as 10,120 and divides it as follows: French and Spanish, 3,760; Anglo-Americans, 5,090; Blacks, 1,270.

Rufus Easton, later Territorial Delegate to Congress from Missouri, in a letter dated at St. Louis, January 17, 1805, to President Jefferson, states that in 1801 the census taken of the inhabitants of Upper Louisiana showed a population of 10,301; and that according to the best informed persons in the district the population at the close of 1804 had risen to over 12,000. Of this latter number he thought that two-fifths were French and the others mostly immigrants from the United States. (Copy of this letter in *State Hist. Soc. of Missouri*; original in MSS. Div., Library of Cong., *Jefferson Papers*, 2d Series, vol. 32.)

(8) "On the 9th day of July, 1803, at seven o'clock p. m.—and the precision with which this date is registered indicates the profound sensation with which the news was received—the inhabitants of St. Louis learned, indirectly at first, that Spain had retroceded Louisiana to Napoleon, and that the latter had *sold* it to the United States." Nicollet, p. 89.

"It is easier to imagine than to describe the astonishment and wonder of the good colonists, when, as a sequel of the sundry official acts by which they were declared *republicans*, and their country a member of the great American

As an historical illustration of how circumstances may alter cases might be noted here the cold reception extended to the United States by these early Missourians of 1804 when they first learned of their newly made connection with the Fed-

confederation *founded by Washington*, they witnessed the arrival of a legion of judges, lawyers, notaries, collector of taxes, etc., etc., and, above all, a flock of vampires in the shape of land speculators. Liberty, with the popular institutions that accompany her, was welcomed; their advantages were soon understood; etc." *Ibid.*, pp. 90f. This last statement by Nicollet is not entirely true. American institutions were not welcomed, especially by the better class of Frenchmen, and however quickly they were understood, their advantages were late in being appreciated. See below the account of the French convention of delegates in September, 1804.

Mr. Primm says:—

"When the transfer was completely effected—when in the presence of the assembled population, the flag of the United States had replaced that of Spain—the tears and lamentations of the ancient inhabitants, proved how much they dreaded the change which the treaty of cession had brought about." Perkins and Peck, *op. cit.*, p. 537.

Mr. Houck does not take the same position on this point. He says: "Without the least objection on the part of the French population of Upper Louisiana, and to the great satisfaction of the American settlers, the jurisdiction of the United States was thus extended over the new territory." (Houck, *Hist. Mo.*, II. 373.) Speaking of the sentiment in Cape Girardeau he adds: "At Cape Girardeau the people, who were all Americans, with the exception of Lorimier and Cousin, were pleased greatly with the transfer of the country and seemed to have been decidedly hostile, if not to the Spanish Government, to the Spanish officers." (*Ibid.*, p. 364.) However, regarding New Madrid he makes the following statement: "But the people of New Madrid were not pleased with the change of government and he [i. e. Don Juan La Vallee, who surrendered the New Madrid fort to Captain Bissell] writes that 'this change has caused the greatest anger among these habitans, who live here, and especially on the day of surrender, during the ceremonies of which they have expressed the greatest grief.' 4" (*Ibid.*, p. 363. The footnote No. 4 gives the authority for the foregoing as follows: "General Archives of the Indies, Seville—Report of La Vallee to the Marquis de Casa Calvo and Don Manuel de Salcedo—dated March 29, 1804.")

Even as regards the inhabitants of Cape Girardeau, Major T. W. Waters, a resident of that town, wrote in a letter dated August 23, 1804, to President Jefferson as follows: "I will observe one thing to you, Sir, that many here do not like the change and every law that is passed that puts them in a worse situation than they would have been under the Spaniards is criticised and the worst construction put on, and those that are fond of the change feel disappointed at the law that Congress has passed for the government of this country." (*Ibid.*, pp. 385f.) It is, however, quite probable that Major Waters referred *purely* to the change in sentiment after the cession was made and after the law of Congress of March 26, 1804, became known.

Regarding the holders of large Spanish land grants and incidentally of the sentiment in St. Louis at the time of the cession, Mr. Houck says: "A few French land speculators, who, ... , had secured large and important concessions of land, no doubt anticipated to reap great benefits. They well understood that land values would greatly increase, because free donations of land to actual settlers would no longer be made. Under the new govern-

eral Union of States, and on the other hand, how impassioned they were fifteen years later in their arguments for admission into that very Union. We believe that the reasons for their first attitude were: their attachment to the Spanish

ment these holders of concessions and their assignees at once became and were regarded as the landed capitalists of the new territory. Such being the case, it is very probable that one of the chief beneficiaries of the favors of the late Spanish authorities became very enthusiastic and called for 'three cheers in honor of his adopted country,' as has been stated. Nevertheless, it is said that Charles Gratiot was about the only man in St. Louis who took a personal interest in the transfer of the country to the United States; that the people as a whole were indifferent. But Gratiot had received large land grants and perhaps understood better than anyone in St. Louis at that time the immense benefit a change of government implied." (*Ibid.*, pp. 373f.) Mr. Heuck further says: "The general apathy of the French inhabitants at the time lead [led] many to think that the inhabitants were not fit for self-government." (*Ibid.*, p. 375.)

Major Amos Stoddard, who certainly was most competent to judge of the sentiment in Upper Louisiana at the time of the cession, wrote as follows: "Indeed, *few of the French, and part of the English Americans only,* were at first reconciled to the change, though they never manifested any discontent. The former did not doubt the justice of the United States; but they seemed to feel as if they had been sold in open market, and by this means degraded; the treaty of 1762, and the change under it in 1769, rushed on their minds, and awakened all their apprehensions. The latter anticipated taxation, many of whom had abandoned their native country to avoid it, and voluntarily became the subjects of a government, careful not to impose any burthens on the agricultural part of the community." (Stoddard, *op. cit.*, p. 311. For an account of some of the actual benefits that did accrue then and later to Upper Louisiana under American rule, *cf. ibid.*, pp. 253f., 266: and Brackenridge, *Views of Louisiana,* pp. 140, 143-145.) (Italics mine.)

An equally reliable authority on this point is Rufus Easton, who on January 17, 1805, wrote the following from St. Louis: "That they, the French inhabitants, are in general enemies to the change of Government requires no argument to demonstrate—it depends on fact. When it was rumoured thro' [*sic*] this Country last summer that a recession to Spain would take place, joy gladden in their hearts—This however must not be taken for a universal sentiment—It is only that of the few who have feasted upon the labors of the more ignorant and industrious and whom they prejudice and influence as they please. Many have sufficient discernment to perceive that the cession to the United States advanced their landed property at least two hundred per centum they thank the stars and are willing to give the praise to whom it is due." (Letter to Pres. Jefferson. Copy in *State Hist. Soc. of Mo.* Original in *MSS. Div., Library of Congress, Jefferson Papers, 2d Series, vol. 32.*)

Darby, although not a contemporary authority, was well acquainted with many who witnessed the transfer of Upper Louisiana in 1804. The following quotation is from his work: "It was Charles Gratiot who requested the inhabitants, in their native tongue, when the ceremony took place, to cheer the American flag, when it was for the first time run up and floated to the breeze on the western bank of the Mississippi. The cheers of the crowd were faint and few, as many, very many of the people shed bitter tears of regret at being transferred, without previous knowledge, from the sovereignty of a government and language to which they had been accustomed and fondly

regime with its practical freedom from taxes and military services, with its swift and generally true justice, its liberal land policy, and its uniform respect for French institutions, customs and language; and their dislike of American laws and institutions, combined with the fear of some attack on slavery, such as the Northwest Ordinance of 1787. (9) Moreover, the French inhabitants felt insecure of their religion under the new Republic. (10) Years later when they perceived the benefits that would flow from statehood and when

---

attached, and under which they had been bred, to that of a strange government, with whose manners, habits, language, and laws they were not familiar. There existed, moreover, in the minds of many of the French inhabitants a deep-rooted prejudice against the Americans, notwithstanding the encouraging and conciliating speech made by their countryman and friend, Charles Gratiot, who was favorable to, and sustained and approved the transfer of the country." . . . "Mr. Jefferson, from his long residence in Paris, understood the French character well, was much attached to the French people, and was aware that the inhabitants of Louisiana disliked and were greatly opposed to the American government." (*Recollections*, pp. 223f.)

Scharff quotes Billon as follows regarding the sentiment in St. Louis in 1804: "On that day [March 9, 1804] the inhabitants witnessed a scene which, to much the largest portion of them, was fraught with sadness and apprehension. These people had been so long contented and happy under the mild sway of all their Spanish commandants, with one exception alone (De Leyba), that it was not surprising they should have entertained those feelings at being transferred, themselves and homes, to a nation whose people were mainly descended from the English, a nation that for generations back they had looked upon as the natural and hereditary enemy of the land from whence they sprung. For it must be borne in mind that they were nearly all of French origin, and although under Spanish dominion, there were but few Spaniards in the country, outside of the officials and soldiery." (*Hist. St. Louis*, I. 259.)

(9) It is here worthy of note that on January 23, 1804, there was communicated to the United States Senate a "Memorial of the American Convention for Promoting the Abolition of Slavery" praying Congress to prohibit by law the importation of slaves into the "Territory of Louisiana, lately ceded to the United States." This memorial actually suggested an enactment on this subject similar to the one in the Northwest Ordinance. *Am. State Papers, Misc.*, I. 386. The chaotic condition of society which had prevailed in the Illinois country after American occupation would also hardly have served to endear the United States in the minds of many of both the French and American settlers who had immigrated to Upper Louisiana from their former homes on the east bank of the Mississippi during the latter eighties and the nineties of the 18th century. *Cf.* also *Kaskaskia Records* 1778-1790, in *Ill. Hist. Collections*, V; especially letter of John Rice Jones, later Justice of Missouri Supreme Court, dated Oct. 29, 1789, at Kaskaskia to Major Hemtramck. (*Ibid.*, pp. 514-517.) The inhabitants of Upper Louisiana, especially the older ones, also undoubtedly resented the manner of cession which appeared to them like a sale in the open market.

(10) Alback's *Annals of the West*, p. 777.

the flood of American immigration poured in, they naturally desired admission into the Union.

The first organic law of American origin that applied to Louisiana was passed at the first session of the Eighth Congress of the United States on October 31, 1803, and provided a temporary government for the new district. This act empowered the President of the United States to take possession of Louisiana and placed under his direction all military, civil and judicial powers that had been exercised by the officials of the existing government. This great power was lodged in his hands until Congress made other regulations. (11) Strange though it seems to us now, this law was not unfavorably received by the French inhabitants of Louisiana. And the reason for this attitute was not because they excused and appreciated it as a temporary makeshift government and therefore as a necessary, initiatory step towards later self-government, but rather because of their natural inclination for a military regime, due to years of training under just such a centralized government. The belief that this act was unpopular in Upper Louisiana is unfounded in fact. In the eyes of the French better classes it must have seemed at the time the ideal type of government for this territory. It was in the following year, after Congress had passed an act annexing Upper Louisiana to Indiana Territory, that these well-to-do Frenchmen petitioned Congress and through their representative, Chouteau, pleaded with President Jefferson for just this kind of government.

Under this law Captain Amos Stoddard was appointed the first American civil commandant of Upper Louisiana. The seat of government remained at St. Louis, and little change in governmental administration was introduced. This was in accordance with the policy of the Washington officials, who wisely tried to pacify the fears of the inhabitants. (12)

(11) *Stat. at Large*, II. 245; *Treaties & Conventions*, I. 508ff.
(12) Captain Stoddard had instructions that "inasmuch as the largest portion of the old inhabitants were strenuously opposed to the change of government, it would go far to conciliate them, and they would much sooner become reconciled to the new order of things, by making little, if any change in the *modus operandi* of the government, at least for a time." Billon, *Annals of St. Louis*, 1764-1804, p. 364.

Congress did not wait long, however, in making provision for the government of Louisiana. By an act of March 26, 1804, Louisiana was divided into two districts or territories. All south of the thirty-third degree of north latitude was to be called the "territory of Orleans"; and all north, the "district of Louisiana"; the line of demarcation being the present southern boundary of Arkansas. The District of Louisiana was placed under the government of Indiana Territory, which then consisted of a Governor, Secretary, and three Judges. The Governor and Judges exercised full judicial, legislative and executive power under certain general restrictions. They were specifically given power to establish inferior courts and prescribe their duties; make laws, etc., except those abridging religious freedom or those contrary to the laws of the United States; and it was also set forth that criminal trials were to be by a jury of twelve and civil trials involving amounts over $100 also to be by jury. The Judges were to hold two annual courts in the district. It was provided, among other things, that the laws in force in the District of Louisiana which were not inconsistent with this act were to remain in force until altered. This act went into effect October 1, 1804, (13) and excepting the attempted legislation bearing on the "Missouri Question" Congress never passed an act which applied solely to Missouri that was more de-

(13) *Stat. at Large*, II. 283-289; *Mo. Ter. Laws*, pp. 5f.
A large part of this act also dealt with the government of the Territory of Orleans. The inhabitants of Lower Louisiana included in the new "Territory of Orleans" were equally incensed by this act. They drafted a memorial protesting against the division of Louisiana into two parts and the lack of self-government. This act gave the "Territory of Orleans" a territorial government of the first or lowest grade. This petition is said to have been signed by over two thousand heads of families of Louisiana. It was entitled a "Remonstrance Of The People Of Louisiana Against The Political System Adopted By Congress For Them", and was communicated to the Senate December 31, 1804. *Am. State Papers, Misc.*, I. 396ff.

This petition was placed in the hands of a committee appointed by the House of Representatives. On January 25, 1805, the committee closed its reports with a resolution "that provision ought to be made by law for extending to the inhabitants of Louisiana the right of self-government." This resolution was passed by the House on January 28, 1805. *Annals of Congress*, pp. 1014-21.

To this same committee was also referred the petition of the inhabitants of the "District of Louisiana", which will next be discussed. *Ibid.*, p. 957.

tested by at least one-half of her population than was this one. It is hardly necessary for us to enter into a discussion of the laws governing the District of Louisiana passed by the Governors and Judges of Indiana Territory. There were sixteen acts passed all together; however, their bearing on our study is unimportant. (14) It should be stated that these laws were well suited to a pioneer community like Missouri, and no criticism of them is found in any of the literature of that day.

From the very beginning of Missouri's connection with the United States there has never existed the least timidity on the part of the people of this State to make known to the nation in a perfectly constitutional way their wants and grievances. The legislation of Congress in 1804 for the inhabitants of the District of Louisiana was received with the greatest disfavor west of the Mississippi, and occasioned the first of a long series of petitions and remonstrances presented to Congress by the inhabitants of the present State of Missouri. These early petitions are characterized by temperate language and a tone of positiveness based on a just cause. Although at the time of the cession there was no considerable open dissatisfaction or opposition, in less than six months after that the discontent was widespread. The people of Upper Louisiana did not like the American regime with its numerous officials, tax gatherers and jury system. They regarded with equal disfavor the method provided for settling the Spanish land grants; (15) the increased expenses under the American regime, e. g., taxes, road and military service without compensation; the absence of all representative government; and the act of March 26, 1804, in whole. As early as August 23, 1804, Major T. W. Waters of Cape Girardeau, a staunch American and a man of influence, wrote President Jefferson that a petition *had been* "drawn up" protesting against parts of that act of Congress. (16) On September 29, 1804, two days before the act of Congress of March 26,

(14) *Cf.* also Loeb, *op. cit.*, I. 59-71.
(15) Stoddard, *op. cit.*, p. 253.
(16) Houck, *Hist. Mo.*, II. 385, 387f.

1804, was to take effect, a "remonstrance and petition of the representatives elected by the freemen of the districts in the District of Louisiana to Congress" was drawn up and signed in St. Louis by sixteen deputies from the five subdivisions now included in the State of Missouri. (17) The sixteen delegates were apportioned as follows: two from each of the districts of New Madrid, Cape Girardeau, and Ste. Genevieve; six from St. Louis and "dependencies"; and four from St. Charles and "dependencies". The dissatisfaction with the law of March 26, 1804, was based on the grievances that it annexed upper Louisiana to Indiana Territory; that it contained no provisions granting self-government; that it did not protect and secure slavery west of the Mississippi River; that it proposed settling the eastern Indians on Louisiana soil; and that section fourteen of that act, the section relating to the Spanish land grants, was unjust and unreasonable. This last grievance was beyond question the most real and deeply seated of all. One prominent contemporary of that day even goes so far as to state that the annexation of upper Louisiana to Indiana Territory was only an ostensible objection to the law of 1804, and that the real ground for dissatisfaction was the land title clause. (17a)

This interesting petition remonstrates at some length against the division of the Louisiana Purchase into two parts and states that the ceded territory if left as one whole had sufficient population to be admitted as a state; that the Northwest Ordinance provided for the admission of States in that district which had a population of sixty thousand and that Ohio when admitted did not have more than from thirty-three to forty thousand free inhabitants; that the third article of the treaty of cession provided that the inhabitants of Louisiana were to be incorporated into the United States as soon as possible; that if Congress could divide Louisiana once, she could subdivide indefinitely whenever the population became sufficient to form a state, and thus would

---

(17) *Am. State Papers, Misc.*, I. 400ff. This petition was presented to Congress January 4, 1805.
(17a) Letter of Rufus Easton, *op. cit.*

Louisiana be always oppressed. This part of the remonstrance against the division of Louisiana was followed by a protest against the form of government provided for the "District of Louisiana". The delegates seriously objected to (1st) being under the government of another territory; (2d) being under a governor of another territory who did not reside or hold a freehold estate in the District of Louisiana; (3d) the seat of government being at Vincennes, which was one hundred and sixty-five miles over impassable roads from them, and the governor sometimes even farther distant; (4th) the laws of Indiana Territory not being similar to those of Louisiana, e. g., slavery existed in Louisiana and was prohibited in the Northwest Territory; (5th) the absence of a Congressional law on slavery, which might make the inhabitants of the District of Louisiana feel that perhaps some day Congress would abolish it, even though by the treaty with France they were protected in their property. In short they objected to the great injustice of being under Indiana Territory; but they also objected, and, we believe, in a more serious way, to the 14th section of the Act of Congress of March 26, 1804, which declared null and void all Spanish land grants made subsequent to the treaty of San Ildefonso, and to the 15th section of this same act which settled Indians from east of the Mississippi on the land in Louisiana District. Further, they objected to the use of the inferior word "District" as applied to Louisiana in contradistinction to "Territory" as applied to Indiana and Orleans. (18) There was really much righteous wrath on the part of the Louisiana inhabitants against that part of the Act of Congress which proposed settling the Indians from the country east of the Mississippi in this district. The necessity of protecting themselves against the Indians already west of the Mississippi imposed labors and hardships on those pioneers. Even President Jefferson, who, we think, lacked here his usual foresight, warmly favored this removal of the savages. (19)

(18) Houck. *Hist. Mo.*, II. 388.
(19) Jefferson's *Writings*, VIII. 249. In a letter to Horatio Gates dated July 11, 1803, speaking of Louisiana Jefferson writes: "If our legislature

The delegates then asked that the act which divided Louisiana into two territories and which provided a temporary government thereof, be repealed; that there be made a *permanent* division of Louisiana legally; that the Governor, Secretary, and Judges of Louisiana District be appointed by the President and reside and hold property there; that the above officers be appointed from those speaking both French and English; that the records of each county and the proceedings of the courts of Louisiana District be kept in both French and English; that Louisiana District be divided into five counties and that the people of each county elect two members for a term of two years to form with the Governor a Legislative Council; that they be protected in their slaves and be given the right to import slaves. They also asked that Louisiana District be permitted to send a delegate to Congress and that funds be apportioned and lands set apart for French and English schools in each county and also for a "seminary of learning". And, finally, they requested that private engagements which had been entered into during the Spanish rule and which were conformable to the Spanish law, be maintained; that former final judgments rendered according to the Spanish law, should not be reversed; and that former judgments which had been rendered under the Spanish law and which according to it were appealable, should still be appealable to the proper United States courts.

This petition was accompanied by a declaration of "the Representatives of the District of Louisiana, in General Assembly met", signed in St. Louis September 30, 1804. There were fifteen deputies from five districts and from Femme Osage in this latter meeting, which was held in St. Louis. The declaration was signed by the President and Secretary of the Convention on the 30th and the authenticity of their signatures was certified by Amos Stoddard, Captain and First Civil Commandant in Upper Louisiana, who added "that respect ought to be paid to what they affirm". (20) The declaration

dispose of it with the wisdom we have a right to expect, they may make it the means of tempting all our Indians on the East side of the Mississippi to remove to the West, and of condensing instead of scattering our population."

(20) *Am. State Papers, Misc.*, I. 404f.

of the fifteen delegates of Upper Louisiana simply stated that "Mr. Augustus Chouteau" and "Mr. Eligius Fromentin" had been "unanimously chosen" to act "as the deputies, delegates, and agents, general and special, for the inhabitants of Louisiana, for the purpose of presenting to the honorable the Congress of the United States" the "humble petition" aforesaid. Of the sixteen names of the delegates attached to the "petition", the document first referred to above, thirteen are the same as are affixed to the "declaration". There was also a slight change in the apportionment of the delegates who signed the "declaration": there being one each from New Madrid and Femme Osage; four from Cape Girardeau; two from Ste. Genevieve; four from St. Louis and dependencies; and three from St. Charles and dependencies. (21)

This memorial or petition as adopted and transmitted to Congress by Auguste Chouteau, was quite different from the one originally prepared. No early public document of Missouri down to the framing of Missouri's First Constitution in 1820 and the Solemn Public Act of Missouri's First Legislature in 1821, has a more interesting history than this one. It involved the first successful wire-pulling in Missouri history, and had it not been for an unnamed schoolmaster, might have resulted very disastrously for Missouri. The inner history of this remarkable document is set forth in a letter of Rufus Easton, dated at St. Louis January 17, 1805, to President Jefferson. He wrote that immediately after the Act of Congress of 1804 became known in Missouri, about twenty of the inhabitants of St. Louis assembled with a view to appoint a committee which was to call a convention of delegates from the different districts, and that this convention was to form a plan of government for upper Louisiana. (22) The whole affair seems to have been arranged by the

---

(21) Houck gives the names of eighteen delegates who signed the petition dated September 29, 1804. This authority seems to have combined the names of all the delegates who signed this petition with the two new members who signed the "declaration" of September 30, 1804. *Cf.* Houck, *Hist. Mo.*, II. 391.

(22) *Op. cit.* Easton said that these twenty inhabitants met on April

French inhabitants, as no American was invited, although there was a number of prominent ones here. It was so slated that a majority of the delegates to be selected was to be of the French interest by having them elected by committees who in turn were chosen principally by French villages. How successfully the plan worked is evident from the result of the election. Of the sixteen signers of the "petition", seven were Americans and nine Frenchmen; and of the total eighteen signers of both documents, nine were Americans and nine Frenchmen. The name of Stephen Byrd, who was a delegate to the Constitutional Convention of 1820, appears in the "declaration" as a delegate from Cape Girardeau. Eligius Fromentin, one of the delegates from New Madrid, seems to have been the framer of the "petition", as he is credited with being the most learned. In 1812 this man was one of the first United States Senators from the State of Louisiana. Practically all the French and American delegates were men of wealth and held large land tracts, and this placed them in perfect accord regarding the Spanish land grants. (23)

The original petition drafted by this convention recommended in reality a "gouvernement militaire". It provided that they have a Governor residing in the territory possessing both civil and military jurisdiction; that there be Commandants for each district possessing like powers, with an appeal to the Governor in certain cases; that there be no trials by jury "except in such cases as in the opinion of the Governor or Commodant justice should absolutely require it for special cause to be shown"; and that the practice of lawyers be entirely prohibited. It compared the Governor and Judges of the Indiana Territory to "foreign Bashaws—to Pro-prætors and Pro-Consuls under the more modest name of Governor and judges sent here to rule over the people and to write liberty as had been done in Venice upon our prison walls—"; and

2, 1804, to peruse the bill of Congress of March 26. The date of this meeting, as given, may be correct, but, if so, it was the proposed bill that was perused, since the law of March 26 could not have reached St. Louis by April 2.
(23) Houck, *Hist. Mo.*, II. 39ff.

declared that the treaty of cession had been broken: and "a motion was made by one of the members to call upon the Emperor of France thro' his Ministers to enforce a fullfillment."

This draft of the petition was presented to Captain Stoddard, who made several slight changes in it so as to obtain for it a reading in Congress. It was then again considered by the convention and singularly failed to pass. Easton gives the following reason for this failure: "But for a person who resided some years within the United States in character of a school-master who understands the French language, catching at the popular declamation of some members of Congress—Governed by the principles advanced in the memorial of Orleans and fired with ambition to distinguish himself in the political world this original plan would not have been changed—The flame of his eloquence and unparallelled knowledge of American politics changed the tone to the whole system and the plan was to ridicule the Majority of Congress for their *professions* of Republicanism and *boasted* love of liberty—". (24)

After the petition had been changed to its present and final form, it was entrusted to Chouteau to take to Washington. There is little doubt that the wealthy French inhabitants favored a military government without civil law and lawyers. Chouteau had presented his views for such a government to Gallatin during the previous summer of 1804, when many of the leading Frenchmen of Louisiana District were in Washington. Gallatin wrote to President Jefferson regarding this interview with Chouteau, and stated, that while he respected the zeal and ability of the Frenchman, he did not endorse his views and those of his business associates. It is by no means improbable that when Chouteau carried this democratic petition of September, 1804, to Washington, he still pleaded for the military system. The democratic ideals

---

(24) Easton's Letter, *op. cit.* *Cf.* also Fortler, *Hist. La.*, III. 16f., and *Am. State Papers, Misc.*, I. 396ff.

After careful searching we have been unable to ascertain who this unique school-master was.

of Jefferson, however, made this plea a vain one, and nothing more was heard of the "gouvernement militaire". (25)

(25) Houck, *Hist. Mo.*, II. 400.
The following very valuable letter is copied from note No. 163, p. 355, vol. II., of Robinson, *Louisiana*, 1785-1807: "The following extract from a letter (entitled Separate observations") dated St. Louis, November 4, 1804 (conserved in the Bureau of Rolls and Library, Department of State, Territorial Papers, vol. I., "Louisiana"), shows conditions in Upper Louisiana or Louisiana Territory:
"I conceive it may not be improper to mention some circumstances concerning the Petition from the Committee held in September last at this Place, before my arrival, for tho' I have not read that Memorial I have heard it much spoken of, and I have reason to think a Paper, said to be a copy of it, may have been sent to the public printer for insertion, in which case it will be found different from the original, that pretended having been taken from the first draft of it before its ultimate correction. It seems the act of Congress of March last concerning Louisiana created some discontent in the minds of People here, they wished and expected a Government of their own. It hurt their pride to be made dependent on Indiana for officers and laws, because their population and territory are much more extensive than those of their neighbours. They conceived the act of Congress infringed some of the Rights insured to them by the Treaty, placing them in a more degraded situation than other territories of the United States. They formed a Convention in which a Committee was chosen to draw up a Petition to Congress. The Member who made the sketch of the Memorial was sent out before my arrival and I have not seen him, but I am told he is a man of warm passions and I conceive him to be probably of a character such as I have known in the French Revolution, who allowed their exalted ideas to run away with their understanding and could not distinguish between the true principles of liberty, and those leading to Anarchy and despotism. . . . I have a particular satisfaction at the time in saying that the inhabitants are much pleased with Govr Harrison now here. His affability and easy access form a strong contrast with what they had been accustomed to—all the *disinterested* sensible men among them are glad of the change of Government, but there are some, as you will easily believe who have prejudices which time and experience will wipe away—there are others who enjoyed, or were directly concerned in, extensive privileges, or had certain advantages which attached them to the former system. I am speaking of the French part of the inhabitants, whose sentiments I know best by their considering me as one of themselves on account of the language and my very long residence in France. The appearance of hostilities—an idea many of them have of this part of the country being about to be receded to that nation for the Floridas, are topics often brought forward which have tended to show me the real inclinations of some and they open their minds with less reserve by not considering me in the light of a stranger."
—Letter unsigned—"From a man who went up Mississippi to become acquainted with Peltry trade."
The dislike of lawyers on the part of the French inhabitants is also seen in the Historical and Political Reflections on Louisiana by Paul Alliot. (Robertson, *op. cit.*, I. 135, 137.) Speaking of St. Louis that physician says: "The magistrate who renders justice does not molest or percesute any citizen. He is a father whose entrails are at all times open to his children." "None of those blood-suckers known under the names of bailiffs, lawyers, and solicitors are seen there." (This was written before the transfer in 1803.)

Within two months after this first petition had been presented to Congress, an act was passed on March 3, 1805, which remedied most of the objections and granted some of the requests set forth by the St. Louis convention of September, 1804. (26) It was rather satisfactory to the French inhabitants, as it established a separate centralized form of government. The act provided: 1st, that the "District of Louisiana" be changed to the "Territory of Louisiana"; 2nd that this territory be separated from the government of Indiana territory; and 3d that a new government of the territory of Louisiana be established. As Missouri by this act became a territory of the lowest grade and from this stage gradually advanced to statehood, it is a matter of importance to notice the plan of government outlined by this second organic act of Congress relating to Missouri.

The executive power was lodged in the hands of the Governor, whose tenure was appointive by the President of the United States, whose term was three years, and who must reside in the territory. His powers were wide, being both executive and legislative in their scope. He was commander of the militia, superintendent *ex-officio* of Indian affairs, had the power of appointment and command of all officers in militia below the rank of general officers, could grant pardons and reprieves under certain limitations, could divide the territory into districts where the Indian titles were extinct, and appoint magistrates for civil and military purposes. Asso-

---

The following report made by Doctor John Watkins to William C. C. Claiborne in 1804 relating to lower Louisiana, shows that the sentiment of the French inhabitants in that part of the country on government and politics was quite similar to what obtained in the upper portion of Louisiana:—"They wish to be allowed a member upon the floor of Congress, to represent their true interests and situations. Sometimes they desire to enter immediately into all the benefits and advantages of a State Government, but they generally stop short at the difficulties of popular representation, in their present State of political knowledge. The expenses of public buildings, Courthouses, Prisons, etc., the increase of taxes, the acrimony of elections, Courts of Justice, Juries, pleadings at Law and Lawyers, with the difficulties of language has made most of the sensible reflecting people fall into the opinion that a Government of Commandancies (at any rate for the Country) is best adapted to their present situations." (Robertson, *op. cit.*, II. 319.)

(26) *Stat. at Large*, II. 331f. Passed at second session of Eighth Congress, March 3, 1805, and went into effect July 4, 1805.

ciated with the Governor was a Secretary, whose duties were clerical, and who became governor when that office was vacant. His term was four years, and he was also required to live in the territory. His tenure was the same as that of the Governor.

The legislative power was vested in the Governor and the three territorial Judges, or a majority of them. This body or Legislative Council had power to establish inferior tribunals and prescribe their duties. It was empowered to make all laws conducive to the good government of the inhabitants of the territory provided no law should be enacted inconsistent with the Constitution and Laws of the United States or abridging the religious freedom of the inhabitants or dispensing with trial by jury in both civil and criminal cases under certain regulations. All laws passed by this council were subject to the ratification of the President and Congress.

The judicial power was vested in three Judges appointed by the President for four years, and in such inferior tribunals as might be established by the Legislative Council. The three Judges or any two of them were to hold two courts annually in the Territory and to have the same jurisdiction as that formerly held by the Judges of Indiana Territory.

The compensation for the five foregoing officers was the same as obtained in Indiana Territory. All were required to take an oath of allegiance to the United States. It was expressly provided that all existing laws were to remain in force until modified.

Such are the general provisions of this act. It did much to mollify the inhabitants of Upper Louisiana, and, although not granting them the elective tenure nor a delegate in Congress, it was far more satisfactory than the previous act. They now had a territory and a government that were not united to or under any other subdivision of the United States, and, although their new officials were appointed in Washington, and subject in every express way to the national government, still they were required to reside in the territory, and this alone was worth a great deal to the inhabitants of a pioneer country where distance played such an important part in law administration. (27)

During the following half decade the Territory of Louisiana made rapid strides in development. The increase of population alone justified a change in the governmental machinery provided for by the act of 1805. The population of the territory in 1810 had risen to 19,976, being distributed among the five districts as follows: Cape Girardeau, 3,888; New Madrid, 2,296; St. Charles, 3,505; Ste. Genevieve, 4,620; and St. Louis, 5,667. (28) This remarkable growth in population naturally created desire for a higher grade of territorial government. It was the wish of a large majority of the inhabitants of this territory that the American policy of self-government be applied to them. And this was soon revealed in the numerous petitions presented to Congress on that subject. Never in the history of Missouri, during neither the French, Spanish, American, Territorial, nor State Period, have her inhabitants framed, signed, and presented so many petitions to Congress as issued from the Territory of Louisiana from 1810 to 1812 inclusive. But, to us even this seems less remarkable than is the failure heretofore of every writer on Missouri history to notice a single petition

(27) Showing the sentiment in Louisiana Territory shortly after this act of Congress of 1805, is the following extract from a letter of Judge Coburn to Madison, dated August 15, 1807, Mayville, Kentucky. (Robinson, *op. cit.*, II. 359f.)

"I would here take the liberty to remark, that altho some of our American Citizens have entertained strong prejudices, against the manners, habits, language and religion of the French settlers in Louisiana. Those settlers appear to me, to be an inoffensive and peaceable people, little disposed to disturb the harmony of Government, and I think they will be found to be easily governed; as they are strangers to riot, tumults and drunkenness. It is true that, they are unhappy at this particular period. And they assign as reasons; that their land claims are unsettled, and that the administration of Justice is dilatory. That there should be some causes of uneasiness is by no means surprising. The change of Government, the prospect that their language, religion, manners and influence are about to be swallowed up in the American character, are some causes of unpleasant sensations. It only requires that a temper of conciliation, mixed with impartial Justice should be observed by the rulers of the Territory—That they should feel and act superior to national, local, religious or civil distinctions; and endeavor to blend in a common mass, the various characters of settlers who may be resident in that country. . . . ."

(28) *U. S. Census*, 1900, *Pop.*, I. 27f.

of that time. This silence can be construed only as the result of a lack of information, since the greatest importance always attaches to those documents that reflect the sentiment of so large a district of people in regard to a change in their organic law. At least fifteen of these petitions appeared, twelve of which are still in existence. These twelve requested that the Territory of Louisiana be raised from a territory of the first to one of the second grade. One of the other petitions, very significantly, prayed that no alteration be made in the form of government. (29)

On January 6, 1810, there was presented to Congress "a petition of sundry inhabitants of the Territory of Louisiana, praying that the second grade of Territorial Government may be established in said Territory." This was probably one of the first of these petitions and, we think, was drawn up and signed in 1809. It based its request for a higher grade of territorial government on the treaty of cession, on the unsatisfactory exercise of both legislative and judicial powers when vested in the same persons, and on the large size of the militia in the Territory of Louisiana compared with the militia in either Indiana or Mississippi territories. This petition was referred to a committee on January 9, 1810, which reported, on January 22d, a bill "further to provide for the government of the Territory of Louisiana." This bill after its second reading was referred to the Committee of the Whole, in which it was not brought up during that session.

---

(29) Six hundred and thirty-six signatures are attached to five of these petitions, the number of signatures on the other seven petitions was not counted. These petitions were first noticed by us in the *Annals of Congress*. We had always wondered at the silence of Missouri historians on this point, and could hardly be convinced that Missouri became a territory of the second grade without there having been an application for same on the part of the inhabitants of Louisiana Territory. An examination of the *Annals* proved our conclusion to be correct. Mr. Parker's *Calendar of Papers in Washington Archives relating to the Territories of the United States* (Carnegie Institution, 1911) showed that these petitions were still in existence. Finally, after having made futile application to the House Librarian we interested Dr. J. Franklin Jameson who at our request placed Dr. N. D. Mereness on the trail of these documents. Dr. Mereness not only located all of these petitions but also made copies of same. These copies are now in the library of *The State Hist. Soc. of Mo.* The original documents are still preserved in the House Files in Washington, D. C.

(30) On January 15, 1810, an exact copy of the foregoing petition was referred in the House. This latter document had attached to it about two hundred and seventy-three signatures, the former had seventy-six. (31) On February 22, 1810, several petitions to Congress "from a number of the inhabitants of the Territory of Louisiana" were presented to the Senate. Their purpose and wording were, we infer, the same as the other two presented to the House. (32) Another duplicate petition, of this year, bearing only nine signatures was presented to the House, (33) but nothing was accomplished by any of these at this time.

At the third session of the Eleventh Congress, on January 3, 1811, a committee, appointed by the House on De-

---

(30) *Annals of Congress*, I. 1157, 1253. Following is a copy of this petition as found in the House Files by Dr. Mereness:

[Dec. 1809 ?] Petition of sundry inhabitants of the territory of Louisiana—Referred Jan. 9th, 1810. [No. 3458 in Parker.]

[This petition is as follows:] To the hon*ble* the Sen. and Ho. of Reps. of the U. S., in Cong. assembled

The petition of the undersigned inhabitants of the Territory of La., most respectfully sheweth.

That they have waited with anxious but silent expectation for the arrival of that period, when pursuance of the treaty by which Louisiana was ceded to the United States, they are to he admitted "according to the principles of the federal constitution, to the enjoyment of all the rights, advantages and immunities of Citizens of the United States." These rights they do humbly conceive cannot be enjoyed while the judicial and legislative powers are vested in the same persons. Where powers are combined which the constitution requires should be separate, [sic] and where the maker of laws, is also obliged to expound, and to decide upon them.

Your petitioners are fully impressed with the idea that legislative powers are never better, nor more satisfactorily exercised than when committed to those persons who are elected for that purpose by the people themselves, whose conduct must be regulated by those very laws thus made. The inhabitants of the territory of Orleans, have already obtained those rights which your petitioners now ask, and to which they deem themselves also entitled. The last returns of the militia of this territory will be found to exceed those of the Indiana and Mississippi territory, and the number is daily increased by rapid emigrations to this territory. Confiding therefore, in the justice and wisdom of your hon*ble* bodies, they most respectfully ask, that a law may be passed for enabling the inhabitants of this territory to have and enjoy the rights and privileges consequent upon a second grade of ter*l* gov't, and that the same may be established in this territory.

And your petit*rs* as in duty bound will ever pray.
[This petit*n* is printed] [76 signatures]

(31) *Ibid.* Found in House Files.
(32) *Ibid.*, p. 578.
(33) *Ibid.* Found in House Files.

cember 11, 1810, "presented a bill further providing for the government of the Territory of Louisiana". After a second reading the bill was lost in the Committee of the Whole and this Congress expired without passing an act on this matter. (34)

During the summer of 1811 numerous petitions of this kind were framed and signed in Louisiana Territory. Some of these originated in the Arkansas country and others in that part that lies within the present boundaries of Missouri. They were all similar in tone and argument to the 1810 petitions. The desire for a second grade of territorial government was strong, and this wish was strengthened by the still unsettled or unsatisfactorily settled condition of the land claims. The inhabitants of Louisiana Territory not only wanted a voice in their territorial or local government, but were equally desirous of having their wishes voiced in Congress by a regularly elected territorial delegate. (35) Not

---

(34) *Annals of Congress*, 3d Sess., 11th Cong. (1810-11), p. 486.
(35) Sometime during the session of 1811-12 five petitions were presented to the House. Each of the five is as follows according to Dr. N. D. Mereness:

[Referred 1811-12.] Each of the "five petitions" listed by Parker under No. 3468 is in part as follows: To the Honble the sen. & Ho of Reps——Sheweth; That convinced as well of their rights in pursuance of the treaty which ceded La. to the U. S., to be admitted "according to the principles of the federal constitution, to the enjoyment of all the rights, advantages and immunities of the citizens of the United States," as of the advantages resulting from representative government, which rights and advantages have not been extended to them. They hope indeed, that as a free people, so far as the policy of territorial government will admit, they may have a partial voice in the government which they support. Their sister territories of Orleans, Mississippi and Indiana, are fast approaching to political manhood, under the fostering hand of the General Government; while La. with a large and fast increasing population have not been admitted to the enjoyment of the same political blessings; all the powers of the government, as well executive and legislative, as legislative and judicial, are blended together, not only contrary to the treaty and "*Federal Constitution*," but also the political safety and happiness of the people. A large majority of your petitioners depend on agriculture for support, *whose claims to land* form the principal hope of themselves and families, and more than two-thirds of their claims have been rejected by the board of commissrs; from whose official representations they have little to hope, and much prejudice to fear; for these reasons which are all important to your petitioners, they now most respectfully ask of your hon*ble* body the passage of a law, which will admit them into what is denominated the second grade of territorial govt, (provided no better can be devised) which entitle them to a delegate in Congress by whom they can make known their

only were many of these petitions presented to the twelfth Congress at its first session but on December 27, 1811, there was also presented to the House "a certified copy of a presentment by the grand jury of the 'District of St. Charles', in said Territory, representing that the second grade of Territorial government ought to be extended to the Territory; that the judges of the general court ought to reside in the Territory; and that further and equitable provisions ought to be made in favor of rejected land claims". (36) These were

unfortunate situation. And your petitioners as in duty bound will ever pray. [Found in House Files.]

Another petition referred December 27, 1811, is an exact copy of the above (House Files, Parker, *op. cit.*, No. 3480.); another duplicate was read January 6, 1812, (Senate Files, Parker, *op. cit.*, No. 3481.); and another bearing one hundred and ninety signatures was also presented to Congress. (House Files, Parker, *op. cit.*, No. 3487.) The following petition, dated Arkansas, 9th Sept. 1811, was referred Dec. 7, 1811:—

Petition (dated Arkansas, 9th Sept*r* 1811) for the Second grade of Government.—No. 3472 in Parker—Referred Dec. 7, 1811 to Com*ee* of the whole House on the bill for the Govt of said Territory. Bill postponed in the Senate April 22, 1812.

This petit*n* is as follows: To the Hon*ble*——The Petition of the undersigned Inhabitants of the Territory of La. Respectfully sheweth: That convinced as well of their rights (in pursuance of the Treaty which ceded La. to th[e] U. S.) to be admitted according to the Principals [*sic*] of the Federal Constitution to the enjoyment of all the rights, advantages, and immunities of Citizens [o]f the U. S.—as of the advantages resulting from a representative Gov't, which Rights and Advantages have not been extended to them—they hope indeed that as a free People so far as the Policy of Ter*l* Gov't will admit they may have a Partial Voice in the Govt wch [which] they support. Their sister Territories of Orleans, Mississippi and Indiana are fast approaching to Political Manhood, under the Fostering hand of the Gen'l Gov't, while La. with a large and fast increasing Population, has not been admitted to the enjoyment of the same Political blessing.—all the Powers of the Gov't as well Executive and legislative, as Legislative and Judicial are blended together not only Contrary to the Treaty and Federal Constitution but also to the political safety and happiness of the People.

A large majority of your Petitioners depend on Agriculture for support whose claims to lands form the Principal hope of themselves and families and more than two thirds [o]f their just Claims have been rejected by th[e] board of Commissioners from whose official Representations they have little to hope.

For these reasons wch are all important to your Petitioners they now most respectfully ask of your Hon*ble* body, the Passage of a Law wch will admit them into what is denominated the second grade of Ter*l* Govt, wch will entitle them to a delegate in Cong. by whom they may make known their unfortunate situation——and your Petit*rs* as in duty bound will ever Pray. [88 signatures. The original of this petit*n* is not printed. Found in House Files.]

Cf. also Annals of Congress, p. 557.

(36) *Annals of Congress*, I. 584f.

referred and undoubtedly were of the greatest influence in the final passage of the law of June 4, 1812.

Although the local pressure on Congress favoring a higher grade of territorial government in Louisiana Territory was strong, we are hardly surprised to discover some undercurrent of opinion in this district that opposed raising the status of the territory. We have noticed how the act of 1805 was satisfactory to most of the inhabitants of Upper Louisiana especially to the French portion, and also why they preferred a centralized form of government. Wherever the French influence was strong whether in Indiana Territory, Louisiana Territory, or the Territory of Orleans, the preference of that race has been for few officials, concentration of power in the hands of a few, and either an indifference or opposition to self-government unless some vital problem could be solved by no other means. (37) In Louisiana Territory the special problem that concerned many, including both French and American inhabitants, was the land claim or land grant problem. Many claims had not been settled and many had been refused. The settlers, both old and new, thought that more lenient laws regulating these claims would be passed if only the Territory had a delegate in Congress. There was also of course a sincere, strong sentiment for self-government in Louisiana Territory, but we believe that the opposition to this self-government or representative government would have been stronger than it was had not there been pressing for settlement hundreds of land claims. At all events we have record of one remonstrance and petition being presented to Congress that opposed a change in government. On December 7, 1811, there was presented to the House a remonstrance and petition of sundry inhabitants of St. Louis

---

(37) Indiana Territory in 1800 was largely French. They cared nothing for self-government. The influx of American settlers created a desire for a higher grade of territorial government. The French joined in this demand for self-government since through it they could make slavery more secure, which was a great object to be attained owing to the provisions of the Northwest Ordinance on that point. Cf. also Webster, Homer J., *William Henry Harrison's Administration of Indiana Territory*, in *Ind. Hist. Soc. Pub.*, IV. 202ff. Cf. Chapter VI. of this work on the peculiar sentiment exhibited in Orleans Territory on the eve of framing a State Constitution.

"stating the many injuries and inconveniences which would result from a change in their form of government, and praying that no alteration may be made in their said form of government". (38) This was referred to a committee from which it was never reported. The demand of the inhabitants of Louisiana for the higher grade of territorial government had become too insistent for Congress to longer delay.

In the year 1812 affairs reached a focus that made necessary at least some kind of action. The Territory of Orleans was admitted into the Union April 8, 1812, under the name of the State of Louisiana. This made expedient, though not essential, as some authorities have supposed, a change in name of the Territory of Louisiana. Action was taken by Congress, and on June 4, 1812, a law was passed changing the name of the Territory of Louisiana to the Territory of Missouri. (39) It was this law which gave to Missouri her present name; and it is very probable that had the Territory of Orleans taken the name of State of Orleans on its admission into the Union, then the Territory of Louisiana would have retained its name and in 1821 would have been admitted as the State of Louisiana. This act of June 4, 1812, raised Missouri to the second grade of territories and not only gave the inhabitants control of the lower house of the legislature through the elective tenure and the election of a delegate to Congress, but also provided in section fourteen for a bill of rights. (40)

The government provided for by this act was far more complex in character than that in the act of 1805. The executive authority was still vested in a Governor whose term, tenure, and powers were the same as before, except that he had some enumerated powers, including that of convening the legislature on "extraordinary occasions". His veto

(38) *Abridg. of Debates of Cong.*, IV. 434.
(39) *Stat. at Large*, II. 743-747; *Cf.* also *Mo. Ter. Laws*, I. 8-13.
(40) There are sixteen sections in this law, but they will not be taken up here in detail, as their importance and influence on Missouri's First Constitution were so great that they will be minutely considered in the chapter dealing with the sources of that instrument.

power was absolute. No change was made in the term, tenure, and duties of the Secretary.

It was in the legislative branch of the new government that the greatest changes are noticed. The legislative power was vested in a bicameral body called the "general assembly". This was composed of a Legislative Council and a House of Representatives. The former consisted of nine members, five making a quorum, appointed for five years by the President of the United States from a list of eighteen persons made by the territorial House of Representatives. Provision was made for filling vacancies by the President appointing one of two persons nominated by the lower house. Their qualifications were: that they should have resided in the territory for at least one year preceding appointment; that they should be at least twenty-five years of age; that they should have property of at least two hundred acres in the territory. They were disqualified from holding any other office of profit under the territorial government except that of justice of the peace. It was in the House of Representatives that the greatest innovation was made. This body was composed of representatives elected for two years by the people of the territory. The apportionment was on the basis of one member to every five hundred free, white, male inhabitants until the number of representatives reached twenty-five, when the ratio was left under the regulation of the general assembly. The qualifications for representatives were lower in nearly every respect than for members of the Council: the age qualification was twenty-one years; the residence qualification was the same as in the case of members of the Council; and the property qualification required one to be a freeholder in the county from which he was elected. Vacancies were filled by a new county election on writ of the Governor. Annual meetings of the General Assembly were provided for. The place of meeting was at St. Louis, and the time the first Monday in December unless the General Assembly set a different date. The Governor was empowered to lay off the territory into convenient counties for the election of thirteen representatives.

The electors of representatives consisted of all the free, white, male citizens of the United States who were twenty-one years of age, had resided in the territory twelve months before the election, and had paid a territorial or county tax assessment made at least six months before the election. It might be noticed in this connection that the tax qualification for electors was purposely omitted from Missouri's first Constitution, and, so far as the later political careers of the delegates that framed that document are concerned, it was a very wise omission. It was provided in the act of 1812 that all free, white, male persons who were inhabitants of Louisiana on December 20, 1803, and all free, white, male citizens of the United States who had immigrated to Louisiana since December 20, 1803, or who might hereafter do so, if otherwise qualified, could hold any office of honor, trust or profit in the territory under the United States or the territory, and vote for members of the General Assembly and a Delegate to Congress during the temporary government provided for by that act.

The powers of the General Assembly were large, comprising the power to make laws, civil and criminal; to establish inferior courts and prescribe their jurisdiction; to define the powers and duties of the justices of the peace and other civil officers of the territory; to regulate and fix fees, etc. There were certain express limitations placed on their power, however, that are important to notice. All bills had to be passed by a majority of each house and receive the approbation (signature) of the governor. They were by implication prohibited from passing any acts which would be inconsistent with the large number of privileges and rights reserved to the people and enumerated at some length in section fourteen of the law. This section fourteen is a very interesting paragraph, as it is the first bill of rights that Missourians ever had, excepting those guaranteed in the United States Constitution, and is an epitome of the one included in the constitution of 1820. The General Assembly was also prohibited by express provision from interfering with the primary disposal of the soil of the United States, etc., and from levying any tax or impost on the navigable waters in or touching the territory. This provision is also found in the constitution of 1820.

The judiciary was composed of a superior court, inferior courts and courts of justice of the peace. The superior court alone was set forth in detail, the others being left under the regulation of the General Assembly and Governor. This court was the same in composition and in term and tenure of members as that provided for in the act of 1805. Certain regulations were provided as regards its jurisdiction, and power was granted it and the inferior courts to appoint their clerks.

Some miscellaneous provisions were also set forth that are important. All officials were required to take an oath to support the Constitution of the United States and discharge faithfully the duties of their office. The citizens of the territory were given the right to elect one delegate to Congress. Schools and education were urged, and encouragement and aid promised from the United States lands in the territory. It was provided that the acts of 1804 and 1805 when inconsistent with this act were repealed.

Pursuant to the power granted him in the seventh section of the act of 1812, Benjamin Howard, Governor of the Territory of Louisiana, by proclamation issued October 1, 1812, divided the new Territory of Missouri into the five counties of St. Charles, St. Louis, Ste. Genevieve, Cape Girardeau, and New Madrid, and gave them their boundaries. (41) Provision was made for the election from these counties of territorial representatives to the General Assembly and also a Delegate to Congress. Appended to this proclamation was a statement setting forth the qualifications of representatives and electors—which was taken from the act of Congress of June 4, 1812. Thus was set in working the new government of the Territory of Missouri.

An attempt was made to amend the law of 1812, and on January 7, 1813, on motion of Mr. Hempstead (of Missouri)

---

(41) *Am. State Papers, Misc.*, II. 202f; Scharf, *op. cit.*, I. 557f.

a committee was appointed by the House of Representatives "to inquire if any, and if any what, amendments are necessary to be made" to that act. (42) On January 29, 1813, this committee reported and recommended no alterations. (43) The problem suggested to the committee was to settle the doubts that some entertained as to whether Missouri's Territorial Delegate to Congress, who had been elected on November 2, 1812, in pursuance of the act of Congress of that year, could hold his seat after March 3, 1813. The committee decided that as he was elected for two years, he could hold his seat for that time, and that no alteration in the law of 1812 was necessary, as it appeared perfectly clear on this point.

Population kept increasing rapidly in Missouri. Lawence county was established by the Territorial Legislature January 15, 1815, (44) and just a little over a year later Howard county, the "mother of counties" and one of the empire counties of Missouri, was erected by act of January 23, 1816. (45) On January 21, 1816, on motion of Mr. Easton in the House of Representatives, the Committee on the Judiciary was instructed to inquire if any, and what, alterations were necessary to be made in the act entitled "An act providing for the government of the Territory of Missouri" approved June 4, 1812". (46) This committee on March 6, 1816, reported a bill to alter certain parts of the act of 1812, which without any amendment finally became the organic act of Congress of April 29, 1816, by which Missouri became a territory of the highest grade. (47) By this law, the elective tenure was also applied to the Legislative Council, one member being elected from each county. The term was reduced to two years and qualifications remained the same as in the act of 1812. A majority of the members constituted a quorum. The regular sessions of the General As-

---

(42) *Annals of Congress*, p. 618.
(43) *Ibid.*, pp. 929f; *Am. State Papers, Misc.*, II. 201f.
(44) *Mo. Ter. Laws*, pp. 354ff.
(45) *Ibid.*, pp. 460ff.
(46) *Annals of Congress*, pp. 1047, 1049, 1358, 1362.
(47) *Stat. at Large*, II. 328; *Mo. Ter. Laws*, p. 14.

sembly were changed from annual to biennial sessions. Everything else of the act of 1812 remained unchanged except the provisions relating to the judiciary. It was the provisions in this act of 1816 relating to the judiciary that was its most objectionable feature to Missourians, as is expressly set forth in the very earliest petitions for statehood in 1817. (48) The General Assembly was authorized to require the judges of the superior court to hold superior and circuit courts; to appoint the times and places for the same; and to make rules and regulations regarding these courts. The circuit court was to be composed of one of the said judges and to have jurisdiction in all criminal cases, exclusive original jurisdiction in capital cases, and original jurisdiction in all civil cases of $100.00 value or over. The superior and circuit courts were to possess chancery powers as well as common law jurisdiction in all civil cases, provided that in matters of law and equity, in all cases, appeal lay from the circuit courts to the superior court of the territory.

The year following this law of Congress of 1816, which made Missouri a territory of the highest rank, saw the inhabitants here petitioning Congress for that greatest of all boons —the privilege of statehood. It will be our purpose in the next chapter to give, in the first place, a short history of these efforts on the part of Missouri's pioneers to obtain permission of the National Legislature to frame a state constitution; and, in the second, to sketch the struggle in Congress itself over this mighty question from 1818 to 1820. It is hardly an exaggeration to say that never in the history of this nation since the adoption of the Constitution has there ever been a purely domestic question, except of course the Civil War of 1861-65, that has so stirred the country from border to border; has been so ominous in so many of its phases; that for so many months literally shook the foundations of the United States and brought forth declarations and prophecies of the most calamitous character from the mouths and pens

---

(48) This will receive further consideration in tho chapter following.

of men who even today rank foremost in the galaxy of American Statesmen and authors, as the famous Missouri Question.

FLOYD C. SHOEMAKER,
Assistant Librarian of The State Historical
Society of Missouri.

Editor's Note: This article forms the first chapter of Mr. Shoemaker's forthcoming publication on "Missouri's Struggle for Admission", and we consider it a very valuable contribution to our knowledge of Middle West history. Mr. Shoemaker has not only made some remarkable researches in bringing to light so many hitherto unknown petitions, documents and letters, but has taken great pains to interpret these in a scholarly and interesting manner. He has by these means cleared up several formerly unsolved problems in the early history of Upper Louisiana and Missouri Territory. The Review has been promised sketches of some of the other chapters of this work and these will appear sometime in the future. The completed chapters will form the most important publication on the constitutional history of Missouri.

TRAVEL INTO MISSOURI IN OCTOBER, 1838.

BY EDUARD ZIMMERMANN.

From among a number of old letters and diaries of some of the German settlers in Missouri the following account of a foot-tour extending about eighty miles into the state is described. The writer was a German, Eduard Zimmermann, who had recently come from Europe. The angle at which he views American conditions is not wholly without interest. This being the time when the great influx of Germans began in Missouri, this man's account doubtless was read with the keenest interest by his friends at home. The translation reads as follows:

"On the twelfth of October, I left my stopping place, which is a few miles east of the Mississippi river in the state of Illinois, in order to go to St. Louis. In company with a friend who had but recently come from Germany, I intend to spend a few weeks in wandering through at least a part of the new promised land of the state of Missouri. We reached the Father of Waters at sunset, just in time to take a steamboat to the Missouri side. From sunrise to sunset the ferry boats do not run because of various dangers.

Previously I had seen St. Louis only during the hottest time of the year. How striking then was the difference between that season and this! Now activity and joyousness was seen on every hand. During my other visit all the shops were closed and empty, the streets forsaken and the places of amusement dead. Cholera and bilious fever raged as for a wager, and the hearse alone was constantly on the go. Sickness, death, burial, these were the themes of all conversation. Precautions and medical directions the sole objects of reflection and thought. How entirely different it was now. The streets were lively, the coffee houses and other places of entertainment were filled with people, the most care-free enjoyment of life had taken the place of deathly anxiety and precaution.

St. Louis is after all a second New Orleans, in spite of Duden's statement to the contrary. This is the place where the inestimable quantities of produce from the entire Missouri Valley and of the upper Mississippi Valley accumulate in order to find a good and speedy market on the Gulf of Mexico. Here is also the gathering place of men and merchandise coming from the Ohio River and the eastern states. The extra distance from the mouth of the Ohio is wholly disregarded because here the shippers and the travelers are certain of finding opportunities of rapid transportation to the mouth of the Mississippi, regardless of the stand of the water. Trade and commerce flourish more and more and will be brought to a still higher degree of efficiency when the proposed waterways through the state of Illinois are completed. Settlers from all the states of North America come here, and the still greater mass of European immigrants arrive here from New Orleans, from the seaports of the Atlantic, from New York, Philadelphia and Baltimore, to pour themselves into the fertile plains of Illinois, into the much-praised Missouri, into the recently opened state of Arkansas, even into southern Texas, where not only the beauties of nature but the exceptionally alluring material inducements attract the agriculturists.

St. Louis numbers at present scarcely more than ten thousand inhabitants, and yet it surpasses in the varied mixture of its population, in the great number of strangers within its midst and in its geographic significance and interest every city of its size in the old and the new world. Beside the many descendants of genuine Indian blood, a large part of the population consists of Frenchmen, Germans and Spaniards. The descendants of the Britons, of course, constitute the majority. Several thousand negro slaves and free colored people live here, and if on Sunday the devout are at their churches, and the care-free inhabitants have been lured to the country, then one might easily imagine himself to be walking on the streets of some city in San Domingo. Only black faces are then seen on the streets, only gaudily dressed groups of colored children play before the houses. In the larger hotels and the 'entertainments' the haggard American gentlemen sit around the hearth in a semicircle, showing an almost Indian-like apathy, their legs crossed, rocking themselves and chewing tobacco, (a custom which in the interior of America is by no means regarded as improper). The Frenchman with lighted cigar hops around the billiard table in the coffee-house and wastes more breath in a minute than an American does in an entire day. The easy-going German, too, finds his place of entertainment, where the beverages are tolerable and the stay homelike and pleasant, and there amid the smoke of the pipes and the clinking of glasses a German song and the sound of musical instruments are heard.

Since the distribution of Duden's book St. Louis has become the main goal and gathering place, especially of the German immigrants. Those who live here or in the neighborhood are well informed regarding the affairs in Germany, and often times know more than their friends at home, because the newspapers are not subjected to censorship.

St. Louis has grown rapidly during recent years. This growth is hastened by the discovery of near-by lead mines, by the rapidly growing population in the interior of Missouri, and especially by the rapidly increasing Illinois town on the opposite bank of the river.

One of the main branches of trade in the city is the fur trade which is carried on by a company of specially privileged private citizens who have one of their main depots here. These special privileges consist, as far as I have been able to ascertain, in this, that other private individuals are not permitted to trade with the Indians for certain definite articles, especially firearms and tomahawks. These articles may be sold only by the company. The sale of intoxicating liquors is forbidden by the United States even to the fur companies, in order to prevent certain avaricious white persons from deriving exorbitant profits from this sort of trade. The enormous basin of the Missouri river which is visited annually by hired hunters who work for the fur companies (among whom there are many Germans but still more French adventurers,) furnishes thousands of buffalo hides and also quantities of the still more valuable beaver pelts. Nothing is more fascinating than the stories of such hunters. The hunting expeditions usually depart from here in April or May. The usual time of service is eighteen months, of which more than half is required for the journey to and from the Rocky Mountains. Eighteen dollars and provisions, which in the far west consists almost solely of buffalo meat, constitutes their monthly wages. But then the hunters must agree to perform all sorts of service. Usually the hunters go by steam-boat as far as Liberty in Clay County, the most western town in Missouri. From there they go either on horseback or in small boats which usually have to be pulled by the men themselves, further into the interior. Council Bluffs, the outmost fortification of the United States, is about five hundred miles above St. Louis. This is said to be the farthest point to which settlements and civilization have thus far penetrated. The so-called forts further up the river on the important tributaries, the LaPlatte and the Yellowstone, have been established by the fur companies themselves, but they are in reality only pallisades not real forts, and must be regarded as simply the offices of the company. Several hundred miles west of the state of Missouri the large herds of buffalo begin. From there on these animals appear in such large herds that their actual number can no longer be accurately determined, but the space of ground which they occupy is taken as the measure of their number. At first I did not believe the stories of the hunters, but books of travel by trustworthy men assure me that the buffalo in those regions are actually counted by the mile. 'I saw five, ten, or fifteen miles of buffalo,' that is the current expression in regard to their number. The buffalo is shot with a rifle. The Indians who have a cunning way of enticing the animals into an enclosed place kill them with the bow and arrow. The buffalo is by no means dangerous and always seeks safety in flight. The beaver is caught with traps in his holes. The manner of trapping them has been learned from the Indians. Concerning the Indians I have heard various contradictory reports. Some depict them as peaceable and even honest, while others cannot tell enough of their wicked intentions and their cunning. The various tribes differ in this regard. The relations of the Indians to the fur-trading companies must necessarily often times be strained because of the passion and the lack of self control on the part of these children of nature on the one hand and the avarice and selfishness of the whites on the other. All accounts agree that the Indians live in constant bloody feuds with one another. The Sioux, the Osages, the Delawares, the Mandans and the Blackfeet are the tribes with which the hunters have most to do on this side of the Rocky Mountains. The Blackfeet are said to be the most hostile and dangerous. In dress and manner of living the western tribes differ vastly from those which are still found in the states of the Union, though there appears to be no essential difference in their customs and their character.

We should have left St. Louis on the day following our arrival there, if we had not found many highly educated and most agreeable German immigrants who had just arrived and in whose company we felt comfortable and at home. Besides this, another cause for my stay was the horseraces which were scheduled to take place at this time, the like of which I had not seen either here or in Europe. The races took place about three miles from the city at the so-called Prairie House, a favorite place of amusement of the St. Louisans. The races were attended by large crowds. I believe indeed that these Americans are happy at such occasions, but we foreigners were not able to detect many evidences of it, for their joy and delight manifests itself in ways so much different from ours. External pomp and finery which make such a pleasing effect at our public gatherings are entirely wanting here. Varying costumes, music, songs and dancing, all that makes an European public gathering so cheerful and lively, one looks for in vain in America. The eye of the foreigner, at least, is able to distinguish only one class of people here. From the Governor to the jockey they all belong to the large class of gentlemen; at least, I was not able to discern any difference between them. But this sort of monotony does not entertain. In this regard it is different among us. At home it is seen what each one is or what he professes to be. Every characteristic is sharply defined. There is the student, the soldier, the clergyman from the country, the merchant, the baron—crowded in a little space one believes to see the whole world before him. Of course we owe this entertaining mixture chiefly to our differences in rank and station, to our prejudices and to our arrangement of state. But who thinks of all this in the moments of joyful intoxication, who concerns himself with sad reflections during these fleeting moments of joy! It is enough that one is entertained and charmed; the question as to what produces this delight does not concern us in the moments of bliss. One thing that gives an amusing touch to the gatherings of the Americans, whether these gatherings be secular or religious in character, is the fact that everybody arrives on horseback. Women and children everybody is on horseback. In the country frequently two, sometimes even three persons, are seen riding one horse. Such a gathering has much in common with a camp of Cossacks, and the lover of horses certainly finds plenty material for entertainment. The Americans, like the English, are much given to betting, and at the horse races hardly anybody is a mere spectator. In the state of Missouri there are apparently no strict laws against gambling, especially against games of hazard, as in most of the other states, or these laws are waived on special occasions, for one roulette wheel stood beside another at these races. The number of persons who took part in the gambling is incomprehensible. Without dismounting from their horses many made a wager with the nearest by-stander and without apparently enjoying the exhilaration of the suspense rode on again when the result was made known.

On the morning of the fifteenth of October we started on our excursion into the valley of the Missouri. We took a westerly direction, slightly toward the north. We had made up our minds to follow the highway toward Jefferson City, the seat of government of the state of Missouri, and to deflect from this road only for the purpose of seeking out the settlements of the educated Germans. Close to St. Louis the country is not especially attractive, but further on it becomes more so. Two German writers, one of whom is Friedrich Schmidt, have written contradictory reports as to the region immediately around St. Louis. The one asserts that it is prairie land while the other claims that it is woodland. Both are right. It is manifest that once everything was prairie. Everybody in the west knows how quickly a prairie is transformed into forest land if it is no longer set on fire in the autumns. Illinois, which is chiefly a prairie state, is constantly in the process of changing into the most attractive forest land. If Mr. Schmidt was here twenty-five years ago, he doubtless saw but little forest land. Even now there are still miles of prairie. The weather was delightful for our journey. The sky and the air reminded us of spring. The prairies are said to be enchantingly beautiful in spring. Even now they are still marvelous. Here and there the young hickory trees glowed in the most livid gold, numerous varieties of sumach glowed in fiery red and caused the wide prairie to appear like a huge carpet wrought in purple. Countless clusters of flowers of bright colors modified by the thousandfold autumnal shading of their leaves adorned the plains. After a few hours of rest with a cultured German family which lives about ten miles from St. Louis, we went about an equal distance further and spent the night with an American, who a few years ago immigrated from Virginia. Inns are found only in the cities and towns, or possibly along the mail-routes. The traveler is therefore obliged to make use of the hospitality of the settlers. This sort of hospitality is perhaps nowhere developed to a higher degree than in this new country where it would indeed be unnatural and inhuman if a stranger were not hospitably and cordially received. For our purpose of becoming acquainted with the land and its people we had chosen the right mode of traveling, for it compelled us to stop several times each day in the huts of the inhabitants. Necessarily we had to enter into conversation, and no theme was nearer at hand for discussion than the nature of the country, the advantages and disadvantages of the settlement, the kind of produce raised, and the means of disposing of it.

By constantly losing our road we went much farther than we ought to have gone, but occasionally we struck upon a shorter way without knowing it. Below the river Au Vasse, which we had to cross in a canoe, the country is for the most part prairie land, except that part which is nearest the river. The cold became painful, and the icy wind which blew across this vast plain, where no elevation offered it resistance, seemed to us to come from the Rocky Mountains, many thousand miles to the northwest. We found no German settlements in this region, but were told that shortly before this time a deputy had bought land for some Germans in Bran (?) County, [perhaps Boone County], above Jefferson City. Before we reached the little town of Pinkney our way led us through Louther Island in Montgomery County. This island has been formed by a creek, which, having divided into two parts, flows in two channels into the Missouri. The island is exceptionally fertile. There are large and beautifully equipped settlements here which have much in common with the plantations of the southern states. Many of the houses of the homesteads are used exclusively as the dwellings of the black slaves. Here the farmers raise tobacco and cotton. Tobacco is said to do exceptionally well in Missouri and to be preferred to all other tobaccos on the market in New Orleans. The practice of cultivating this crop, however, might easily bring the condition of the slaves near to that condition which their unfortunate fellows suffer in the southern states. Up to this time the treatment of the slaves, who are in the country districts, is very good. Their material condition is very endurable. As a rule they live in families, have their own dwelling houses, their own live stock and till a certain amount of land for themselves, in which way they have their own earnings. This tolerable condition of the Missouri slaves by no means excuses the shameful practice of slavery, however, and against this sin committed against humanity one must strive with all energy. The Germans who live in Missouri have no slaves as yet, and are still opposed to the institution of slavery. However, it is possible that in time this feeling may become dulled, and their posterity may grow up with the idea that it is a necessary institution. No German ought to live in a slave state. Illinois, a free state, has a great advantage over its neighboring states. The breech between the free states and the slave states is inevitable, and who should then like to be found on the wrong side? Near Louther Island we met with a slight adventure. In the darkness of the night we had lost our way, and finally came to a broad creek. The icy coldness of the water rather than its depth repelled us from wading it. Finally our calling and shooting was answered by the barking of dogs in the distance. We went in the direction from which the barking came and were so fortunate as to find a sort of a bridge which had been made of felled logs, which brought us to a very new little settlement. The cold became more intense day by day, so that our hands became very cold on the rifle barrels. With every degree that the mercury fell our faith in Duden's pleasant winters in these western states vanished more and more. [A footnote states that the winters of the previous years were very severe.] To be sure there are many days which make us feel that we are ten and more degrees further south than we were in our old home, but there is no such thing in Missouri as a winter which approaches the rainy season of the tropics. There will be no change in the climate of the state until clearings and tilling of the soil have done their work.

Pinkney, a little town of a few houses, is prettily located. Here many Germans have settled and some of them have chosen very romantic locations. The Americans reproach the Germans for selecting the very poorest land at times, and this is on the whole true. The Germans prefer high lying regions because they are more healthful, open and attractive. This the Americans do not comprehend. They call only that land pretty which is rich in fertility. They never become attached to a given region. If they can sell their property to any sort of advantage, they are certain to do so, regardless of the fact that it may be the scene of their happy childhood with its dearest memories. This characteristic of the Americans is not beautiful, but for the rapid settling of a new state it is very advantageous. It is also beneficial to the political condition of the Republic that the American is less susceptible to moral and ethical impressions. The more self-satisfied a people is the more easily it is governed, provided the right cords are touched. The so-called man of feeling is the toy of every ambitious person.

Ten miles below Pinkney is the new town of Marthasville in the newly created County of Warren which was formerly a part of Montgomery County. Here the German settlements are numerous. The settlers seem to think that their fortune is made if they are close to Duden's old home. All the Germans whom we met in Missouri belong to the educated classes, and in spite of the short time they have lived here many of them are already handsomely arranged in their homes. Most of them have forgotten the disappointment which at first gave them so many sad hours, and they fare better here than they did in their oppressed home country. Duden's place itself is not as poorly situated as some people say. But the wanderer seeks in vain for something that might with due apology be called a dwelling house. Neither are there any arbors and beautiful vistas to be observed. However, it must be remembered that the settlement has been lying idle for several years and on this account it makes an unattractive and unpleasant impression.

A beautiful road led us from Lake Creek to Missouritown, a very small, dead village, which, however, boasts of a very beautiful situation on the river. There are many German settlements along Lake Creek.—Limestone constitutes the greater part of all bluffs along the Missouri. Sandstone occurs more rarely. Granite is not found at all between the Alleghany and the Rocky Mountains. Our plan to return by way of St. Charles was frustrated when we again lost our road. It would have taken us too long to have found the right road again, so we returned to the right side of the Missouri at Lewis' Ferry. For a while we followed the river valley, crossing Bon Homme creek and Creve Cœur creek and on the twenty-second of November we again reached St. Louis, our starting place, after three weeks of wandering."

Translated by William Godfrey Bek,
  University of North Dakota.

INDIAN MODE OF LIFE IN MISSOURI AND KANSAS.

Fort Osage was located near present site of the town of Sibley, Mo. This post was established for military purposes as well as a permanent trading post and Sibley was in charge of it. Previous to this time trappers did not care to have the geography of their rich hunting grounds known and they were more interested in keeping this vast territory the "unknown". Perhaps they fostered the belief that a journey into it was full of peril. It is true that explorers in this new country had to endure enormous toil, perpetual care to avoid marauding bands of Indians, swollen streams to be crossed, no roads and few trails. After the reports of Lewis and Clark's expedition and Zebulon Pike's return, attention was called to a country of possibilities known to only a few venturesome traders and voyageurs. Soon posts began to spring into existence, and every stream of any consequence had its local trader. To bring trade into legitimate and safe lines the government established Fort Osage. The trade at this fort was drawn from the tribes along the Missouri and Kansas Rivers, and from the Osage tribes to the south and southwest. Sibley had spent several years among these people and understood them thoroughly.

Today this country is settled by an industrious and energetic people, full of resources, living their lives in plenty without much thought of the struggles of the aborigine or even of their forbears that took the place from this original people. We may glimpse back a hundred years and see the vast changes that have occurred in this comparatively short period of time. I believe the letter which here follows presents the best view of the mode of life of the aborigines inhabiting this country that I have ever seen. It is taken from Moore's Report on Indian Affairs, page 203, Appendix.

DAVID W. EATON,
Versailles, Mo.

Letter from Geo. C. Sibley, Esq., Factor at Fort Osage, to Thomas L. McKenney, Esq., in which he gives a good description of the mode of life of the Indians then living in Missouri and Kansas.

"Fort Osage, 1st., Oct., 1820.

Sir: Your letter of the 9th. Aug. was received three days ago, I hasten to reply to the queries therein contained.

The tribes of Indians, who usually hold intercourse with this trading house, are

1st. The Kansas, residing about three hundred miles up the Kansas river, in one village. They hunt all through the exterior country watered by the Kansas River, and on the Missouri, south side, above this place to the Nodaway. I rate this tribe at somewhere about eight hundred souls, of whom about two hundred and thirty are warriors and hunters, thirty or forty superannuated old men, and the rest women and children.

2nd., The Great Osages, of the Osage River.

They live in one village on the Osage River, seventy-eight miles (measured) due south from Fort Osage. They hunt over a very great extent of country, comprising the Osage, Gasconade and Neeozho rivers and their numerous branches. They also hunt on the heads of the St. Francis and White Rivers, and on the Arkansaw. I rate them at about one thousand two hundred souls, three hundred and fifty of whom are warriors and hunters, fifty or sixty superannuated and the rest women and children.

3d., The Great Osages of Neeozho, on about one hundred and thirty or forty miles southwest of Fort Osage; one village on the Neeozho River. They hunt pretty much in common with the tribe of the Osage river, from which they separated six or eight years ago. This village contains about four hundred souls, of whom about one hundred are warriors and hunters, some ten or fifteen aged persons, and the rest women and children.

4th. The Little Osages.

Their villages on the Neeozho River, from one hundred and twenty to one hundred and forty miles south of this place. This tribe, comprising all three villages, and comprehending about twenty families of Missouris that are intermarried with them, I rate at about one thousand souls, about three hundred of them are hunters and warriors, twenty or thirty superannuated, and the rest are women and children. They hunt pretty much in common with the other tribes of Osages mentioned, and frequently on the head waters of the Kansas, some of the branches of which interlock with those of the Neeozho.

5th. The Ioways, only visit this place occasionally. This tribe is about as numerous as the Kansas. They are latterly much divided, so that I am unable to state precisely how many villages they occupy, or where they are located. About half the tribe, I understand, joined the Ottoes, near the Council Bluffs, last year, with the intention of remaining there. I am not sure whether they still remain there or not. The other part of the tribe remains in two villages, I believe, on the Des Moines and Grand Rivers. The Ioways hunt principally between the Missouri, north of it, and Mississippi rivers, from the heads of the two Charatons, up to the Nodaway, and sometimes still farther up.

6th. Of the Chaneers, or Arkansaw tribe of Osages, I need say nothing, because they do not resort here to trade. I have always rated that tribe at about an equal half of all Osages. They hunt chiefly in the Arkansaw and White Rivers and their waters.

It must be understood, that the above is merely an estimate of numbers founded on the general knowledge I have of the several tribes mentioned, and without any pretension to accuracy, though I do not believe I am far from the truth;

if any thing I am over the mark. As relates to the Osages; it is next to impossible to enumerate them correctly. I have made several attempts in vain. They are continually removing from one village to another quarrelling or intermarrying, so that the strength of no particular village can even be correctly ascertained. I do not believe that any of the tribes, named above, increased in numbers, take them in the aggregate, and I think they are rather diminishing. They are always at war and not a year passes when they do not lose some in that way. Epidemic diseases attack them now and then, and sweep them off by families.

I proceed to answer your 4th. query. The main dependence of each and every of the tribes I have mentioned, for clothing and subsistence, is hunting. They would all class alike in respect of their pursuits; therefore, one general remark will suffice for all.

They raise annually small crops of corn, beans, and pumpkins, these they cultivate entirely with the hoe, in the simplest manner. Their crops are usually planted in April, and receive one dressing before they leave their villages for the summer hunt, in May. About the first week in Aug. they return to their village to gather their crops, which have been left unhoed and unfenced all the season. Each family, if lucky, can save ten to twenty bags of corn and beans, of a bushel and a half each; besides a quantity of dried pumpkins. On this they feast, with the dried meat saved in the summer, till September, when what remains is cached, and they set out on the fall hunt, from which they return about Christmas. From that time, till some time in February or March, as the season happens to be mild or severe, they stay pretty much in their villages, making only short hunt excursions occasionally, and during that time they consume the greater part of their caches. In February or March, the spring hunt commences; first the bear, and then the beaver hunt. This they pursue till springtime, when they again return to their village, pitch their crops, and in May set out for the summer hunt, taking with them their residue, if any, of their corn, Etc. This is the circle of an Osage life, here and there indented with war and trading expeditions; and thus it has been, with very little variation, these twelve years past. The game is very sensibly diminishing in the country, which these tribes inhabit; but it has not yet become scarce. Its gradual diminution seems to have had no other effect on the Indians than to make them more expert and industrious hunters, and better warriors. They also acquire more skill in traffic, become more and more prone to practice fraud and deception in their commerce; are more and more dependent upon the traders, and consequently more and more debased and degraded.

I ought to have stated that these people derive a portion of their subsistence regularly from the wild fruits their country abounds with. Walnuts, hazelnuts, pecans, acorns, grapes, plums, papaws, persimmons, hog potatoes and several other very nutritious roots; all of these they gather and preserve with care, and possess the art of preparing many of them, so that they are really good eating. I have feasted daintily on the preparation of acorns (from the small white oak,) and Buffalo grease. I had the advantage, however, of a good appetite, well whetted by nearly two days abstinence from food. The acorns and fat agree with me, however, and convinced me that a man may very well subsist upon it, if he can get nothing better. This dish is considered as last resort, next to a corn alone. From these facts you will not be surprised to learn, that the arts of civilization have made but little progress, as yet among the Indians of this quarter, knowing as you do, the natural propensity of the Indians to live without toil, upon the bounties of wild nature, rather than to submit to what he considers the degradation of labor, in order to procure subsistence. So long as the facilities, I have enumerated, exist, so long will exist the propensity to rely chiefly on them. This is nature. Art assumes the reins when nature gives them up, and we cling to nature as long as we can. So long as her exhuberant bosom affords us sustenance, there we tenderly repose, free and untrammelled. On the failure of that resource we are obliged to resort to art for support. The whole history of man shows that art never gets the ascendancy of nature, without a desperate struggle, in which the object of contention is most piteously mangled, and often destroyed, and a compromise is always obliged to be effected; which compromise, if I understand the subject, is the very thing we call civilization, in reference to the Indian nations; an object we are all aiming at, and what I feel as anxious as any one to effect.

I have often noticed Indians observing, with much apparent interest the effects of our agricultural skill, our fine gardens, and crops, and our numerous comforts and conveniences. A very sensible Osage, The Big Soldier, who had twice been at Washington, once said to me, when I was urging the subject of civilization to him, "I see and admire your manner of living, your good warm houses, your extensive fields of corn, your gardens, your cows, oxen, workhorses, wagons, and a thousand machines, that I know not the use of. I see that you are able to clothe yourself, even from weeds and grass. In short you can do almost what you choose. You whites possess the power of subduing almost every animal to your use. You are surrounded by slaves. Everything about you is in chains, and you are slaves yourselves. I hear I should exchange my presents for yours, I too should become a slave. Talk to my sons, perhaps they may be persuaded to adopt your fashions, or at least to recommend them to their sons; but for myself, I was born free, was raised free, and wish to die free." It was in vain to combat this good mans opinions with argument. "I am perfectly content", he added, "with my condition. The forests and rivers supply all the calls of nature in plenty, and there is no lack of white people to purchase the surplus products of our industry". This is the language that is held by the Indians in this quarter generally. Like all people in state of ignorance, they are bigoted, and obstinately adhere to their old customs and habits. Tis in vain to attempt to bend the aged oak to our purposes. The tender sapling, however, can be made to yield to our effort, and bend to our will. The missionary establishment now forming near Osage, I have no doubt will tend very much to promote the civilization of these tribes, so far at least as regards the rising generation. Few, if any, of these now above the age of fifteen, will ever wholly abandon their present savage pursuits.

It is a singular fact, however, that although the Indians who have attained the age of twenty five years and upwards, generally refuse instruction, yet they seem by no means averse to have their children taught our arts.

I will conclude this communication with the following proposition, which you may make use of as you think proper. It is for the government, by compact with the Indians, to cause to be surveyed certain districts of the Indian lands suitable for the purpose, in the same manner that the United States lands are surveyed, only that I would recommend that the lines should be more distinctly marked. Whenever an Indian evinced a serious disposition to settle himself permanently, and to pursue civilized habits, a portion of this land, from 160 to 640 acres, as might be proper, should be allotted to him and family forever. He should not have the right to sell, or alienate it in any manner, except by the express permission of the President of the United States, nor should it be held for debts. I believe that by locating each Indian family, disposed to adopt our mode of living, on a tract of land, of their own distinctly marked out, and permanently secured to them, government would greatly promote the scheme of civilization. You would thus give then, at once, a distinct and permanent property, and interest in the soil, instead of a vague, transient, undivided property in a vast extent of country, from which the art of a few of his leaders may expel him forever at any time. Each individual may thus be secured in his own right. He may have a house where he and his family may live securely on the fruits of their own industry. Each may sit down in despair, they have no longer a home or a country. Yet have we pursued them, and importuned them to become farmers, after their spirits are broken and after they have unwillingly deprived themselves of the power of possessing what a farmer values most, an independent home.

I forbear any further remarks on this subject for the present. A little reflection, will, I am sure, satisfy you that it is worthy of consideration.

(signed) GEO. SIBLEY.

THE ORIGIN OF "O. K."

(From the Evening Post.)

Jeffersonville, Ind.—People constantly write the letters O. K. on bills or other statements to signify that they are all right. How did this practice originate?

Answer—The practice got its start in the days of Gen. Jackson, known to the men of his time as Old Hickory.

It is said that Gen. Jackson was not as proficient in spelling as he was in some other things, and so in the abbreviating which he practiced he made O. K. stand for all correct—"oll korrect."

This is as near as our data at present enables us to come to the origin of the now wide practice.

Editor Evening Post:

I note what you say about the origin of the practice of using the letters "O. K." to signify "Correct" or "All right." It seems to me that your informant is wrong. I am quite sure that this practice originated during the Clay and Polk campaign. At that time the writer was a boy, living in Boonville, Mo. You all know what a lively campaign the Clay and Polk campaign was. Mr. Clay was the idol of the Whigs, and was affectionately called "Old Kentucky." Those who favored his election put up their flags on ash poles, at all the crossroads, country taverns and wood yards on the river, while the Democrats put up hickory poles with poke bushes at the top, the Whigs using for a flag a square of whole cloth with the letters "O. K." signifying "Old Kentucky." The Democrats used a streamer with "Polk and Dallas, Oregon and Texas."

The town of Boonville boasted two newspapers, one the Observer, a Whig paper, conducted by one Caldwell, a very brilliant young man, the other the Boonville Register, conducted by one Ira Van Nortrick. Toward the close of the campaign the editor of the Register came out in a very salty editorial, denouncing the ignorance of the Whigs and demanding to know "What does 'O. K.' mean anyhow?" Caldwell came back at him with the information that he would find out that "O. K." meant "Oll Korrect" in November. The expression took like wildfire; the boys yelled it, chalked it on the fences. Like other slang, it seemed to fill a want, and upon the inauguration of the telegraph, in '46, the adoption of "O. K.," I was informed by one of the first operators in the country, Mr. E. F. Barnes, introduced it to the business public, as he was one of the parties organizing the system of signals used by the company. Then it passed into general use. Of course Missouri was not the only place where Mr. Clay was called "Old Kentucky." A favorite song of the Whigs, both in Missouri and Kentucky, only a line or two of which I can now call to mind, sung to the tune of "Old Dan Tucker," ran about thus:

"The balky hoss they call John Tyler,
We'll head him soon, or bust a biler!"

Chorus:
"So get out of the way, you're all unlucky.
Clear the track for 'Old Kentucky!' "

J. W. B.

BOOK NOTICES.

Eleven Roads to Success charted by St. Louisans who have traveled them. By **Walter B. Stevens,** St. Louis, 1914.

The above work was published "to the memory of Joseph Pulitzer who rose by tireless industry and high ideals from a St. Louis reporter to a foremost place in the journalism of the world." It consists of a series of talks with notably successful St. Louisans, showing how they started and to what they owed advancement in life, and these talks were suggested by Mr. Pulitzer to the author. The talks were had with E. C. Simmons, Samuel Cupples, James Campbell, Adolphus Busch, Festus J. Wade, Elias Michael, Chas. P. Johnson, John Scullin, W. K. Bixby, D. R. Francis and J. J. Glennon. Our readers know the roads these eleven men traveled, and the success each one made in the road selected by him.

The Methodist Episcopal Church and the Civil War. By **William Warren Sweet,** Ph. D., Assistant Professor of History, Ohio Wesleyan University. Methodist Book Concern Press, n. d.

The above was a Doctor's Thesis at the University of Pennsylvania, and its object was to show the importance of the churches as an aid to the government during the civil war. The material used had been practically untouched by the regular historian, and the sources of it had been such as the church periodicals, minutes of the General and Annual Conferences, church records, minutes of preachers' meetings, histories of individual churches, and biographies of prominent church officials.

The first two bishops of the Methodist Episcopal Church, Coke and Asbury, were the earliest ecclesiastical officials to tender to the president of the United States the unanimous support of their church immediately upon its organization, and that church has ever since given the State its hearty support.

Of many things treated by the author there were controversies, but in all the author has especially tried to be impartial, and to record the true facts. His work will be found of great value.

Out of the Shadow. How a Missouri banker conquered tuberculosis out in Colorado. By **J. L. Woodbridge,** a victim. 1914. Fowler, Colo. 30 p.

The above author was a member of the Historical Society and a contributor to the first volume of the Review. His account of getting out of the shadow that was constantly becoming darker is a valuable one.

BOOK NOTICES

The Spanish Domination of Upper Louisiana. By Walter B. Douglas. Reprint from Proceedings of the State Historical Society of Wisconsin, Madison, 1914.

This paper of 17 pages by Judge Douglas is a historical account of the country from 1762 to 1803, while under Spanish rule.

The Waters of Lethe. By Lida L. Coghlan. With illustrations by Clara M. Coghlan. Baltimore and New York. John Murphy Company (C. 1904).

The above is an interesting novel by a Missouri authoress of Maplewood, Missouri, and for which we are indebted to her.

The Wood-Using Industries of Missouri. By Charles F. Hatch and Hu Maxwell, U. S. Forest Service. Reprint from St. Louis Lumberman, March 15, 1912.

Manufacturers reported to the authors fifty-six species of Missouri woods used by them, and this reprint is full of interesting information concerning them, their uses and their manufacture.

In this number of the Review is an account of the origin of "O. K.," differing from the commonly accepted one. It is given by J. W. Baird, of Louisville, Kentucky, a descendant now past eighty-two years old, of James Baird, who was the first to engage in the Santa Fe trade, an account of which we will give later.

NECROLOGY.

Hon. Samuel Byrns was a member of the Missouri State Senate in the Thirtieth General Assembly, 1879, and also in the Thirty-first; and was a member of Congress in the Fifty-second Congress. He and Martin L. Clardy were intimate friends, having served together in the Confederate army, and a few minutes after being informed of Mr. Clardy's death he suffered a stroke of paralysis, and died at Fulton, Missouri, July 9, at the age of sixty-eight years.

Mrs. Louise Norwood Fitch, daughter of Dr. J. G. Norwood, formerly of the University of Missouri, and of the Missouri Geological Survey, for the last fifteen years Matron of the University, died at her home in Columbia June 21, 1914.

James Mickleborough Greenwood, a member and valued friend of this Society, died suddenly as he sat in his office chair in the public library building in Kansas City, August 1, 1914, after a life of active and leading work in the field of education and educational methods, since 1874 as Superintendent of the public schools of Kansas City. He was born November 15, 1837, in Sangamon county, Illinois, and came to Adair county, Missouri, in 1852, where at the age of sixteen years he began his life work of teacher, and at the time he was made Superintendent of the Kansas City schools he was a member of the faculty of the Kirksville Normal School. May 15, 1913, he retired from the superintendency of the Kansas City schools, and was made adviser to the board of education of the city. Since that date he was also engaged in writing a history of Missouri, which was just completed. He had been president of the Missouri State Teachers' Association, a member of the National Educational Association from its formation, and had been its treasurer and president.

Professor Charles M. Harvey, one of the Trustees of this Society, and for many years associate editor of the Globe-Democrat, died in St. Louis August 17th. He was born in

Boston sixty-six years ago, and came to St. Louis soon after completing his education. Because of his knowledge of historical and scientific subjects he was referred to as "the walking encyclopedia," and after his retirement from active editorial work was often consulted by other writers. For the past year and a half since his retirement from active editorial work, he has written for magazines, and had applications for work beyond his ability to perform.

The second volume of the Review had a valuable paper by Prof. Harvey on "Missouri from 1849 to 1861."

Judge Elijah H. Norton was born in Logan County, Kentucky, November 21, 1821, and educated at Cantrall College and Transylvania University. He came to Missouri in 1842, and was elected a Circuit Judge before the war, and in 1861 was elected as a Whig to the Thirty-seventh Congress. He was a member of the Constitutional Convention of 1875, and in 1876 was appointed to the Supreme Court. In 1878 he was elected Judge of the Supreme Court for a term of ten years, and since the end of his term has lived in retirement. He died at Platte City, August 6, 1914.

Rev. Jesse B. Young died in Chicago, July 30, aged seventy years. He graduated from Dickinson College in 1868, was a Captain in the Eighty-fourth Pennsylvania Volunteers, was in the ministry of the Methodist Episcopal Church at Kansas City and other cities, and for eight years was editor of the Central Christian Advocate at St. Louis. His latest volume as an author was on the battle of Gettysburg.

√

56

GARLAND CARR BROADHEAD.

MISSOURI HISTORICAL REVIEW.

Vol. IX. JANUARY, 1915. No. 2.

GARLAND CARR BROADHEAD.

Garland Carr Broadhead was born October 30, 1827, near Charlottesville, Albermarle County, Virginia. His father, Achilles Broadhead, emigrated to Missouri in 1836, and settled at Flint Hill, St. Charles County. Educated at home and in private schools, his fondness for the natural sciences, history and mathematics, early in life shaped his sphere of labor.

He entered the University of Missouri in 1850, a proficient scholar in History, Latin and Mathematics. With the close of the school year of 1850-51 he shifted to the Western Military Academy of Kentucky, where he continued his studies in Geology, Mathematics and Engineering under the able guidance of Richard Owen, Professor of Geology and Chemistry, and General Bushrod R. Johnson and Colonel Williamson, they then occupying the chairs of Mathematics and Engineering in the Academy.

Early in the year 1852 he accepted a position with the Missouri Pacific Railroad as surveyor on their lines, then being projected in western Missouri. In May, 1853, he was made Assistant Engineer in charge of location of lines, which position he held until 1855, when, on account of ill health, he had to give up his work as a builder of railroads. With the beginning of the year 1857, he was again with the Missouri Pacific Railroad Company as resident Engineer of Construction, located at Hermann, Missouri.

During the year 1857 he was chosen by Professor Swallow, then State Geologist, to assist in making a Geological Reconnaissance along the line of the Southwest branch of the Pacific Railroad, and as Assistant State Geologist he continued with Professor Swallow until 1861, when the Civil War put a stop to the activities of the survey.

In 1862 he was commissioned Assistant Adjutant General on the staff of General J. B. Henderson. During the same year he was appointed Deputy Collector of Internal Revenue for the First District of Missouri, where he continued until the close of 1864, when he again returned to the employ of the Missouri Pacific Railroad Company as Assistant Engineer in charge of Construction on the road then building between Kingsville and Lee's Summit. In this capacity he continued until near the close of 1866, when he was appointed by President Andrew Johnson, Assessor of Internal Revenue for the Fifth District of Missouri. Under this appointment he served until 1868, when he was commissioned Assistant Geologist on the Illinois Geological Survey.

After two years work on the Illinois Survey he submitted reports on seven counties, which were published in Volume 6, 1875, and the economic portions republished in "Economical Geology of Illinois," Volume 3, 1882. This task completed, he returned to his work as a railroad builder, and during the period of 1870-1871 he was engaged as Engineer in Charge of Construction in western Missouri.

During the month of October, 1871, he was again called to become Assistant State Geologist of Missouri. As Assistant State Geologist he continued with the Survey until June, 1873, when, with the resignation of State Geologist Raphael Pumpelly, he was elected as head of the Survey. With the termination of his commission, May, 1875, the remaining months of the year were spent in assembling a collection of Missouri minerals for the State, and Smithsonian Institution, for their exhibits at the Philadelphia Centennial Exposition, and during the Exposition he was one of the twenty Jurors, foreign and American, who were charged with making awards, for the division of Mines and Geology.

In 1879 Professor Broadhead again turned his attention to railroad work, and was employed in surveys and construction in western Missouri and Kansas. During the year 1881 he acted as Special Agent of the Census Bureau, investigating the building stones of Missouri.

During the years 1883-1884 Professor Broadhead was employed as a special assistant in the Department of Geology in the State University, classifying and arranging collections. In 1884 he received the appointment as member of the Missouri River Commission. In 1887 he was elected by the Board of Curators, Professor of Geology in the University of Missouri, where he labored for ten years. At the time of his resignation in 1897, he was made Professor Emeritus in Geology. With the reorganization of the Geological Survey, August, 1885, Governor Francis appointed Professor Broadhead member of the Board of Managers, and during the period of 1889-1893 Professor Broadhead worked zealously in the interest of the survey.

In 1858 Professor Broadhead was elected corresponding member of the Academy of Science of Saint Louis; in 1879 a Fellow of the American Association. He was a charter member of the Geological Society of America, being one of the ninety-eight who had complied with all the requirements of the "Provisional Constitution" of 1888. In the field of Geology Professor Broadhead was best known by his work on the Pennsylvanian, and we feel safe in asserting that his work on the stratigraphy of the Missouri Coal Measures is more nearly in accord with fact than any contempory work.

When in the field he observed not the geology alone, but his eye caught every object of natural history in the region he was studying; the animals were noted, plants were catalogued, size and growth of the trees given, general surface and typographic features discussed, and through this method of note writing, his note-books were, to the geologist, botanist and zoological student, a mine of valuable data.

He was intimately acquainted with the early history of the State, and his knowledge of events, distinguished men, historic spots, local and state politics was remarkable. During the last years of his life, while not actively engaged in research, his interest in his favorite studies was keen to the last, and his memory of places and events as vivid as ever. After a short illness, Professor Broadhead died at his home in Columbia, December 15, 1912.

BIBLIOGRAPHY OF PUBLICATIONS BY PROFESSOR G. C. BROADHEAD.

Report on Copper Prospects (examined by).—Geological Report on Southwestern Branch, Pacific Railroad, pp. 67-68, St. Louis, 1859.

On Ancient Graves in Pike County (Missouri).—Transactions Academy of Science, St. Louis, Volume 2, Number 2, page 223, 1862.

Coal Measures in Missouri.—Transactions Academy of Science, St. Louis, Volume 2, Number 2, pages 311-333, 1862.

The Caves of Missouri.—The Missouri Republican, November, 1863.

Distribution of Trees and Shrubs in Missouri.—Missouri State Board of Agriculture, Second Annual Report, 1866, pages 97-99. 1867.

Mineral Springs of Missouri.—Missouri State Board of Agriculture, Second Annual Report, 1866, pages 99-103. 1867.

Cass County (Missouri).—Missouri State Board of Agriculture, Second Annual Report, 1866, pages 226-229. 1867.

Paints and Clays (of Missouri).—Missouri State Board of Agriculture, Third Annual Report, 1867, pages 200-201. 1868.

Caves in Missouri.—Missouri State Board of Agriculture, Third Annual Report, 1867, pages 201-204. 1868.

Fossil Horse in Missouri.—American Naturalist, Volume 4, page 60. 1869.

Bones of Large Mammals in Drift.—Transactions Academy of Science, St. Louis, Volume 3, page xxiii, November 15, 1869.

Fossil Horse in Missouri.—Transactions Academy of Science, St. Louis, Volume 3, pages xx-xxi, October 4, 1869.

Maple Sugar.—Missouri State Board of Agriculture, Fourth Annual Report, 1868, pages 116-119. 1869.

Quaternary Deposits.—American Naturalist, Volume 4, page 61. 1869.

Mineralogy of Cole County (Missouri).—Transactions Academy of Science, St. Louis, Volume 3, pages xxxiii-xxxiv, November, 1870.

Note on Coal Measure Fucoids.—American Journal of Science, Volume 2, pages 216-217, Third Series. 1871.

Maries County, Missouri (Geology of).—Missouri Geological Survey, Report of 1855-1871, pages 1 to 23. 1873.

Osage County (Missouri) (Geology of). Missouri Geological Survey, Report of 1855-1871, pages 25-36. 1873.

Warren County, Missouri (Geology of).—Missouri Geological Survey, Report of 1855-1871, pages 37-64. 1873.

Shelby County, Missouri (Geology of).—Missouri Geological Survey, Report of 1855-1871, pages 65-73. 1873.

Macon County (Missouri) (Geology of).—Missouri Geological Survey, Report of 1855-1871, pages 74-92. 1873.

Randolph County (Missouri) (Geology of).—Missouri Geological Survey, Report of 1855-1871, pages 93-110. 1873.

Area and Topographical Features of the Coal Field.—Missouri Geological Survey, Report on Iron Ores and Coal Fields, 1872, part 2, pages 5-10. 1873.

The Lower Coal Measures.—Missouri Geological Survey, Report on Iron Ores and Coal Fields, 1872, part 2, pages 11-44. 1873.

The Middle Coal Measures.—Missouri Geological Survey, Report on Iron Ores and Coal Fields, 1872, part 2, pages 45-87. 1873.

The Upper Coal Measures.—Missouri Geological Survey, Report on Iron Ores and Coal Fields, 1872, part 2, pages 88-135. 1873.

Economic Geology of the Coal Measures.—Missouri Geological Survey Report on Iron Ores and Coal Fields, 1872, part 2, pages 135-156. 1873.

Geological Report on the Country adjacent to the Pacific Railroad from Sedalia to Kansas City.—Missouri Geological Survey, Report on Iron Ores and Coal Fields, 1872, part 2, pages 157-213. 1873.

Geology of Livingston County.—Missouri Geological Survey, Report on Iron Ores and Coal Fields, 1872, part 2, pages 290-316. 1873.

Geology of Clay County.—Missouri Geological Survey, Report on Iron Ores and Coal Fields, 1872, part 2, pages 317-326. 1873.

Geology of Platte County.—Missouri Geological Survey, Report on Iron Ores and Coal Fields, 1872, part 2, pages 327-343. 1873.

Geology of Buchanan County.—Missouri Geological Survey, Report on Iron Ores and Coal Fields, 1872, part 2, pages 344-358. 1873.

Geology of Holt County.—Missouri Geological Survey, Report on Iron Ores and Coal Fields, 1872, part 2, pages 359-375. 1873.

Geology of Atchison County.—Missouri Geological Survey, Report on Iron Ores and Coal Fields, 1872, part 2, pages 376-387. 1873.

Geology of Nodaway County.—Missouri Geological Survey, Report on Iron Ores and Coal Fields, 1872, part 2, pages 388-402. 1873.

Notes on such rocks of Missouri as admit of a fine polish. Missouri Geological Survey, Report on Iron Ores and Coal Fields, 1872, part 2, pages 414-415. 1873.

Report on the Geological Survey of the State of Missouri, including field work of 1873-1874.—Published by the authority of the Bureau of Geology and Mines, G. C. Broadhead State Geologist, pages 1-734, 91 illustrations and an Atlas, Jefferson City, 1874.

Historical notes on early mining in Missouri.—Missouri Geological Survey, Report on Field work of 1873-1874, pages 11-17. 1874.

General Geology (of Missouri).—Missouri Geological Survey, Report on Field work of 1873-1874, pages 18-34. 1874.

Caves (of Missouri).—Missouri Geological Survey, Report on Field work of 1873-1874, pages 35-39. 1874.

Soils (of Missouri).—Missouri Geological Survey, Report on Field work of 1873-1874, pages 40-43. 1874.

Minerals (of Missouri).—Missouri Geological Survey, Report on Field work of 1873-1874, pages 46-56. 1874.

Topographical features of the Southwest Coal Field.—Missouri Geological Survey, Report on Field work of 1873-1874, pages 57-61. 1874.

Geology of Cedar County.—Missouri Geological Survey, Report on Field work of 1873-1874, pages 62-76. 1874.

Geology of Jasper County.—Missouri Geological Survey, Report on Field work of 1873-1874, pages 77-96. 1874.

Geology of Barton County.—Missouri Geological Survey, Report on Field work of 1873-1874, pages 97-118. 1874.

Geology of Vernon County.—Missouri Geological Survey, Report on Field work of 1873-1874, pages 119-154. 1874.

Geology of Bates County.—Missouri Geological Survey, Report on Field work of 1873-1874, pages 155-178. 1874.

Geology of Howard County.—Missouri Geological Survey, Report on Field work of 1873-1874, pages 179-221. 1874.

Geology of Sullivan County.—Missouri Geological Survey, Report on Field work of 1873-1874, pages 222-241. 1874.

Geology of Adair County.—Missouri Geological Survey, Report on Field work of 1873-1874, pages 242-256. 1874.

Geology of Linn County.—Missouri Geological Survey, Report on Field work of 1873-1874, pages 257-271. 1874.

Geology of Andrew County.—Missouri Geological Survey, Report on Field work of 1873-1874, pages 303-311. 1874.

Geology of Daviess County.—Missouri Geological Survey, Report on Field work of 1873-1874, pages 312-321. 1874.

Geology of Cole County.—Missouri Geological Survey, Report on Field work of 1873-1874, pages 322-341. 1874.

Geology of Madison County.—Missouri Geological Survey, Report on Field work of 1873-1874, pages 342-379. 1874.

Mineral Springs (of Missouri).—Missouri Geological Survey, Report on Field work of 1873-1874, pages 701-704. 1874.

Area and Topographic Features of Southwest Coal Fields.—Mines, Metals and Arts. 1874.

Review of Reports of the Geological Survey of the State of Missouri, 1855-1871, by Broadhead, etc.—Geological Magazine, Volume I n.s., pages 368-369. 1874.

Note on Pickeringite from Missouri.—American Journal of Science, Volume 7, Third Series, page 520. 1874.

Iron Ores of Carboniferous Age.—Mines, Metals and Arts, February, 1875.

Mines of Morgan and Benton Counties.—Mines, Metals and Arts, July, 1875.

Mines of Cole County, Missouri.—Mines, Metals and Arts, August, 1875.

Morgan County Lead Mines.—Mines, Metals and Arts, September, 1875.

Meteoric Iron in Missouri.—Mines, Metals and Arts, September, 1875.

Meteoric Iron, with reference to Doctor Shumard's notes.—Mines, Metals and Arts, October, 1875.

The St. Joe Mines, Southeast Missouri.—Mines, Metals and Arts, October, 1875.

A visit to Southeast Missouri Mines.—Mines, Metals and Arts, October, 1875.

Drift Formation and Gold in Missouri.—Mines, Metals and Arts, December, 1875.

Geology of Bond County (Illinois).—Geological Survey of Illinois, Volume 6, pages 128-134. 1875.

Geology of Fayette County.—Geological Survey of Illinois, Volume 6, pages 135-148. 1875.

Geology of Montgomery County.—Geological Survey of Illinois, Volume 6, pages 149-155. 1875.

Geology of Christian County.—Geological Survey of Illinois, Volume 6, pages 156-162. 1875.

Geology of Shelby County (Illinois).—Geological Survey of Illinois, Volume 6, pages 163-174. 1875.

Geology of Effingham County.—Geological Survey of Illinois, Volume 6, pages 175-184. 1875.

Geology of Moultrie, Macon and Pratt Counties.—Geological Survey of Illinois, Volume 6, pages 185-196. 1875.

On the Well at the Insane Asylum, St. Louis County, Missouri.—American Journal of Science, Volume 9, pages 61-62, Third Series. 1875.

On a Discovery of Meteoric Iron in Missouri.—American Journal of Science, Volume 10, Third Series, page 401. 1875.

On the Height of the St. Louis Directrix.—American Journal of Science, Volume 10, Third Series, page 75. 1875.

The Geology of Missouri—in Article on "Missouri."—The American Cyclopaedia, pages 665-666. 1875.

Physical Geography of the Mississippi Valley.—Mines, Metals and Arts, February, 1876.

Geographical Notes on Southeast Missouri, Reynolds County.—Mines, Metals and Arts, March, 1876.

Callirrhoe digitata (Notes on).—Botanical Gazette Volume 1, Number 3, page 9. 1876.

Quercus heterophylla (Note on).—Botanical Gazette, Volume 1, Number 3, page 9. 1876.

Oenothera speciosa (Note on).—Botanical Gazette, Volume 1, Number 3, page 10. 1876.

Ancient Mounds of Saline County, Missouri.—Transactions Academy of Science, St. Louis, Volume 3, page lxxxvi. 1876.

Meteor of January 3, 1877.—Transactions Academy of Science, St. Louis, Volume 3, page cclviii. 1876.

The Rocky Mountain Locust and the Season of 1875.—Transactions Academy of Science, St. Louis, Volume 3, Number 3, pages 345-349. 1876.

Meteor of December 27, 1875.—Transactions Academy of Science, St. Louis, Volume 3, Number 3, pages 349-352. 1876.

Age of Our Porphyries.—Transactions Academy of Science, St. Louis, Volume 3, Number 3, pages 366-370. 1876.

Porphyritic rocks of Southeast Missouri Huronian.—The Western, Volume 2, pages 241, 243 and 248. 1876.

Age of our Porphyries.—Transactions Academy of Science St. Louis, Volume 3, Number 3, page ccxix, June, 1876.

Drift Formation and Gold in Missouri.—American Journal of Science, Volume 11, Third Series, page 150. 1876.

Bituminous Shales.—Mines, Metals and Arts, February, 1877.

Southeast Missouri Lead District.—American Inst. Mining Eng. Trans., Volume 5, pages 100-106. 1877.

Coal of Southwest Missouri.—Mines, Metals and Arts, December, 1877.

On Barite Crystals from the Last Chance Mine, Morgan County, Missouri; and on Goethite from Adair County, Missouri.—American Journal of Science, Volume 13, Third Series, pages 419-420. 1877.

Note on Fall of Meteor in Warren County, January 3, 1877.—The Western, Volume 3, N. S., pages 245 and 246. 1877.

Mineralogy; (a Paper on Various Hydrocarbons).—Kansas City Review of Science and Industry, Volume 1, Number 4, pages 209-224. 1877.

Thickness of the Missouri Coal Measures.—Kansas City Review of Science and Industry, Volume 1, Number 7, pages 392-393. 1877.

On the Range of the common Huckleberry in Missouri.—Botanical Gazette, Volume 3, Number 2, page 24. 1878.

On the Distribution of certain Plants in Missouri.—Botanical Gazette, Volume 3, Number 6, pages 51-53. 1878.

On the Distribution of certain Plants in Missouri.—Botanical Gazette, Volume 3, Number 7, pages 58-61. 1878.

(Erratic) Boulders South of the Missouri (River).—Transactions Academy of Science, St. Louis, Volume 3, page xxiii. 1878.

Occurrence of Bitumen in Missouri.—Transactions Academy of Science, St. Louis, Volume 3, pages 224-226. 1878.

On the Well at the Insane Asylum, St. Louis County.—Transactions Academy of Science, Volume 3, Number 2, pages 216-223. 1878.

Baldwin's Prehistoric Nations (Review).—Kansas City Review of Science and Industry, Volume 1, pages 370-372. 1878.

Missouri Iron Ores of Carboniferous Age.—Kansas City Review of Science and Industry, Volume 1, Number 11, pages 650-654. 1878.

Growth of Minerals.—Kansas City Review of Science and Industry.—Volume 1, Number 11, pages 693-694. 1878.

Meteoric Stones and Shooting Stars.—Kansas City Review of Science and Industry, Volume 1, Number 12, pages 724-742. 1878.

Meteors (observed by, with dates).—Kansas City Review of Science and Industry, Volume 2, Number 2, page 100. 1878.

Ancient Earthworks in Saline County, Missouri.—Kansas City Review of Science and Industry, Volume 2, Number 3, pages 166-167. 1878.

Jackson County, Missouri, a few notes on its Geology.—Kansas City Review of Science and Industry, Volume 2, Number 4, pages 204-210. 1878.

Prehistoric Evidences in Missouri.—Annual Reports, Smithsonian Institute, Report 1879, pages 350-359. 11 Figs. 1879.

Missouri (Geological formation in).—McFarlanes Geological Railroad Guide, pages 154-158. 1879.

Melanthium virginicum (Note on).—Botanical Gazette, Volume 4, Number 11, page 232. 1879.

Origin of the Loess.—American Journal of Science, Volume 18, Third Series, page 427. 1879.

Geologists Traveling Hand-book and Geological Railway Guide, by James Macfarlane. (Review.)—Kansas City Review of Science and Industry, Volume 2, Number 10, pages 628-629. 1879.

Remarks on Hunt's and Dana's Sections.—Kansas City Review of Science and Industry, Volume 2, Number 11, pages 664-668. 1879.

Notes on Surface Geology of Southwest Missouri and Southeast Kansas.—Kansas City Review of Science and Industry, Volume 3, Number 8, pages 460-461. 1879.

Geological Report upon the Mineral Lands of Major R. H. Melton.—Sedalia, pages 1-12. 1880.

Missouri (Building Stones of).—The U. S. Census Report for 1880, Report on the Building Stones of the United States and Statistics of the Quarry Industry for 1880. Part of Volume 10, pages 265-274. 1880.

Geology of Southern Missouri.—St. Louis Immigration Society, Convention of April, 1880.

A Buried Race in Kansas.—Kansas City Review of Science and Industry, Volume 3, Number 9, pages 530-534. 1880.

Geographical Distribution of Certain Trees and Plants in Missouri and Kansas.—Kansas City Review of Science and Industry, Volume 3, Number 10, pages 608-611. 1880.

A Review of "Contributions to Paleontology," Numbers 2-8, by C. A. White.—Kansas City Review of Science and Industry, Volume 4, Number 7, pages 448-449. 1880.

Prehistoric Remains in Missouri.—Missouri Historical Society, Bulletins Number 2-3, pages 21-22, St. Louis. 1880.

The Southeast Missouri Lead District.—Engineering and Mining Journal, Volume 22, pages 59-60. 1881.

The Carboniferous Rocks of Southeast Kansas.—American Journal of Science, Volume 22, pages 55-57, July, 1881.

The Mastodon.—Kansas City Review of Science and Industry, Volume 4, Number 9, pages 519-530. 1881.

Extracts and Notes from an Old Book (of Travel).—Kansas City Review of Science and Industry, Volume 4, Number 9, pages 563-565. 1881.

Fort Orleans, Where Was It?—Kansas City Review of Science and Industry, Volume 5, Number 1, pages 22-23. 1881.

"Sniabar."—Kansas City Review of Science and Industry, Volume 5, Number 1, pages 23-24. 1881.

The Carboniferous Rocks of Southern Kansas (Abstract).—Kansas City Review of Science and Industry, Volume 5, Number 5, pages 273-275. 1881.

Geological Notes on the Central Branch, Union Pacific Railroad.—Kansas City Review of Science and Industry, Volume 5, Number 3, pages 129-132. 1882.

Geology of Bond, Fayette, Montgomery, Christian, Shelby, Effingham, Moultrie, Macon and Platt Counties.—Illinois Geological Survey, Economical Geology of Illinois, Volume 3, pages 467-544. 1882.

The Chalk Beds of Wakeeney, Kansas.—Kansas City Review of Science and Industry, Volume 5, Number 10, page 616. 1882.

Missouri Historical Notes (Compiled by).—Kansas City Review of Science and Industry, Volume 5, Number 10, pages 629-630. 1882.

Archaean Rocks of Missouri.—Kansas City Review of Science and Industry, Volume 5, Number 12, pages 735-738. 1882.

Marbles of Southeast Missouri.—Kansas City Review of Science and Industry, Volume 5, Number 9, pages 523-526. 1882.

North Park, Colorado.—Kansas City Review of Science and Industry, Volume 6, Number 4, pages 197-204. 1882.

Geological Notes on a Part of Southeast Kansas.—Kansas City Review of Science and Industry, Volume 6, Number 5, pages 172-175. 1882.

Jura-Trias.—Kansas City Review of Science and Industry, Volume 6, Numbers 9-10, pages 534-540. 1883.

Southwest Missouri Lead Interest—A Proposed Lead Combination.—Engineering and Mining Journal, Volume 25, page 73. 1883.

Missouri Lead Smelters.—Engineering and Mining Journal, Volume 25, page 91. 1883.

Missouri Minerals.—Engineering and Mining Journal, Volume 25, pages 276-277. 1883.

Old Granby Mines, Newton County, Missouri.—Engineering and Mining Journal, Volume 25, page 406. 1883.

Old Maps.—Kansas City Review of Science and Industry, Volume 7, Number 1, pages 56-58. 1883.

Steatite Quarries and Utensils.—Kansas City Review of Science and Industry, Volume 7, Number 3, pages 188-189. 1883.

Explorers of Western America.—Kansas City Review of Science and Industry, Volume 7, Number 6, pages 407-412. 1883.

Note on Egyptian Stone Dressing.—Kansas City Review of Science and Industry, Volume 7, Number 7, pages 430-431. 1883.

Geology of Bates County.—History of Bates County. 1883.

The Relation of the Soils of Missouri to Geology. (Lecture delivered in the University Chapel, March 29, 1884).—Annual Report of State University, Report of 1883-1884, pages 72-79. 1884.

The Relation of the Soils of Missouri to Geology.—Missouri State Board of Agriculture, Seventeenth Annual Report, 1883, pages 159-168. 1884.

Flint Chips.—Kansas City Review of Science and Industry, Volume 7, Number 10, pages 599-602. 1884.

Mines of Carterville, Jasper County, Missouri.—Kansas City Review of Science and Industry, Volume 8, Numbers 2-3, pages 70-77. 1884.

Black Bird.—Kansas City Review of Science and Industry, Volume 8, Number 7, pages 362-364. 1884.

Gravel Beds of Southern Kansas.—Kansas City Review of Science and Industry, Volume 8, Number 8, pages 453-454. 1884.

Sketch of Geology of Missouri.—Missouri State Board of Agriculture, Eighteenth Annual Report, 1885, pages 250-259. 1885.

Distribution of Plants in Missouri.—State Horticultural Society of Missouri, Twenty-eighth Annual Report, pages 263-269. 1886.

Carboniferous Rocks of Eastern Kansas.—Transactions Academy of Science, St. Louis, Volume 4, Number 3, pages 481-492. 1886.

Missouri Geological Surveys, Historical Memoir.—Transactions Academy of Science, St. Louis, Volume 4, Number 4, pages 555-568. 1886.

Discourse on "Trees."—State Horticultural Society of Missouri, Twenty-ninth Annual Report, pages 403-408. 1887.

Mitchell County, Texas.—American Geologist, Volume 2, pages 433-436, December, 1888.

The Geological History of the Ozark Uplift.—American Geologist, Volume 3, pages 6-13, January, 1889.

Missouri, its Mineral Resources.—Report of U. S. Commissioner of Statistics, 1889, pages 461-468. 1889.

The Missouri River.—American Geologist, Volume 4, pages 148-155. September, 1889.

Missouri (Geological formation in).—Macfarlane's Geological Railway Guide, Second Edition, pages 267-273. 1890.

Fruit Growing in Missouri.—State Horticultural Society of Missouri, Thirty-second Annual Report, pages 241-244. 1890.

The Ozark Series.—American Geologist, Volume 8, pages 33-35. 1891.

The Black Earth of the Steppes of Russia, a paper by A. N. Krassnof. (Discussion by G. C. Broadhead, et al).—Bulletin of the Geological Society of America, Volume 3, pages 80-81. 1892.

The Correct Succession of the Ozark Series.—American Geologist, Volume 11, pages 260-268. April, 1893.

The Settlements West of the Alleghenies Prior to 1776.—Magazine of American History, Volume 29, Number 4, pages 332-337. April, 1893.

A Critical Notice of the Stratigraphy of the Missouri Paleozoic.—American Geologist, Volume 12, pages 74-89. 1893.

Production of Zinc in Missouri.—American Geologist, Volume 12, page 274. 1893.

The Cambrian and the Ozark Series.—American Journal of Science, Volume 46, pages 57-60. July, 1893.

Geological History of the Missouri Paleozoic.—American Geologist, Volume 14, pages 380-388. December, 1894.

A Plea for our Native Plants.—State Horticultural Society of Missouri, Thirty-sixth Annual Report, pages 25-26. 1894.

The Coal Measures of Missouri.—Missouri Geological Survey, Volume 8, pages 353-395. 1895.

Biography of Joseph Granville Norwood, M. D., LL.D.—The American Geologist, Volume 16, Number 2, pages 69-74, August, 1895.

The Devonian of North Missouri, with Notice of a New Fossil.—American Journal of Science, Volume 2, pages 237-238. 1896.

Native Fruits of Missouri.—State Horticultural Society of Missouri, Thirty-ninth Annual Report, pages 150-153. 1897.

Missouri Nuts.—State Horticultural Society of Missouri, Thirty-ninth Annual Report, pages 153-154. 1897.

Geology of Boone County, Missouri.—Missouri Geological Survey, Volume 12, pages 375-388. 1898.

The Ozark Uplift and Growth of the Missouri Paleozoic.—Missouri Geological Survey, Volume 12, pages 391-409. 1898.

Major Frederick Hawn (Biography).—American Geologist, Volume 21, pages 267-269, May, 1898.

Biographical Sketch of G. C. Swallow.—American Geologist, Volume 24, pages 1-6, July, 1899.

Aboriginal Antiquities.—Encyclopedia History of Missouri, Volume 1, page 3. 1901.

Geological Surveys (of Missouri).—Encyclopedia of Missouri, Volume 3, pages 27-31. 1901.

Indian Wars.—Encyclopedia History of Missouri, Volume 3, pages 358-369. 1901.

Indian Legend.—Encyclopedia History of Missouri, Volume 3, page 353. 1901.

Indians in Missouri.—Encyclopedia History of Missouri, Volume 3, page 369. 1901.

Mineralogy (of Missouri).—Encyclopedia History of Missouri, Volume 4, pages 390-393. 1901.

Roads and Trails.—Encyclopedia History of Missouri, Volume 5, pages 361-369. 1901.

Stage Lines.—Encyclopedia History of Missouri, Volume 6, page 53. 1901.

The New Madrid Earthquake.—American Geologist, Volume 30, pages 76-87. August, 1902.

Obituary Notice of R. A. Blair.—American Geologist, Volume 30, pages 398-399. 1902.

Abram Litton, M. D. (Biography).—Transactions Academy of Science, St. Louis, Volume 12, pages xxiv-xxvii. 1903.

Bituminous and Asphalt Rocks of the United States.—American Geologist, Volume 32, pages 59-60. July, 1903.

Bitumen and Oil Rocks.—American Geologist, Volume 33, pages 27-35. January, 1904.

The Loess.—American Geologist, Volume 33, pages 393-394. June, 1904.

Surface Deposits of Western Missouri and Kansas.—American Geologist, Volume 34, pages 66-67. July, 1904.

The Saccharoidal Sandstone.—American Geologist, Volume 34, pages 105-110. August, 1904.

Edwin Harrison (Biography).—Transactions Academy of Science, St. Louis, Volume 15, pages xxxv-xxxvii. 1905.

Cone in Cone.—Science, New Series, Volume 26, page 597. 1907.

A Few of the Leading People and Events of Early Missouri History.—Missouri Historical Review, Volume 1, pages 284-292. 1906-1907.

Notes on the Jones Family in Missouri.—Missouri Historical Review, Volume 3, Number 1, pages 1-4. 1908.

The Location of the Capital of Missouri.—Missouri Historical Review, Volume 2, Number 2, pages 158-163. 1908.

Interesting Extracts from old Newspapers.—Journal of the Illinois State Historical Society, Volume 2, Number 2, pages 37-42. 1909.

The Fossil Fields of Wyoming.—Geology of the Laramie Plains.—Report on U. P. Exped. to the fossil fields of Wyomming. Issued by Passenger Department of Union Pacific Railroad, pages 1-61. Omaha. 1909.

Albert G. Blakey (Biography).—Missouri Historical Review, Volume 4, Number 1, pages 36-37. 1909.

The Pinnacles.—Missouri Historical Review, Volume 4, Number 3, pages 202-203. 1910.

The Sante Fe Trail.—Missouri Historical Review, Volume 4, Number 4, pages 309-319. 1910.

Missouri Weather in Early Days.—Missouri Historical Review, Volume 4, Number 4, page 320. 1910.

Missouri Grasses. (Posthumous, edited by F. A. Sampson). —Missouri Historical Review, Volume 6, Number 3, pages 153-154. 1912.

Early Railroads in Missouri. (Posthumous, edited by F. A. Sampson—). Missouri Historical Review, Volume 7, Number 3, pages 149-150. 1913.

Early Missouri Roads. (Posthumous, edited by F. A. Sampson).—Missouri Historical Review, Volume 8, Number 2, pages 90-92. 1914.

Harmony Mission and Methodist Missions. (Posthumous, edited by F. A. Sampson).—Missouri Historical Review, Volume 9, Number 2, pages ——. 1915.

DARLING K. GREGER.

THE CABELL DESCENDANTS IN MISSOURI.

William Cabell, son of Nicholas, was born in Warminster, Wiltshire, England, March 20, 1699, and graduated in the Royal College of Medicine and Surgery in London. After several years of successful practice he entered the British Navy as surgeon. His vessel came to Jamestown, Virginia, and being detained there some time, he visited the interior of the Colony and was so well pleased with the country that he determined to make it his home. He resigned from the service, married Elizabeth Burks, settled up his affairs and came to Virginia about 1725, locating in Goochland County. Their children were Mary, William, Joseph, John, George, who died young, and Nicholas. Dr. Cabell was a man of great ability, high moral character, liberal education and possessed of considerable wealth. "He lived to see every one of his sons occupy honorable positions in society and become the foremost men in their section." His wife died September 21, 1756, and on September 30, 1762, he married Margaret, the widow of Samuel Meredith. He died April 12, 1774. The descendants of no other immigrant include so many noted families. Among them may be named the Breckinridges, Browns, Callaways, Carringtons, Carters, Castlemans, Dabneys, Dickinsons, Flournoys, Garnetts, Gordons, Harrisons, Henrys, Hills, Letchers, Lewises, McClellands, McCullochs, McDowells, Marshalls, Mayos, Merediths, Merriwethers, Monroes, Pages, Penns, Pollards, Prestons, Randolphs, Riveses, Shackelfords, Talliaferros and Tuckers. In 1895 Alexander Brown of Union Hill, Nelson County, Virginia, the home of Dr. Cabell's son William, author of "The Genesis of the United States," published a memorial volume entitled "The Cabells and Their Kin." From it and other sources I have compiled the following data of the Cabell descendants in Missouri.

Mary Cabell, oldest child and only daughter of Dr. William Cabell, born February 13, 1726, married William Horsley who had been a tutor in Dr. Cabell's family. Their oldest daughter, Elizabeth, born March 22, 1749, married Roderick McCulloch who was born November 17, 1741, in Westmoreland County, a soldier of the Revolution, " a fine scholar with high literary culture," a son of Rev. Roderick McCulloch of Scotland and a relative of Elizabeth McCulloch who married Thomas Scott, brother of Sir Walter Scott. Their ninth and youngest child, William H. McCulloch, born December 10, 1791, a captain in the war of 1812, married Mary Douglas of Alexandria, Virginia, daughter of James Douglas of Scotland, and who died eighteen months later, leaving a child, Roderick Douglas McCulloch, father of Colonel Robert McCulloch of St. Louis. William H. McCulloch's second wife was Mary Champe Carter, whose father, Edward Carter, jr., was the great grandson of Robert Carter, called "King Carter of Corotoman."* He went to Callaway County, Missouri, in 1834 with his next older broth-

---

*Robert Carter was the son of John Carter, the first of that name and the great ancestor of many bearing that name in Virginia, under whose direction the old Christ Church in Lancaster County, was built in 1670. It becoming too small, Robert Carter built, at his own expense, the present edifice which was completed about the time of his death, that is, about the year 1732. "The tombs of 'King' Carter, his two wives and several children are in the churchyard. The 'King's' once magnificent tomb is sadly mutilated—the work of the ubiquitous relic hunter. The top is covered with Latin inscriptions, which refute the tradition that he who lies buried there ruled with an iron hand. The following is a translation:

'Here lies buried Robert Carter, Esq., an honorable man, who, by noble endowments and pure morals, gave luster to his gentle birth.

'Rector of William and Mary, he sustained that institution in its most trying times. He was Speaker of the House of Burgesses and Treasurer under the Most Serene Princes William, Anne, George I and II.

'Elected by the House its Speaker six years and Governor of the Colony for more than a year, he upheld equally the regal dignity and the public freedom.

'Possessed of ample wealth, blamelessly acquired, he built and endowed at his own expense this sacred edifice, a signal monument of his piety toward God. He furnished it richly.

'Entertaining his friends kindly, he was neither a prodigal nor a parsimonious host.

'His first wife was Judith, daughter of John Armistead, Esq., his second, Betty, a descendant of the noble family of Landons. By these wives he had many children, on whose education he expended large sums of money.

'At length, full of honors and of years, when he had performed all the duties of an exemplary life, he departed from this world on the 4th day of August, in the sixty-ninth year of his age.

'The unhappy lament their lost comforter, the widows their lost protector and the orphans their lost father.' "—"Old Ministers, Churches and Families of Virginia," by Bishop Meade.

er, Robert Horsley McCulloch who was a soldier in the war of 1812 and who died unmarried in 1839, moved about 1840 to St. Clair County where he bought a fine estate called "Westwood." He died March 5, 1855, and his widow died near Springfield, October 10, 1879. Of their nine children two went into the Confederate army. Richard Ellis McCulloch, born in Callaway County, was killed at Prairie Grove, near Fayetteville, Arkansas, December 7, 1862, in a bloody but indecisive battle between the Federal forces under Generals Blunt and Herron and the Confederates under Generals Hindman, Marmaduke and Shelby; (1) Champe Carter McCulloch, born 1841, near Osceola, was captain and assistant adjutant Second Cavalry Brigade, Missouri State Guard, under Colonel Cawthron at Wilson's Creek, promoted major and adjutant in place of Major Charles E. Rogers of St. Louis, killed in the battle; was in the battles of Lexington, Lone Jack, Elk Horn, Prairie Grove (where his older brother was killed), and Cedar Creek; later was transferred to the ordnance department, and after the war settled in Waco, Texas. Lucy C. McCulloch, the oldest and only married daughter of William H. McCulloch, married Colonel Robert E. Acock who served four terms in the lower house of the legislature from Polk County, from 1838 to 1842 and from 1852 to 1856, in the State senate from 1842 to 1846; was presidential elector in 1853 for the Seventh Congressional District and, with E. D. Bevitt, Alexander Keyser, H. F. Gary, William D. McCracken, Claiborne F. Jackson, John D. Stevenson, C. F. Holly and J. M. Gatewood, cast the vote of Missouri for Franklin Pierce. Acock and Jackson had been prominent in the anti-Benton forces and Stevenson equally prominent on the other side. Acock died in 1862 leaving an only child, Bertie, who married in Waco, Texas, 1889, Rev. William Wilson DeHart, rector of St. Paul's Episcopal church, and a

---

(1) Here General Alexander Early Steen, commanding a Missouri brigade, and Colonel Grinstead, commanding a Missouri regiment, were killed. Steen was a native Missourian, brevetted for meritorious conduct in the battles of Contreras and Churubusco, Mexico; resigned from the regular army May 10, 1861, appointed brigadier-general in the Missouri State Guard, and distinguished himself in battle at Wilson's Creek and at Pea Ridge.

relative of Abagail DeHart who, as Mrs. John Mayo, became the mother of Mrs. General Winfield Scott.

William H. McCulloch's only child by his first marriage, Roderick Douglas McCulloch, came to Missouri with his father, went into business two years later at Osceola and married February 25, 1840, Elizabeth McClanahan Nash, daughter of Dr. Gabriel Penn Nash of Osceola. Dr. Nash was one of the earliest settlers of Lincoln County. He was appointed by the governor probate judge for four years in 1825; before that time and since until 1871 the county court exercised probate jurisdiction. In the same year he was instrumental in having Waverly Township organized out of the territory of Union, one of the four original townships. His grandfather, Colonel Gabriel Penn, of Amherst County, Virginia, was a member of the Revolutionary Convention, and first cousin to John Penn, who was a delegate from North Carolina to the Continental Congress, a signer of the Declaration of Independence and of the Articles of Confederation. Colonel Penn's wife was Sarah Callaway, daughter of Colonel Richard Callaway of Bedford County, Virginia, major in the French and Indian wars, 1755-63, who went to Kentucky in 1775 and raised that year the first corn grown in Madison County. His daughters Elizabeth and Frances with Jemima, daughter of Daniel Boone, were captured by the Indians July 14, 1776, and retaken by Boone and Callaway the next day. On August 7, following, Elizabeth Callaway married Samuel Henderson, one of her rescuers, and their daughter Fanny, born May 29, 1777, was the first white child born in Kentucky of parents married in Kentucky. Colonel Callaway was killed by the Indians near Boonesborough March 8, 1780. A county in Kentucky was named for him. Dr. Nash's wife, Elizabeth Madison McClanahan, was the oldest daughter of Colonel Elijah McClanahan and Agatha Lewis of Botetourt County, Virginia. The statue of her great grandfather, General Andrew Lewis, the hero of Point Pleasant, is among the group around the equestrian statue of Washington in the capitol grounds at Richmond.

Mrs. Elizabeth McClanahan McCulloch died April 17, 1848; her husband died March 8, 1853, at Gonzales, Texas, leaving three children: Robert, Mary Douglas, and Elizabeth Virginia. Robert was born in Osceola September 15, 1841, educated at Virginia Military Institute; entered the Confederate army as lieutenant "Danville Grays," promoted captain; adjutant 18th Virginia; wounded in first and second battles of Manassas, at Gaines's Mill and at Gettysburg, where he was taken prisoner, sent to Johnson's Island and paroled March, 1865; married June 18, 1868, Emma Paxton of Rockbridge County, Virginia; moved to St. Louis January, 1869, and is largely interested in street railways. With him in business is his son, Richard, a graduate of St. Louis University.

Frances McCulloch, sister of William H. McCulloch and ten years his senior, married in 1799 Benjamin Shackelford who represented Amherst County in the Virginia House of Delegates, moved to Richmond, Kentucky in 1817 where he died two years later. Mrs. Shackelford and her fourth daughter, Belinda, came to Hannibal where she died. Her oldest child, Elizabeth M., married Robert Clark, and her second child, Frances A., married Patterson Clark of Clark County, Kentucky, soldiers in the war of 1812, brothers, and first cousins to General John B. Clark, sr., of Fayette, Missouri. Her third oldest, Roderick S., born June 13, 1804, represented Macon County in the Thirteenth General Assembly of Missouri, 1844-6. Mrs. Francis A. Clark's daughter Frances married, 1860, in St. Louis Robert Cook, a retired merchant, who moved to Philadelphia. Belinda Shackelford married 1839, Dr. Jerman of Madison County, Kentucky, moved to Hannibal, then to St. Louis where he died in 1874, and she in 1879. Her brother, George H. Shackelford, a merchant of Hannibal, married Miss Hill of St. Louis and died about 1850, leaving three children, Emma, who married John Hewitt of St. Louis, David and Minnie. Benjamin Shackelford's youngest child, Richard C. Shackelford, was a merchant of St. Louis. Of his two daughters, Frances, the older, married April 22, 1875, Charles W. Knapp, of the St. Louis Republic, and Genevieve married Henry H. Kellar, a Confederate soldier, of Lexington, Kentucky, and later of St. Louis.

Dr. William Cabell's oldest son, William, born March 13, 1730, in Goochland County, represented Amherst with his brother Joseph in the first Revolutionary Convention held in Virginia. They with Roderick McCulloch, the great grandfather, and Gabriel Penn, the great, great grandfather, of Colonel Robert McCulloch of St. Louis, and seventeen others were elected the Revolutionary Committee for Amherst County at the November Court, 1775, as "twenty-one of the most discreet, fit and able men of the county." Colonel Cabell held many responsible offices and for the last one—presidential elector—he received every vote cast in his county. His last official act was casting his vote as an elector for Washington in 1789. Colonel William Cabell married Margaret, daughter of Colonel Samuel Jordan. Their second son, William, born March 25, 1759, was a lieutenant-colonel in the Revolutionary army. He married Ann, daughter of Colonel Paul Carrington. Their second daughter, Margaret, born November 24, 1785, married Thomas Stanhope McClelland, a native of Gettysburg, Pennsylvania, a classmate at Dickenson College of Chief Justice Taney and a cousin of Dr. George McClelland of Philadelphia, the father of General George B. McClellan. Thomas S. McClelland studied law under Judge Archibald Stuart of Staunton, Virginia, whose younger brother, Alexander Stuart, was Speaker of the Fourth General Assembly of Missouri and according to Houck's History (volume 3, page 10), was Judge of the Northern Circuit, composed of the counties of St. Charles, St. Louis, Franklin, Jefferson and Washington, in 1826. He came to St. Louis in 1808. The record of the second session of the Circuit Court of Lincoln County held August 2, 1819, states that "Peyton R. Hayden produced a license from Honorable Alexander Stuart, one of the Judges of the Superior Court, authorizing him to practice law in the several courts of the Territory; he also presented a deputation from John S. Brickey, circuit attorney for the Northwestern Circuit, author-

izing him to officiate as deputy, whereupon he took the oath."
Judge Stuart was born May 11, 1770, and died while on a visit to Staunton, Virginia, December 9, 1832. His oldest son, Archibald, a major in the war of 1812, was the father of James Ewell Brown Stuart, the famous Confederate general, commanding the cavalry of Lee's army, who was wounded in battle at Yellow Tavern near Richmond May 11, 1864, and died the following day. Thomas S. McClelland's twelfth child, James Bruce McClelland, married Nannie L., daughter of Dr. William Leftwich Otey. Their third son, Edmund L. McClelland, married July 11, 1882, Eleanor Barclay, daughter of Judge D. Robert Barclay, of St. Louis, and granddaughter of Elihu H. Shepard.

Colonel William Cabell's third daughter, Anne Carrington, born September 20, 1787, married John James Flournoy, a soldier in the war of 1812. Their oldest daughter married Henry Wood, a successful lawyer. Their second son, William Walter Wood, entered the Confederate army as lieutenant, and rose to the rank of colonel in Pickett's Division; member of the Virginia legislature in 1870; moved to St. Louis in 1874 and practiced law with Colonel Edward Carrington Cabell. He died unmarried.

Colonel William Cabell's fifth daughter, Clementina, born February 26, 1794, married Jesse Irvine. Their fourth daughter, Sarah Cabell, married Judge Asa D. Dickinson of Prince Edward County, "one of the most deservedly popular men in Virginia," author of the famous "Address of the Virginia Assembly to the Virginia Soldiers." Their second son, Clement Cabell Dickinson, came to Clinton in 1872, elected prosecuting attorney of Henry County, to the General Assembly as representative one term, senator one term and to Congress to succeed David DeArmond in the Sixth District.

Colonel William Cabell's third son, Landon, born February 21, 1765, "was a man both of brilliant genius and high cultivation, particularly excelling in the art of conversation. He was offered a place in the cabinet by President Madison, to whom he was allied by marriage, but he declined this, as he did many offices of distinction in his State. "He married

Judith Scott Rose, daughter of Colonel Hugh Rose. Their youngest child, Elizabeth Cabell, married December 23, 1819, William Radford Preston and went to Missouri. Their second daughter, Paulina, married Dr. William Talley, a prominent physician of Wentzville, St. Charles County, a native of Virginia. Their third daughter married Joseph A. Talley, also of Wentzville, a brother of Dr. William Talley.

Colonel William Cabell's second daughter, Margaret Jordan, born 1769 or 1770, married Robert Rives. Henry County, Missouri, was first named Rives, in honor of their second son, William Cabell Rives. Their eleventh child, Alexander, a man of distinguished ability, married Isabella Bachem Wydown. Their ninth child, Adela Bertha Rives, married December 8, 1869, Thomas Keith Skinker of St. Louis, a native of that city but of Virginia parentage, a prominent lawyer and for many years a reporter of the Supreme Court of the State.

Dr. William Cabell's second son, Colonel Joseph Cabell, September 19, 1732, married at the age of twenty Mary, daughter of Dr. Arthur Hopkins. Their oldest son, Joseph, born January 6, 1762, was a member of his father's regiment at Yorktown, married Pocahontas Rebecca, daughter of Colonel Robert Bolling, a descendant of the Indian king, Powhatan. Their second daughter, Sarah Bolling Cabell, born May 29, 1786, married Elisha Meredith. Their second daughter, Mary Ann, born Fayette County, Kentucky, October 27, 1821, married Shelby Wayne Chadwick. Their third son, Robert Alvin Chadwick, born Greensboro, Alabama, 1844, a Confederate soldier, married 1868 Nannie Wright and lives in St. Louis.

Sarah Bolling Meredith's brother, Edward Blair Cabell, born May 29, 1791, married, 1812, Harriet Forbes Monroe, a niece of President Monroe, and removed to Chariton County, Missouri, in 1818. He had the respect and confidence of the Indians and he was frequently the arbiter of their disputes concerning property. He once said that without any legal authority he had on many occasions given judgment in from fifteen to twenty cases in one day in the midst of large bodies of Indians, whose deportment was always grave and decorous, when there was not another white man nearer than four miles. He visited his native county in 1842, and concerning him Major Charles Yancey wrote, February 18, to President Tyler: "Permit me to introduce to notice Mr. Edward B. Cabell, of Missouri, who, I presume, is now in the city of Washington, having left here a few days since. Mr. Cabell seeks the office of Register of the Land Office, which is contemplated to be established in what is called the Platte country in Missouri. I think I can say he is a man of integrity, which is hazarding much to say in these days of great moral depravity. You know the Cabell family, and, I presume the Bolling; his mother was sister to Powhatan and Senacus, and he married a daughter of Joseph J. Monroe. You now have his heraldry; and I rate people very much by their stock, as I do the blooded horse. He is honest, moral, sober, and of business habits. If you cannot do better, take him." He died at Keytesville August 29, 1850, and his wife March 22, 1857. Their oldest child, Charles Joseph Cabell, married Susan Allin, and died October 10, 1882, and was buried at Brunswick. His widow was living in 1895. Their oldest child, Mary Allin Cabell, married John S. Kuykendall and lived in Brunswick. Their second child, Pocahontas Cabell, married Charles Hammond, a lawyer of Brunswick, who with Wesley Halliburton represented the Sixth Senatorial District in the Constitutional Convention of 1875, and who represented Chariton County in the Twenty-Ninth General Assembly. Their fourth child, Robert Boyd Cabell, was a physician in Carroll County. Their sixth child, William Allin Cabell, was a farmer living near Glasgow.

Edward Blair Cabell's second child, Emily Monroe Cabell, married in Chariton County, 1835, Peter T. Abell. Their fifth child, Addison Slye Abell, born April 21, 1844, died in the Confederate army. Edward Blair Cabell's third child, Jane Browder Cabell, married Thomas Parke Wilkinson of Keytesville and their only child, John Cabell Wilkinson, born December 13, 1846, served in the Confederate army; after the war went into business in St. Louis and married,

1877, Margaret Ewing, daughter of Judge Ephraim Barnett Ewing who was brought from Kentucky to Missouri when only a few months old, whose father, the Rev. Finis Ewing, was one of the founders of the Cumberland Presbyterian Church, and whose mother, Margaret Davidson, was the daughter of General William Lee Davidson, killed at the battle of Cowan's Ford, North Carolina, 1781, after rendering distinguished service in the Revolution, and for whom a county in North Carolina and one in Tennessee were named. Edward Blair Cabell's fifth child, Pocahontas Rebecca Cabell, married Adamantine Johnson, a merchant of Brunswick, and his sixth child, Robert Hervey Cabell, was a practicing physician of Grundy County, whose second wife bore him three daughters and two sons and his third wife four daughters and one son.

Colonel Joseph Cabell's second daughter, Mary Hopkins Cabell, born February 22, 1769, married, 1785, John Breckinridge. Their sixth child, John, brother of the great Presbyterian preacher, Robert Jefferson Breckinridge, was himself an eloquent preacher and able writer. He married, 1823, Margaret, daughter of the Rev. Samuel Miller, professor of ecclesiastical history in Princeton Theological Seminary. Their son, Samuel Miller Breckinridge, born in Baltimore November 3, 1828, began the practice of law in St. Louis. With Frank Blair, B. Gratz Brown, J. Richard Barrett, Benjamin Farrar and eight others, he represented St. Louis in the Eighteenth General Assembly. This, with the exception of the Eighth General Assembly, was, perhaps, the ablest legislature that ever met in the State. In the Senate there were, in the order of their districts, R. H. Parks, Peter Carr, Robert Wilson, Robert M. Stewart, Benjamin J. Brown, John D. Stevenson, Solomon G. Kitchen, James Lindsay, Miles Vernon, Charles Sims, James S. Rains, John Gullet, Henry T. Blow, Daniel M. Frost and Walter B. Morris. In the House, besides the St. Louis delegation, there were James Sidney Rollins and Odon Guitar from Boone, Charles H. Hardin from Callaway, William Heryford from Chariton, Alexander Willam Doniphan from Clay, John T. Hughes from

Clinton, Robert C. Harrison and W. C. Ewing from Cooper, J. W. Kelley from Holt, Edward Cresap McCarty and John W. Reid from Jackson, Marton E. Green from Lewis, James H. Britton and Dr. Marcus H. McFarland from Lincoln, Abner L. Gilstrap from Macon, J. M. Bean and Samuel Drake from Monroe, William Moseley from New Madrid, John C. Layton from Perry, George Rappeen Smith from Pettis, Thomas Jefferson Clark Fagg and Edward C. Murray from Pike, D. D. Burnes, John Doniphan and George P. Dorris from Platte, Robert E. Acock from Polk, William Newland, the Speaker, from Ralls, Dabney C. Garth from Randolph, Charles F. Fant and Josiah Pratt from St. Charles, Lewis Vital Bogy from St. Genevieve, Joshua Chilton from Shannon, John McAfee from Shelby and James H. McBride from Texas. Two of these had distinguished themselves in the war with Mexico; four had a distinguished career as Confederate and two as Federal generals; three afterwards became governors, four United States senators, five members of the Lower House of Congress and two candidates for vice-president on the Democratic ticket. In ability and character Judge Breckinridge was the peer of any. He served one term as judge of the circuit court, beginning in 1859. "He was a close friend of President Lincoln and a strong Republican. He was an elder in the Presbyterian Church, and a leading member of its General Assemblies. His death, on the floor of the General Presbyterian Assembly, at Detroit, on May 28, 1891, of apoplexy, was one of the tragic scenes ever beheld. In the debate he had just made a speech against the Rev. Dr. Briggs; the excitement in the body was intense; he said: 'Now, gentlemen, I feel that I have discharged my duty, and wish to be excused from further speaking.' Then reaching for a glass of water, he threw up his hands and fell dead." He married, 1850, his cousin, Virginia Harrison Castleman. Their oldest child, Margaret Miller Breckinridge, married William S. Long; their second, Virginia Castleman Breckinridge, married, 1892, Onward Bates, son of Judge Barton Bates; their fourth, John Breckinridge, educated at West Point, resigned from the army and lived at Huntsville, Randolph County.

John Breckinridge who married Mary Hopkins Cabell, mentioned in the preceding paragraph, was a member of the Virginia House of Delegates and author of the celebrated Kentucky Resolutions of 1798-9; moved to Kentucky and elected in 1801 to the United States Senate; was Attorney General in the cabinet of President Jefferson from December 23, 1805, to his death December 14, 1806. His oldest son, Joseph Cabell, was the father of Vice President John Cabell Breckinridge. His eighth child, William Lewis Breckinridge, born July 22, 1803, was for forty-five years a zealous minister of the Presbyterian Church. His last charge was in Cass County, Missouri, where he died. He married, 1823 or 1824, Frances C., daughter of Judge Prevost of Louisiana son of Mrs. Aaron Burr, by her first husband, General Augustin Prevost, a British officer who died in the West Indies. Their fifth child, William Lewis Breckinridge, married Anna P. Clark of Kentucky and their oldest son, Charles Clark Breckinridge, lived in St. Louis.

Ann, third daughter of Colonel Joseph Cabell, born February 15, 1771, married, 1788, Robert Carter Harrison, first cousin to President William Henry Harrison and nephew to Benjamin Harrison, the signer of the Declaration of Independence. They went to Fayette County, Kentucky and died there July and September, respectively, 1840. Their second daughter, Mary Hopkins Harrison, married, 1812, Samuel Q. Richardson, a colonel in the war of 1812. Their second daughter, Sarah Bainbridge Richardson, married, 1844, at Palmyra, the Rev. John Leighton, one of the pioneer Presbyterian ministers of Missouri, pastor in Palmyra thirteen years and Hannibal seventeen years; he died in St. Louis August 16, 1885. Of their two children the older, Mary Harrison Leighton, married, 1866, George Howell Shields, one of Missouri's foremost lawyers, captain in the Missouri Federal militia, 1863-4, (his brother, Dr. D. Howell Shields, was a member of my company, Confederate army, 1861;) and the younger, Josephine Walker Leighton, married, 1866, John

B. Shepherd, a captain of Ohio volunteers, then living in Hannibal.

Mary Hopkins Breckinridge Richardson, the third daughter of Colonel Samuel Q. Richardson, married, 1845, Colonel Richard Fell Richmond of Hannibal. "He was born in Kentucky; studied law under Governor Owsley; was at one time junior partner in the law firm of which John J. Crittenden was the head. He moved to Hannibal, Missouri early in the history of the State, rose to the head of the northeast Missouri Bar; was Democratic nominee for Congress in 1858, (2) but was defeated by Colonel Thomas L. Anderson, and died soon after from fever induced by the hardship of the campaign, leaving two sons: Bainbridge and William Samuel; the latter studied law under Judge Samuel M. Breckinridge and died a young lawyer of great promise."

Ann Cabell Harrison, fifth child of Robert Carter Harrison and Ann Cabell, born August 28, 1798, married, 1818, Samuel Mansfield Brown, a native of Baltimore, "a lawyer of distinction, decision and courage, at the Lexington, Kentucky, Bar;" was blown up in the Ohio River steamboat, the Lucy Walker, near New Albany, Indiana, October 22, 1844. Their first three children, two daughters and a son, died under nine years of age. Their fourth child, George Mason Brown, born September 21, 1824, was second lieutenant in Captain Cassius M. Clay's company of Humphrey Marshall's regi-

---

(2) This date is wrong. Colonel Richmond was nominated for Congress in 1856. The campaign that followed was one of the most memorable ever fought in Missouri. Anderson stood in the front rank of Missouri's eloquent speakers and Richmond was one of the most forceful. Anderson was elected. He had been a Whig, but he then belonged to the American or Know-Nothing party. The storm that burst in 1861 was then gathering and both parties in the old Second Congressional District were overwhelmingly Southern in sentiment. Anderson's record in Congress was guided by this sentiment and he had the full confidence of the Southern Democratic members. For this reason the Democratic party of the Second District made no nomination in 1858, but endorsed that of Anderson. John Brooks Henderson, then an ultra Southern Democrat, ran as an independent Democrat but was defeated. The Bell and Everett party, in 1860, nominated James Sidney Rollins and the Democrats nominated Henderson. The contest was one of giants; Rollins was elected. Lincoln County was then in the Second District. My father was a political and personal friend of Colonel Anderson, but refused to follow him into the Know-Nothing party because it proscribed his religion and he cast his first Democratic vote for Richmond, but voted again for Anderson in 1858.

ment in the Mexican war, greatly distinguished himself at Buena Vista; married August 20, 1849, Mrs. Sarah A. Hicklin of Bourbon County, Kentucky, moved to Saline County, Missouri, 1850; captain in the Missouri State Guard, killed in the second battle of Boonville, September 13, 1861. Their fifth child, William Breckinridge Brown, born February 5, 1828, went to California in the spring of 1846 with Colonel William H. Russell, where he joined the battalion of Colonel John Charles Fremont; was sent back as commander of escort, with Colonel Russell who was bearer of dispatches in 1847; was summoned as a witness in the trial of Colonel Fremont, returned by land to California in 1849, remained till 1852; came back to Saline County where he married, February 14, 1853, Lenora V. Thompson. "He was an extraordinary man." Was colonel of a Missouri Confederate regiment and was killed in battle at Boonville September 13, 1861. Their sixth child, Samuel Mansfield Brown, born April 30, 1830, a soldier in Captain Robertson's company, Kentucky volunteers, Mexican war, went to California and was buried under an avalanche. Their seventh child, Ann Mary Cabell Brown, died aged nineteen; then a daughter and two sons died in infancy. It is thus seen that Colonel Brown and Captain Brown, killed at Boonville, were the last of the family. Captain Brown left six children: Jane S., Robert Harrison, Alexander, Ann Mary Cabell, Perry Beard and Carter Henry, born between the years 1850 and 1857. Colonel Brown left three children: George Washington, Robert Harrison and Lucy Cabell, born 1853, 1855 and 1857.

The author of the Cabell genealogy does not mention the fact that Samuel M. Brown was stabbed almost to death by Cassius Marcellus Clay, ambassador to Russia from 1862 to 1869. Collins in his History of Kentucky mentions it and gives the date as August 1, 1843. Clay in his Memoirs refers to it and says that he saw Brown only once after the affair; that Brown bowed politely without speaking and that he did the same. The difficulty occured at a political meeting held in the woods at Russell's Cave six miles northeast of Lexington and was caused by Brown questioning a statement made by Clay. Both men were armed with pistols but Clay always had a bowie knife beneath his coat collar behind. He immediately drew the knife, sprang upon Brown and slashed him horribly. It was a month or more before there appeared any chance for Brown's recovery. Not long after that a man named Turner interrupted Clay's speech by saying, "Now, Cash, you know that's a lie." Quick as a flash Clay was on him knife in hand, cutting him so severely that he never recovered. During the Mexican war, in which he was a captain, Clay kept his sword ground as sharp as a razor. One day he had a quarrel with Edward Marshall, brother of Thomas F. Marshall, the great orator. Clay seized his sword and bore down upon Marshall who, being unarmed, ran and jumped in a river. Sometime after they became reconciled, Clay mentioned having made Marshall run. "You did," replied Marshall, "but you didn't make me cry out, 'Help me, Cassius, or I sink.'" When Price's army was encamped on Cowskin Prairie, July, 1861, a mass meeting was held one evening to rejoice over some good news from the Confederate army in Virginia. Several officers made speeches, among them Colonel Bill Brown, as he was commonly called. He was a ready and forceful speaker. After a clear presentation of the issues involved, he told with great gusto of his battles with the Kansas abolitionists and said that his intense hatred of abolitionists began when, at the age of fifteen, he had seen the great Kentucky abolitionist, Cassius M. Clay, cut his father to pieces. I thought for many years that the words "cut my father to pieces" had no other meaning than that his father had been killed by Clay. There was another Colonel Brown, Division Inspector in Price's army—Benjamin J. Brown of Ray County, prominent in politics, then in his second term as State senator. He was killed at the battle of Wilson's Creek, while acting as aide to General Slack.

One of the brothers of the wife of Judge Samuel M. Breckinridge, Lewis Castleman, educated at Washington

College, Pennsylvania, a Confederate soldier (as were two other brothers and a brother-in-law), "a farmer and a man of affairs" lived near Bunceton, Cooper County. Another brother, George Alfred Castleman, the youngset of fourteen children, was a member of the Thirty-third General Assembly from St. Louis, and of the State Senate in the Thirty-fourth and Thirty-fifth General Assemblies; Democratic candidate for Congress, 1888, defeated by Nathan Frank, appointed by Governor Francis judge of the criminal court, 1892.

Robert Carter Harrison's youngest child, Pocahontas Rebecca Peyton Harrison, born August, 1809, married Dr. Samuel Sloane of Jacksonville, Illinois, moved to Palmyra, where they both died before 1850. Their oldest daughter, Mary Sloane, married three times and "traveled all over the world."

Dr. William Cabell's son, Colonel John Cabell, married Pauline Jordan. Their seventh son, Samuel Jordan Cabell, born 1777, married Susanna Ewing. Their second daughter, Jenneta Cabell, born 1803, married James Simpson of Marion County, Kentucky. Their youngest son, George Simpson, married, 1861, Nannie B. Gordon; their oldest daughter, Elizabeth, married Dr. Nathaniel M. Baskett of Moberly, member of the Missouri Senate in the Thirty-seventh and Thirty-eighth General Assemblies. Samuel Jordan Cabell's daughter Elizabeth married, December 8, 1824, William McElroy of Marion County, Kentucky; their youngest daughter, Mary, married Wilson Vaughan of Shelbyville, Missouri. Mrs. Vaughan had only two brothers, Edwin and Samuel McElroy, both killed in the Confederate army.

Dr. William Cabell's youngest son, Colonel Nicholas Cabell, married, 1772, Hannah Carrington. Their oldest child, William Cabell who inserted the letter H in his name to distinguish it from others was a member of the Assembly of 1798 and voted for the celebrated resolutions of that Assembly, was elector in the first and second elections of Thomas Jefferson, and his brother, Joseph Carrington Cabell, an elector in the first election of James Monroe. William

H. Cabell was governor of Virginia, 1803 to 1808, succeeding John Page and succeeded by John Tyler. His second wife, Agnes Sarah Bell Gamble, married March 11, 1805, was sister to the second wife of William Wirt, Attorney General of the United States, 1817 to 1829, who received in 1832 the electoral vote of Vermont for President. Their son Edward Carrington Cabell, born February 5, 1816, in the old Gamble mansion, Richmond, was elected to Congress from Florida as a Whig in 1844; his seat given to W. H. Brockenborough, Democrat, January 28, 1846, on a contest, but at the three succeeding elections was elected by large majorities, although the State was Democratic. He left the Whig party on account of the nomination of General Scott whom he strongly opposed. He married in St. Louis, November 5, 1850, Anna Maria Wilcox, a native of Columbia, Missouri. Her father Dr. Daniel Pinchbeck Wilcox, represented Boone County in the Sixth General Assembly, dying at Jefferson City during his term of office in 1831. Her mother, Elizabeth, daughter of Dr. James W. Moss, married, 1833, General William H. Ashley, a native of Powhatan County, Virginia, who came to Missouri in 1808, (3) settling in Cape Girardeau County where he married a daughter of Ezekiel Able who was probably the brother of Wilson Able, second lieutenant in the company of Captain Peter Craig who was killed in battle with Black Hawk at the Sink Hole near Fort Howard, Lincoln County, May 24, 1815.

Wilson Able was the father of Captain Barton and Daniel Able, of St. Louis. Ashley's second wife was Elizabeth Christy. He served in the war of 1812, was general of militia in 1822; the first lieutenant-governor of the State; ran for governor at the August election, 1824, but defeated by Frederick Bates; elected to Congress to succeed Spencer Pettis who fought a duel with Major Thomas Biddle of the

---

(3) Houck's History of Missouri says 1805, but Lanman's Annals of the Civil Government says 1808, and this date is given in a letter to the Missouri Republican, dated August 1, 1877, by John F. Darby, long a political and personal friend of General Ashley, and who represented the St. Louis District in the Thirty-second Congress. Mr. Darby was, perhaps, better informed about prominent Missourians than any other man of his time.

United States army, August, 1831, in which both were mortally wounded. Ashley was twice re-elected; he died in St. Louis (4) March 26, 1838. In February, 1853, his widow married John Jordan Crittenden, then Attorney General of the United States, and three times before that and once since a Senator from Kentucky. He died in Louisville, 1863, and his widow in St. Louis, 1873.

Through the efforts of Mr. Cabell the first railroad of Florida was built. In January, 1860, he opened a law office in St. Louis. After the fall of Fort Sumpter, Governor Jackson commissioned him to confer with President Davis at Montgomery. Reporting to Governor Jackson, he was despatched to Richmond with full power to act for Missouri. On his way from Jefferson City he reached St. Louis the day Camp Jackson was captured. His negotiation with the administration was a failure. Mr. Davis was an extreme strict constructionist and no advantage of a policy differing from his conviction could influence him. He demanded what Missouri, in the grasp of military power, could not give. Undismayed, Mr. Cabell made a personal appeal to every member of the Confederate Congress, the result that an act was passed August 20, 1861, relating to Missouri and providing that when the "Constitution for the Provisional Government of the Confederate States shall be adopted and ratified by the properly and legally constituted authorities of said State, and the governor of said State shall transmit to the President of the Confederate States an authentic copy of the proceedings, touching said adoption and ratification by said State of said Provisional Constitution, upon receipt thereof the President, by proclamation, shall announce the fact." (5). The Missouri Legislature met at Neosho, a quorum of both houses being present, and on October 31, 1861, passed an act "declaring the political ties heretofore existing between the State of Missouri and the United States of America dissolved," and an act "ratifying the Constitution of the Provisional Government of the Confederate States of

(4) Houck's History; Lanman and Darby both say "near Boonville."
(5) Messages and Papers of the Confederacy, volume 1, page 144.

America. "These acts were attested by John T. Crisp, secretary of the Senate and Thomas M. Murray, clerk of the House, forwarded by Governor Jackson, November 5, received and transmitted to Congress by President Davis November 25. (6) Had Mr. Cabell been as successful with the administration as he was with Congress, Price's army would have been properly supported and, in the opinion of Champ Clark, "he would have rescued Missouri from the Unionists." (7)

Mr. Cabell was appointed aid to Governor Letcher with the rank of lieutenant colonel and participated in the battles around Richmond. Near the close of 1862 he was transferred to the West and served on the staffs of Generals Price and Kirby Smith to the end of the war. He returned to St. Louis November, 1873. He represented the Thirty-second District in the Thirtieth and Thirty-first General Assemblies. At the time of his death in 1896 he was the oldest living Cabell and one of the very few surviving great grandchildren of Dr. Cabell, the immigrant. Mrs. Cabell died November 21, 1873. They have children and grandchildren living in St. Louis.

JOSEPH A. MUDD,
HYATTSVILLE, Md.

(6) Messages and Papers of the Confederacy, volume 1, page 144; Confederate Military History, volume 9, part 1, page 69.
(7) Speech in Congress on the acceptance of the statues of Benton and Blair.

BOOKS OF EARLY TRAVELS IN MISSOURI.
LONG—JAMES.

"Account of an Expedition from Pittsburg to the Rocky Mountains, performed in the years 1819 and '20, by order of Hon. J. C. Calhoun, Sec'y of War: under the command of Major Stephen H. Long. From the notes of Major Long, Mr. T. Say, and other gentlemen of the exploring party. Compiled by Edwin James, Botanist and geologist for the expedition. In two vols., with an atlas.
Philadelphia: H. C. Carey and I. Lea, Chestnut St., 1823.

The title page tells sufficiently the origin of the journey whose details are given in this work. On the first of June 1819 the boat containing the party had reached the Mississippi river opposite the Missouri shore, and having a heavy current to contend with, several of the passengers went ashore and walked some miles, passing several "Shawnee" Indian encampments. These Indians had very little acquaintance with the English language, and appeared reluctant to use the few words they knew. "The squaws wore great numbers of trinkets, such as silver arm bands and large ear rings. Some of the boys had pieces of lead tied in various parts of the hair. They were encamped near the Mississippi, for the purpose of hunting on the islands. Their village is on Apple creek, ten miles from Cape Girardeau." "On the 3d of June we passed that insular rock in the middle of the Mississippi, called the Grand Tower. It is about one hundred and fifty feet high, and two hundred and fifty in height." "The Grand Tower, from its form and situation, strongly suggests a work of art. It is not impossible that a bridge may be constructed here, for which this rock shall serve as a pier. The shores on both sides are substantial and permanent rocks, which undoubtedly extend across, forming the bed of the river."

On the 5th they were ascending the river by the aid of sails, when the boat struck a snag and sprung a leak, on account of which they had to lay by till the next day, and raise the stern of the boat to make repairs. On the beach opposite where they were was a large flock of pelicans, which remained in sight several hours. The prediction was made that the American Bottom would become one of the most populous places of the country. The Missouri side of the river is quite different, the highlands approaching the river, presenting abrupt declivities, prominent points and perpendicular precipices from one to two hundred feet high. In these precipices the three shot towers at Herculaneum were built. This place depended on the lead mines for its support, the lead region commencing some thirty or forty miles southwest. Another stop had to be made to allow the engineer to clean the mud out of the boilers, and some of the party returned along shore "to the Merameg, a beautiful river, whose limpid and transparent waters present a striking contrast to the yellow and turbid Mississippi."

They found many objects of interest, among them being various flowers, and a rat which was made the type specimen of the Florida rat. On the 8th they arrived at St. Louis, and were received by a salute from a six pounder stationed on the bank of the river.

"Saint Louis, formerly called Pain Court, was founded by Pierre LaClede and his associates in 1764, eighty-four years after the establishment of Fort Crevecœur, on the Illinois river. Until a recent period, it was occupied almost exclusively by people of French extraction, who maintained a lucrative traffic with the Indians. The history, and present conditions of this important town, are too well known to be dwelt upon in this place. Its population has been rapidly augmented within a few years, by the immigration of numerous families, and its wealth and business extended by the accession of enterprising merchants and mechanics from the Eastern states. As the town advances in importance and magnitude, the manners and customs of the people of the United States are taking the place of those of the French and Spaniards, whose numbers are proportionally diminishing."

The impressions of a human foot in the limestone rock underlying St. Louis were seen, and believed to belong to a time later than the formation of the subcarboniferous rock in which they were found. (1) On the prairies west of St. Louis there were some fine farms. Mr. John Bradbury, well known as a botanist and author of a book describing his travels in the interior of America, was then preparing to erect a home upon one of them. (2) Indian tumuli were numerous, twenty-seven being within a short distance to the northward, and these were carefully measured and described. Various Indian graves were opened, and a grave yard on the Meramec said to be of a race of pigmies was visited, and found to be of persons of ordinary stature.

June 21st the party started on the trip to ascend the Missouri, and were glad to find that the engine had power enough to propel the boat against the current, without the aid of the cordelle. They were surprised to see a flock of blackheaded terns, a bird whose range along the Atlantic is confined to the immediate neighborhood of the sea. Finding that the boiler would have to be cleaned of mud daily, and the method of taking off the end to admit a man to clean it required much delay, a tube was adjusted to the boiler so that the mud could be blown out without stopping.

St. Charles was said to have had one hundred houses in 1804, but the Indian trade having failed, the town had declined for several years. However, within two or three years, the town had begun to prosper again, and substantial brick buildings were replacing the frame ones. The record the author gives is that of a town of about one hundred houses, "two brick kilns, a tan yard, and several stores."

At this place arrangements were made by Say and others to ascend the Missouri by land with horse and pack sad-

---

(1) Various specimens of human footprints in solid stone have been noticed in the scientific publications. The popular supposition has been that they were actual impressions of human feet. The one mentioned above has been noticed by Dr. Owen and by Schoolcraft in the Americal Journal of Arts and Science. Dr. Owen's opinion that they were carved by the aborigines was confirmed in his opinion by specimens in rocks of older formation, from Moccasin-track Prairie, in Missouri, where the slabs had many carvings of human feet, and of other animals, and which clearly showed tool marks.

(2) John Bradbury arrived in St. Louis on the last day of 1809, and his "Travels in the Interior of America" covered the years 1809, 1810, and 1811. In December of 1811 he was near New Madrid, and in his book described the earthquake of that year.

dle, keeping near the steamer, so that they could rejoin it whenever they desired, as this arrangement allowed them better opportunities for investigating the natural history of the country. This party traveled over a somewhat hilly country, and suffered much for water to drink. Finally their horse got away from them, and they had to carry their baggage. Being unaccustomed to marching several of them became lame, so that after nine days they were glad to rejoin the boat at Loutre Island. Near this place were several forts, for protection from the Indians, "chiefly the Kickapoos and Sankees who were most feared in this quarter."

Nearly opposite the mouth of the Osage was the village of Cote Sans Dessein, containing about thirty families, mostly French. "At the time of the late war, the inhabitants of this settlement relying on mutual protection, did not retire, but erected two stockades and block houses for their defense; the Sauks, assisted by some Foxes and Ioways, having by a feigned attack and retreat, induced the greater part of the men to pursue them, gained their rear by means of an ambuscade, and entering the village, raised their war cry at the door of the cabins. The women and children fled in consternation to the block houses. At this juncture, a young man was seen, who would not abandon his decrepid mother, even though she entreated him to fly and save his own life, leaving her, who could at best expect to live but a few days, to the mercy of the savages. The youth, instead of listening to her request, raised her upon his shoulders, and ran towards the stockade closely pursued by the Indians. They fired several times upon him, and he must have been cut off had not a sally been made in his favor." After killing the villagers who fell into their hands the Indians kept up the attack on the stockade all the day, but finally withdrew without capturing it.

"The river of the Osages, so called from the well known tribe of Indians inhabiting its banks, enters the Missouri one hundred and thirty-three miles above the confluence of the latter river with the Mississippi. Its sources are in the

Ozark mountains, opposite those of White river of the Mississippi, and of the Neosho, a tributary of the Arkansas. Flowing along the base of the north-western slope of a mountain range, it receives from the east several rapid and beautiful rivers, of which the largest is the Yungar (so named, in some Indian language, from the great number of springs tributary to it,) entering the Osage one hundred and forty miles from the Missouri. (3)

Within a few miles of this island Captain Callaway with a company of mounted rangers were attacked by Indians, and he was killed. Several families lived on the island, which was in a high state of cultivation.

"The first dwellings constructed by the white settlers, are nearly similar in every part of the United States. Superior wealth and industry are indicated by the number and magnitude of corn-cribs, smoke houses, and similar appurtenances; but on the Missouri, we rarely meet with anything occupying the place of the barn of the northern states. The dwellings of people who have emigrated from Virginia, or any of the southern states, have usually the form of double cabins, or two distinct houses, each containing a single room, and connected to each other by a roof, the intermediate space, which is often equal in area to one of the cabins, being left open at the sides, and having the naked earth for a floor, affords a cool, and airy retreat, where the family will usually be found in the heat of the day. The roof is composed of from three to five logs, laid longitudinally, and extending from end to end of the building; on these are laid the shingles, four or five feet in length; over these are three or four heavy logs, called weigh poles, secured at their ends by withes, and by their weight supplying the place of nails."

"The black walnut attains, in Missouri bottoms, its greatest magnitude. Of one, which grew near Loutre Island, there had been made two hundred fence-rails, eleven feet in

---

(3) The present Niangua river; another Indian name for it was Nehemgar, a stream supplied by many springs. The latter is the name of a literary club in Sedalia that for the past eighteen years has been one of the most successful in the State.

length, and from four to six inches in thickness. A cotton tree in the same neighborhood produced thirty thousand shingles, as we were informed by a credible witness.

In point of magnitude, the Osage ranks nearly with the Cumberland of Tennessee. It has been represented as navigable for six hundred miles, but as its current is known to be rapid, flowing over great numbers of shoals and sand bars this must be considered an exaggeration. In the lower part of its course it traverses broad and fertile bottom lands, covered with heavy forests of sycamore and cotton trees. We may expect the country along the banks of this river will soon become the seat of a numerous population, as it possesses a fertile soil and a mild climate, advantages more than sufficient to compensate for the difficulty of access, and other inconveniences of situation."

"Almost every settler, who has established himself on the Missouri, is confidently expecting that his farm is, in a few years to become the seat of wealth and business, and the mart for an extensive district."

On the 13th they arrived at Franklin. "This town, at present increasing more rapidly than any other on the Missouri, had been commenced but two years and a half before the time of our journey. It then contained one hundred and twenty log houses of one story, several frame dwellings of two stories, and two of brick, thirteen shops for the sale of merchandise, four taverns, two smiths' shops, two large steam mills, two billiard rooms, a court house, a log prison of two stories, a post office, and a printing press issuing a weekly paper. At this time bricks were sold at ten dollars per thousand, corn at twenty-five cents per bushel, wheat one dollar, bacon at twelve and a half cents per pound, uncleared lands at from two to ten or fifteen dollars per acre. The price of labor was seventy-five cents per day." There were then more than 800 families above Cote Sans Dessein. He thought it probable that at some future time the bed of the river would occupy the then site of the town.

Boonville, on the opposite side of the river had eight houses, and was destined to rival if not surpass its neighbor.

Salt was manufactured at Boon's Lick, four miles away.

"A Mr. Munroe of Franklin related to the party that in 1816 he found on a branch of the Lamine, (4) the relics of the encampment of a large party of men, whether of whites or of Indians he did not know. Seeing a large mound near by which he believed to be a cache for the spoils of the party, he opened it and found the body of a white officer, apparently a man of rank, which had been interred with extraordinary care. The body was placed in a sitting posture, upon an Indian rush mat, with its back resting against some logs, placed around it in the manner of a log house, enclosing a space of about three by five feet, and about four feet high, covered at top with a mat similar to that beneath. The clothing was still in sufficient preservation to enable him to distinguish a red coat trimmed with gold lace, golden epaulets, a spotted buff waistcoat, furnished also with gold lace, and pantaloons of white nankeen. On the head was a round beaver hat, and a bamboo walking stick, with the initials J. M. C., engraved upon a golden head, reclined against the arm, but was somewhat decayed where it came in contact with the muscular part of the leg. On raising the hat, it was found that the deceased had been hastily scalped. To what nation he belonged, Mr. Munroe could not determine. He observed, however, that the button taken from the shoulder, had the word Philadelphia moulded upon it. The cane still remains in the possession of the narrator, but the button was taken by another of the party."

It was reported that in 1815 a fight had taken place between some Spanish dragoons and Pawnee Indians on one side and Sauks and Foxes on the other, and that a Spanish officer pursued an Indian boy, who shot and killed him.

Dr. Baldwin, the botanist of the expedition became sick, and was left at Franklin, where he died a few weeks later.

After six days stay they resumed their journey, and on the fourth day arrived at "Charaton," a flourishing town,

---

(4) Tradition says that this was on the farm of Mr. Warren, on Flat Creek, three miles south of Sedalia.

commenced in 1817, having fifty houses and five hundred inhabitants.

"The Sauks, Foxes and Iowas, hunt in the plains towards the sources of Grand River, where elk, and deer are still numerous, and the latter dispose of their peltries to the traders on the Missouri."

On the first of August they arrived at Fort Osage, 105 miles above the mouth of Grand river, and there they found a party which had come overland from Franklin. They found a cabin on Fire Prairie creek, where a black wolf was chained to the door. The hunter had lived there two years, had killed seventy deer and fifty bear. In the winter of 1818 he saw a large herd of bison near Grand Pass.

Fort Osage was established in 1808 by Gov. Lewis, and was at this time the extreme frontier of the settlements.

The journey was continued to and beyond the limits of the state, but we here leave them. Various notes on the geology and paleontology would be of interest to those conversant with those subjects.

F. A. SAMPSON.

HARMONY MISSION AND METHODIST MISSIONS.

About the year 1820 a delegation of the Osage Indians, being in Washington City, expressed a wish to have Missionaries sent to them. The A. B. C. F. M. made up a party in 1821 to go among them. The party consisted of the Rev. N. B. Dodge, Superintendent; Rev. Wm. B. Montgomery, Rev. Mr. Pixley, D. H. Austin, a millwright, Dr. Belcher, a physician; S. D. Bright, a farmer; M. Colley, a blacksmith; and Ainara Jones. All of them were married, and all took their families with them. Also a Miss Ethap, a teacher. The party passed down the Ohio, and up the Mississippi in keelboats in the spring of 1821. The boats were flat bottomed and had neither sails nor oars, and poles were used in going up stream, on the Mississippi and the Osage. On August 9th they reached Papinville, being six months on the way from Pittsburgh. They found French and half-breed traders at Papinville, also Mrs. Sibley, wife of an Army Officer. July 15th, 1806, Captain Z. M. Pike, with a party, left Bellefontaine on the Missouri and passed up stream. July 27th they reached the Osage. August 19th they reached the trading post of Manuel Lisa near where Pupinville now is. The Grand Osages had a village near by, and the Little Osages on Little Osage River. There had formerly been a trading post of the Chouteaus here, but it had been abandoned, and Manuel Lisa, a Cuban succeeded. Later he moved up the Missouri.

The Missionary party selected a location a mile northwest of the Indian Village, and pitched tents until November; then they built rude cabins and covered them with boards, and laid puncheon floors, but had no glass. The hardships endured caused many to become sick, and some died. The cabins were made by Colonel Henry Renick, a Kentuckian, who had settled in Lafayette County in 1819.

Holes were bored in the walls and frames placed and covered with prairie hay for beds, and blankets laid on.

HARMONY MISSION AND METHODIST MISSIONS 103

Schools were soon established. Great patience had to be practised in teaching the Indians. The pupils were chiefly Osages, with some Delawares, Omahas and Cherokees. The mission improved a large farm, and planted an orchard. Their supplies were first brought by wagon from Jefferson City, but as steamboats reached Independence the supplies were hauled from Independence to the Mission. Along the eastern part of Cass County there is still seen parts of an old road running north and south called the Harmony Mission Road.

The Mission was kept up until 1837 when the Indians were moved west. The government paid $8,000 to the A. B. C. F. M. for the improvements on the land. The Missionaries then scattered to various places. Most of them were Congregationalists, but some moved to Henry County, and there organized a Presbyterian Church.

The Methodist Conference of 1830, at its meeting in St. Louis, resolved to establish four Missionary Stations among the Indians in the territory just West of Missouri. Two brothers, William and Thomas Johnson, were placed in charge. They were born in Nelson County, Virginia, but were then residing in Howard County, Missouri, and had just begun preaching in Missouri.

They were placed in charge of Missions among the Shawnees, Delawares, and Kansas. The Stations were located on Kansas River, not far from Kansas City.

An old trace passes north and south from Springfield, by Clinton, Kingsville near Lone Jack, Independence and Westport, known as the Shawnee trace. Along this road the Shawnee Indians passed when moved from the South. In the counties of Johnson, Cass and Jackson it is very near the Harmony Mission Road.

G. C. BROADHEAD.

CARROLL COUNTY MARRIAGE RECORD.
THE FIRST 530, 1833–1852.

Lewis Mears and Salome Eppler, Jan. 29, 1833.—By Jonathan Eppler.

James Philips and Mary Philips, Mar. 10, 1833.—By Jonathan Eppler.

George W. Mullen and Sarah Harvey Cleer, May 4, 1833.—By Jonathan Eppler.

Buckner Smart and Nancy Gentry, Mar. 14, 1833.—By Thos. Hardwick.

Hiram Bryans and Missouri Parmer, Mar. 30, 1833.—By Thos. Hardwick.

Benjamin Ashley and Alvira Stanley, Jan. 25, 1833.—By Patrick Darcy.

William Cable and Temperance Webb, Aug. 4, 1833.—By Hugh R. Smith.

Nevil Arterburn and Caroline Fair, Nov. 24, 1833.—Geo. W. Folger.

Jeremiah Maston Ellis and Peggy Jenkins, Feb. 11, 1834.—By Jonathan Eppler.

William Casner and Sarah Woolsey, Feb. 27, 1834.—By Geo. W. Folger.

James Stone and Charlotte Casner, Feb. 27, 1834.—By Geo. W. Folger.

Samuel Hill and Lucretia Parmer, Mar. 13, 1834.—By Geo. W. Folger.

C. C. Staton and Mary Adkins, Apr. 13, 1834.—By Geo. Hardwick.

William Haney and Polley Bailey, May 22, 1834.—By Henry Winfrey.

Jacob S. Rodgers and Elizabeth Talbert Scott, June 5, 1834.—By John B. Wood.

Robert C. Campbell and Polly Ann McGaugh, Feb. 26, 1834.—John B. Wood.

George Daugherty and Mary Lucas, May 29, 1834.—By Hugh R. Smith.

CARROLL COUNTY MARRIAGE RECORD, 1833-52   105

Thomas J. Hardwick and Nancy D. Farr, July 31, 1834. —By Geo. Hardwick.

William James and Ritiance Booth, Aug. 21, 1834.— By Geo. Hardwick.

Joshua Clements and Mariah Cooley, Oct. 23, 1834.— By Geo. Hardwick.

Clifton Parmer and Elvira Johnson, Oct. 26, 1834.— By Geo. W. Folger.

Henderson Work and Juley Hendrin, Oct. 2, 1834.— By Reuben McCaskrie.

Jacob Gabin and Lucinda Lisk, Nov. 20, 1834.—By Reuben McCaskrie.

Bartlett Curl and Betsey Hardwick, Feb. 12, 1835.— By Sarshal Woods.

William Ewell and Polly Blann, Feb. 27, 1835.—By Samuel Todd.

Joseph Spaulding and Melvina Parmer, Jan. 25, 1835.— By Thomas Minnis.

Callaway Bavns and Cynthia Mears, Dec. 2, 1835.— By Jonathan Eppler.

Creed Carey and Polley Beaty, Mar. 15, 1835.—By Geo. Hardwick.

Washington Grubb and Amanda Kees, Mar. 13, 1835. —By Reuben McCaskrie.

Jesse McMahan and Emily Cunningham, Apr. 12, 1835. —By Reuben McCaskrie.

Noah Woolsey and Sally Harvey, June 27, 1835.—By Thomas Booth.

Samuel Gee and Martha Tinnea, Sept. 3, 1835.—By William Martin.

Patrick H. Thompson and Letitia Shelby Thompson, Aug. 24, 1835.—By Jesse Newlin.

John Margan and Emeline Turner, Oct. 14, 1835.—By Patrick M. Darcy.

James Garman and Eliza Turner, Oct. 3, 1835.—By Geo. Hardwick.

Burrell Godsey and Nancy Millsaps, Sept. 24, 1835.— By Sashal Woods.

Sampson Gentry and Sarah Gentry, Nov. 18, 1835.—By Sashal Woods.

Willis G. Adkins and Polly G. Adkins, Jan. 10, 1836.—By Geo. Hardwick.

Joseph Dickson and Pamole Warren, Jan. 31, 1836.—By Thos. Minnis.

Azariah Parker and Anny Wilkerson, Dec. 10, 1835.—By Jesse Newlin.

Geo. Washington Martin and Nancy Jane Liggett, Nov. 19, 1835.—Wm. Martin.

Gilbert Parman and Olive Gumpstock, Dec. 31, 1835.—By Reuben McCaskrie.

Jacob Riffe and Sarah Shannon, Apr. 28, 1836.—By William Barbee.

Daniel Mathaney and Susan Ewell, Feb. 22, 1836.—By Samuel Todd.

Alfred Rockhold and Eliza Fisk, Mar. 3, 1836.—By Samuel Todd.

James Austin and Rosey Maupin, Mar. 20, 1836.—By Samuel Todd.

Daniel Shives and Margaret J. Maberry, Feb. 17, 1836.—By Samuel Venable.

James Johnson and Melvina Parmer, Apr. 12, 1836.—By Reuben Harper.

John A. Cunningham and Amy Carc, May 8, 1836.—Jesse Newlin.

John N. Johnson and Elizabeth Beaty, Aug. 7, 1836.—Geo. Hardwick.

William Smart and Elizabeth Thomas, Nov. 3, 1836.—By Sashal Woods.

Manly Turner and Nancy Philips, Dec. 1, 1836.—Geo. W. Folger.

Henry Cooke and Ann W. Sullers, Dec. 4, 1836.—By Reuben Harper.

John Gudgell and Lovey Gregory, Jan. 3, 1837.—By Samuel Todd.

Thomas McMuntry and Charlotte Maupin, Jan. 3, 1837.—By Samuel Todd.

CARROLL COUNTY MARRIAGE RECORD, 1833-52

James Tipet and Ann Biles, Dec. 13, 1836.—James A. Davis.

Henry Reynolds and Lavina Comstock, Nov. 10, 1836.—By James W. Parmon.

Lind G. Ayres and Susan Hargrove, Feb. 2, 1837.—By James A. Davis.

James Fulton and Nancy Tinney, Jan. 8, 1837.—James A. Davis.

George Parmer and Elizabeth Cooley, Apr. 4, 1837.—By Geo. W. Folger.

James Trotter and Cynthia Carey, May 13, 1837.—By John Thatcher.

Govey Pitts and Phebe Ann Woolsey, June 28, 1837.—By Geo. W. Folger.

Martin Davis and Eveline Vilet, May 18, 1837.—By W. Staton.

Christopher C. Crizler and Melinda Warren, July 16, 1837.—By Sashal Woods.

William Irons and Mary Huffstutter, July 30, 1837.—By John Thatcher.

James Wethers and Polly Ann Tull, July 4, 1837.—By Sashal Woods.

Jonah B. Bassett and Katharine Monroyn, Aug. 30, 1837.—By Geo. W. Folger.

Joshua Whitney and Julia Raundy, Sept. 19, 1837.—By Geo. W. Folger.

John Gentry and Dorcas Anderson, Oct. 15, 1837.—By W. Staton.

John Adkins and Sarah Winfree, Oct. 22, 1837.—By W. Staton.

William Kirkpatrick and Mary Winfree, Nov. 28, 1837.—By Sashal Woods.

Stephen Woolsey and Abigail Woolsey, Jan. 21, 1838.—By Thomas Arnold.

James M. Staton and Nancy Adkins, Jan. 24, 1838.—By W. Staton.

Walter H. Courts June and Malinda Northcut, Mar. 10, 1838.—By Sashal Woods.

John Gardner and Matilda Bennett, Mar. 24, 1838.—By Sashal Woods.

Stephen Smart and Margaret Trotter, Mar. 28, 1838.—By Sashal Woods.

James Barns and Polly Rusher, Mar. 25, 1838.—By W. Staton.

Elisha W. Thomas and Ailsey McKinney, May 15, 1838.—By Geo. Hardwick.

Sundane Moore, Nancy Thomas, July 15, 1838.—Geo. Hardwick.

Joseph Hill and Nancy Gentry, Aug. 6, 1838.—By W. Staton.

Harvey Beaty and Elizabeth Campbell, Aug. 7, 1838.—By Sashal Woods.

Nathaniel Banks and Mary Umphries, Aug. 8, 1838.—By James M. Waldon.

William A. Bricken and Susan C. Brock, Sept. 8, 1838.—By Sashal Woods.

William Mann and Sarah Stearns, Sept. 7, 1838.—By A. B. Garland.

Thomas J. Hardwick and Louisa Brickens, Oct. 18, 1838.—By Sashal Woods.

Stephen C. Woolsey and Elizabeth A. Caton, Oct. 28, 1838.—By Reuben Harper.

Benjamin D. Kendrick and Elizabeth Thomas, Dec. 4, 1838.—By David Enyart.

Joseph Dickson and Charlotte Austin, Jan. 15, 1839.—By Abbot Hancock.

Zebolin Gay and Sarah Titus, Jan. 5, 1839.—By James M. Waldon.

Jesse Parker and Mary Ann Pearson, Jan. 16, 1839.—By James M. Waldon.

Hamilton Wallace and Elizabeth Smith, Nov. 15, 1838.—By W. Smith.

James Adkins and Nancy Simpson, Jan. 13, 1839.—By W. Smith.

Benjamin D. Midiett and Elizabeth Barbee, Apr. 9, 1839.—By James M. Walden.

CARROLL COUNTY MARRIAGE RECORD, 1833-52   109

David Hardwick and Sarah Cooley, Sept. 12, 1839.—By Danid Enyart.

Charles Powell and Ann Crocket, Sept. 13, 1839.—By Sashal Woods.

George W. Graham and Jane Braden, July 30, 1839.—By Abbot Hancock.

Reece Paynter and Martha Freeman, Nov. 18, 1839.—By Geo. Hardwick.

William Maloy and Sarah Glaze, Sept. 1, 1839.—By Abbot Hancock.

Thorton H. Freeman and Statira Arnold, Jan. 23, 1840.—By Abbot Hancock.

Anderson Barns and Elizabeth Gentry, Dec. 29, 1839.—By James M. Walden.

Osborn Anderson and Sarah Davis, Aug. 29, 1839.—By James L. Forsythe.

Josiah Goodson and Malinda Shirley, Jan. 21, 1840.—By Elijah McDaniel.

Benjamin Harrison and Elizabeth Adkins, Dec. 4, 1839.—By W. Staton.

David Gregory and Martha Ann Brock, Feb. 18, 1840.—By L. W. Gehcath.

Charles M. Minnis and Martha Ann Caskey, Mar. 12, 1840.—Elijah McDaniel.

Amariah Hanna and Matilda Chesney, Feb. 5, 1840.—By Wm. Ketron.

Lewis N. Rus and Hannah Tull, Mar. 26, 1840.—By Abbot Hancock.

John Minnis, Ann Beaty, Apr. 21, 1840.—By Sashal Woods.

George Craig and Sarah Chriswell, May 28, 1840.—Sashal Woods.

Stephen Shives and Margaret Barbee, May 28, 1840.—By James Reed.

David B. Bayles and Elvina West, May 28, 1840.—By James Reed.

Thomas Mathews and Sarah Caskey, June 1, 1840.—By Abbot Hancock.

Charles Stern and Sarah Blackwell, June 1, 1840.—Abbot Hancock.

Abraham Cresswell and Matilda Malvina White, July 2, 1840.—By Th. H. Freeman.

William Adkins and Elizabeth Brickens, July 16, 1840.—By Sashal Woods.

William P. Jones and Artetitha Wookey, July 16, 1840.—By Wm. Sparks.

Hiram McCall and Harriet Graham, Sept. 26, 1840.—By Sashal Woods.

John Newlin and Minerva Hardwick, Oct. 31, 1840—By Henry Winfrey.

Barry Jones and Sally Titus, Oct. 19, 1840.—By Henry Winfrey.

Pleasant Newton and Jane Cross, Sept. 26, 1840.—By Henry Winfrey.

James Fielder and Monica Pitts, Oct. 29, 1840.—By Wm. Sparks.

Samuel Clinkscales and Harriett Hancock, Jan. 12, 1841.—By Sashal Woods.

Isaac Cuppy and Elizabeth Jackson, Nov. 11, 1841.—By James M. Goodson.

Richard S. Downy and Mary Lewis, Feb. 7, 1841.—By Geo. Hardwick.

William Jobe and Viney Bowers, June 15, 1841.—By Jacob Francis.

William D. Permell and Elizabeth Cusher, July 27, 1841.—By Th. H. Freeman.

John C. Smith and Mary Stovall, May 31, 1841.—By Geo. Hardwick.

William P. Winfrey and Eliza A. Hardwick, Sept. 3, 1841.—By Sashal Woods.

George Hardwick and Christina Taylor, July 29, 1841.—By Wm. Staton.

Robert Emily and Mary McCollum, Dec. 7, 1841.—By Jacob Francis.

Bargillai D. Lucas and Sarah Ann Staton, Dec. 22, 1841.—By Wm. Ketron.

CARROLL COUNTY MARRIAGE RECORD, 1833-52

John Glaze and Lucinda Ferris, Nov. 10, 1841.—By James M. Goodson.

John Anderson and Elizabeth Ferris, Dec. 7, 1841.—By James M. Goodson.

John G. Hardwick and Eliza Mason, Nov. 7, 1841.—By James M. Goodson.

Tipton Findley and Sarah Ann Berry, Jan. 13, 1842.—By Abbot Hancock.

Elisha Thomas and Caroline Isem, Jan. 16, 1842.—By Abbot Hancock.

James W. Cox and Margaret Wallice, Feb. 1, 1842.—By Wm. Ketron.

John Beaty and Rosanna Graham, Feb. 4, 1842.—Wm. Ketron.

Dudley Thomas and Elizabeth Miles, Feb. 4, 1842.—By Wm. Ketron.

Thomas Williams and Delilah Swinney, Feb. 20, 1842.—By Bartley Pitts.

Johnston Adkins and Mariah Page, Jan. 1, 1841.—By H. Winfrey.

David H. Walker and Elizabeth E. Thomas, Mar. 9, 1841.—By H. Winfrey.

Isaac Cox and Minerva Dumm, Mar. 17, 1842.—By Wm. Ketron.

Thomas Boswell and Eliza Mears, Feb. 15, 1842.—By James L. Walden.

Benjamin F. Baker and Serfrony Ann Merrill, June 4, 1841.—By Abbot Hancock.

Abram Riffe and Polly Cooley, Jan. 16, 1842.—By Sashel Woods.

Harris Vanhook and Nancy Campbell, May 31, 1842.—By James M. Goodson.

John Crocket and Dressella Pitts, May 22, 1842.—By A. C. Blackwell.

Richard Downey and Mary Barrier, June 26, 1842.—By Jas. M. Goodson.

William Taylor and Rachel Woolsey, June 30, 1842.—By Bartley Pitts.

Hugh M. Caton and Nancy Ann Harvey, Aug. 25, 1842.—By Bartley Pitts.

Wylee Dumm and Catharine Eaker, Mar. 31, 1842.—By Wm. Ketron.

John Stemme and Eady Colman, Oct. 21, 1842.—By Abbot Hancock.

Lewis O'Ry and Eunice Titus, Aug. 24, 1842.—By Wm. Ketron.

Charles Berry and Parthena Brock, Oct. 26, 1842.—By Abbot Hancock.

Furdinand Gentry and Margaret Brock, Nov. 29, 1842.—By Sashel Woods.

Jesse Anderson and Unity Johnson, Jan. 7, 1843.—By L. W. Gilreath.

Franklin Merideth and Mariann Standley, Jan. 11, 1843.—By Samuel Brock.

William Tull and Martha Ann Partlow, Dec. 1, 1842.—By Abbot Hancock.

Samuel Turner and Martha Jane Bailey, Feb. 23, 1843.—By Abbot Hancock.

John W. Brock and Elizabeth Beaty, Mar. 2, 1843.—By Abbot Hancock.

Benjamin T. Turner and Nancy Jane McCoy, Dec. 11, 1842.—Th. H. Freeman.

Foster Demasters and Permelia Falant, Mar. 1, 1843.—By Hiram McCall.

Samuel Mears and Piney Gentry, Feb. 24, 1843.—By James M. Walden.

John Merril and Elizabeth Adkins, Nov. 19, 1841.—By H. Winfrey.

Joseph Riffe and Emily Cooley, Dec. 22, 1841.—By H. Winfrey.

John Campbell and Sarah Jane Fisk Graham, Apr., 1843.—By John A. Tutt.

William Winfrey and Frankey Smart, Apr. 16, 1843.—By David Enyart.

Solomon Davis and Mary Wilson, Mar. 23, 1843.—By John Daughterty.

CARROLL COUNTY MARRIAGE RECORD, 1833-52   113

Amos A. Logston and Cynthia Barnes, Feb. 9, 1843.—By John Daugherty.

James A. Hancock and Mary E. Lineis, June 1, 1843.—By Abbot Hancock.

Miller Cooley and Elizabeth Hill, June 8, 1843.—By Abbot Hancock.

William Snider and Mary King, June 11, 1843.—By L. W. Gilreath.

William Helton and Celia Ann Enyart, Aug. 11, 1843.—By Th. H. Freeman.

Norman P. Holsey and Elizabeth Staton, Aug. 17, 1843.—By John A. Tutt.

John Freeman and Eliza Kilgor, Feb. 16, 1843.—Jacob Francis.

John Chase and Harriet Holsa, Aug. 22, 1843.—By John A. Tutt.

Martin Glaze and Emily Morgan, Sept. 25, 1843.—By Abbot Hancock.

James Burton and Dicy Phillips, July 16, 1843.— By J. W. Lumpkin.

Howell L. Heston and Ester E. Austin, Nov. 14, 1843.—By John L. Yontis.

Joseph H. Freeman and Harriet Johnson, Dec. 7, 1843.—By Thos. Arnold.

Franklin S. Bryant and Sarah Morris, Apr. 13, 1843.—By Samuel Grove.

John Jinkins and Matilda Wheeler, Jan. 1, 1843.—By Wm. Ketron.

Lilburn M. Barns and Mary Logston, Apr. 13, 1843.—By Wm. Ketron.

Thomas Crop and Mary Miles, June 27, 1843.—By Wm. Ketron.

James H. Lane and Elizabeth Ann Browning, Nov. 14, 1843.—By Wm. Ketron.

Benjamin Maggard and Elizabeth Peyton, Dec. 23, 1843.—By Sashel Woods.

Pleasant M. Hill and Levina Mares Booth, Sept. 21, 1843.—By James M. Walden.

Zebulon Gay and Sary Ann Maston, Oct. 12, 1843.—By James M. Walden.

Newton Halsey and Mary Ann Gentry, Oct. 16, 1843.—By James M. Walden.

Edwards S. Williams and Mary Brown Austin, Jan. 2, 1844.—By John L. Yontis.

Aaron Cooley and Martha Turner, Jan. 3, 1844.—By Thos. Arnold.

William Lewis and Louisa Jane Carr, Feb. 10, 1843.—By James Brents.

Benjamin Franklin Owens and Sary Sereen, Taylor, Aug. 8, 1843.—By James Brents.

Warren McDaniel and Rachel Taylor, Mar. 22, 1844.—By George Craig.

James Gentry and Della Standley, Jan. 14, 1844.—By James M. Walden.

Sterling W. Mohley and Malinda E. Woolsey, May 23, 1844.—By Reece Paynter.

Henry A. Waid and Roxly Havens, May 25, 1844.—By John Cooly.

Robert D. Ray and Francis V. Prosser, May 28, 1844.—By Abbot Hancock.

William F. H. Shaw and Rachael Sipears, July 23, 1844.—By Reece Paynter.

Holeman Sneed and Sarah Catharine Austin, Aug. 14, 1844.—By John L. Yontis.

Robert Thompson and Mary Hill, July 9, 1844.—By E. P. Noel.

Augustus Redwine and Mary Turner, May 7, 1844.—By David Enyart.

Zebidee Roberts and Elizabeth Parmer, Aug. 19, 1844.—By Samuel Turner.

Nathaniel Ellis and Francis Elizabeth Haines, May 23, 1844.—By John Daugherty.

William O'Neal and Nancy Wilson, Mar. 29, 1844.—By John Daugherty.

Gove M. Pitts and Martha Fielder, July 1, 1844.—By George Craig.

CARROLL COUNTY MARRIAGE RECORD, 1833-52   115

Thomas Lewis and Juliet Roy, July 16, 1844.—By Abbot Hancock.

Harden Rogers and Sarah Ann Thomas, Aug. 13, 1844. —By Abbot Hancock.

Jesse Tull and Mary Carico, Aug. 20, 1844.—By Abbot Hancock.

William Turner and Francis Ann Johnson, Aug. 7. 1844.—Thos. Arnold.

Thomas G. Dobbins and Charlotte Dickson, Nov. 2, 1843.—By Wm. C. Legon.

Nathaniel H. Price and Susan C. Branch, Oct. 5, 1844.— By John P. Bennett.

Thomas House and Hannah P. Coleman, Sept. 12, 1844.—By Ephram P. Noel.

Wesley Gentry, Jr. and Malinda Ann Harper, Jan. 5, 1845.—L. W. Gilreath.

Bennett Brock and Rebecca Standley, Feb. 13, 1845. —By William Brown.

James Caloway and Ann E. Lewis, Jan. 11, 1845.—By J. W. Langkin.

David Crocket and Evaline Johnson, Feb. 20, 1845.— By Jno. R. Harris.

Thomas McCan and Verlinda Boaman, Jan. 23, 1845.— By Abbot Hancock.

John Galette and Harriet Frances Thomas, Dec. 10, 1844.—By Abbot Hancock.

Christopher Phillips and Louise Ball, Dec. 12, 1844.— By Samuel Carson.

William Standley and Sarah Maggard, Mar. 2, 1845. —By Thos. Arnold.

Ingram Standley and Sarah I. Hale, Mar. 5, 1845.— By Sashal Woods.

Lycurgus N. Smith and Mary Simpson, Dec. 22, 1844.— By John Daugherty.

Jonathan McKinny and Elizabeth Henslèy, Apr. 8, 1845.—By B. H. Spencer.

Richard Withers and Ann Critzer, Sept. 17, 1844.—By John Watson.

Thomas W. Morris and Balinda Barnett, Mar. 18, 1845.—By Abbot Hancock.

Harrison Wilcoxson and Nancy Jane Clinkscales, Mar. 27, 1845.—By Abbot Hancock.

Willis Davis and Isabella Squires, Apr. 29, 1845.—By Abbot Hancock.

John P. Winkler and Martha Woolsey, Apr. 3, 1845.—By Christopher P. Caton.

William Ballew and Polly Ann Taylor, May 8, 1845.—By Joseph Riffe.

Robert Kilgore and Mary Cole, June 8, 1845.—By B. H. Spencer.

Samuel Titus and Elizabeth Harris, July 1, 1844.—By John Daughterty.

Garret Maupin and Martha A. Poindexter, May 16, 1845.—By James Grove.

Thomas H. Thurman and Mary A. Framin, May 14, 1845.—By James Grove.

John A. Carey and Mary Jane Thomas, Aug. 4, 1845.—By David Enyart.

Allen Lampkin and Mary Ann Maggard, July 1, 1845.—By Reece Paynter.

George W. Jones and Sally Standley, July 16, 1845.—By Joseph Riffe.

Jesse Ashly and Lorinda Bunce, Aug. 21, 1845.—By Hiram McCall.

Leander Strode and Susan Turner, July 22, 1845.—By Joseph Winfrey.

Jacob Francis and Sarah Kilgore, Sept. 10, 1845.—By B. H. Spencer.

William Phillips and Malinda Meads, June 11, 1845.—By Wm. Staton.

John Casner and Lucinta Williams, Sept. 16, 1845.—By Christopher P. Caton.

George W. Bricken and Margaret Buckhart, Sept. 7, 1845.—By Jas. M. Goodson.

James A. Messer and Arabelle B. Smith, Nov. 13, 1845. —By C. B. Wilcox.

CARROLL COUNTY MARRIAGE RECORD, 1833-52

James L. Leeper and Elizabeth Hooper, Nov. 20, 1845.—By Abbot Hancock.

Levin Bower Smith and Evaline Crouch, Nov. 23, 1845.—By James M. Walden.

Alton F. Martin and Ann M. Ely, Nov. 11, 1845.—By Jas. M. Goodson.

John Jones and Louisa Jane Sharp, Aug. 8, 1845.—By Samuel Carson.

Strangeman Johnson and Harriet Haines, Dec. 11, 1845.—By Jas. M. Goodson.

Ignace Heidel and Amanda Folger, Jan. 27, 1846.—By Reece Paynter.

David Al. Robinson and Caroline Rogers, Nov. 7, 1845.—By Powhatan B. Darr.

Levi Shinn and Rebecca Trotter, Jan. 15, 1846.—By Jas. M. Goodson.

John Hill and Eliza Sapp, Feb. 1, 1846.—By Reece Paynter.

William W. Tommerson and Ann I. Austin, Aug. 6, 1845.—By John R. Bennett.

Harden Simpson and Mariah Winfrey, Sept. 11, 1845.—By Henry Winfrey.

Nicholas B. Little and Elizabeth Winfrey, Oct. 30, 1845.—By Henry Winfrey.

William Davis and Catharine Powers, Feb. 22, 1846.—By John W. Shively.

Archibald Austin and Lucy Newman, Jan. 6, 1846.—By Henry Renock.

Wm. H. Graham and Nancy J. Minnis, Mar. 31, 1846.—By B. H. Spencer.

David Haynes and Elizabeth Enyart, Apr. 10, 1846.—By Joseph Winfrey.

Henry Hase and Mrs. Tinny, Apr. 25, 1846.—By John W. Shively.

Isaac A. Lauck and Susan Farr, Feb. 10, 1846.—By James M. Walden.

Bartin Arnold and Elizabeth Harriett Cunningham, Feb. 26, 1846.—By Thos. Arnold.

Joel Turner and Cinthia Johnson, Feb. 18, 1846.—By Samuel Turner.

Andrew J. Ellis and Margaret Merrill, May 17, 1846.—By Henry Renock.

Coleman Hill and Nancy Nuson, Sept. 7, 1845.—By Joseph Riffe.

Jesse Franklin and Sarah Ann Guilete, May 19, 1846.—By Johny Porter.

Daniel Sharp and Nancy Kasky, July 13, 1846.—By Reece Paynter.

Jesse Anderson and Martha Cook, July 16, 1846.—By John P. Harris.

Thomas Hardwick and Elizabeth Mabery, July 16, 1846.—By John P. Harris.

Sidney C. Farr and Cintha Ann Allen, May 16, 1846.—By John Cooly.

James Night and Susanah Young, June 18, 1846.—By George Craig.

William Reed and Nancy White, June 23, 1846.—By George Craig.

Harmond Lee Booth and Martha Cooly, June 4, 1846.—Samuel Turner.

William New and Melinda Toberman, July 6, 1846.—Henry Renock.

John Mogg and Emaline Brown, May 28, 1846.—By Christopher P. Caton.

Asa M. Brooks and Lucy Hudson, Sept. 20, 1846.—By Abbot Hancock.

Wm. R. Allen and Martha Ann Tull, Sept. 24, 1846.—By T. N. Gaines.

J. M. Hardwick and Lucinda Mason, Sept. 3, 1846.—By James M. Goodson.

John S. Farr and Nancy Hurlock, Oct. 14, 1846.—By Thomas Hardwick.

Flemmings Adison and Jane Morris, Oct. 14, 1846.—By John W. Shively.

William H. Isem and Lucy Appleberg, Oct. 1, 1846.—By Joel Appleberg.

CARROLL COUNTY MARRIAGE RECORD, 1833-52 119

Green Gentry and Elvina Stanley, Aug. 2, 1846.—By James M. Walden.

Richard Bowers and Louisa Thomas, Oct. 29, 1846.—By James E. Drake.

Robert Gentry and Serilda Ashby, Aug. 26, 1846.—By E. W. Smith.

Daniel Ranson and Amy Owens, Aug. 30, 1846.—By E. W. Smith.

Dorsay Miles and Martha Jane McKenny, Nov. 22, 1846.—By W. T. Ellington.

James H. Frazell and Nancy J. Sparks, Oct. 15, 1846.—By C. B. Wilcox.

Henry Winfrey and Matilda McCann, Dec. 24, 1846.—By Joseph Winfrey.

John Staunton and Louisa Brown, Jan. 2, 1847—By Christopher P. Caton.

William Price and Elizabeth Prather, Oct. 25, 1846.—By S. S. Edgar.

James Smith and Mary Ann Havens, Feb. 14, 1847.—By Reece Paynter.

Lewis E. Scott and Jemima Gentry, Feb. 23, 1847.—By William Smart.

Jacob Maggard and Lucy Williams, Mar. 7, 1847.—By Reece Paynter.

Burton Godsey and Sarah Heartless, Mar. 3, 1847.—By Abbot Hancock.

Noah Gilreath and Nancy Suttles, Feb. 7, 1847.—Abbot Hancock.

Emanuel Flenner and Sarah Jane Simons, Feb. 5, 1847. By John Daugherty.

Jonathan S. Knox and Emaline Frazzier, Jan. 3, 1847.—By C. B. Wilcox.

John Mabberry and Tilpha Newson, Dec. 13, 1846.—By Phillip Jackson.

Thomas Standley and Sarah Harper, Mar. 14, 1847.—By James M. Goodson.

John Maggard and Susan Trussel, Mar. 2, 1847.—By James M. Goodson.

Thomas I. Bricken and Martha C. Winfrey, Feb. 21, 1847.—By Thos. Hardwick.

James W. Bailey and Elizabeth Tull, Dec. 29, 1846.—By T. N. Gaines.

John I. Martin and Amanda B. Smith, Jan. 7, 1847.—By C. B. Wilcox.

James H. Taney and Lydia Ann Harvey, Mar. 20, 1847.—By Christopher P. Caton.

Jefferson Phillips and Nancy Lathom, July 21, 1847.—By Henry Winfrey.

Ellis Gennings and Nancy Heartless, Apr. 24, 1847.—By Joseph Winfrey.

William Smart and Elizabeth Temperance, May 15, 1847.—By Jas. M. Goodson.

Samuel Henthorn and Laney Crouch, Mar. 21, 1847.—By James M. Walden.

John Epperson and Sarah Flewors, July 7, 1847.—By Reece Paynter.

John Campbell and Elizabeth Godsey, June 8, 1847.—By Severn Bristoe.

Daniel Sharp and Lochy Squires, July 11, 1847.—By James M. Walden.

James C. Miller, and Mary Ann Sampkins, July 25, 1847.—By T. N. Gaines.

John Gambel and Jane Lucas, Aug. 1, 1847.—By James M. Walden.

Vansant Britton and Louisa Benson, July 10, 1847.—By John Daugherty.

Charles Rogers and Sarah Smith, Aug. 19, 1847.—By John Daugherty.

W. I. Polland and Mary Oliver, Oct. 7, 1847.—By T. N. Gaines.

Benjamin Bowman and Permelia Higgins, Nov. 7, 1847.—James B. Calloway.

Richard G. Adkins and Lyctia V. Harden, Nov. 20, 1847.—By David Enyart.

Samuel S. Miller and Martha Young, Sept. 30, 1847.—By Abbot Hancock.

CARROLL COUNTY MARRIAGE RECORD, 1833-53

George Davis and Elizabeth Hall, July 1, 1847.—By Abbot Hancock.

John Bunch and Patcy Cooly, Dec. 2, 1847.—By Joseph Riffe.

Liman McNall and Polly Harden, Aug. 27, 1847.—By Thomas Hardwick.

Wiley Clark and Angetine Burrow, Jan. 16, 1848.—By Abbot Hancock.

Nevil Artaburn and Mickey Gentry, Nov. 22, 1847.—By David Enyart.

Walter Squires and Frances Hancock, Jan. 16, 1848.—By John Daugherty.

Flanders Calloway and Mary Ann Banks, Nov. 18, 1847.—By James M. Walden.

Elias Hubbard and Hulda Jane Morgan, Jan. 20, 1848.—By James M. Walden.

Elmore W. Squires and Louisa Smith, Mar. 1, 1848.—By B. D. Lucas.

Jonathan Zooke and Margaret Ellen Harris, Mar. 20, 1848.—By Marcus Stevenson.

Samuel Simpson and Nancy Manning, Mar. 16, 1848.—By John Daugherty.

William Mears and Mary Morris, Feb. 3, 1848.—By John Daugherty.

Washington Zuck and Abigail Woolsey, Mar. 26, 1848.—By James Craig.

Martin Wheat and Ann Daniels, Mar. 1, 1848.—By C. P. Caton.

Thacker M. Lucas and Mary Catharine Banks, Apr. 20, 1848.—By John Y. Porter.

Abner G. Squires and Sarah Winfrey, Apr. 16, 1848.—By Kemp Scott.

Burvadus C. Woods and Nancy Calloway, May 18, 1848.—By Abbot Hancock.

Daniel Peyton and Louisa Jane Farr, June 1, 1848.—By Thomas Hardwick.

Mark Hallsey and Eliza Parr, June 1, 1848.—By Thomas Hardwick.

Jno. M. Howell and Elizabeth Herndon, June 1, 1848.—By Wm. S. Sigon.

Samuel Brock and Nancy Vint, May 16, 1848.—By James M. Goodson.

Henry Knipskiett and Elizabeth Stem, June 18, 1848. By James M. Goodson.

James Ezra and Sarah Rouse, July 6, 1848.—By David H. Dewey.

Ablasom Wolf and Ann Tussy, July 6, 1848.—By James M. Goodson.

Nathan S. Cooley and Polly Cary, June 4, 1848.—By Joseph Riffe.

James Carpenter and Matilda Landon, Apr. 3, 1848.—By Joel Appleberry.

Mathew Jones and Mary Elder, July 14, 1848.—By Joel Appleberry.

Robert G. Martin and Katharine E. H. Tull, July 25, 1848.—B. Anderson.

Thomas Sparks, Martha Morris, Apr. 13, 1848.—By John Dorherty.

Isaac F. Ball and Aelia Simpson, June 4, 1848.—By James M. Walden.

Foster Rhodes and Nancy Mathias, June 8, 1848.—By John W. Smith.

George W. Baker and Adelia A. McBrier, Aug. 28, 1848.—By B. Anderson.

Thomas Wilson and Rachael Tilery, Aug. 10, 1848.—By Isaac A. Lauck.

Kenion Newson and Sarah Barbee, Aug. 1, 1848.—By James S. Ashby.

Anthony Arnold and Martha Cunningham, Sept. 11, 1848.—By R. Paynter.

John B. Calvert and June Ann Scott, Aug. 24, 1848.—By James M. Goodson.

Edmund Thomas and Elizabeth Staton, Sept. 20, 1848. —By James E. Drake.

John Cole and Jane Craig, Oct. 3, 1848.—By James Baird Calloway.

CARROLL COUNTY MARRIAGE RECORD, 1833-52

Cornelius N. Blauvelt and Susan Hunter, Aug. 15, 1848.—By Abbot Hancock.

Zepeniah Reed and Mary Adkins, Nov. 27, 1848.—By P. V. Darr.

John N. Braden and Sarah Ann Minnis, Nov. 7, 1848.—By R. R. Dunlap.

Warren Minnis and Sarah Ann Campbell, Nov. 3, 1848.—By R. R. Dunlap.

William Millsaps and Martha Jane Coop, Nov. 29, 1848.—By Abbot Hancock.

George W. Morris and Rebecca Hill, Sept. 21, 1848.—By John W. Smith.

Thomas Tetham and Centhia Philips, Aug. 28, 1848.—By Henry Winfrey.

Dewey Elder and Mary Tearaunt, Nov. 7, 1848.—Joel Appleberry.

Andrew Jackson Thompson and Sarah Parmelia Parmer, Sept. 14, 1848.—By John Daugherty.

Charles Winfrey and Savina Hall, Oct. 5, 1848.—By John Daugherty.

Jonathan Miles and Caroline Reed, Sept. 19, 1848.—By John Daugherty.

Jeremiah Smith and Nancy Cline, Dec. 20, 1848.—By John Daugherty.

Peter Stemn and Elizabeth Norman, Nov. 16, 1848.—By James M. Goodson.

Thomas Game and Frances Jane Farries, Jan. 13, 1849.—By Jas. M. Goodson.

William Beaty Jun and Nancy Jane Shirley, Jan. 11, 1849.—By Jas. M. Goodson.

Isaac Harmon and Orleany Wallace, Dec. 21, 1848.—By David H. Dewey.

John Tathan and Polly Ann Adkins, Dec. 31, 1848.—By David H. Dewey.

George C. Brown and Mary G. Hardin, Dec. 31, 1848.—By Kemp Scott.

Lewis Mears and Ailsey L. Dotz, Oct. 26, 1848.—By Kemp Scott.

Fleming J. Birch and Nancy Hardwick, Jan. 16, 1848.—By James E. Drake.

Philey Schook and Sarah Jane Woodward, Jan. 18, 1849.—James M. Goodson.

John F. Houston and Sarah Stafford, Nov. 31, 1848.—By Wm. C. Sigon.

Benjamin F. White and Sarah Ann Proper, Dec. 12, 1848.—By Wm. C. Sigon.

James Nite and Elizabeth Harrier. Jan. 9, 1848.—By P. Caton.

John C. Arterburn and Mary Adkins, Jan. 18, 1848.—By David Enyart.

Charles C. Hancock and Alpha Jane Sharp, Nov. 19, 1848.—By James L. Ashby.

Alexander Triplett and Ann Eliza Cothran, Jan. 19, 1849.—James L. Ashby.

Levi Fawks and Eliza Carr, Feb. 28, 1849.—By James E. Drake.

Oliver Perry Appleby and Mary Ann Brock, Feb. 7, 1849.—By James M. Goodson.

John Noland and Elizabeth F. Curtis, Feb. 20, 1849.—David H. Dewey.

Samuel Wheelbergar and Mary Gentry, Jan. 4, 1849.—By Simon W. Louch.

John Elder and Racheal Morris, Dec. 28, 1848.—By Joel Appleberry.

John Murphy and Ann E. Hensley, Dec. 15, 1848.—By William G. Caples.

William Tomlenson and Sally Harmon, Jan. 5, 1849.—By P. B. Darr.

Saunders Brook and Herrietta Hancock, Jan. 2, 1849.—By Kemp Scott.

Green Short and Jane E. Bugg, Feb. 5, 1849.—David H. Dewey.

Fleming Courts and Elizabeth Winfrey, Mar. 1, 1894.—By James E. Drake.

William Taylor and Margaret Hopkins, Jan. 14, 1849.—By Alfred Stevenson.

Jackson Phillips and Lucy Harmon, Mar. 10, 1849.—By F. A. Redwine.

Daniel Hoover and Elizabeth Rankin, Apr. 24, 1849.—By R. R. Danlap.

George W. Harlow and Racheal E. Charlton, Mar. 22, 1849.—By Samuel Grove.

Walker Trussell and Mary Frances Settles, May 10, 1849.—By Abbot Hancock.

William P. Dulary and Celia Ann Colaway, July 6, 1849.—Abbot Hancock.

Samuel Elliot and Sarah Francis Williams, June 16, 1849.—By Jas. M. Goodson.

Tilford Busby and Sally A. Hardwick, May 3, 1849.—By James E. Drake.

John Hill and Polly Cary, June 25, 1849.—By James E. Drake.

John Wiswell and Julian Van Rensatea, Apr. 3, 1849.—By Alfred Stevensen.

Repps Bedford Hudson and Catharine Orear, June 5, 1848.—By R. R. Dunlap.

William M. Chapman and Catharine Higgins, Apr. 12, 1849.—By Kemp Scott.

Daniel N. Hill and Sarah Broyles, June 3, 1849.—By Kemp Scott.

James Craig and Hannah Boyd, Mar. 6, 1849.—By C. P. Caton.

Thomas Merideth and Mary Ann Baker, June 3, 1849.—By James M. Goodson.

Jeffory D. Staton and Lucy I. Velette, May 2, 1849.—By Philip Jackson.

John Hammom and Mary Evella Halsey, May 10, 1849.—By Philip Jackson.

Elza Hardwick and Charity Bailey, Aug. 23, 1849.—By James E. Drake.

Jeremiah Francis and Rachael Marphew, July 1, 1849.—By Alfred Stevensen.

John Kenton and Hester Kilgon, July 4, 1849.—By Alfred Stevensen.

Churchill Davis and Edny Norman, Sept. 2, 1849.—By M. Goodson.

William Standley and Martha Ann Kennedy, Sept. 17, 1849.—By Seven Briston.

John Riffe and Margaret Damron, Sept. 30, 1849.—By William Smart.

Charles Wilcox and Catharine J. Bone, Oct. 21, 1849.—By Alfred S. Cooper.

Alexander Shell and Elizabeth Snowden, Oct. 20, 1849.—By James M. Goodson.

James M. Farris and Caroline Trotter, Nov. 15, 1849.—By James M. Goodson.

Edmund Thomas and Nancy Staton, Oct. 28, 1849.—By James E. Drake.

Thomas W. Drake and Sally Thomas, Nov. 7, 1849.—By James E. Drake.

William C. Fauks and Lucinda Caroline Thomas, Aug. 16, 1849.—By John W. Smith.

F. B. Atwood and Louisa Barnett, Sept. 20, 1849.—By William C. Sigon.

Lewis B. Ely and Martha Herndon, Nov. 29, 1849.—By William C. Sigon.

Miles Appleberry and Mahaly Powers, Nov. 22, 1849.—By Aaron Baker.

William Z. Darr and Cynthia C. Plemmons, Nov. 16, 1849.—By Kemp Scott.

Marcus Stevenson and Mary Ann Miller, Jan. 1, 1850.—By H. Brown.

James G. Plemmons and Euphamy Hall, Dec. 4, 1849.—By William Henson.

John House and Malinda Coleman, Jan. 3, 1850.—Josiah Goodson.

John Deitrick and Catharine Stamm, Jan. 20, 1850.—By James M. Goodson.

James Casky and Dicy Ann Standley, Nov. 20, 1849.—By James M. Goodson.

Sampson C. Casky and Elizabeth Branden, Nov. 22, 1849.—By James M. Goodson.

CARROLL COUNTY MARRIAGE RECORD, 1833-52

James M. Minnis and Malinda New, Dec. 11, 1849.—By James M. Goodson.

William Knox and Sarah Ann Haines, Jan. 6, 1850.—By James M. Goodson.

John M. McCaslin and Sarah Flenner, Dec. 9, 1849.—By Isaac A. Sauck.

Henry Havins and Elizabeth Titus, Nov. 4, 1849.—By Philip Jackson.

John Coop and Nancy Wallace, Feb. 7, 1850.—By James E. Drake.

William Hudson and Hannah Yates, Feb. 28, 1850.—By Alfred Cooper.

John S. Winfrey and Sarah Ann Thomas, Mar. 14, 1849.—By Jas. E. Drake.

William Payne and Elizabeth J. Dulany, April 8, 1850.—By Elijah Jeffries.

William H. Jeffries and Eliza Jane Hubbard, Mar. 13, 1850.—By Elijah Jeffries.

James F. Reeves and Mary Jane Stevenson, Mar. 31, 1850.—By R. R. Dunlap.

Samuel Williams and Rebecca Flowers, Feb. 14, 1850.—By Simon M. Sauck.

Reuben Winfrey and Sarah Jones, Feb. 24, 1850.—By Simon M. Sauck.

James Cochran and Mary C. Mears, June 6, 1850.—By Kemp Scott.

John W. Staton and Elizabeth Cundiff, Nov. 15, 1849.—By Isaac A. Sauck.

William Smart and Mary Jane Scott, Aug. 5, 1850.—By William Smart.

John B. Sea and Mary Ann Henderson, Apr. 11, 1850.—By Alfred Stevenson.

William Zuck and Malinda Sea, June 30, 1850.—Isaac A. Sauck.

Thomas J. Atkinson and Polly Ann Hardwick, Aug. 28, 1850.—By James E. Drake.

Samuel Smith and Melinda Clark, June 6, 1850.—By Philip Jackson.

William James Smith and Manerva Smith, Sept. 8, 1850.—By P. B. Darr.

John Burkhart and Ann Winford Goodwin, Oct. 21, 1850.—By David H. Dewey.

Nelson McRunnells and Martha Brinegar, July 21, 1850.—By C. P. Caton.

Mark Runion and Charity Roscon, Sept. 23, 1850.—By John W. Smith.

Wm. D. A. Griffith and Eliza Ann Ulry, Nov. 7, 1850.—By Isaac A. Sauck.

William Jackson Wooden and Nancy Short, Sept. 5, 1850.—By John W. Smith.

William Powers and Sarah Jane Shirley, Oct. 10, 1850.—By Aaron Baker.

William McDaniel and Nancy Jane Turner, Oct. 24, 1850.—By William Smart.

William Sugg and Elizabeth Smith, Jan. 9, 1851.—By A. B. Poindexter.

John Harvoid and Salinda Halsey, Nov. 24, 1850.—By P. B. Darr.

Bennett M. Hartgrove and Mary Catharine Winfrey, Feb. 6, 1841.—By David H. Dewey.

William Zuick and Mary Mills, Feb. 13, 1851.—By Isaac A. Sauck.

Benjamin LeMasters and Mary John Ely, Mar. 8, 1851.—By James M. Goodson.

Larkin Standley and Mary Mahany, Feb. 9, 1851.—By Marcus Stevenson.

John Casner and Louisa Stanton, Mar. 10, 1851.—By Wm. Rea.

Deel Seeton and Seeny Newsorns, Mar. 4, 1851.—By Alfred Cooper.

Haziel McKenly and Lucy Jane Jeffries, Jan. 29, 1851.—By Elijah Jeffries.

Joel S. Harper and Glaphin Kavenkapuch, Rush, Mar. 26, 1851.—By Jas. Goodson.

Joseph Street and Sarah Satlent, Apr. 15, 1851.—By Wm. Rea.

CARROLL COUNTY MARRIAGE RECORD, 1833-52 129

Isaac O. Herndon and Mary Brent Sterne, Feb. 18, 1851. —By Fletcher Riggs.

John Toberman and Hannah Jones, Oct., 1851.—By Fletcher Riggs.

Frederic Fait and Susanna Musen, Apr. 11, 1851.—By Josiah Goodson.

Gabriel B. Brents and Mary E. Trussell, Apr. 17, 1851. —By Jas. M. Goodson.

Charles Smith and Elizabeth Fisher, Apr. 14, 1851.—By R. A. Taylor.

Francis M. Appleby and Elvira Standley, May 11, 1851. —By R. A. Taylor.

John L. Moberly and Elizabeth J. Woolsey, May 29, 1851.—By C. P. Caton.

Zadock Yater and Elizabeth Shin, May 25, 1851.—By Alfred Cooper.

Quintius C. Atkinson and Louisa Ann Cooly, July 9, 1851.—By James E. Drake.

John W. Wells and ——— Petes, May 2, 1851.—By Fletcher Riggs.

Thomas W. Morris and Miriam E. Barnes, July 17, 1851.—By Fletcher Riggs.

William Dunkle and Jane Corbin, Sept. 29, 1851.—By Jas. M. Goodson.

Alfred M. Hay and Harriet E. McKinzee, Sept. 14, 1851.—By Fletcher Riggs.

David Blue and Sarah Burchett, Aug. 12, 1851.—By James Kenton.

John W. I. Sern and Sarah I. Street, Aug. 30, 1851.— By A. P. Poindexter.

Alfred Richardson and Melissa S. Ivine, Aug. 24, 1851.— By A. B. Poindexter.

Charles Berry and Louisa Appleberry, July 9, 1851.— By Jas. M. Goodson.

James P. Haines and Susan T. Daugherty, July 31, 1851. —By Jas. M. Goodson.

Irving P. Long and Rebecca Teavantt, Apr. 15, 1851.— By Samuel Grove.

John Teavantt and Sarah Jane Davis, July 27, 1851. —By Aaron Baker.

Montgomery Johnson and Latilda Wallis, July 20, 1851.—By William Smart.

William Hudson and Ann Young, Oct. 6, 1851.—By C. P. Caton.

Lazarus Underwood and Cindrilla Parkenson, July 28, 1851.—By John B. Winfrey.

Archilles Riffe and Caroline Glaze, Sept. 14, 1851.—By R. Paynter.

Johathan H. Walker and Tabitha Isom, Oct. 10, 1851.—By A. B. Poindexter.

David K. Scott and Elizabeth Doty, Oct. 9, 1851.—By Jas. M. Goodson.

Thomas Cook and Mary Ann McClary, Aug. 21, 1851.—By L. H. Ballew.

William N. Brogg and Menerve Emerson, Sept. 27, 1851.—By L. H. Ballew.

John Abuns and Rebecca Collins, Oct. 5, 1851.—By Reuben A. Taylor.

James F. Battons and Nancy Brown, Sept. 25, 1851.—By James E. Drake.

Daniel H. Cary and Sarah Jane Dewey, Oct. 9, 1851.—By James E. Drake.

John Broils and Rhoda Hill, Sept. 11, 1851.—By Kemp Scott.

Jefferson L. Harry and Sarah Hatfield, Nov. 23, 1851.—By Joseph Devlin.

Joshan S. Crouch and Mary E. Haines, Nov. 27, 1851.—By James M. Goodson.

William H. Trotter and Mary Jane Hill, Dec. 2, 1851.—By James M. Goodson.

Reuben Park Williams and Liddy Catharine Whitworth, Nov. 19, 1851.—Kemp Scott.

John A. Pile and Elizabeth Zeater, Jan. 4, 1852.—By Josiah Goodson.

Thomas Rhodes and Polly Mathews, Dec. 9, 1851.—By Reuben A. Taylor.

CARROLL COUNTY MARRIAGE RECORD, 1833-52

William Cunningham and Susan A. Hendricks, Nov. 25, 1851.—By James E. Drake.

Williams W. Bottoms and Elizabeth Brown, Dec. 3, 1851.—By James E. Drake.

Thomas Cunningham and Elizabeth Bottoms, Dec. 11, 1851.—By James E. Drake.

James E. Drake and Nancy Cary Goodson, Dec. 23, 1851.—By Wm. C. Atkinson.

Josiah Hudson and Mary E. Green, Feb. 3, 1852.—By James Devlin.

David B. Hudson and Lucy R. Hudson, Feb. 3, 1852.—By James Devlin.

Samuel Cole and Agnes Pulliam, Oct. 8, 1852.—By Fletcher Riggs.

Craig F. Robberson and Margaret A. Stovall, Feb. 23, 1852.—By James E. Drake.

William D. Cox and Mary Jane Thomas, Mar. 2, 1852.—By James E. Drake.

John Miller and Martha Jane Sandusky, Jan. 18, 1852.—By John W. Smith.

Littleton Tull and Ruth S. Clinkscales, Feb. 24, 1852.—By Jas. Devlin.

Francis Shirley and Miriam Smith, Feb. 26, 1852.—By Josiah Goodson.

Harmon L. Booth and Nancy Anderson, Jan. 13, 1852.—By Joseph Winfrey.

A. Sparks and Mary Elizabeth Rolston, Feb. 19, 1852.—By R. S. Humphries.

John W. Waddell and Bettie R. Austin, Mar. 9, 1852.—By D. L. Rupell.

Bennet Banning and Telitha Latham, Feb. 19, 1852.—By Logan H. Ballew.

Willis Powell and Lucretia King, Apr. 7, 1852.—By P. B. Darr.

Jabez Calvert and Nancy Ann Mitchell, Apr. 22, 1852.—By William Smart.

(Mrs. Robert W.) Mary G. Brown, Historian.
The Carrollton Chapter Daughters of the American Revolution. Carrollton, Missouri.

NOTES.

CHURCH MINUTES.

The State Historical Society of Missouri has always made special efforts to get the minutes of the various church organizations of the State, and it now has several thousand of them. Lately it had twenty-eight volumes bound, which contain 504 minutes of seven denominations and twenty-three organizations, and will bind the others as rapidly as it can get missing numbers. From the fact that so few persons preserve these publications they seem to be looked upon as of small value, and even the secretaries or clerks do not act as if they thought any one would ever want to bind them in volumes; so that of these twenty-three organizations only a single one had all of the minutes of the same size or nearly enough of the same size so that the volumes could be trimmed except on the top. Yet when these publications become old the general appreciation of them increases, and a late catalog of a leading book firm in London offers for sale a collection of eleven American Baptist Associations from 1770 to 1818 bound in eleven volumes for $87.00.

MISSOURI TRAVEL AND DESCRIPTION.

The Society is making a special effort to obtain all books of travel and description that include Missouri, although it may be of only a few pages. It has a list of two hundred and fifty such books, and has in its library a large part of these, and is obtaining others from dealers in this country and also from Europe. On some of the latter it now has to pay an added war tax imposed by the countries now at war.

In the October number of the Review was printed an account of travels into Missouri by Edward Zimmermann, which was translated from manuscript into English by Prof. Wm. G. Bek of the University of North Dakota, and by a mistake in print the time of the travels was given as five years later than it was. It should have been given as 1833 instead of 1838.

IGNATIUS DONNELLY COLLECTION.

The Minnesota Historical Society has been fortunate in getting a splendid collection of manuscript and publications, from the library of Hon. Ignatius Donnelly, of Minnesota, of letters received by Mr. Donnelly during all his life in Minnesota, 1857 to 1900, and as member of Congress, 1863-1869. There were about 30,000. More than 2,200 pamphlets, of addresses, reports and publications relating to the state and national politics, were bound in 72 volumes. There were also 18 scrapbooks containing much Minnesota history from 1870 to 1896. The Society is to be congratulated on the public spirit disposition that caused this donation.

MISSOURI RIVER BOATS IN 1841.

"During this year, there were twenty-six steamboats engaged in the trade of the Missouri River, named and commanded as follows:

Shawnee	Clifford.
Smilie	Keiser.
Col. Woods	Knox.
Gen. Leavenworth	White.
Bowling Green	Roe.
Iatan	Eaton
Platte	Hughes.
Pre-Emption	Harris.
Thames	Dennis.
Omega	Weston.
Gen. Brady	Hart.
Trapper	Chouteau.
Oceana	Miller.

Roebuck	Elk.
Manhattan	Dohuman.
Little Red	Price.
Malta	Thockmorton.
Lehigh	Pierre.
Osage Valley	Young.
Gloster	Williams.
Amazon	McLean.
Mary Tompkins	Beer.
Glaucus	Field.
Huntsville	
Warsaw	

These boats made 312 arrivals and departures at Glasgow, during the year; and have been employed in delivering freight and passengers at the various landings and towns from the mouth to the head of navigation for steam.

The Iatan (regular packet) made, during the year, twenty-four regular weekly trips from St. Louis to Glasgow, besides several trips farther up.

During the present season, there will be two boats in this line, which will regularly leave St. Louis and Glasgow twice a week. The Emilie will also run as a packet upon this river.

The Missouri River, from having been for a long time considered as hardly navigable for keels, is now run upon, night and day, by some of the most splendid, yes, splendid —steamboats upon the western waters; and, although there were five boats engaged in running the trade in '36, there have been, for the last two or three years, from twenty-five to thirty transporting during the year '41, forty-six thousand tons of freight of various kinds, as near as can be ascertained by the size of the boats and their average freight up and down.

The eleven tobacco stemmeries and factories at and in the vicinity of Glasgow, furnish a vast amount of freight."

COLUMBIA PATRIOT.
March 19, 1842.

BOOK NOTICES.

The relationship between the library and the public school. Reprints of papers and addresses, with notes by **Arthur E. Bostwick, Ph. D.** The H. W. Wilson Company, White Plains and New York City, 1914. 331 pages.

The above is the first of a series of "Classics of American Librarianship," to be edited by Mr. Bostwick, librarian of the St. Louis Public Library. The various papers have been published in the Library Journal, the N. E. A. Proceedings, and other publications, and are here put in accessible shape. All librarians will find a mass of information connecting their work with the public schools.

Readings in Indiana History, compiled and edited by a committee of the History Section of the Indiana State Teachers' Association, Published by Indiana University, 1914. 470 pages with 10 maps and 29 illustrations. Price, 70 cents, cloth bound.

The State University has recently published, through its Extension Division, a volume entitled "Readings in Indiana History." As the name implies, the book is a compilation of extracts from original sources, such as autobiographical sketches, state papers, early works on Indiana History, reminiscences, personal narratives, and newspaper items and sketches. Interspersed with narratives of lively incidents are vivid descriptions of the new country, its swamps and thickets, reptiles and wild animals. Many of the incidents are related in the first person and are sprinkled with dialogue, so attractive to juvenile readers, and perhaps to their elders as well. The quaint dialect of the "poor lone woman body" who sheltered the circuit preachers and of the woman who warned Baynard R. Hall of the "most powerfulest road" has an interest for all Hoosiers.

Perhaps one of the most interesting features of the book is the description of travel and transportation in those days. The Pullman traveler of today, stopping at modern hotels, can scarcely conceive of conditions as they existed less than a hundred years ago. Buffalo traces, plank and corduroy roads were the first routes. Some of the taverns beggar description. The health, civic ideals, schools, and religious life are depicted in interesting sketches. The pioneer physician bleeding his patients, the circuit judge sentencing a man to suffer thirty stripes for stealing horses, the schoolmaster who was "barred out" for his failure to "treat," the camp-meeting converts completely overcome by their religious fervor—all these have passed into history.

This book was compiled and edited by a committee from the History Section of the State Teachers' Association of which Mr. Oscar H. Williams, Assistant Professor and Critic Teacher in History in the University, was chairman.

The aim of the compilers was to prepare a book which would render available materials for the study of Indiana History in the schools of the state, in anticipation of the centennial celebration in 1916. The publication of this work has appropriately fallen to the Extension Division of Indiana University, the aim of which is "to bring the University to the people where the people cannot come to the University." In putting into the hands of the younger generation—and making available for their elders also—a narrative of the struggles of the forefathers against adverse conditions, their efforts to found a commonwealth where civic liberty and righteousness should prevail, the University has discharged a useful function.

NECROLOGY.

Joseph E. Baldwin was born in Indianapolis, and died in Topeka, Kansas, October 5, 1914, aged eighty-eight years. He was admitted to practice in Indiana in 1856, and came to Missouri before the Civil War. He was a member of the Senate in the Twenty-third General Assembly, 1864, from the twenty-third district. He held firmly to a belief that he would live to be a thousand years old.

Judge Elijah H. Norton, son of William F. Norton, a Pennsylvanian Quaker, was born in Russellville, Kentucky, November 21, 1821, came to Platte County, Missouri in 1845; was elected County Attorney in 1850; Circuit Judge in 1857; Member of Congress in 1860; member of the Missouri Constitutional Conventions of 1861 and 1875; and appointed Judge of the Supreme Court of Missouri in 1876 and elected in 1878. He became an Odd Fellow in 1844, and was the oldest one in the United States In 1882 William Jewell College conferred the degree of Doctor of Laws upon him. He died at his home in Platte City, July 7, 1914, at the ripe age of ninety-three years.

Professor James Love, son of Granville Love, was born September 30, 1820, at Manchester, Clay County, Kentucky. For a time after coming to Missouri he taught school at Fulton, and then went to the State University from which he graduated in 1853. In 1853 and for two years afterwards he taught in William Jewell College at Liberty, and then organized Clay Seminary for girls, and conducted it till after 1865, not missing a day during the Civil War. Professor Love was a candidate for Congress in 1888 against A. M. Dockery, and polled the largest Republican vote that had ever been cast for a Republican in the district. The State Historical Society received from him a large collection of old St. Louis and other newspapers, and for years had promised it books and pamphlets, which he wished to handle and select for it, but the infirmities of age prevented his doing this. He died at his home in Liberty, September 10, 1914.

MISSOURI HISTORICAL REVIEW

Vol. IX.   April, 1915.   No. 3.

NATHANIEL PATTEN, PIONEER EDITOR.

It is recorded of American newspaper editors that in the Westward Movement they were always in the vanguard, setting up their presses and issuing their sheets before the forests had been cleared or the sod turned. Of such editors were John Bradford of the Kentucke Gazette, the first paper issued in Kentucky; William Maxwell of the Centinel of the Northwestern Territory, the first paper north of the Ohio; and Joseph Charless of the Missouri Gazette (the present St. Louis Republic), the first west of the Mississippi river. And of such also was Nathaniel Patten of the Missouri Intelligencer, first editor of a newspaper west of St. Louis or north of the Missouri river, Missouri's best example of the pioneer editor.

Nathaniel Patten was born at Roxbury, Massachusetts, in 1793. (1) His family had been prominent in New England for several generations. His father, also named Nathaniel, had received a good education, and spent much time in cultivating the minds and morals of his five children, (2) of whom Nathaniel, Jr., was eldest. In 1808 the family moved west,

---

(1) The date of his baptism was September 9, 1793, as stated in a letter from Thomas W. Baldwin, compiler of the Patten geneology. (Boston, 1908.) A number of interesting details of the Patten family have kindly been furnished by Mr. Baldwin.

(2) Missouri Intelligencer, Oct. 9, 1821. Obituary of Mary B. Patten.

and in 1812 settled at Mount Sterling, Montgomery County, Kentucky, where in all probability young Patten had his first experience as an editor. (3) Then for some reason he left his father's family and joined the great caravan of Kentucky immigrants to the frontier of Missouri, arriving there in 1818. (4)

Only a short time before his arrival, the whole frontier region known as the Boon's Lick Country had been unorganized and unsurveyed, and with the exception of a few hardy pioneers, unsettled. In 1816, however, Howard county was formed, consisting of that portion of Missouri west of St. Louis and St. Charles counties, with an area of about 22,000 square miles, one-third as large as the present State of Missouri. In the same year, the town of Franklin was laid off on the bottom lands across the river from the present town of Boonville, and the next year was made the seat of government of this extensive county. In 1818 the land office for central Missouri was located at Franklin, and an immense migration to that region followed. Franklin quickly became the economic center of the Boon's Lick country, being rated second only to St. Louis among all the towns of Missouri Territory. (5) It had a population of about one thousand in 1819, and gave better promise for rapid growth than any other town west of St. Louis. (6) Many of its inhabitants belonged to the best families of Virginia, Kentucky and Tennessee, and became prominent in the later history of the State. This high standard of its population made the town noted on the frontier for its hospitality, intelligence and enterprise. (7)

---

(3) In later years Patten was charged by a rival editor with having been an opponent of the War of 1812, and an advocate of the Hartford Convention; in reply, he branded the charges as false, and declared that he had always upheld the war "and as the editor of a newspaper during the last year or two of its continuance, gave it his decided support." Mo. Intel., Sept. 20, 1827.

(4) In an editorial in 1829, he writes of himself as residing "permanently in this county for the last twelve years." Mo. Intel., Oct. 2, 1829. This is the only indication as to his time of arrival.

(5) Mo. Intel., April 1, 1820.

(6) J. M. Peck's Memoirs, quoted in History of Howard County, p. 117.

(7) History of Howard County, p. 166.

It was to this thriving, vigorous community that Nathaniel Patten determined to contribute his part,—education by the use of printer's ink.

Patten formed a partnership with Benjamin Holliday, a Virginian, who had arrived in Franklin in February, 1819, (8) and together they issued the first number of The Missouri Intelligencer and Boon's Lick Advertiser, April 23, 1819. (9)

The paper consisted of four pages, each twelve by eighteen inches, five columns to a page. The contents of this first issue, interesting after the lapse of nearly a hundred years, must have held the absorbed attention of the readers of that day from the editorial announcements to the last advertise-

(8) History of Boone County, p. 135.

(9) This partnership continued until June 17, 1820, when notice of its dissolution was given, debtors and creditors to make settlement with Holliday who continued as publisher. From occasional later references however, it appears that Patten continued in actual charge of the typographical work through this and all subsequent changes. (For instance, in the issue of Sept. 4, 1821, a note in the editorial column ascribed a delay in the appearance of the paper to "the indisposition of Mr. Patten, who prints it." And in the issue of Aug. 24, 1826, Patten said editorially: "We established this press when the whole Boon's Lick country was literally a wilderness, and have conducted it ever since.") Holliday appeared as nominal publisher from June 17, 1820, to May 28, 1821, following which for two months neither publisher nor editor was named in the paper, although it was published regularly.' From July 23 to August 28, 1821, John Payne, a young lawyer of Franklin, was publisher, following which a reorganization made Payne editor and Holliday publisher again. The death of Payne eleven days later left the position of editor unfilled as far as any notice in the paper shows. Holliday continued as publisher, however, until June 18, 1822, when he severed his connection with the paper, and four numbers appeared without any announcement of publisher or editor. In the issue of July 23, 1822, a long editorial over the names of Nathaniel Patten and John T. Cleveland announced that they had become joint proprietors of the Intelligencer and would continue its publication. (Cleveland was a teacher; in the issue of the Intelligencer of June 4, 1821, he had advertised a summer school which he was about to start in Franklin, and years after his connection with the Intelligencer ceased he reappeared as an advertiser in its columns, in charge of Fayette Academy. Mo. Intel., April 11, 1828.)

This partnership continued until April 17, 1824, when notice of its dissolution appeared, together with the announcement that the paper had come under the exclusive control of Patten. After the removal of the paper to Fayette, a notice appeared in the issue of June 28, 1827, that henceforth the editorial department of the paper would be conducted exclusively by John Wilson (a strong partisan of John Quincy Adams.) But he surrendered his editorial duties July 18, 1828, and thereafter, until the Intelligencer ceased publication in 1835, Patten was its editor, publisher, printer and proprietor.

A fairly complete file of the Intelligencer is in the possession of the State Historical Society of Missouri.

ment. Almost two columns were given to a list of unclaimed letters at Franklin, the only postoffice in the whole Boon's Lick country; four columns were devoted to Washington news and gossip; about five columns to general literature, such as Benjamin Franklin's caution to young printers; nearly five columns more to advertisements of one kind and another, legal and commercial; the rest of the space was given to editorial announcements, a contributed article, and two or three items of local news.

The future policy of the paper was announced in the following high sounding and somewhat stilted phraseology: "—Truth being the first principle of virtue,—and virtue being the only sure basis upon which any government can rest, it will be the first object of this paper to make truth, on all occasions, its polar star.

"One firm and steady course—unshackled by the influence of any party—will dictate the discharge of their editorial functions. Respect for public sentiment will always be held in estimation.

"As the tendency of our government is towards aristocracy, the enroachment of our rulers on the constitutional rights of the people, will never be viewed in silence. But, to maintain unalloyed the right of suffrage; the liberty of conscience in matters of religion; the liberty of the press, and the freedom of speech; and to keep separate and distinct ecclesiastical and civil concerns, will always be subjects enlisting the exertions of the editors.

"Public measures, and the public characters and acts of individuals in office will always be considered just subjects of investigation; but no private quarrels, or the aspersion of private characters, will find admission into the columns of the Intelligencer."

It was also one of Patten's ambitions to make the paper neat in its appearance, and typographical and grammatical errors seldom appeared. During the seventeen years of its existence, these policies and principles were admirably carried out by the editor. Few papers can boast any higher standards than those outlined in the first number of the Intelligencer, and steadfastly accepted as guiding principles in its later publication.

The paper was to be published weekly, its price per annum being three dollars if paid in advance, or four dollars at the end of the year, the former being preferable. Some years later, in order to lengthen the subscription list, the editor offered one free subscription to any one obtaining seven new subscribers. (10) He also advertised regularly in the autumn of the year that produce would be taken in payment for subscriptions, pork especially being desired, although wood, corn, flour and vegetables were welcomed. (11) But even with such special inducements, the subscription list never was large, perhaps a few hundred at the most. An editorial at the beginning of the fifth year declared that three hundred new subscriptions had been secured during the previous year, but that the total number of subscribers was still only four hundred. (12)

With a small circulation the advertising rates could not be high—one dollar for the first insertion consisting of not more than fifteen lines, and fifty cents for each subsequent appearance. Obviously the paper by itself was scarcely a paying proposition. As was customary therefore, the newspaper plant became also a job printing plant; hardly an issue failed to advertise "job printing neatly done at this office."

Even so Editor Patten found it difficult to keep the wolf from the door, perhaps chiefly because of the non-payment of subscriptions and bills for advertising and job printing. There was a constant appeal for the settlement of old debts, and the editor frequently was obliged to place his accounts in the hands of constables to collect "without suit." For this service he had to pay liberally. This method of collection was objectionable to many, and Patten writes regretfully of "the necessity which obliged him to adopt it—but he must have money to carry on his business and to support his family."

(10) Mo. Intel., June 2, 1832.
(11) Mo. Intel., Dec. 9, 1823; Oct. 28, 1825.
(12) Ibid., Aug. 5, 1823.

(13) The loss from bad debts must have amounted to hundreds of dollars in the course of a few years. Indeed the income was so precarious during the early history of the Intelligencer that the editors had to engage in various other forms of business to make sure of a living. In an early issue it was announced that Patten and Holliday were prepared to do a storage, commission and land agency business, (14) and a week later appeared the notice that they had received by steamboat [the first steamboat to ascend the Missouri river to Franklin] 150 barrels of excellent superfine flour which they would sell for less than the regular Franklin price. They also had for sale a few barrels of "excellent whiskey," as well as salt in wholesale or retail quantities. (15) Patten also seems to have been somewhat of a land speculator, offering for sale through the columns of his paper over fifteen hundred acres situated in Chariton and Randolph counties. (16) From time to time as long as the Intelligencer was published a rich variety of notices called attention to this same land, for which there seemed to be no market.

Finally, he had reason to expect a regular even though a small income by holding the position of postmaster, The office at Franklin, known at first in the government records as Howard Court House, was established February 8, 1817, Alexander Lucas being the first postmaster. He was succeeded by Patten September 7, 1819. (17) That was before the day of postage stamps, and since small change also was scarce it was customary for postmasters on their own responsibility to give credit for postage. Patten followed this unbusiness-like custom until he found upwards of two hundred

(13) Ibid., Sept. 20, 1827. See also Jan. 18, 1826 and May 12, 1826.
(14) Ibid., May 28, 1819.
(15) Ibid., June 4, 1819.
(16) Ibid., March 13, 1829.
(17) Postoffice Department Records, Washington, D. C. (From information furnished by the First Assistant Postmaster General.) In the History of Howard county, p. 171, it is stated that "Augustus Stores" [Storrs] was the first postmaster at Franklin, and that April 20, 1821, was the date of the establishment of the office. This is manifestly incorrect. The government records do not show any actual change of name of the office, the change in the records being simply to correspond to the common name given to the office in the vicinity of Franklin.

dollars due to him in very small sums, the most of which probably never were paid. In November, 1820, the office was robbed of $800; Patten as postmaster was held responsible for the stolen money, and though he later petitioned Congress over and over for relief his petition never was granted. (18) This loss was a hard blow financially, and together with the manner of his removal from office embittered his experience as postmaster. The only reason given for his removal was the charge that he had violated a department regulation which required postmasters to notify newspaper publishers of the death or removal of any of their subscribers. In this case Gales and Seaton of the National Intelligencer made the charge, which Patten denied. (19)

The financial burden was not the only one the proprietor of the Missouri Intelligencer had to bear. There were other disheartening difficulties. The irregularity of the mail kept him in a constant state of suspense; in 1819 it was scheduled to be received once in two weeks, on horseback, but occasionally a month went by without news from the outside world. (20) In 1824, the carrier was under contract to deliver the St. Louis mail in three days—he seldom did it in less than seven. (21) On one occasion, apologizing for only a half sheet, Patten said: "We do not know that our readers would be much benefitted, the present week, had we issued a full sheet, as we have no news." (22) Sometimes the shipments of paper or ink were weeks overdue, and their failure to arrive made it almost impossible to issue the full-sized sheet. Good

---

(18) A complete history of the affair, with much sidelight material on frontier conditions and on Patten himself, is given in various Senate and House documents as a result of the petitions. See particularly House Report 59, 21st Cong., 1st Ses. From these Reports it appears that Patten was very small, very deaf, in ill health, and poor. Notwithstanding, there were numerous statements from some of the most prominent citizens of Missouri as to his integrity of character, honor, probity, and careful attention to business. Among those who bore witness for him were General Thomas A. Smith, Receiver of Public Money, Charles Carroll, Register of the Land Office, Duff Green, and Senator Thomas H. Benton.
(19) Mo. Intel., April 23, 1821.
(20) Ibid., Dec. 5, 1835.
(21) Ibid., Dec. 25, 1824.
(22) Ibid., Jan. 15, 1831.

workmen were hard to secure and were usually addicted to intemperance, occasionally leaving the editor with no help at all. (23) Patten also had an annoying experience with one of his partners, Cleveland, into whose hands fell the business of collecting the firm's debts when their partnership was dissolved. To do this, he took disagreeably coercive measures, presumably with the chief object of hurting the Intelligencer's subscription list. Patten thereupon ran a notice in the paper to the effect that persons wishing to discontinue as subscribers must send him the order, as he would pay no attention to orders received through Cleveland. (24)

In addition to all these annoyances and difficulties in the publication of the paper, Patten had some personal griefs while residing at Franklin. When he came from Kentucky to Missouri, his father's family had remained at Mount Sterling. In 1820 the father died, leaving the mother and two sisters alone. (25) They soon left Mount Sterling to join the son and brother in Franklin, but had lived in their new home less than a year when the younger of the sisters was taken sick of "the prevailing fever," presumably typhoid, and died a few days later. (26) Patten himself was almost at the point of death at the same time, and during his whole residence at Franklin suffered from what he considered its poor climate. Writing of this afterwards, he said he was "almost annually brought to the gates of death." (27)

By 1826 it was apparent that the earlier prophecies of Franklin's future greatness would not be fulfilled; Howard county had been reduced almost to its present size, and Fayette instead of Franklin made the county seat. Boonville, across the river, was drawing trade from Franklin. Worst of all, the river had changed its current and was swiftly eating away the ground upon which Franklin stood. Under these

(23) Ibid., Feb. 12, 1831.
(24) Mo. Intel., May 15, 1824.
(25) One sister had died in infancy, and another had married and was living in Indiana. Nothing is known of the later life of his mother or of the fourth sister.
(26) Mo. Intel., October 9, 1821.
(27) Ibid., Sept. 25, 1829.

conditions, and with the desire to enjoy better health, Patten determined in June, 1826, to remove the Intelligencer to Fayette. (28) During the seven years of its publication in Franklin, he had constantly kept in mind the fine principles outlined in the first issue, and had continued to put forth the paper regularly in the face of delicate health, annoyances, and difficulties almost unknown to his brother printers in other parts of the Union.

At Fayette, where the Intelligencer was published for nearly four years, Patten enjoyed in some respects more prosperity and happiness than had been his lot at Franklin. At the time of his removal he was nearly thirty-four years old, and still a bachelor. But shortly afterwards he met Miss Matilda Gaither whom he married in the summer, presumably, of 1827. (29) He was too reticent when it came to his personal affairs to even mention the marriage in his paper. The bride was a cultured, educated lady, originally from Maryland, a favored guest at the White House during Madison's presidency, and must have exerted a powerful influence upon her husband.

It was at Fayette, however, that Patten experienced for the first time the rivalry of another newspaper, rivalry of a most sordid and bitter nature. This rival, The Western Monitor, appeared in mid-summer, 1827. The new paper was evidently established because of dissatisfaction with the political course of the Intelligencer. Previously the Intelligencer had been non-partisan in the sense that its editorials had not favored any particular candidate, while its colums had been open to contributions from all sides. (30) In the issue of June 29, 1826, Patten said that his course in regard to the next presidential election was undetermined, but in the issue of May 3, 1827, he came out in favor of John Quincy Adams, his editorials through the previous months showing that he had gradually come to that conclusion. The Jackson adherents thereupon decided to establish a rival paper, with

(28) Ibid., June 16, 1826.
(29) The date is approximately established by a notice in the Intelligencer of Jan. 8, 1830.
(30) Mo. Intel., Aug. 5, 1823.

James H. Birch from the St. Louis Enquirer as its editor. Before doing this, they proposed to Patten that the new paper should unite with his and be published upon "Jacksonian Principles." Patten gave "an unhesitating refusal" (to use his own words) defending himself afterwards by declaring that he did not "feel disposed to abandon a good and just cause, for the support of a bad one." (31) Moreover, he did not like Birch and would have no connection with him of any sort. (32)

After the establishment of the Monitor, the two papers began a bitter quarrel which lasted, with short intermissions, during the rest of Patten's residence at Fayette. As there is no known file of the Monitor in existence at the present time, we have only Patten's side of the quarrel; and judging from his editorials, Birch was doing everything possible to destroy the Intelligencer and drive him away. On one occasion Birch went to the postoffice and counting the papers Patten had deposited there to be forwarded by mail, used the information to belittle the latter. Birch reported the Intelligencer on the verge of failure and Patten on the point of moving to Indiana. "We never expressed such an intention in our life," exclaimed Patten; "it is true our residence here may not be permanent, for the reason that, for several years (in consequence of the great personal labor which has constantly devolved on us—our continued ill state of health, and a wish to be aloof from the quarrels and contentions of party) we have been willing to dispose of our establishment; and would still do so if a suitable offer were made. As to its being discontinued, there is not the remotest possibility of it." (33)

According to Patten, Birch went to the extreme of waylaying and assaulting him. "It is this dark, insidious, assassin-like conduct that we have had to contend against, and which has excited our horror and indignation." (34)

(31) Ibid., March 14, 1828.
(32) Ibid., March 28, 1828.
(33) Ibid., June 27, 1828.
(34) Ibid., Birch had a reputation over the State as being among "the most reckless and abusive" of editors. See Mo. Argus, April 14, 1837.

Writing later of his life at Fayette, Patten called it unspeakable misery, to endure which again no earthly consideration could tempt him. (35)

After the election of 1828 the bitterness between the two papers seems to have abated somewhat, and by the summer of 1829 Patten could write: "Altho' the billows have dashed around us, threatening to overwhelm us, yet, through the interposition of Providence, aided by the support and kindness of personal and political friends, together with our own unwearied personal industry and economy, we have emerged from the waves. The sun of prosperity has dissipated the impending clouds, and now shines upon us, inviting to renewed exertion." (36)

It was about this time that Birch sought again to form a business connection with Patten, a proposition which the latter repelled. He would have nothing to do with Birch, but his refusal seemed to stir up the animosity more fiercely than ever, and the last months of 1829 were among the most bitter of Patten's life. It was in the midst of his professional trouble that his wife's health failed, and after a lingering illness of three months she died December 27, 1829. (37)

Nearly a year before this bereavement, Patten had received pressing invitations from a neighboring county (Boone presumably), accompanied by assurances that his subscription list would be three times as long, to transfer his business there. (38) He had evidently seriously considered making the change, for he tried to sell his real estate in Fayette. (39) This he was unable to do even at less than cost. Following the death of his wife, however, he determined to stop the publication of the Intelligencer at Fayette, and then to resume it after a time in Columbia, the seat of Boone county. In the issue of February 26, 1830, notice of

(35) Mo. Intel., Dec. 5, 1835.
(36) Ibid., July 17, 1829.
(37) Ibid., Jan. 1, 1830. In an editorial of Oct. 30, 1829, Patten speaks of ilness in the family, causing all of his editorial writing to be done after the hour of midnight.
(38) Ibid., Jan. 23, 1829.
(39) Ibid., Jan. 2, 1829.

this intended suspension appeared, the reasons therefor being the editor's impaired health, domestic affliction, and the desire personally to collect debts due to him in the surrounding country. The last numer of the paper at Fayette appeared April 9, 1830.

At the time Patten intended to take a long rest, but his enemies spread false reports as to the cause of suspension, to refute which he resumed publication at Columbia May 4, 1830. Undoubtedly his chief reason for removing from Fayette was to get away from the "demon of contention" with the rival paper. He was not of a combative nature and never courted disputes even of a friendly character. Moreover, he never was completely satisfied to make his paper an exponent of any party; in fact he represented a new spirit in newspaper journalism, the spirit of independence in politics. "We have labored hard, very hard," he wrote later, "that we might at all times pursue an independent course, and speak our thoughts without 'fear, favor or affection.'" (40) And he let it be distinctly understood in his first issue at Columbia that he wished to conduct a paper impartially, though he would permit discussion on both sides of questions "if conducted with candor and moderation." (41)

Columbia at that time had a population of about six hundred (42) and appeared to be growing rapidly, and its citizens had confidence in its future. Patten's six years there formed the most contented, prosperous and influential period of his life. Among Missouri editors he was the dean in point of service, and at Columbia he quickly improved the reputation already made for himself and his paper; and though the abuse from the Western Monitor continued it was like the rumbling of a receding storm. On February 27, 1831, he married for his second wife Mrs. Eliza Holman, widow of Dr. John Holman. (43) As in the case of his first

---

(40) Ibid., Oct. 3, 1835.
(41) Ibid., May 4, 1830.
(42) History of Boone Co., p. 802.
(43) Ibid., p. 138. The only known child of this marriage was Nathaniel Patten, Jr., date of birth unknown.

marriage, no notice of this appeared in the Intelligencer. At the end of his first year in Columbia, in an appeal for increased support in the way of more subscribers, his contentment with his new residence was shown as follows: "It is the wish of the Editor that his residence here should be permanent. It has thus far been rendered pleasant and agreeable—the hand of friendship and good will has been extended to him by the inhabitants generally—if he has a personal enemy in Boone he does not know it. Certain he is, that none other than the kindest feelings towards every individual, has a place in his breast. He therefore hopes it will be made his interest to remain here." (44)

In 1832 some of Patten's friends proposed an increase in the size of the paper, but he deemed it unwise, pointing out that he was already giving more reading matter than any other paper in the State, having usually sixteen solid columns, and only four of advertisements. (45)

In politics, the Intelligencer, during the time of its publication in Columbia, was inclined to oppose the Jacksonians, but it was never subsidized by the Whigs. "We have never," wrote Patten, "at any period, or under any circumstances, levied contributions upon our political friends." (46) He usually thought out political problems for himself, "unshackled by the influence of any party," and frequently lost friends and patrons, even among distinguished politicians, because he could not agree with them. (47) He severely denounced the "demoralizing and slavish" practice of the treating of voters by candidates, little caring whether the denunciation hit Whig or Democrat; in fact, the custom seemed so pernicious that he favored the adoption of an amendment to the state constitution, making officials take oath that they furnished no voter with meat or drink during the canvass." (48)

(44) Mo. Intel., April 16, 1831.
(45) Ibid., Dec. 22, 1832.
(46) Ibid., Dec. 22, 1832.
(47) Ibid., Dec. 5, 1835.
(48) Ibid., Oct. 18, 1834.

Patten's unusual and keen appreciation of the interrelations of government and politics frequently proved itself. Upon one occasion a long editorial discussed the relations of the people to the legislature and to the constitution. (49) Again, to take the place of the discredited caucus, he suggested a method of making nominations for local offices: "Let the people of each township choose from amongst themselves, one or more discreet persons, who shall meet those chosen in the other townships, at the center of the county, who shall nominate as many candidates as shall be necessary, regarding only their qualifications." (50) At another time he gave his views as to the relation of the State government to banks and currency, one of the great problems of the day. (51) As to slavery, he held the opinion prevailing in Missouri. He strongly opposed abolitionism, and although a New Englander by birth himself owned slaves. (52) On the subject of nullification he was outspoken, refusing to print a contributed article advocating it and upholding South Carolina. "We cannot consent," he wrote, "that this press shall be made a vehicle for disseminating a doctrine which aims so deadly a blow at the Union of the states—we cannot reconcile it to our feelings—to that ardent attachment which we have felt for our beloved country, to countenance, directly or indirectly, the pernicious principles, advocated in this communication." (53)

On the subject of taxation for public education, Patten took a progressive stand, one which apparently was not approved by his readers. In the August election of 1835 an amendment providing a school tax was badly defeated, and Patten writes that although the county was almost unanimously against the measure he voted for it, "being willing to encourage any project having for its end, the promotion of education." (54) The finer, more cultured side of Patten's

(49) Ibid., July 20, 1826.
(50) Ibid., Jan. 25, 1827.
(51) Ibid., Feb. 2, 1835.
(52) Ibid., Sept. 24, 1819. Nov. 13, 1824.
(53) Ibid., Feb. 23, 1833.
(54) Ibid., Aug. 29, 1835.

nature was shown not only in his encouragement of educational progress, but also in the genuine literary ability frequently appearing in his editorials. He became eloquent over the return of fair October weather after days of rain. He placed a high valuation upon art, and his description of the work of George C. Bingham, the Missouri painter, showed an unusual knowledge of the Italian schools of painting as well as a deep and artistic appreciation of Bingham's work. (55)

As to his own function in the community, Patten had very definite ideas. "The appropriate duties of an editor," he wrote, "are, to enlighten, to improve, and ennoble the minds of the people; to elevate public sentiment, and to infuse kind and generous feelings into the bosoms of their patrons." He believed that editors in general were to be criticised for the low order of material published in their papers. "Our newspapers form so large a proportion of the reading of the community, that they have a controling influence in forming public sentiment, and directing the movements and energies of the nation. It is then very desirable that the press should be conducted with more judgment, and with a different temper than has usually been displayed of late by American Editors." (56) In giving the news he considered it his duty as an impartial journalist to present the facts, so far as he could ascertain them, to his readers, leaving them to draw their own conclusions. (57)

Patten's sanity, abstention from abuse, and liberalism gained many friends for his paper throughout the State, even among the Jacksonian Democrats. Since the establishment of the Intelligencer in 1819, Missouri newspapers had multiplied rapidly, but it still easily held a leading place. The Missouri Argus, a Democratic paper published at St. Louis, classified the Intelligencer as "decidedly the best conducted and most influential opposition journal in the State," only

---

(55) Ibid., March 14, 1835.
(56) Quoted in Mo. Argus, May 26, 1837, from the St. Charles Clarion.
(57) Mo. Intel., April 17, 1824.

excepting the St. Louis Republican. (58) The editor's ill health continued, however, and towards the close of the year 1835 it became known that he was anxious to dispose of his paper. (59) The approach of the presidential and state elections of 1836 made its ownership of considerable importance to the two political parties. Each made an active attempt to secure the property, a group of Whigs under the leadership of James S. Rollins and Thomas Miller finally being successful. (60) The last number of the Missouri Intelligencer was issued December 5, 1835, its successor, the Columbia Patriot, appearing a week later.

In answer to the inquiries of friends, Patten announced publicly that he was undecided as to his future, though he hoped to remain permanently in Columbia. (61) But he was only in his forty-third year, still in the prime of his intellectual life, and within a few months he decided to re-enter his profession, this time at St. Charles. (62) According to his prospectus, published in other newspapers, his new venture, "The St. Charles Clarion and Missouri Commercial and Agricultural Register," was to commence publication October 12, 1836. (63) Little is known of the success of the Clarion, no file of which seems to be in existence, but occasional Clarion editorials quoted in other Missouri papers indicate in their author the same hopeful buoyant spirit as of old. (64)

Patten's experience on the St. Charles Clarion, however, was short. His life had been a constant struggle against disease and he finally succumbed November 24, 1837, in the

---

(58) Mo. Argus, Nov. 13, 1835.
(59) Nearly a year before, a parenthetical expression in an editorial, "—we expect, in the course of twelve months, (if we are then the proprietor) to procure another and larger press,—" seemed to indicate that he was considering the sale of the paper at that time. See Mo. Intel., Feb. 21, 1835.
(60) History of Boone County, p. 136.
(61) Mo. Intel., Dec. 5, 1835.
(62) "We understand that a newspaper is to be established at St. Charles, to be called the 'Clarion,' by N. Patten, Esq. We have room only to say that it will be one of the most liberal of opposition papers." Mo. Argus, Sept. 23, 1836.
(63) Mo. Argus, Sept. 30, 1836.
(64) Ibid., Sept. 8, 1837, Oct. 18, 1837.

forty-fifth year of his age. (65) One of his characteristics, maintained to the last, was his loyalty to his adopted state. Always expressing faith in its future, he was willing to spend himself in its service. As a young man at Franklin, he had given a toast at a Fourth of July celebration to "Our Own State—Destined by Nature to become a Star of the first magnitude in the constellation of the Union." (66) Later in his career he had written, "We have devoted seventeen years of our life in unceasing toil to advance the best interests of Missouri." (67) In his "Valedictory," in the last number of the Missouri Intelligencer, he wrote of himself, in the third person: "It has been his aim, throughout his long career, to act consistently, honestly and disinterestedly. He has also the satisfaction to believe........that he has 'done the State some service.'" (68)

F. F. STEPHENS.

BIBLIOGRAPHY OF THE MISSOURI PRESS ASSOCIATION.

Having lately been called upon for a paper that was read before the Missouri Press Association, and on hunting for it I was struck by the forgotten or unknown value of the papers that have been read before that Association, and immediately set to work to put the facts in shape so that every one who reads will come to the same conclusion that I did. The papers are not all technical or shop papers of the editor or publisher, but a large number are valuable for the historical, biographical, educational or literary contents. Probably

(65) Mo. Republican, Nov. 29, 1837. The short obituary notice there published is rather inaccurate: Patten's only heirs were his widow and son. See Report 164, 32nd Cong., 1st Ses. Also Court records in St. Charles, kindly looked up by Mr. B. L. Emmons of that city. Mrs. Patten afterwards married Major Wilson L. Overall, and of that marriage there were three children.
(66) Mo. Intel., July 9, 1825.
(67) Ibid., Oct. 3, 1835.
(68) Ibid., Dec. 5, 1835.

very few of the editors remember or realize the importance of these papers, or the number of prominent men who have read them. Of the Governors of Missouri there were Marmaduke, Brown and Dockery; Lieutenant Governors Colman, Johnson and Painter; Cabinet members Bryan; Members of Congress, Champ Clark, Cowherd and Burnes; Judges Dillon, Given, Hawthorne and Wallace; University Presidents, Laws and Jesse; State officials, Cook, Lesueur, Roach, Gass and Swanger; United States Ambassador Child; Poets, Eugene Field, Child and Garrett; and of others Walter B. Stevens, Col. Switzler, William Marion Reedy, and others well known in the State.

The State Historical Society has a complete set of the proceedings of the Association, which was finally completed after more than twenty-five years search for copies. The late president of the Society, H. E. Robinson, had a set complete to the time of his death, but that has probably been scattered, and no other complete set is known unless the Editorial Library at Newark, New Jersey, has one.

The following list of the papers read, and of the addresses made at the meetings of the Association, has been prepared to direct attention to the value of the publications and to make them available to research workers.

F. A. SAMPSON.

ADDRESSES OF WELCOME.

Carthage. Mayor T. T. Luscombe. 17th, 1883.
Columbia. Col. W. F. Switzler. 13th, 1879.
———. Mayor Dr. Woodson Moss. 19th, 1885.
Fredericktown. Judge Jno. B. Robinson. 11th, 1877,
Fulton. Mayor Don P. Bartley. 43rd, 1909.
Hannibal. Geo. A. Mahan. 24th, 1890.
———. Jno. A. Knott. 40th, 1906.
———. Mayor Chas. T. Hays. 46th, 1912.
Jefferson City. Hon. H. Clay Ewing. 15th, 1881.
———. Mayor John G. Riddler. 21st, 1887.
———. Acting Gov. J. F. Gmelich. Winter, 1910.

Lebanon. Judge Wallace. 28th, 1894.
Lexington. Col. John Reid. 8th, 1874.
Mexico. Mayor M. Y. Duncan. 20th, 1886.
Nevada. Mayor Chas. O. Graves. 23rd, 1889.
———. Hon. W. J. Stone, 23rd, 1889.
St. Joseph. Hon. James M. Burnes. 16th, 1882.
St. Louis. Hon. Norman J. Colman. 25th, 1891.
Sedalia. Mayor Dr. E. C. Evans. 14th, 1880.
Springfield. Mayor H. F. Fellows. 12th, 1878.
———. Mayor Ralph Walker. 18th, 1884.

ANNUAL AND PRESIDENTIAL ADDRESSES.

Ovid Bell. 47th, 1913.
Prof. J. P. Blanton. 2nd, 1888.
Gov. B. Gratz Brown. 13th, 1879.
E. P. Caruthers. 36th, 1902.
W. D. Crandall. 21st, 1887.
Howard Ellis. 10th Winter, 1903.
———. 37th, 1903.
Henry W. Ewing. 31st, 1897.
J. West Goodwin. 25th, 1891.
Omar D. Gray. 42nd, 1908.
H. J. Groves. 33rd, 1899.
John W. Jacks. 29th, 1895.
Capt. Henry P. King. 14th, 1880.
I. H. Kinley. 21st, 1887.
Jno. A. Knott. 28th, 1894.
W. R. Painter. 34th, 1900.
E. L. Purcell. 46th, 1912.
Wes. L. Robertson. 30th, 1896.
———. 35th, 1901.
E. W. Stephens. 24th, 1890.
Geo. W. Trigg. 32nd, 1898.
J. H. Turner. 13th, 1879.
T. T. Wilson. 38th, 1904.

POEMS.

Mrs. Julia M. Bennett. 13th, 1879.
Col. J. T. Child. Poesy. 19th, 1885.
Miss M. Josephine Conger. 33rd, 1899.
Miss Elizabeth Dugan, *pseud.* Rosa Pearle. 16th, 1882.
Mrs. Geo. E. Dugan, *pseud.* May Myrtle. 17th, 1883.
Maj. J. N. Edwards. 6th, 1872.
Geo. W. Ferrel. 9th, 1875.
———. 11th, 1877.
———. 15th, 1881.
Eugene Field. 10th, 1876.
———. 11th, 1877. Also given in 30th, 1896.
Thomas E. Garrett. 3rd, 1869.
John W. Hatton. 13th, 1879.
Mrs. Jennie M. Hicks. 14th, 1880.
"Jenks." 4th, 1870. (Published in 5th.)
Mrs. D. C. Kelley. 16th, 1882.
Geo. A. M'Donald. 17th, 1883.
R. M. Morrow. 8th winter. 1901.
Mrs. Annie Robertson Noxon. 18th, 1884.
Dudley A. Reid. 8th Winter, 1901.
B. F. Russel. 14th, 1880.
D. F. Thompson. 37th, 1903.
J. H. Turner. 10th, 1876.
———. 12th, 1878.
C. B. Wilkinson. 5th, 1871.
Byron Williams. 42nd, 1908.
C. M. Zeigle. 35th, 1901.

PAPERS.

D. L. Ambrose. The Country Press. 22nd, 1888.
Jim G. Anderson. Big puffs for little tickets, with special reference to shows, entertainments, etc. 20th, 1886.
Dr. J. C. Armstrong. Not outside the realm of Ethics. 6th Winter, 1898.

Arthur Aull. Advertising, 12th Winter, 1906.

———. Establishing a daily in a small city. 46th, 1912.

George Bartholomaeus. Missouri's Agricultural exhibit at the World's Fair. Extra, 1904.

John Beal. The subscription list. 6th Winter, 1898.

———. The editor's joy. 37th, 1903.

———. Some things the country editor should do. 46th. 1912.

Edward E. Bean. What is a newspaper. 29th, 1895.

J. H. Bean. The business end of a newspaper. 45th, 1911.

Ovid Bell. Responsibilities of a country editor. 37th, 1903.

———. Suggestions for making the Association of greater benefit to its members. 41st, 1907.

———. Farm news for farmers. Journalism week, 1912.

Mark Bennett. Missouri at the World's Fair. 37th, 1903.

L. A. Bird. Correspondence. 12th Winter, 1906.

Milo Blair. Essay. 8th, 1874.

Jack Blanton. How I keep in touch with my readers. 42nd, 1908.

———. A fair rate per thousand circulation for advertising. Winter, 1910.

———. Our fraternity immortals. 45th, 1911.

———. Anticipation and realization and story of the Legislature. 47th, 1913.

A. J. Blethen. Modern journalism. 18th, 1884.

Mrs. T. D. Bogie. A trenody for the times. 17th, 1883.

———. The country editor. 23rd, 1889.

———. Writers, old and new, their labors and characteristics. 26th, 1892.

T. D. Bogie. What is editorial? 4th Winter, 1893.

Mrs. Bonfils, *pseud.* Winifred Black. The American Newspaper and the American Home. 44th, 1910.

G. M. Booth. Cost system. 45th, 1911.

J. W. Booth. Advertising from a newspaper standpoint. 42nd, 1908.

Euphrates Boucher. The old and new journalist. 9th Winter, 1902.

W. R. Bowles. Politics in the Association. 37th, 1903.

Clark Brown. Hyperboles, pardonable and otherwise. 37th, 1903.

W. V. Brumby. The making of a good reporter. 44th 1910.

Joe H. Bryan. Cash subscriptions. 21st, 1887.

Hon. Wm. J. Bryan. The weekly newspaper. 35th, 1907.

W. M. Bumbarger. Personal column. 2nd Winter, 1891.

A. C. Cameron. Printing office management. 2nd Winter, 1891.

E. E. Campbell. The ethics of the newspaper profession. 37th, 1903.

John P. Campbell. Dignity and honor of the country press. 37th, 1903.

John L. Cannon. Country and City—their unity necessary. 34th, 1900.

E. P. Carthurs. Ethics of journalism. 4th Winter, 1893.

———. Legal advertising. 34th, 1900.

———. Some more about legal advertising. 36th, 1902.

———. Some more about legal advertising. 42nd, 1908.

———. Business methods in the county newspaper office. Journalism week, 1912.

Col. T. S. Case. The Newspaper the borderland between romance and history. 12th, 1878.

W. G. Chappell. The causes for the increased cost of printing material. 7th Winter, 1900.

Hon. J. T. Child. Poetry of journalism. 14th, 1880.

―――――. Early journalism of the Missouri Valley. 16th, 1882.

Col. T. J. Child. Address. 25th, 1891.

H. F. Childers. Interesting report on advertising contracts. 24th, 1890.

―――――. An association advertising agent. 25th, 1891.

―――――. Importance of preserving the Association's history. 5th Winter, 1898.

―――――. Response to Fulton address of welcome. 43rd, 1909.

E. H. Childers. Making prices on printing. 47th, 1913.

O. W. Chilton. Getting business. 47th, 1913.

H. C. Chinn. Business management. 25th, 1891.

―――――. Business management. 4th Winter, 1893.

Levi Chubbuck. Farmer's advertising. 25th, 1891.

―――――. Relations of the country editor to the farmer. 7th Winter, 1900.

―――――. A pod of peas. 9th Winter, 1902.

Hon. Champ Clark. The necessity for political morality. 15th, 1881.

Roy T. Cloud. News. 47th, 1913.

J. G. Coe. Country newspapers and clubbing propositions. 12th Winter, 1906.

Ex-Gov. Norman J. Colman. Address. 3rd, 1869.

―――――. Address. 19th, 1885.

C. J. Colden. Needed newspaper legislation. 12th Winter, 1906.

F. J. Conger. The mechanical department. 28th, 1894.

E. J. Conger. The newspaper. 31st, 1897.

―――――. The mechanical department of a country newspaper. 32nd, 1898.

Hon. Sam B. Cook. Newspaper piracy. 23rd, 1889.

Hon. W. S. Cowherd. My experience with and advice to the press. 33rd, 1899.

W. D. Crandall. The lights and shadows of journalism. 13th, 1879.

———. Journalistic personalities. 20th, 1886.
R. B. Crossman. Personal journalism. 9th Winter, 1902.
C. W. Crutsinger. Printers' inking rollers. 21st, 1887.
———. Mechanical department. 1st Winter, 1890.
———. Printers' rollers. 30th, 1896.
Sam W. Davis. Advertising. 42nd, 1908.
R. T. Deacon. Personality plus system. Journalism week, 1912.
Mark L. DeMotte. Address. 9th, 1875.
Clint H. Denman. The undignified use of a dignified office. 46th, 1912.
W. M. Denslow. Personals and the personal column. 31st, 1897.
Judge John A. Dillon. The Future of Missouri. 17th, 1883.
J. W. S. Dillon. Methods of gathering the news. 11th Winter, 1904.
———. Best method of getting subscriptions. 42nd, 1908.
D. P. Dobyns. The editorial management of the country newspaper. 25th, 1891.
Gov. A. M. Dockery. Address. 38th, 1904.
John Dopf. Address. 10th Winter, 1903.
R. E. Douglas. Material equipment—its purchase, care and use. 43rd, 1909.
Howard Ellis. District Associations—their relation to the State Association. 8th Winter, 1901.
Henry W. Ewing. Reminiscences and suggestions. 30th, 1896.
Excursion to Pilot Knob. 3rd, 1869.
Excursion to Yellow Stone Park. 24th, 1890.
Excursion to Lebanon. 25th, 1891.
Hon. Phil. G. Ferguson. The local reporter. 16th, 1882.
Eugene Field. Page set apart to his memory. 30th, 1896.
Bernard Finn. The editorial page. 47th, 1913.

Theo. D. Fisher. Association literature. 12th, 1878.
———————. The Advertising department, 20th, 1886.
Mrs. Theodore Fisher. Sketch of Ste. Genevieve. 30th, 1896.
Mrs. Susie McK. Fisher. Women in journalism. 15th, 1881.
———————. The literary crazy quilt. 19th, 1885.
A. J. Fleming. Comic phases of journalism. 17th, 1883
Joseph Flynn. Early history of Cape Girardeau. 3th, 1896.
W. B. Folsom. The business department of a country newspaper. 32nd, 1898.
B. Ray Franklin. How to make a weekly pay in a small town. 46th, 1912.
Mrs. Lily Herald Frost. Our town. 42nd, 1908.
J. G. Gallemore. Boom editions. 29th, 1895.
———————. A newspaper's obligations to its constituancy. 5th Winter, 1898.
Philip Gansz. The duty of the newspaper to the public. 32nd, 1898.
———————. What importance should be given to country correspondence. 11th Winter, 1904.
———————. The press club house. 42nd, 1908.
———————. Home advertising. 43rd, 1909.
Corydon Garrett. Serum contra mortem. 36th, 1902.
Thomas E. Garrett. Field and work. 14th, 1880.
E. S. Garver. The advertising agent. 4th Winter, 1893.
Joseph L. Garvin. The social value of the country newspaper. 47th, 1913.
H. A. Gass. The local press and the schools. 36th, 1902.
———————. Missouri's educational exhibit at the World's Fair. Extra, 1904.
Judge S. A. Gilbert. Address. 11th, 1877.
Robert Gillham. The press in the eyes of a citizen. 5th Winter, 1898.
Judge Noah M. Givan. "Temple of Fraternity" at St. Louis World's Fair. 9th Winter, 1902.

Joe Goldman. Kidding. 45th, 1911.

M. S. Goodman. Newspaper policy. 28th, 1894.

J. West Goodman. Newspaper legislation. 22nd, 1888.

—————. What is a model press association. 24th, 1890.

—————. Fifty-seven years in a printing office. 41st, 1907.

J. A. Graham. The home newspaper. 7th Winter, 1900.

W. O. Graham. The real mission of the country newspaper. 42nd, 1908.

Omar D. Gray. How to make a country weekly pay. 28th, 1894.

—————. The newspaper—its news. 31st, 1897.

—————. How to induce country merchants to advertise everlastingly. 10th Winter, 1903.

—————. County Magazines. 10th Winter, 1904.

—————. The benefits of county press associations and how to organize them. 41st, 1907.

—————. Response to welcome address at Excelsior Springs. 42nd, 1908.

John Harris. Advertising a country newspaper. 9th Winter, 1902.

C. M. Harrison. A newspaper's obligation to its constituancy. 5th Winter, 1898.

—————. Newspapers in Europe. 42nd, 1908.

Frank Hart. Metropolitan journalism. 24th, 1890.

M. C. Harty. Local news. 9th Winter, 1902.

Judge J. H. Hawthorne. Missouri's exhibit at St. Louis World's Fair. 38th, 1904.

Col. B. B. Herbert. National Editorial Association. 23rd, 1889.

—————. A course of journalistic reading. 30th, 1896.

—————. Journalism founded on truth. 31st, 1897.

—————. Paper. 42nd, 1908.

Ewing Herbert. Self-effacement. 43rd, 1909.

J. J. Heifner. Insurance laws. 10th Winter, 1903.

Chas. J. Henninger. The Press. 41st, 1907.

—————. How to make a newspaper pay. 46th, 1912.

State Historical Society. 35th, 1901; 9th Winter, 1902; 10th Winter, 1903; Extra, 1904; 39th, 1905; 12th Winter, 1906; 40th, 1906; 41st, 1907; 42nd, 1908; 43rd, 1909; 46th, 1912.

R. Earle Hodges. The Missouri Press Association's "Hell Box." 37th, 1903.

J. N. Holmes. The Country Editor. 7th Winter, 1900.

E. S. Horn. Associated advertising clubs of America. 42nd, 1908.

J. A. Hudson. Practical printing. 19th, 1885.

——. The best methods of business management. 24th, 1890.

——. The business department. 29th, 1895.

——. Journalism. 45th, 1911.

Harvey W. Ingham. Newspaper leadership. 47th, 1913.

Harry S. Jacks. Business management. 43rd, 1909.

John W. Jacks. An historical sketch. 22nd, 1888.

Rufus Jackson. Of interest to stockmen and farmers. 45th, 1911.

W. T. Jenkins. Relative value of editorial and local columns. 32nd, 1898.

President R. H. Jesse. Address. 31st, 1897.

——. Education. 5th Winter, 1898.

——. Address. 40th, 1906.

Hon. W. O. L. Jewett. Legislation affecting newspapers. 23rd, 1889.

——. Why we are here. 28th, 1894.

——. What constitutes a country newspaper. 5th Winter, 1898.

George S. Johns. The essential thing in a newspaper. 7th Winter, 1900.

——. Newspaper power—its use and abuse. 44th, 1910.

Ex-Gov. Chas. P. Johnson. The art of printing; its relation to intellectual development, with observations on the character and influence of the press of America. 15th, 1881.

——. Personal recollection of some of Missouri's eminent statesmen and lawyers. 10th Winter, 1903.

Joe P. Johnston. Party organs *vs.* independent journalism. 25th, 1891.

———. Use and abuse of the second class mailing privilege. 46th, 1912.

Hon. J. Ed. Jones. The Missouri Press. 18th, 1884.

C. H. Jones. Journalism and journalists. 23rd, 1889.

J. H. Kerby. Response to welcome address. 27th, 1893.

Hon. Chas. W. Knapp. The metropolitan press. 6th Winter, 1898.

———. Postal rates and regulations. 41st, 1907.

Jno. A. Knott. Advertising. 1st Winter, 1890.

———. The unpurchasable press. 31st, 1897.

Lewis Lamkin. Local organization. 20th, 1886.

———. Our first meeting. 30th, 1896.

Dr. S. S. Laws Presentation of badge address. 16th, 1882.

———. Sovereignty as realized in our American system of government. 16th, 1882.

A. L. Lawshe. Postal laws regarding newspapers. 42nd, 1908.

Mrs. S. E. Lee. The woman editor's opportunity. Journalism week, 1912.

Hon. A. A. Lesueur. Response to address of welcome. 16th, 1882.

———. The opportunities of journalism. 17th, 1883.

———. Editorial ethics. 20th, 1886.

———. The literary and personal features of country journalism. 25th, 1891.

———. The office cat. 28th, 1894.

———. The ethics of journalism. 32nd, 1898.

Chas. S. Lewis. The country press. 42nd, 1908.

W. H. Lighty. Historical societies and social progress. 10th Winter, 1903.

R. H. Lindsay. The relation of the metropolitan to the country press. 5th Winter, 1898.

Geo. R. Lingle. The needs of the country press. 27th, 1893.

John M. London. The nobler aims of the profession. 11th, 1877.

J. R. Lowell. How much should an editor engage in politics. 8th Winter, 1901.

――――. Response to Joplin address of welcome. 45th, 1911.

B. F. Lusk. Newspaper observations. 9th Winter, 1902.

Lon Luther. Rural mail delivery and the country press. 36th, 1902.

――――. Commercial politics and its effects upon the body politic. 10th Winter, 1903.

E. K. Lyles. Which is of the greatest value to the country newspaper—the editorial, local or correspondence department. 34th, 1900.

J. B. McCullogh. Modern journalism. 12th, 1878.

E. E. E. McJimsey. Editorials—how much and what about. 6th Winter, 1898.

R. W. McMullen. Should an editor hold office. 29th, 1895.

――――. Independent journalism. 34th, 1900.

Edmond McWilliams. Value of the editorial pag. Journalism week, 1912.

Mrs. Elizabeth Mantiply. Women as newspaper men 47th, 1913.

Mark Twain. Acceptance of honorary membership. 47th, 1913.

Gen. John S. Marmaduke. Address. 7th, 1873.

A. J. Martin. Circulation—how gained and maintained. 43rd, 1909.

Dewitt Masters. Getting the news. 47th, 1913.

Will H. Mayes. Health, wealth and happiness. 32nd, 1898.

Jewell Mayes. The work of the Missouri Commission. Extra, 1904.

――――. How special features help. Journalism week, 1912.

E. O. Mayfield. The relation twentieth century ready prints bear to publications outside large cities. 42nd, 1908.

Wm. Maynard. The printer's devil of the future. 14th, 1880.

J. B. Merwin. Spelling reform. 14th, 1880.

Chas. L. Miller. How to make money in the job office of the average country shop. 43rd, 1909.

R. W. Mitchell. Newspaper controversies, wise and otherwise. 5th Winter, 1898.

———. A peculiar profession. 34th, 1900.

J. F. Mitchin. Advertisements—how written and displayed. 8th Winter, 1901.

A. D. Moffett. The near-city daily. Journalism week, 1912.

Col. J. C. Moore. Address, 5th, 1871.

W. L. Moorhead. Newspaper influences. 37th, 1903.

C. D. Morris. Free rural mail delivery. Effects of the local paper. 8th Winter, 1901.

———. Do we need a new capitol? Winter, 1910.

J. S. Morton. Advertising from the standpoint of a country merchant and newspaper man. 37th, 1903.

L. T. Moulton. Some phases of newspaper work. 8th Winter, 1901.

W. G. Musgrove. The editor as a politician. 32nd, 1898.

Edgar C. Nelson. Shop equipment. 47th, 1913.

J. G. Nelson. The business of job printing. 39th, 1905.

L. O. Nelson. Job printing axioms. 6th Winter, 1898.

———. The special feature of a country newspaper made necessary by surroundings. 36th, 1902.

———. My experience with a country newspaper. 42nd, 1908.

W. L. Nelson. The real mission of the country newspaper. 42nd, 1908.

Miss Frances Nise. The woman reporter's work. Journalism week, 1912.

I. L. Page. Personal journalism. 9th Winter, 1902.

Hon. W. R. Painter. The Missouri book. Extra, 1904.

———. The postal laws, the postal department and the newspapers, 41st, 1907.

J. C. Patterson. Our office. 7th Winter, 1900.

Wright A. Patterson. How the country newspaper may help itself. 47th, 1903.

J. E. Payne. Should newspapers lead or follow public opinion. 20th, 1886.

C. Pearson. The real mission of the country newspaper. 42nd, 1908.

Rev. W. F. Perry. The Church and the newspaper. 39th, 1905.

S. A. Pierce. Reason for the advance costs. 7th Winter, 1900.

J. K. Pool. Editorials in a country newspaper. 4th Winter, 1893.

J. W. Powell. County correspondence and how to handle it. 4th Winter, 1893.

J. B. Powell. Advertising rates. 47th, 1913.

James B. Price. Address to the Press of Missouri. 15th, 1881.

W. C. Price. Getting and keeping circulation. 47th, 1913.

E. L. Purcell. The editor and the preacher. 36th, 1902.

————. Job printing in the country office. 12th Winter, 1906.

————. County correspondence. 43rd, 1909.

Miss Georgiana Raby. The newspaper woman. 10th Winter, 1903.

P. S. Rader. Plea for State pride. 26th, 1892.

————. The editorial department. 29th, 1895.

————. The boundaries of the Louisiana Purchase. 10th Winter, 1903.

Wm. Marion Reedy. The myth of a free press. 42nd, 1908.

Dudley A. Reid. The ideal newspaper. 35th, 1901.

W. L. Reid. The country editor. 23rd, 1889.

Report on foreign advertising. 2nd Winter, 1896.

Report of legislative committee. 24th, 1890.

Hon. Cornelius Roach. Newspaper legislation. 29th, 1895.

―――――. Newspaper controversies, wise and otherwise. 5th Winter, 1898.

―――――. The new primary law. 42nd, 1908.

J. J. Rice. Brain work. 24th, 1890.

Luther H. Rice. Some familiar faces. 9th Winter, 1902.

S. D. Rich. Our Association. 11th, 1877.

Chas. Richards. Success in the small town. 43rd, 1909.

Walter Ridgeway. My experience with the small daily. 42nd, 1908.

―――――. Province of the press. 44th, 1910.

L. P. Roberts. Does the sensational pay in the country newspaper. 37th, 1903.

Wes. L. Robertson. What is pay matter. 4th Winter, 1893.

―――――. The subscription department. 29th, 1895.

―――――. County correspondence. 31st, 1897.

H. E. Robinson. What should an editor read, and why? 5th Winter. 1898.

―――――. Foreign advertising―cause of decrease. 7th Winter, 1900.

―――――. Historical of the Association. 35th, 1901.

―――――. State Historical Society books. Extra, 1904.

Adam Rodemyre. The country editor. 23rd, 1889.

N. G. Rogers. The small city daily. 12th Winter, 1906.

B. A. Roy. Tribulations of an editor. 36th, 1902.

―――――. Success of country newspapers. 37th, 1903.

Col. Sidney J. Roy. The value and necessity of advertising Missouri. 46th, 1912.

Justin A. Runyan. Public men. 32nd, 1898.

Francis A. Sampson. See State Historical Society.

Lon Sanders. The relation of the engraver and printer. 30th, 1896.

Miss L. M. Sargent. The assistant editor. 7th Winter, 1900.

Judge E. L. Scarritt. The law of libel. 5th Winter, 1898.

Geo. Schulte. The relation of the country to the mail order business. 41st, 1907.

Geo. H. Scruton. The partisan party newspaper. 47th, 1913.

Lee Shippey. The grip of fellowship. 43rd, 1909.

———. Special features in the country weekly. Journalism week, 1912.

Mrs. H. J. Simmons. The editor's rib. 47th, 1913.

Sam Slawson. Job work. 1st Winter, 1890.

E. H. Smith. The country editor. 36th, 1902.

E. A. Snively. The uses of editorial associations. 24th, 1890.

Wm. Southern, Jr. Papers, politics and patronage. 10th Winter, 1903.

———. President's annual report. 39th, 1905.

———. Legal advertising and legal rates. 42nd, 1908.

———. The editorial page. 44th, 1910.

———. The independent party newspaper. 47th, 1913.

R. B. Speed. Subscriptions. 1st Winter, 1890.

E. W. Stephens. The Country newspaper. 18th, 1884.

———. Some of the practical features of country journalism. 23rd, 1889.

———. Response to address of welcome. 24th, 1890.

———. The newspaper and its relations to the public. 2nd Winter, 1891.

———. School of journalism. 30th, 1896.

———. What the Missouri Press Association can do for Missouri this year. 45th, 1911.

———. Address on journalism. 46th, 1912.

Hugh Stephens, Job work. 7th Winter, 1900.

———. Estimating. 36th, 1902.

Walter B. Stevens. Missourians and the World's Fair. 9th Winter, 1902.

Rev. Parker Stockdale. Liberty and the press. 9th Winter, 1902.

C. H. Streit. The advertising agent and his directory. 26th, 1892.

H. S. Sturgis. Our State Association. 32nd, 1898.

———. Some mistakes I've made in the business. 34th, 1900.

———. The news in the county paper. Journalism week, 1912.

O. P. Sturm. The local editorial. 6th Winter, 1898.

———. The journalistic quack. 33rd, 1899.

Hon. John E. Swanger. The dignity of the profession. 40th, 1906.

Col. W. F. Switzler. The country newspaper. 10th, 1876.

———. Who has been conspicuous characters in Missouri journalism. 24th, 1890.

———. History and progress of newspaper work in Missouri. 25th, 1891.

———. Words—printed words. 37th, 1903.

Fred H. Tedford. Limiting the number of newspapers. 45th, 1911.

G. H. Ten Brock. Cost of second-class mail. 40th, 1907.

S. G. Tetweiler. The local department. 24th, 1890.

Wm. L. Thomas. A short history of the Missouri Press Association. 1st Winter, 1890.

W. D. Thomas. Causes of the increase in cost. 7th Winter, 1900.

———. Response to address of welcome. Extra, 1904.

J. B. Thompson. The Hell-box. 13th, 1879.

R. P. Thompson. The independent and the dependent press. 20th, 1886.

W. J. Thornton. Early history of railroads in Missouri. 10th Winter, 1903.

James Todd. What constitutes a country newspaper. 5th Winter, 1898.

Geo. W. Trigg. The literary and personal features of country journalism. 25th, 1891.

———. Business system. 28th, 1894.

———. How to solicit, secure and create business. 31st, 1897.

———. Address at reception at Kansas City Commercial Club. 5th Winter, 1898.

———. The party paper and the politician. 8th Winter, 1901.

Capt. Joseph H. Turner. The duty of the press toward the public school system. 19th, 1885.

J. P. Tucker. What the publisher owes the advertiser. 37th, 1903.

———. What do you owe your town? 45th, 1911.

W. C. Van Cleve. The relation of the newspaper to the home candidate. 32nd, 1898.

C. P. Vandiver. How to increase advertising patronage. 4th Winter, 1893.

———. Mending our nets. 10th Winter, 1903.

———. Missouri's horticultural exhibit at the World's Fair. Extra, 1904.

Robert Walker. Press liberties. 34th, 1900.

Judge Wm. H. Wallace. "Grand old Missouri." 40th, 1906.

R. S. Walton. Typesetting machines. 12th Winter, 1906.

E. M. Watson. The small city daily. 43rd, 1909.

W. W. Waters. The legislator and the press. 36th, 1902.

Frank A. Weimer. Legal advertising. 21st, 1887.

R. G. Welsel. Paper. 28th, 1894.

F. L. Wensel. Typesetting machines. 34th, 1900.

L. M. White. Soliciting advertisements. 47th, 1913.

Mitchell White. A look ahead in the profession. 46th, 1912.

R. M. White. The duty of the press during preliminary canvasses toward candidates for public position. 20th, 1886.

————. Subscription to newspapers. 25th, 1891.

————. Newspapers and news. 27th, 1893.

————. Doing Europe in four days. 33rd, 1899.

T. B. White. Co-operation among country newspapers. 25th, 1891.

H. J. Wigginton. The dignity of journalism. 33rd, 1899.

Hon. C. B. Wilkinson. Address. 2nd, 1868.

Wallace Williams. Hints on practical printing. 20th, 1886.

Walter Williams. The profession of journalism from a business, moral and social standpoint. 20th, 1886.

————. Relations of national and state associations. 22nd, 1888.

————. What should an editor read, and why? 5th Winter, 1898.

————. The supreme mission of the editor. 32nd, 1898.

————. A plea for the editor. 34th, 1900.

————. The American editor and his foreign brother. 37th, 1903.

————. The Missouri School of Journalism. 42nd, 1908.

————. This year in the School of Journalism. 43rd 1909.

————. The practice of journalism. 44th, 1910.

E. H. Winter. Business methods. 47th, 1913.

Ben. F. Wood. Up-to-date advertising. 37th, 1903.

————. Increased rates for advertising and job work. 41st, 1907.

C. L. Woods. Missouri's mineral exhibit at the World's Fair. Extra, 1904.

R. P. Yorkston. Story of the printing press. 19th, 1885.

R. M. Yost. The editorial department. 1st Winter, 1890.

Will H. Zorn. Discontinuing the daily in a small town. 46th, 1912.

PORTRAITS.

There were no portraits in the proceedings until 1895. Afterwards there were the following:

29th meeting, 1895. John W. Jacks, H. E Robinson, R. S. Burckhart, E. E. Bean, H. T. Childers, W. L. Thomas, Lon Luther, R. M. White, and a group of the Association.

30th, 1896. Henry W. Ewing, Geo. W. Trigg, E. J. Conger, E. Boucher, Wm. L. Thomas, H. C. Chinn, H. E. Robinson, Jas. Flynn, J. West Goodwin, a plate of the retiring officers: Robinson, Burckhart, Bean, Childers, Thomas, Luther and White, and a group of the Association.

31st, 1897. Geo. W. Trigg, H. W. Ewing, R. B. Speed, W. M. Denslow, Dr. J. N. Holmes, John W. Jacks, H. J. Groves, J. H. Blanton, C. W. Barrett, C. M. Harrison, E. K. Lyles, C. C. Hilton, F. A. Leonard, Tom Tarboe, W. R. Painter, C. W. Crutsinger, W. R. Bowles, E. J. Conger, H. J. Wigginton, Wes L. Robertson, J. F. Childers, Omar D. Gray, John A. Knott, J. T. Bradshaw, W. L. Reid, C. M. McCrae, James Todd, Winfred Melvin, W. L. Thomas, A. J. Adair and wife, and R. M. White.

5th Winter, 1898. Geo W. Trigg, James Todd, W. O. L. Jewett, Cornelius Roach, H. W. Mitchell, C. M. Harrison, J. G. Gallemore, W. R. Painter, W. R. Bowles, R. M. White, H. F. Childers, H. E. Robinson, Walter Williams, and H. J. Groves.

32nd, 1898. W. T. Jenkins, Hon. A. A. Lesueur, Philip Gansz, Justin A. Runyan, W. L. Thomas, W. C. Van Cleve, W. G. Musgrove, H. S. Sturgis, Wes L. Robertson, J. T. Bradshaw, and groups of the Association.

6th Winter, 1898. H. J. Groves.

33rd, 1899. W. R. Painter, Miss M. Josephine Conger.

7th Winter, 1900. W. R. Painter.

34th, 1900. Wes L. Robertson.

8th Winter, 1901. Wes L. Robertson.

35th, 1901. E. P. Caruthers, Howard Ellis and small groups.

9th Winter, 1902. E. P. Caruthers, Levi Chubbuck, B. F. Lusk, E. W. Stephens, Euphretes Boucher, R. B. Crossman, R. M. White, John Harris, I. L. Page, Rev. Parker, Stockdale, W. D. Thomas, L. H. Rice, W. L. Thomas, Howard Ellis.

36th, 1902. T. T. Wilson, W. D. Thomas, L. O. Nelson, H. A. Gass, E. H. Smith, Hugh Stephens, E. L. Purcell, W. W. Watters, Corydon Garrett, Lon Sanders, C. W. Crutsmger, Jno. M. Sosey.

10th Winter, 1903. Howard Ellis, Jno D. Dopf.

37th, 1903. T. T. Wilson.

11th Winter, 1904. T. T. Wilson.

38th, 1904. W. D. Thomas.

39th, 1905. Wm. Southern, Jr., J. V. Bumbarger, Philip Gansz, Jno. P. Campbell, E. K. Lyles, R. M. White, H. A. Gass, six children of editors, page of wives and children.

12th Winter, 1906. Wm. Southern, Jr.

40th, 1906. Page of seven officers of Association, Mark Twain in front of boyhood home, page group of Directors of Merchants Association of Hannibal, Judge Wm. H. Wallace, Hon. John E. Swanger.

41st, 1907. Omar D. Gray, James Todd, W. L. Thomas, H. E. Robinson, Adam Rodemyre, J. West Goodwin, Lewis Lamkin, E. H. Smith, Jr.

42nd, 1908. H. F. Childers, C. M. Harrison, J. R. Lowell, Mrs. Lily Herald Frost, J. P. Campbell, J. R. Pool, Howard A. Gass, William Marion Reedy, A. L. Lawshe.

43rd, 1909. J. R. Lowell, C. M. Harrison, E. L. Purcell, Ovid Bell, Howard A. Gass, J. P. Campbell, J. K. Pool, R. E. Douglas, Lee Shippey, Chas. L. Miller, Walter Williams, Ewing Herbert, W. L. Jenkins.

47th, 1913. Clint H. Denman, H. S. Sturgis, Fred Naeter, B. Ray Franklin, J. P. Tucker, H. J. Blanton, E. H. Winter, Gov. Norman J. Colman.

BOOKS OF EARLY TRAVEL IN MISSOURI.

BRADBURY.

"Travels in the interior of America, in the years 1809, 1810, and 1811; including a description of Upper Louisiana, together with the states of Ohio, Kentucky, Indiana and Tennessee, with the Illinois and Western Territories, and containing Remarks and Observations useful to persons emigrating to those countries. By John Bradbury, F. L. S., London, Corresponding Member of the Liverpool Philosophical Society, and Honorary Member of the Literary and Philosophical Societies, New York, United States, America. Liverpool: Printed for the Author, By Smith and Galway, and published by Sherwood, Neely and Jones, London, 1817." 367 pp.

The author arrived at St. Louis on the last day of 1809, intending to make that place his headquarters while collecting natural history specimens. During the next spring and summer, he made frequent excursions to points within one hundred miles of St. Louis. In the fall he decided on joining the party under Mr. Wilson P. Hunt, which was going to cross the continent to Astoria, being sent out by John Jacob Astor in connection with his fur trade, some account of which is given in our article from Washington Irving.

Mr Hunt decided to take his party to some point on the Missouri, where they could winter with less expense than in St. Louis, and they proceeded to the mouth of the "Naduet" (Nodaway). In March Mr Hunt returned to St. Louis in a boat with ten oars, and on the 12th he started to return to his camp. The author waited for the mail to arrive the next morning from Louisville, a distance of more than 300 miles through the wilderness, and from various causes the mail had been delayed some weeks. Learning that a writ for debt would be issued against the interpreter of the expedition by some one who wished to cripple it, he and

Thomas Nutall, both Englishmen, and both of whom published accounts of their travels in the West, started at two o'clock in the morning, and finding the boat, had the interpreter and his squaw wife put on shore, to walk to some point above St. Charles and there join the boat again. Soon after leaving St. Charles, they found Dorion, but alone, he having whipped his wife and she had run into the woods. A man was sent to find her, but he returned without her. Before day the next night she hailed the boat, having relented, and decided on joining her husband. On the third day after, they reached the French village Charette, near which an old man standing on the bank was pointed out to him as Daniel Boone. He went ashore and talked with him for some time. Boone was then eighty-four years old. At Cote sans Dessein, two miles below the mouth of the Osage, they learned that there was a war party of Indians in the neighborhood, consisting of "Ayauwais, Potowatomies, Sioux, and Saukee nations, amounting to nearly three hundred warriors." They were going against the Osages, and there was danger to the company of sixteen in the boat, from some of the bands of Indians that they would meet, and a few days later they heard of the Great Osages having killed a white man at their village. At the Bonne Femme the Boone's Lick settlement commenced. It extended along the river 150 miles, and back about 50 miles, and was supposed to be the best land in Western America for so great an area. The Lick settlements were the last on the river, except those occupied by one or two families near Fort Osage. On the last day of March it suddenly turned colder, so that the water in a tin cup of about one pint measure was nearly solid ice on the morning of the first of April.

On the 2nd they passed the site of a former village of the Missouri tribe, and four miles above it were the remains of Fort Orleans, formerly belonging to the French. On the 8th they arrived at Fort Osage. A village of the Petit Osage Indians was close to the fort, and bout 200 of them were at the landing. The village consisted of one hundred lodges of an oblong form, the frame of timber and the covering mats made of leaves of the flag.

"I inquired of Dr. Murray concerning a practice which I had heard prevailed amongst the Osages, of rising before day to lament their dead. He informed me that such was really the custom, and that the loss of a horse or a dog was as powerful a stimulus to their lamentations as that of a relative or friend; and he assured me, that if I should be awake before day the following morning, I might certainly hear them. Accordingly on the 9th I heard before day that the howling had commenced; and the better to escape observation, I wrapped a blanket around me, tied a black handkerchief on my head, and fastened on my belt, in which I stuck my tomahawk, and then walked into the village. The doors of the lodges were closed, but in the greater part of them the women were howling and crying in a tone that seemed to indicate excessive grief. On the outside of the village I heard the men, who, Dr. Murray had informed me, always go out of the lodges to lament. I soon came within twenty paces of one, and could see him distinctly, as it was moonlight; he also saw me and ceased, upon which I withdrew. I was more successful with another, whom I approached nearer unobserved. He rested his back against the stump of a tree, and continued for about twenty seconds to cry in a loud and high tone of voice, when he suddenly lowered to a low muttering, mixed with sobs; in a few seconds he again raised to the former pitch."

Here he found a man dressed as a squaw, and engaged in work with the squaws. This was for a punishment of one who showed want of bravery, and when once the sentence was passed it lasted for life. The men do not associate with them, nor are they allowed to marry. On the 10th they again continued their journey, and on the 15th passed the site of a former village of the Kansas Indians, and two days later they arrived at the winter camp on the Nodaway river. On the bluffs near by were many flat stones, and under these were many snakes in a half torpid condition. He killed a number of eleven different species.

On the 21st they broke camp and to the number of sixty started across the continent. The author continued daily to make observations as to the soil, the geology or the productions of the country. On the 27th the night was so cold that the sides of the boats and the oars were covered with ice.

A few days after the author passed beyond the limits of Missouri. He finally decided to not cross the mountains with Mr. Hunt's party, but to return with a boat that was to carry furs back to St. Louis, and for fear that the furs would be captured by the Indians, orders were given to make the most rapid time possible, and not to make any stops, so that there were few opportunities for collecting on the way down. At Boon's Lick they saw three neatly dressed white women, whom they contrasted with the squaws they had for some time been seeing. In due time they arrived safely in St. Louis.

Here he was placed in charge of a boat with 30,000 pounds of lead to take to New Orleans. The crew consisted of five French creoles, and on December 5, 1811 they started on their long journey. Near New Madrid they saw four Choctaw Indians, who beckoned them to come ashore, and from whom they bought three turkeys and two hind quarters of venison for seventy-five cents.

At New Madrid there were only a few straggling houses, with two poorly stocked stores. When they came to the dangerous part of the river known as the Devil's Channel, it was sun down, and they resolved to wait until morning, and the boat was moored to a small island, and the interesting account of the New Madrid earthquake is extensively quoted as follows:

"After supper, we went to sleep as usual; about ten o'clock, and in the night I was awakened by a most tremendous noise, accompanied by an agitation of the boat so violent, that it appeared in danger of upsetting. Before I could quit the bed, or rather the skin upon which I lay, the four men who slept in the other cabin rushed in crying in the greatest terror. I passed them with some difficulty, and ran to the door of the cabin, when I could distinctly see the river as if agitated by a storm; and although the noise was inconceivably loud and terrific, I could distinctly hear the crash of falling trees and the screaming of the wild fowl on the river, but I found that the boat was still safe at her moorings. * * * *

By the time we could get to our fire, which was on a large flag, in the stern of the boat, the shock had ceased; but immediately perpendicular banks, both above and below us, began to fall into the river in such vast masses, as nearly to sink our boat by the swell they occasioned. * * * * I sent two of the men with a candle up the bank, in order to examine if it had separated from the island, a circumstance that we had suspected, from hearing the snapping of the limbs of some drift trees, which were deposited betwixt the margin of the river, and the summit of the bank. The men told us that there was a chasm formed already, so wide that it would be difficult to pass it to attain the firm ground. I ordered them to go upon the island and make a fire, and desired Mr. Bridge and the patron to follow them; and as it now occurred to me that the preservation of the boat in a great measure depended on the depth of the river, I tried with a sounding pole, and to my great joy, I found it did not exceed eight or ten feet.

Immediately after the shock we noticed the time, and found it was near two o'clock. It was now nearly half past, and I determined to go ashore myself, after securing some papers and money, and was employed in taking them out of my trunks, when another shock came on, terrible indeed, but not equal to the first. I went ashore, and found the chasm really frightful, as it was not less than four feet in width, and besides the bank had sunk at least two feet, I took the candle, and examined to determine its length, and concluded that it could not be less than eighty yards; and where it terminated at each end, the banks had fallen into the river. I now saw clearly that our lives had been saved by having moored to a sloping bank. Before we had completed our fire, we had two more shocks, and they occurred during the whole night, at intervals from six to ten minutes, but slight in comparison with the first and second. At four o'clock I took a candle, and again examined the banks, and found to my great satisfaction that no material alteration had taken place; I also found the boat safe, and secured my pocket compass. I had already noticed that the sound which we heard at the time of every shock, always preceded it at least a second, and that it always proceeded from he same direction. I now found that the shock came from a little northward of east, and proceeded to the westward. At daylight we had counted twenty-seven shocks, during our stay on the island, but still found the chasm so that it might be passed. The river was covered with foam and drift timber, and had risen considerable, but our boat was safe. Whilst we were waiting till the light became sufficient for us to embark, two canoes floated down the river, in one of which we could perceive some Indian corn and some clothes. We considered this as a melancholy proof that some of the boats we passed the preceding day had perished. Our conjectures were afterwards confirmed, as three had been overwhelmed, and all on board perished. When the daylight appeared to be sufficient for us, I gave orders to embark, and we all went on board. Two men were in the act of loosening the fastenings, when a shock occurred nearly equal to the first in violence. * * * I walked down the island, in company with Morin, our *patron*, to view the channel, in order to ascertain the safest part, which we soon agreed upon. Whilst we were thus employed, we experienced a very severe shock, and found some difficulty in preserving ourselves from being thrown down; another occurred during the time we were at breakfast, and a third as we were preparing to embark. In the last Mr. Bridge, who was standing within the declivity of the bank, narrowly escaped being thrown into the river, as the sand continued to give under his feet. * * * We continued on the river till eleven o'clock, when there was a violent shock, which seemed to affect us as sensible as if we had been on land. The trees on both sides of the river were most violently agitated, and the banks in several places fell in within our view, carrying with them innumerable trees, the crash of which falling into the river, mixed with the terrible sound attending the shock, and the screaming of the geese, and other wild fowl, produced an idea that all nature was in a state of dissolution."

They continued their journey, and other, but less severe shocks succeeded, until the 21st when the last occurred, and they were now beyond the limits of Missouri.

The book contains a very interesting description of forty-five pages of Missouri Territory.

F. A. SAMPSON.

HARMONY MISSION. (1)
MORSE'S REPORT ON INDIAN AFFAIRS. Page 222.

(Note.—Harmony mission was commenced in 1821 (built) and school commenced in 1822, and by May had 16 scholars. It was supported by the United Foreign Missionary Society of New York, and the U. S. government appropriated $1,000 towards the construction of buildings. The school was in a progressive state, and some of the children could read in words of two syllables. The Chiefs are very friendly, and willing to give up their children to become as white men and women. The children are pleasant, listen to instruction with interest and shrewd in their remarks on our customs and manners.)

Harmony. The best view of the location and present state of the Education Establishments at this station, is given in the letter and journals of its principal members. Mr. Newton writes to General Steele, from Harmony, State of Missouri, September 27th, 1821, thus: Morse's Rep. 222.

---

(1) The following letters and notes are contributed to follow the article in the last Review by the late Garland C. Broadhead. Some names, in addition to the ones given by Mr. Broadhead, may be found in these letters.

The site of this Mission on the Maries des Cygnes is an historical one to Missourians and worthy of being marked. The letter from Mr. Newton to Gen. Steele and the letters of Mr. Sprage and others furnish a good description of the site.

Contributed by David W. Eaton, Versailles, Mo.

"Harmony is situated on the margin of the Maries de Cygnes River, about six miles above its junction with the Osage. This place was granted to us by the Indians in council, on the 13th of August.

Our limits embrace excellent timber in abundance; first rate prairie for plowing, pasturing, and mowing; the only mill-seat known in this vast country; stone coal on the surface of the ground, and within a few rods of our buildings; and a large ridge, sufficiently near for our convenience. Our river bottoms are rather low for cultivation, without drainage; but our prairies are high, and inclining toward the creeks, which receive and carry off the surplus water. The soil of our prairies is a dark rich loam, about two feet thick, beneath which we have clear clay, as deep as we have yet penetrated. We shall depend on deep wells for water for family use. The grass of the prairies varies from two to seven feet in heighth, and forms an average to travelling equal to that of snow from eight to ten inches in depth.

Cattle are raised in this country without much expense. Indian corn can be bought for fifty cents a barrel, of about five bushels. Pork in the hog is advertised at seventy-five cents per hundred weight. This abundance is within a hundred miles from us, and there is a wagon way from our Station to Fort Osage, seventy-eight miles of the distance."

Mr. Sprage writes about the same time to his brother: Ibid. p. 225. "Our buildings will be erected on the river bank, but sufficiently remote to give us a spacious and handsome green in front. In the rear we have a vast prairie, covered with grass, yielding in the uncultivated state, from one and a half to two tons of hay on the acre. On either side of us we have good timber in great plenty. We have, also, near at hand, an excellent spring of water, stone coal, limestone, and clay of the first quality for making bricks. Our mill seat is about a mile below us, and is directly opposite to the United States trading house, which was commenced in July, and which is to be completed by the first of next month. We are within fifteen miles of the Great Osage village.

The Indians appear very friendly. They frequently visit us; and we feel the assurance, that some of their children will be sent to us as soon as we are able to accomodate them. Mr. Williams, the interpreter, talks of giving us his little daughter, who can speak both the English and the Osage languages, and who, of course, would be a great help to us."

The latest accounts from Harmony, are up to this year. (1882). Mr. Dodge writes thus to the Domestic Secretary: Ibid. p. 223.

"Jan. 1822.

"We have already 12 children who are given to us for instruction. We have not as yet built a school house, but at present, occupy one of our houses for the use of the school. We calculate to build accommodations for the school, as fast as they are needed, so as not to reject one Indian child that may be offered for our instruction. As our family is now large, and we have the prospect of a numerous school, we think it would promote the interests of the mission if the Board were to send us a carpenter and joiner, a thorough workman at tanning and shoemaking, an additional farmer, and a man acquainted with brick making. Some, or all of these would be very useful at this station immediately.

We have several hands employed in assisting us in erecting some necessary outbuildings, preparing us a well, splitting and hauling rails to fence our field, etc. We calculate to commence building a saw mill, and a grist-mill, early this spring, with the hope of having them finished in the fall. We have fitted up a room, which will probably have forty scholars; and our school is now in operation under as favorable circumstances as we could expect. We find much difficulty in persuading the natives to give up their children, and in keeping them after they have been given up.

Brother Sprage is doing very well in the blacksmith department; but he very much needs an assistant, which we wish you would procure for us, one who is a real substantial workman; for we have not only our own work to do, which we find must be considered; but we find the Indians are determined to come here for their work also, although they have a blacksmith under pay from the United States. Some of the principal men among the Osages have manifested a wish that the Government would establish their blacksmith at our station.

The mode of building in this country, if it is ever settled, will undoubtedly be with brick, as there is abundance of the best of clay to make them, and of limestone for lime; and there is but little timber, the country being principally open prairie. If economy is used in this country with timber, there may be enough to finish brick buildings, and no more. We have concluded, if we ever erect permanent buildings in this place, they must be of brick."

Rev. Mr. Pixley to the Domestic Secretary: Ibid. p. 223.

"Previous to our coming out to this distant country, the public mind had been prepared, to suppose these Osages were very different from what they are; but, however things may have been presented to our minds about the condition and desires of this people, a better knowledge of their case, from actual observation, does not less excite our pity, nor make us wish we had not come out for their instruction. They pray, indeed, if it may be called prayer, as we were told; and even now, as the day dawns, while I am writing in my house, I can hear them at their orgies, where their lodges are set up more than a mile from me. They begin very high in a sing-song note, as loud as they can halloo, and then run their voice, as long as they can carry breath, to the lowest key. Thus they continue the strain, until they are wrought to a pitch, wherein you will hear them sob and cry, as though their hearts would break. I have not yet learned whether it be some particular individuals, who make this their business, as mourning men and women, or whether they are all adepts in this. In such a case they put mud upon their faces and heads, which, as I understand, they do not wash off till their desire is in some measure answered. Thus, you will often see men, women and children, bedaubed with black mud. But this is more especially the case when they are going off upon an expedition to shoot game, or to fight their enemies, or when they hear bad news, or have lost some friend or relative. In warm weather, the men go quite in a state of nature, except a clout around their waists. Many, and indeed most of their children, are seen going about naked, even at this cold season of the year, notwithstanding the thermometer has sometimes stood below zero, and the ground is frozen six or eight inches deep. Their villages are nothing more than what they can remove on the shortest notice, one horse being capable of carrying house, household furniture, and children all at one load. From this period of the year to the time of planting their corn, they generally reside together at one place, which they call their village. The rest part of the time, they separate into parties, and stay but a few days in proportion to the abundance or scarcity of the game where they happen to set up their lodges.

Our school went into operation about two weeks since; and we have now twelve children from the natives, of both sexes, and of all sizes; five of the full-blooded, and seven half-breed. These children are certainly as interesting and active as the generality of children among the whites, and I have sometimes thought they are more so; and the Lancasterian method of instruction is peculiarly calculated to interest them. We are now all turning our attention to the more particular business of our designation; and mine is the laborious undertaking of becoming master of the Indian language. It is not, however, that which I dread. Strange as it may seem, never did I enter upon the Latin or Greeks with more desire than I do upon this language; and the thought of being able to speak to them fluently in their own tongue, makes no sacrifice or privation appear great or difficult, to compass such an object; and when this is gained, I am not certain but what a translation of some part of the Scriptures, and readers sent out from the school, as soon as they should be prepared, would be a most valuable method of advancing the mass of the nation in knowledge, and of improving their morals."

Miss Comstock to her friend in Connecticut: Ibid. p. 226.

"I have a little girl, twelve years old with me. She has only been with me six days, and has learned all the letters, and will write them very well. She is, as far as I can judge, a very amiable girl. She is a daughter of a Chief; and, of course, quite distinguished among them. She was obtained by the instrumentality of our interpreter, who gave her the name Ballariah. It is my prayer, and let it be yours, that she may prove a second Catherine Brown. We have the promise of several more children of the tribe when they return from their winter hunt.

We receive visits from the natives almost daily. Sans Neuf was present last Sabbath during our worship. He expressed much satisfaction that he could see so many children with us. How frequently do I weep over the moral blindness, and pray that Christians may do much to remove it; and by their prayers, strengthen our hands, and encourage our hearts. This is an ardous, self-denying work, but the most interesting in which I was ever engaged."

From Harmony—Mr. Sprage. Morse Rep. p. 228.

"It is painful to reflect on the condition of the Indians to whom we have come. The moon they call heaven, to which we are all going at death. The sun they call the Great Spirit, which governs the moon and earth. When asked, "Where do the bad white men go?" they answer "to the moon."

On the 14th of August we began to cut hay, which is produced at about one and one-half tons to the acre. On Monday the 27th, Brothers Chapman and Fuller arrived from Union Mission on the Arkansaw; which is about one hundred and fifty miles from us."

* * * * * * * * * *

Note.—"Union is situated on the west bank of Grand River (Neosho) about 25 miles north of its entrance into the Arkansaw. The buildings are erected on an eminence, about one mile from the river." Morse's Report, p. 217.

"In report of the Union Mission, Oct. 30th, 1821, to the Sec. of War, the following statement appears:

"In the month of August, it was ascertained, that the great Osage Mission had arrived at *Harmony*, and that a skillful interpreter had been found at the U. S. factory, in the immediate vicinity of that station. It was thought expedient that two of the brethren should repair thither, and pursue their study, in company with the assistant of the other mission. Under date of the 28th, of December, Mr. Chapman states that they had finished a dictionary, and the most important part of a grammar, and were then attending to the construction of sentences in the Osage language."

Mrs. Jones—Harmony, August 11th, 1821.

"While I write this, five of my white brethren and sisters are seated by my side. One woman, with a smiling countenance, sits viewing me, and says, she cannot write, but can speak some English. On our first interview, about fifteen men, women and children unexpectedly came on shore to see us. They appeared much pleased. We visited their wigwams. They gave us green corn and watermelons.

Some of the Indians have pleasant, intelligent countenances. They appear to have great confidence in us. They say our hearts appear good outside now, but they wish to try us three years, and in that time they can judge whether they are good inside. They appear fond of our children, often clasp them in their arms, and bring them presents of nuts. The chiefs and the Big Warrior assure us, that they will protest us from injury from their nation, and that our smallest child shall experience no harm."

Mr. Jones—Harmony.

"From the time we left New York to the time we reached our station, was something more than five months. The distance not far from two thousand miles. When the council assembled at Harmony, we found it a truly interesting season to all present. The Indians discovered to us minds as well stored with knowledge, as could be expected of the children. of nature. They seemed to be happy that we had come, and expressed much willingness to give up their children to be instructed in the arts of civilization. They promised to give to us whatever land we should mark out. Since that time they have frequently visited us, and seem to be happy in our society. They are in appearance as noble a race of people as I have ever seen. We are hoping in the spring to be able to put our school into operation, and then we shall be able to find what abilities they have to learn.

The men are large and well built—not many of them are less than six feet in height. I think we have great encouragement to believe that it will not be long before their habits will be changed, and they become both civilized and christianized."

Dr. Belcher—Harmony, December 21st, 1821.

"The season is cold. Snow, two or three inches deep, has lain upon the ground for more than two weeks. We find our flannels in this climate, not only acceptable, but very beneficial to health. In addition to a good kitchen, and warehouse, we have finished ten small, but comfortable log houses; and as soon as the weather will permit, we shall erect a school house. We hope soon to enter upon our missionary labors. From present appearances, we have no doubt of obtaining as many of the Osage children for the school, as we shall be able to accommodate. Several of the tribe have called on us, and offered their children, expressing a wish that they might be taught to read and live like white people."

The Superintendent—Harmony, April 2nd, 1822.

"Our family now consists of eighty persons in our school. We have sixteen Osage children, who are making pleasing progress in their learning, some of them can spell readily in words of two syllables. I have under my care here five little girls, the oldest seven years of age, and the others about three, they began to speak English, and can understand all that is said to them. We have a sabbath school; most of the hired men attend it, and appear quite engaged in their studies. We have a garden of four acres, fenced and plowed a part of it is planted, and several kinds of seeds are up. The brethren are preparing to plant forty acres of corn. They are also engaged in erecting a grist mill and a saw mill about a mile below us, and the latter they expect to put in operation in the month of June. Our labors are arduous and our situation responsible. Pray for us, that we may be strengthened to a faithful discharge of our duties.

Journal of the Mission in the month of December—Friday, Dec. 28th, 1821.

"Saw White Hair again today. He says that the meddling traders who are among them will be a great hinderance to our success in obtaining their children, as they are scattering the people. It appears evident that there are some traders among them that contrive every plan and adopt every kind of artifice and intrigue to lead or drive the Indians away from the trading houses established by the government, in order to gain the trade themselves. White Hair says he thinks we shall obtain some children; but until these things can be regulated by government, we can not expect very much success."

PIKE COUNTY MARRIAGE RECORD.

1818–1837.

The following list gives the names of the groom and bride, with the date of marriage, and the official who performed the ceremony. If the office of such person is not stated it will be understood that he was a minister.

James Templeton—Jenny Mackey. Jan. 26, 1818. John Mathews, Presbyterian.
James Venable—Lucinda Walker. Feb. 6, 1818. John Mathews.
Andrew Jordan—Peggy Henry. Oct. 6, 1818. John Mathews.
Carroll Moss—Miss Mackey. Dec. 10, 1818. John Mathews.
Tyra A. Haden—Unice Fisher. Dec. 31, 1818. Leroy Jackson, Baptist.
Joseph Walker—Sarah Patterson. Jan. 28, 1819. Leroy Jackson.
John Hynen—Betsy Moss. Feb. 24, 1819. John Mathews.
James Orr—Betsy Campbell. May 11, 1819. John Mathews.
Jacob Lames—Maria Phillips. June 22, 1819. John Mathews.
Joseph Basye—Ann Watson. Nov. 18, 1819. Alex. McAlister.
John Kincaid—Susanna McCune. Dec. 13, 1819. Leroy Jackson.
Mathew Byrnside—Anna Booth. Dec. 23, 1819. John Mathews.
George Campbell—Polly Benz. Jan. 2, 1820. Leroy Jackson.

William Oustott—Frances Harper. Jan. 7, 1820. Dabney Jones, J. P.
Meek Watson—Betsy Jordan. Jan. 20, 1820. John Mathews.
John Denny—Rosanna Walker. Jan. 20, 1820. Stephen Ruddell, Baptist
Daniel Hendrick—Darkus Conaway. Mar. 5, 1820. Leroy Jackson.
Robert Muse—Margaret Frier. Mar. 16, 1820. Leroy Jackson.
John Gossaline—Peggy Templeton. June 1820. John Mathews.
William K. Pickens—Margaret Jordan. Apr. 20, 1820. John Bryson, J. P.
John Watson—Ann Rogers. July 6, 1820. John Bryson, J. P.
——Allison—Mrs. Love. Aug. 8, 1820. John Mathews.
James Johnson—Nancy Horsley. Aug. 24, 1820. John Mathews.
Notley Burch—Nellie Brown. Aug. 31, 1820. John Bryson, J. P.
Thomas Burbridge—Margaret Chilton. Sept. 12, 1820. M. J. Noyes, J. P.
Joseph Thomas of Kentucky—Elizabeth Goldsberry. Sept. 14, 1820. John Bryson, J. P.
Jesse Roberts—Nancy Green Watson. Oct. 3, 1820. M. J. Noyes, J. P.
John Scott—Betsy Lewellin. Oct. 1820. Davis Biggs, Baptist.
John Barnett—Ann Stith. Nov. 12, 1820. Stephen Ruddell.
Joseph McConnel—Cynthia Gordon. Dec. 7, 1820. John Mathews.
Joseph Gash—Sally Longmire. Dec. 1820. Davis Biggs.
Christopher Columbus Easton—Margaret Mountjoy. Dec. 28, 1820. Stephen Ruddell.
James Glenn—Betsy Watson. Jan. 18, 1821. John Mathews.
John S. Ferguson—Rebena Stephenson. Jan. 25, 1821. M. J. Noyes, J. P.
Levi Newman—Catharine Jordan. Feb. 15, 1821. M. J. Noyes, J. P.
John Donovan—Patsy Ford. Feb. 22, 1821. ———
Josiah Henry—Jane Jordan. Mar. 1, 1821. M. J. Noyes, J. P.
Moses Kelly—Nancy Small. Mar. 15, 1821. John Mathews.
John Reading—Sally Maxfield. Mar. 22, 1821. John Mathews.
Canada Frier—Rebecca Williams. June 26, 1821. Davis Biggs.
Fisher Petty—Sally Jackson. Oct. 28, 1821. Davis Biggs.
Robert Maconnel—Jean Turner. Nov. 15, 1821. John Mathews.
Adam Mace—Maximila   . Nov. 22, 1821. Davis Biggs.
John Conley—Betsey Wattihouse. Dec. 25, 1821. Benj. Mun.
Joseph Mackey—Betsy Davis. Jan. 31, 1822. John Jordan, J. P.
John Shwim—Nancy Johnson. Feb. 25, 1822. John Mathews.
Samuel Shaw—Phebe Mann. Apr. 23, 1822. John Mathews.
Benson Bailey—Eva Kelly. Jan. 30, 1823. Wm. McLoed, J. P.
John Venable—Elizabeth Bryson. Dec. 4, 1823. John Jordan, J. P.
Ephraim W. Beasley—Rebecca Ruddell. Feb. 5, 1824. R. Kerr, J. P.
James Venable—Polly Bryson. June 10, 1824. John Jordan, J. P.
Absalom Sutton—Matilda Tribue. July 15, 1824. Davis Biggs.
William S. Brimer—Hannah Venable. Nov. 11, 1824. John Jordan, J. P.
Willis Whitley—Polly Swain. Feb. 15, 1825. Samuel Rubey, Presby.
Benj. Ealy—Patsy Layne. Mar. 10, 1825. Caleb Weeden.
Nathaniel Montgomery—Patsy Mitchell. Mar. 10, 1825. Davis Biggs.

Jeremiah Penix—Perthana South. Mar. 24, 1825. Caleb Weeden, Presby.
John Jordan—Jane South. Apr. 1825. Davis Biggs.
Elijah Hudson—Polly Montgomery. Aug. 30, 1825. Caleb
  Weeden.
David A. Briggs—Polly Parks. Aug. 30, 1825. Samuel G. Briggs.
Christian Lighter—Matilda Keithley. Sept. 8, 1825. Dabney Jones, J. P.
Bartholomew Grogin of Howard Co.—Mary Fraker. Sept. 22, 1825.
  Thomas Kerr, J. P.
William McCune—Jane Guy. Nov. 6, 1825. Thomas McQueen, J. P.
Richard Brewer—Polly McCune. Nov. 13, 1825. Jeremiah Taylor,
  Baptist.
Nathan Swift—Sally Campbell. Nov. 24, 1825. Caleb Weeden.
Peter Offe—Lucy Kelly. Nov. 24, 1825. Davis Biggs.
Jordan McClellan—Marilla Burns. Dec. 13, 1825. John Jordan, J. P.
Arthur Burns—Sally Moore. Dec. 14, 1825. John Jordan, J. P.
James Patton—Elizabeth Jamison. Dec. 14, 1825. Caleb Weeden.
Maryland Jones—Sally Anderson. Dec. 22, 1825. Thos. Kerr, J. P.
James Reed—Elizabeth Harlow. Dec. 25, 1825. C. C. Eastin, J. P.
Daniel Ferguson—Susanna Sinclair. Jan. 4, 1826. Jos. B. Yeater, J. P.
James Hobbs—Sally Davis. Jan. 12, 1826. M. J. Noyes, J. P.
Joseph Miller—Polly White. Feb. 26, 1826. Robert Rennek.
Heman Wallace—Sally Mellheizer. Feb. 28, 1826. M. J. Noyes, J. P.
John Watson—Nancy Hutton. Mar. 7, 1826. John Jordan, J. P.
Isaac Orr—Joanah Campbell. Mar. 16, 1826. Caleb Weeden.
John Guiley—Sarah Ann Kennady. Apr. 27, 1826. Davis Biggs.
William Simpson—Pamelia Burns. May 7, 1826. Wm. McLoed, J. P.
James E. Glenn—Susan Foster. May 25, 1826. M. J. Noyes, J. P.
Joel Campbell—Rosanna Love. June 8, 1826. Davis Biggs.
John M. Jordan—Sarah Jones. June 22, 1826. Thos. Kerr, J. P.
James Grimes—Rebecca Mulherrin. Aug. 6, 1826. Thos. McQueen, J. P.
Thomas Kerr, Esq.—Susan Kincaid, Aug. 15, 1826. David M. Kirk-
  patrick.
Robert B. Jordan—Isipheny Allison. Aug. 24, 1826. Robert Renick.
Solomon Fisher—Susannah Thompson. Sept. 5, 1826. Dabney Jones, J. P.
William Harper—Jane Walker. Sept. 14, 1826. Jos. Yeater, J. P.
Augustus H. Evans—Mildred M. James. Oct. 9, 1826. Samuel Lewellen,
  J. P.
Matthew Moss—Jane Mackey. Nov. 2, 1826. Wm. McLoed.
Wilson Cook—Patsey Jones. Nov. 9, 1826. Davis Biggs.
Joshua White—Ann Triplett. Dec. 5, 1826. Wm. McLoed, J. P.
Wm. Walker—Emily Moore. Dec. 21, 1826. M. J. Noyes, J. P.
Zachariah Hogan—Polly McClane. Dec. 24, 1826. Wm. McLoed, J. P.
Pleasant Hudson—Polly Mase. Jan. 4, 1827. Dabney Jones, J. P.
Milton Finley—Sally Grant. Jan. 4, 1827. Davis Biggs.
John Liter—Susan Clark. Jan. 14, 1827. Samuel G. Briggs.

Wm. Irvine—Kitty House. Jan. 18, 1827. Thos. Kerr, J. P.
Alexander Oldham—Lydia Williams. Mar. 1, 1827. C. C. Eastin, J. P.
Richard Addis of Fulton Co., Ill.—Sarah Ann Davis. Mar. 4, 1827. M. J. Noyes, J. P.
Washington Dunham—Nancy Griffee. Mar. 18, 1827. Davis Biggs.
John Layne—Ann Porter. Apr. 5, 1827. Dabney Jones, J. P.
Robert Williams—Amelia Beasley. April 15, 1827. C. C. Eastin, J. P.
Granville Cothron—Mary Ann Williams. Apr. 29, 1827. James McBride.
Franklin Burnet—Jane Johnston. May 17, 1827. Davis Biggs.
John J. McCloskey—Drusilla Turbit. May 20, 1827. C. C. Eastin, J. P.
Noah Beasley—Catherine Boothe. May 31, 1827. M. J. Noyes.
William Bryson—Liza Yates. June 7, 1827. James W. Campbell, Presbyterian.
Thomas Jackson—Julian Mefford. Aug. 2, 1827. Samuel G. Briggs.
Willis Hutton—Cassandra Humphrey. Aug. 16, 1827. M. J. Noyes, J. P.
William Eoff—Patsy Rowland. Aug. 23, 1827. M. J. Noyes.
Richard Worsham—Elizabeth Triplett. Aug. 30, 1827. Wm. McLoed, J. P.
William Hayden—Parthenia Fisher. Sept. 9, 1827. Rev. Samuel G. Briggs
Richard Yale—Liza Bonham. Sept. 13, 1827. Rev. James W. Campbell.
Matthew Smith—Susanna Layne. Sept. 25, 1827. Dabney Jones, J. P.
Thomas Buchanan—Siana Fisher. Oct. 24, 1827. Samuel Lewellen, J.P.
Dudley Butler—Matilda Liter. Oct. 25, 1827. Samuel Briggs.
Samuel C. Rubey of Cooper Co.—Elizabeth Alison. Nov. 6, 1827. James W. Campbell.
John Trewitt—Margaret Hayden. Nov. 8, 1827. Samuel Briggs.
Thomas Bramble—Amelia Butler. Nov. 22, 1827. Francis Watts, J. P.
William Parks—Leura Moore. Nov. 29, 1827. Samuel Briggs.
Owen Doyle—Sally Humphrey. Nov. 29, 1827. Davis Biggs, Baptist.
Eluathan Wicks—Elizabeth Karr. Dec. 16, 1827. S. Lewellen, J. P.
John Jones—Lydia Sidener. Dec. 18, 1827. Dabney Jones, J. P.
James McClellan—Elizabeth Grant. Jan. 3, 1828. John Jordan, J. P.
Ayers Layne—Polly Sidener. Jan. 8, 1828. Dabney Jones, J. P.
John A. Cobb—Eleanor Cleaver. Feb. 28, 1828. Dabney Jones.
John Mitchell—Patsy Watson. Mar. 9, 1828. Davis Biggs.
Sampson Anderson—Patience Spears. Mar. 27, 1828. Wm. McLoed, J. P.
John Burnett—Sally Johnson. Mar. 30, 1828. M. J. Noyes, J. P.
Wm. Brown—Malvina Pearce. May 18, 1828. S. Lewellen, J. P.
Woodson Blankenship—Mahala Oustot. July 3, 1828. S. Lewellen.
Alfred Mefford—Betsey Pritchard. July 10, 1828. Davis Biggs.
James Smith—Eliza Findley. July 10, 1828. Davis Biggs.
John Kincaid of Lincoln Co.—Caroline Campbell. July 22, 1828. James W. Campbell.

PIKE COUNTY MARRIAGE RECORD

Matthew Anderson—Sally Hinton. Aug. 5, 1828. Harrison Hendrick, J. P.
Samuel W. Parsons—Margaret Hinton. Aug. 7, 1828. Slade Hammond, J. P.
Charles Williams—Margaret Carpenter. Aug. 12, 1828. Davis Biggs.
Robert Brown—Patsey McGarey. Sept. 16, 1828. Davis Biggs.
Thomas McMillen—Ursula Humphrey. Sept. 25, 1828. Davis Biggs.
Ezekiel Ferrell—Ann Burch. Oct. 7, 1828. S. Lewellen, J. P.
Thomas Hudson—Polly Hammond. Oct. 23, 1828. Harrison Hendrick, J. P.
Daniel Bolling—Sally St. Clair. Oct. 30, 1828. Dabney Jones.
Jesse Humphrey—Hannah McMillen. Nov. 2, 1828. M. J. Noyes.
George Jackson—Melinda Jacks. Nov. 6, 1828. Davis Biggs.
Solomon Ouslott—Mary Ann Fugate. Nov. 13, 1828. S. Lewellen.
Charles Blankenship—Mary Lewellen. Nov. 18, 1828. S. Lewellen.
Charles Williams—Margaret Carpenter. Nov. 21, 1828. Wm. McLoed.
William Taylor—Polly Tumolt. Nov. 27, 1828. Davis Biggs.
John S. Craig—Nancy McKey. Dec. 4, 1828. Thos. McQueen, J. P.
William Brimer—Mrs. Polly South. Jan. 15, 1829. M. J. Noyes.
Reuben McCroskey—Betsey Benus. Jan. 22, 1829. Davis Biggs.
Chappell Gregory—Penelope Moore. Feb. 1, 1829. David Hubbard, Baptist.
James I. Elliott—Jane Griffith. Feb. 3, 1829. Wm. McLoed.
Thomas Dunkin—Emelia Williams. Feb. 5, 1829. Francis Watts, J. P.
Abram Hostetter—Polly Mefford. Feb. 5, 1829. S. Lewellen.
Isaac Hills—Elizabeth Swain. Feb. 12, 1829. Wm. Tompkins, J. P.
William Penix—Nancy Thompson, Feb. 19, 1829. Davis Biggs.
Lewis James—Mary Vail. Feb. 19, 1829. B. S. Ashley, Methodist.
Elijah Williams—Polly Purdom. Mar. 1, 1829. G. P. Nash., J. P.
John Watt—Catherine Sealy. Mar. 12, 1829. Harrison Hendrick, J. P.
Jeptha Ousley—Eunice Brown. Mar. 12, 1829. Davis Biggs.
John Claton—Susanna Tribue. Mar. 31, 1829. Davis Biggs.
Napoleon Thompson—Matilda L. Lindsey. Apr. 9, 1829. Davis Biggs.
James Pharr—Lucy B. Fortune. Apr. 21, 1829. Samuel Pharr, Presbyterian.
Norman Boothe—Sarah Jane Lindsey. May 29, 1829. Davis Biggs.
James Roach—Paulina Frier. June 4, 1829. M. J. Noyes, J. P.
James Scott—Elizabeth Purdon. June 23, 1829. Robert Irvine, J. P.
Joseph Burbridge—Sally Jordan. July 2, 1829. M. J. Noyes.
Mastin Arthur—Basheba Butt. July 23, 1829. Wm. McLoed.
Robert Allison—Louisa Jane Carroll. July 30, 1829. M. J. Noyes.
James R. Hayden—Purlina Williams. Aug. 20, 1829. Slade Hammond J. P.
Gad Chapan—Nancy Turner. Sept. 3, 1829. James W. Campbell.
Wilkerson W. W. Watts—Leones Jacoby. Sept. 10, 1829. Davis Biggs.

Moses Hendrick—Amanda Daniel. Sept. 15, 1829. Harrison Hendrick, J. P.
Francis Campbell—Indiana Boone. Oct. 22, 1829. Davis Biggs.
Samuel Epperson—Catherine Robertson. Oct. 29, 1829. William Tompkins, J. P.
Henry Crow—Susan Ripperton. Nov. 5, 1829. Robert Irvine, J. P.
Greenlee Hayes—Elizabeth Jane Keith. Dec. 8, 1829. G. P. Nash, J. P.
George Miller—Betsey Adams. Dec. 10, 1829. Davis Biggs.
Samuel Grooms—Ann Sidwell. Dec. 10, 1829. James W. Campbell.
James Kinney, son of Hugh Kinney and Judith Major and Jane Williams, daughter of Isaac Williams and Margaret Hunter. Dec. 20, 1829. F. F. L. Vevseydt, Catholic Priest.
Joseph Hayden—Nancy Williams. Jan. 20, 1830. G. P. Nash, J. P., Lincoln Co.
Thomas South—Margaret South. Jan. 26, 1830. James Campbell.
William Drummond—Emeline Rowland. Jan. 31, 1830. Samuel Pharr.
William H. Jones—Mary Jane Williams. Feb. 3, 1830. M. J. Noyes.
James Renny—Rosannah Brow. Feb. 4, 1830. Davis Biggs.
Caleb Mefford—Mary Pritchett. Feb. 11, 1830. R. Q. Stark, Methodist.
Samuel W. Finley—Cynthia Ann Carroll. Feb. 18, 1830. M. J. Noyes.
Jacob W. Thomas—Miss Jane Thomas. Mar. 7, 1830. Thos. McQueen.
John C. Jordan—Nancy Underwood. Mar. 23, 1830. James W. Campbell.
Joel Griffeth, Jr.—Nancy Moore. Apr. 1, 1830. David Hubbard.
Adam Jamison—Nancy Sherwood. Apr. 8, 1830. Samuel Pharr.
Robert Anderson—Mrs. Anna Burbridge. Apr. 15, 1830. M. J. Noyes.
Cyrus Watson—Betsy Mitchell. Apr. 29, 1830. Davis Biggs.
James A. Jordan—Julian Smith. Apr. 29, 1830. James W. Campbell.
John Turner—Margaret Gordon. May 11, 1830. James W. Campbell.
Joseph D. Tapley—Jemima C. Watson. May 13, 1830. R. Q. Stark, Methodist.
Simon White—Mahala Gibson. May 13, 1830. James W. Campbell.
Samuel Thomas—Elizabeth Wells. May 13, 1830. Francis Watts, J. P.
John Turpin—Betsy Moore. June 3, 1830. Davis Biggs.
Marville Oustot—Charlotte Hayes. June 3, 1830. George Waters.
Johnson Hendrick—Levicy Standford. June 10, 1830. Harrison Hendrick, J. P.
Wm. Cornelius—Hannah Ann Hays. June 14, 1830. Robert L. McAfee.
Bennett Nally—Jane Anderson. June 15, 1830. Samuel Pharr.
John Duncan—Sally Kilby. July 14, 1830. Robert Irvine, J. P.
George Hughlett—Syrena Duncan. Aug. 3, 1830. Robert Irvine.
John Jordan—Elizabeth Underwood. Aug. 17, 1830. Wm. S. Lacy, Presbyterian.
Clayton Allcorn—Eleanor Haff. Aug. 19, 1830. James W. Campbell.
James McMillen—Tabitha Unsell. Aug. 26, 1830. Davis Biggs.

PIKE COUNTY MARRIAGE RECORD

Morris James—Mary Beasley. Sept. 5, 1830. Francis Watts.
Samuel Benn—Mary Ann Mefford. Sept. 5, 1830. R. Q. Stark.
Rev. Thomas Johnson—Sarah T. Davis. Sept. 7, 1830. William Ketron, Methodist.
Parsons Brown—Orpha Bogges. Oct. 21, 1830. Davis Biggs.
William Googe—Naomi Bogges. Oct. 21, 1830. Davis Biggs.
Hampton Weed—Mary Irvine. Oct. 22, 1830. Davis Biggs.
William Gibson—Pasy Swift. Nov. 7, 1830. James W. Campbell.
William Browning—Elizabeth Mefford. Nov. 14, 1830. R. Q. Stark.
Matthew B. Moore—Amanda Lain. Nov. 14, 1830. Frederick B. Leach, Methodist.
Cyrus Mackey—Malinda Jones. Nov. 23, 1830. Thomas McQueen, J. P.
George Burns—Sarah Turner. Nov. 25, 1830. James W. Campbell.
Sanders H. Bartlett—Margaret Hobbs. Dec. 9, 1830. M. J. Noyes.
Ephraim Jinkins—Margaret McDowell. Dec. 16, 1830. Stephen Ruddell.
William Colliver—Polly Grooms. Dec. 21, 1830. Samuel Pharr.
Francis H. Bonham—Mary Ann Neville. Dec. 23, 1830. George Waters.
John Worsham—Martha McQuary. Jan. 6, 1831.
John Scott—Margaret Givens. Jan. 20, 1831. David McAlister, J. P.
John Long—Liza Ann Grymes. Jan. 25, 1831. Stephen Ruddell.
Joseph H. Thomas—Sally Ann Sidwell. Jan. 27, 1831. Thos. McQueen.
Thomas Triplett—Jane E. Bradley. Feb. 13, 1831. Thos. McQueen.
Phillips J. Thomas—Verlinda Duncan. Feb. 24, 1831. Frederick B. Leach.
George Miers—Milly Anderson. Mar. 20, 1831. Francis Watts.
Edmond Tucker—Betsy Colwell. Mar. 24, 1831. Davis Biggs.
John Montgomery—Elizabeth Ravenscraft. Mar. 27, 1831. James W. Campbell.
Belitha G. Long—Margaret Thomas. Mar. 28, 1831. Thos. McQueen.
Robert Dillard—Susannah Seely. Mar. 29, 1831. Isaac J. Nowell.
Hiram Petree—Mary Carr. Mar. 31, 1831. Davis Biggs.
John Leeper—Mahala Hobbs. June 9, 1831. James M. Watson, J. P.
Levi Pettibone—Martha Rouse. June 14, 1831. James W. Campbell.
Wm. Brown—Mary Love. June 16, 1831. Davis Biggs.
Solomon Fisher—Elizabeth Welthy. June 26, 1831. R. Q. Stark.
Alexander Sinclair—Lucinda Boling. July 3, 1831. Alexander Waggener, J. P.
John Chilton—Rachel Jackson. July 17, 1831. James W. Campbell,
James Harvey Davis—Letitia R. Staley. July 26, 1831. Davis Biggs.
John Purdon—Catherine Jane Weatherford. Aug. 11, 1831. F. B. Leach.
Thomas J. Mackey—Sarah Griffith. Aug. 11, 1831. James W. Campbell.
Dayton Crider—Polly Emison. Aug. 25, 1831. Willis Mitchell, J. P
Merriam Moore—Permelia Evans, Farmer. Aug. 31, 1831. Davis Biggs.
Abraham Davis—Sally Burns. Sept. 1, 1831. James M. Watson.
Peter Anson—Lorinda Grooms. Sept. 1, 1831. James W. Campbell.

Turner Hayden—Sallena Fisher. Sept. 4, 1831. Gabriel Phillips, J. P.
Judson M. Keath—Sarah Hammer. Sept. 6, 1831. Gabriel Phillips, J. P.
John Mitchell—Sarah Prichard. Sept. 11, 1831. James W. Campbell.
Alfred Swaringin—Amanda McCloar. Sept. 15, 1831. James W. Campbell.
Ivy Sumolt—Sally James. Sept. 18, 1831. Davis Biggs.
Benjamin Allen—Margaret McAlister. Sept. 29, 1831. Wm. Tompkins, J. P.
William Bradshaw—Drucilla Harvey. Oct. 3, 1831. Samuel Findly, Presbyterian.
Hezekiah Gibson—Terissa Bishop. Oct. 13, 1831. S. W. Finley, J. P.
Wm. Fletcher—Rachel Burrows. Oct. 13, 1831. Gabriel Phillips, J. P.
Isaac Orr—Susan Darby. Oct. 20, 1831. Samuel Findly.
Joshua Blankenbaker—Elizabeth Linyard. Oct. 23, 1831. David McAlister, J. P.
Richard Oldham—July Williams. Oct. 25, 1831. Francis Watts, J. P.
Peter Grant—Martha Hollad. Nov. 10, 1831. Davis Biggs.
Peter Sap—Patience Wells. Nov. 22, 1831. Francis Watts, J. P.
Lenus H. Watson—Louisa Carr. Dec. 1, 1831. Willis Mitchell, J. P.
John C. Basye—Penina Watson. Dec. 1, 1831. James W. Campbell.
William Alexander—Jane Kennady. Dec. 5, 1831. Davis Biggs.
Freeman Elmore—Martha Orr. Dec. 20, 1831. Samuel Findly.
Joseph Barnett—Mary Fry. Dec. 23, 1831. James W. Campbell.
James Trimble—Ruth Wells. Jan. 5, 1832. Francis Watts, J. P.
Myaman Templeton—Mary Mackey. Jan. 5, 1832. James W. Campbell.
Samuel K. Campbell—Elizabeth Darby. Jan. 12, 1832. Samuel Findly.
Johnson Barnard—Nancy Colliver. Jan. 23, 1832. James M. Watson, J. P.
Richard Ayres—Isabella Findley. Feb. 3, 1832. James W. Campbell.
John Nichols—Mary Ann Brown. Feb. 5, 1832. Gabriel Phillips, J. P.
William Fisher—Eliza Hostetter. Feb. 16, 1832. Gabriel Phillips.
Pleasant Mabray—Barshaba Ingram. Mar. 1, 1832. Harrison Hendrick, J. P.
John Mase—Louisa Harris. Mar. 8, 1832. Harrison Hendrick.
Mastin Moore—Margaret Parsons. Mar. 8, 1832. David Hubbard.
Madison Farquer of Louisville, Ky.—Mary Ann Jane Martin, Mar. 21, 1832. F. B. Leach.
Abraham E. Kilby—Rhodea Parsons. Mar. 22, 1832. F. B. Leach.
Silas M. Doyle—Lavicy Keithley. Apr. 8, 1832. George Waters.
David Oustot—Katherine Gibson. Apr. 12, 1832. Isaac G. Nowell, J. P.
Thomas C. Wells—Susan Dawson. Apr. 26, 1832. Francis Watts.
Thomas R. Vaughan—Lucy L. Edmonds. May 2, 1832. F. B. Leach.
Cullen Tinker of St. Louis—Polly Ann Biggs. May 7, 1832. Davis Biggs.
Spencer Wood—Relief McConnell. May 10, 1832. John Price, J. P.
Washington Watts—Marietta Gray. May 17, 1832. Davis Biggs.

PIKE COUNTY MARRIAGE RECORD 199

James D. Tisdell—Martha Ann Boxley. June 7, 1832. L. Rogers, J. P.
Samuel E. Nevil—Charlotte Boone. June 7, 1832. F. B. Leach.
Ignatius Burns—Elizabeth Bailey. June 21, 1832. Gabriel Phillips.
Wm. M. Swain—Francis Walker. July 8, 1832. Isaac J. Nowell, J. P.
Eli Keithley—Nancy Aulman. Aug. 9, 1832. Gabriel Phillips.
Joseph Shanks—Patsey Davis. Aug. 9, 1832. James M. Watson.
James Brown—Elmira Merrit. Aug. 14, 1832. Gabriel Phillips.
Nicholas Murrow, Sr.—Mrs. Mary Owens. Aug. 22, 1832. Andrew Forgey, J. P.
James Stevens—Mary Love. Aug. 23, 1832. Davis Biggs.
Thomas B. Whitledge—Susan Jacoby. Aug. 30, 1832. Jeremiah Vardeman, Baptist.
John Wesley Gillum—Wilmina Suddith. Sept. 6, 1832. F. B. Leach.
William Spencer—Elizabeth Decamp. Sept. 23, 1832. William Bryson, J. P.
Israel N. Bust—Susan H. January. Oct. 4, 1832. S. W. Finley, J. P.
Thomas Anson—Polly Burbridge. Oct. 4, 1832. John H. Hughes, Christian Church.
Daniel Stark—Eliza M. Campbell. Oct. 6, 1832. Stephen Ruddell.
Washington Sterrett of St. Louis Co.—Margaret Graffort. Oct. 7, 1832. John Price, J. P.
Robert Barnett—Matilda Prichard. Oct. 16, 1832. James W. Campbell.
Chappel Gregory—Polly Underwood. Oct. 18, 1832. Davis Biggs.
Aaron Vanvickel—Catherine Mase. Oct. 23, 1832. Gabriel Phillips, J.P.
Caswell Kilby—Patsy Standford. Oct. 25, 1832. F. B. Leach.
John Mulherrin—Jane Griffith. Oct. 25, 1832. John H. Hughes.
James Boone—Matilda Wainscott. Oct. 27, 1832. Lewis Rogers, J. P.
George Brown—Irenia Merrit. Nov. 1, 1832. G. Phillips.
Lafranier C. Musick—Jane D. Haden. Nov. 4, 1832. Thomas R. Musick, Baptist.
Lunsford Lewellen Louis—Eliza Jane Louis. Nov. 4, 1832. Davis Biggs.
Henry C. Draper—Mary Jones. Nov. 11, 1832. James W. Campbell.
Thomas Smith—Mahala Cast Steel. Nov. 18, 1832. John Price, J. P.
Lewis Haden—Mary E. Bellum. Nov. 18, 1832. Thomas R. Musick.
Micajah Thompson—Elizabeth Mefford. Nov. 20, 1832. Gabriel Phillips.
Foreman Long—Harriet Crow. Nov. 27, 1832. James W. Campbell.
Napoleon B. Van Winkle of Illinois—Sarah Crow. Nov. 27, 1832. James W. Campbell.
Elihu Watson—Elizabeth Watson. Nov. 27, 1832. Joseph J. Basye, M.E.
William Morrow of Lincoln Co.—Polly Hughes. Nov. 29, 1832. David Hubbard.
Robert Watson—Elizabeth McQuie. Dec. 13, 1832. Samuel Findly.
Flemming Holloway of Montgomery Co.—Ann Hagood. Dec. 20, 1832. David Hubbard.
Carson King—Nancy Humphrey. Dec. 20, 1832. F. B. Leach.

William Igo—Mary C. Montgomery. Dec. 20, 1832. J. H. Hughes.
William McDowan—Damarins Bradley. Dec. 23, 1832. J. H. Hughes.
William Cossy—Mrs. Sarah M. Calister. Dec. 23, 1832. William Bryson, J. P.
Asa Luck—Lucy Fitsue. Dec. 27, 1832. James W. Campbell.
Thomas Smith—Nancy Hickoson. Jan. 3, 1833. Davis Biggs.
James D. McElwee—Mary Mills. Jan. 3, 1833. Lewis Rogers, J. P.
James McCloed—Sally Kelly. Jan. 3, 1833. Davis Biggs.
John Oliver—Elender Carpenter. Jan. 6, 1833. James M. Watson, J. P.
Willis Sidwell—Eliza Brown. Jan. 10, 1833. James W. Campbell.
James H. Stewart—Mary H. Young. Jan. 20, 1833. Lewis Rogers, J. P.
Elijah Harper—Sally Roberts. Feb. 19, 1833. G. Phillips.
Samuel Abbot—Mary Hagood. Feb. 21, 1833. David Hubbard.
William Dobyns—Lucinda Peper. Feb. 24, 1833. Samuel Pharr, Presbyterian.
John McLaughlin—Martha Ann Sidwell. Feb. 28, 1833. James W. Campbell.
Claybourn M. Thermon—Rebecca Mackey. Mar. 14, 1833. James M. Watson.
Irvine Davis—Margaret Kerr. Mar. 18, 1833. George W. Bewley, Methodist.
William Hutchison—Nancy Biggs. Apr. 3, 1833. J. Vardeman.
John C. Bowles—Mileta A. May. Apr. 3, 1833. F. B. Leach.
John S. King—Harriet Oden. Apr. 5, 1833. F. B. Leach.
Asa Todd—Elizabeth Whitledge. Apr. 11, 1833. J. H. Hughes.
Solomon Fisher—Elizabeth Welty. Apr. 18, 1833. G. Phillips, J. P.
Irvine Guy—Nancy L. Vaughan. May 2, 1833. J. H. Hughes.
Alfred Oden—Francis Ann Brown. May 23, 1833. F. B. Leach.
Benjamin Hawkins—Ailsey Loury. June 6, 1833. Davis Biggs.
Flemming House—Sally Humphrey. June 6, 1833. F. B. Leach.
James McKee—Elizabeth Mulherrin. June 9, 1833. J. H. Hughes.
John Kerr—Sally Wells. June 13, 1833. F. B. Leach.
Booker P. Edwards—Polly Lacy McCune. June 13, 1833. James W. Campbell.
Caleb Brown—Cinthia Hughes. June 23, 1833. David McAlister, J. P.
Daniel Haden—Mary Ann Musick. June 24, 1833. J. J. McCloskey, J. P.
Richard Wells—Levilda Kerr. June 30, 1833. R. K. Jordan.
Felix Smith—Barbara Dismukes. July 18, 1833. James W. Campbell.
Catton Mun—Eliza Elmore. Aug. 1, 1833. Samuel Findly.
Lewis Parsons—Louisa Moore. Aug. 1, 1833. David Hubbard.
Robert T. Cassell—Nancy Butler. Aug. 3, 1833. S. W. Finley, J. P.
Jabez E. Dougherty—Haughn. Aug. 8, 1833. J. H. Hughes.
Harvey Mitchell—Harriet Hendrick. Aug. 8, 1833. F. B. Leech.
Richard Lewellen—Kitty Brice. Aug. 11, 1833. G. Phillips.
John J. McCloskey—Olive Tolbert. Aug. 21, 1833. J. H. Hughes.

PIKE COUNTY MARRIAGE RECORD 201

F. C. Todd—Mary Ann Buford. Aug. 23, 1833. J. H. Hughes.
James McCord—Edna Pepper. Sept. 5, 1833. J. H. Hughes.
Dearborn Delaney—Matilda Alvis. Sept. 12, 1833. F. B. Leach.
John Shaw—Elizabeth Davis. Sept. 12, 1833. J. W. Campbell.
Hiram Ward—Elizabeth Hughes. Sept. 19, 1833. Francis Watts.
Milton Ravenscroft—Frances Luck. Sept. 19, 1833. Davis Biggs.
Edward Huntsman—Mary Ann Orr. Sept. 26, 1833. Samuel Findly.
David C. Purseley—Elizabeth Zumalt. Oct. 1, 1833. F. B. Leach.
Hezekiah Robey of Marion Co.—Magdalina Tillett. Oct. 7, 1833. J. M. Watson, J. P.
Reuben Underwood—Nancy Fry. Oct. 10, 1833. James W. Campbell.
Rolly Dickson—Tempa McCoy. Oct. 10, 1833. J. H. Hughes.
John Hughlett—Mrs. Dianah Willis. Oct. 17, 1833. Robert Irvine, J. P.
Orvel Crenshawe—Mavinda Norton. Oct. 24, 1833. James W. Campbell.
Francis Jacoby—Telitha Bondurant. Oct. 31, 1833. Davis Biggs.
John Brown—Catherine Brison. Nov. 7, 1833. Davis Biggs.
Edward Emerson—Isabella Shields. Nov. 23, 1833. Peter J. Lefevre, Catholic Priest.
James Colvin—Sarah Brown. Nov. 28, 1833. J. H. Hughes.
Richard Owens—Elizabeth Lindsey. Nov. 28, 1833. J. H. Hughes.
Joseph Counts—Edith Griffith. Dec. 5, 1833. J. H. Hughes.
James Lamb—Elizabeth Crow. Dec. 5, 1833. James W. Campbell.
James Frier, Sr.—Mary P. Luck, Sr. Dec. 8, 1833. Walter McQuie, Baptist.
Ammon Hostetter—Matilda Jackson. Dec. 15, 1833. G. Phillips.
Smiley Miller—Eleanor Gentle. Dec. 15, 1833. Isaac G. Nowell, J. P.
Isaac Rigsby—Catherine Anson. Dec. 20, 1833. J. W. Campbell.
James M. Frier—Mary P. Luck (minors). Dec. 26, 1833. Walter McQuie
Elijah Cole of Morgan Co., Ill.—Amanda Swearingen. Dec. 29, 1833. F. B. Leach.
Wm. D. Grant—Loucintha Moore. Dec. 29, 1833. G. W. Bewley.
John Jones—Mary Ann Landlin. Jan. 19, 1834. S. W. Finley, J. P.
Simon Branstetter—Jane P. Branstetter. Jan. 28, 1834. F. B. Leach.
John Turnbong—Ruth McLane. Jan. 1834. Francis Watts.
Martin H. Berry—Jane Brown. Feb. 13, 1834. Wm. Bryson, J. P.
William Brice—Tharnea Miller. Feb. 18, 1834. Davis Biggs.
Richard Estes of Lincoln Co.—Sarah Martin. Feb. 26, 1834. Sandy E. Jones, Christian Church.
Dr. William C. Hardin—Louisa M. Pettibone. Mar. 13, 1834. Samuel Findly.
Joseph Stanford—Fanny Williams. Mar. 20, 1834. Davis Biggs.
Tiry Martin—Elvira Thompson. Mar. 26, 1834. William W. Waddell, J. P.
Stephen Jett—Patsy Parker. Apr. 1, 1834. James W. Campbell.
William Hunter—America Fry. Apr. 13, 1834. James W. Campbell.

Enoch Hostetter—Sarah Floyd. Apr. 20, 1834. Isaac J. Nowell, J. P.
William F. Watson—Amelia McQuie. Apr. 30, 1834. James W. Campbell.
Drury Christian—Nancy Tillett. May 18, 1834. James M. Watson, J. P.
Samuel Galaspie—Mahala Dickerson. May 22, 1834. Elijah Williams.
Miles Price—Luannah Baxter. May 22, 1834. James W. Campbell.
Boone Elliott—Permelia Anderson. May 25, 1834. Francis Watts, J. P.
Daniel Draper of Lincoln Co.—Mary Orr. June 12, 1834. J. W. Campbell.
John Spencer—Amanda Melvina Brice. June 19, 1834. G. Phillips.
David Watson—Mary Nevil Edmunds. July 3, 1834. G. W. Bewley.
Dr. Beverly T. Coalter—Elizabeth J. McQueen. July 24, 1834. J. H. Hughes.
John R. Gilmore—Rebecca Frier. July 26, 1834. Geo. T. Ashburn, J. P.
Briant W. Obanison—Nancy Liles. Aug. 7, 1834. David Hubbard.
Elijah Sidwell—Martha Todd. Aug. 7, 1834. J. W. Campbell.
John Hobbs—Polly Lemasters. Aug. 10, 1834. James M. Watson.
Shelton Kennerly—Catherine Hays. Aug. 27, 1834. Samuel Findly.
William Steel—Mary Kerr. Aug. 28, 1834. Andrew Forgey, J. P.
Peter T. Vaughan—Mary Jeans. Sept. 4, 1834. J. H. Hughes.
William Vannoy—Nancy Mackey. Sept. 11, 1834. F. B. Leach.
James Greer—Martha Mullikin. Oct. 2, 1834. Samuel Pharr.
Wilbourn Neal—Susan Butler. Oct. 2, 1834. Geo. Waters.
Martin Harlow—Eunice Lyles. Oct. 2, 1834. J. H. Hughes.
John A. Mackey—Sarah Sinclair. Oct. 7, 1834. Samuel Pharr.
Isaac Uptegrove—Elizabeth Ann Ingram. Oct. 9, 1834. Harrison Hendrick, J. P.
Eaton Turner—Nancy Weldy. Oct. 23, 1834. Elijah Williams.
Alexander McNair—Dincy McCoy. Oct. 25, 1834. J. H. Hughes.
Nathaniel T. Pierce of Ralls Co.—Harriet Roberts. Oct. 30, 1834. Samuel Pharr.
William McCune—Jane Edwards. Oct. 30, 1834. J. W. Campbell.
Elisha Louis—Jane Hagewood. Nov. 5, 1834. Davis Biggs.
William Devin—Elizabeth Lewellen. Nov. 6, 1834. Elijah Williams.
Wesley Jackson—Elizabeth Waddell. Nov. 9, 1834. Wm. W. Waddell, J. P.
John Thomas—Darcus Munday. Nov. 13, 1834. Andrew Forgey, J. P.
Dan McElwee—Nancy Bradley. Nov. 20, 1834. Samuel Findly.
John Pit—Patsey True. Nov. 23, 1834. Francis Watts, J. P.
Morton Bowen—Evaline Smith. Nov. 27, 1834. Francis Watts.
Lawson V. Lafferty—Hester Ann Martin. Dec. 2, 1834. John B. Hays, J. P.
James Chamberlain—Martha Wright. Dec. 4, 1834. F. B. Leach.
James Branstetter—Elizabeth Branstetter. Dec. 11, 1834. F. B. Leach.

PIKE COUNTY MARRIAGE RECORD 203

Thomas Cleaver of Ralls Co.—Margaret McCune. Dec. 16, 1834. James W. Campbell.
Samuel Hamilton—Nancy Reed. Dec. 29, 1834. J. H. Hughes, Christian Church, Paynesville, Mo.
Eliselett Pulaskay—Betsey Kane. Dec. 30, 1834. Davis Biggs.
William W. Waddle—Lois Goldsberry. Jan. 1, 1835. Davis Biggs.
John Calvin—Rosanah Sherwood. Jan. 6, 1835. J. H. Hughes.
John G. Givens—Mary Ann Stewart. Jan. 8, 1835. Lewis Rogers, J. P.
Philander Draper of Lincoln Co.—Eliza Ann Clark. Jan. 18, 1835. James W. Campbell.
William Shellhorse—Betsey Griffith. Jan. 20, 1835. Davis Biggs.
John R. Jordan of Morgan Co. Ill.—Mrs. Laura Parks. Jan. 22, 1835. F. B. Leach.
John G. Shields—Elizabeth Emerson. Jan. 29, 1835. Wm. W. Waddell, J. P.
Moses Fuqua of Kentucky—Harriet Irvine, daughter of Mrs. M. Irvine of Louisiana, Mo. Feb. 5, 1835. Samuel Findly.
Axum Farmer—Sally Estis. Feb. 12, 1835. J. M. Watson, J. P.
Jasper Jewell—Mrs. Mary Williams. Feb. 18, 1835. J. H. Hughes.
Rawleigh Bryson—Julian Lindsey. Feb. 26, 1835. S. G. Patterson.
George Biggs—Margaret Jackson. Mar. 3, 1835. James W. Campbell.
Robert Jones—Alcy C. Whitledge, daughter of Lyne Whitledge. Mar. 5, 1835. Samuel Findly.
Samuel McMillen—Ann Calwell. Mar. 12, 1835. Davis Biggs.
Wm. C. Downing of Lincoln Co.—Margaret Ann Reading. Mar. 26, 1835. J. W. Campbell.
Perry Johnson—Mary Jane Linbrick. Mar. 26, 1835. J. W. Watson, J. P.
James Boothe—Sally Ann Tillett, daughter of James Tillett. Mar. 29, 1835. J. Lindsey, J. P.
Noah Hendrick Jr.—Nancy Kilby. Apr. 9, 1835. Thomas T. Johnson, Baptist.
Jacob Leer—Catherine Ewing. Apr. 9, 1835. J. M. Watson, J. P.
Presley Neville—Delila Keithley. Apr. 9, 1835. Elijah Williams.
Henry Palmer—Nancy McGowan. Apr. 14, 1835. J. H. Hughes.
Joshua Fisher of Ralls Co.—Mariah A. Lard. Apr. 19, 1835. F. B. Leach.
James Jamison, Jr.—Esther Brown. Apr. 23, 1835. Andrew Forgey, J.
Joseph Keithley—Pelina Barshears. Apr. 23, 1835. S. Lewellen, J. P.
Henry Williams—Jamima Carpenter. Apr. 30, 1835. Francis Watts, J. P.
David W. Fuqua—Jane S. Mifford. May 1, 1835. S. G. Patterson, Methodist.
Franklin Anson—Polly M. Robbins. May 5, 1835. F. B. Leach.
Abraham M. Thomas—Lucinda Munday. May 7, 1835. Thos. McQueen, J. P.
Pleasant C. W. Edwards— . May 14, 1835. J. H. Hughes.
Edward Tribue—Lydia Neville. May 23, 1835. Jeremiah Vardeman.

John N. Burton—Susan McCord. May 24, 1835. John A. Ivie, Christian Church.
James Jamison—Mrs. Elizabeth Steel. May 27, 1835. Andrew Forgey, J. P.
William Pointer—Elizabeth Morrison. May 31, 1835. J. M. Watson, J. P.
David H. Hemphill—Elizabeth Turner, June 23, 1835. J. M. Watson, J. P.
Marshall Barbey—Susan Browning, June 26, 1835. Francis Watts, J. P.
James E. Glenn—Sarah Love, July 2, 1835. Samuel Findly.
Francis Watts—Ellen Todd, July 16, 1835. J. H. Hughes.
Robert Lindsey—Elizabeth Ford, July 30, 1835. J. H. Hughes.
Joseph Ford, Jr.—Nancy Benus, July 30, 1835. Davis Biggs.
Singleton W. Boyd of Ralls Co.—Nancy Ellis, Aug. 9, 1835. Elijah Williams.
Henderson Branstetter—Patsy Adams. Aug. 30, 1835. John B. Hays, J. P.
William Thompson—Sarah Ann Shields. Oct. 1, 1835. G. Phillips, J. P.
Zachariah Lovelace—Mary Lovel. Oct. 8, 1835. Samuel Pharr.
James Watson—Emily A. Franklin. Oct. 5, 1835. Samuel Findly.
John D. Mulherrin—Theodosia Beauchamp. Oct. 15, 1835. J. H. Hughes.
Merrimon Rutterford—Nancy Orr. Oct. 22, 1835. Samuel Pharr.
William B. Baxter—Catherine Mase. Oct. 25, 1835. G. Phillips, J. P.
Solomon Hughlett—Parthenia Willis. Nov. 1, 1835. Robert Irvine, J. P.
Nicholas Wells—Mandy Williams. Nov. 17, 1835. Andrew Forgey, J.P.
Mason Brown—Lucinda Unsell. Nov. 18, 1835. J. Vardeman.
Charles Tinker—Luceta Roberts. Nov. 19, 1835. Davis Biggs.
Joseph Blackwood—Catherine W. Jones. Nov. 19, 1835. Samuel Pharr.
James Baxter—Lavina Price. Nov. 28, 1835. J. W. Campbell.
Zedekiah Merit of Ralls Co.—Caroline Smith. Dec. 10, 1835. J. W. Campbell.
Benjamin Sallee—Susan Cooley. Dec. 14, 1835. Thos. McQueen, J. P.
John Purkin—Sarah Tally. Dec. 14, 1835. S. Lewellen, J. P.
Thomas Cash—Martha Parks. Dec. 24, 1835. S. GPatterson, Methodist.
Elisha Ingram—Priscilla Henderson. Dec. 24, 1835.. F. B. Leach.
Sterling Turner—Lydia Allchon (?) Dec. 24, 1835. S. W. Finley, J. P.
William Davis—Elizabeth Price. Dec. 24, 1835. J. H. Hughes.
Adam Gourley—Maranda Norton. Dec. 27, 1835. J. W. Campbell.
Moses Sidwell—Amanda Dunn. Dec. 31, 1835. J. W. Campbell.
Robert Ware—Nancy Margaret Gray. Dec. 31, 1835. J. W. Campbell.
Scott Shaw—Mary Jane Thompson. Jan. 12, 1836. James McCord, J. P.
John Furney Wright—Elizabeth Goodman. Jan. 21, 1836. F. B. Leach.
Rev. Learner B. Stateler of Mo. Conference—Malinda S. Purdon. Jan. 26, 1836. F. B. Leach.
Fielden House—Mrs. Nancy Lane. Feb. 2, 1836. Robert Irvine, J. P.
John Guy—Lucy Ann Dameron. Feb. 18, 1836. J. H. Hughes.
William Mulherrin—Ann McCoy. Feb. 25, 1836. J. H. Hughes.

PIKE COUNTY MARRIAGE RECORD

Aaron Ginkins—Mrs. William Ann Willis. Mar. 3, 1836. Robert Irvine, J. P.
James Brown—Abby Lindsey daughter of John Lindsey. Mar. 3, 1836. Thomas T. Johnson, Baptist.
Sylvester Holmes—Nancy Hull. Mar. 6, 1836. J. M. Watson, J. P.
John Shores—Eliza Burch. Mar. 20, 1836. Samuel Lewis, J. P.
Stephen B. Gordon—Lydia L. Quick. Apr. 3, 1836. F. B. Leach.
Benjamin Fanning—Mary Nicholas. Apr. 7, 1836. Francis Watts.
Wm. McDowell—Jane Hughs. Apr. 7, 1836. Francis Watts, J. P.
Martin Mays—Cordelia Palmer. Apr. 7, 1836. J. H. Hughes.
Henry Trower—Matilda Ann Keith. Apr. 10, 1836. Slade Hammond, J. P.
Joel M. Weatherford—Mary B. Standford. Apr. 20, 1836. F. B. Leach.
James L. Bradley—Sarah Ann Smith. Apr. 26, 1836. Geo. T. Ashburn, J. P.
John Swimmer—Jane McQuary. May 3, 1836. Davis Biggs.
Oliver Harris—Mary Ann Catherine Dudley. May 12, 1836. Samuel Findly.
Birdem H. Carroll—Margaret Watson. May 12, 1836. Walter McQuie, Baptist.
John W. Wilbarger—Lucy Ann Anderson. May 26, 1836. F. B. Leach.
James Parks—Alezar Benning. June 3, 1836. Davis Biggs.
Samuel C. Savage—Elizabeth L. Brown. June 5, 1836. Sandy Jones, Christian Church.
Daniel G. Reel—Elizabeth Boone. June 9, 1836. J. H. Hughes.
Linaray Todd—Viletta Beardsley. June 11, 1836. Andrew Forgey, J. P.
Thomas Thornton Johnston—Margaret Watson. June 14, 1836. Davis Biggs.
Arthur S. Broadley of Ralls Co.—Harriet Alvis. June 16, 1836. F. B. Leach.
Warren Allison—Elizabeth Smith. June 16, 1836. S. Findly.
Thomas Cash—Permelia Shotwell. June 30, 1836. G. Phillips.
John Lewellen—Martha Ann Pritchett. July 7, 1836. James W. Campbell.
William Hawkins—Martha Bondurant. July 19, 1836. Davis Biggs.
James Finley—Polly Dodds. July 26, 1836. Thomas T. Johnson.
Benjamin F. Brown—Harley A. Kilby. July 28, 1836. Sandy E. Jones.
Nathaniel Scoggin—Sally Love. July 28, 1836. Geo. L. Ashburn, J. P.
Jeremiah Stark—Mary Ann Jones. July 30, 1836. S. Lewellen, J. P.
Wesley Hendrick—Huldah G. Clempsten. Aug. 16, 1836. F. B. Leach.
James May—Patience Wells. Aug. 16, 1836. J. H. Hughes.
Thomas Wilson—Rebecca Reading. Aug. 25, 1836. James W. Campbell.
James Love—Polly Bennett. Aug. 25, 1836. Geo. T. Ashburn, J. P.
Samuel Crutcher of Montgomery City —Eliza A. Holliday. Sept. 8, 1836. Sandy E. Jones.

Andrew Love, Jr.—Mary Ann Muir. Sept. 29, 1836. M. J. Noyes, J. P.
John Lovell—Elizabeth Lovelace. Sept. 29, 1836. Samuel Pharr.
John Briscoe—Emily Biggs. Sept. 29, 1836. Davis Biggs.
John B. Strange—Mary J. Shaw. Oct. 5, 1836. F. B. Leach.
Thomas Reading—Elizabeth Beauchamp. Oct. 6, 1836. Samuel Findly.
Wm. M. Inlow—Elizabeth Roberts. Oct. 9, 1836. Samuel Lewis, J. P.
Francis E. Elgin—Dorcas Ann Limberick. Oct. 13, 1836. James McCord.
Samuel Jameson—Caroline Sherwood. Oct. 13, 1836. J. H. Hughes.
Daniel Ellis—Jane Hazleton. Oct. 20, 1836. Tyrus L. Watson.
Beverly B. Foster—Adaline T. Beherst. Oct. 31, 1836. J. H. Hughes.
John Baxter—Mahala Stadley. Nov. 1, 1836. James W. Campbell.
James M. Coleman—Martha Turner. Nov. 2, 1836. J. H. Hughes.
Thomas J. Parker—Melissa Ann Almond. Nov. 10, 1836. Samuel Lewis, J. P.
Harvey L. McCune—Mary Watson. Nov. 24, 1836. James W. Campbell.
John Thompson—Martha A. Saunders. Nov. 29, 1836. James W. Campbell.
John J. Miles—Susan McCune. Dec. 1, 1836. James W. Campbell.
Isaac L. Mills—Eliza Ann McDowell. Dec. 4, 1836. Francis Watts, J. P.
William Cummans—Elizabeth W. Tally. Dec. 8, 1836. Samuel Lewis, J. P.
John Jenkins—Elizabeth Woodson. Dec. 8, 1836. Harrison Hendrick, J. P.
Robinson McCoy—Elizabeth Amos. Dec. 15, 1836. J. H. Hughes.
Hardin McGinnis—Cyntha Ann Thurmond. Dec. 20, 1836. J. H. Hughes.
Lloyd B. Goll—Eleanor Mathews. Dec. 22, 1836. J. H. Hughes.
Andrew J. Davis—Gresilla W. Staley. Dec. 22, 1836. James H. D. Henderson, Presbyterian.
Robert Neal—Eliza Hammer. Dec. 22, 1836. S. Lewis, J. P.
Henis Worsham—Cathrine Triplett. Dec. 29, 1836. Francis Watts, J. P.
Sanford Crow—Nancy Jane Brown. Jan. 5, 1837. James M. Watson, J. P.
Johnson Givens—Ellen Tribble(minor). Jan. 5, 1837. Walter McQuie.
William P. Shehonney of Ralls Co.—Verlinda Benn. Jan. 18, 1837. Sandy E. Jones.
William Figgins—Sarah Alvis. Feb. 2, 1837. F. B. Leach.
Joseph McCune—Martha Edwards. Feb. 15, 1837. James W. Campbell.
Robert Herring—Triphany Jordan. Feb. 19, 1837. James W. Campbell.
Robert J. Haygood—Amanda M. F. Jackson. Feb. 21, 1837. S. W. Finley, J. P.
Royal Flynn—Luvica Hall. Feb. 25, 1837. S. W. Finley, J. P.
John Jones—Mrs. Margaret Kingston. Mar. 1, 1837. James M. Watson, J. P.
Owen Lewellen—Margaret Ellen Pritchett. Mar. 9, 1837. James W. Campbell.

PIKE COUNTY MARRIAGE RECORD

Francis McCord—Mary Weatherford. Mar. 12, 1837. James W. Campbell.
Jackson Gordon—Sally Gordon. Mar. 12, 1837. James M. Watson, J. P.
James Davis—Ellen Tisdale. Mar. 14, 1837. J. W. Campbell.
Abraham Litter—Rebecca Bonham. Mar. 14, 1837. Geo. Waters.
John Branstetter—Jane Woodson. Mar. 21, 1837. Harrison Hendrick, J. P.
Wesley Scoby of Lincoln Co.—Lydia Orr. Mar. 30, 1837. F. B. Leach.
William Moss—Louisa Mackey. Apr. 11, 1837. James M. Watson, J. P.
Samuel South—Redonia Irvine. Apr. 11, 1837. Samuel Pharr.
David Peterbaugh—Elizabeth Anderson. Apr. 13, 1837. G. L. Adams, J. P.
Samuel King—Ann Willbarger. Apr. 13, 1837. F. B. Leach.
Nathaniel Abbylys—Rachel Block. Apr. 23, 1837. S. W. Finley, J. P.
John P. Fisher—America Gilaspie. May 18, 1837. Timothy Ford, Methodist.
James Macmahale—Almeda Pigg. June 3, 1837. Davis Biggs.
William Kling—Eliza A. Allen. June 8, 1837. S. W. Finley, J. P.
William Hough—Martha Jacoby. June 8, 1837. J. H. Hughes.
George Wright of Ralls Co.—Cyntha Fowler. June 22, 1837. Timothy Ford.
John R. Morris of Montgomery Co.—Lucinda Adams. June 25, 1837. B. H. Lovelace, J. P.
Jesse Prichard—Sarah McHugh. June 25, 1837. G. L. Adams.
Lewis Jones—Mary Willbarger. June 28, 1837. James W. Campbell.
Richard S. Smith—Elizabeth Shaw. June 29, 1837. James W. Campbell.
Archibald Worsham—Alsey Swift. July 4, 1837. Thos. R. Musick.
Lanson T. Musick—Irena Middleton. July 4, 1837. Thomas R. Musick.
John D. Field of Ralls Co.—Eunice Hostetter. July 6, 1837. Timothy Ford.
Benoni Brice—Elizabeth Hammond. July 13, 1837. Timothy Ford.
Pallis Neal—Mary Ann Dowell. July 20, 1837. Geo. Waters.
Nicholas Cooper—Jane E. Long. July 20, 1837. J. H. Hughes.
Robert A. Browday—Diana Taylor. July 21, 1837. S. W. Finley, J. P.
John Kingston—Harriet Holland. July 27, 1837. James M. Watson, J. P.
Ichabod J. Davis—Elizabeth Haygood. Aug. 3, 1837. Robert Gilmore, Baptist.
William Hammond—Elizabeth Neal. Aug. 20, 1837. S. Lewis, J. P.
Joseph Oneal—Nancy Baldridge. Aug. 23, 1837. Francis Watts.
Thomas Price—Rosanna Lard. Aug. 24, 1837. Constantine F. Dryden.
William Colans—Margaret Scott. Sept. 7, 1837. Samuel Lewis, J. P.
John Love—Ruth Hobbs. Sept. 7, 1837. S. W. Finley. J. P.
John A. Masterson—Nancy James (minors). Sept. 9, 1837. Geo. T. Ashburn, J. P.

Melza Norton—Mildred Ann Haff. Sept. 14, 1837. Samuel Pharr.
John Allison—Elizabeth Waddell. Sept. 21, 1837. Timothy Ford.
John A. Norton—Ellen Amanda Haff. Oct. 1, 1837. Samuel Pharr.
John Ferrell—Mary Doyle. Oct. 1, 1837. Thos. T. Johnson.
Edwin McQuie—Margaret Smith. Oct. 8, 1837. J. W. Campbell.
Ambrose Crutcher of Monroe Co.—Mary Holliday. Oct. 12, 1837. Sandy E. Jones.
John Lewis—Elizabeth Miles. Oct. 13, 1837. J. H. Hughes.
John Smith—Martha Yeater. Oct. 19, 1837. Thos. T. Johnson.
John Griffith—Katherine Amos. Oct. 19, 1837. J. H. Hughes.
Frederick A. A. Heison—Ann Paxton. Oct. 22, 1837. J. W. Campbell
John G. Turpin—Cynthia Madison. Oct. 23, 1837. James W. Campbell.
John B. McDowell—Letitia Birch. Oct. 26, 1837. F. B. Leach.
John McRees—Jane M. Jordan. Nov. 5, 1837. Walter McQuie.
Joel S. Griffith—Roannah B. Dodds. Nov. 5, 1837. Robert H. Allison, J. P.
John B. Dodds—Nancy Griffith. Nov. 6, 1837. R. H. Allison.
William Fisher of Ralls Co.—Electa Watson. Nov. 8, 1837. James W. Campbell.
William Britt—Clementine Hopwood. Nov. 14, 1837. J. H. Hughes.
Jacob Fry of Marion Co.—Emily Fry. Nov. 28, 1837. James W. Campbell.
Henry W. Bibb—Judith Ann Mundy. Nov. 30, 1837. J. H. Hughes.
Findley Branstetter—Mrs. Lucretia Goodman. Dec. 7, 1837. Robert Irvine, J. P.
William Eoff—Cordelia Mifford. Dec. 17, 1837. M. J. Noyes, J. P.
Harrison Wisdom—Virginia Turner. Dec. 21, 1837. J. W. Campbell.
Samuel Jacoby—Ann Givens. Dec. 21, 1837. J. H. Hughes.
Uriah Neil of Lincoln Co.—Sarah Calvin. Dec. 21, 1837. Hugh L. Dodds.
William H. Smith—Mary Edwards. Dec. 27, 1837. James W. Campbell.
George W. Fielder—Mariah M. Ford. Dec. 28, 1837. J. H. Hughes.
 Copied by (Mrs. W. J.) Harriet V. Rowley,
  Regent Bowling Green Chapter, D. A. R.,
   Bowling Green, Mo.

NOTES.

In the October number of the Review was a paper on early travel in Missouri by Zimmermann, translated by Dr. Wm. Bek, in which the date was given as 1838. It should have been 1833. The Society has a large and valuable collection of books of Missouri Travel and Description, and notwithstanding the war in Europe is constantly getting from England, France, Germany and Italy old books of this character.

One member has expressed a preference to have the numbers of the Review cut or trimmed before sending them out, to save the reader the trouble of cutting the leaves. They have not been trimmed because if that should be done close, there might not be margin enough for binding the volumes as large as persons might want to have them. Then, too, some enjoy the cutting of a magazine as they read the articles. The society would be pleased to hear from members as to their preferences in the matter.

The State Historical Society has a complete set of the Proceedings of the State Press Association. However, one is a defective copy—the 31st for 1897—pages 33 to 38 are missing, and a paper or two may be omitted from the Bibliography on account of it. It is to be hoped that some editor will give the Society a perfect copy.

The Missouri Valley Historical Society of Kansas City, at a meeting January 12, 1915, elected the following officers: John B. White, re-elected President; Dr. W. L. Campbell, Vice-President; Henry C. Flower, Treasurer; Mrs. Nettie C. Grove, Secretary. Directors: Mrs. John B. White, Mrs. R. Wornall, Mrs. Homer Reed, J. F. Richards, W. R. Nelson, Charles S. Keith, R. A. Long, C. R. Pence and M. C. Long.

Missouri Historical Society Collections.—The number issued for 1914 by the Society in St. Louis is of 131 pages, and contains interesting papers, with quite a number of portraits and other plates. It is the third number of the fourth volume of the Society's Collections.

A tablet to pioneer Missourians was unveiled at the Jefferson Memorial building, February 16, 1915, the tablet being allegorical of the Missouri pioneers, and a brass scroll by it with names of one hundred of these pioneers. On what theory this particular hundred was selected over the other hundreds is not stated.

El Comino Real (the King's Highway). The Missouri Daughters of the American Revolution Old Trails Road Committee have published a sketch and map of the above road from Little Prairie, now Caruthersville, north thru New Madrid, Cape Girardeau and Ste. Genevieve to St. Louis, the road which connected those four military posts established by the Spanish, and known as El Camino Real— (the King's Highway), and at a later date as the Illinois road.

The five places above named were settled at dates from 1733 to 1794, and the road connecting them, at first a mere bridle path, can now be definitely located at various places along the line, and the efforts of the D. A. R to permanently mark the trail or road should be encouraged, and financial help given them in so doing.

Shields Monument. In the 47th General Assembly a bill introduced by Senator Wm. G. Busby was passed, appropriating $10,000 for a monument to General Shields to be erected on the court house square in Carrollton, Missouri. The bill provided for the appointment of three commissioners and that they should keep a record of their proceedings and deposit the record with the State Historical Society of Missouri.

This record has been kept in typewritten manuscript on sheets 14 by 11 inches, and specially bound for preservation by the Society. It shows that the bronze statue of General Shields was made by Frederick C. Hibbard of Chicago, and mounted upon a base of Missouri red granite, the whole standing nineteen feet high.

The inscriptions upon the monument are:

Front.
General James Shields.

Born in County Tyrone, Ireland, May 10, 1810.
Died at Ottumwa, Iowa, June 1, 1879.
Erected by the State of Missouri in recognition of his distinguished public service and exemplary private virtues.

Back.
Soldier
Statesman
Jurist.
:—:—:—:—:—:
Cerro Gordo
Chapultepec, (1)
Brigadier General Mexican and Civil Wars
Winchester
Port Republic.
:—:—:—:—:—:
United States Senator from
Illinois
Minnesota,
Missouri.
Governor Oregon Territory,
Commissioner U. S. Land Office,
Justice Supreme Court of Illinois
Act Missouri General Assembly, 1913.
Senator Wm. G. Busby, Author.

Edward A. Dickson,
Harry C. Brown   } Commissioners.
Hiram J. Wilcoxson

There is included in the report a twenty-one page biography of General Shields by Henry A. Castle, and also a photograph of the monument as it stands in front of the court house at Carrollton.

(1) This name is incorrectly spelled in the report, but a letter received states that it is correct on the monument.

BOOK NOTICES.

The Book-plate Booklet. Vol. 4, 1911-1912. 4 numbers.
The Ex Libran, Kansas City. Vol 1, 1912. 4 numbers.
The Biblio. Kansas City. Vol. 1, 1913. 4 numbers.
The Miscellany. Kansas City. Vol. 1, 1914. 4 numbers.
The Canticle of the Sun by St. Francis of Assisi.
Lincolniana Book Plates and Collections. Kansas City. C, 1913.

The above delightful publications have been issued by H. Alfred Fowler, Board of Trade Building, Kansas City. The Canticle of the Sun by St. Francis of Assisi is printed throughout from blocks of drawings by Rev. Arthur Howard Noll in the style of the old mediaeval manuscripts in an edition of 300 at $1.25 per copy. The other publications are principally about book plates. In Europe there were many Ex Libris Societies, publishing journals devoted principally to the book plates of their own nationality. The American Ex Libris Journal was in existence but one year, and the English Ex Libris Journal ceased after eighteen years, so that the above publications were the only ones current in the English language. The current publication by Mr. Fowler is The Miscellany at one dollar for four numbers, and no book plate collector can afford to do without it.

An incomplete genealogy of the Fowler family. By H. Alfred Fowler, Kansas City, 1913. 27 pp., 7 plates.

The above is a welcome addition to our genealogies by Missouri authors, and is by the editor of the book plate periodicals noticed above.

Ha Ha Tonka. In the Ozarks. K. C. [1915.]

A finely illustrated pamphlet has been issued, describing the tract of land in Camden county which contains the finest scenery of a varied character to be found in the State of Missouri. Its purchase by the State will do more towards the improvement of roads to it from all directions than anything else that can be done. If taken by the State it will finally become noted thruout the whole country, and will be the pride of the State.

Missourians in review. Address of **Rollin J. Britton** at the ninth annual banquet of Gallatin Commercial Club, Tuesday, February 23rd, 1915. Gallatin, n. d. 31 p.

For a hasty review of persons and events notable in the history of Missouri, and no inconsiderable number of them from the place where the address was delivered, we have never seen a better one than the above. If the facts in it were told to all the high school scholars of the State it would be a benefit to them and to the State.

Fifty years a detective by **Thomas Furlong.** n. p., n. d. (C. 1912.)

Mr. Furlong was well known as Chief of the Secret Service of the Missouri Pacific Railway, and his book contains thirty-five detective stories, stories of real detective work done by the author in the long period during which he did excellent work.

Personal Recollections of President Abraham Lincoln, General Ulysses S. Grant and General William T. Sherman. By **Major-General Grenville M. Dodge,** Council Bluffs, 1914. 8°., 237 p. Portraits.

Not many books are now being printed written by prominent actors in the Civil War, and this one by a Major-General is an important and an interesting one, and covers the time from 1859, when he first met Lincoln. We are indebted for the book to the author who is a valued member of the Society.

A Glimpse of the Enchanted Valley, June, 1914. By **James M. Breckenridge.** [St. Louis, 1914.]

The above is a pleasing account of a trip made by the author to the Yosemite Valley, and reminds the editor of a similar trip that he made to that wonderful valley, and also of the fact that a publication of the San Francisco Academy of Science says he was the first person who ever found a living shell in that valley.

General Wilkinson and his later intrigues with the Spaniards.

The **Pan-American** policy of Jefferson and Wilkinson.

The two above papers were by Professor Isaac Joslin Cox of the University of Cincinnati, the first a reprint from the American Historical Review of July, 1914, and the other from the Mississippi Valley Historical Review of September, 1914.

The researches in the Cuban papers, and in the archives of the Indies at Madrid have furnished abundant proofs of the corruption of General Wilkinson, who was commander of the army of the United States in the early part of the last century. They show that he was promised, and for a time received from the Spanish government two thousand dollars a year, and that for this and other financial considerations he was acting the traitor to his country, and working in the interest of Spain. Professor Cox is entitled to much credit for his thorough investigation into the double dealings and intrigues with the Spaniards.

Among the holiday publications of periodicals two of similar character from St. Louis deserve special mention—Reedy's Mirror and the Censor, of 248 and 206 pages. Each of them has many portraits of prominent Missourians, and articles on special Missouri subjects, and each is well worthy of preservation.

The Warrenton Banner of December 18, 1914 celebrates its fiftieth anniversary, and is full of historical matter. It has a history of Warren county, of the different towns in it, of Central Wesleyan College, the Emmons Asylum, the Wesleyan Orphan's Home, and portraits of many of the residents of the town and county, and is full of matters of historical interest. The editor and publishers are to be congratulated on their creditable work.

The Euclidean or Common Sense Theory of Space. By **John Newton Lyle.** Portrait. n. p., n. d.

Prof. Lyle, now of Bentonville, Arkansas, was formerly in Westminster College in Fulton, Missouri. The above work will be welcomed by those interested in higher mathematics, and his conclusions in regard to space and to the circle cannot well be disputed.

The General Education Board. An account of its activities, 1902-1914. With 32 full page illustrations and 31 maps. New York General Education Board, 61 Broadway, 1915.

The United States Department of the Interior has published annual reports of the above Board, and the above is an interesting one covering the time from its organization to date.

Peter Hurst Sangree. In memoriam. An address by Judge Henry Lamm, to the Pettis Bar, at Memorial Exercises, October 5, 1914. Sedalia, [1914].

Judge Lamm for many years was the law partner of Mr. Sangree in Sedalia, and his address was an appreciation of the partner to whom he was greatly attached.

Longevity in Saturnid Moths and its relation to the function of reproducction by Phil. Rose and Nellie Rose. And **The History of Science in St. Louis,** by Mary J. Klem have just been issued as the first and second parts of the transactions of the Academy of St. Louis. The first shows painstaking investigation of moths, and the second laborious research in many publications to show what has been done in St. Louis or by St. Louisans in the cause of science.

Printed Samples. Black and White and Multi-Colors. The Hugh Stephens Printing Company, Jefferson City, [1915].

A note in the above pamphlet says it is sent to those who believe in printing of good quality. Good quality hardly expresses it, and those who see it cannot help but be pleased to know that they can get within the State work equal to that done in any of the large cities. The firm is to be congratulated on its work of more than good quality.

The Tecnic of the Speaking Voice—its development, training and artistic use. By **John R. Scott,** A. M. Emeritus Professor of Elocution, University of Missouri. Columbia, Stephens Co., 1915. XXIII. 660 pp.

The author has a goodly library of dozens of books on elocution, but to the one who needs but one, and wants that to be the best one, the choice would easily fall on the above.

Simeon North, first official pistol maker of the United States. A memoir, by **S. N. D. North,** LL. D., and **Ralph H. North,** Concord, N. H. The Rumford Press, 1913.

The authors, great grandsons of Colonel North, unearthed for this volume a mass of forgotten or unrecorded achievements of their ancestor, from 1799 to 1852, in the progressive advance in the character and quality of the arms manufactured by him.

Memorial Address on the life and character of Judge Elijah Hise Norton by **Robert P. C. Wilson.** Delivered before the Missouri State Bar Association, 1914.

Judge Norton was a member of the Supreme Court of Missouri so long that the opinions of the court written by him are found in thirty-three volumes of the Missouri Reports. He was also a member of two Constitutional Conventions, those of 1861 and 1875, and wielded an influence in the work of both conventions.

Report of the Old Settlers Resolution Committee, (Jefferson County, Missouri.) By **Samuel A. Reppy.**

In the Missouri Historical Review for October, 1913, was a paper by Judge John L. Thomas on the telegraph line thru Jefferson county, the first telegraph line west of the Mississippi, which was made in 1850. In the above paper Mr. Reppy advocates making the 27th of July a legal holiday, to be called Telegraph Day, and the creation of a State park in Jefferson county, in which he pictures a great group of museums. Whether any part of the picture becomes a reality depends, perhaps, on the people of that county organizing and pushing the matter actively enough to bring to the county what outsiders will not thrust upon it.

Report of Committee on Marking Historical Sites in Rhode Island, made to the General Assembly at its January session, 1913, Providence, 1914.

The above is an official State report of 183 pages, and nineteen plates of places of historic interest. It is to be hoped that Missouri will appoint a similar committee, and make appropriation for marking the sites in Missouri that should not be forgotten.

The Missouri Persecutions, by **Elder B. H. Roberts,** Salt Lake City, Utah. Cannon & Sons, 1900.

The State Historical Society has a large collection of books and pamphlets on the Mormons in Missouri, and the Mormon troubles, and these have been and are now being made use of by a number of persons investigating these matters. The Church of Latter Day Saints at Salt Lake City on request presented the above volume. Professor Violette of Kirksville is now writing a history of those troubles, and to do it truthfully without making it offensive to either side will be indeed a difficult task.

NECROLOGY.

Lucien Carr, author of "Missouri a Bone of Contention" and "Mounds of the Mississippi Valley, Historically considered," lately died at Cambridge, Massachusetts. The St. Louis Republic said of him "born when Andrew Jackson was President, he was an observant youth when Kit Carson was a young man, when Doniphan marched to Mexico and when Thomas Benton was one of the mighty men of this country. He was in Washington as the representative of The Missouri Republican, now the Republic, when Zachary Taylor was President, and the chain of events which were soon to lead to civil war made the material of his daily copy."

He was born in Troy, Lincoln county, Missouri, December, 1829, and graduated from St. Louis University in 1846. He was Assistant Curator of the Peabody Museum at Cambridge from 1877 to 1894. He died January 27, 1915.

Rear Admiral Wells Laflin Field, a native of St. Louis, born January 31, 1846, died in Washington, D. C., November 27, 1914. He graduated from the Naval Academy in 1867, was appointed Rear Admiral June, 1902, and retired November, 1902.

Hon. John H. Flanigan, a member of the House from Jasper county, in the Thirty-fifth General Assembly, and who then became extensively known as "Fire Alarm" Flanigan, died at his home in Carthage, January 24, 1915. His nickname came from the fact that he was a ready and enthusiastic speaker on all matters that came before the House.

He was born at Almont, Michigan, July 3, 1857, and moved to Jasper county when nine years old. He was admitted to the bar in 1881, and in 1883 was City Attorney of Carthage, Missouri. He was a prominent figure in Jefferson City at all sessions of the General Assembly after the time when he was a member.

Judge John Cutler Gage of Kansas City, a member of this Society, died of Pneumonia, February 27, 1915. He was born in Pelham county, New Hampshire, April 20, 1835, and graduated from Harvard in 1856; was admitted to the bar in Boston in 1858, and came to Kansas City the following March. He was the first president of the Kansas City Bar Association and of the Law Library Association, and in 1884 was the president of the State Bar Association. His ancestors came from England to Boston in 1630.

Col. Elijah Gates came to Missouri in 1847, and to Buchanan county in 1857. During the Civil War he was Colonel of the First Missouri Confederate Cavalry, and lost an arm in service. He was sheriff from 1874 to 1878, and was appointed United States Marshal for the Western District of Missouri. He was elected State Treasurer in November, 1876. He died at St. Joseph, March 4, 1915 at the age of eighty-eight years.

Dr. William W. Mosby was born in Scott county, Kentucky, June 1, 1824, and came to Richmond, Missouri when four years old. He graduated from the Medical Department of Transylvania University in 1845. In 1862 he was elected a member of the State Senate of the 22nd General Assembly, and re-elected two years later. He died at Richmond, February 26, 1915.

Ripley D. Saunders, dramatic and literary editor of the Post-Dispatch of St. Louis, died on the operating table at St. John's Hospital in St. Louis, March 16, 1915. It was supposed that he was suffering with an acute attack of gastritis, but the operation showed it was a cancer. He was 59 years old, and had been connected with the St. Louis newspapers since 1888. In addition to his literary newspaper work he published two books "John Kenadie" and "Col. Todhunter of Missouri."

Hon. Thomas Martin Spofford was born at Pulaski, Tennessee, and came to Kansas City in 1895. Two years afterwards he was elected a member of the House in the 39th General Assembly from the fourth district of Jackson county. He was a graduate of Washington and Lee University, and of the law department of Columbia University. He was married in 1898, was president of the upper house of Kansas City one term, and died in New York, February 24, 1915, aged 52 years.

Frederick Oakes Sylvester, formerly instructor in art at the Central High School of St. Louis, and a well known landscape painter, died in St. Louis, March 2, 1915. He was born in Brockton, Massachusetts, October 8, 1869, and came to St. Louis in 1892. He was Secretary and later President of the St. Louis Artists' Guild, and was awarded medals at the St. Louis World's Fair, the Portland Exposition and by the Society of Western Artists.

In the landscapes painted by him he made a specialty of the Mississippi river, and the book of poems and pictures published by him was called "The Great River." A splendidly bound copy of this work was presented to the Society by Mr. and Mrs. C. R. Meston of St. Louis, containing an original water color painting by the author, and an original manuscript poem on "History" signed by him.

THE MISSOURI HISTORICAL REVIEW

SIX PERIODS OF MISSOURI HISTORY.*

Floyd C. Shoemaker.

Recorded Missouri history covers three hundred and seventy-four years and divides itself into six periods. During these years that part of the Mississippi Valley that lies within the present limits of Missouri, was first claimed by Spain, possessed by France, again became subject to Spain, was later retroceded to France, and finally sold to the United States. If the Indians' dominion is included, legal sovereignty over Missouri changed hands five times.

The first period in Missouri history was one of discovery and exploration and covered nearly two centuries,—from 1541 to 1732. This was a period of romance, filled with heroic deeds and striking characters. The first two years of this period belong to the familiar story of the Spaniard's quest for American gold; the next one hundred and seventeen years are a blank; and the remaining seventy-three years are the prized possession of France. To Spain this period in Missouri history is but a brilliant incident; to France it is one of the fascinating pages in her story of the St. Lawrence, the Great Lakes, the Mississippi and the Gulf.

---

*An address delivered on November 13, 1914, at the St. Joseph meeting of the Missouri Society of Teachers of History and Government.

In April, 1541, less than half a century after Columbus founded the New World, DeSoto, a Spaniard, discovered the Mississippi River. He and his successor, Moscoso, traversed much of the present State of Arkansas and probably set foot on Missouri soil. Neither DeSoto's remarkable discovery nor his journey through the Arkansas and Missouri swamps and over the Ozarks, is of importance in Missouri history except to mark a beginning. The first white men had arrived, but not until the latter half of the seventeenth century did others follow. It might be noted that the same year that witnessed DeSoto's discovery of the Mississippi River and his probable entrance into Missouri, also marked the approach towards Missouri of the famous Spanish expedition of Coronado from Mexico. To Spain belongs the honor of discovering the Mississippi River; to France the greater honor of rediscovering it and of exploring and settling the great Mississippi Valley.

Between the coming of DeSoto and the appearance of the French, nearly a century and a quarter elapsed. During this time the English had established a fringe of settlements along the Atlantic; the Spanish had settled themselves in the West Indies, Florida, Mexico and for hundreds of miles to the south and north of the latter country; and the French had occupied a strip along the St. Lawrence and made a few settlements on the Great Lakes. Not until the latter half of the seventeenth century did the French begin rapidly pushing westward and southwestward from eastern Canada, although it is reported that as early as 1634, Jean Nicolet, acting under the command of the great Champlain, visited Lake Michigan, Green Bay and Fox River in Wisconsin, and perhaps reached the upper Mississippi River. French missionaries, traders, soldiers and adventurers, then commenced traversing the country lying between the Ohio, Mississippi and Wisconsin rivers. Two daring French traders, Sieur Radisson and Sieur des Groseilliers, passed Lake Huron and Lake Michigan in 1659, traversed the Wisconsin country, rediscovered the Mississippi River and, according to one authority, discovered the Missouri River. Radisson and Groseilliers were remarkable men,—being among the

SIX PERIODS OF MISSOURI HISTORY.   223

first recorded Frenchmen to view the Mississippi River and being possibly the discoverers of the Missouri River, being the founders of the great Hudson Bay Company in 1670, and both serving twice under France and twice under England. The important travels and explorations of these two adventures in New France have curiously been overshadowed and in fact almost forgotten in the public mind by the better known expedition of Joliet and Marquette. The reason for this, however, is not hard to find. In the first place, the journals of Radisson were not brought to light even in part until 1750, were not entirely collected until 1839, and were not copied and published until 1885. On the other hand, the reports or journals of Marquette were widely known, soon after their compilation, and their vividness and definiteness of language combined with their author's tragic death, immediately attracted attention.

The so-called expedition of Joliet and Marquette was, indeed, a noteworthy one and followed closely that of Radisson and Groseilliers. Acting under the direction and aid of Count Frontenac and Talon, the Governor and Intendant respectively of New France, Louis Joliet, a Canadian-born trader, led a small company through the Illinois country, and on June 17, 1673, reached the Mississippi River. Floating down that stream, Joliet passed the present eastern boundary of Missouri and viewed the great river that bisects this State. On arriving at the mouth of the Arkansas River, the company disembarked, made peace with the Indians, and having learned that the Mississippi River emptied into the Gulf, which information was the main object of the trip, returned north the same summer. One of the members of the expedition was a Jesuit missionary, Father Marquette, who had obtained permission from his Superior to accompany Joliet. To Marquette we are indebted for his account of the exploration of Joliet as the journal kept by the latter was lost. Marquette's reports to his Superior naturally made prominent the activity of Marquette and told little of Joliet, and as a result the expedition has been generally though erroneously known as that of Marquette and Joliet.

The leading spirit of all this expansion movement was, however, the patriotic French soldier, Robert Cavelier de La Salle, who in 1671 had discovered the Ohio River and probably the Illinois River. Acting under the direction and aid of this great empire-builder, Father Hennepin traversed the Illinois country and in 1680 reached the Mississippi River. The Great Lakes had by this time become more or less familiar to the Canadian-French traders and missionaries, and this is also true of the Wisconsin, the Illinois, the St. Joseph and the upper Mississippi rivers. In 1682 La Salle himself succeeded in leaving New France for the great Mississippi Valley, and to him is the honor of being the first white man to navigate the Mississippi River from its upper course to the Gulf. And on April 9, 1682, at the mouth of that river, he took possession of the country for France and named it Louisiana, in honor of Louis XIV. La Salle was the greatest of the French explorers in the Mississippi Valley. He saw the opportunity to build up here an empire for France and his early death in 1687 was a great loss to his country. La Salle was ably aided by his friend and lieutenant, the "iron-handed" Italian, Henri de Tonty, who, later proved the valued lieutenant of another of France's great empire founders, Bienville. Tonty, in 1685, also made the trip to the Gulf but not finding La Salle, returned to the Illinois country.

From now on French activity increased, principally in the Illinois country and the Great Lakes region. The principal motives were missionary zeal, the fur trade, the dream of an empire for France, and the love of adventure,—the first two motives being the most important. At the time of La Salle's death in 1687, no French settlement had been made on the Gulf; but the Illinois country could boast of a number of wandering French traders and missionaries, and a temporary fort or two,—perhaps even a settlement. At least by 1700 two permanent settlements had been made close to Missouri soil, Kaskaskia and Cahokia, both located in the Illinois country just south of St. Louis on the east bank of the Mississippi River. About the same time the great French-Canadian soldier, Iberville, established a settlement at Biloxi

(1699) on the Gulf. The latter was abandoned in 1705 and the population moved to Mobile, which had been established in 1702. In 1706 the population of lower Louisiana was only eighty-two and possessed only forty-six cattle. This shows that, contrary to popular opinion, upper Louisiana,—the Illinois country,—developed first, as its population was larger at this time. Not until 1718 was New Orleans founded, or two decades after the founding of Cahokia and Kaskaskia.

During this time no permanent settlements or forts had been made within the present boundaries of Missouri. The first fort, Fort Orleans, was not built here until 1720 and was destroyed in 1724; and the first permanent settlement was not made until about 1732. Missouri was not, however, an unknown country to the French. From the beginning of the 18th century the French had explored Missouri and her great river; had traded with the Indians; had mined lead; and perhaps made salt. In fact it is not improbable, though not authentic, that a permanent settlement was made in Missouri in 1719 at the present town of "Old Mine" in St. Francois County. It appears somewhat strange that earlier settlements were not made in Missouri. The reason is found in the more favorable conditions that prevailed in the Illinois country. The land and water routes of travel between the Great Lakes and the Gulf were through Illinois; the Illinois Indians were friendly to the French; and the east bank of the Mississippi River below St. Louis was more favorable for early settlements. Owing to the trade routes, the character of the aborginal inhabitants, and the nature of the country, the Illinois country was first in settlement and development despite the well known valuable lead deposits in Missouri. It was during this period, however, that Missouri was explored as far west as the mouth of the Kansas River and the way was open for permanent settlements. It need hardly be added that little is known of what the French did in Missouri during these years. Missouri history at this time is obscure. The actual extent of the French exploration is uncertain, and the same can be said of the fur and lead business, forts and settlements. If we except a few well ascertained events and facts it may be stated, that the most important fact in Missouri history at this time, is that Missouri was but an appendage or province of the Illinois-French, who regarded it with the eyes of the exploiter.

Beginning about 1732 Missouri history, proper, took on a definite form. Events and dates were more or less accurately recorded and individual names appeared. The second period in Missouri history began at this time and ended in 1804. This period was one of *early settlements*, during which Missouri was still essentially an Indian country. This second period like the first was fundamentally a French period despite the sovereignty of Spanish rule and law during half of this time. The inception of this period was the founding at Ste. Genevieve in 1732 of the first authentic permanent settlement in Missouri. During this period Missouri history was still very closely connected with Illinois history and practically every important event that influenced the latter reacted on the former. This even extended to Indiana history to some degree, and towards the close of the period the American colonists pushing westward also became important factors here. Although this period falls into several divisions, based either on the character of the immigrations or on the sovereignty exercised over Louisiana, it was still a unit, the fundamental characteristic of which was the establishing of a relatively small number of permanent settlements.

The first of these permanent settlements that history has recorded, was in southeast Missouri near the present town of Ste. Genevieve. The exact date of the founding of the old town of Ste. Genevieve is still a matter of dispute among historians, but this much appears credible: Ste. Genevieve was well established by the middle of the eighteenth century and probably was settled by 1732 or even prior to that year. Several lead mines in Missouri had been worked by the Illinois-French for three or four decades before this, and the fame of these valuable mines was not unknown even in Paris, France, at the dawn of the eighteenth century. Hundreds of the Illinois-French had probably taken up a more or less permanent residence here long before 1732, but the records are in-

SIX PERIODS OF MISSOURI HISTORY. 227

definite on this point. The founding of Ste. Genevieve was due almost entirely to its proximity to the lead mines combined with a favorable location for obtaining salt and for small farming.

Thirty-two years elapsed after the founding of Ste. Genevieve before the second permanent settlement was made in Missouri. In 1764 under the direction of Pierre Laclede Liguest and his stepson, Auguste Chouteau, St. Louis was founded. The sole cause of this settlement was a desire to establish a well located trading post.

It is almost certain that if European politics had not intervened, the next fifty years of the development of Missouri would have been as slow as during the preceding half century. But the chancellories of France, England, and Spain, were to unconsciously settle Missouri. On November 3, 1762, France by secret treaty, offered to cede to Spain, as a reward for past services, all the territory she possessed west of the Mississippi River and also New Orleans. Spain accepted this princely donation ten days later. At the Treaty of Paris on February 10, 1763, between England, France and Spain, France ceded all her continental American possessions east of the Mississippi River except New Orleans to England. The Illinois country, lying east of the Mississippi River, thus passed into English hands. The Treaty of Paris was soon known in the Mississippi Valley, but almost two years elapsed before even New Orleans heard of the secret treaty of 1762. As a result of the Treaty of Paris, hundreds of Illinois-French crossed to the west bank of the Mississippi River into Missouri territory, and on June 15, 1764, the French commander of Illinois, St. Ange, moved to St. Louis. When the English occupied Fort Chartres in Illinois in 1765, the French continued to show their hatred of England by immigrating to Missouri soil, and as a result several new settlements sprang up here, the most important being St. Charles. The coming of the Spanish officials was also distasteful to the French of both upper and lower Louisiana, and in the latter country resulted in the expulsion in 1768 of Ulloa, the first Spanish Governor of Louisiana. Upper Louisiana was not formally acquired by

Spain till 1770. From that time to 1804 Missouri was governed by a Spanish lieutenant-governor, who resided at St. Louis and who was under the Governor of Louisiana in New Orleans. The government of Spain in upper and lower Louisiana was a mild, benevolent and, on the whole, a liberal administration. Laws were simple, the French customs and language respected, taxes practically nothing, and court procedure just and quick without either lawyers or juries. Land was plentiful and to be had for the cost of surveying. Although neither the government nor its officials were perfect, the province was prosperous and the people happy and contented.

The population of Missouri in 1770 was not large, but new events caused another tide of immigrants to pour in. The campaign of George Rogers Clark in the Illinois and Indiana countries in 1778 gave the American colonies a claim to the Northwest Territory, and the treaty of peace with England in 1783 secured this territory to the United States. Three causes operated, however, that drove hundreds to Missouri soil: 1st, the slavery prohibition in the Northwest Ordinance; 2nd, the reign of lawlessness succeeding the attempted establishment of American rule in Illinois and Indiana; and 3rd, the shortsighted land policy of the United States regarding old French land claims there. This new influx of settlers may be considered as the second great immigration to Missouri, and was composed of both Frenchmen and Americans: the first in the sixties having been entirely French. New settlements sprang up in Missouri at this time and within the next fifteen years, the most important being at New Madrid, Potosi, and Cape Girardeau.

The third immigration into Missouri during the period of Spanish rule, was caused by the liberal land grants offered to settlers by the Spanish officials. This induced hundreds of Americans from Kentucky, Tennessee, Virginia and the Carolinas, to settle west of the Mississippi River. By 1804 the new American immigration to Missouri had been under way for ten years.

The year 1800 marked the cession of Louisiana to France, but Spanish officials remained in actual command of upper

Louisiana until within twenty-four hours of the transfer to the United States in 1804. This transfer of upper Louisiana in 1804, based on the purchase of United States in 1803, marks the end of the second period in Missouri history.

The third period in Missouri history began in 1804 and closed in 1820. During these years Missouri was essentially *a pioneer territory*. The year 1804 witnessed the passing out of foreign rule in upper Louisiana and the incoming of American rule. Contrary to popular opinion, this change was not welcomed by the inhabitants of this territory even though more than half of the population was American, and to the French part the change caused much grief. American rule brought many taxes and officials, slow court procedure with jury trials, scores of lawyers, and hundreds of hungry landsharks. All these were distasteful to even many native-born Americans and were detested by the French. The government was at first a military one and lasted only a few months. Upper Louisiana, whose white population was contained in Missouri, was then joined as the District of Louisiana in 1804 to Indiana Territory. This change was so opposed by the inhabitants of upper Louisiana that in 1805 the District of Louisiana was made the Territory of Louisiana, and was given the first or lowest grade of territorial government. The population having increased from ten thousand to twenty thousand between 1804 and 1810, petitions were sent to Congress to raise the rank of government, and in 1812 the second grade of territorial government was applied to Louisiana Territory and the name changed to Missouri Territory. A further advance to the highest grade of territorial government was made in 1816, and a year later petitions for statehood were circulated.

This third period of Missouri history found Missouri a province with five districts and left it a state with fifteen counties. Settlements had been made along the Mississippi from New Madrid to as far north as the present county of Ralls, and up the Missouri to the present county of Ray. The great Boone's Lick Country in central Missouri, and the Salt River district lying between the Mississippi and Missouri rivers, had been settled. Settlers had also pushed their way a little into the Ozark region. But Missouri was still essentially a pioneer territory despite the great increase of two hundred and nineteen per cent in population from 1810 to 1820. The main occupations were fur-trading, salt making, merchandising, agriculture, and lead mining. Land speculation reigned supreme. Agriculture was still very limited, and the gathering of wild-bee honey perhaps netted some frontier communities more money income than the produce of the farm.

This was the day of big lawyers, of duels, of contested Spanish land claims, and of Indian struggles. Regarding the latter, however, Missouri was fortunate compared with many states. During this period the bar of Missouri was a remarkably able one. Such public men as the Bateses and Bartons, Benton, Buckner, Scott, the Cooks, Evans, and at least two scores of talented lawyers served Missouri in assemblies and in courts. Missouri's public life for over three decades was entirely in the hands of these men. Some were native of Wales, England, and Ireland; others of France; but most were from the States, principally from the South.

During this period two private banks were established, but neither succeeded. Several individual Masonic lodges were founded, which survive today, and the Methodists in 1816 established a General Conference here. By 1820 five weekly newspapers were issuing regularly, but these reached a comparatively small population owing to the poor transportation facilities and to mechanical difficulties. Life was simple, and both economic and social conditions were essentially pioneer.

In 1820 Missouri, with a population of sixty-six thousand, organized a state government, and in 1821 was admitted into the Union. This change in itself broadened the Missourian's horizion, but the mere framing of a state constitution and the establishing of a state government did not work remarkable transformations in either Missouri's political, social or economic life. In fact from 1820 to 1836, Missouri was essentially a *pioneer state*. These sixteen years embraced the fourth period in Missouri's history.

SIX PERIODS OF MISSOURI HISTORY. 231

In many respects the third and the fourth periods in Missouri history had more in common than any other two periods. Each covered sixteen years of development and each was essentially a pioneer stage. If it were not for a single great event, we would be persuaded to consider the two periods as one. This event was, however, of such commanding importance that it is difficult to refuse placing it at the beginning of a new period. We refer to the change in Missouri's political status from a territory to a state. The fourth period of development in Missouri history, that this event inaugurated, included, however, many other noteworthy events. It marked the inception and growth of the great steamboat traffic. It witnessed the final departure of the Indian from Missouri soil in 1832. During its span of sixteen years, Missouri as a political unit for the first time extended money aid and credit to her inhabitants. This period also saw the beginning of political parties in Missouri, although the personality of candidates, and especially that of Benton, still had the strongest hold on the voters. In the field of finance no systematic advance was made. Nevertheless the finances of Missouri and of her inhabitants were in a prosperous condition. This was due to the fur trade, the lead mines, and the Mexican trade. The later, or as it is familiarly known, the Santa Fe Trade, was at its height during this time and was then one of the greatest industries of Missouri. Agriculture was the livelihood of most of the people, but it was still in its pioneer stage although the State's rapidly increasing population was aiding greatly in developing this. The tobacco and hemp industries also became important during this period. In social and educational development some progress was made, principally in the field of churches and fraternities. Private and religious schools of worth, though on a small scale, were established, the most important of which was St. Louis College in 1828, now St. Louis University. In religion three great sects, following the example of the Methodists of 1816, established state-wide organizations in Missouri. The Catholic diocese of St. Louis was formed in 1826; the Presbyterian Synod was organized in 1832; and the Baptist General

Conference in 1834. The Missouri Temperance Society was organized in 1832. Two great fraternal orders also effected state organizations: the Masonic Grand Lodge was organized in 1821, and the Odd Fellows in 1834. If we include with the foregoing events the Morman tragedies in the thirties in Missouri, and the immigration of Missourians to Texas in the twenties and thirties, we have perhaps reviewed the striking and most important developments of Missouri history during this period. It was essentially a *pioneer period*, but towards its close it merged into a more advanced and progressive stage of civilization, though not necessarily a happier one.

This new epoch constituted the fifth period in Missouri history and extended from approximately 1836 to about 1870. During these thirty-four years Missouri was a *state in the making*. A word of explanation is perhaps necessary to illustrate. This period marked the transition of Missouri from colony to to colonizer; from a pioneer community to a settled commonwealth; from a frontier state to a state of national importance; from a district of little wealth and population to one great in industries and people. However, there were lacking several important lines of development and activity, except towards the close of this period, that are essential to the modern, fully realized American state. The latter not only progresses and meets the needs of her citizens through the enterprise of individuals, but, as a political unit, as a master organization, she takes over those activities that can be handled best by her under our democratic ideals of government. Except in the economic field, Missouri as a corporate whole did not realize these ideals of government activity until about 1870. Nor did the cooperative social life of Missouri, taken as a whole reach a state stage of development until about 1870, except in the field of religion, although the social life of individuals and of districts was perfected years before. A brief survey of this period is necessary to appreciate and perhaps even to agree with these generalizations. In fact it is almost an act of temerity to publicly declare that from 1836 to 1870 Missouri was *a state in the making*, and certainly it is inviting discussion to include the years 1861 to 1865 in anything else than a period by themselves. I hope my reason for doing this will be clear,—at least suggestive.

The year 1836, the beginning of this period, is noteworthy in Missouri history for two great events: the Platte Purchase, which rounded out Missouri's territorial boundaries, was acquired then; and the first railroad convention of Missouri was held in St. Louis in that year. From that time to 1870 the State's development was rapid. In 1836, fifty-five of Missouri's counties had been established, in 1861 the one hundred and fourteenth one, the county of Worth, was organized. Corresponding with the increase in counties, was the growth of population. In 1840, which ended the last decade in Missouri history when her population doubled, there were three hundred and eighty-three thousand persons on Missouri soil, and Missouri ranked sixteenth in population among the States: in 1870, Missouri's population had increased to one million seven hundred and twenty-one thousand and her rank was fifth. During this period the great German and Irish immigrations set in, especially during the forties and fifties; and after 1865, northern and eastern immigrants settled here. Missouri's rise in importance in national affairs coincided with this great growth in population. This was true not only in politics, but also in war and in colonization. Missouri's part in the Seminole Indian war was prominent; and the same is true regarding both the Texas War of Independence and especially the Mexican War. And in the Civil War few border states were more prized by both sides than Missouri. As a colonizer during this period Missouri's influence was felt to some extent in Wisconsin, Iowa and Arkansas: later in Texas, Oregon, California, Kansas and Nebraska; and still later in Colorado and Montana. Some of the latter states were settled largely by Missourians. In short Missouri had passed the stage of a colony, and had herself become a colonizer.

The economic development of Missouri during this period was remarkable. Her first State Bank was established in 1837, and in 1857 the foundation of her present state banking law was enacted. In 1851 the State and her citizens entered on an extensive railroad construction policy. By loaning her credit to individuals Missouri enabled this line of work to progress rapidly, and this in turn greatly developed the State. The five miles of wooden railroad in Missouri in 1851 had by 1870 increased to over two thousand miles of iron roads. This early railroad history of Missouri was an important factor in Missouri's development, but it finally entailed a debt of nearly twenty-five million dollars on the State government at the time that a large war debt was incurred. The effect of these two debts was to raise the state taxes as never before nor since in the history of Missouri. In 1856 the State's revenue was about five hundred thousand dollars; in 1870 it was nearly three million dollars a year. In 1860 the state tax rate for revenue and interest purposes was thirty cents on the hundred dollars assessed valuation; in 1870 it was fifty cents, being equally divided for revenue and interest purposes; and in 1867, the high tide of state taxation in Missouri, the rate was sixty-five cents.

During this period agriculture advanced with the railroads. In 1850 the value of farm land in Missouri was eighty-seven million dollars, and only seven per cent of Missouri land was improved; in 1870, farm wealth had risen to three hundred and ninety-four million dollars and twenty per cent of Missouri land was improved. Factories had their inception during these years, but only a small part of Missouri's wealth was in a corporation form. The increase in the total taxable wealth in Missouri was almost miraculous, increasing from forty-seven million dollars in 1850, to five hundred seventy-five million dollars in 1870. To summarize, it may be stated that the beginning of the period found Missouri a sparsely populated, almost undeveloped state, and the close left her a population of over a million and a half, and a taxable wealth assessed at over one-half billion dollars. The period was essentially one of great economic development.

In the field of state wide social development, little was accomplished outside of religious organizations. All important State church organizations were completed. In 1840 the Episcopal Church effected this; in 1845 the South Methodist;

SIX PERIODS OF MISSOURI HISTORY.   235

in 1847 the Catholic Archdiocese was established; in 1855 the First Catholic Provincial Council, and the Evangelical Lutheran; in 1864 the Congregational; and in 1866 the Christian. A beginning was made in state wide voluntary associations such as the Medical in 1850, the 1836 association having been premature and failed; the Agricultural in 1853; the Teachers in 1856; the Horticulturists in 1858-59; the Dentists in 1865; and the Press in 1867. The inception of Women's Clubs is found at the latter part of this period, the first being the Missouri Woman's Suffrage Club of 1867, the Woman's Christian Organization of St. Louis in 1868 and of Kansas City in 1870. These clubs were, however, all for a particular object and were not of the cultural and social character of today. The fraternal orders made some advance in their state organizations; the Knight Templars in 1847 and the Knights of Pythias in 1870. Two voluntary institutions of a cultural and educational character and of great worth and importance were established but accomplished little at this time: The Missouri Historical and Philosophical Society in the forties, which soon died; and the St. Louis Missouri Historical Society in 1866.

This period was the great day of private schools and colleges. In fact until 1850 more children were receiving their education in these than in the public schools. At least two-thirds of the prominent private colleges and schools in Missouri today were founded between 1836 and 1870. In the field of public education, however, and especially higher public education, the progress of Missouri was very slow. The first separate State Superintendent of Public Instruction was not appointed until 1839, and after two years the office was assumed by the Secretary of State, who held it until 1853. The first report on public schools in 1839 showed only one hundred and fourteen school districts in Missouri where one hundred and sixty-three months of school was taught altogether and at which only five thousand of Missouri's 100,000 children attended. The amount of State money expended for public education was two thousand three hundred dollars. In 1856, three years after the second establishment of a separate State

Superintendent of Schools, the number of school districts had increased to three thousand eight hundred, the number of children enrolled to ninety-eight thousand, and the salaries of teachers to three hundred and seventy-nine thousand dollars. A great advance in common public school education was made from 1856 to 1860. In the latter year there were five thousand two hundred school districts in which one hundred and seventy thousand children or nearly one-half of Missouri's school population were enrolled, and the teachers of which received six hundred and sixty-seven thousand dollars. During the war, education was greatly retarded, and many of the district schools closed. The office of State Superintendent of Schools was again in the Secretary of State's hands, and Missouri received a great intellectual setback. In 1870, the public schools had, however, more than recovered what they had had in 1860, and the number of school districts was seven thousand five hundred with two hundred eighty thousand pupils, or nearly one-half Missouri's school population, enrolled. In the field of higher public school education, little was accomplished. The State University, founded in 1839, was not supported by State appropriations, except two thousand five hundred dollars a year interest on the Seminary Fund, until 1867 when ten thousand dollars was given. As a result of this lack of state support the State University in 1870 had only ten teachers, with two hundred and forty-three students enrolled, one-third of the latter being in the preparatory department. The day of the public schools had just begun to dawn.

In the field of eleemosynary institutions the State prior to 1870 had accomplished little. A state hospital for the insane had been established at Fulton in 1847, a school for the blind in St. Louis in the fifties, and for the deaf in 1851. The work of caring for the unfortunate of Missouri prior to 1870 was largely in the hands of private institutions and under the churches, especially the Catholic. Equally tardy was Missouri in establishing state boards and commissions. During this period only four important ones were met with: the Board of Public Works in 1855; the Geological Survey in 1853; the Board of Agriculture in 1863; and Board of Statistics in 1866.

In short the fifth period of Missouri history was one of remarkable economic development aided greatly by the State Government. The great day of higher intellectual progress; of public education; of state care of the unfortunate; of state boards of information, inspection and regulation; of women's clubs; voluntary state societies of a vocational character: had just begun by 1870. And until a state has these in a flourishing degree, it is still a state in the making, a commonwealth that has not fully realized itself. In closing this period a word about the war is essential. Costly as it was to Missouri both in men and money, in misery and sorrow; and prized as it is for Missouri's unselfish devotion to her ideals and convictions; still to the historian the war in Missouri represents essentially a partial paralysis of her intellect. The point I would emphasize is not, however, educational retrogression even though this was present in many counties, but it is educational stagnation. Missouri's public educational system was in a deplorable condition in 1860, and the war, in the main, simply prevented an improvement owing to the stopping of the state school-money apportionment and to the disturbed peace. The war worked no revolution in industry and no great change in social life, except during two or three years in certain districts. The three greatest things it produced, excepting the settlement of slavery, were: 1st, Missouri's stagnation in intellectual pursuits especially in the field of education; 2nd, Missouri's semi-political martyrdom from 1861 to 1870; and 3rd, the piling up of a large war debt on top of the railroad debt. The evils that these three things eventually, though indirectly caused, are too many and too complicated for this paper. From 1860 to 1870 Missouri grew in wealth and population by leaps and bounds, but partly offsetting both of these were the blows that had been delivered to Missouri's intellectual, political, and financial condition as a State.

About the year 1870 a new period began in Missouri history. This was her sixth period and extended to the present. It is very probable, however, that a historical prospectus taken twenty or thirty years from now will make apparent the necessity of closing this period before the year 1914. In fact to all thoughtful men and women it is obvious that for several years there has been coming into existence a new mode of thinking; a new attitude towards social, educational, religious, political and industrial problems; a new appraisement of everything; and even a new position in international affairs. We are now too close to all this new birth to accurately analyze it; we are unable to even pick out the big factors and say which are the most important. Who has the temerity to prophesy what is the main thing that has started, and which will spell progress or retrogression. Is it clean government and business administration in city, state and nation? Is it reform of our judiciary? Is it woman suffrage? Is it prohibition? Is it Single Tax? Or is it Socialism? Is it the great impulse just given to education? Or is it free trade? Is it a score of reforms? Or is it a feeble, unconscious grasping after information on everything? Missouri as one of the greatest states in this nation is in the midst of all this, and Missouri's present history is, therefore, too uncertain for accurate interpretation. The following are, however, the most patent generalizations.

The sixth period of Missouri's development from 1870 on, is one of almost unlimited individualistic progress combined with a conservative advance of the State as a political organism along utilitarian lines. I shall say but a word regarding the former. This was the great day of corporations, the growth of cities, the development of factories, the rise in population and wealth, the increase of land values. Between 1870 and 1900 Missouri's taxable wealth doubled, and her population did nearly this; Missouri's improved land area jumped from twenty per cent to fifty-one per cent; Missouri's agricultural land rose in value from four hundred million dollars to over a billion dollars and by 1910 to over two billion dollars; and her two thousand miles of railroads in 1870 had grown to over ten thousand miles in 1910. This was also the day of unlimited individualism in cooperative associations of a cultural, vocational and social character. Women's clubs and lodges have their beginning and rapid growth during these years; and practically all voluntary vocational societies and organizations were formed then. In short except in the field of education, care for the unfortunate, a few regulating boards, and the machinery of government, the individual by himself or in cooperation with others, was supreme and almost unlimited in his activities at this time. From an individualistic standpoint Missouri during this period reached a remarkably full realization of herself in both social and economic affairs. We have just indicated in a general way her sphere of activity as a political organization.

In this latter sphere, although her advance was remarkable, Missouri failed to keep pace with her citizens in their work. Missouri was unfortunate in being so circumscribed by self-imposed limitations in her present constitution of 1875. That document very naturally limited the state revenue tax to twenty cents on the one hundred dollars assessed valuation, and then to still further limit the state's progress, declared that this rate should be reduced to fifteen cents when the assessed wealth of the state reached nine hundred million dollars. This was equivalent to saying, and this is practically what happened in 1892, that when Missouri's assessed wealth was eight hundred and ninety-nine million dollars her state revenue tax should yield one and three-fourths million dollars, but that when Missouri's assessed wealth reached nine hundred million dollars, this tax should be decreased twenty-five per cent or about one-half million dollars. A true illustration would be given if a man were to declare that when his income reached two thousand dollars, he would reduce it to one thousand five hundred dollars; or if a corporation were to rule that when its business had reached a certain mark, it would curtail its own development. The reason for this limitation in the constitution of 1875 is as clear as that the limitation is today unfortunate. The enormous state railroad and war debt had entailed the most burdensome of taxes on Missourians during the latter sixties and early seventies. In fact the state revenue and interest taxes in 1867 yielded a larger income on less than five hundred million dollars assessed taxable property than these did in 1910 on over one billion five hundred million dollars. I have enlarged on this subject because it was this lack of revenue after 1875 that caused the very conservative development of Missouri as a political, economic unit. Between 1870 and 1875, five large state institutions were established, which include two normals, two hospitals and a school of mines; from 1875 to 1880, Lincoln Institute was established; between 1880 and 1890, two hospitals and two training schools; the next decade saw the establishment of a virtually new state university, two soldiers' homes, a home for the feeble-minded, a fruit experiment station, and a state historical society; and between 1900 and 1910, a state sanatorium and two normals. It is thus seen that between 1870 and 1875, nearly as much progress was made in establishing state institutions as during any census decade thereafter.

However, considering her binding tax limitations, Missouri made remarkable progress from 1870 to 1910. She advanced wonderfully in education, both higher and elementary; she took care of her unfortunate; and she established numerous boards and commissions for gathering information and some for inspection. In fact even with her limited income combined with the rise in local taxes, Missouri by 1910 has become a great, cooperative and progressive commonwealth.

Note: The statements made regarding the first and second periods are based on Fortier, *History of Louisiana;* Houck, *History of Missouri, and Spanish Regime in Missouri;* the Illinois State Historical Library, *Collections* and *Publications;* and the State Historical Society of Wisconsin, *Collections.* Extensive use was also made of the valuable publications of the various historical societies of Canada. The third and fourth periods rest on the official publications of the United States Government and of Missouri; newspapers; Houck, *History of Missouri;* Billon, *Annals of St. Louis;* Stoddard, *Sketches of Louisiana;* accounts of various travelers, as Brackenridge, Darby, Flint, Schoolcraft, and others; together with a manuscript of mine on *Missouri's Struggle for Statehood.* The fifth and sixth periods are based on information obtained principally from the laws of Missouri and the official reports of the State's officials, institutions and boards; the various Civil War histories of Missouri; church minutes; school and college catalogues; association reports; and club programs.

FLOYD C. SHOEMAKER.

"MISSOURI DAY" PROGRAMS FOR MISSOURI CLUB WOMEN.

Floyd C. Shoemaker.

In response to a growing interest in the study of Missouri history on the part of Missouri schools, clubs and reading circles, the State Historical Society has compiled these programs. Topics have been selected upon which there is available literature and information of a satisfactory character. There has been no attempt to cover the entire field of Missouri history, but a study of the subjects here presented will contribute much towards an appreciation of the richness and interest of this kind of work. No state offers a more absorbing and valuable story than Missouri.

In addition to the references given, much information can be obtained by a careful examination of both the county and city newspapers. Special articles of a historical or biographical character are constantly appearing in the press, and many of of these are well worth the time and trouble to clip and preserve. An aid to this kind of material will be found in each number of the *Review* under *Historical Articles in Missouri Newspapers*. A further aid will be found in the first article in this number of the *Review*. In fact all persons interested in Missouri history should obtain a set of *The Review* and should have their names entered as members of *The State Historical Society of Missouri*.

"Missouri Day" Programs for Missouri Club Women will be found useful to persons who desire information on specific Missouri topics, to teachers of history, to students, and to clubs. Public, school and college libraries in Missouri are advised to secure the more important publications herein listed. These programs can in many cases be advantageously divided into several programs, or portions can be selected for study. Such division or selection will depend largely on the extent of references and information obtainable.

I. Discovery and Early Settlements of Missouri, 1541-1804
   1. Spanish exploration—De Soto.
   2. French exploration—Joilet and Marquette.
   3. Early settlements—Fort Orleans, Ste. Genevieve, St. Louis, St. Charles, New Madrid, Cape Girardeau and other towns.
   4. Social and economic Missouri of the 18th century.

   > Bryan's *Daniel Boone*, *Review*, Vols. III and IV.
   > Bourne's *The Romance of Western History*, *Review*, Vol. I.
   > Carr's *Missouri*, Chs. I-III.
   > Chouteau's *Journal of the Founding of St. Louis*, in *Mo. Hist. Soc.*, (St. Louis) *Coll.*, Vol. III.
   > Davis and Durrie's *Missouri*, Chs. I-III.
   > Finkelnburg's *Under Three Flags*, in *Mo. Hist. Soc.*, (St. Louis) *Coll.*, Vol. III.
   > Houck's *History of Missouri*, Vols. I and II.
   > Missouri county histories, first part.
   > Mss., *The Spanish Forts at the Mouth of the Missouri River*, in *Mo. Hist. Soc.*, (St. Louis) *Coll.*, Vol. III.
   > Primm's *Early History of St. Louis*, in *Mo. Hist. Soc.*, (St. Louis) *Coll.*, Vol. IV.
   > Rader's *History of Missouri*, Part I.
   > Shoemaker's *Six Periods of Missouri History*, *Review*, Vol. IX.
   > Stipes' *Fort Orleans*, *Review*, Vol. VIII.
   > Switzler's *History of Missouri*, Chs. I-VI.
   > Viles' *The Story of the State*, in *The State of Missouri*, edited by Walter Williams, pp. 9-14.
   > Viles' *Population and Extent of Settlement in Missouri before 1804*, *Review*, Vol. V.
   > Violette's, *Early Settlements in Missouri*, *Review*, Vol. I.

Information on the various topics in this program is easily obtainable. Much of the subject matter is widespread in its nature and can be found in many books not listed with the foregoing. The *Missouri Historical Review* has enlarged on many of these subjects and reprints of some of these articles can be obtained from the Historical Society.

II. Lewis and Clark Expedition, 1804
   1. Story of the expedition.
   2. Biography of Merriweather Lewis and William Clark.
   3. National importance of the expedition.
   4. Special significance to Missouri.

   > (All standard encyclopedias contain accounts of this expedition and the lives of its leaders. Similar articles are found in United States histories.)
   > Coues' *History of the Expedition under the Command of Lewis and Clark*.
   > (Mrs.) Dye's *The Conquest: The True Story of Lewis and Clark*. (A historical novel.)

Hosmer's *History of the Expedition of Lewis and Clark.*
Houck's *History of Missouri*, Vol. III, pp. 140-143.
Lighton's *Lewis and Clark.*
Southern History Co., *Encyclopedia of the History of Mo.*, Vol. II, pp. 7-9; Vol. III, pp. 36-38.
Switzler's *History of Missouri*, Ch. X.
Thwaite's *Original Journals of the Lewis and Clark Expedition;* Ibid. *Wm. Clark*, in *Mo. Hist. Soc.*, (St. Louis) *Coll.*, Vol. II.
Wheeler's *The Trail of Lewis and Clark.*
Williams' *History of Missouri*, Part III, Ch. IV.

The Lewis and Clark Expedition was not only the most famous of its kind undertaken by the United States government but its importance to the Nation was perhaps greater than any other. This expedition was a factual justification of the Louisiana Purchase, an official herald of the extent and opportunities of the far trans-Mississippi, Rocky mountain and Oregon country, and a forerunner of American immigration to those sections. Perhaps in the history of the country no other single peaceful enterprise that employed so few men and cost so little, had such an effect in broadening the intellectual horizon of Americans as did the Lewis and Clark Expedition. The expedition was organized in St. Louis and disbanded there: its leaders later entered public life in Missouri and became her governors. In leaders, men, and equipment, it was largely Missourian.

III. Early Missouri Trails and Roads
   1. Indian warpaths and hunting trails.
   2. El Comino Real.
   3. Boone's Lick Trail.
   4. Salt River Road.
   5. Santa Fe Trail—history and significance to Missouri.
   6. Hannibal and St. Joseph Road.
   7. Missouri Avenue or the "Lottery Road."
   8. Plank roads.
   9. Early mail routes.
   10. Military roads.

Bicknell's *Missouri-Santa Fe Trade*, in *Mo. Hist. Soc.*, (St. Louis), *Coll.*, Vol. II.
Broadhead's *Early Missouri Roads, Review*, Vol. VIII.
Broadhead's *Roads and Trails*, in *Encyclopedia of the History of Missouri*, Vol. V., pp. 366-369.
Broadhead's *The Santa Fe Trail, Review*, Vol. IV.
Gregg'e *Commerce of the Prairies.*
Harvey's *Story of the Santa Fe Trail* in *Atlantic Monthly.* Vol. 104, No. 12.

Hayes' *New Colorado and its Santa Fe Trail.*
Houck's *History of Missouri,* Vol. I, pp. 224-231. (Other articles indexed in this work.)
Missouri county histories.
Napton's *Over the Santa Fe Trial,* 1857.
Ravenel's *Riverways and Roadways, in History of Northeast Missouri* Vol. I, Ch. V.
Sampson's *Santa Fe Trail—M. M. Marmaduke Journal, Review,* Vol. VI.
Sampson's *The Journals of Capt. Wm. Becknell from Boone's Lick to Santa Fe, etc., Review* Vol. IV.
Stephen's *Major Alphonso Wetmore's Diary of a Journey to Santa Fe, Review,* Vol. VIII.
Wetmore's *Santa Fe Trade and Santa Fe Trail.*

Scarcely a county in Missouri but possesses an aboriginal or pioneer path, trail, trace, or road. Only some of the familiar ones have here been given. Local research work will bring to light equally interesting ones in every quarter of the State. Consultations with early settlers will reveal a deer path here, an Indian trail there, and pioneer traces ramifying in all directions. No community is at any time too young to have some past, and to have some record of that past in the memories of its pioneers. An exceedingly pleasant entering wedge to develop an interest in the life of the community is to interview the old pioneers, a practice that will often prove as profitable as pleasant. The memories of pioneers, while sometimes treacherous as to dates and persons, may yield items of much value about each settlement.

IV. Missouri's Struggle for Statehood
  1. Early petitions to Congress.
  2. First Missouri Compromise.
  3. Missouri's first constitutional convention.
  4. Second Missouri Compromise and admission into the Union.

Carr's *Missouri,* Chs. VII-VIII.
Davis & Durries' *History of Missouri,* Chs. VI-VIII.
Hodder's *Side Lights on the Missouri Compromise, Review,* Vol. V.
Houck's History of Missouri, Vol. I, Ch. I; Vol. III, Ch. XXIX.
Missouri county histories.
School histories of Missouri, as Rader's, Viles', and Williams' give brief accounts.
Shoemaker's *Missouri's Struggle for Statehood.*
Shoemaker's *The First Constitution of Missouri, Review,* Vol. VI.
Switzler's History of Missouri, Ch. XVII.
Trexler's *Slavery in Missouri Territory, Review,* Vol. III.
United States histories.

"MISSOURI DAY" PROGRAMS. 245

The national aspect of Missouri's Struggle for Statehood is set forth in every history of the United States. The local aspect of this subject is briefly treated by Professor H. A. Trexler and Professor F. H. Hodder, and is handled in detail by Floyd C. Shoemaker. Few subjects in Missouri history are more interesting than this one and fortunately there is no difficulty in obtaining information on it.

V. Early Missouri Statesmen
1. John Scott—Missouri's first United States Representative.
2. David Barton—president of the first constitutional convention of Missouri, Missouri's first United States Senator.
3. Thomas H. Benton—United States Senator from Missouri from 1820 to 1850, greatest statesman from west of the Mississippi River.
4. Edward Bates—one of the framers of Missouri's first constitution, Unites States Representative from Missouri, first United States Cabinet official from west of the Mississippi River.
5. Lewis F. Linn—the "Model Senator of Missouri."

(All standard encyclopedias contain biographical articles on one or several of these men.)

Allen's *Col. Alexander W. Doniphan.*
American Biographical Publishing Co., *The Bench and Bar of Missouri Cities.* (Indexed)
Bates' *Bates et al. of Virginia and Missouri.*
Bay's *Bench and Bar of Missouri.* (Indexed)
Britton's *Col. Alexander W. Doniphan.*
Broadhead's *A few of the Leading People....of Early Missouri History, Review,* Vol. I.
Collier's *Recollections of Thomas H. Benton, Review,* Vol. VIII.
Darby's *Personal Recollections.* (indexed)
Dyer's *Great Senators,* pp. 190-217.
Flagg's *Thomas Hart Benton, Review,* Vol. I.
Gibson's *Memoir of Edward Bates,* in *Mo. Hist. Soc.,* (St. Louis), *Coll.,* Vol. II.
Greenwood's *Lewis Fields Linn.*
Hughes' *Doniphan's Expedition.*
Legal Publishing Co., *Hist. of the Bench and Bar of Mo.* (Indexed)
Meig's *Life of Thomas Hart Benton.*
Ravenel's *Hon. David Barton, Review,* Vol. VIII.
Rogers' *Thomas H. Benton.*
Shoemaker's *Famous Missourians,* in *Mo. Red Book, 1913,* pp. 144-147.
Shoemaker's *Missouri's Struggle for Statehood,* Ch. V.
Southern Hist. Co., *Encyclopedia of the History of Missouri.* (Indexed)

Ray's *The Retirement of Thomas H. Benton from the Senate*, etc., *Review*, Vol. II.
United States Biographical Publishing Co., *The U. S. Biographical Dictionary, Missouri Volume*. (Indexed)
Van Nada's (editor) *The Book of Missourians*. (Indexed)

The lives of these five Missouri statesmen are the prized possession of this State. These men did much to give Missouri a leading place in the halls of Congress. They strove to express the will of the people in Missouri. Each has been honored by having his name perpetuated in a Missouri county, except Edward Bates whose brother, Frederick—the second governor of the State—obtained this honor. All were men of eminent ability and served well their constituents.

VI. Military Missouri
  1. Indian wars.
  2. Mexican War—Alexander W. Doniphan, Sterling Price.
  3. Civil War—Nathaniel Lyon, Frank P. Blair, Franz Sigel, Sterling Price, J. O. Shelby, J. C. Porter.
  4. So called "Wars"—Mormon war, Hetherly war, Slicker war.

Allen's *Life of Col. Alexander W. Doniphan*.
Alvord's *The Conquest of St. Joseph, Mich., by the Spaniards in 1781*, *Review*, Vol. II.
Anderson's *Brig. Gen. Nathaniel Lyon*.
Bios' *Denkwurdigkeiten des Generals Franz Sigel*.
Borland's *General Jo. O. Shelby*, *Review*, Vol. VII.
Britton's *Alexander W. Doniphan*.
Britton's *The Civil War on the Border*.
Bryan and Rose's *Pioneer Families of Missouri*.
Carr's *Missouri*, Chs. X, XII-XVI.
Clark's *Frank P. Blair*.
Davis and Durrie's *History of Missouri*, Chs. III, VI, XI, XII, XIV, XVIII, XIX.
Edward's *Shelby and his Men*.
Ferril's *Missouri Military in the War of 1812*, Review, Vol. IV.
Grover's *Civil War in Missouri*, *Review*, Vol. VIII.
Grover's *The Price Campaign of 1864*, *Review*, Vol. VI.
Grover's *The Shelby Raid, 1863*, *Review*, Vol. VI.
Histories of the Mormans.
Houck's *History of Missouri*, Vols. II and III. (Indexed)
Hughes' *Doniphan's Expedition*.
Missouri county histories.
(Mrs.) McCausland's *The Battle of Lexington*, *Review*, Vol. VI.
McElroy's *The Struggle for Missouri*.
Mudd's *What I Saw at Wilson Creek*, *Review*, Vol. VII.
Mudd's *With Porter in North Missouri*.
Peckham's *Gen. Nathaniel Lyon*.
Robinson's *Two Missouri Historians*, *Review*, Vol. V.

School histories of Missouri.
Shoemaker's *The Story of the Civil War in Northeast Missouri Review*, Vol. VII.
Smith's *Morman Troubles in Missouri, Review*, Vol. IV.
Sneed's *The Fight for Missouri*.
Snyder's *The Capture of Lexington, Review*, Vol. VII.
Southern Hist. Co., *Encyclo. of Missouri History*. (Indexed)
Switzler's *History of Missouri*, Chs. VII, XI, XII, XX-XXII, XXVI-XXXI.
Teggert's *The Capture of St. Joseph, Mich., by the Spaniards in 1781, Review*, Vol. V.
Vincent's *The "Slicker War", Review*, Vol. VII.
Violette's *The Battle of Kirksville, Review*, Vol. V.
Ware's *The Lyon Campaign in Missouri*.
Webb's *Battles and Biographies of Missourians*.
Wherry's *The Campaign of Missouri and Battle of Wilson's Creek*, in *Mo. Hist. Soc.*, (St. Louis) *Pub.*, Vol. I.
(Mrs.) Whitman's *Mormon Troubles in Carroll Co., Review*, Vol. VIII.
Wight's *Gen. Jo. O. Shelby, Review*, Vol. VII.
Woodward's *Life of Gen. Nathaniel Lyon*.

This program could easily be broken up into a number of divisions and each division made a separate study. The references listed are by no means complete. Only those books and articles have been given that are well known and accessible. Valuable supplementary information can be obtained from Civil War vetrans and from current newspaper articles. Many Federal and Confederate commanders and public men in Missouri could be added to those listed above and it is desirable to do this if more information can thereby be obtained or more local interest aroused.

Missouri military history has never been fully written. Her early settlers engaged the Indians in almost daily combats; Missouri sent her sons to subdue the aborigines in Wisconsin, Iowa, and on the plains; she aided Texas in her struggle for independence; she helped conquer the Seminole chief, Osceola, in the swamps of Florida; she added pages of honor to the military annals of the Nation on the fields of Brazito, Sacramento and Durango; and she enlisted one hundred and fifty thousand strong under the Stars and Stripes and the Stars and Bars to give her brave to the North and the South.

"Missouri Day" Programs for Missouri Club Women in the October number of the *Review* will treat of literature and education in the State.

HISTORICAL ARTICLES IN MISSOURI NEWSPAPERS.
April-May 1915.

Adair County. Kirksville, *Journal*
    April 15. Sketch of the life of A. B. Lyon, pioneer.

Atchison County. Rock Port, *Atchison County Mail*
    April 16. Sketch of the life of Capt. Cannon, old settler.
    April 30. Sketch of the life of Joel W. Hoover, old settler..

Audrain County. Mexico, *Intelligencer* (Weekly)
    April 8. Sketch of the life of Dr. John F. Cowan, 53 years pastor of Auxvasse Church, Callaway County pioneer.
    April 15. History of the Benton City Presbyterian Church, by Rev. H. B. Barks.
—————————— *Ledger* (Weekly)
    April 8. Sketch of the life of former Mayor Eli D. Graham.
    April 15. Sketch of the life of Patrick H. Gantt.
    History of the Benton City Presbyterian Church.
    May 17. Sketch of the life of Mrs. J. E. Hutton, widow of Col. J. E. Hutton, Congressman from 9th District of Missouri and for years editor of the *Mexico Intelligencer*.
—————————— *Missouri Message*
    April 8. Sketch of the life of J. E. Lewis, St. Charles Co. pioneer.
    April 15. Churchmen in the Jesse family.
—————————— Vandalia, *Leader*
    April 2. Where Bill-Anderson died, by R. J. Allen

Barton County. Lamar, *Republican-Sentinel*
    May 13. Sketch of the life of Joel Yancey, born 1826 in Howard Co.

Bates County. Butler, *Bates County Record*
    April 21. Sketch of the life of Joel M. Sallee, pioneer.
    May 16. The News and Other things in vol 1, no. 1, of *Bates County Record*, July 9, 1866.
    May 16. Reminiscence by Dr. W. P. Hall.
    Talks and Tales of Old Times, by Clark Wix.
    May 29. Reflections of an Old Timer, by J. H. Rayborn.
—————————— *Times*
    April 8. Sketch of the life of Robert Plummer, pioneer.
—————————— Rich Hill, *Mining Review*
    April 8. Sketch of the life of Judge George P. Huckeby, pioneer.
    April 15. Sketch of the life of Edward Allison, pioneer.
—————————— *Western Enterprise*.
    April 23. Sketch of the life of Rev. James Stephen Porter, Rich Hill, oldest minister and oldest Mason in point of service in Mo.

Benton County. Warsaw, *Benton County Enterprise*
    April 2. Sketch of the life of J. Henry Junge, pioneer.
—————————— *Times*
    April 22. Sketch of the life of Francis B. Babbitt, Mo. Civil War veteran.

HISTORICAL ARTICLES. 249

Boone County. Ashland, *Bugle*
April 1. Sketch of the life of Robert Franklin Pearman, pioneer.
———————— Centralla, *Courier*
May 21. Sketch of the life of John J. Hulen, Randolph and Boone Co. pioneer and Confederate veteran.
————————————— *Fireside Guard*
April 2. Hildebrand the Outlaw.
Centralia Forty Years Ago. (Ch. X.) Reminiscences by J. A. Townsend. See prior and later issues.
April 16. A Personal Sketch of "Bill" Anderson.
May 14. Remembers Mt. Zion (Church) Battle.
———————— Columbia, *Alumnus*
May 15. In State Coach Days, by Thomas B. King, son of Austin A. King, Governor of Mo., 1848-52.—A sketch of Mo. University days in the 50's.
————————————— *Herald-Statesman*
April 2. Sketch of the life of Liberty Henry Gibbs, pioneer.
April 7. Finely illustrated Anniversary Edition on Columbia and Boone County,—many historical and descriptive articles.
————————————— *Times*
April 18. Sketch of the life of T. J. Durk, aged 90, veteran of Balaklava and soldier of Sebastopol.
————————————— *Tribune*
April 3. Was a Hornet Without a Sting—Account of the *Columbia Daily Hornet* established in 1899, edited by Dr. Jerome Johnson.
April 2. Boone County History, a series of articles by Hon. E. W. Stephens. See prior and later issues.
May 4. Old Boone Co. Record that contains political and historical information—A deed from Henry Clay in 1823.
May 5. Pioneer Bishop, Daniel S. Tuttle, Recounts Works as missionary bishop in Montana, Idaho and Utah fifty years ago.
May 12. Description of Lake Ha Ha Tonka and scenery in Camden Co., by E. W. Stephens.
May 18. When the Missouri Went on a Rampage—Account of famous flood of 1844.
May 19. Arrow Rock Day and Night Ferry—Some points of historic interest along cross-state highway.
————————————— *University Missourian*
April 5. Mo. U. has two new curators—Biographical sketch of H. B. McDaniel, Springfield, and John Bradley, Kennett.
April 13. Democracy's Idol—Tribute to Thomas Jefferson and the story of his original monument which now stands on campus at Mo. U.
Y. W. C. A. organizer aid in 25th Anniversary Celebration—Dr. Henry N. Chapman tells of early struggles of Association.
April 14. Edwin M. Rayle tells story of early University of Mo.
April 23. Find Historic Chair in Academic Hall.—Picture of the chair made to order for Prof. R. Thomas who taught in the old brick academy—property of four M. U. presidents.
April 20. Lindenwood College, St. Charles, Mo. History of oldest girls school west of Mississippi, established in 1831.
April 27. Who's Who Journalism Week.—Sketches of Karl Walters, of *Kansas City Star*, and A. B. Chapin, of *St. Louis Republic*— First of a series of articles on Journalism Week speakers.
April 28. Stephens College One of the Oldest—Story of Columbia woman's school established 1853.
May 4. A "Katy" Engineer on Road Since 1861—W. H. Willis, oldest man on M. K. & T. knew Thos. A. Edison as a newsboy.

May 5. Built Stockade to Protect Bank.—Reminiscences by R. B. Price, Sr., of banking in Columbia during the Civil War.
Columbia Statesman second paper (?) in Missouri—History of early journalism in Mo.
May 24. Records of Pioneer Days Found in Attic—Account books and Diary of Moses Payne found in old Rocheport house date back to 1828.
May 25. Tom Sawyer's cave at Hannibal—Picture of entrance to cave made famous by Mark Twain.
———————— Rocheport, *Progress*
April 2. Sketch of life of Elijah Inman, pioneer.
Sketch of the life of James M. Gregory, pioneer.
———————— Sturgeon, *Missouri Leader*
April 1. Sketch of the life of Dr. A. J. Harris.

Buchanan County.   St. Joseph, *Gazette*
April 15. Capt. Greer of Macon saw Booth shoot Lincoln.
April 25. Dr. Knox Miller, Missourian, Gave Hookworm Hook.
April 25. To Revive Leafy Isles in Lover's Lane that Field Wrote of.—D. A. R. tree planting program with reminiscences of Eugene Field.
April 26. Aged Preacher Back to First Pastorate—Sketch of the life of Rev. J. M. Regan, minister in 1853 at Albany, Mo.
May 2. Oregon, Typical "Old Missoury" Town, is progressive—Sketch of Oregon, Holt Co.,—Town established before St. Joseph.
May 16. Sketch of Mound City, Holt County.
May 23. Women of Mo. to Own St. Joseph for next Six Days—Sketches and pictures of Women leaders in Mo.
May 30. When St. Joseph Mourned Her Soldier Dead—Recollections of Battle of Franklin, Tenn., in which 44th Mo. regiment lost half its number.
May 31. Tarkio College in Forefront of Mo. Institutions—Pictures and sketch of college founded in 1883.
———————— ———————— *News-Press*
April 13. Sketch of the life of Mrs. Elizabeth Baker whose husband was law partner of former Governor Silas Woodson.
April 15. "Huck" Finn at 90.—Mark Twain's famous character now living in Oregon. [State]
April 25. Lived in St. Joseph since 1841.—Death of Clark Deppen who came to Mo. when there was only one house in St. Joseph.
April 18. Chillicothe Landmark Razed—Old opera house erected in 1869 where the author of Ben Bolt gave his last performance.

Caldwell County.   Breckenridge, *Bulletin*
April 16. Sketch of the life of Enoch Plummer, pioneer.

Callaway County.   Fulton, *Gazette*
April 2. Sketch of the life of Mrs. Josephine B. A. Harriss, pioneer.
Sketch of the life of Mrs. Sue T. Scott, pioneer.
Sketch of the life of Mrs. Elizabeth Suggett, pioneer.
April 9. Sketch of the life of Dr. John T. Cowan, pioneer minister, educator and author.
April 16. Sketch of the life of J. D. West, grave the oldest at White Cloud Cemetery, 1846.
April 23. Sketch of the life of Mrs. E. W. Wood, pioneer.
April 30. Sketch of John C. Newson, pioneer and Mo. Civil War veteran.
Sketch of the life of J. C. Douglass, pioneer and Mo. Civil War veteran.

HISTORICAL ARTICLES.

May 14. Sketch of the life of Mrs. Alice Harrison, one hundred years old.
———————— ———————— *Missouri Telegraph*
April 2. Sketch of the life of David A. McCleery, pioneer.
April 30. Sketch of the life of James S. Henderson, pioneer.

Camden County. Linn Creek, *Reveille*
May 22. Sketch of the life of Henry K. Vincent, 82 years, pioneer and Mo. Civil War veteran.
Sketch of the life of William H. Hilhouse, 75 years, Laclede Co. pioneer.

Cape Girardeau County. Cape Girardeau, *Republican* (Weekly)
April 2. Old King's Highway Will Become Missouri's Most Noted Road.
April 30. Sketch of the life of Col. P. R. VanFrank, southeast Mo. pioneer, Mo. Civil War veteran, and pioneer Mo. railroad builder.
May 28. Sketch of the life of Judge Alexander Ross, pioneer lawyer and Mo. Civil War veteran.
A Reminiscence, Richard Berry, Foreman of First Railroad Construction Force into Cape Girardeau, by Hon. Louis Houck.
Sketch of the life of Dr. Alfred Peironnet, 86 years, pioneer.

Carroll County. Carrollton, *Democrat*
April 2. Sketch of the life of Robert Hopkins, pioneer.
April 9. Sketch of the life of Mrs. Margaret Squires, first woman ever elected in Carroll County.
April 30. Sketch of the life of John C. Montgomery, pioneer.
May 14. Sketch of the life of Mrs. Mary J. Jartung, old settler.
May 28. Sketch of the life of Jas. A. Christy, 84 years, pioneer.
———————— ———————— *Republican-Record*
April 8. Reminiscences of Battle of Shiloh and of Co. K. 23 Mo., by J. D. Parsley.
April 15. More of Co. K. 23 Missouri, Mo. Civil War regiment.
April 22. Sketch of the life of F. M. Miller, Benton and Carroll Co. pioneer.

Cass County. Pleasant Hill, *Times*
May 14. Sketch of the life of Henry Gibson, Marion Co. pioneer.

Chariton County. Keytesville, *Chariton Record.*
April 30. Meeting of General Sterling Price Monument Commission.
———————— Salisbury, *Press-Spectator*
April 9. Sketch of the life of George McDonald, pioneer.
Remembrances of Salisbury from 1869 to 1885, by E. T. Ammerman.

Clark County. Kahoka, *Clark County Courier*
April 2. Sketch of the life of Wm. H. Cain, pioneer.
Sketch of the life of John Herberth, pioneer.
Sketch of the life of John Kerr, pioneer.
Sketch of the life of A. J. McAfee, pioneer.
Sketch of the life of W. R. Wilson, pioneer.
April 16. Sketch of the life of John Scollins, pioneer.
April 23. Sketch of the life of M. H. Resor, pioneer.
Sketch of the life of P. H. Bennett, pioneer and Mo. Civil War veteran.
April 30. Sketch of the life of Capt. W. Galland, Mo. veteran of Mexican and Civil Wars.

May 7. Sketch of the life of Dr. Frederick I. Beard, pioneer.
May 28. Sketch of the life of Charles H. Dyer, Civil War veteran and early Clark County settler.

Clay County. Excelsior Springs, *Standard*
April 5. History of the Public Schools of Excelsior Springs.
——————— Liberty, *Advance*
April 23. Sketch of the life of W. E. Bell, pioneer.
April 30. Sketch of the life of G. W. Winn, pioneer.
——————————— *Tribune*
April 16. Sketch of the life of Hiram Warren, pioneer.
Sketch of the life of Reuben B. Allen, pioneer.

Clinton County. Cameron, *Sun*
April 15. Sketch of the life of John C. Divinia, pioneer.
April 22. Sketch of the life of J. Q. A. Kemper, pioneer.
Sketch of the life of Harrison Blacketer, pioneer and Mo. Civil war veteran.
——————— Plattsburg, *Clinton County Democrat*
April 2. Sketch of the life of John T. Shoemaker, pioneer.
April 9. Sketch of the life of T. B. Tyer, pioneer.
Sketch of the life of Patrick Shehan, pioneer.

Cole County. Jefferson City, *Democrat-Tribune*
April 13. Picture of Judge Ephriam C. Ewing, presented to Supreme Court by Judge Marshall of St. Louis.
April 20. Sketch of the life of Major J. H. Fink (s), Mo. Civil War veteran and legislator.
——————— *Post*
April 1. Industrial Section with biographical sketches of Jefferson City citizens and business men.
April 3. Negroes are taught many useful things—Write-up of Lincoln Institute with picture of President B. F. Allen.

Cooper County. Boonville, *Advertiser*
April 23. An old Church to be Perpetuated—Article on New Salem Church near Prairie Home, one of oldest Presbyterian churches in Missouri, founded 1822.
May 28. Frank James' Ambition, by Hon. Ed. T. Orear, Kansas City.
——————— *Central Mo. Republican*
April 1. Judge John F. Philips Tells of Central Missouri Lawyers.
April 8. Fifty Years Have Brought Perfect Peace—Historical address of Joseph Leiber of G. A. R., and Lieut. S. W. Ravenal of U. C. V.

Dade County. Greenfield, *Dade County Advocate*
April 1. Sketch of the life of Thomas V. Speer, Mo. Confederate veteran.
Autobiographical sketch of Daniel W. Scott, 1826—date—See April 8, 15, 22—Historical sketches of Dade County.
April 15. Autobiographical sketch of Samuel J. Weir, 1830—date. See April 22.
May 13. Autobiographical sketch of Samuel N. McMillen. See later dates.

Daviess County. Gallatin, *Democrat*
April 15. Sketches of the lives of Mr. and Mrs. Dave Youtsey, pioneers—Mr. Youtsey was a Civil War veteran.

HISTORICAL ARTICLES. 253

———————— ————— *North-Missourian*
April 15. Sketch of the life of E. H. Cravens, pioneer.
April 22. Sketch of the life of David Manville, aged 93 years.
——————————— Pattonsburg, *Call*
April 6. Sketch of the life of John P. Crump, pioneer.
April 13. Sketch of the life of Jacob M. Poage, pioneer.
April 20. Sketch of the life of Freeland Boyer, a centenarian and resident of Daviess Co. since 1831.

DeKalb County. Maysville, *Pilot*
May 13. Sketch of the life of John L. Johnson, northwest Mo. pioneer.
Sketch of the life of W. R. Browning, Civil War veteran.

Dent County. Salem, *Monitor*
April 29. Sketch of the life of Wm. Miller, pioneer.

Douglas County, Ava, *Douglas County Herald*
April 8. Sketch of the life of Wm. Hood, pioneer.
May 13. Sketch of the life of Robert Huffman, pioneer.

Franklin County. Pacific, *Transcript*
April 23. Sketch of the life of Henry Westmeyer, Civil War veteran.
——————————— Union, *Franklin County Tribune*
April 9. Sketch of the life of S. W. Coleman, pioneer.
May 7. Fiftieth Anniversary Edition—Fine historical sketch of Franklin County, by Clark Brown.

Gasconade County. Hermann, *Advertiser-Courier*
April 21. Sketch of the life of Carl Heck, pioneer.

Gentry County. Albany, *Capital*
April 22. Sketch of the life of S. S. Austin, pioneer.
May 20. Sketch of the life of Jonas Cook, age 91 years, resident of Gentry County 71 years.
——————————— King City, *Chronicle*
April 2. Sketch of the life of John Wheatley, pioneer.
May 28. Sketch of the life of W. M. Haynes, Clinton & Gentry Co. pioneer.
——————————— Stanberry, *Herald*
April 29. Sketch of the life of Thos. McCarthy Simpson, pioneer.

Greene County. Springfield, *Leader*
April 2. Sketch of the life of M. L. Crum, pioneer.
April 4. Sketch of the life of Henry Cooper, pioneer.
April 6. Biographical sketch of General James H. McBride, Mo. Confederate veteran.
April 8. Sketch of the life of Joseph H. Speer, southwest Mo. pioneer.
April 15. R. H. Collins, Inventor, Springfield Man Will Receive Royalties over one Million Yearly.
May 3. The first piano in south Missouri Ozarks.
May 13. Early days in Dallas County, Missouri, by C. A. Cummins.
May 27. Mr. and Mrs. Kannon Gilmore, Greene Co. pioneers, celebrate 66th wedding anniversary.
May 30. An Ozark literary colony—Sketch of lives of prominent Ozark authors.

────────── ────────── *Republican.*
April 4. Mrs. Savala Vandaveer, Montgomery City, Owns Ax Lincoln Split Rails With.
April 6. Sketch of the life of Joseph H. Speer, pioneer and overland freighter in early days.
April 11. Early History of Springfield, by Mrs. A. B. McAfee.
April 14. How Springfield Received Lincoln Assassination News, as recalled by Matt Simms.
April 21. Early Days of Springfield Congregational Church, by A. M. Haswell.
May 2. Valley of Jordan Once Recreation Ground for City—Reminiscences of Early History of Springfield.
May 12. Sketch of the life of Col. Daniel N. Fulbright—Born in 1830, believed to have been first white child born in Greene Co. Mo.
May 23. Old Wire Road of 1852—History of famous telegraph line from Rolla, Mo., to Ft. Smith, Ark., constructed by Federal government to keep Mo. in the Union. (*Cassville Democrat.*)

Grundy County. Trenton, *Republican* (weekly)
May 13. Sketch of the life of Eli R. Overman, pioneer and Mo. Civil War veteran.

Harrison County. Bethany, *Clipper*
May 13. Sketch of the life of James Russell, pioneer and Mo. Civil war veteran.

Holt County. Mound City, *News-Jeffersonian*
April 8. Sketch of the life of William Kelly, pioneer of Kearney, Mo.
Sketch of the life of James B. Payne, 81 years, whose father entered the land on which Missouri University is located.
────────── Oregon, *Holt County Sentinel*
April 16. Sketch of the life of Capt. W. S. Canon, 81 years, pioneer.
April 23. History of Pioneer Days of Methodism in Holt County.
Sketch of Capt. Grinstead, Civil and Spanish-American Wars veteran.
April 30. The Sentinel's Golden Jubilee—Fine illustrated sketch of Holt County and of the *Sentinel*.
May 14. Historical sketch of the *Sentinel* and its editors.
May 21. History of Company "F," 4th Mo. State Militia Cavalry, Holt Co. Company.

Howard County. Fayette, *Howard Co. Advertiser*
April 29. Sketch of the life of Major Joseph Hughes Finks, Marshall of Missouri Supreme Court for 20 years. Confederate veteran, Circuit Clerk of Howard Co., and Representative from Howard Co.
────────── Glasgow, *Missourian*
April 11. Sketch of the life of Frank P. Fuoss, prominent Missouri-born journalist of Kansas City, St. Louis, Chicago and Los Angeles.

Howell County. West Plains, *Howell Co. Gazette*
May 20. Sketch of the life of John Goldsberry, pioneer Ozark hunter and preacher,—established town of Mountain View, Howell County, made overland trip to gold fields in 1849.

HISTORICAL ARTICLES.

———————— ———— *Journal*
 April 8. Passing of the Last Log School House in Howell County.
 April 29. Sketch of the life of John Rogers, Mo. Civil War veteran.

Iron County. Ironton, *Iron County Register*
 April 22. An Episode at Pilot Knob, 1865.

Jackson County. Independence, *Jackson Examiner*
 April 2. To Mark Daniel Boone's Grave.
 April 9. Sketch of the life of Henry Harper, Kansas City pioneer.
 April 16. Sketch of the life of John Bishop, Indiana Mexican War veteran and Mo. pioneer.
 May 14. Sketch of the life of Mrs. A. J. Henley, pioneer.

Kansas City, *Independent*
 May 15. History and Descriptive number on Kansas City.
——————— *Journal*
 April 5. Dr. Dibble Tells of Santa Fe Trail in 1857.
  Mrs. Josephine G. Ragan, daughter of pioneer Missourian, born in Jackson County, dies.
 April 23. John Donnelly, veteran employee of City quits.
 May 1. Anniversary of Rothschild Store established in Kansas City in 1855.
 May 3. Anniversary of first Baptist Church in Kansas City, established 1855.
 May 5. "Old Gobbler" zinc mine near Carthage is revived. Once belonged to Frank Rockefeller, brother of oil king.
 May 10. Sketch of the life of George H. Barse, Civil War lieutenant and veteran railroad man.
 May 13. Sketch of the life of Adam Woolf, hero of the Civil War and Federal office holder under President Grant.
 May 19. Elias Perry of De Witt, Mo., travels in a Pullman car over the route he traversed in an ox-cart in Pike's Peak gold rush of 1859.
 May 20. Sketch of the life of Col. Robert T. Van Horn, for 40 years owner of *Kansas City Journal*, who celebrates 91st birthday.
——————— *Post*
 April 3. Old Missouri Packets Once Numbered 150, by V. G. Whelan.
 April 18. Speaker Champ Clark in his Lighter Vein.
 April 28. Reminiscences of George A. Wilcox, Kansas City pioneer.
 April 9. Where Kansas City History Was Made—Views of old Shawnee Missouri near Kansas City built by Rev. Thomas H. Johnson, missionary to the Indians in 1839.
——————— *Star*
 April 1. Old Union Depot Down Next Week. See April 5.
  Santa Fe Trail Trip by Oxen in 1857, by Dr. Leroy Dibble, Kansas City pioneer, see April 4.
 April 2. Sketch of life of Jacob Crosby, 90 years old, pioneer.
 April 4. A Half Century Since Lee Up Up His Sword at Appomattox.
  When Kansas City Heard The Word From Appomattox.
 April 6. Sketch of the life of Charles Lewis Dew, pioneer.
 April 10. Sketch of the life of Mrs. Nancy Dorman, Kansas City pioneer.
 April 10. Sketch of the life of Isaac J. Baldwin, K. C. pioneer.
  Description of Duels of Early Missouri Days—Benton-Lucas.
 April 11. Fifty Years Have Passed Since Lincoln Was Slain.
  Champ Clark, Writer.
  To Mark Fort Osage at Sibley.

April 13. Death notices and comments of William Rockhill Nelson—
See April 13, 14, 15, 16, 17, 18.
April 18. Sketch of the life of L. J. MacGillis, K. C. pioneer.
Sketch of the life of Jere T. Dew, Kansas City pioneer.
April 25. Lessons of the Civil War, by Edwin J. Shannahan.
Description of How the Yankees Wiped Out a Town—Bloomington, Macon County, Mo.
May 2. The "Old Trails" road through Missouri as seen by Colorado motorists—Some points of historic interest.
Sketch of Park College, Parkville, Mo., occasion of 42nd anniversary.
Schools honor memory of Audubon upon anniversary of his travel through Missouri in 1842—Extract from his journal.
Howard C. Sykes, a former Kansas City newspaper man, writes of the Singapore Mutiny.
Views and sketches of Excelsior Springs.
Sketches of William H. Hamby of Chillicothe.
May 3. The rise of Missouri's first millionaire, John Mullanphy.
John Lewis first English speaking farmer to locate in Missouri River Bottoms, 1795—Historical account.
How German Militarism saved Missouri in 1861, by John William Burgers.
May 6. Account of attempt to recover 500 barrels of whisky from the steamer Arabia, sunk in the Missouri River near Parkville in 1856.
May 9. John C. Caps, the Kansas City man who almost beat Henry Ford to motor car millions.
Historical sketch of the town of Hume, Mo.
May 14. Some historic routes through Missouri to the Pacific Coast.
May 16. Major S. G. Brock of Macon, Mo., tells of the chase of a Confederate blockade runner in 1863.
May 20. Sketch of the life of David C. King, pioneer and Civil War veteran.
May 23. How war rubbed the Aladdin lamp for Joplin in the zinc mining district of Mo.

———————— *Times* ————————

April 6. Sketch of the life of Mathew B. Mullins, Kansas City pioneer.
April 7. Sketch of the life of Mathew Harris, Civil War veteran and Kansas City pioneer.
Sketch of the life of T. W. Gillam of Brunswick, Mo., Chariton County pioneer.
April 8. Sketch of the life of W. O. Cox, Civil War veteran and former Kansas City banker.
April 9. E. W. Railey, Weston, Mo., a Missouri Banker for 50 years.
Only 900 Civil War Veterans Here—Kansas City.
April 13. William Rockhill Nelson—death notices and comments, 4:13-30.
Sketch of the life of C. C. Connely, Cass Co. pioneer and Civil War veteran.
April 16. Sketch of the life of Edward P. Garnett, pioneer Mo. lawyer and State representative of Jackson Co.
April 17. Sketch of the life of John H. Knoepher, pioneer.
April 19. Sketch of the life of Mrs. Mary M. Ragland, Lafayette Co. pioneer.
April 22. Sketch of the life of James H. Carter, Mo. pioneer plainsman and freighter.
May 6. L. A. Allen took first herd of cattle out of Kansas City over the Old Santa Fe Trail in 1863.

May 11. Sketch of Col. Jared L. Sanderson, Boulder, Colo., who organized the first stage line out of Kansas City.
Sketch of the life of Noah Fyock, a Missouri River steamboat engineer before the Civil War.
May 28. Ozark scenery equals that in Scotland says Charles Phelps Cushing in *Leslie's Weekly.*
Sketch of the life of John Priest Green, Liberty, Mo., president of William Jewell College since 1892.
May 31. The Diamond & Times buildings, old Kansas City landmarks, dating back to 1870 and 1885, are torn down.

Jasper County. Carthage, *Press* (Weekly)
April 15. Sketch of the life of W. J. Senall, Editor for 25 years of the *Press.*
April 22. Sketch of the life of John Fairfield, Mexican—Civil War veteran.
May 27. Sketch of the life of John W. Burch, Jasper county pioneer and official.
———————— Joplin, *Globe*
April 11. Sketch of the life of Mrs. Elizabeth A. Bartlett, widow of late Capt. E. A. Bartlett, Joplin mine owner.
———————— ———————— *News-Herald*
April 4. Sketch of the Real "Trail of Lonesome Pine"—Road Winding to Ozarks south of Joplin.
April 13. Spanish-American War "Vets" of 1898 to Organize in Joplin. Capt. McDowell elected commander.
April 18. Joplin Man Was Left for Dead on Chickamauga Field—Sketch of the life of Capt. L. French Williams now living in Joplin.
April 21. Diagram of Ozark Trails Route with officers and plans of Ozark Trails Association.
May 2. Woman 101 Holds Open House—Joplin Woman born in Scotland—a war nurse under Gen. Sherman; her husband a civil engineer under Grant.
May 9. Sketch of the life of W. B. Halyard, Civil War veteran and twice Mayor of Joplin, 80 years old.
May 20. "For Old Times Sake"—Tales of early days related by old Joplin citizens.
May 30. Stories of the Ozark Hills.

Laclede County. Lebanon, *Rustic*
April 29. Sketch of the life of Senator John W. Farris, Civil war veteran, editor, county official, state senator and representative.
Feb. 28. Literary Landmarks of Lebanon.

Lafayette County. Higginsville, *Advance*
April 2. Sketch of the life of Charles Hoefer, Franklin and Lafayette Co. pioneer, banker.
April 23. Sketch of the life of Philip E. Ayers, pioneer.
Sketch of the life of Julius Vogt, Civil War veteran.

Lincoln County. Troy, *Free Press*
April 23. Sketch of the life of William H. Bryan, 81 years, Mo. Civil War veteran.
May 21. Sketch of the life of Francis L. Hewitt, pioneer and Mo. Confederate veteran.

Linn County. Brookfield, *Gazette*
- April 22. A Civil War Story—A marching and fighting Missouri regiment.
- May 1. That First Circus—Description of first circus in Linn County in 1857 and reminiscences of early days.
- May 8. In the Early Fifties—Historical sketch of Linn county and of the construction of H. & St. Jo. R. R., by John McGowan.
- May 22. In the Early Fifties—Pioneer Road Builders.
- May 29. In the Early Fifties—"A land of Milk and Honey, of Hog and Hominy".

Livingston County. Chillicothe, *Constitution* (Weekly)
- April 1. Sketch of the life of Frank H. Leaver, pioneer.
- April 8. Sketch of the life of John Walker, pioneer.
- April 29. Sketch of the life of Isadere Sisk, pioneer.

Macon County. Macon, *Republican*
- April 16. Sketch of the life of Jacob Schienker, pioneer.
- April 23. Sketch of the life of Capt. Bill Stephens, Mo. Civil war veteran
- May 7. To Colorado in 1865, by Macon men.
  First Call to Arms—Sketch of Rally Day in Bloomington, Mo., in 1861.
- May 21. Lincoln Spanked Him—Reminiscences by F. M. Wilson.

Chronicle
- April 17. Something about the Men of the Macon County Bar.
- April 19. Something about Macon and the County—Points of interest to tourists.
- April 22. Account of early journalism, by Chas. H. Grasty of *Baltimore Sun* who began newspaper work in Mexico, Mo.
- April 26. The Old Time Spellin' Match—Short Story by Homer Croy.
- April 30. Reminiscences by M. C. Tracy of Missouri Journalism of the 40's and 50's.
- May 6. New Cambria Heads all for Long Life—Sketch of New Cambria.

Marion County. Hannibal, *Courier-Post*
- April 9. To Restore Birthplace of Mark Twain at Florida, Mo.
- May 3. Sketch of Edward Gerald, former member of Courier-Post editorial staff.
- May 12. Thirty-fourth G. A. R. Encampment Convenes in Hannibal—Jas. B. Dobyns, St. Louis, elected commander for 1915.
- May 19. Sketch of the life of Mrs. Mary Hornback, age 94 years, one of the oldest women in northeast Missouri.

Palmyra, *Spectator*
- April 14. Old-Time Songs.
- April 21. Sketch of the life of Wm. Crane, pioneer.
  Then and Now—The Autobiography of a Kid by Uncle James.

Mercer County. Princeton, *Post*
- April 29. Knew Princeton's First Printer—Sketch of the life of James Scarborough.
- May 6. Cornbread Day in North Missouri, by I. B. Stover.

Telegraph
- April 14. Sketch of the life of Cyreneus Bain, 87 years, pioneer.
- May 5. Old Pioneers Write Letters of Early Days.
- May 12. Sketch of early days in north Missouri, by Rev. J. H. Burrows, former Mo. Congressman.

HISTORICAL ARTICLES. 259

Moniteau County. California, *Democrat*
   April 8. Sketch of the life of Mrs. S. Finke, 95 years old, pioneer.
            Sketch of the life of John M. Crum, 90 years old, Miller Co., pioneer.
            Sketch of the life of Buford Russell, Mo., Confederate veteran.
———————— ———————— *Moniteau County Herald*
   April 8. Sketch of the life of Dr. H. C. Klueber, pioneer physician.
   April 15. Recollections of Appomatox, by J. M. Williams.

———————— ———————— *Times*
   April 22. Sketch of the life of Judge John G. Knox, pioneer.

Nodaway County. Maryville, *Tribune*
   April 19. Boyhood Companion of Lincoln Is Dead—Sketch of the life of E. B. Yeaman, who split rails with the Emancipator in his youth.
   April 20. Sketch of the life of Theodore Gwin, first Union soldier to enter fortress at surrender of Vicksburg.

Oregon County. Alton, *South Missourian-Democrat*
   April 17. Sketch of the life of Thos. Batman, 83 years old, pioneer.
   April 22. Sketch of the life of D. J. Lane, pioneer.
            Letter From An Old Timer On Early Days.
   May 20. Sketch of the life of J. W. Bruce, pioneer.

Pettis County. Sedalia, *Capital*
   April 1. Sketch of the life of Mrs. Jane B. Wilson, former Edina, Mo. poetess.
   April 9. Missourian Whose Bugle Blast Ended Civil War Still Survives—Sketch of the life of Capt. Nathaniel Sisson, Maryville, Mo.
   May 6. James R. Major, pioneer Missourian, tells of trip across plains to California in 1850.
   May 19. Old Time Bandits meet for the Last Time—Kit Dalton comes from Mississippi to pay a last visit to his life-long friend, Cole Younger, at Lees Summitt.
   May 23. Sketch of Judge Rush Leaming pioneer and Civil War veteran.

Phelps County. Rolla, *Herald*
   May 6. Sketch of the life of Joe Daugherty—Phelps county pioneer and official.

Pike County. Bowling Green, *Times*
   April 8. Sketch of the life of T. M. Guthrie, pioneer.
            Champ Clark as a Rail Splitter.
———————— Louisiana, *Press-Journal*
   April 1. Sketch of the life of Prof. A. Slaughter, 87 years old, pioneer.
            Roll of the Dead—Memento of Maj. Johnston, killed by Guerrillas in 1864.
   April 8. World's Greatest Nursery, will celebrate its centennial in 1916—Stark Bros., Louisiana, Mo.
   April 22. Sketch of the life of Capt. A. J. Lovell, pioneer and Mo. Civil War veteran.

Putnam County. Unionville, *Republican*
   April 7. Sketch of the life of John Probasco, 86 years old, pioneer.
   April 28. Sketch of the life of Thomas Aitken, pioneer.

Ralls County. New London, *Ralls County Record*
   April 9. Red Wing's Captive—Early Indian and Pioneer tale.

Randolph County. Huntsville, *Herald*
   April 2. Sketch of the life of Benj. L. Cockrell, pioneer.
   May 28. Sketch of the life of John A. Heether, State and Co. official.
           Sketch of the life of Uncle John Cockrell, Randolph county pioneer and relative of Senator Cockrell.
——————— Moberly, *Democrat* (Daily)
   April 13. Sketch of the life of W. H. Emerson, pioneer citizen of Moberly and Mo. Confederate veteran.

Ray County. Richmond, *Missourian*
   April 1. Biographical sketch of Col. A. W. Doniphan.
   April 15. A True Picture by Mrs. James B. Gantt Writes of Mrs. Helen Morton, mother of Senator J. B.
           Sketch of the life of Mrs. Rebecca Thompson, 87 years old, pioneer.
   April 22. Sketch of the life of James C. Endicott, 81 years old, pioneer.

St. Charles County. St. Charles, *Cosmos-Monitor*
   April 28. Out Population in the year 1791—Translation of the census of San Carlos Del Misury.
   May 19. Sketch of the life of Wm. F. Broadhead, pioneer and official of St. Louis Co.

St. Clair County. Osceola, *St. Clair County Republican*
   May 20. Sketch of the life of Judge B. F. Copenhaver, pioneer and Co. official.

St. Francois County. Farmington, *Times*
   April 9. Battle of Shilo as seen by Capt. W. A. Kennedy.
           Brief History of the Farmington Times, 1874—date.
   April 23. Hon F. P. Graves Surmounts Difficulties—Letter by "A Friend" on pioneering.

St. Louis City, *Globe-Democrat*
   April 2. Melford's Oldest Eating House in St. Louis closed.
   April 4. Historical Article on Kaskaskia.
   April 12. Missouri Society of Washington, D. C., Elected Officers in Washington—Willard N. Holmes, president.
   April 14. Sketch of the life of John A. Holmes, financier.
   April 15. Sketch of the life of Mrs. B. C. Jones, 79 years old—Was the oldest sister of D. M. Houser, head of Globe-Democrat.
   April 19. Sketch of the life of Elbridge G. Newell, St. Louis broker, 89 years old.
   April 24. Steps Taken For State Centennial Observance in 1918 by the Missouri Historical Society of St. Louis.
   April 27. Washington University to Honor Memory of Dr. Wm. Beaumont, pioneer St. Louis physician.
   May 9. Biographical sketch of B. F. Bush, St. Louis, president of Missouri Pacific.
           Facsimile reproduction of telegram received by Marc J. Gautier, St. Louis, April 13, 1861, telling of the fall of Ft. Sumpter.
   May 10. Sketch of the life of Joseph McDonnell, captain of a Missouri regiment in Spanish-American War.
           Sketch of the life of Joseph T. Mouell, St. Louis mining engineer and scientist.

————————— *Republic*
April 11. J. P. Johnson of Missouri Appointed Superintendent of U. S. Railway Mail Service.
April 10. Lincoln and Booth, by Winfield M. Thompson—A series of articles on the "Inner Story of the Great Tragedy of Fifty Years Ago."
April 11. Women of the Missouri Legislature—Mrs. Elliott W. Major, by Mrs. James B. Gantt—Other Articles in former Sunday editions of Republic.
April 11. Biographical sketch of Mrs. Emily Newell Blair, by Robertus Love.
April 25. Biographical sketch of Judge Frank P. Divilbiss, by Robertus Love.
April 12. Copy of Missouri Republican "Extra," 1865, on Surrender of Lee.
April 18. Ozark Boys, Led by Gen. McBride, Among South's Bravest Soldiers—Biographical sketch of Gen. James H. McBride.
April 20. "St. Louis Made Me What I am"—Tribute by William M. Chase, foremost painter in America.
April 25. Sketch of the Missouri Author, Wm. H. Hamby, by Robertus Love.
Two Pike County Couples, Mr. and Mrs. Marion E. Motely, and Mr. and Mrs. W. T. Jacobs, Celebrate Golden Weddings—Biographical sketches.
April 30. Missourian's Pardon, George Vaughn's, Last of Lincoln's Official Acts.
May 2. America's First Jewish Governor is for Prohibition and Equal Suffrage—Autobiographical sketch of Gov. Moses Alexander of Idaho who began life in Missouri on $10 a month.
May 3. Minister McGoodwin's Achievement—Editorial on work of Preston McGoodwin, Joplin newspaper man, who is minister of U. S. to Venezuela.
May 9. Lover's Lane, St. Joseph—An incident in life of Eugene Field, by Robertus Love.
Journalism Week at University of Missouri—Feature story by Love and Chapin.
Striking it Rich—True stories of the southwest Missouri lead and zinc fields.
Mrs. Margaret B. Downing, St. Louisan, wins High Rank in Newspaper Field—Sketch of Missouri author now living in Washington, D. C.
May 16. Evolution Bordering on Revolution in St. Louis Banking Circles—Short history of banking in St. Louis.
May 14. Sketch of the life of J. L. Griswold, of St. Louis, millionaire owner of Laclede Hotel.
May 30. Points of interest on Grand Avenue and Olive Street, St. Louis, by Betty Boyd, illustrated by A. B. Chapin.

Saline County. Marshall, *Democrat-News* (Weekly)
April 1. Sketch of the life of W. H. Chick, 90 years old, pioneer of Saline County and Santa Fe Trader, by Mr. T. C. Rainey.
Washington Irving Here 1832—The seventh of a series of historical articles written by Judge W. B. Napton.
Mr. Rainey Came Here 1865—Historical article.
April 15. Sketch of the life of Judge R. C. Hanna, pioneer.
——————————— *Saline County Progress*
Mar. 26 Pioneers of Saline County, by Dr. Chastain—A series of historical articles appearing weekly.

Schuyler County. Lancaster, *Excelsior*.
    April 2. Sketch of the life of Frances J. Cowan, 89 years old, pioneer.
    April 23. Sketch of the life of Isaac W. Stanley, 84 years old, pioneer.

Shelby County. Shelbina, *Democrat*
    May 26. Sketch of the life of Felix M. Allison, pioneer and "Forty-nine."

Stoddard County. Bloomfield, *Vindicator*
    May 7. Historical Sketch of Early Settlement and Organization of Stoddard County.
    May 14. Further Events in Early History of Stoddard Co. See latter issues.

Sullivan County. Milan *Standard*
    May 13. Sketch of the life of M. E. Franklin, 86 years, pioneer.
    ——————— ——————— *Republican*
    April 8. Sketch of the life of Jas. B. Dunlap, Mo. Civil War veteran.

Taney County. Branson, *White River Leader*
    April 9. The Tale of An Old Pioneer, by James Blankenship.
    May 7. Stories of the Pioneers—Number Fourteen. See prior and later issues.

Texas County. Houston, *Herald*
    April 16. Sketch of the life of Hon. Thomas N. Bradford—Native pioneer Texas County, County official, Confederate veteran, Member of 32nd and 39th Mo. General Assembly.
    Sketch of the life of General James H. McBride.
    May 6. Sketch of the life of J. M. Hilderbrand, Moniteau Co. pioneer and Mo. Confederate veteran.

Warren County. Warrenton, *Banner*
    May 21. Sketch of the life of Thomas Mills, 80 years old, pioneer.
    May 28. Sketch of the life of Joseph A. Humphreys, Mo. Civil War veteran.

NOTES AND DOCUMENTS.

NATHANIEL PATTEN: In the biographical sketch of Nathaniel Patten, published in the April, 1915, number of the *Review*, it was stated (p. 140) that in all probability Patten had his first experience as a newspaper editor at Mount Sterling, Montgomery County, Kentucky. Since that sketch was written, a bibliography of early Kentucky newspapers has appeared in Part 2 of Volume XXIV of the *Proceedings of the American Antiquarian Society*. This bibliography shows Patten's career as a newspaper man in Kentucky to have been as follows: As junior member of the firm of Martin (William W.) and Patten, he helped to establish the Winchester Advertiser, August 5, 1814. [Patten at that time was 21 years of age. Winchester was the county seat of Clark County, fifteen miles southwest of Mount Sterling, the home of his father.] In July, 1815, this firm was succeeded by Patten and Finnell, and the name of the paper changed to "Kentucky Gazette." August 3, 1816, Finnell retired and the paper was published by Patten alone. "With the issue of July 26, 1817, vol. 3, no. 156, Patten apparently suspended the paper on account of arrears in subscription." It was soon after this that he came to Missouri (though the Winchester paper was afterwards revived by N. L. Fennell).

It thus appears that Patten had three years' experience as an editor of a newspaper before he became editor of the Missouri Intelligencer.

F. F. STEPHENS.

* * * * *

SANTA FE ROAD: An article in the March, 1915, number of *The Mississippi Valley Historical Review*, by Professor W. R. Manning of the University of Texas, is of considerable interest to the Missouri student of history. The article deals with the diplomacy between the United States and Mexico relative to the Santa Fe Road. During the early part of 1825, a bill fathered by Senator Benton, providing for the survey and marking of a road from Missouri to the international boundary on the Arkansas river, had passed Congress. This work was commenced the following July 17, (instead of "June 17"), and completed in September. The diplomatic negotiations had to do chiefly with the attempt to secure co-operation from Mexico, and the construction by her of the road from the Arkansas River to Santa Fe. The negotiations ended with the refusal of the Mexican government to undertake the work, though with its permission to the American commissioners to survey the route.

Of the three commissioners, Benjamin H. Reeves was the most prominent from the Missouri point of view. He was lieutenant-governor of the state, and seems to have resigned that office to accept this new position. G. C. Sibley was a fur trader, and had been a United States Factor at Fort Osage previous to the abolition of the Factory system. Pierre Menard, of Kaskaskia, Illinois, the third member of the commission as first constituted, had been in public life for many years, and had been particularly interested in various Indian questions. Indeed, at this very time, he was assisting in the negotiations for the removal of the Indians living north of the Ohio to the region west of the Mississippi and hence Thomas Mather was appointed on the commission in his place. [See *Missouri Intelligencer*, April 19, 1825.] Mather was not with the other commissioners when they left Franklin, July 4, 1825, [*Mo. Intel.*, July 9, 1825], but seems to have joined them before the following August 10, the date of the treaty with the Osage Indians, as his name is signed to that document.

In connection with the Santa Fe trade, attention should be called to a magazine entitled *"Old Santa Fe"*, published quarterly by The Old Santa Fe Press, Santa Fe, New Mexico. Volume 1, number 1, appeared July, 1913. The leading article since the beginning of the publication has been a continued history of *"New Mexico under Mexican Administration, 1821-46"*. This contains frequent reference to the importance of the Santa Fe trade, and to the relations between Santa Fe and Missouri.

F. F. STEPHENS.

* * * * *

The Bates, et al. of Virginia and Missouri, by Onward Bates, which has lately been donated to the State Historical Society, is a compact book of 160 pages devoted to the genealogy of a family that has done much in shaping the history of Missouri and of even the Nation. The Virginia-Missouri Bates family was remarkable for the number of prominent public men it produced. The first member of this family to link his fortunes with Missouri was Frederick Bates, who came to the Territory of Louisiana, upper Louisiana, in 1807. He served as Secretary of this Territory and of the Territory of Missouri from 1807 to 1820, and was acting Governor during part of this time. In 1824 he was elected Governor of the State of Missouri and died a year later. His youngest brother, the able lawyer, Edward Bates, was a member of the convention that framed Missouri's first state constitution, was appointed her first Attorney-General in 1820, and served Missouri both in the General Assembly and in Congress. After refusing an appointment to the United States Cabinet in the fifties, he became Attorney-General under President Lincoln in 1861, being the first man from the states west of the Mississippi River to hold a Cabinet position. Edward Bates was not only an able legislator but he achieved distinction as a political leader, orator, and lawyer. His son, Barton Bates, also followed the profession of the law and in 1862 became a member of the Supreme Court of Missouri.

This book by Onward Bates is essentially a genealogy but the author has not, fortunately for the biographer, confined his work to genealogy tables. Many interesting facts are set forth and some of the most valuable of these are revealed in "*Letters a Hundred Years Old*", written by different members of this Virginia-Missouri family of pioneers. The random style of presentation is easily excused by the reader who appreciates the public spirit of the author in compiling and distributing this book at his own expense.

* * * * *

The Lewis Publishing Company has again invaded the field of local Missouri history and published a fine morocco bound set of three quarto volumes on the *History of Northwest*

Missouri. The first Missouri venture of this company was a *History of Southeast Missouri*, compiled under the editorship of Professor R. S. Douglass, Cape Girardeau Normal. We have never seen a copy of this work. It must have proved a success as this company soon published a *History of Northeast Missouri*, compiled under the editorship of Dean Walter Williams, Missouri writer and editor, who is also the editor of the recent work on the northwest counties of the State.

In workmanship and mechanical make-up, these last two sectional Missouri histories are the finest that have appeared in the State. Each set devotes two volumes to biographical sketches and one volume to general Missouri history and county histories. In one respect the work on northwest Missouri marks a distinct improvement over its companion work on the northeast counties. It excels in those articles on the general history of the State and of the section under consideration. The separate histories of counties in both works are of practically equal value. The space allotted to each county has not been sufficient to enable the contributing editors and authors to do more than make summaries of what had been more fully written up in former works. This unfortunate condition is today almost inevitable, and involves a point that the critics of county histories fail to appreciate.

One of the most unprofitable kinds of literary activity is the writing of a local history that does not largely feature biography. Even then financial success is not assured. So well known is this that no one but a philanthropist has the temerity to venture to disprove it in practice. It even applies to state histories unless they are purposed for school textbooks. The most valuable work that has been published on Missouri history, Houck's *History of Missouri*, is a classic illustration of this. None but an author of the public spirit and wealth of Hon. Louis Houck would have attempted this and, despite a well ascertained future financial loss, have succeeded. Owing to this poor recompense for perhaps years of labor and thousands of dollars of expense, the author of a local history has been compelled to change his arrangement of subject matter. Instead of the local history occupying the major portion of his work, he has been forced to feature biographical sketches.

The county history of today is valuable. Its worth does not, however, rest on the story told of a particular county, but on its concise and generally accurate articles on the lives of the prominent men and women in that county. The latter is important. Biography has ever been one of the most useful tools of the historian. The county histories of today will in this respect be the treasure house of the histories of tomorrow.

In volume one of the *History of Northwest Missouri* are four chapters on the history of the State that are of special value. These are: *The Life of the Pioneer, In the Good Old Times, The Men Who Laid the Foundations,* and *The Missouri River.* One feature of this work, which also appeared in the *History of Northeast Missouri,* that deserves commendation is a chapter on *The Part Woman Played.* Another noteworthy chapter is on *The Literature of the Land.* Miss Minnie Organ's paper on *The County Press,* which had appeared in the *Review,* is of much value and could well bear reprinting.

The *History of Northwest Missouri* is commendable in having a well arranged index—an aid invaluable to the reader and research worker. Dean Williams is also to be congratulated on this and his former work in having written a history that is interesting and that will be read—both laudable but frequently missing qualities in books of this nature.

* * * * *

Reminiscences of One Who Suffered in the Lost Cause, by C. H. Hance, "dedicated to relatives and friends", has been recently donated to the Society by the author. Mr. Hance is a native Missourian, born in 1837 at old Lewiston. He was a county official and business man in Randolph county for many years and before the Civil War engaged in the overland trade to Colorado. During the war he served under General Porter, the "Stonewall Jackson of Missouri", was wounded at the battle of Moore's Mill, and taken prisoner by the Federals. His acquaintanceship with prominent lawyers of the State was wide and much of this is reflected in this book, which is an interesting and valuable autobiography. Mr. Hance's residence is now at Los Angeles, California, where he has engaged both in private business and public life.

* * * * *

The Archaeological Bulletin for March-April, 1915, published by The International Society of Archaeologists, Somerset, Kentucky, contained the following interesting articles relating to recent archaeological activity in Missouri: *An Unusual Indian Flint Notched Hoe*, by Dr. H. M. Whelpley, St. Louis; *Trailing the Firt Settlers*, by Ernst J. Palmer, Webb City, Missouri,—a description of many prehistoric articles of peace and war found in a cave three miles southwest of Webb City; and several short items on Missouri mounds.

* * * * *

The first number of the *Tennessee Historical Magazine*, published by the Tennessee Historical Society of Nashville, appeared in March of this year. The last publication of this Society was the *American Historical Magazine*, which had its beginning in 1896 and continued until 1904. The high character of that magazine and its able editors gave it a standing in the historical world which made its discontinuance the more regrettable. The present *Tennessee Historical Magazine* promises to be a valuable publication. The first article, of special interest to Missourians, is on *Colonel Burr's First Brush With the Law*. This article is an account of the affidavit made by Joseph Hamilton Daveiss, United States District Attorney in Kentucky, on November 5, 1806, preferring implied charges against the machinations of Aaron Burr. Daveiss was a brother-in-law of Chief Justice Marshall and held the distinction of being the first western attorney to argue a case before the United States Supreme Court. He was a noted lawyer and enjoyed a wide-spread popularity. Counties in Indiana, Illinois, Kentucky and Missouri perpetuate his name as Daviess. The old newspapers of that day spelt his name both ways—Daviess and Daveiss. Daviess County, Missouri, was named in his honor. The people of northwest Missouri, and especially those in Daviess County that are interested in western history, will find this first number of the *Tennessee Historical Magazine* interesting.

* * * * *

The *Society* has received a fine shipment of laws from C. S. Hook, Staunton, Virginia. These consist of Georgia session acts of the Civil War period and of Indiana laws from 1838 to 1870. Another large addition to the law books of the *Library* has been obtained from the Cincinnati Law Library. The *Society* now has a set of Ohio laws complete from 1840 to 1914 except for the years 1849, 1850 and 1851.

* * * * *

Dr. J. F. Feaster, Columbia, Missouri, has donated to the *Society* a file of the old *University Missourian* from October, 1874 to April, 1875. One of the many interesting notes in this file states that Miss Lulie Gilette, Hannibal, Missouri, was the first female graduate of the University. She completed her work in the Normal Department in 1870. Miss S. A. Ware, Spring Hill, Missouri, class of 1872, was the first woman graduate in the Scientific Department.

* * * * *

A complete file of *El Cosmopolita*, Kansas City, Missouri, has been donated by the publisher to the *Society*. This is the only current Spanish paper in the State. It contains data on the Latin-American population and features Mexican conditions. The paper is making an exhaustive study of the teaching of Spanish in Missouri schools. Its report on this work will appear later.

* * * * *

Valuable in its associations and its history is a scrap of paper only eight by three inches in size recently donated to the *Society* by Mr. James O. Thornton, Hamilton, Missouri. This paper reads: "Received of Joseph T(h)ornton the sum of Five Dollars and ——— Cents, it being the balance in full of the amount subscribed by him to the State of Missouri for the use and benefit of the State University, this 18th day of January, 1842.   James M. Gordon,
                                                                Collector."

The family tradition in the Thornton family is that Joseph Thornton donated twenty-five dollars towards obtaining the location of the State University in Boone County. The donor lived in the western part of the county across from the Howard County line. Here he reared a family of fourteen children and was very poor.

This small offering of Joseph Thornton for education was in many ways a monument to him. His grandson, James O. Thornton writes: "My grandfather—also the grandfather of Dr. J. E. Thornton of Columbia—was a resident of Boone County for many years preceding the establishment of the University, and........ it is a matter of some pride to us that Joseph Thornton was among those who made our great state University possible for Columbia and Boone County."

* * * * *

Four special editions of Missouri newspapers and periodicals have lately appeared valuable for historical and descriptive information on Missouri. The *Holt County Sentinel*, Oregon, Missouri, of April 30, celebrated the semi-centennial of its founding with a finely illustrated historical edition replete with information relating to Holt county. The *Columbia Herald-Statesman*, Columbia, Missouri, of May 7, issued a centennial souvenir number of fifty-three pages devoted to the agriculture and commerce of Boone county. This number is commemorative of the first settlement of white men made in that county in 1815. The *Franklin County Tribune*, Union, Missouri, of May 7, published a "Fiftieth Anniversary Edition" devoted to the history of Franklin county and the vicinity. Especially valuable was a "Brief History of Franklin County", written by Mr. Clark Brown, who is compiling a local history to be published next year. *The Independent*, Kansas City, Missouri, of May 15, was a special illustrated number devoted to the Kansas City of today. Many biographical sketches of prominent Kansas Cityans were included.

BOOKS RECEIVED FROM MISSOURI AUTHORS.

Bates et al. of Virginia and Missouri. By Onward Bates. Chicago: Printed for private distribution. 1914.

The Four Gates. By Edward Gareschè, S. J. New York: P. J. Kennedy and Sons. 1913.

Your Neighbor and You. By Edward F. Garesche, S. J. St. Louis: The Queen's Work Press. 1912.

Henry Cooley Ives, LL. D., 1847-1911, Founder of the St. Louis School of Fine Arts, etc. Edited by Walter B. Stevens. St. Louis: The Ives Memorial Association. 1915.

History of Northwest Missouri. Edited by Walter Williams. Chicago: Lewis Publishing Company. 1915.

Reminiscences of One Who Suffered in the Lost Cause. By C. H. Hance. (n. d., n. p.)

Sunshine and Roses. By Edwin P. Haworth. Kansas City: Rockhill Art Publishers. 1914.

The Twentieth Century Epic. By R. B. Garnett. Boston: The Roxburgh Publishing Company. (n. d.)

The Yoke. By David Roy Piper. Minneapolis: The Nunc Licet Press. (n. d.)

When To Lock The Stable. By Homer Croy, with illustrations by Monte Crews. Indianapolis: Bobbs-Merrill Company. 1915.

HISTORICAL NEWS AND COMMENTS.

Mr. F. A. Sampson, who has been editor of this journal since October, 1906, resigned in May. The *Review* is greatly indebted to Mr. Sampson's devotion and good judgment to its interests. Under his guidance the *Review* completed nearly nine years of publication and is being sent to one thousand members of the Society. Mr. Sampson will devote his efforts in the future to the collecting of Missouri historical material for the Society and to the compiling of Missouri bibliographies. Mr. Floyd C. Shoemaker, former Assistant Librarian of the Society, succeeds Mr. Sampson as Secretary and Librarian.

THE STATE HISTORICAL SOCIETY OF MISSOURI.

The new fireproof Library Building of the University of Missouri is nearing completion. Half of this building will be used to house the library of the Society. Arrangements are being made to transfer the one hundred and fifty thousand books and pamphlets from their present shelving in Academic Hall to the new quarters. The task of moving this large library will probably not be ended before September.

The first article in this number of the *Review* was printed in obedience to requests received from members of the Society. Some of the information in it is quite familiar to all, social and economic development of the State is not, however, so well known. This article may also be of value to those who desire a general perspective of Missouri history but who lack the time and facilities for intensive study.

The second article was written under the pressure of self-defense. The requests of Missouri club women and of Missouri reading circles for Missouri programs, have so increased during the last year that the time of the officials of the Society was endangered. *"Missouri Day" Programs For Missouri Club Women* is a general answer to these requests.

PERSONAL.

Hon. Edward P. Garnett, Missouri lawyer and legislator, died in Kansas City on April 16. Born on May 7, 1850, in Culpepper county, Virginia, he was reared with his father's family in Saline county, Missouri. His father was a pioneer Missouri physician and practiced in Saline, Boone and Jackson counties. Edward P. attended William Jewell College in 1871, practiced law in Howell and Jackson counties, and represented the latter county in the General Assembly of 1889. He is known especially for his authorship of the Kansas City park and boulevard system bill, which he championed and put through the Legislature.

Jere T. Dew, sixty-eight years old, a pioneer attorney of Kansas City, died at his home on April 17. Mr. Dew was born and educated in Illinois and was a veteran of the Civil War. The last gave him various G. A. R. honors in later life, among them that of commander of the Missouri State Encampment. For years he was a member of The State Historical Society of Missouri.

Judge G. P. Huckeby, Bates County pioneer and Civil War veteran, died in Rich Hill, Missouri, in April. In 1880 Judge Huckeby established the Gazette, the first paper published in Rich Hill.

Senator John W. Farris, Civil War veteran and Missouri legislator, died at his home in Lebanon in April. Born in Marion county, Illinois, in 1846, Senator Farris was under sixteen years of age when the Civil War began. He enlisted, served four years, and was promoted to adjutant of his regiment. In 1867 he moved to Lebanon, Missouri, and founded the *Lebanon Signal*. He held the following public offices in Laclede county: County assessor, 1870; clerk of probate court, 1872; circuit clerk, 1874; state senator, 1882; prosecuting attorney, about 1884; state representative and speaker of the House, 1897.

Hon. Thomas N. Bradford, Missouri pioneer, Civil War veteran and legislator, died at Wagoner, Oklahoma, on

April 4. He was born in Texas county, Missouri, on April 22, 1841. In 1861 he crossed the plains to California and later in the same year joined Frasier's Missouri Cavalry (Confederate). He was twice elected sheriff of Texas county and was state representative in the 32nd and the 39th General Assemblies of Missouri. Mr. Bradford was a merchant and landowner and was well known in Texas, Dent and Phelps counties. He was a Democrat and a Mason.

Major Joseph Hughes Finks, aged seventy-seven, died at Fayette on April 24. Major Finks' long political career made him one of the best known men in central Missouri. He was a major in the Confederate army and served on the staff of Generals Frost, Clark, Drayton and Parsons. He was circuit clerk of Howard County from 1874 to 1882 and state representative in 1879. He had been marshal of the Missouri Supreme Court since 1895.

Dr. John F. Cowan, pastor of the Old Auxvasse Presbyterian Church for fifty-three years and professor emeritus of modern languages in Westminister College, died at Fulton on April 5. Born in Washington county, Missouri, on March 8, 1837, the son of a pioneer minister of southeast Missouri, Dr. Cowan was graduated at Westminister College in 1857 and at the Princeton Theological Seminary in 1861. He was professor at Westminister College for twenty-three years and was a poet of both English and German verse. Dr. Cowan had been a member of the State Historical Society for several years and had donated to it a number of his productions.

William Rockhill Nelson, editor of the *Kansas City Star* and *Times*, died at his home on April 13. Mr. Nelson was born in Fort Wayne, Indiana, on March 7, 1841. He was educated in that state, and practiced law, edited the *Fort Wayne Sentinel*, and was a contractor there. Mr. Nelson moved to Kansas City, Missouri and founded the *Star* in 1880. Through this newspaper he became a national character. Not only did the *Star* take its place as one of the leading newspapers in Missouri, but it became one of the leading papers in the Nation. Mr. Nelson was one of the greatest of such eminent Missouri journalists as Joseph Pulitzer, Carl Schurz, Henry King, Walter Williams, and other nation-wide editors. He was a trustee of the State Historical Society.

Captain Washington Galland, Missouri pioneer, lawyer, veteran of the Mexican and Civil wars and Iowa legislator, died on April 22 at the Lee county (Iowa) home, where he was admitted in 1912. Capt. Galland was born in Illinois on July 20, 1827, and was reared in that state. He studied law in St. Louis and was admitted to the bar in 1859. At the age of nineteen years he had enlisted in the Mexican war and had served in old and New Mexico under Col. Alexander W. Doniphan and Gen. Sterling Price. Having moved to Iowa he enlisted in the Sixth Iowa Volunteer Infantry during the Civil War and was captured at the battle of Shiloh. He served one term in the Iowa Legislature in 1863 and held several county offices in that state. Capt. Galland was a Master Mason, a member of the K. P. lodge and of the Iowa G. A. R.

GENERAL.

The *Bates County Record*, Butler, Missouri, was sold on April 12 by Mrs. Florence M. Austin to W. O. Atkinson. The *Record* is the oldest paper in Bates county. It was established by O. D. Austin in 1866 and for forty-seven years was owned and edited by its founder.

The distinction of having been the first white child born in Linn county, Missouri, is claimed for Thomas Benton Bowyer of Linneus. Mr. Bowyer, who is now seventy-seven years old, was born during one of Senator Thomas H. Benton's campaigns and so received his name.

The following article relating to Eugene Field's poems was copied from the *Kansas City Star* of May 20: "New York, May 20.—At a sale today of first editions, manuscripts and letters of Eugene Field and other American writers, from the library of the late Frank L. Hanvey of Washington, a presentation copy of Field's first book, 'The Tribune Primer,' printed by the Denver Tribune in 1881, was sold to Van Dusen for $314. George D. Smith paid $195 for Field's manuscript of

'Ye Diuell (*sic*) and Ye Miller Hy-S Wiffe,' written after the style of an old English ballad and not intended for publication. In the Stedman sale a folio of Field verses, rewritten for Stedman, which included this item, brought $1,700. J. F. Drake paid $151 for Field's manuscript of his verses 'Some Time', and $80 for one of thirty copies of Field's 'echoes from the Sabine Farm,' printed by Francis Wilson and distributed among the Wilson's friends. Drake also bought the manuscript of James Whitcomb Riley's poem, 'Rest,' for $29 and another untitled manuscript of Riley's verse for $38."

JOURNALISM WEEK: The sixth annual Journalism Week was held in Columbia May 3-7, in connection with the School of Journalism of the University of Missouri. Editors from all sections of the State were present as well as editors of note from other states. The Missouri Press Association and the Missouri School of Journalism have made Missouri's Journalism Week perhaps the most popular and instructive of its kind in the United States. Col. John H. Sleicher, editor of *Leslie's Weekly*, said in this connection that the Missouri School of Journalism was much more widely known, even in New York, than any other, not excepting the Pulitzer school at Columbia University in the heart of the metropolis.

The sixth annual Journalism Week was especially noted for two historical movements that it originated: One, the founding on May 4 of the first state-wide organization of Missouri Authors, the Missouri Writers' Guild; the other, the first "Made-in-Missouri" Banquet. The author of both of these distinctively Missouri movements was Walter Williams, bard of Missouri and Missourians.

Owing to the absence of President A. Ross Hill, the toastmaster's duties devolved on Dean Williams. The speakers were the eminent Missourians, Hon. Champ Clark, Lieutenant Governor Painter, and Judge Henry Lamm, Ex-Governor David R. Francis, Walter B. Stevens, and Charles S. Keith. The banquet was even more than a "Made-in-Missouri" banquet, it was a Missouri History Banquet. All the speakers had as their theme Missouri and Her History. Missourians are conversant with the greatness of Missouri, but many are not so well versed in her history. No greater stimulus toward obtaining a knowledge of the story of the State has been lately felt than were the speeches delivered at this banquet. State pride in Missouri and her history was the spirit of the evening and for this will the "Made-in-Missouri" banquet of May 7, 1915, be remembered.

MISSOURI WRITERS' GUILD—The inception of few statewide associations has attracted more attention, and justly, in the State than the founding of the Missouri Writers' Guild at Columbia on May 4. Letters and press notices of this proposed organization had been sent over the State and a hearty response was made by Missouri authors. Writers with the pen and the brush—poets, novelists, humorists, playwrights, composers, artists,—from all parts of Missouri gathered in Switzler Hall, University of Missouri, on Tuesday afternoon, May 4, to meet, greet and organize.

Dean Walter Williams, author, speaker, traveler, and journalist, introduced the program with remarks on Missouri's claims to greatness from the viewpoint of her literature and her writers. Papers of value and interest were read by J. Breckenridge Ellis, Plattsburg, novelist of national repute and author of a "best-seller"; by Miss Elizabeth Waddell, Ash Grove, poet; by Robertus Love, St. Louis, poet-humorist; by Mrs. Wm. H. Hamby, Chillicothe, magazine writer; and by Mrs. Emily Newell Blair, Carthage, magazine writer and editor of the *Missouri Woman*.

Permanent organization was effected with the adoption of a constitution and the election of the following officers: President, Wm. H. Hamby; first vice president, J. Breckenridge Ellis; second vice president, Mrs. Emily Newell Blair; secretary and treasurer, Floyd C. Shoemaker.

The following qualifications for members were set forth in the constitution: "First, any one who has had published by a reputable publisher a book or books of general literary nature on a regular royalty basis; second, any writer who has sold at least three articles or stories to magazines of general circulation or who has written a play that has been produced, shall be entitled to (active) membership. Any person ambitious to be a writer may become an associate member. The dues (for either) shall be $1.00 a year."

A banquet was served in the evening to sixty persons who were members of or interested in the Guild, and plans were made for the annual meeting next year to be held in Columbia during Journalism Week.

The founding of the Missouri Writers' Guild on May 4, 1915, in a sense marks the closing of that social cycle in Missouri history that began with the organization of the Missouri Medical Society in 1850. The latter was the first statewide organization that had a continuous existence for years and that was not religious or fraternal in its essential character. Its object was both social and utilitarian. From 1850 to 1915 state wide organizations and clubs of a vocational nature have been founded in Missouri on all lines of important activities. The cultural and social elements have become more and more prominent without loss, however to the utilitarian. It is surprising, therefore, that a Missouri authors' association was not effected during these years. Missouri's pioneer poet and perhaps the first in the Mississippi Valley, Augus Umphraville, published his first book of poems in St. Louis in 1821. He was followed by scores of Missouri writers including such eminent ones as Mark Twain and Eugene Field. Delayed by nearly half a century in their organizing, Missouri authors have this year tried to atone for this delay by founding in the shadow of Missouri's State University and under the auspices of the State Press Association, a Missouri Writers' Guild truly representative of Missouri literature.

The Missouri division of the G. A. R. held its thirty-fourth annual encampment in Hannibal during May together with the Sons of Vetrans, the Women's Relief Corps and the Ladies of the G. A. R. James B. Dobyns of Ransom Post, St. Louis, was elected department commander. The next meeting will be held in Kansas City in 1916.

The eighth annual meeting of the Mississippi Valley Historical Association was held at New Orleans, April 22 to 24, 1915, upon invitation of the Louisiana Historical Society.

HISTORICAL NEWS AND COMMENTS. 279

There were seven meetings of the Association, at which many topics relating to the history of the Mississippi Valley were discussed.

Twenty-five hundred delegates attended the seventy-seventh annual session of Missouri Odd Fellows, held at Cape Girardeau in May. The sessions of the Grand Lodge were held in the historic old Common Pleas Court building on the site presented to the district by Don Louis Torimer more than a century ago. A number of other Missouri fraternal orders held their annual meetings in May.

The May issue of The Cosmopolitan Student, Ann Arbor, Michigan, was a University of Missouri number. The principal articles were written by professors in that institution and were on the following subjects: *Intellectual Pan-Americanism*, by Professor J. Warshaw; *Nationalism*, by Professor R. J. Kerner; *International Public Opinion*, by Professor W. J. Shepard; *The Cosmopolitan Ideal*, by Professor Max M. Meyer; *The Provincialism of the American Student*, by Professor M. S. Handman; and *Cosmopolitanism and the Peace Movement*, by Rodolfo Petrucci. In the mass of literature that has appeared since last summer on the European war, we have not read more concise and scholarly articles than the foregoing by Professor Kerner and Shepard.

RECENT MISSOURI HISTORY LEGISLATION—The increased interest of Missourians in the history of the State and her people is apparent in the appropriations and laws set forth in the session acts of the Forty-eighth General Assembly of Missouri for 1915. The appropriations made by this body for furthering this field of work totaled $59,557.67, of which $6,000, for the collecting of Missouri folk-lore tales, was vetoed. The following items were carried in this appropriation: Missouri State memorial, Missouri regimental and battery monuments and makers, and expenses of the Missouri-Vicksburg natural military park commission at the Memorial National Park at Vicksburg, Mississippi, $17,298.15; State Historical Society of Missouri, $13,600; Mark Twain monument at Hannibal and marker at Florida, Missouri, $10,

462.72; Alexander W. Doniphan monument at Richmond, Missouri, $10,000; completion of Sterling Price monument at Keytesville, Missouri, $2,196.80; gathering stories of the earlier history of Missouri and preserving the same under the State Historical Society of Missouri, $6,000. Although this appropriation bill as signed by the Governor carried only $53,557.67 for Missouri history activities as compared with $73,176.42 appropriated in 1913 by the Forty-seventh General Assembly of Missouri, the former provided for $36,259.52 to be spent within the State while the latter included only $25,800 for this specific purpose. The Missouri-Vicksburg monument commission was granted $47,376.42 in 1913 as compared with its grant of $17,298.15 in 1915.

The Forty-eighth General Assembly also enacted a law designating the twelfth day of February in each year as a public holiday, to be known as "Lincoln Day". The first Monday of October of each year hereafter was designated as "Missouri Day" and, in the words of the statutes, "shall be and is hereby set apart as a day commemorative of Missouri history to be observed by the teachers and pupils of schools with the appropriate exercises." The "people of the State of Missouri, and the educational, commercial, politic, civic, religious and fraternal organizations of the state of Missouri" are requested to devote some part of the day to the consideration of the resources of the State, the achievements of Missourians in commerce, literature, statesmanship, science and art, "and in other departments of activity in which the state has rendered service to mankind." The October number of the *Review* will contain an account of the history of "Missouri Day."

COMMUNICATIONS.

Mr. J. C. Fisher, editor of *The Monetary Record*, St. Louis, Missouri, writes under date of May 7, the following valuable sketch of the life of the late Hon. Dr. Wm. A. Curry. The *Review* failed to notice the death of Dr. Curry and Mr. Fisher kindly calls attention to this. The *Review* appreciates such interest.

"Dr. William A. Curry, born in Culpepper county, Virginia, on March 12, 1827, died in Kansas City, Missouri on July 28th, 1914. He came to Missouri with his father in 1837 and lived in Jefferson City until 1880. Dr. Curry was one of the first and youngest to enlist in the Mexican War in 1846. He marched from Ft. Leavenworth with Col. Alexander W. Doniphan. While in the Mexican service he fought several battles and was present at the surrender of Santa Fe. At the close of the War he went to the University of Virginia where he graduated in medicine in 1850. Locating in Jefferson City he was appointed physician of the State Prison by Governor Sterling Price. When the Civil War broke out he quit the practice of medicine and entered politics, holding the offices of factor at the State Prison, representative in the Legislature from Cole county, and public printer. At the close of the war Dr. Curry moved to St. Louis and engaged in the contracting business. Four years later he returned to Jefferson City and organized the banking house of Curry, Kirby and Cooper. The panic of 1870 swept this bank away and Dr. Curry lost his entire fortune surrendering all of his property to his depositors.

At the age of fifty-four years, Dr. Curry moved to Texas. In that State he rebuilt another fortune, which he distributed between his children before his death. Dr. Curry was survived by his daughters, Mrs. Bradbury, Kansas City, Mrs. Roy, Hannibal, and Mrs. Wintersmith, Louisville, Kentucky, and by his son, William A. Curry, Kansas City, Missouri. Although a slave-holder Dr. Curry was a strong Union man during the war. Almost to the very hour of his death his clear mind remained with him and he had the war news read to him and also the result of the election of the governor of Texas. The night before he died he felt his own pulse, and remarked to his daughter, Mrs. Bradbury: "My pulse is mighty strong to be as near death as I am. I can't live more than a few hours."

* * * * *

Rev. Almer Pennewell, a former Missourian and at present pastor of the Euclid Avenue Methodist Episcopal Church, Oak Park, Illinois, writes under date of June 7, the following:

"Mr. L. C. Frasier, a former resident of western Missouri, and a friend of mine, has told me this story which I thought might be of interest to you, as it was to me. In 1867 or 1868 a steamboat loaded with six hundred barrels of whisky en route from Kentucky to Lexington, Missouri, sank about one and one half miles below Waverly. General Joe Shelby and a certain mill owner, by name Lawton, purchased the bill of lading, and in 1881 or 1882, when a sand bar had formed where the boat went down, they attempted to raise it. The work began when the ice was on the river and promised to be successful, but a sudden thaw broke up the ice and the river flooded the excavation. I have not been able to verify this story, but give it to you for what it is worth."

STATE OF MISSOURI.

State Historical Society of Missouri.

COLUMBIA, MISSOURI.

F. A. SAMPSON, Secretary.

CIRCULAR NO. 17.

MISSOURI HISTORICAL REVIEW.

The above society has completed eight volumes of a historical quarterly under this title, the volumes averaging about 330 pages to the volume. The quarterly is sent to all members without charge. Full sets of the eight volumes can be furnished at price given to enquirers.

The principal papers of the eight volumes have been:

Vol. I, 1906-1907.

The Romance of Western History, by the late Prof. E. G. Bourne of Yale University; Thomas Hart Benton, by Thos. J. C. Fagg, Ex-Supreme Court Judge of Missouri; Early Settlements in Missouri, by Prof. E. M. Violette of Kirksville Normal School; The Beginnings of Missouri Legislation, by Dr. Isidor Loeb, Professor in the University of Missouri; The Lincoln, Hanks and Boone Families, by the late H. E Robinson, President of the Society; Bibliography of Missouri State Publications, by F. A. Sampson, Secretary of the Society; Constitutional Conventions of Missouri, 1865-1875, by the late Col. Wm. F. Switzler; The Shackelford Amendment, by the late Judge Thomas Shackelford, Glasgow, Mo.; Col. Benj. Whiteman Grover, by Capt. Geo. S. Grover, St. Louis, Wabash Railroad Law Department; Historic Landmarks of Jefferson County, Mo., by John L. Thomas, Ex-Judge Supreme Court of Missouri, (three papers); A Few of the Leading People and Events of Early Missouri History, by the late Prof. G. C. Broadhead, formerly State Geologist of Missouri; Battle of Wilson Creek, letter of Gen. F. Sigel; Missouri History as Illustrated by Geo. C. Bingham, by May Simonds, Mercantile Library, St. Louis; Documents Illustrating the Troubles on the Border, 1858, by Prof. Jonas Viles, University of Missouri, also for 1859, by same; Glimpses of Old Missouri by Explorers and Travelers, by F. A. Sampson; Presbyterianism in Saline County, Mo., by J. L. Woodbridge, Marshall, Mo.

Vol. II, 1907-1908.

The Retirement of Thomas H. Benton from the Senate and its Significance, by Prof. P. O. Ray, State College of Penn.; Historic Landmarks of Jefferson County, by Judge Jno. L. Thomas (two papers); Missouri from 1849 to 1861, by Prof. Chas. M. Harvey, St. Louis Globe-Democrat; A History of Westminster College, by the late

Judge John A. Hockaday; Origin of the Christian Chirch at Westport, by the late Stephen C. Ragan; Documents Illustrating the Troubles on the Border, 1860, by Prof. J. Viles; Names of Revolutionary Soldiers buried in Missouri, by the late Mary Louise Dalton, Missouri Historical Society; The Democratic Convention of Missouri in 1860, by Dr. J. F. Snyder, ex-President Illinois Historical Society; Bibliography of Missouri Biography, by F. A. Sampson; The Location of the Capital of Missouri, by the late Prof. G. C. Broadhead; Ethan Allen Hitchcock, by the late H. E. Robinson; The Conquest of St. Joseph, Mich., by the Spaniards in 1781, by Prof. Clarence Walworth Alvord, of the Illinois History Commission; Rufus King and the Missouri Compromise, by Prof. H. C. Hockett, of Central College, Fayette, Mo.; Civil War Reminiscences, by Col. Warner Lewis, Montgomery, Mo.; Bibliography of Slavery and Civil War in Missouri, by F. A. Sampson and W. C. Breckenridge of St. Louis; Rev. Jesse Walker, the Apostle of the Wilderness, by Rev. J. Spencer, Slater, Mo.; The Archives at Jefferson City, by Prof. J. Viles; Missouri Old Settlers' Day Tales, by Col. Wm. F. Switzler; Bibliography of Missouri State Publications, 1906-07, by F. A. Sampson.

Vol. III, 1908-09.

Notes on the Jones Family in Missouri, by the late Prof. G. C. Broadhead; Historic Lines of Missouri, by Judge Jno. L. Thomas (two papers); Bryant's Station and its Founder, William Bryant, by Thomas William Bryant of Iowa.; A German Communistic Society of Missouri, by Dr. Wm. G. Bek, of the University of Missouri; Daniel Boone, by Wm. S. Bryan, of St. Louis (three papers); A Decade of Missouri Politics—1860 to 1870, from a Republican Viewpoint, by Judge H. C. McDougal, of Kansas City; Muster Roll of Company B, First Mo. Cav. C. S. A.; The Settlement of Columbia, Mo.—a Type Study, by James M. Wood, President Stephens College, Columbia, Mo.; Slavery in Missouri Territory, by Harrison A. Trexler, of Hardin College, Mexico, Mo.; Missouri's Aborginal Inhabitants, by Rev. J. Spencer; Historical Sketch of the Presbyterian Church in Columbia, Missouri, by the late Col. W. F..Switzler; A few of the Colonial and Revolutionary Ancestors of Mrs. Jessie Benton Fremont, by Mrs. Emma S. White, of Kansas City; Missouri Folk-lore Society, by Prof. H. M. Belden, University of Missouri.

Vol. IV. 1909-10.

Historical Sketch of Kansas City, by Judge H. C. McDougal, of Kansas City, Mo.; Missouri's Aboriginal Inhabitants, by Rev. J. Spencer; Daniel Boone in Missouri, by Wm. S. Bryan, St. Louis (two papers); Albert G. Blakey, by the late Prof. G. C. Broadhead; Missouri Military in the War of 1812, by W. C. Ferril, Denver, Colo.; Sessions of the Missouri Legislature, by F. A. Sampson; The Journals of Capt. Wm. Becknell from Boone's Lick to Santa Fe and from Santa Fe to Green River, Notes by F. A. Sampson; Col. Robert T. Van Horn, by Supt. J. M. Greenwood, of Kansas City; A Short Biographical Sketch of Gov. Lilburn W. Boggs, by W. M. Boggs, of California; History of the County Press of Missouri, by Miss Minnie Organ, of the State Historical Society (three papers); Bibliography of Missouri State Publications, 1908-09, by F. A. Sampson; The Pinnacles, by the late Prof. G. C. Broadhead; Bryant's Station and its Founder, by T. J. Bryant (second paper); Mormon Troubles in Missouri, by Heman C. Smith, Historian of the Mormon Church, Lamoni, Iowa; The Santa Fe Trail, by the late Prof. G. C. Broadhead; Missouri Documents for the Small Public Library, by Miss Grace Lefler, University Library, Columbia.

Vol. V. 1910-11.

Hamilton Rowan Gamble and the Provisional Government of Missouri, by Judge John F. Phillips, formerly of the U. S. Court, Kansas City; Washington Irving—Travels in Missouri and the South, Notes by F. A. Sampson; Old Newspaper Files in the State Historical Society; Monumental Inscriptions in Missouri Cemeteries (four papers); Administration of Missouri Governors—Gov. Willard Prebel Hall, by Judge John F. Philips; Recollections of the First Catholic Mission Work in Central Missouri, by Rev. Joseph H. Schmidt; The Battle of Kirksville, August 6, 1862, by Prof. E. M. Violette; Two Missouri Historians, by the late H. E. Robinson; Side Lights on the Missouri Compromise, by Frank H. Hodder; Bryant's Station and its Founder, William Bryant, by T. J. Bryant; John Clark, Pioneer Preacher and Founder of Methodism in Missouri, by Rev. J. Spencer; Population and Extent of Settlement in Missouri before 1804, by Dr. J. Viles; The Capture of St. Joseph, Michigan, by the Spaniards in 1781, by Prof. Fred J. Teggart; Christ Church Parish, Boonville, by Capt. S. W. Ravenel; Livingston County, Missouri, by L. T. Collier.

Vol. VI. 1911-12.

Santa Fe Trail—M. M. Marmaduke Journal, Notes by F. A. Sampson; Cities That Were Promised, by F. A. Sampson; Early History of the M. E. Church and M. E. Church, South, in Saline County, Missouri, by Rev. J. Spencer; Monumental Inscriptions in Missouri Cemeteries (four papers); The First Constitution of Missouri, by Floyd C. Shoemaker, State Historical Society; Bibliography of Books of Travel in Missouri, by F. A. Sampson; "Battle of Osawatomie," by Col. J. F. Snyder; Reminiscenses of Wm. M. Boggs; New Madrid Earthquake, by Col. John Shaw; The Shelby Raid, 1863, by Capt. Geo. S. Grover; The Battle of Lexington, Missouri, as Seen by a Woman, by Mrs. Susan A. Arnold McCausland, of Lexington; Daniel Boone, by T. J. Bryant; Scenic and Historic Places in Missouri, by F. A. Sampson; Administration of Missouri Governors—Gov. Joseph W. McClurg, by J. S. Botsford, Kansas City; Livingston County Pioneer Settlers and Subsequent Events, by L. T. Collier; Manuscript Collection of Gen. Thos. A. Smith belonging to the Society, by F. A. Sampson; Mississippi Valley Historical Association Meeting; Speech of Judge Thomas Shackelford; The Price Campaign of 1864, by Capt. Geo. S. Grover.

Vol. VII. 1912-13.

The Capture of Lexington, by Dr. J. F. Snyder; General Jo. O. Shelby, by Hon. Wm. P. Borland, M. C., Kansas City; The Province of Historical Societies, by the late H. E. Robinson; Sketches of Livingston County, No. 3, by L. T. Collier; Old Time News (two papers); State Publications of Archives, by F. A. Sampson; Monumental Inscriptions in Missouri Cemeteries (three papers); The State Historical Society of Missouri, by F. A. Sampson; The Story of the Civil War in Northeast Missouri, by Floyd C. Shoemaker (two papers); History of Missouri Baptist General Assembly, by E. W. Stephens, Moderator of the Assembly, Columbia, Mo.; What I Saw at Wilson Creek, by Joseph A. Mudd, Maryland; Van Bibber Tavern, by Huron Burt; Old Landmarks of Jefferson County, by Judge Jno. L. Thomas; Gen. Jo. O. Shelby, by Hon. S. A. Wight; Early Railroads in Missouri, by the late Prof. G. C. Broadhead; The New Madrid Earthquake by F. A. Sampson; Life and Influence of Danville and Danville Township, by Miss Olive Baker, of St. Louis; Missouri's Eleven State Capitals, by Hon. Cornelius Roach, Secretary of State; The Columbia Library, 1866-1892, by H. O. Severance, University Librarian; Hon. John Brooks Henderson, by F. A. Sampson.

Vol. VIII. 1913-14.

Civil War in Missouri, by Capt. George S. Grover; Report by Committee on Old Landmarks, by Judge John L. Thomas; Sketches of Livingston County, by L. T. Collier; Schuyler Letters from Mowry Collection; First Threshing Machine Across the Mountains, by H. F. Grinstead; Monumental Inscriptions in Missouri Cemeteries, 12th and

13th papers; The Value and Sale of the Missouri Slave, by Harrison A. Trexler; The Old Town of Elizabeth, by Ovid Bell; Early Missouri Roads, by G. C. Broadhead; Echoes of Indian Emigration, by David W. Eaton (three papers); Famous Goose Case, by N. T. Gentry; Soldiers of War of 1812; Fort Orleans, the First French Post on the Missouri, by M. F. Stipes; Recollections of Thomas H. Benton, by L. T. Collier; Historical Sketch of Shelby County, by W. O. L. Jewett; Major Alphonso Wetmore's Diary of a Journey to Santa Fe, 1828, by F. F. Stephens; A Running Glance Over the Field of Music in Missouri, by Mrs. Susan A. Arnold McCausland; An Old Missouri Town, Napton, Saline County, by Rollins Bingham; Hon. David Barton, by Capt. Sam'l W. Ravenel; Mormon Troubles in Carroll County, by Susan H. Whiteman; The First Soldier Paper, by Edgar White; From Senator Doolittle's Papers, by Duane Mowry.

All of the thirty-two numbers also had notes, and book and necrology notices.

The second number of Vol. IX, 1914-1915 is now in press.

Lightning Source UK Ltd.
Milton Keynes UK
UKHW012010080920
369574UK00001B/85